تحفۂ دلهن

*A Gift for*

# Muslim Bride

تحفۂ دلہن

# A Gift for Muslim Bride

**A Guide for Joyous and Successful Married Life**

(A Complete English Translation of the Famous Book *"Tohfa-e-Dulhan"*)

***Rendered into English by:*** **Mufti Afzal Hoosen Elias**

MUHAMMED HANEEF ABDUL MAJEED

idara

**www.idaraimpex.com**

# A Gift for Muslim Bride

**Compiled by: M. Haneef Abdul Majeed**

***Rendered into English by:*** **Mufti Afzal Hoosen Elias**

9788171014323 00000

Edition 2019

ISBN: 81-7101-432-1

TP-787-19

*Published by Mohammad Yunus for*

**IDARA IMPEX**

D-80, Abul Fazal Enclave-I, Jamia Nagar
New Delhi-110 025 (India)
Tel.: +91-11-2695 6832 & 085888 33786
Email: **info@idara.in | www.idarastore.com**

*Retail Shop:* **IDARA IMPEX**

Shop 6, Nizamia Complex, Gali Gadrian, Near Karim's Hotel
Hazrat Nizamuddin, New Delhi-13 (India) Tel.: 085888 44786

# Contents

## A Gift for Muslim Bride

# How to read this book

This book deals with people's domestic life. Since one's domestic happiness has a direct bearing on one's happiness outside the home, we advise that the contents of this book should be read with great earnestness and that the failings cautioned against should be avoided. Although these failings may result from immaturity and inexperience, they are nevertheless extremely harmful. One should read this book with the intention of reforming oneself. One will be able to avoid these failings if one reads this book with the following advices in mind:

1. Before reading the book, make *Du'a* to Allah saying, "O Allah! Make this book a means for my guidance and make me the delight of my husband's eyes and make me his most valuable asset."
2. Set aside such time for reading this book, which is free from disturbances and worries, because a mind that is preoccupied with other concerns will soon become weary with the subject matter of any book.
3. An important advice is that this book should be read in sequence from cover to cover even though this may take months. In fact, one should never grow

despondent even if it takes longer than a few months. An easy way to ensure that one completes the book is to calculate a specific number of pages that one will read daily, based on the total number of pages in the book. A book mark should always be used to mark the page where one stops.

4. Another extremely important advice is that one should keep a pencil handy to mark places that mention something especially pertinent to one. These parts should be read many times and *Du'a* should be made to Allah to grant one the ability to practise accordingly.

Another benefit of keeping a pencil handy is that when reading, it may occur to one that some subject matter which may satisfy the thirst of some Muslim sister has not been included in this book. It may be that this subject pertains to a woman's life as a Muslim woman or as a wife or as a mother, or it may even be something that could terminate disputes. Should such a though occur to one, one should make a note of it under the heading of "Clarification" and bring it to the attention of the publisher or the compiler, specifying the page number and line number where it is to be added.

While reading the book, one should make *Du'a* to Allah that He creates love and affection between all married Muslim couples and that He makes them all a means of rearing pious children. One should make *Du'a* daily that Allah keeps them all happy together with all those getting married. Together with reading this book and progressing spiritually and morally, one should also pass these advices on to other women.

The final request to the reader is to make *Du'a* for the compiler of this book, the people who authored the books from which information was taken and all those who assisted in this publication in any way. Of course, the person making the *Du'a* will never be deprived of the good of the *Du'a*. May Allah reward you all tremendously.

تمهيد

# Introduction

This book cites the sterling examples of six women during the time of Rasulullah ﷺ. The lessons that this book teaches include:

- Obeying the husband
- True love for the husband
- Honouring and serving the husband
- Being loyal towards the husband
- Making one's husband a Muslim or a pious person
- Qualities of a good wife
- How to remain the beloved of one's husband
- Bad habits of women and ways of losing them
- How to live in harmony with one's in-laws
- The rights that women owe to their husbands
- Advice for the married couple
- Formulas to avoid disputes between a bride and her

husband, mother-in-law and sisters-in-law, which often lead to premature separations and bitter feelings between entire families.

Besides the above there are many other subjects and solutions discussed. By practising the teachings of this book, a home can become a garden of *Jannah* and means of attaining success in this world and in the *Aakhirah* (Hereafter).

## AN IMPORTANT NOTE

We will be greatly indebted to scholars of *Deen* and reviewers who bring errors and omissions to our notice.

## Save your Husbands from Sin

Our Muslim sisters are generally negligent of attracting their husbands to themselves sufficiently by beautification and by other means. As a result, even if they are physically close to the husband, it is as if they are not there at all. Whether the consequences of this are light or serious, it is unfortunate that the woman will have to bear the brunt of it all. Allah has made the wife a garment of her husband and vice versa. However, many women do not seem to give this enough thought. Whereas an important function of garments is to conceal the body, another very important purpose of clothing is to beautify a person.

Just as clothing wraps a person, a woman should beautify herself so that she wraps her husband's attention exclusively for herself. She should captivate his attention and imagination by fulfilling all his permissible desires. A person is open and unrestricted beneath his clothing, yet he appears well covered in front of people. Similarly, a married man's chastity is well protected in society because he has a wife. However, he is open and unrestricted to satisfy himself with her in a permissible manner. She therefore has an extremely important function to fulfil because she is the only means by which her husband can satisfy his sensual passions. Now if a woman has to be dressed like a street-sweeper and is careless about personal hygiene, her husband will have no interest in her. His eyes will then start roving and it should never occur that the poisonous arrows of infatuation penetrate his heart.

Is the cure for this situation not that a woman should keep herself attractive so that her husband's eyes stay riveted to her? If a wife neglects this, she will soon find her husband enamoured with the parading masqueraders adorned with the artificial beauty and false glitter all manufactured by beauty parlours. The evil effect of this will even distract him from remembering Allah. We therefore appeal to our Muslim sisters to ensure that their bodies, their clothing and their permissible means of beautification should all harness the complete attention of their husbands. In this manner, they will secure their dominion. It should be borne in mind that if they resort to impermissible means of beautification, they will drive their husbands further from them.

When the wife takes the time and effort to beautify herself, she will be saving her husband from major sins. In addition to this, she will also be saving herself from unnecessary grief.

Many women complain to the *Ulama* and *Muftis* that their husbands do not love them and have no feelings for them. They lament about how their husbands meticulously carry out the orders of their parents without any consideration for her feelings. These husbands have no time for their children and continuously scold their wives. The best "*Ta'weez*" (amulet) for this situation is that the wife should use whatever means of beautification she has at her disposal to ensure that she remains attractive. She should be grateful for the natural beauty that Allah has given her and do her best to captivate the husband's attention. When this is achieved, all her worries will disappear. She will then have her husband eating out of her hand and he will even ignore her major faults. He will then do nothing against her wishes and no other woman will appeal to him irrespective of her beauty and charm.

If a wife fails to charm her husband, the consequences will be devastating. When at his office or company, another woman needs only to affectionately ask, "What is the matter that you seem so sad today?" thereafter even a married man's heart melts. Then, she leads him into sin. It may even happen that the most unattractive prostitute is waiting on a side street for someone to pick her up. However, the passing man does not realise what she is hiding beneath the layers of make-up until after he has committed the most despicable sin and she has washed her face. In many cases, the man realises only after marrying a second wife that she was previously married and that he was foolish to cause grief to his first wife. All these situations may well have been averted if the man's wife did not dress like a maid-servant at home and if she had taken better care of herself.

This piece of advice to women is given with conviction based on the experiences of thousands of women. When a woman fails to maintain a high standard of personal hygiene and fails to adorn herself for her husband, the couple may face serious problems. You may try it for yourself. Whenever your husband looks at you, you should appear like a bride to him. In this manner, you will avert many difficulties and unpleasant situations that leave a bitter taste even though they may be permissible. May Allah grant all Muslim women the ability to take heed and to practise.

We will now present to you some advices that an Arab poetess gave to her daughter who was to be married. A brief explanation has been given in English. It is anticipated that if a woman in any age practises the teachings taught in these advices, *Insha'allah* her home will be like a garden of *Jannah.*

A Saudi Arabian artist has presented these advices with beautiful illustrations so that the messages are portrayed more vividly. In fact, you may even understand the messages without the English explanations. We have dedicated these advices to every Muslim woman in the world. Please read them in conjunction with the illustrations and try to practise what is being said.

## The First Advice

My beloved daughter! Lead a life of contentment. Be content even with simple foods. The dry bread and water eaten with contentment is better than a sumptuous meal eaten after your persistent complaints forced him to grudgingly provide it for you.

## The Second Advice

My beloved daughter! Always listen attentively to what your husband says, give importance to what he says and do as he says. In this manner, you will soon win a place in his heart because it is not really a person who is beloved, but what the person does that is most loved.

## The Third Advice

My beloved daughter! Be his confidante and never disobey him. If you disclose his secrets, he will lose trust in you and if you disobey him, you will not be safe from his wrath.

## The Fourth Advice

My beloved daughter! Never display your happiness when he is grieved i.e. share his sorrow. Never reveal any hidden grief when he is happy and never complain about any of his qualities. Be happy when he is happy (never spoil his happiness) because you will then be counted among those who bring sadness to his heart.

## The Fifth Advice

My beloved daughter! If you want him to honour you, you should have great respect for him and do as he pleases. He will then also be your best companion throughout every stage of your life.

## The Sixth Advice

My beloved daughter! Guard this advice with your life. The bud of happiness will not blossom in your life unless you suppress the desires of your heart to please him and you prefer him above yourself in every situation. With these advices, I leave you with Allah. May Allah destine good for you and protect you from every evil. *Aameen.*

بسم الله الرحمن الرحيم

# Foreword

All praises belong to Allah and may His choicest mercies and blessing be on His noble Nabi Muhammad ﷺ.

We present to our Muslim sisters the lives of six exemplary Muslim ladies from the best era who displayed excellent qualities as wives and lifelong friends to their husbands. Islām has taught us perfect guidelines to lead our domestic lives and Rasulullah ﷺ and the Sahabah ؓ have displayed excellent examples for us to emulate. However, we have ignored these teachings and therefore instead of being happy, content and successful, we have become miserable, dissatisfied and unsuccessful. Married life has become a scourge for many. Disputes between couples, bickering between daughters-and-mothers-in-law, jealousy between sisters-in-law and couples failing to fulfil the rights of each other have become common place nowadays. The repercussions of this have adversely affected not only the married couple, but entire families and communities.

By the infinite grace of Allah and the direction of Hazrat Mufti Ahmadur Rahmaan (A.R), I managed to diagnose the principle causes for divorce and friction between married couples while serving at the *Ifta* department of the *Jaami'atul Uloom Islãmiyya.* These are:

❖ Problems with mothers-in-law and sisters-in-law (husband's sisters as well as husband's brothers' wives)

❖ Unreasonable mothers-in-law

❖ Ill-tempered husbands

❖ Couples blaming each other for mishaps and constantly quarrelling.

Of course, wives are also to blame for such problems because of their immaturity, discourteous speech and inconsiderate behaviour. Fanning the flames of such squabbles are the insolent lessons that women learn from their mothers and other women coupled with the solidarity that mothers-and-sisters-in-law display in these situations.

It has therefore been my aspiration for some time to compile for the Muslim wife a book containing advices that would ensure that such disputs never arise. If (Allah forbid!) such a fire does catch on, these advices would serve to extinguish it without destroying the beautiful garden of marriage and without even uprooting a single flower from it.

By Allah 's grace, I also managed to read the book of Shaikh Muhammad Ibraheem Saleem, titled "An Nisaa Howla Rasulullah ﷺ". It then occurred to me that based on this book and taking our present-day situation into consideration, I should compile a book dealing with the marital lives of six *Sahabiyat* رضي الله عنهن women so that their lives become role models for Muslim women to follow. In addition to this, the advices and experiences of our leading Muslim scholars will also be brought to the attention of our sisters, especially the gems from the lips of Hazrat Maulana Ashraf Ali Thanwi (A.R).

Because this book has been compiled with people's current state of affairs in mind, the advices of various books have been randomly quoted in the best interests of today's woman. Therefore, the traditional arrangement and classification of subject matter has not been employed. Scholars of literature are therefore requested not to judge the book according to their standards. However, should they detect any errors or omissions, they will do me a great favour by bringing this to my notice.

Admitting my incompetence and many faults, I present this book for all readers. Should any reader find any literary or subjective errors, s/he will share in the rewards gained through this book by bringing the same to our notice. These will Insha Allah be corrected in future editions. Everyone who benefits from this book is requested to remember us in their *Du'as*.

We sincerely pray to Allah to make this humble effort a means of salvation in both worlds for us and for every couple. May Allah also end all domestic disputes because this is the secret formula for success and for love to develop between couples. In this manner, future generations will be able to live peacefully under the graceful shadow of their parents, ensuring happiness for all.

# An Offering of Thanks to Rasulullah ﷺ from all Muslim Women

[Adapted from the "Kaarwaan Madinah" by Maulana Sayyad Abul Hasan Nadwi (A.R)]

We invoke the special mercies of Allah and peace on you, O Rasulullah ﷺ. With the help of Allah, you removed us from the shackles of ignorance, from foolish customs and traditions. You have delivered us from the oppression of society and the tyranny of men. You stopped the burying of little girls alive and you warned against disobeying mothers. You even said that *Jannah* lies under the feet of mothers. You have given us a share in inheritance as mothers, sisters, daughters and wives. You did not even forget us when you delivered the momentous sermon at Arafah. You said, "Fear Allah with regard to your women because you acquired them with Allah 's name." You also reminded men on numerous occasions to treat us kindly and to fulfil our rights.

On behalf of all women, may Allah grant you the best reward that He bestows on any of His Ambiyaa (*Alaihimus Salãm*) and on any of His chosen servants.

*"The most Precious thing in the world is a pious wife."* *(Hadith)*

## The Six Exemplary Women

1) Ummul Mu'mineen Hazrat Khadija رضي الله عنها bint Khuwaylid.
2) Ummul Mu'mineen Hazrat Sowda رضي الله عنها bint Zam'ah.
3) Hazrat Zainab رضي الله عنها bint Muhammad ﷺ bin Abdullaah.
4) Hazrat Ruqayya رضي الله عنها bint Muhammad ﷺ bin Abdullaah.
5) Ummul Hakeem رضي الله عنها bint Haarith .
6) Hazrat Khowla رضي الله عنها bint Maalik bin Tha'laba.

May Allah abundantly reward every Muslim sister who reads this book and encourages others to do the same.

# Why Women were Created

Hazrat Adam ﷺ lived in *Jannah* where he enjoyed every type of bounty and he was immersed in Allah's mercy at every step. However, he still yearned for something else. It was only when Allah created his spouse Hazrat Hawwa (R.A) that Hazrat Adam ﷺ experienced the joys of *Jannah* to their fullest and *Jannah* became a true paradise for him. The beautiful appearance of a delicate flower, the fragrance of a rose, the singing of a nightingale, the chirping of birds, the vivid colours of the setting sun and everything else that brings delight to the heart seem incomplete to the person who is without a spouse. With companionship, every bounty gives one true joy. Without a wife, man's life is empty and shapeless. A wife blows enthusiasm and colour into his life.

A wife is the true beauty of a man's life and his primary source of comfort and solace. She lights up his life and his life will be dull and dark without her. Women are the nucleus of society and the embellishment of mankind. She adds flavour to man's life. Without her, civilizations would be disorganised and stagnant. She blows the spirit into man's activities and her presence keeps him going. As a result, man is always progressing and exploring new ground.

Allah has given women beauty and the ability to calm the roughest waters. She is therefore a great source of comfort for the husband and dispels his loneliness. She instils zest in his life so that he continues doing what he has to do and never becomes bored with his daily routine. Without her, he would become frustrated with his mundane activities and may stop altogether.

The charm women add to life equates her to the petals of a rose, the delicate gems of a necklace, a sparkling dewdrop, the ripples of a stream and everything else that lends beauty to another. A wife cheers up her depressed husband and can turn hell into heaven. In fact, every king, minister, saint and even Allah's beloved Rasul ﷺ called woman a mother. He also declared that *Jannah* lies beneath the feet of mothers.

Just as the world would be deserted without people, a house without a pious woman would be deserted and fraught with problems. A good woman is the queen of her home and can command her husband to do anything within the ambit of the *Shari'ah.* However, before taking the reins of command into her hands, some sacrifices will have to be made. The crown of this queen is a crown of roses. Just as roses have thorns to contend with, a wife will have to be a humble bonds-women before she becomes a queen. She will have to wear a crown of thorns before adorning the crown of roses. Such is the system of this world.

While a man was busy pounding kohl fine, the kohl asked him, "Why are you pounding me so fine?" The man replied, "So that you may become worthy of finding a place in the best organ of the best of creation (i.e. in man's eyes)."

Dear lady, because you are the ray of hope in every man's life, you have to make yourself pious. You have to ensure that you are particular about all your five *Salaahs*, that you don the Islamic *Hijaab*, that you encourage the ladies in your locality to lead a religious life together with making an effort for this way of life to spread throughout the world. May Allah make you pious and the delight of your husband's eyes. Aameen.

## The Testimony of the Qur'ãn

With concise words, the Qur'ãn has explained the purpose of woman's creation. If a wife fulfils this purpose, her husband will be the most fortunate man in the world. Otherwise, his life on earth will be reminiscent of *Jahannam*. According to the *Ahadith*, such a wife will make a person old before his time. Allah says in the opening verse of *Surah Nisaa* (*Surah* 4) that He had created man's spouse from himself. Allah says in *Surah Roum*,

> **"And from His signs is that He has created spouses for you from your own species so that you may find solace with her and He has placed love and mercy between you. There are certainly signs in this for people who contemplate."** [*Surah* 30, verse 21]

This solace and mutual love underpins the happiness and stability of a family and oils the wheels of civilization.

The woman is therefore the cradle of comfort for her husband. It is with her that he may satisfy his passions and stay away from sin so that his chastity may remain untainted.

A pious wife is the greatest bounty any man can have and nothing can be more valuable and special than her. She is there to love, to be loved and to care for her husband. When a man returns tired and frustrated after a hard day at work, he will forget all his fatigue and worries when he is welcomed home by a smiling and charming wife. A good wife gives a man vigour and enthusiasm and a few words from her are more revitalizing than glucose and vitamins.

The married couple ease the worries and concerns of each other by displaying mutual compassion. In this manner, they make life pleasant for each other. May Allah make every bride the source of comfort for her husband. *Aameen.*

## The Du'a of Allah 's Sincere Bondsmen

Describing the qualities of His chosen bondsmen, Allah says that they always make *Du'a* for good wives and children. Quoting their *Du'a* in *Surah Furqaan*, Allah says,

> **"Those who say, 'O our Rabb! Accord to us the coolness of our eyes from our spouses and children, and make us leaders of the pious.'"** (*Surah* 25, verse 74)

This *Du'a* is a reminder to all *Mu'mineen* that they should also ask the same from Allah. It is obvious that if a woman is not good-natured and pleasant, the couple cannot live happily together. A woman can be the coolness of a man's eyes only when she is good and pious. A man is therefore extremely fortunate if he finds a wife who is well-groomed, compassionate and intelligent. Insha Allah, if a bride or wife reads this book and sincerely practises the advices mentioned, the couple will quickly become the coolness of each other's eyes.

If a wife inculcates within herself the qualities which Islãm teaches, she will soon conquer her husband's heart and he will attain the contentment of heart that a good wife should provide for him. He will then be prepared to make sacrifices for her and do whatever she asks. Nothing she asks will be too much for him.

---

**Note:** Every Muslim male and female should read the *Du'a* taught in the above verse of the Qur'ãn after every *Fardh Salãh*. Especially boys and girls who have come of age should recite this *Du'a*.

> ***"The most precious thing in the world is a Pious Wife."*** ***(Hadith)***

# The Pious Wife

When Rasulullah ﷺ received the first revelation, he was overcome with natural anxiety because it was the first time that he experienced something of that nature and it was the first time that he met an angel. During this troubled and difficult stage, it was his wife Hazrat Khadija رضي الله عنها who provided the comfort and courage he needed.

Similarly, when Rasulullah ﷺ was leaving this world and experiencing what every dying person regards as *Qiyaamah*, who was there to tend to him and comfort him? Although thousands of *Sahabah* رضي الله عنهم were present in Madinah, the books of history and *Ahadith* make it clear that none of them were present with Rasulullah ﷺ then. At this time when Rasulullah ﷺ was departing to meet Allah, whose lap had the privilege to serve as a pillow for him? Neither was Hazrat Abu Bakr رضي الله عنه nor Hazrat Umar رضي الله عنه nor Hazrat Usman رضي الله عنه nor Hazrat Ali رضي الله عنه nor any perform the other *Sahabah* رضي الله عنهم present there. The good fortune belonged to none other than Rasulullah ﷺ's beloved wife Hazrat A'isha رضي الله عنها.

Islãm accords and exceptionally high esteem to women which one will not find in other cultures and nationalities regardless of the lip service they offer in support of women's rights. We will present to you the lives of some wives who reached tremendous heights and who engraved their undying love in the hearts of their husbands. We shall describe the excellent qualities of these women and discuss how they became the pride of their husband's lives and how they made their children worthy of entering *Jannah.*

If you inculcate these qualities in your life, you will also become the light of your husband's eyes and the most precious thing in the world for him. You will be the queen of your home, enjoy true love and respect and be his companion in public and in private.

## Islãm's Standard of Judging a Good Wife

In Islãm, the standard by which a good wife is judged is not her university degrees or college diplomas, all of which really do not matter to the husband. The most truthful Rasulullah ﷺ has mentioned, "If I were to command anyone to prostrate to another (human), I would have certainly commanded a wife to prostrate to her husband." A good wife would therefore be one who suppress all her desires for her husband, prefer him above herself and sacrifice her own pleasures for him. She is one who would be prepared to lay down to sleep on the bed of thorns her husband provides, imagining it to be a bed of roses.

Dear wives! Regard the dry bread he gives you to be a delicious meal from *Jannah* and imagine the old clothes to be finery and jewellery. Turn a deaf ear to his scolding and imagine that the insults from your mother-and-sister-in-law are the kind words of your mother. Keep smiling though all the difficulties. Pass your life with tolerance and contentment. This will demonstrate that even in this fourteenth century after *Hijrah* women can be born who will not disgrace the names of their forebears, who were the true slaves of Allah and who would sacrifice themselves at the mere gestures of Hazrat Khadija رضي الله عنها and Hazrat A'isha رضي الله عنها. It will be seen that obedience to Allah, fear for Allah can be rolled into one person together with obedience to the husband.

We make *Du'a* to Allah to allow us all the ability to practise what we will read in the ensuing narratives and the ability to do whatever pleases Him. May Allah make every Muslim wife the most precious thing in the world to her husband and may He make every Muslim husband the best of people who behaves excellently towards his wife. *Aameen*

# Hazrat Khadija رضي الله عنها

## Her Lineage

Her name was Khadija, her family name was Ummu Hind and her title was *Taahira.*

Her father was Khuwaylid, who was the son of Asad, who was the son of Abdul Uzza, who was the son of Qusay. It is from Qusay that her lineage meets that of Rasulullah ﷺ.

When Rasulullah ﷺ was being harassed by the Quraish, only two women supported him. They were Hazrat Khadija bint Khuwaylid رضي الله عنها and Hazrat Faatima bint Asad رضي الله عنها. It is because of her loyal support that she is regarded as one of the world's best women. Recalling her loyalty and support, Rasulullah ﷺ mentioned, "She believed in me when the people falsified me, she regarded me to be truthful when people called me a liar and she gave me financial assistance when people denied me wealth." During the time when none were prepared to stand by the side of Rasulullah ﷺ, it was Hazrat Khadija رضي الله عنها who echoed his message whilst she was the first person to accept Islãm.

## Hazrat Khadija رضي الله عنها Comforts Rasulullah ﷺ

Hazrat Khadija رضي الله عنها was always there to console Rasulullah ﷺ whenever the *Mushrikeen* harassed him. The comfort she provided would dispel his worries and relieve him of his burden. When Rasulullah ﷺ received the first revelation, he felt natural fear because it was the first experience of such a super-nature. He was visibly shaken when he arrived home. It was then that Hazrat Khadija رضي الله عنها consoled him with words worth writing in gold. If every Muslim woman could console her husband so effectively, he will always refer to her when he experiences any anxiety, which is a prized certificate of merit for any woman.

Hazrat Khadija رضي الله عنها said to Rasulullah ﷺ, "Allah shall never disgrace you and never forsake you because you maintain good family relations, assist people, provide for the needy and destitute, entertain guests and support all good causes." A person with qualities like these cannot be influenced by *Shaitaan* because Allah would never allow it to happen. She said this with such conviction that it consoled Rasulullah ﷺ.

**Note:** These words display true love and true loyalty that any husband would cherish. Only a person with true love can utter such comforting words. It is evident that his grief was her grief; his happiness, her happiness; his illness, her illness; his health, her health. A person like this recognises every good quality in her spouse and accommodates these in her heart. Therefore, when the occasion arose, she was able to express these to comfort him.

It is difficult to imagine that such wise, consoling and loving words could come from someone who grew up in the harsh desert of Arabia where there were neither schools, universities or finishing schools. In fact, a bit of thought would reveal that these words detail exactly how a person should lead her life.

All thanks are for Allah Who gave us the perfect example of a woman like Hazrat Khadija ﵂ to follow. Although a woman cannot be a Nabi, Allah has made the means for a woman's way of life to be emulated if she so desired it. The lives of all the wives of Rasulullah ﷺ provide women with perfect examples and lessons for leading their lives. Before doing something, Muslim women ought to first think about what the *Sahabiyaat* ladies ﵅ would do in the same situation. They should think about the homes of these *Sahabiyaat*, their food, their clothing, their relationships with their husbands and every other aspect of their lives.

Reflect once again over her words. She said, "Allah shall never disgrace you and never forsake you because you maintain good family relations, assist people, provide for the needy and destitute, entertain guests and support all good causes."

It is actually possible for a woman to develop all these qualities in her husband. If a wife does not complain to her husband about his parents, his brothers, his sisters and other relatives and if she encourages him to associate with them cordially and to overlook their faults, she will be making him a person who maintains good family relations. Allah has also given the wife the ability to purge her husband's heart of any enmity and ill feelings he may have towards another family member. By eradicating any friction between him and his family members, she will be immensely rewarded in this world and in the Hereafter. In this manner, all will live in peace and harmony and Allah's mercy and blessings will continue to shower upon the entire family.

With love and understanding, a wife may explain to her husband that if he does not maintain good relations with his family, it would be very difficult if not impossible for her and their children to foster good relations with them. If the husband is the eldest brother, she may tell him that because he enjoys the status of the father, it is unbecoming of him to get upset about trivial matters as women do. In fact, his father would be disappointed with such behaviour. If he is a younger brother, she should tell him to forgive and overlook because those who are younger ought to listen to and respect their elders. She should explain to him that if he exercises tolerance and listens to his elders, his children will respect and obey him in future. In addition to this, Allah has promised tremendous rewards for the patient.

She should always encourage her husband to exercise patience irrespective of the difficulty that others give him. Even if (for example) his brothers have deprived him of his share of inheritance or if they have seized complete control of their shared property, the wife should stop him from severing relations with them by telling him that the commodities of this world are temporary. If the others want it for themselves, they may have it with pleasure. Everything a person receives in this world is predestined and Allah provides for all. If one door of sustenance seems to be closed, Allah will open another. Allah holds the treasures of the heavens and the earth in His hand and He grants what He wants to whom He wants. Allah will soon grant what is best in this world. Otherwise, He will surely give the full reward in the Hereafter - a reward that is everlasting.

It is not befitting of a Muslim to fight and to severe ties with others because of the perishable commodities of this world, especially if the others are his blood. In this manner, a wife can make her husband emulate the first *Sunnah* that Hazrat Khadija رضي الله عنها mentioned, viz., maintaining good family relations.

A wife can also influence her husband to practise the second *Sunnah* mentioned above viz., assisting others. If a wife reduces her household expenses to a minimum, there will be enough money left over to assist others and to earn the everlasting rewards of the Hereafter. The needy and destitute will find a haven with such a family and guests will also have the best entertainment. A wife may also encourage her husband to employ the unemployed or to assist in finding them employment. In this way, she will share his rewards. Of course, if she earns her own money, she is at liberty to spend this also to assist the needy and support good causes.

Whenever a female guest visits, the wife should ensure that she does not leave without having something, even if it is a glass of plain water. The guest should be met with a smiling face, reminded about some aspect of *Deen* while talking and she should be encouraged to practice and propagate the Deen.

When the husband brings a guest home, the wife should prepare to the best of her ability, giving preference to the guest over herself. It is permissible and even encouraged that she prepares special meals that are normally not served at home. Of course, wastefulness is not encouraged. Although every guest attracts blessing to the home, pious people bring untold good and blessings to the home. The same attitude of selflessness should be displayed to all types of guests, irrespective of their standing. In fact, Rasulullah ﷺ even entertained *Kuffaar* guests.

One should never think that one is doing the guest a favour by entertaining him/her. It is in fact the guest doing one a favour by eating his own predestined sustenance at one's home and allowing one to share in the reward.

Guests should never be regarded as a burden. Although keeping the house clean, cooking and entertaining guests is no easy task, doing this solely for Allah's pleasure earn rewards that are too great to mention. In addition to this, the guests make heartfelt *Du'as* for the host and hostess. Especially when the guest is a traveller, his *Du'as* are most readily accepted.

If one's husband is not accustomed to bringing guests home, one should encourage him to do so. According to one's means, one should occasionally invite pious people home and feed them. One should also feed those in Allah's path. The food should not be extravagant, but something that the guests will enjoy even though it is simple and easy to prepare. Just as it is wrong for a guest to think that the host fed him something very simple, it is also wrong for the host to think that the guest will feel this. These notions should be removed from our minds. Everything should be done to please Allah. One should serve whatever one can afford and whatever can be easily prepared so that Allah should be pleased, irrespective of what people think.

We make *Du'a* to Allah makes every Muslim wife a splendid flower in the flourishing garden of the *Deen* of Hazrat Muhammad ﷺ through the sterling example of Hazrat Khadija رضي الله عنها. *Aameen*

## Sacrificing One's Wealth for One's Husband

Describing the qualities of Hazrat Khadija رضي الله عنها, Rasulullah ﷺ said, "she gave me financial assistance when people denied me wealth." It is common knowledge that people love their wealth. It follows therefore that the person on whom one spends one's wealth is more beloved than the wealth. If one's husband requires one's financial assistance for any necessity of *Deen* or for some permissible worldly need, one should regard giving assistance as an honour. In fact, spending one's wealth or jewellery on one's husband when needed will win his heart and earn one tremendous rewards. Being generous with this is better than storing it in one's cupboard, looking at it occasionally and then losing it to someone else after one's death. The rewards of whatever one provides for one's husband to spend shall be made available on the Day of Qiyaamah, when one will most need it.

If a woman's husband spends her wealth to spread Deen and to ensure that the orders of Allah and the teachings of Rasulullah ﷺ are practised throughout the globe, one will share a most elevated platform with Hazrat Khadija رضي الله عنها. *Insha'allah* , when Allah will raise the wives of the Prophets (*Alaihimus Salãm*) on the Day of Qiyaamah and reward them for assisting their husbands in propagating the belief of *Tauheed* and for eradicating *Kufr* and *Shirk*, the Muslim wife who spent her wealth for her husband's *Deeni* activities will also be rewarded with them. She will be rewarded with all these women who boosted the spirits of their husbands who in turn sacrificed their possessions and their faculties so that Allah's *Deen* reigns supreme on earth. Needless to say, it is also necessary for such a woman to lead a pious life reminiscent of the lives of all these women.

A wife has to be prepared to sacrifice everything for her husband, a quality which Hazrat Khadija رضي الله عنها displayed on so many occasions. When she was to marry Rasulullah ﷺ, her father was unhappy that his daughter should marry the poor orphaned nephew of Abu Taalib. To win her father's approval, Hazrat Khadija رضي الله عنها sent two Awqiya of silver or gold to Rasulullah ﷺ, telling him to buy material, a sheep and certain other items with it. She told Rasulullah ﷺ that he should then give these things to her as a gift. When Rasulullah ﷺ sent these gifts, she showed them to her father, telling him that Rasulullah ﷺ had sent them. Seeing the expensive gifts, her father was pleased. This is an excellent example to all women, echoing the message that everything of this world pales into insignificance before the status of the husband.

It is necessary for every Muslim woman to display the same kind of selflessness for her husband and to spend whatever she can with love and affection. A poet says:

> "Dear friend! If you need my life, it is at your disposal
> And if you need anything that may be more valuable than my life,
> Do inform me of it so that I may offer it to you as well." [This poem has been translated from Urdu]

Learn to sacrifice for your husband, obey him, respect him, try to understand him and shower your love on him instead of making demands. Make him feel that he is most honoured, that he is more valuable to you than everything else and that everything has value because of his presence. When treated in this manner with love, together with *Du'as* after every *Farz Salaah*, even the most ill tempered and ungrateful husband will be conquered. He will then appreciate everything that his wife does and will repent for his past behaviour. He will even remember his wife fondly long after her demise. His attitude will then resound the following words:

> "My dear candle of honour, light of my dreams!
> When you left, four hundred layers of darkness arrived

Now I can only wipe the tears that flow
Destiny has it that the ship is being thrust towards the shores of patience
The children gather up the tears flowing from my eyes
We think that we can turn and look away
But still lying there is the bed and the couch,
On which you would spend entire nights teaching the children
I now appreciate you now after you have left
Destiny has shattered with wasted tears
Come! Return to fill my home just one more time" [This poem has been translated from Urdu]

## Advising the Husband Correctly

Another responsibility of the Muslim wife is to influence her husband to consult with her in all matters, whether religious or otherwise. In fact, when a Muslim carries out any worldly activity, it is also regarded as a *Deeni* activity because he does everything for the pleasure of Allah. The husband should seek his wife's assistance in all matters and discuss these with her so that both of them can be happy about the outcome. A husband should never think that he may dictate matters because he is in a position of authority.

The Qur'ãn stipulates that a child should be breast-fed for two years. During this period, it is compulsory for the father to pay for the suckling mother. However, the couple have the prerogative to wean the child off milk before two years on condition that they have consulted with each other. Allah says about this in *Surah Baqara*,

> **"If the couple decide to wean the child by mutual consent and consultation, there shall be no sin upon either of them."** (*Surah2*, verse 233)

This verse makes it clear that the couple should make domestic decisions after consultation.

The Qur'ãn also mentions that "*Mashwara*" (mutual consultation) is among the characteristics of the *Mu'mineen.* Allah says in *Surah Shura* that the *Mu'mineen* are people,

> **"Who respond to (the commands of) their *Rabb*, who establish *Salaah*, whose affairs (are decided) by mutual consultation between themselves, and who spend from what We have provided for them."** (*Surah* 42, verse 38)

The matter of consultation is given so much importance in the *Shari'ah* that the Qur'ãn mentions it together with *Salaah* and *Zakah.*

Rasulullah ﷺ has mentioned[1], "Consult with your women concerning your daughters." This *Hadith* enjoins fathers to consult with their wives concerning the marriage of their daughters.

The *Seerah* (biography) of Rasulullah ﷺ written by Ibn Hishaam (A.R) describes Hazrat Khadija رضي الله عنها as a

1. Ahmad and Abu Dawud, Page 285

woman who "was a true advisor to Rasulullah ﷺ in the matters of *Deen.*" Together with deep insight and excellent character, Hazrat Khadija رضي الله عنها was endowed with sound intelligence. She had many years of experience with people and understood them well. Her opinions were therefore very sensible and valuable. She always gave Rasulullah ﷺ advice that lessened his grief and gave him all the support he needed.

This should be the behaviour of all Muslim women. Whenever her husband requires her advice, she should give the matter the attention it deserves, make *Du'a* to Allah and offer her best advice. If the matter is beyond her, she should ask advice from pious people in her family who are capable of providing some direction. If no one from her family is able to assist, advice should be sought from a pious person in the appropriate field. The husband should be referred to such a person or persons, just as Hazrat Khadija رضي الله عنها referred Rasulullah ﷺ to her cousin Waraqa bin Naufal, who was learned in the previously revealed divine scriptures. Therefore, when Hazrat Jibra'eel عليه السلام came to Rasulullah ﷺ with the first revelation, Hazrat Khadija رضي الله عنها told Rasulullah ﷺ as much as she knew and then directed him to Waraqa bin Naufal, who knew much more than her.

After signing the Treaty of Hudaybiyyah, when Rasulullah ﷺ instructed the *Sahabah* رضي الله عنهم to slaughter their animals and to shave their hair, no one responded. The *Sahabah* رضي الله عنهم found it difficult to do this because they found it difficult to return without performing *Umrah* and they expected that the command might be reversed at any time.

When Rasulullah ﷺ consulted his wife Hazrat Ummu Salma رضي الله عنها about the issue, she advised Rasulullah ﷺ that he should do it first and that the *Sahabah* رضي الله عنهم would soon follow his example. When Rasulullah ﷺ did as she had advised, the *Sahabah* رضي الله عنهم followed suit. Her valuable advice therefore averted an extremely inconvenient and uncomfortable situation.

Today's women are also required to sometimes advise their husbands on *Deeni* issues like their pious predecessors. In this way, they will also share the rewards of spreading *Deen* throughout the world. In fact, every Muslim wife should be concerned about how *Deen* should spread in her locality, her country and throughout the entire world. She should continue advising her husband in this regard. At the same time, she should also offer him sincere advice in matters of this world as well.

Some people are of the opinion that women should not be consulted when taking decisions. This opinion is incorrect because the advice of a pious, sensible and intelligent woman should be accepted. Besides the above two examples, the books of history are full of incidents in which the advice of Muslim women has tremendously benefited the *Ummah* and saved them from great difficulty. Of course, this does not mean that the wife should make the decisions in the house. Ultimately, it is the husband who takes the decisions. What his wife says shall be her opinion.

## Making Sacrifices for the Husband

When faced with any domestic crisis, the wife should bear with her husband and stand with him. She should not behave disloyally by forsaking him when times are tough. She should not fit the description of someone who said, "Gobble up the gifts and spit out the sacrifices." The wife should never remind the husband that something would not have happened if he acted on her advice. Let alone a Muslim wife, such behaviour is unbecoming of even a *Kaafir* wife. Everything happens by Allah 's command. Neither a calamity nor a bounty that Allah ordains can be averted.

Allah says in the *Surah Taubah,*

> **"Tell them, 'Only what Allah had ordained for us will affect us. He is our Protecting Friend and the believers should trust only in Him.'"** (*Surah* 9, verse 51)

Allah is All Knowing and will never abandon one in distress. When one pleads for his mercy, it is sure to come rushing to one's side.

The wife should be especially patient when her husband earns less because he is serving the *Deen* or engaged in some *Halaal* occupation. Patience must also be exercised when she experiences difficulty during his absence. She should never complain of these difficulties to others because speaking ill of the husband shall not alleviate the problem. In fact, the problem will be compounded and Allah will also be displeased with such a wife. She should perpetually make *Du'a* to Allah to alleviate the difficulty and also ask her children to make *Du'a*.

During the seventh year after Rasulullah ﷺ announced his prophethood, the Quraish decided to banish the family of Rasulullah ﷺ to a valley near Makkah and to completely ostracise them. This was done to stop Rasulullah ﷺ from propagating Islãm. Consequently, Abu Taalib and all his family members joined Rasulullah ﷺ in what was referred to as the Valley of Abu Taalib. At his side was Hazrat Khadija رضي الله عنها. Although the condition was so harsh that the Muslims were forced to eat the leaves of trees, Hazrat Khadija رضي الله عنها stayed with Rasulullah ﷺ and never deserted him. Because of Hazrat Khadija رضي الله عنها's influence on the people of Makkah, food was sometimes brought to the Muslims. However, this was scarce and the children were so starved that their cries could be heard from very far off.

Despite the hardship, Rasulullah ﷺ could not stop propagating Islãm and the message continued. All this while, Rasulullah ﷺ's family the Banu Haashim and Hazrat Khadija رضي الله عنها patiently bore the hardship without once complaining and without blaming Rasulullah ﷺ for their predicament. This boycott lasted for three long years. Hazrat Khadija رضي الله عنها displayed her loyalty to Rasulullah ﷺ for approximately thirty years, patiently enduring all the difficulties that came to them. May Allah reward Hazrat Khadija رضي الله عنها abundantly on our behalf for the tremendous sacrifices she made for the spread of Islãm.

It is therefore the duty of every Muslim wife to emulate the example of this *Ummul Mu'mineen* (Mother of the

Mu'mineen). She should be her husband's deputy and aide in the propagation of Islãm and should be prepared make every sacrifice in this cause. By doing this, they can also earn the great rewards that Hazrat Khadija رضي الله عنها earned.

## Serving the Husband

Although Hazrat Khadija رضي الله عنها was an influential, well-established and wealthy woman of the Quraish, she personally served Rasulullah ﷺ. A narration of *Bukhari* mentions that Hazrat Khadija رضي الله عنها was once serving something to Rasulullah ﷺ in a dish when Hazrat Jibra'eel عليه السلام came and informed Rasulullah ﷺ that Allah had sent *Salaams* (greetings of peace) to her. Rasulullah ﷺ said, "O Khadija! Here is Hazrat Jibra'eel عليه السلام conveying the *Salaams* of your Rabb to you." Hazrat Khadija رضي الله عنها replied, "Allah is Himself the Giver of peace, all peace if from Him and peace be to Hazrat Jibra'eel عليه السلام as well."

This narration shows the elevated status of Hazrat Khadija رضي الله عنها because Allah Himself send greetings to her. It can only be a chosen servant of Allah who can have this honour. According to another narration, she was also given the glad tidings that she would have a palace in *Jannah* where there shall be neither noise nor fatigue.

Because of her devotion and dedication, Rasulullah ﷺ, said,

> "The best women of this world are Maryam bint Imraan and Khadija bint Khuwaylid."

The lives of the wives of Rasulullah ﷺ are recorded for Muslim women of every age to emulate. The manner in which they served Rasulullah ﷺ is a lesson for every Muslim wife so that every woman can earn the same rewards. Although we are presently discussing Hazrat Khadija رضي الله عنها, it is appropriate to mention a bit of the life of Hazrat A'isha رضي الله عنها because the discussion revolves around serving one's husband.

In his biography of Hazrat A'isha رضي الله عنها, Allaama Sayyid Sulaymaan Nadwi (A.R) states that although Hazrat A'isha رضي الله عنها had a servant, she personally served Rasulullah ﷺ. She personally crushed the wheat to make flour, cooked the food herself, made the beds and brought water for Wuzu. She would also twine the garlands that were hung on Rasulullah ﷺ's sacrificial animals. In addition to this, she used to comb his hair, perfume his body and wash his clothes all by herself. She used to keep his *Miswaak* and water ready at night and would always keep the *Miswaak* clean. Whenever Rasulullah ﷺ received any visitors, she would also attend to entertaining them.

Hazrat Qais Ghifaari رضي الله عنه, who was one of the Sahabah رضي الله عنهم of the Suffa[1] narrates that Rasulullah ﷺ once told them all to accompany him to the room of Hazrat A'isha رضي الله عنها. When Rasulullah ﷺ asked Hazrat A'isha رضي الله عنها to serve some

1. Suffa was a platform in the masjid of Rasulullah ﷺ where many poor *Sahabah* رضي الله عنهم lived. Their number always varied and their sole occupation was to learn from Rasulullah ﷺ. They ate only when Rasulullah ﷺ could provide something for them and often went hungry. One of the most famous Sahabah رضي الله عنهم of the Suffa was Hazrat Abu Hurairah رضي الله عنه.

food, she served something that she had already cooked. When Rasulullah ﷺ asked for something else, she served a dish made of dates. When Rasulullah ﷺ asked for something to drink, she brought a large container of milk and smaller container of water.

This was an example of a good wife. She considered it an honour to serve her husband and to do things herself. When a woman does this with the intention of fulfilling her husband's rights and pleasing Allah, her service will be regarded as *Ibaadah.* Of course, a wife should not be so engrossed in domestic work that she neglects her other acts of worship. It often occurs especially in *Ramzaan* that women become so occupied with preparing several types of dishes, savouries, deserts and drinks that they find no time to engage in *Ibaadah.* As a result, they carry out no *Nafl* acts of *Ibaadah* and if they manage to perform their *Fardh Salaah,* they perform it very late. Women should take heed not to invest all their energies in decorating their tablecloths because this will rob them of valuable time which could be invested in earning the rewards of the Hereafter; especially the valuable hours of *Ramzaan.* Allah did not send women to this world only to tend to domestic chores. They also need to prepare for their lives in the Hereafter. A single moment wasted in this world will be a source of regret in the *Aakhirah* (Hereafter), even if a person enters *Jannah.* A *Hadith* mentions that the only regret of a person entering Jannah will be the moments that he spend without *Zikr.*

It is therefore important for every Muslim wife to spend as little time as possible in cooking and to devote the majority of her time to *Ibaadah, Zikr,* learning and teaching *Deen* and propagating *Deen* for Allah 's pleasure.

## Obeying the Husband Completely

Hazrat Khadija ﷺ was such an obedient wife that even before the five daily salaah were made obligatory , she used to perform optional salaah with Rasulullah ﷺ. The historian Ibn Sa'd (A.R) writes, "Rasulullah ﷺ and Hazrat Khadija ﷺ secretly performed salaah for a long time."

Hazrat Khadija ﷺ had cast herself into the mould of her husband ﷺ. According to a narration of Imaam Ahmad (A.R)'s "*Musnad*", Hazrat Khadija ﷺ stopped worshipping idols long before Rasulullah ﷺ even declared his prophethood. It is the trait of a good wife that when her husband is practising the truth, she should do as he does and think as he thinks. Her husband should view her as he wants her to be. This is advice to all Muslim women from the first Muslim of this *Ummah*, the first Mother of the *Mu'mineen*, the first wife of Rasulullah ﷺ.

Dear sister! If you also cast yourselves in the mould of Hazrat Khadija ﷺ and obey every instruction of your husband when his instructions conform with the *Shari'ah*, Allah will be extremely pleased with you. When Allah is pleased with one, difficulties will disappear and one's affairs will be manageable.

One should always bear in mind that after marriage, nothing is done for oneself. One then eats for one's husband, dresses for him and does everything else to please him because he is one's lifelong companion and the crown on one's head. When one does this, one will find that just as Allah sent greetings of peace to Hazrat Khadija ﵂, Allah bless one's home with peace and comfort. As a result of this peace, the children will live in harmony and an atmosphere of love will exude from the home. Such a home will then be reminiscent of *Jannah.*

If one's husband performs *Tahajjud* and other *Nafl Salaahs,* one should make an effort to do so as well. One should recite Qur'ãn with him and join in him in his acts of *Ibaadah.* One should never think that one's responsibilities are restricted to managing the home and rearing the children. Fix a time to engage in *Zikr* and teach the children how to make *Zikr*. Teach them Allah's names, make them recite Qur'ãn daily and fix a time for making *Du'a* daily.

If one's husband is not inclined towards Ibaadah, one should make *Du'a* to Allah to make him pious and also consult with one's seniors so that they may advise one how to influence him. Encourage him first to be regular with his *Farz Salaah* and the *Waajibaat* and *Nawaafil.* Encourage him to spend time in Allah 's path and Insha Allah he will soon change for the better.

## Some Ahadith Concerning Obeying the Husband and Fulfilling his Rights

The following *Ahadith* make it clear that it is extremely important for a wife to obey the instructions of her husband. Ponder over these *Ahadith* and make the intention to practise. Also make *Du'a* to Allah to assist one in practising.

- Rasulullah ﷺ said, "The woman who performs her five daily *Salaah*, who fasts during Ramzaan, who protects her chastity and who obeys her husband has the choice of entering *Jannah* from whichever door she pleases." ["*Mishkaat*" Pg. 281]

Here are so many ways of entering *Jannah*. By obeying the lawful commands of one's husband, one will live harmoniously in this world and be able to enjoy the bliss of *Jannah* eternally in the Hereafter. Irrespective of what a woman looks like in this world, if she performs her *Salaah*, fasts during *Ramzaan*, safeguards her chastity and obeys her husband, she will be more beautiful and honoured than the damsels of *Jannah*.

In his *Tafseer* "*Ruhul Ma'aani*"[1], Allaama Aalusi (A.R) has quoted a narration in which Hazrat Ummu Salma رضي الله عنها asked Rasulullah ﷺ whether the "*Hoor Een*" (damsels of Jannah) or the *Mu'min* wives of this world will be more beautiful. Rasulullah ﷺ told her that the *Mu'min* wives of this world will be made more beautiful than the "*Hoor Een*". When she asked the reason for this, Rasulullah ﷺ replied, "Because of their *Salaah*, their fasting and their *Ibaadah*, Allah shall cover their faces with *Noor* (celestial light)." The beauty of a person whose face exudes *Noor* cannot be imagined. While the "*Hoor Een*" will not have this privilege, it will be exclusive to the believing women of this world.

- Tabraani has narrated that some women during the time of Rasulullah ﷺ sent one of them to pose a

1. "Ruhul Ma'aani", Vol. 27, Pg. 126.

question to Rasulullah ﷺ. When the lady arrived, she said, "O Rasulullah ﷺ! I have been sent on behalf of the other women. *Jihaad* has been made *Farz* on men. They are rewarded when they are victorious of if they are injured. If they are martyred, they attain a great status and their *Rabb* feeds them and allows them to live peacefully in the next life. We wish to know what will be our reward for serving these men?" Rasulullah ﷺ replied, "Tell every woman you meet that when a woman obeys her husband and acknowledges the rights of her husband, her reward will equal that of her husband. However, few of you do this."

If a woman learns to obey all her husband's lawful instructions, she will attain the reward of enduring hunger, thirst, injuries, illness and even martyrdom although she has not left her home. If her soul leaves her while she is lying on her comfortable bed, she can attain the status of a *Shaheed* (martyr) who has laid down his life for the *Deen* of Allah.

When a woman obeys her husband, she will be saving the family from ruination and her husband will have true love for her in his heart. The family will then be saved from the endless quarrels and bitterness that destroy even the most respectable homes.

- Rasulullah ﷺ has mentioned that a woman will enter Jannah if she passes away when her husband is pleased with her. [*Tirmidhi* Vol. 1 Pg. 219]

- Rasulullah ﷺ said, "If I were to command anyone to prostrate to another, I would have commanded wives to prostrate to their husbands. If a husband commands his wife to move a rock from one mountain to another mountain and then back to the first mountain, she should do as he says."
["*Mishkaat*" Pg. 281 from Ibn Majah]

- *Tirmidhi* (Vol. 1 Pg. 219) reports that Rasulullah ﷺ said, "If a husband calls his wife to bed, she should respond even if she is busy at the stove." This means that she is obliged to respond to his call even if she is tending to something important.

- According to another *Hadith*, the angels curse the wife who does not respond when her husband calls her to bed and he spends the night angry with her.
[Muslim Vol. 2 Pg. 1059]

- Rasulullah ﷺ said that when a woman troubles her husband, his wife in the Hereafter says to her, "Woe to you! Do not bother him so! He is only your guest. After a few days he shall leave you to return to us."
[*Ibn Majah* Vol. 1 Pg. 649; *Ahmad* Vol. 5 Pg. 242; *Jaami'ul Usool* Vol. 6 Pg. 497]

- Rasulullah ﷺ said that there are three categories of people whose *Salaah* and every good act is not accepted. The three are: (1) The slave who escapes from his/her master, (2) the woman whose husband is displeased with her and (3) the person who is drunk until he becomes sober. ["*At Targheeb wat Tarheeb*" Vol. 4 Pg. 128; *Fat'hul Baari* Vol. 9 Pg. 294]

- Someone asked, "O Rasulullah ﷺ! Who is the best woman?" Rasulullah ﷺ replied, "The woman who pleases her husband when he sees her, who obeys him when he speaks to her and who does not betray him with regard to her chastity and his wealth."

## The Advice of a Pious Father to his Daughter to be Married

The above *Ahadith* outline the characteristics of a good wife. They may be translated in the following:

> "A good wife gives her all for her husband. Her happiness is when her husband is happy. She is prepared to sacrifice her spirit, her ambitions, her desires and her comfort for her husband. She regards herself as a wife and a slave. For the sake of her husband, she regards disgrace as honour and a bed of thorns as a bed of flowers. Listen well O my innocent daughter! You will soon be a new bride and a daughter-in-law. You are entering a new phase in your life. Until now, you have been playing and eating and sleeping without a worry. You was happy and laughing all the time. Things will be changing now. You will now have responsibilities and you will be living under a new rule. Until now you have been living for yourself. From tomorrow, you will be serving others. The one who was the charm people's eyes and who grew up in a cradle of hopes will now be handed over in the service of others."

"Remember that whatever good or bad happens will be for that day. Take things a step at a time. You will need to restrain yourself because the journey ahead is not going to be an easy one. The responsibilities will be difficult but, O Muslim, remember that the rewards and glad tidings are also tremendous."

"Hazrat Ummu Salma رضي الله عنها narrates from the one who was sent as a mercy to the universe, 'The woman who passes every stage of her life and finally reaches the final stage while her husband is pleased with her, she will surely enter *Jannah.* It is as if there is no barrier between *Jannah* and her.' Dear daughter! Even the worst difficulties of life are temporary. Keep the final stage of life in front of you and Allah will turn every thorn into a flower and every stone into water."

## An Obedient Wife

The personality of Hazrat Umar bin Abdul Azeez (A.R) needs no introduction. He is regarded by many as the fifth with the four *Khulafa Raashideen*[1]. His wife Faatima bint Abdil Malik has mentioned that although there may be others who performed more *Salaah* and *Wuzu* than Hazrat Umar bin Abdul Azeez (A.R), she has never seen anyone who feared Allah more than him. He used to remain on

1. These were the rightly guided successors of Rasulullah ﷺ viz. Hazrat Abu Bakr رضي الله عنه, Hazrat Umar رضي الله عنه, Hazrat Usman رضي الله عنه, and Hazrat Ali رضي الله عنه.

the *Musalla* after the *Isha Salaah* and continue making *Du'a* and weeping until sleep overcame him. When he awoke, he used to continue in this manner the entire night.

His wife was the daughter of the famous king Abdul Malik. Among the fortune of jewellery that her father had given her was a necklace that no other woman possessed. When Hazrat Umar bin Abdul Azeez (A.R) became the Khalifa, he gave his wife the choice of either separating from him or depositing all her jewellery in the public treasury because he disliked living in a house with so much wealth. She replied, "What is the worth of all these treasures? I shall never part from you in exchange for even more than this." All her jewellery was then deposited in the state treasury for the benefit of the masses.

Here was a woman whose father, grandfather, brother and husband were all kings. Despite growing up in the lap of luxury, she was prepared to forsake everything to please her husband. Her sacrifices were so great that the pages of history still mention her name and she will always remain a role model for all women.

After the demise of her husband, her brother Yazeed became king. He told his sister that he could return her jewellery to her if she pleased. She said, "I was not happy with it during my husband's lifetime, how can it bring me any pleasure now?" With this sentence she expressed her sincere loyalty by not doing anything that would displease him even after his demise. May Allah make all Muslim wives loyal and obedient to the husbands. *Aameen.*

## The Demise of Hazrat Khadija ﵂

Hazrat Khadija ﵂ remained in Rasulullah ﷺ's wedlock for twenty-five years. She passed away in *Ramzaan* ten years after Rasulullah ﷺ announced his prophethood, which was three years before the *Hijrah*. She was then 64 years old. Because the *Janaazah Salaah* was not ordained at that time, no *Janaazah* salaah took place and Rasulullah ﷺ himself lowered the body of his companion, advisor and aide into the grave. The moment was so heart-rending that no pen can describe. In carrying out his tremendous task of propagating Islãm, Hazrat Khadija ﵂ had always been invaluable to him. She would console him in his distress, advise him when he needed advice and sacrifice everything she had for him.

An innumerable amount of stones and pebbles break off from mountains and hills. Without any regard for them, people and animals merely trample on them. If one of these stones has to become a ruby or a diamond more precious than the kingdoms of the world, how distressed will one become if it has to be destroyed?

The number of raindrops falling on the ocean every year is also countless. From all of these, one enters an open oyster and is transformed into a priceless pearl which is worthy of being set in the crown of a king. If someone casts this pearl back into the ocean, one cannot imagine the grief it will cause to those who realise its value.

The leaves, roots and plants of the wild are also plenty for animals to feed on. If among these there is an extremely rare and delicate rose that can produce a most exquisite perfume, one cannot imagine the loss to mankind if this rose falls prey to harsh weather and wilts away.

Spiritually, time is neither measured by man's calendar nor by the earth's orbit around the sun. The appointed time for a soul to return to Allah is when it has perfected itself. There is therefore no necessity to grieve excessively when a person leaves this world. To Allah do we belong and to Him shall we all return.

Rasulullah ﷺ himself declared the year in which Hazrat Khadija رضي الله عنها passed away as the year of grief. Although Allaama Sayyid Sulaymaan Nadwi (A.R) was not a poet, he wrote the following couplet in memory of his wife to whom he was very attached:

"Upon your departure, it appeared as if time would be thrown into chaos
It is strange that the Last Day did not end time when you left."

[This poem has been translated from Urdu]

## *Du'a*

"O Allah! Make our girls and women like Hazrat Khadija رضي الله عنها. Grant them her pure habits, her character, her chastity, her love, her obedience, her concern for the *Aakhirah*, her *Taqwa* and her loyalty. O Allah! Make the pure personality of Hazrat Khadija رضي الله عنها common among the new generation of Muslims. Grant us all the ability to do as she did. O Allah! Fill her grave with peace and tranquillity and elevate her stages abundantly. Grant her the best of rewards on our behalf. *Aameen.*"

## Salutations of Peace from Us All

Every Muslim sends salutations of peace to Hazrat Khadija, the first believer of this *Ummah,* the first "Mother of the *Mu'mineen*" and the honoured lady who received greetings of peace from none other than the *Rabb* of the universe.

There is a lesson for Muslims in every detail of her pure life. By following her noble example, every wife can become the delight of her husband's eyes and the most precious thing for him in this world. She will then become a source of solace and comfort for him and thus fulfil the purpose of her creation.

Therefore, every wife should sincerely try to follow her example and make the following *Du'a* after every *Salaah*: "O Allah! Grant me the same character, understanding, obedience and self-sacrifice that you blessed Hazrat Khadija with. Also bless my daughters, sisters and all Muslim women with the same sterling qualities. Aameen."

This *Du'a* should be made as often as possible. If Allah accepts this *Du'a,* one will be the most fortunate person both in terms of this world and in terms of the Hereafter. Hazrat Ummu Salma has narrated that she heard Rasulullah say that a woman will enter *Jannah* if she passes away when her husband is pleased with her.

[*Tirmidhi* Vol. 1 Pg. 219]

Can a woman have any desire greater than that she should be Allah's guest in *Jannah*? This is the ultimate aspiration. Allah declares in His Qur'ãn ,

> "Whoever is saved from the fire and entered into *Jannah* shall truly be successful."
>
> (*Surah A'al-Imran, Surah* 3, verse 185)

One should constantly ponder over this *Hadith* and Qur'ãnic verse. By doing so, it will become easy for one to carry out the responsibilities of being a good wife and a good daughter-in-law. Allah will then assist one every step of the way.

You may say that everything being said seems biased. Everything said thus far is definitely directed at women because they are being addressed in this book. Men have a separate set of responsibilities. When a woman fulfils her responsibilities, her husband will automatically discharge his. The advices to men have been published in a separate book titled "Gift to a Husband".

Life with one's in-laws can really be difficult. While the insults of a mother-in-law cut the heart more effectively than a knife through butter, the presence of the husband's elder and younger sisters can be a terrible nuisance. The husband's affection towards his wife often seems to cause hurt to his sisters for no good reason whatsoever. What makes all of this unbearable is when the husband is ill-tempered. However, patience will soon win the day.

The *Ummah* has been shown the examples of exemplary wives like Hazrat Khadija رضي الله عنها and Hazrat A'isha رضي الله عنها. Keeping their lives in mind, every Muslim wife should also not forget the words of Rasulullah ﷺ when he said that nothing can stop her from *Jannah* if she passes away when her husband is pleased with her. Keep this *Hadith* in mind at all times and every bitterness will be sweet. The thorns that people throw at you will then seem like rose petals and Allah will be your Protector and Assistant. May Allah save every Muslim woman from the bane of a temperamental husband and inconsiderate mothers-and-sisters-in-law. *Aameen.*

We will now discuss the exemplary life of Rasulullah ﷺ's second wife Hazrat Sauda bint Zam'ah رضي الله عنها. Before reading, one should make *Du'a* to Allah to make one like her. *Aameen*

الله

May Allah abundantly reward every Muslim sister who reads this book and encourages others to do the same.

# Hazrat Sauda bint Zam'ah رضي الله عنها

## Conversion to Islãm

Hazrat Sauda bint Zam'ah رضي الله عنها accepted Islãm during the very early stages and therefore had the honour of being included among the earliest Muslims. She was also among the early immigrants to Abyssinia. After Hazrat Khadija رضي الله عنها passed away, Hazrat Khowla bint Hakeem رضي الله عنها the wife of Hazrat Usman bin Madh'oon رضي الله عنه asked Rasulullah ﷺ whether he needed another wife. Rasulullah ﷺ told her that Hazrat Khadija رضي الله عنها always tended to the children and the house. Hazrat Khowla bint Hakeem realised from this that Rasulullah ﷺ certainly needed a wife to tend to these matters. She therefore set out to find a lady who was experienced enough to care for Rasulullah ﷺ's daughters and to manage domestic affairs. The lady she found was Hazrat Sauda bint Zam'ah رضي الله عنها.

Hazrat Sauda bint Zam'ah رضي الله عنها belonged to the Banu Najjaar tribe of Madinah and was married to Rasulullah ﷺ in Ramzaan, ten years after Rasulullah ﷺ announced his prophethood. When Rasulullah ﷺ performed Hajj during the 10th year after Hijrah, he sent Hazrat Sauda bint Zam'ah رضي الله عنها ahead of the others from Muzdalifa because she had difficulty manoeuvring through the crowds on account of her size.

## Forfeiting her Turn for the pleasure of her Husband

A person may take his own right and simultaneously fulfil the rights of others without infringing on theirs. On the other hand, a person may also surrender all or part of his right to others. This is referred to as preferring others above oneself, an act which Hazrat Sauda bint Zam'ah ﷺ displayed when she gave over her turn to be with Rasulullah ﷺ to Hazrat A'isha ﷺ.

**Note:** Every woman who is a co-wife should bear in mind that she will receive from her husband only that which is predestined for her. Similarly, what was not destined for her shall never reach her irrespective of the number of co-wives she shares her husband with. She will receive whatever she is receiving even if she were the only wife. Of course, if the husband behaves unjustly towards the wife, he will be answerable to Allah. The *Ahadith* have mentioned severe warnings against displaying partiality towards one's wives.

Hazrat Sauda bint Zam'ah ﷺ awarded her turn to Hazrat A'isha ﷺ because she understood that Rasulullah ﷺ had great love for Hazrat A'isha ﷺ. She therefore pleased her husband and became worthy of the glad tidings of *Jannah* that are promised for the woman whose husband is pleased with her.

## Sincerely Obeying the Husband

After performing the Farewell *Hajj*, Rasulullah ﷺ instructed his wives saying, "Stay within your homes after my demise." Hazrat Sauda bint Zam'ah رضي الله عنها took this instruction to heart and never performed *Hajj* again even though she had the means. She said, "I have performed both *Hajj* and *Umrah*. I am now staying at home in conformance with the instruction of Rasulullah ﷺ."

[Tabaqaat Ibn Sa'd Vol. 8 Pg. 37]

Although *Hajj* and *Umrah* are great acts of *Ibaadah*, Hazrat Sauda bint Zam'ah رضي الله عنها opted not to perform them because they entailed leaving the home. The condition of women today is indeed a far cry from that of the women during the time of Rasulullah ﷺ. Nowadays, let alone not obeying the husband who prevents his wife from something virtuous (like *Hajj* or *Umrah*), many women do not even obey their husbands who tell them not to carry out acts that are sinful.

When the husband issues an instruction to his wife, she will earn the reward of *Ibaadah* by obeying his instruction. By obeying his instructions she will therefore earn the rewards earned for *Sadaqah* or for *Tahajjud Salaah*. In fact, her reward will be even greater because avoiding a *Haraam* act (such as disobedience) is a sign that one's *Imãn* is sincere (and this earns one the reward of carrying out a *Farz* act). When a woman keeps this in mind, it will be easy for her to obey any instruction that her husband issues.

If one's husband prevents one from carrying out any of one's permissible desires, one should make *Du'a* to Allah saying, "O Allah! You are the only One Who fulfils needs. Fulfil this desire of mine and make my husband the means of fulfilling it. Change his 'No' into 'Yes'. O the One in Whose control is the hearts of man! Nothing is difficult for you." When the subject arises and he is adamant about not allowing one, the matter should not be debated. It should be left to be until another time when he is in a good mood. The matter should then be discussed amicably. *Insha'allah,* Allah will certainly soften his heart and if your desire cannot be adequately realised, he will ensure that he pleases you in some other way.

The wife who adorns herself with the robe of obedience and who learns to obey every lawful instruction of her husband shall convert this mundane existence into a garden of *Jannah.* Such a wife makes her pauper husband a king without a throne or crown. Whether one believes this or not, experience will prove it beyond doubt.

If only women will understand this. When a man enters his shack on a sweltering day and finds his obedient wife smiling with him, he will feel such delight in his heart which even air-conditioning and ice-cream cannot provide. In fact, even all the riches of a monarch cannot provide such inner delight. Every difficulty will be considerably eased for such a husband and nothing will be too much for him to handle. Everything will have flavour for the husband as well as for the children. Their simple food will be delicious, their simple home will provide the comforts of a palace and they will enjoy contentment without possessing the visible means.

The first quality of a good wife that Rasulullah ﷺ mentioned is that she is obedient to her husband when he instructs her to do something. May Allah make all women obedient to their husbands so that these men can have *Jannah* in both worlds. *Aameen*

## Generosity

It was not the general habit of women during the early days of Islãm to collect money because they were always conscious of the fact that the things of this world are temporary. Hazrat Umar رضي الله عنه once sent a bag to Hazrat Sauda bint Zam'ah رضي الله عنها. When it was brought to her, she asked the carrier what was in it. When he told her that the bag was full of *Dirhams*, she remarked, "Are *Dirhams* sent in bags like dates?" She then distributed all the money to the needy. Hazrat Sauda bint Zam'ah رضي الله عنها used to treat skins from Taa'if, sell them and use the profits generously in good cause.

[*Isaabah* Vol. 8 Pg. 918]

When one has great concern for the *Aakhirah*, one will find it easy to spend in good causes because one realises that what is amassed and remains in the cupboard will be of no benefit to one and will be left behind for someone else. One then knows that whatever is being spent in Allah's way shall certainly be rewarded in the Hereafter and will please Allah tremendously.

## An Easy Way of Becoming Generous

At the outset, it is necessary for a woman to identify which items in the house belong to her and which items belong to her husband. Even the smallest and largest items in the house should accounted for. The *Shari'ah* requires this specification of ownership for every item to avoid disputes. Even if the husband brings four cups into the house, it should be made clear whether they are a gift to his wife or whether they belong to him.

Once this is done, the mate should clean her cupboards every month and single out all items that she does not need or which she uses very scarcely. Such items should immediately be given away to deserving people, especially deserving Muslims. One should also have the conviction that if one ever needs such an item in future, Allah will provide it after one performs two *Rakaats* of *Salaah.*

## The Testimony of a Co-Wife

Referring to her magnanimity, Hazrat A'isha رضي الله عنها mentioned, "Besides Sauda رضي الله عنها, there is no person in whose body I would prefer my soul to be instilled." It is a tremendous accolade to a woman when her co-wife praises her. May Allah instil the qualities of Hazrat Sauda bint Zam'ah رضي الله عنها in every Muslim woman. Aameen.

## Her Demise

Hazrat Sauda bint Zam'ah رضي الله عنها passed away during the closing years of Hazrat Umar رضي الله عنه's *Khilaafah.* This was in the 32nd year after *Hijrah.* The wives of Rasulullah ﷺ once asked him which of them would pass away first. Rasulullah ﷺ replied, "The first of you to meet me shall be the one with the longest arms." Taking the literal meaning of the statement, they started measuring the length of their arms and found that the arms of Hazrat Sauda bint Zam'ah رضي الله عنها were the longest. However, when Hazrat Zainab bint Jahash رضي الله عنها was the first to pass away after Rasulullah ﷺ, they realised that Rasulullah ﷺ was referring to the wife who was the most generous.

**May Allah abundantly reward every Muslim sister who reads this book and encourages others to do the same.**

# Hazrat Zainab رضي الله عنها bint Muhammad ﷺ

## A Loyal Wife

Fifteen centuries have passed since the personality of Hazrat Zainab رضي الله عنها bint Muhammad ﷺ graced the earth with her presence. However, her name is echoed even today because of her sincere *Imãn* and her loyalty and love for her husband. She is an example of self-sacrifice to every Muslim woman until *Qiyaamah*.

Hazrat Zainab رضي الله عنها was the eldest daughter of Rasulullah ﷺ. She was born ten years before Rasulullah ﷺ announced his prophethood when he was thirty years old. When she was married to her cousin (mother's sister's son) Abul Aas, her mother gave her a valuable necklace to take with her.

The couple lived happily together. When the light of *Islãm* lit the earth darkened by *Kufr*, she accepted the religion brought by her father ﷺ. However, her husband did not accept Islãm then. She exhorted him to accept, but he refused to do so. She then told him that despite her profound love for him, she could not live with him if he did not accept Islãm. She made it clear to him that although it would be a painful separation, she would tolerate this rather than live with him when he would not accept the oneness of Allah.

## Separation from her Husband

Addressing her husband, Hazrat Zainab رضي الله عنها said, "Think awhile. I am not lawful for you. Either hand me over to my father or accept Islãm with me. Zainab is not yours after this day unless you believe in what Zainab believes."

Although the *Sahabiyaat*[1] had great love for the husbands, they did not compromise on their Islamic beliefs. Remaining staunch Muslims, their love for their husbands made them try their best to make their husbands Muslims. It was because of this love and concern that Allah reunited these couples once again.

When Hazrat Zainab رضي الله عنها's husband Hazrat Abul Aas رضي الله عنه was captured by the Muslims during the Battle of Badr and a delegation left for Madinah to ransom the captives, Hazrat Zainab رضي الله عنها sent her cherished necklace with them to free her husband. Not only was she fulfilling the rights of the love she had for her husband, but she also realised that a man becomes the slave of someone who does him a favour. This favour was to become the means of her migrating to Madinah and meeting her beloved father ﷺ. When Rasulullah ﷺ saw the necklace that once belonged

1. the word *Sahabiyaat* is the plural of the word *Sahabiyyah,* referring to Muslim women who saw Rasulullah ﷺ and who passed away as Muslims.

to Hazrat Khadija ﷺ, he consulted the *Sahabah* ﷺ and they decided that the necklace should be sent back to Hazrat Zainab ﷺ and that Hazrat Abul Aas ﷺ should be set free on condition that he sent Hazrat Zainab ﷺ to Madinah.

Upon his return to Makkah, Hazrat Abul Aas ﷺ told Hazrat Zainab ﷺ that she was to return to her father. Although Hazrat Abul Aas ﷺ had not accepted Islãm by then, Hazrat Zainab ﷺ had already instilled the love of Islãm in his heart. Consequently, Hazrat Abul Aas ﷺ told his brother Kinaana to accompany Hazrat Zainab ﷺ out of Makkah where Hazrat Zaid bin Haaritha ﷺ and a few other Muslims were waiting to escort her to Madinah. He could not accompany her personally because he was unable to bear the separation. He said to his brother, "I do not wish any other woman of the Quraish to be in exchange for Zainab. I cannot bear to be parted from her." He also instructed his brother not to allow anyone to approach her even if he had to use all his arrows in her defence. However, because of resistance from the Quraish, Hazrat Zainab ﷺ was unable to leave Makkah that day. It was only at night that she was handed over to the Muslim escort and proceeded with them to Madinah.

## Loyalty to her Husband

While Hazrat Zainab ﷺ was living in Madinah, a Muslim contingent under the leadership of Hazrat Zaid bin Haaritha ﷺ attacked a Makkan caravan at a place called Ees and captured the *Mushrikeen* manning the caravan.

Among these captives was Hazrat Abul Aas ﷺ. Upon reaching Madinah, Hazrat Abul Aas ﷺ requested Hazrat Zainab ﷺ to grant him amnesty. Still loyal to him, she acceded to his request and announced to all the Muslims that they could not harm Hazrat Abul Aas ﷺ because he was now under her protection. Rasulullah ﷺ sanctioned her amnesty and advised her saying, "Beloved daughter! Look after your guest but do not have any relations with him because you are not lawful for him as long as he is still a *Mushrik.*"

Out of respect for Rasulullah ﷺ and Hazrat Zainab ﷺ, the *Sahabah* ﷺ returned the captured wealth to Hazrat Abul Aas ﷺ and prepared to send him back to Makkah. During this time, someone told him that if he accepted Islãm, he could remain in Makkah and keep all the wealth of the caravan which belonged to the Makkans. In response to this, Hazrat Abul Aas ﷺ replied, "It would be a bad start to my Islãm if I were to betray a trust."

He then left for Makkah and after returning all the goods of the caravan to their respective owners, he announced, "O gathering of the Quraish! Is the wealth of any person still with me?" "No," they responded, "may Allah reward you abundantly. We have found you to be one who delivers the trusts given to him and one who is honourable." He then declared, "I testify that there is none worthy of worship but Allah and I testify that Muhammad ﷺ is Allah's bondsman and messenger. The only factor that prevented me from accepting Islãm in Madinah was the thought that you would say that I accepted Islãm so that I could usurp your wealth. I now declare my *Imãn* after Allah has allowed me to return your trusts." He then returned to Madinah where his marriage to Hazrat Zainab رضي الله عنها was renewed and the couple were reunited. However, Hazrat Zainab رضي الله عنها was preparing to leave this world by then and she passed away a short while after being reunited. Nevertheless, Allah made her realise her dream of seeing her husband accepted Islãm and thus being rescued from eternal damnation in *Jahannam*.

When she passed away in the 8th year after Hijrah, Hazrat Ummu Ayman رضي الله عنها, Hazrat Sauda رضي الله عنها, Hazrat Ummu Salma رضي الله عنها and Hazrat Ummu Atiyya رضي الله عنها bathed her body under direction from Rasulullah ﷺ. Rasulullah ﷺ performed the Janaazah salaah and placed the body in the grave. Rasulullah ﷺ was extremely grieved upon her demise.

["*Tabaqaat Ibn Sa'd*" Vol. 8 Pg. 24, *Bukhari* Vol. 1, Pg. 167, Muslims Vol. 1, Pg. 324 and "*Asadul Ghaaba*" Vol. 5 Pg. 468]

**Note:** If women inculcate certain important qualities in their lives, they will be able to convert their homes to gardens of *Jannah*. These qualities are clearly displayed in the life of Hazrat Zainab رضي الله عنها. The first is that the wife should be deeply in love with her husband. It is obvious that Hazrat Zainab رضي الله عنها possessed such love because, to free her husband, she was prepared to part with her expensive necklace which her mother had given her as a legacy, and which was handed down from generation to generation. After undergoing hardships and separation because of her husband's refusal to accept

Islãm, she immediately accepted his request for amnesty.

It was because of her excellent qualities that Hazrat Abul Aas ﷺ said to his brother Kinaana, "I do not wish any other woman of the Quraish to be in exchange for Zainab. I cannot bear to be parted from her." However, Hazrat Abul Aas ﷺ had to send Hazrat Zainab ﷺ to Madinah because he had promised Rasulullah ﷺ that he would and the Arabs (though *Mushrikeen*) always honoured their word. May Allah grant every Muslim the quality of keeping promises. Aameen.

## Testimony of the Husband

The status of a loving wife is at its height when her husband testifies that there is none as good as she and if he has to search for a wife with her sterling qualities, he will be unable to find someone. The life of Hazrat Zainab ﷺ is an example for all women to follow. Her excellent behaviour towards her *Mushrik* husband is exemplary and won him over to Islãm.

Many Muslim women swayed the sword of love on their husbands to convert them to Islãm. This sword proved effective even against men who had sworn that were prepared to commit suicide rather than accept Islãm. This incident of Hazrat Zainab ﷺ teaches the wives of the world how to love their husbands and to sacrifice everything for them. A wife should be content with what her husband provides and she should not complain when she does not have something. At the same time, every wife needs to be concerned that her husband should be saved from *Jahannam.* She should therefore encourage him to carry out good deeds and to refrain from sin. At the same time, she should ensure that she does not become the cause for her husband or her children suffering any loss in the Hereafter.

The *Sahabah* once expressed the desire to know which type of wealth was best. Rasulullah told them that the best wealth was a tongue that engages in Allah 's *Zikr*, a heart that is grateful and a Muslim wife who assists her husband in his faith. This *Hadith* makes it clear that money, property and businesses are not the real wealth of this world. True wealth is a tongue that engages in Allah 's *Zikr*, a heart that is grateful and a Muslim wife who assists her husband in his faith.

Therefore, together with making an effort to reform herself inwardly and outwardly, a Muslim wife also has the responsibility of rejuvenating her husband's *Imãn.* Her daily effort should be to deepen the roots of his conviction in Allah so that he becomes totally convinced that Allah is All Knowing and Capable of doing whatever He pleases. She should also send him to gatherings where his *Imãn* is refreshed and where he is reminded about death and the Hereafter. Where possible, she should also attend such gatherings when attendance does not violate any laws of the *Shari'ah.* She should consolidate the conviction that everything happens by the will of Allah. Even is a glass breaks or some other greater disaster takes place, she should immediately say:

{Translation: To Allah do we belong and to Him shall we return. O Allah ! Reward me in my calamity and grant me something better."}

One should reflect on the meaning of this *Du'a* and explain it to one's husband and children to console them.

A good wife should remind her husband about his five daily salaahs, fasting and reciting the Qur'ãn daily. She should explain the virtues of these and other acts of *Ibaadah* and encourage him with wisdom and love. By encouraging her husband and children to fulfil their duties to the *Deen* and to practise the *Sunnahs* of Rasulullah ﷺ, she will be doing them all a great favour.

She should also stipulate a time during the day to gather and recite *Deeni* books to them. Excellent books for this purpose are "*Fadhaa'ile A'maal*", "*Fadhaa'ile Sadaqaat*" and "*Bahisti Zewar*".[1] Such a woman receives the *Du'as* of Rasulullah ﷺ. People usually request pious people and saints for their *Du'as* whenever they have the opportunity and regard this to be a source of great fortune. One cannot imagine the fortune of a person who receives the *Du'as* of the greatest of all saints and pious people, Rasulullah ﷺ. Rasulullah ﷺ made the following *Du'a*, "May Allah shower His mercy on the woman who wakes up for *Tahajjud*, performs her *Salaah* and wakes her husband up as well. If he does not wake up, she lovingly sprinkles some water on his face." A man who marries someone who performs

1. All these books have been translated into English and are easily available from good Islãmic book store, i.e., **Idara Ishaa't-E-Diniyat**

*Tahajjud* and wakes him up as well should certainly regard himself as a king even though he has no throne or crown.

## Love for the Husband

A couple can truly enjoy happiness in their marriage when they are compatible. Without this, their lives would become miserable and bland. Irrespective of a woman's education and beauty, she will never really be the true beloved of her husband if she is not obedient to him. The most effective manner of harnessing the husband's sincere love is to obey him and serve him with love and devotion.

Homes in which the wives sincerely love their husbands and obey them are not tainted by quarrels and friction. On the other hand, life becomes hell in the homes of women who disobey their husbands and who have a terse reply for everything he says. Such homes are speedily deprived of blessings and good. One should always remember that love for his wife is the elixir which adds happiness to a husband's life. It ensures that his health remains sound, that his youth is perpetuated and that his *Imãn* is fortified. Even though Hazrat Adam عليه السلام had every bounty he could imagine in *Jannah*, his heart was still not content until Allah created Hazrat Hawwa to be Hazrat Adam عليه السلام's wife.

When the Qur'ãn[1] states that women have been created so that man "may find solace with her", it refers to every conceivable thing that provides comfort such as peace, contentment, cure from anxiety, cure from physical illnesses

1. Surah 30, verse 21.

and a boost to one's *Imãn*. It is only with a good wife that a person experiences true pleasure in everything he does. Therefore, Rasulullah ﷺ said, "There is nothing better for two lovers than marriage."

Every husband looks for love in the heart of his wife and searches every act and gesture of hers to detect the love she has for him. When he finds this, he will be comforted. A wife should therefore put on a smiling face whenever she meets her husband. If he upsets her in any way, she should exercise patience and continue speaking sweetly because he finds comfort in her words. When deprived of this, he will wilt away and fade.

Every wife should understand that her affection is sufficient to dissolve her husband's fatigue and dispel his every difficulty. This is what her husband wants from her. When the wife is a devout Muslim, the husband becomes pleased. He wants her to display excellent character so that his children can have a good upbringing. He wants her to have a friendly disposition so that the couple can earn the *Du'as* of his parents and family. He wants her to treat the wives of his friends and neighbours well so that he can enjoy a respectable position among them. He wants her to be content with what he provides for her so that he does not have to tire himself earning more and more. He wants her to maintain a high standard of personal hygiene and to dress smartly so that he may protect his eyes from gazing at other women. He wants her to keep herself beautiful to safeguard his chastity. He wants her to conceal herself from strange men so that he can have faith in her.

He wants her to wear the earrings of obedience. He wants her to apply the henna of thriftiness to her hands so that his wealth is not wasted. He wants her to wear the necklace of trustworthiness so that he can trust her in his absence.

The wife who inculcates all these good qualities in her life will be everything to her husband. All she as to do besides this is to be concerned about how she will face Allah on the Day of *Qiyaamah* and make an effort to spread *Deen* among her family and among other women.

Wise men always maintain that the most unfortunate person is he who feels unfortunate with his wife and children. On the other hand, the most fortunate man is he who feels fortunate and happy with his wife and children. May Allah make every person as fortunate as this.

## Women who make Men old before their Time

Rasulullah ﷺ used to make the following *Du'a*, "O Allah ! I seek Your protection from a wife who makes me old before my time." May Allah safeguard every woman from qualities that make her destroy the youth of her husband, and may Allah save every man from such a wife. My grandfather Haaji Ayyoob used to say that when the lunch and supper of a family burns, it causes instant difficulty and hunger for the entire family for that day. However, when a wife is ill tempered and disobedient, the family is put through a lifetime of difficulty, bordering on the brink of destruction.

Haafiz Yusuf who is a friend of mine often speaks about his friend Habeeb who used to tell his wife to get married after his death. When asked why he told her this, he would say, "So that the other husband should know why Habeeb died so soon."

A humorous tale is related about a person whose lips were black. When asked the reason for this, he said, "My wife left for Lahore today. I was so happy when she left that I kissed the coaches of the train that carried her."

Her sons and daughter-in-law were having an argument when an old lady heard the sound of breaking glass. Hurrying downstairs to see what had happened, the old lady saw that the pieces of an expensive vase were scattered about. "Who broke this antique?" she said in disbelief. "Your daughter-in-law," replied her son. "Nonsense!" blurted his wife. "It hit the wall and broke only because he moved when I threw it at him."

After divorcing his wife, a poet wrote:

"Umamah left with a divorce and I have been delivered from a suffocating yoke

Neither does my heart grieve with her parting, nor do my eyes tear

It (divorce) was the only cure (for her insolence), a cure that no one really wants to use because of its instant results

Life is not life for a couple with incompatibility on the prowl

Were she not separated like this, I would have
had relief only by running off somewhere."

[Translated from an Arabic poem]

A poor Arab poet was distraught because his wife constantly nagged, insulted him, quarrelled with him and never behaved cordially with him. Neither did she bother to keep herself tidy, nor was she particular about her *Salaah*. In fact, she did everything that displeased Allah. This led him to write:

"Get away! Stay far away from me! May Allah
save the men of the universe from you
In my knowledge, your life has been an evil life
(because you have displeased Allah and people)
Your death shall certainly give joy to every good
person."

[Translated from an Arabic poem]

A person approached a renowned poet in Delhi and requested that the poet teach him the art of poetry. The poet said, "Poetry cannot be taught. A person says poetry when in ecstasy. When he is afflicted by a calamity or overcome by intense love, poetical words flow from his lips and he becomes a poet."

It is perhaps the calamity of a terrible wife that prompts many men to become poets. An Arab poet whose wife was causing him untold grief once wrote:

"I am desperately awaiting her death
but I fear that an evil companion lives very long
How I wish that she leaves soon for her grave

Where she should be punished by *Munkar* and *Nakeer*." [Translated from an Arabic poem]

A bad wife has often been described in classical works as a yoke which Allah casts on the necks of whoever He pleases.

## The Good Influence that a Pious Mother has on her Daughter

It is hardly surprising that Hazrat Zainab رضي الله عنها was so loyal and compassionate towards her husband because her mother Hazrat Khadija رضي الله عنها was the same. Because daughters learn from their mothers, our saintly predecessors always advise people that when they are looking for a girl for the son, they should investigate the relationship between the girl's parents. They should enquire about the conduct of the girl's mother from her relatives because behaviour of the mother almost always rubs off on the daughter.

Our pious predecessors have emphasised that girls should always be taught to speak softly, even when they are young. Whenever a young girl speaks loudly, the mother should affectionately place her hand on the child's head and explain to her that girls ought to speak softly.

The result of being raised by a pious mother we see in *Umamah* the daughter of Hazrat Zainab رضي الله عنها who grew up with the excellent qualities of her mother and grandmother. By being a good wife, a woman not only teaches her daughters to be good wives, but she also raises many generations of good wives in her granddaughters and great granddaughters. Not only will her husband and sons-in-law remember her fondly in their *Du'as*, but so too will men of many generations who marry her descendants. Even as a *Mushrik*, Hazrat Abul Aas ﷺ used to say on his journeys to Shaam, "May Allah abundantly reward the daughter of Ameen ﷺ on behalf of every husband who comes to know of her."

If a woman does not take heed, the opposite will take place. If a woman behaves insolently with her husband, is ungrateful and does not honour him as she should, the ill effects of her behaviour will certainly rub off onto her daughters, grand daughters and great grand daughters. She can then expect no good *Du'as* to reach her.

We make *Du'a* to Allah to cast the graceful shadow of Hazrat Zainab ﷺ on all our daughters and that Allah shower her with His mercy. May Allah also fill our hearts with sincere love for our husbands.

We shall now discuss the life of Rasulullah ﷺ's second daughter Hazrat Ruqaiyya ﷺ.

**When someone asked Hazrat Ali ﷺ about what marriage really is, he replied:**

1) Luzoom-ul-Mahar (fixing a dowry).
2) Suroorsh-Shahar (rejoicing for a month).
3) Ghumoom-ud-Dahar (perpetual grief).
4) Kusooru-dh-Dhahar (breaking one's back).
5) Nuzool-ul-Qabar (laying one in his grave).

# Hazrat Ruqaiyya رضي الله عنها bint Muhammad ﷺ

## The Wife of Hazrat Usman رضي الله عنه

Hazrat Ruqaiyya رضي الله عنها was the second daughter of Rasulullah ﷺ and the third daughter of Hazrat Khadija رضي الله عنها. She had an only son by the name of Abdullaah and made *Hijrah* with Hazrat Usman رضي الله عنه to the distant land of Abyssinia, leaving behind her hearth and home for the protection of her *Deen*. She set a sterling example to the women of the world, teaching them love for their *Deen* and devotion to their husbands.

Hazrat Ruqaiyya رضي الله عنها was first married to Utba who was the son of Abu Lahab. However, she had not yet started living with her husband when Abu Lahab instructed his son to divorce her because Rasulullah ﷺ had announced his prophethood. She was then married to Hazrat Usman رضي الله عنه. Five years after Nabuwwah (i.e. after Rasulullah ﷺ announced his prophethood), Hazrat Usman رضي الله عنه and Hazrat Ruqaiyya رضي الله عنها migrated to Abyssinia. For a long while afterwards, Rasulullah ﷺ received no news from his daughter until a woman of the Quraish informed him that the couple were well. Rasulullah ﷺ said:

{Translation: "May Allah be their companion."}

This is a *Du'a* that every parent should make for their children, especially for those children who are travelling. Rasulullah ﷺ then remarked, "Usman is the first person since Loot عليه السلام to migrate with his family." When Hazrat Ruqaiyya رضي الله عنها returned to Makkah, her beloved mother رضي الله عنها had already left this world, a shock that she had to endure with patience.

## The Second Migration

The time soon arrived when all the Muslims were commanded to migrate to Madinah because the Muslims now had a place of their own where they could consolidate and use as a base to spread Islãm. From here they were able to send people throughout the world to carry the message of Islãm to mankind so that they could be saved from the fire of *Jahannam*. Here they could practise Islãm in peace and extend invitations to Islãm to people near and far. As for those *Kuffaar* who refused to accept Islãm, they were not forced to do so and merely had to pay a small tax called "*Jizya*" so that they could continue living in the Muslim state. By living with the Muslims, they were given the opportunity to be first-hand witnesses to the lives and practices of the Muslims. This attracted them to Islãm and encouraged them to become Muslims.

Madinah had become a centre for the propagation of Islãm and a place where new Muslims could learn Islãm and have the opportunity to practise it before transmitting the message to others. The *Hijrah* (migration) to Madinah was extremely difficult for the Muslims because it meant leaving their homes, their properties, their kith and kin and everything that had sentimental value. The trial was immense. Notwithstanding all of this, Hazrat Ruqaiyya ﵂ had made *Hijrah* to Abyssinia and then again to Madinah so that this *Deen* of Islãm could be preserved and become a means of saving mankind from *Jahannam*. Every Muslim during those times had the burning desire in their hearts that every Arab, every non-Arab, every Jew, every Christian, every Hindu, every fire-worshipper, every black and every white should be saved from *Jahannam*.

When Hazrat Usman ﵁ and Hazrat Ruqaiyya ﵂ reached Madinah, they stayed at the home of Hazrat Aws bin Thaabit ﵁. They now had the opportunity to recover from the fatigue of long travels and to settle down. The duty of Rasulullah ﷺ was close to realisation. However, Allah had decided that it was time to call Hazrat Ruqaiyya ﵂ back from this world so that He may confer on her the great rewards she deserved after the suffering she endured for Islãm, for living in a foreign land for the sake of Islãm, for separating from her beloved mother, for suffering the pain of divorce for Islãm and for everything she did to please Allah.

## The Demise of Hazrat Ruqaiyya ﵂

Hazrat Ruqaiyya ﵂ left to meet Allah during the 2nd year after Hijrah when Rasulullah ﷺ had left for the Battle of Badr. She fell seriously ill before the Battle and

Rasulullah ﷺ instructed Hazrat Usman رضي الله عنه to stay behind to tend to her. At the precise moment when Hazrat Zaid bin Haaritha رضي الله عنه announced in Madinah that the Muslims were victorious at Badr, this jewel of Rasulullah ﷺ's eye left the world. This was not a journey like the one to Abyssinia from where she returned. She left on the journey from which none has ever returned.

Because Rasulullah ﷺ had been at Badr, he was not present for the burial, but when he returned to Madinah, he visited her grave. No pen can express the grief of a father who lost his daughter. Her two sisters wept at her departure and her little son Abdullaah was without his mother. She may have dreamt of seeing her little son grow up into a young boy full of life and then into a strong man like his grandfather ﷺ. However, these dreams ended when she had to respond to the call of death. She had let this world just when the time had arrived to settle and find happiness in Madinah, when the Muslims were gaining a strong foothold and were getting poised to conquer not only Makkah, but the entire Arabian peninsula and territories beyond.

May Allah bless her with peace and His mercy on behalf of every Muslim present today and every Muslim to come until the Day of Qiyaamah. May Allah bless our women with her noble and pure qualities. *Aameen*

# Hazrat Ummu Hakeem bintul Haarith رضي الله عنها

## Sacrifice

Together with being a woman of great courage and making tremendous sacrifices for *Deen*, Hazrat Ummu Hakeem رضي الله عنها had great love for her husband. Before accepting Islãm, she fought along side her husband in the Battle of Uhud against the Muslims. When the Muslims conquered Makkah, the understanding of Islãm that she had by then developed made her accept Islãm very quickly. However, her husband, who was the son of the notorious Abu Jahal, refused to accept Islãm and fled to Yemen.

## Concern for her Husband

Like a true loyal and loving wife, she sought amnesty from Rasulullah ﷺ on behalf of her husband. The magnanimous Rasulullah ﷺ accepted her request and like he had given amnesty to people who were his sworn enemies, he did the same for her husband. Armed with love for her husband and the intense determination to save him from *Jahannam*, Hazrat Ummu Hakeem رضي الله عنها searched for him until she found him in Yemen. She called for him just as he was about to board a ship and leave the Arabian shores. Addressing him with great love and compassion, she called out, "O my uncle's son!" This address was sufficient to harness his attention because people readily respond to family members.

She said to him, "I have come to you from one who is most particular about maintaining good family ties, one who treats people most kindly and one who is the best of people. Do not destroy yourself. Accept Islãm and come with me. I have sought amnesty from Rasulullah ﷺ on your behalf and he has granted it." "Did you really do this?" he asked. When she confirmed that she had, he accepted Islãm and returned to Makkah. Thereafter, he proved to be a great warrior of Islãm and fought fiercely in all the consequent battles, laying his life down for the *Deen* each time. During the Khilaafah of Hazrat Abu Bakr t, Hazrat Ummu Hakeem رضي الله عنها and her husband Hazrat Ikrama رضي الله عنه left to fight at Yarmook, a place bordering Syria. It was there that her husband was martyred and entered into the mercy of Allah.

## Her Second Marriage

After completing her *Iddah* (waiting period after her husband's death), Hazrat Ummu Hakeem رضي الله عنها married Hazrat Khaalid bin Sa'eed رضي الله عنه in an area of Damascus called Marjus Safar. As her husband prepared to make the customary marriage arrangements, she said to him, "The Romans may attack at any time so why don't we spend some time together." Hazrat Khaalid bin Sa'eed رضي الله عنه agreed and told her that he was sure that he was going to be martyred in the battle against the Romans. The couple therefore met in a tent near a bridge, which is still referred to as the bridge of Ummu Hakeem رضي الله عنها.

As he had anticipated, her husband was martyred in the battle. Being the niece of Islãm's great warrior Hazrat Khaalid bin Waleed رضي الله عنه (her mother was his sister), she stood up to fight against the *Kuffaar*. She took a tent peg in her hand and single-handedly killed seven *Kuffaar* soldiers.

Hazrat Sheikh Zakariyya (A.R) writes: "Let alone the women of our times, even the men would not be prepared to get married under such circumstances. Even if a woman married at such a time, she would have mourned for a very long time after her husband's death. Notwithstanding the loss of her husband, this pious servant of Allah participated in the *Jihaad* herself and even killed seven enemy soldiers."

## It is the Responsibility of the Wife to Make her Husband Lead a Pious Life

Hakeemul Ummah Maulana Ashraf Ali Thanwi (A.R) has mentioned[1] that one of the greatest failings of women in respect of the rights they owe to their husbands is that they make no effort to save them from *Jahannam.* They do not care whether their husbands are earning *Halaal* or *Haraam* wealth to sustain their lavish lifestyles. If the husband is engaged in earning *Haraam*, the wife should advise him to desist and to fulfil all the obligations due

1. *"Tuhfa Zaujain", Page 58.*

from him to others. In the same way, she should advise him to fulfil all his obligations to Allahf he is negligent of this. It is regrettable that a woman will do everything to convince her husband to do something when there is benefit in it for her. However, she is negligent of convincing him to fulfil his obligations towards Islãm, which is her *Deen* as well.

It is not at all difficult for a woman to make her husband religious. However, it is necessary for her to be religious as well. When she is a practical Muslim who is particular about her religious obligations, *Insha'allah* her words will soon take effect. A good wife and mother should not send her husband and sons out to work without explaining that earning a living is not the reason and objective of their creation. She should therefore encourage them to give some time for *Deen* and to spend some time in the Masjid. She should also encourage them to assist those serving the *Deen*, to visit their relatives, to visit the sick, to recite *Surah Yaaseen* daily and to engage in efforts to ensure that every person in the community becomes a good Muslim who practises the *Sunnah*.

She should emphasise that it is not befitting of a Muslim to spend all his valuable time in mundane pursuits. She should tell them that no prophet will come after Rasulullah ﷺ, so it is the responsibility of every Muslim male and female to save mankind from *Jahannam* as the *Ambiya* (*Alaihimus Salãm*) did. The effort of a Muslim should be directed at eliminating *Kufr* from the world and making every person someone who does everything to please Allah only. Of course, some time will have to be spent for this.

One should also say these things to one's visitors so that they may also be encouraged to practise and propagate *Deen*.

Just as the men and women *Sahabah* ﷺ made sacrifices for this *Deen* to be elevated, every male and female Muslim living today should also make some sacrifices. Every Muslim wife should apply herself to the task of reviving the spirit of Islãm within her home and within her community and she should continue making *Du'a* to Allah for this objective to be realised. She should also make *Du'a* to Allah to grant her the ability to sustain such efforts and to forgive her for her shortcomings in this regard.

## Making her Husband a Muslim through Marriage

Hazrat Anas ﷺ narrates that his mother Ummu Saleem ﷺ had received a marriage proposal from Hazrat Abu Talha ﷺ before he accepted Islãm. She said to him, "Abu Talha, do you realise that you are worshipping a tree that grows from the ground?" When he admitted that he did realise this, she said, "Are you not ashamed at worshipping a tree. If you accept Islãm, I shall not ask you for a dowry to marry me." He then took leave to think about the matter. He returned later and declared, "I testify that there is none worthy of worship but Allah and I testify that Muhammad ﷺ is Allah 's messenger." Hazrat Ummu Sulaym ﷺ then asked her son Hazrat Anas ﷺ to perform the *Nikaah* (marriage) and the two were married.

## An Example of a Woman Changing her Husband for the Better

A important lesson that we learnt from the story of Hazrat Ummu Hakeem ﷺ is that after she converted to Islãm she greatly exerted herself to convince her husband to accept Islãm as well. She was therefore responsible for saving him from *Jahannam* and allowing him to enter *Jannah.* Being a courageous woman herself, she encouraged him to fight in *Jihaad* until he met with martyrdom and earned the highest positions in the Hereafter. The same occurred with her second husband. Allah therefore granted Hazrat Ummu Hakeem ﷺ the honour of being the wife of two martyrs. Her life was a great lesson to all Muslim women until *Qiyaamah.*

There are many women whose husbands may be Muslims but are neglecting their duties to Islãm or may be committing sins. Because of this behaviour they may be taking themselves to *Jahannam.* It is therefore the duty of the wife to guide him towards righteousness. For achieving this aim, she should first win his love and confidence by obeying his instructions and not back-chatting. She should then make *Du'a* to Allah saying, "O Allah ! Make my husband/son/brother pious men who are particular about their *Salaah* and who stay away from sin. Give them the love for good deeds and make them warriors and preachers of *Deen* who will water the flourishing garden of Rasulullah ﷺ. Grace them with martyrdom as they strive to propagate your *Deen* to the far corners of the world. Remove the handcuffs of cowardice from their hands and the yoke of fear from their necks. Extract from their hearts the notion of living eternally in this world. Make their hearts and minds evergreen with love for you and your Rasul ﷺ. Make it easy for them to sacrifice for your *Deen* and give their lives for it." *Aameen*

After adopting piety yourself, winning his love and making sincere *Du'a* to Allah, start encouraging him towards righteousness with love and respect. Turn him away from evils such as interest, cheating and lying in business, selling stolen goods, denying creditors their money and giving and accepting bribes. Keep reminding him in an appropriate manner, keep sending him to good environments and cry to Allah *Du'a* at night so that Allah may guide him.

If the son of Abu Jahal could be convinced by his wife to accept Islãm, there is no reason why the heart of a Muslim husband, brother or son cannot be changed to practise the injunctions of the *Shari'ah.* If a woman sincerely cries to Allah for guidance, lovingly gives encouragement and despite being treated shabbily, she treats kindly, she will Insha Allah be able to effect a positive change.

At a time when there were no cars or trains, Hazrat Ummu Hakeem رضي الله عنها crossed the mountains of Makkah and travelled hundreds of miles over rocky terrain in the scorching desert heat to reach her husband in Yemen. From there she still travelled with him all the way back to Makkah.

In addition to fulfilling the rights of her husband, Hazrat Ummu Hakeem رضي الله عنها also fulfilled the rights of Islãm by assisting in *Jihaad* so that Islãm could spread throughout the world. She understood that the responsibility of Muslim women is not confined to her home. When the need arose for her to leave hearth and home to make *Hijrah* (migrate) to Shaam for the sake of Islãm, she did not hesitate to accompany her husband. In the same way, Hazrat Ruqaiyya made Hijrah to Abyssinia, Hazrat Khansa made *Hijrah* to Iraq with her sons and Hazrat Ummu Haraam made *Hijrah* to Cyprus where she passed away and was buried. Like these, there were many other *Sahabiyaat* who made *Hijrah* with their husbands or with other family members to distant parts of the world, where they passed away.

Their graves in these foreign lands address women to come until *Qiyaamah*, telling them that they made *Hijrah* for Allah's pleasure to these lands, enduring the hardships of journey and resettling. Eventually, when Allah called for them to surrender their souls, they did so while still striving to elevate the *Kalimah* of Islãm. Muslim women of today are also encouraged to create the spirit of Islãm within their hearts and to apply themselves to the propagation of Islãm. They should apply their minds, bodies, wealth and zest to the propagation of Islãm so that it reaches every home in the world. This enthusiasm should be passed on to the entire family and imbued in the hearts of every mother and daughter.

## There is no Harm for a Widow to Remarry

An important lesson that we glean from the story of Hazrat Ummu Hakeem is that instead of mourning for years after her husband's death, a woman should continue serving the *Deen* as soon as her *Iddah* expires. Because Nikaah is a command of Allah, she should not be ashamed of remarrying if the opportunity arises. Rasulullah ﷺ has mentioned that when a suitable person of good character and piety proposes for a woman, her family should get her married. If they do not, there will be a calamity and widespread anarchy on earth.

The books of history cite the incidents of many Sahabiyaat رضي الله عنهن who married after being widowed, thereby setting an example for all women until *Qiyaamah.* Hazrat Aatika bint Amar bin Nufayl Adawiyya رضي الله عنها was first married to Abdullaah, the son of Hazrat Abu Bakr رضي الله عنه. When he was martyred at Taa'if, she was extremely grieved and said, "I swear that grief shall never part from my eyes nor will dust leave my body." Later on, she married Hazrat Zaid bin Khattaab رضي الله عنه, who was martyred at Yamaamah. She then married Hazrat Umar رضي الله عنه, who was also martyred as he led the *Fajr Salaah.* She recited the following words of poetry when Hazrat Umar رضي الله عنه passed away:

**"Generously pour your tears forth, O eyes**

And do not tire from weeping over the chosen leader

The sudden death of the skilled horseman has shocked me

On a day of war and revenge

Announce to the poor and dejected

'You all may as well die' because death has claimed the soul of he who assisted the poor and who was a friend to the dejected."

After the demise of Hazrat Umar رضي الله عنه, she was married to Hazrat Zubayr bin Awaam رضي الله عنه. When he was also martyred, Hazrat Ali رضي الله عنه proposed for her hand in marriage. However, she declined the offer saying, "I cannot be so generous with your life (i.e. it should not be that you are also martyred)." It has been narrated that her first husband gave her some wealth on condition that she does not remarry. However, Hazrat Umar رضي الله عنه told her that such a bequest was not permissible because nobody can forbid something that is *Halaal.* He advised her to give the money to her late husband's heirs and then to get married.

("*Al-Isaabah*" Vol. 4 Pg. 357)

This incident makes it clear that a husband's bequest for his wife not to remarry is not permissible. In fact, if she fears falling into sin by remaining single, it is compulsory for her not to abide by the bequest.

Besides Hazrat Aatika رضي الله عنها, there were many other *Sahabiyaat* رضي الله عنهن who remarried after their husbands passed away or after being divorced from their husbands. Hazrat Asma bint Umays رضي الله عنها was first married to Hazrat Ja'far رضي الله عنه. When he was martyred in the Battle of Mauta, she married Hazrat Abu Bakr رضي الله عنه and then Hazrat Ali رضي الله عنه when Hazrat Abu Bakr رضي الله عنه passed away. ("*Al-Isaabah*" Vol. 4 Pg. 231)

Hazrat Ummu Kulthoom رضي الله عنها was first married to Hazrat Zaid bin Haaritha رضي الله عنه. When he was martyred in the Battle of Mauta, she married Hazrat Zubayr bin Awaam رضي الله عنه and then Hazrat Abdur Rahmaan bin Awf رضي الله عنه after Hazrat Zubayr رضي الله عنه divorced her. When Hazrat Abdur Rahmaan bin Awf رضي الله عنه passed away, she married Hazrat Amar bin Al Aas رضي الله عنه. ("*Al-Isaabah*" Vol. 4 Pg. 491)

Marrying widows and divorcees was not looked down upon during the time of Rasulullah ﷺ. Neither did the widowed or divorced women look down on remarrying, nor did the men who married them. It is common knowledge that besides Hazrat A'isha رضي الله عنها, all Rasulullah ﷺ's wives were widows and divorcee. If this practice were common today, there would be no brothels and such dens of vice. Women would have someone to take care of them and their children if they ever lost their husbands. At the same time, if a wife is unable to satisfy her husband on reasonable grounds, he will not have to resort to illicit means of satisfying himself because his other wife/wives will surely be able to satisfy him. In this manner the chastity of men and women will be safeguarded and there would not be the flood of illegitimate children we see today. This will effectively purge our communities of the many physical and spiritual diseases that are so common. Men and women alike will be saved from sin and immoral behaviour and widows and orphans will not be left destitute. According to Allah's promise, there will then be abundant blessings in sustenance.

When such an environment is created, women will not even find it difficult to allow their husbands to take other wives. There will bring great joy in everyone's lives when men fulfil the rights of all their wives and provide equally for all. The situation will be even more blessed when men do this with the intention of assisting widows, divorcees and orphans. Such are the teachings of the *Shari'ah* and the practice of Allah's chosen servants. It is a cure for social ills, a shield against sin and a guarantee for success in both worlds. Likewise, it will also eliminate poverty and open the doors to prosperity.

## A Woman without a Husband is a Pauper

Men and women should always bear in mind that Rasulullah ﷺ said, "A man without a wife is a pauper." "Even if he is wealthy?" asked the *Sahabah* ﷺ. Rasulullah ﷺ replied, "He is a pauper even though he is wealthy." Rasulullah ﷺ then added, "A woman without a husband is a pauper." "Even if she is wealthy?" asked the *Sahabah* ﷺ. Rasulullah ﷺ replied, "She is a pauper even though she is wealthy." (*Jam'ul Fawaa'id*, Vol. 1 Pg. 216)

Rasulullah ﷺ once asked Hazrat Ukaaf bin Bishr Tameemi ﷺ whether he was married. When he replied in the negative, Rasulullah ﷺ asked him whether he owned a slave woman. When he again replied in the negative, Rasulullah ﷺ said to him, "If you have not married despite having the ability and the wealth to marry, you must be one of *Shaitaan's* brothers." (*Jam'ul Fawaa'id*)

When a man or woman is ready for marriage, the *Shari'ah* of Islãm does not approve of their decision to remain single. The *Shari'ah* has laid tremendous emphasis on marriage so that many evils and sin should not take place at all. Marriage seals the avenues to immorality, fornication and a range of other evils that have devastating consequences. Rasulullah ﷺ once mentioned, "I also marry. Whoever is averse to my practices is not from me." In saying this, Rasulullah ﷺ has warned Muslims that they should not regard themselves as one of his followers if they choose to remain single. Rasulullah ﷺ has also described such people as *Shaitaan's* brothers i.e. *Shaitaan's* assistants in spreading evil and corruption.

Together with emphasising the importance of marriage to safeguard people's chastity, Allah has also promised poor people that He shall grant them wealth if they marry. Allah says:

> **"Marry those from you who are unmarried and those slave men and women who are righteous. If they are poor then Allah will make each of them wealthy by His grace. Allah is of ample means, All Knowing."**
>
> (*Surah Noor*, verse 32)

It is therefore incorrect to stay single because even if one does not possess enough wealth, Allah shall grant one the wealth when one marries. Hazrat Abdullaah bin Mas'ood رضي الله عنه has mentioned, "Even if I had only ten days of life left, I would prefer getting married instead of being single."

Both wives of Hazrat Mu'aadh bin Jabal رضي الله عنه passed away in a plague and he was also afflicted by it. Despite this, he told his friends to get him married because he did not want to meet Allah as an unmarried person. (*Sharh Ihyaa*)

After his first wife passed away, Hazrat Maulana Fadhlul Rahmaan (A.R) remarried when he was over a hundred years old. He was then suffering from fistulas because of a disease that had afflicted him. The diligent wife used to tend to him and regularly clean his wounds as no other person would. Hazrat Haaji Imdaadullaah (A.R) also married a second wife towards the end of his life. This conscientious wife served him as well as his first wife who had become blind.

## Marriage brings Wealth and Averts Poverty

Hazrat Abdullaah bin Mas'ood رضي الله عنه reports that Rasulullah ﷺ said, "Seek wealth through marriage."

Hazrat A'isha رضي الله عنها narrated that Rasulullah ﷺ said, "Get married because women will be a source of wealth for you." This means that a wife will bring blessings in one's earnings. There were many incidents during the time of Rasulullah ﷺ when poor people were blessed with wealth after marrying. In fact, Rasulullah ﷺ would encourage poor people to marry so that they could be self-sufficient. Rasulullah ﷺ told a *Sahabi* رضي الله عنه to get married when all he possessed was an iron ring. Rasulullah ﷺ married another *Sahabi* رضي الله عنه who had no possessions and stipulated that the dowry should be that he teaches his wife what portion of the Qur'ãn he knew. Rasulullah ﷺ permitted another person to get married when all he possessed was the upper and lower garments that he wore. Another *Sahabi* رضي الله عنه could afford to give his wife when they married was a pair shoes. In fact, Rasulullah ﷺ also permitted another person to get married when all he had to give his wife was some dates and a barley drink. Refer to the chapters of dowry in *Ahadith* books like "*Mishkaat*", "*Bukhari*" and "*Muslim*" for more details. These are being omitted in the interest of brevity. One may also refer to the Urdu booklet titled "*Islãm ka Nizaame Ismat aw Iffat*" written by Hazrat Maulana Burhanud-Din Sambhali.

The purpose of stating the above is to inform all Muslim widows and divorcees that they should try to get married as soon as their *Iddah* expires. Other women should assist them in this and none should prevent their husbands from marrying other women especially when they intend marrying widows, divorcees or women who were unable to get married for valid reasons. When a man is capable of marrying other wives in strict conformance with the *Shari'ah* and with the intention of assisting them, his wife becomes an obstacle instead of assisting him. This indicates that his wife has no compassion for other distressed women.

Islãm lays emphasis on marriage so that the chastity of Muslim societies may be protected, so that modesty may prevail and so that children are conceived legitimately. In this manner, the world would be free from immorality and promiscuity.

## Why is it Necessary for a Widow to Remarry?

In his book "*Mukhzin Akhlaaq*", Hazrat Maulana Subhaani (A.R) recounts the incident of a women from Azeemabaad who was widowed at an early age. She spend her entire days and nights reciting the Qur'ãn and also fasted every day. She used to break her fast every day with dry bread or leftover wheat grains. She continued this practice until her old age. Because of her extreme piety, hundreds of women became her devotees. Before she passed away, she called for her devotees and asked them, "How do you think I lived a life of chastity and abstinence?" The women expressed their surprise that anyone could have led such a morally upright life without even seeing the face of a man and subsisting on dry bread and some wheat or barley. She then said to them, "Listen to the condition of my heart. From my young days until I became old, I often heard the voice of the night watchman as I recited Qur'ãn and I always thought of how I may reach him. However, fear for Allah and fear for being disgraced always stopped me. I implore you to never allow a young widow to remain single."

This incident makes it clear that regardless of a woman's piety and abstinent lifestyle, instinctive passions will always prey on her. The same applies to men. When such instincts seize hold of a person, even the animals are not safe from him/her. When their sons or daughters grow up, people usually busy themselves saving money for extravagant trousseaus and weddings receptions. Together with this, they also make elaborate preparations for useless customary practices like "*Mehndi*" nights etc. These are all futile and wasteful and not required by the *Shari'ah*. All the *Shari'ah* requires for marriage is that the man pays dowry to his wife. This dowry is a small amount which any man can afford and which does not necessarily have to paid immediately on marriage. If the bride agrees, payment can be deferred to a later time. It is therefore imperative that a woman should be married as soon as she finds a suitable partner. If a man can fulfil the rights of multiple wives, his first wife should not be an obstacle.

## An Incident of a Saint

It has been related that a saint lost his wife. While someone was assisting him to make *Wuzu* towards the end of his life, he cried out in a pain-filled voice, "O Allah! Only You are excellent Alone." Despite being a great poet, *Aalim* and philosopher, he also felt that his life was empty without his wife. One's husband or wife is the valuable factor that gives substance and worth to one's life, without whom life will be lustreless and without spirit. The person who lives without a spouse opposes man's nature and this nature shall soon exact revenge from him.

> *"Looking at a beautiful wife pleases only the eyes, but looking at a pious wife gives pleasure to the heart."*

# Khowla bint Maalik bin Tha'laba ﷺ

Hazrat Khowla bint Maalik ﷺ was an extremely eloquent and well-spoken person. Her story is being related to teach all Muslim women what to do when they have problems with their husbands. She has mentioned, "By Allah ! The opening verses of *Surah Mujaadala* (*Surah* 58) were revealed concerning myself and my husband Hazrat Aws bin Saamit ﷺ." When he grew old, he became irritable. One day, when he became angry with her, he blurted out the words, "You are like the back of my mother to me."[1] When he made advances to her, she exclaimed, "Never! By the Being in whose control is my life, you shall never approach me!" She therefore forbade him from engaging in any relationship with her until they clarified the matter with Rasulullah ﷺ. As hard as he tried to get her to submit to his advances, she fought him off and he was left helpless.

1. This statement was commonly used by the Arabs to divorce their wives and it is referred to as Dhihaar. When Hazrat Aws bin Saamit ﷺ used the words on this occasion, it was the first time that a Muslim had done so. Consequently, the opening verses of *Surah Mujaadalah* were revealed to clarify the issue.

She then went to Rasulullah ﷺ and presented her case thus, "O Rasulullah ﷺ! My husband has consumed my youth and I have given birth to his children. I have served him all my life and now that I am an old woman and my children have left me, he has carried out *Zihaar* with me. If my small children are left with me, they would probably die of starvation and if they are left with my husband, they would be destroyed." As she was saying this, she raised her eyes to the heavens saying, "O Allah! I plead my case before You. Reveal a command to Your Nabi ﷺ so that my difficulty is alleviated."

Allah then revealed the opening verses of *Surah Mujaadalah*[1] saying,

> "Allah had certainly heard the speech of the lady who debated with you concerning her husband and who complained to Allah. Allah was listening to your discussion. Verily Allah is All Hearing, All Seeing." (*Surah* 58, verses 1)

Rasulullah ﷺ then addressed Hazrat Khowla رضي الله عنها saying, "O Khowla! Your cousin (husband) has grown old, so fear Allah with regard to him (i.e. exercise patience with him)." When the verses pertaining to *Dhihaar* were revealed, Rasulullah ﷺ told Hazrat Khowla رضي الله عنها to inform her husband that he would have to free a slave in expiation of his act (of *Dhihaar*). When she told Rasulullah ﷺ that he was unable to do this, Rasulullah ﷺ said that he will then have to fast

1. *Ma'aarif-ul-Qur'ān*, vol. 8, Page 331)

for two consecutive months. When she submitted that he was unable to do this also, Rasulullah ﷺ mentioned that he should then feed two meals to sixty poor people. When she informed Rasulullah ﷺ that her husband would not be able to afford this either, Rasulullah ﷺ offered to assist by supplying some dates. Hazrat Khowla رضي الله عنها then said that she would also supply some dates to assist her husband. Thereupon, Rasulullah ﷺ said, "You have done well. Go and act charitably towards him and treat him kindly."

Hazrat Khowla رضي الله عنها was such a distinguished woman in Islamic history that Allah responded to her plea and the Ummah will remember her as long as the Qur'ãn is recited. Hazrat Umar رضي الله عنه was once riding his donkey when an old lady stopped him to say something. When Hazrat Umar رضي الله عنه stopped, the people asked him why he stopped for a frail old woman. Hazrat Umar رضي الله عنه said to them, "Don't you know who this old lady is? She is Khowla bint Tha'laba. Allah listened to her from above the seven heavens. How can Umar not listen to her when Allah did."

The story of Hazrat Khowla رضي الله عنها displays the perfect confidence that a Muslim should have in Allah. Allah will always provide the solution for every problem because He brings ease after every difficulty. Everything comes from Him. Allah says in the Qur'ãn,

> "It is certainly Him (Allah) Who makes (people) laugh and cry. It is only He Who gives death and life. Verily He grants affluence and poverty."

Allah creates every favourable condition just as he creates every unfavourable condition. He makes people happy just as He can make them sad. He gives wealth to whoever He pleases and takes wealth from whoever He pleases.

There is therefore no need for anyone to be despondent. When faced by any difficulty, all that one needs to do is to perform *Wuzu*, perform two *Rakaahs* salaah with concentration and then plead to Allah. One should supplicate to Allah by saying what Hazrat Khowla ﵂ said. She said, "O Allah! I complain only to You. O Allah! I plead my case to you. O Allah! My home is deserted and my children are distressed. Reveal a command to Your Nabi ﷺ so that my difficulty is alleviated."

Allah says in the Qur'ãn ,

> "O you who believe! Seek help by means of patience and *Salaah*. Verily Allah is with the patient ones." (*Surah Baqarah*, verse 153)

It is therefore necessary for every woman to plead to Allah for the solutions to all her domestic problems. Allah is the Only One who can solve one's problems. Whenever a woman is faced with a serious problem, she should seek counsel from a reliable person so that it may be addressed. This is necessary because when certain problems are pent up, they cause one's mental and physical health to deteriorate. Although Allah is the One who solves all problems, Allah has instructed us to consult with others. Even Rasulullah ﷺ consulted with the Sahabah ﵃. When

Rasulullah ﷺ received the first revelation, he did not keep the anxiety to himself and bottle it up within himself. Instead, he told Hazrat Khadija رضي الله عنها about it and together with consoling him, she took him to her cousin Waraqa bin Naufal who was learned in the previous scriptures. In this manner, Rasulullah ﷺ's found comfort and reassurance.

If a woman's husband is extremely short-tempered, she should recite "*Bismillaahir Rahmaan nir Raheem*" seven times and blow on his food or drink. When blowing, tiny droplets of sputum should also be allowed to fall into the food/drink. Mulla Ali Qaari (A.R) has expressly mentioned this in is commentary of "*Mishkaat*". The same prescription can be used for one's children and mother-in-law if they are short-tempered. If this is done diligently, Insha Allah the results will be visible after forty days. Tempers will be cooled and love will be generated between the members of the family. Such are the blessings of Allah's pure names.

## Being Patient with an Aged Husband

The incident of Hazrat Khowla رضي الله عنها also teaches us that when one's husband becomes irritable and difficult as he becomes old, one should exercise patience even though he may sometimes become intolerable. When Hazrat Khowla رضي الله عنها complained of this to Rasulullah ﷺ, he advised her saying, "O Khowla! Your cousin (husband) has grown old, so fear Allah with regard to him (i.e. exercise patience with him)." This means that a woman should be even more patient when her husband ages and will therefore receive greater rewards.

When a person is young and healthy, everyone is prepared to be with him. However, when he grows old and becomes sickly and temperamental, people stay far from him because they will have to offer some services. At this stage, it will be only a good wife who will stay loyal to her husband. Only a good wife will agree with everything her husband says at this stage and who will fulfil his every wish before he expresses it. It is only such a dedicated wife who will refrain from anything he dislikes and who will take the blame for anything that he finds unpleasant.

If she becomes frustrated with his behaviour, she should think that Allah readily forgives when people fail to fulfil the rights they owe to Him. Similarly, she should also forgive him. If she does this, the spiritual benefit she will receive shall be tremendous and so too will be the rewards she will receive.

## What Should the Wife do When her Husband is at Fault?

Hakeemul Ummah Maulana Ashraf Ali Thanwi (A.R) tells women that if they also become angry when their husbands do, it means that they regard themselves equal to or better than men. This is so because a person usually gets angry with someone lower in status. One never gets angry with someone higher in rank. A woman should therefore not backchat when her husband is angry. If the husband is angry for no good reason, she should remain silent and explain his folly to him when he has calmed down. She should then kindly tell him that he ought to listen to her side to the story before drawing conclusions. This approach will prompt the man to show regard for his wife because he will realise that she is sensible and intelligent. He will then appreciate her much more and respect her.

("*Wa'z Huqooqul Bayt*" Pg. 51)

## The Failing of Husband and Wife and a Word of Caution to Both

When Hazrat Khowla رضي الله عنها became angry just as her husband had become, he uttered the words of *Dhihaar*, which they both regretted. Fortunately, all he had to do to have her back as his wife was to pay the *Kaffaara* (expiation), after which their marriage was restored to normal. However, there are many instances when a woman does not keep quiet and is not prepared to admit her mistake. She rants and raves incessantly until the husband resorts to violence or he divorces her. This tragedy can be easily averted if the wife says that the mistake was hers and that she will not repeat it (even if the mistake is his). However, many women tend to prolong the argument to prove their point until the husband does something regrettable.

The consequences of the husband's reaction are not confined to the couple, but affect the families of both. The ill effects of this permeate the fabric of both families and are even felt by the children and grandchildren of the couple. People then have the opportunity to fabricate tales and publicise them, thereby bringing disgrace to the families involved. People will then be heard saying that a certain person's daughter could not run a home or that someone's mother is a divorcee, causing hurt to the person.

Therefore, Hazrat Maulana Thanwi (A.R) has written that it is unfortunate that many women fail to understand the temperament of their husbands and speak out of turn when his mood is not at its best. If one party keeps silent, the argument will end. However, instead of stifling the argument, they give it more impetus by prolonging it, eventually leading to a divorce. Both end up regretting the consequences, which affects not only the couple, but their entire families.

("*Aadaab Insaaniyat*" Pg. 213 and "*Tuhfa Zowjayn*" Pg. 181)

There are also many foolish women who become widows by daring their husbands to divorce them. Divorce should never be mentioned. It should be borne in mind that divorce will be effective whether it is said in jest or in anger. It is like pulling the trigger of a loaded gun. When the bullet kills someone, claiming that the gun was fired in jest or in anger will not bring the person back to life. Losing one's temper is not a valid excuse. Every person should learn to control his temper using the methods that the *Shari'ah* has prescribed.

We will now quote two cases where matters would have not reached where they did if the husband and wife had exercised more caution. Correspondence of this nature reaches the *Daarul Ifta*[1] daily. May Allah save us and all

---

1. A faculty of a *Daar-ul-Uloom* (Islamic University) staffed by Muftis who respond to queries from the public.

Muslims from the evils of *Shaitaan* and the *Nafs*, which plague family life with bitterness, enmity, animosity, ridicule and disgrace. We will present these cases in the form of a dialogue for easier understanding. A common fault of women is highlighted in these cases, which seems insignificant but which brings destruction to everyone belonging to their families. A plea is made to all women to avoid the behaviour displayed in these incidents. Among these are the evil traits of justifying a wrong, using fire to fight fire and refusing to admit one's mistake.

## The First Incident

Tired after returning from working long in the sun, the husband rings the bell of his home. Still busy in the bathroom, the wife takes some time before opening. When she eventually, lets him in, he is irritated and bangs the door closed. The ensuing argument is as follows:

**Husband:** I've been ringing the bell for the past half hour. Don't you care that I have been standing in the heat for so long?

**Wife:** Couldn't you wait for two minutes? I was in the bathroom and heard the doorbell only now. Besides, you don't even know how to close a door quietly!

**Husband:** You know very well that I return at this time yet you decide that it's necessary to have a bath now!

Wife: You have no idea how much work I have! The children have not given me a moment's rest the entire day. Now you return to make my life a bigger misery. Do my work for a day and you will know what it's like?

**Husband:** I cannot live with you! Go to your mother's!

The Second Incident

The husband asks for some tea. The wife serves the tea, unmindful of the many tea leaves that have remained behind after straining.

**Husband:** Don't you know how to make tea, or do I have to teach you?

**Wife:** What's the matter?

**Husband:** Look at how many tea leaves have remained behind in the cup!

**Wife:** Can't you even take this much? Make the tea yourself and you will come to know! It is very easy for you to give orders. I have to look after you, care for the children, cook the food and do everything in this house!

**Husband:** Is that how you speak to me? Get out of my house!

Hearing the commotion, the neighbours gathered and in their presence, the husband said things that he wished he had never spoken. The couple were then separated never to be reunited.

You decide. If either the husband or the wife in either situation had remained silent at the outburst of the other, they would have remained husband and wife. If you are a husband, you should take heed not to behave as the men in the above incidents did. If you are a wife, you should beware not to do what the wives in these incidents did. May Allah save all couples from kindling the fires of disunity. The flames of discord in a home destroy one's devotion to *Deen* as well as one's performance in one's worldly affairs.

**Ruling:** Ulama have mentioned that after ringing the bell or knocking at the door, the husband should wait for as long as it takes his wife to perform four *Rakaahs* of *Salaah* and come to the door. Thereafter, he should ring the second and the third time. The etiquette of seeking permission to enter a room or a house have been discussed in my book "*Islãm Aur Tarbiyyat-e-Awlaad*", which examines the upbringing of children in Islãm. It was thought appropriate to quote the excerpt from that book here for the benefit of our readers.

## THE ETIQUETTE OF ENTERING A HOME

### First Greet with Salaam and then ask Permission to Enter

Imam Abu Dawood (A.R) has narrated that a person from the Banu Aamir tribe came to meet Rasulullah ﷺ while Rasulullah ﷺ was at home. When he arrived at the door, he called out, "May I enter?" Rasulullah ﷺ said to his attendant, "Go and teach him the method of seeking permission for entry and tell him to say, '*As Salaamu*

*Alaykum*. May I enter?'" The person heard this and immediately said, "*As Salaamu Alaykum*. May I enter?" Rasulullah ﷺ then permitted him to enter.

## Identify Yourself when Requesting Permission to Enter

In the famous *Hadith* of Bukhari and Muslim concerning the *Mi'raaj*, Rasulullah ﷺ had mentioned that when he and Hazrat Jibra'eel عليه السلام approached the gates of the first heaven and requested permission to enter, the gatekeeper asked who it was. When Hazrat Jibra'eel عليه السلام identified himself, the gatekeeper asked who was with him. Hazrat Jibra'eel عليه السلام replied that Hazrat Muhammad ﷺ was with him. The gates were then opened for them. The same procedure took place at the gates of every heaven.

Another *Hadith* of Bukhari and Muslim is related from Hazrat Abu Moosa Ash'ari رضي الله عنه. He says that he once accompanied Rasulullah ﷺ to an orchard and acted as gatekeeper of the orchard. When Hazrat Abu Bakr رضي الله عنه arrived and knocked, Hazrat Abu Moosa رضي الله عنه asked who it was. He let Hazrat Abu Bakr رضي الله عنه in after he had identified himself. The same happened when Hazrat Umar رضي الله عنه and Hazrat Usman رضي الله عنه arrived shortly afterwards. They were all required to identify themselves before being allowed to enter.

Bukhari and Muslim have reported another *Hadith* in this regard from Hazrat Jaabir رضي الله عنه. He narrates that he once knocked on Rasulullah ﷺ's door. When Rasulullah ﷺ asked who it was, he replied, "It is me." Rasulullah ﷺ said, "What is 'It is me', 'It is me'?" Rasulullah ﷺ disliked this ambiguous reply. It is therefore necessary for a person to state who s/he is and who s/he wishes to meet.

## One Should Thrice Seek Permission to Enter

Hazrat Abu Moosa رضي الله عنه narrates that Rasulullah ﷺ said, "Permission to enter should be sought thrice. If permission is granted then all is fine. Otherwise, one should leave." It is preferable that the duration between each of the three knocks should be equal to the time that it takes a person to perform four *Rakaahs* of *Salaah* because the person in the house could be performing *Salaah* or answering the call of nature.

## Never Knock the Door too Loudly

One should be especially cautious about this when the person in the house is one's father, one's teacher or some other person to whom great respect ought to be shown. In his book "*Adabul Mufrid*", Imam Bukhari (A.R) narrates from Hazrat Anas رضي الله عنه that whenever he wished to enter the residence of Rasulullah ﷺ, he would knock with his fingers. It has also been reported that our pious predecessors used to knock on the doors of their elders using only the nails of their fingers. This displays the immense respect that they showed towards their seniors.

The above applies when the person in the house is near to the door. However, when he is far from the door, one should knock as loud as it is necessary for him to hear the knocking. When there is a doorbell to be rung, the visitor should ring it gently so that the people of the house may sense that the visitor is a gentle and cultured person.

## REDUCING ANGER

In her best interests and in the best interests of her children and family, the wife should immediately ask for forgiveness as soon as she notices her husband lose his temper even though she is not at fault. When he scolds her, she should neither reply to him nor remain absolutely silent because either option would make matters worse. She should rather admit that the fault was hers (even it was not) and then ask for forgiveness. Besides this, the following guidelines are valuable for reducing anger.

1. Teach the *Du'as* for entering the home to your husband and children and ensure that they recite these *Du'as* every time they enter. When entering they should recite, "*A'oodhu Billaahi Minash Shaitaanir Rajeem*", "*Bismillaahir Rahmaan nir Raheem*", *Surah Ikhlaas, Durood Shareef* and the following *Du'a*:

   {Translation: "O Allah! I ask you for the good of entering and the good of leaving. We enter with the name of Allah and we leave with the name of Allah and in Allah Alone do we trust."}

   (*Abu Dawood* Vol. 2 Pg. 339)

The family should also learn the meaning of this *Du'a* so that they may consciously ask Allah for what the *Du'a* entails. When the family enters the home after reciting "*A'oodhu Billaahi Minash Shaitaanir Rajeem*", no *Shaitaan* can enter the house to cause disputes and problems in the household.

Hazrat Jaabir ﵁ has narrated from Rasulullah ﷺ that when a person takes Allah's name at the time of entering his home and at the time of eating, Shaitaan says to his companions, "There is neither accommodation nor food for us here." On the other hand, when a person does not take Allah's name when entering his house, *Shaitaan* tells his companions, "You have found accommodation for the night." Thereafter, when he fails to take Allah's name before eating, *Shaitaan* tells his companions, "You have food for the night." (*Muslim, Abu Dawood* and *Ibn Majah*)

**Note:** To be able to remember Allah at all times and using the correct words, one should keep the following two books handy:

A) "*Masnoon Du'as*" by Mufti Aashiq Ilaahi (*Daamat Barakaatuh*)

B) Translation and commentary of "*Hisnul Haseen*", also by Mufti Aashiq Ilaahi (*Daamat Barakaatuh*)

One should learn the *Du'as* mentioned in these books and teach them to one's children. One should also keep with one a book with a collection of things to recite (referred to as Wazaa'if).

2. Another course of action to follow is that when one becomes extremely angry, one should recite, "*A'oodhu Billaahi Minash Shaitaanir Rajeem*" and

immediately drink water. If one's husband is also angry, he should also be given water to drink.

## The First Cure For Anger : Wuzu

The *Ahadith* mention that when one becomes angry while standing, one should sit down. If one is sitting, one should then lie down. When the couple are having an argument, each one should try to remind the other to either sit down, lie down, drink water or make *Wuzu*.

Anger is extremely destructive and can cause many physical ailments. In addition to this, it also causes enmity and hatred between people. One is tremendously rewarded for swallowing one's anger. On the other hand, if one's does not control one's anger, one will become a criminal instead of a reformer. It is therefore imperative that one maintains a balance of mind when anger begins to set in. This is important for every husband, mother and teacher.

The Qur'ãn teaches us that instead of doing something hastily without thought, one should ponder over one's course of action and plan a strategy that will be in the best interests of all involved. Therefore, the solution to a problem should be such that the wife/employee/student realises his/her mistake while the husband/employer/teacher is still filled with love and concern for them instead of resorting to anger and violence. In this manner, the problem will be solved without an ill feelings being created. In fact, after the problem is solved in this amicable manner, one's spouse and children will have even more love and respect for one than they had previously. This principle should always be kept in mind.

Any evil should always be repelled with something good and not with something equally evil. If this is done, the result will be that even an archenemy will become a bosom friend. This is the teaching of the Qur'ãn.

## The Second Cure

Rasulullah ﷺ said, "Whoever swallows his anger while in the position to vent it, Allah shall call him before the entire creation on the Day of *Qiyaamah* and permit him to choose whichever damsel of *Jannah* he pleases."

(*Tirmizi* Vol. 2 Pg. 22; *Abu Dawood* Vol. 2 Pg. 33)

Describing the true *Mu'min* in the Qur'ãn, Allah says that they are people "who pardon when they are angry."

(*Surah Shura, Surah* 42, verse 37)

In *Surah Al-e-Imraan* , Allah describes the pious and abstinent *Mu'mineen* when He says that they are

> "Those who spend in ease and adversity, swallow their anger and forgive people. Allah loves those who do good..." (*Surah* 3, verse 134)

Discussing this verse in his book *Fadhaa'il Sadaqaat*, Hazrat Sheik Muhammad Zakariyya (A.R) writes that swallowing one's anger and forgiving people are exceptionally noble qualities which are used to praise the *Mu'mineen*.

Ulama have mentioned that whenever a *Mu'min* errs, one should make excuses for the error and then explain to one's heart that it should not harbour ill feelings towards the person because s/he had so many excuses for the error. If one's heart still refuses to accept, one should censure one's heart for being so hard and unrelenting. One should tell oneself that a *Mu'min* ought to accept the excuse of another. Rasulullah ﷺ has mentioned that the person who does not accept his brother's excuse shall be very sinful.

According to another *Hadith*, the sip that Allah most loves is the sip that a person takes as he swallows his anger.

## The Third Cure

Imam Ahmad (A.R) has reported a *Hadith* in which Rasulullah ﷺ said, "When any of you becomes angry, he should remain silent." Therefore, when husband and wife start getting angry, the wife should remind her husband about this instruction of Rasulullah ﷺ and encourage him to abide by this instruction because one's success in this world and in the Hereafter shall be guaranteed when one follows the commands of Rasulullah ﷺ. She should admit her fault and tell him that it will not happen again. The couple should then engage in some other activity so that the matter is forgotten.

## The Fourth Cure

When the couple are about to start an argument, they should leave the place immediately. The wife may step awhile outdoors and the husband may go to the *Masjid*.

They may then perform *Salaah* or recite a bit of the Qur'ãn until their anger subsides.

Rasulullah ﷺ said, "Behold! Anger is a burning coal that ignites the heart of a person. Do you not see the dilation of the angry person's veins and the redness of his eyes? Whoever senses this happening to him should resort to the earth. He should resort to the earth i.e. he should lie down and think about his final abode in the grave."

## The Fifth Cure

A person who frequently gets angry should write the following sentence on a paper and hang it on where he will see it often. The sentence is:

> "Allah has more power over you than you have over others."

This will remind one that Allah has more power over one than one has over one's wife, children, employees, students and everyone who is one's subordinates. Despite this, Allah does not punish anyone more than the person deserves. A person shall be accountable for any injustice that he perpetrates in this world. Allah's at liberty to punish a person for this in this world as well as in the Hereafter.

Cowardly indeed is the person who becomes angry with someone weaker than himself, but when confronted by someone stronger than himself he manages to control his anger. By writing down the above sentence and keeping it in mind, one will be able to keep one's temper well under control.

## The Sixth Cure

Rasulullah ﷺ said, "When any of you becomes angry, he should sit and if his anger still persists, he should lie down." (*Abu Dawood* Vol. 2 Pg. 303)

After this prescription to brings one's anger under control, there is no need for another prescription. When standing, one is far from the ground. When sitting, one will be closer to the ground and when lying down, one will be closest to the ground. This proximity to the ground is effective in reducing anger because Allah has imbued the ground with the quality of humility. When sitting and lying down, this quality will rub off onto the angry person and reduce anger because humility is the converse of anger and pride.

Experience shows that when a person becomes angry, he is inclined to get himself into a position to grab or hit the object of anger. Therefore, if he is lying down, he will instinctively sit up or stand up. It follows therefore that by reversing the instinctive position of anger, it will be considerably reduced. ("*Tuhfa Zowjayn*" Pg. 162)

By employing these methods, one will be able to control one's anger. When this is achieved, one will no longer darken the happiness of others and one will no longer deprive oneself of the friendship of good friends. Families will not be wrecked and one will neither be responsible for extinguishing the candles of joy blazing in the hearts of others nor for silencing the nightingales singing songs of mirth in their bosoms.

Besides employing the above methods of reducing one's anger, one should also consult pious people. At the end of this book we will include the names, addresses and contact numbers of some eminent Ulama and Muftis whom one may consult. *Insha'allah,* one will receive the necessary guidance from them.

## THE DEADLY POISON OF BACKCHATING

Hakeemul Ummah Maulana Ashraf Ali Thanwi (A.R) writes that if women learn to control their tongues, they would be damsels of *Jannah* walking on earth. The tongue holds a sting more harmful than a scorpion. Even when her husband is holding a sensible discussion with her, she continues saying whatever pleases her just so that she may have her say. If merely speaking without relevance entailed constructive debate, the donkey would be the best debater.

("*Islaah Khawateen*" Pg. 183)

If women exercise patience and keep silent when their husbands scold them in anger, they will soon become like the pure damsels of *Jannah.* When their husbands gain control over themselves, they will feel ashamed of their behaviour and they will stop getting angry so often. If the wife backchats, the situation can get out of control and her husband may say or do something that both will regret.

("*Behisti Zewar*" Pg. 41)

Hakeemul Ummah Maulana Ashraf Ali Thanwi (A.R) is quoted as saying that a woman's acid tongue is the root of rot setting into marriages. He adds that if this evil trait can be removed from women, they will become damsels of *Jannah.* This is the advice of Hakeemul Ummah Maulana Ashraf Ali Thanwi (A.R) has written hundreds of books and who is regarded as the reformer of his century and a great Imaam. He possessed a thorough understanding of the Qur'ãn and the *Ahadith* and understood the psychology of women. If women practise what he advised, they will convert their homes into gardens of *Jannah*.

All women achieve by backchat is to make their husbands lose their feelings of sympathy and compassion. When a woman relentlessly harps on an issue and nags, her husband's heart becomes detached from her even though he is a good and caring person. No man can tolerate his wife's backchat. Therefore, she should never entertain the hope that he will swallow her insolence thinking it to be a drink of honey.

One of the best attributes that women possess is their ability to talk sweetly. Talking sweetly is a charm that can win over the hardest hearts. An adage is common in Urdu which states that a sweet tongue captures nations and can tie an elephant by a strand of hair. By speaking sweetly to her husband, a woman can make him forget all her faults. On the contrary, the husband of a woman who has every virtue will quickly forget all her virtues if she speaks insolently.

## BE CONCERNED ABOUT YOUR HUSBAND'S COMFORT

A wife should always be conscious about her husband's food, clothing, health, rest and amenities. His happiness should be hers and his grief should also be hers. It is therefore imperative that every wife acquaints herself with her husband's likes and dislikes. She should know exactly what pleases him and what does not. Her most vital task is fulfilling his instructions and seeing to his every need. Intelligent women win over their husbands by diligently serving their husbands. The husband will then be cognisant of her every desire and will do anything to please her. Life then becomes pleasurable for both.

Women who think that they can rule their husbands with their beauty are grossly mistaken. A man is slave to the wife who serves him and not to the wife who is only beautiful. After a tiring day at work, the sight of a dutiful wife is enough to make any man forget his fatigue.

## MAKE YOUR HUSBAND YOUR FRIEND

To lead a happy life, a woman has to make her husband her friend. Only one's spouse can be one's true friend. The couple's hearts cannot be united if the wife does not regard her husband as her friend. Once their hearts are united, love will grow between the couple and they will be comforted by each other.

### How to Make Your Husband your Friend

1. By convincing yourself that you have no friend truer than your husband.
2. Have complete trust in him.
3. Never lie to him and never hide anything from him.

4. Never interfere in his matters especially when he is away.
5. Make every effort to increase your respect for him. One of the methods of doing this is to praise him in front of others.
6. Assist him with mind, money and matter when he is in difficulty. Forget your personal needs during such times and do everything possible to give him relief. These are the occasions to win his love and trust.
7. Express happiness when he is happy and sadness when he is sad.
8. When he is worried about something, do everything in your power to relieve his worry and tell him things to make him happy.
9. Always be conscious of things that please him and things that upset him.
10. Be thrifty with the money he gives you and be content with it.
11. Never make unreasonable demands on him for things that are not necessary. Make do with whatever he gives.

## FACTORS THAT ATTRACT THE HUSBAND

Women should inculcate the following qualities in their lives to win their husbands over:

1. Refrain from all major and minor sins. If a sin is committed, repent immediately.

2. Treat him according to his disposition.
3. Keeping within the bounds of the *Shari'ah,* be the woman he wants you to be.
4. Always be patient and tolerant.
5. Speak sweetly and always wear a smiling face.
6. Beautify yourself for him without disregarding the constraints of the *Shari'ah.*

## A WIFE SHOULD NEVER LOOK DOWN ON HER HUSBAND

Irrespective of the husband's status in society, it is compulsory for his wife to obey his instructions. Just as a nation is constrained to obey its leader, a wife must also do the same. When good Muslims like the *Sahabah* رضي الله عنهم had to obey a tyrannical governor like Hajjaaj bin Yusuf, why should a woman not obey her husband? There is no doubt in the fact that husbands can neither be worse than Hajjaaj nor can wives be better than the *Sahabah* رضي الله عنهم.

The fact that the *Shari'ah* regards men to be senior in status than women is explicitly mentioned in the Qur'ãn and the *Ahadith.* When every woman has witnesses to attest to her marriage, why then should she not obey her husband? Of course, the husband cannot stop his wife from her *Farz* obligations and she may not obey him if he stops her from these. However, she is obliged to obey him if he orders her not to carry out any *Nafl* act of worship. The *Shari'ah* has attached so much importance to obeying the husband that if he instructs her to delay her *Salaah* when there is ample time to perform it in its proper time, she should obey him.

If a woman's husband instructs her to commit a sin, she is obliged not to obey him. If (Allah forbid!) he carries out an act of *Kufr* or says words of *Kufr*, she needs no *Fatwa* to decide that she should be immediately separated from him.

When a woman's husband tells her to leave aside her *Wazeefas* (optional daily recitation of the Qur'ãn or *Du'as*) to render him some service, she should do as he says. She should never think that her piety will be reduced if she forsakes these *Wazeefas*. On the contrary, her piety will be increased by serving him. Piety is acquired by fulfilling the injunctions of the *Shari'ah* and not by doing what one merely thinks is good. Obeying one's husband is a command of the *Shari'ah* and therefore putting aside one's optional acts of worship for the explicit command of the *Shari'ah* will definitely earn Allah's pleasure and augment one's piety.

("*Islaah Khawateen*")

**Note:** It often occurs that women are more academically educated than their husbands, either in religious education or in secular education. This gives her no reason to look down on him because she still owes him the high level of honour and respect that a husband deserves.

## DIAGNOSIS AND TREATMENT OF TWO EVIL TRAITS IN MANY WOMEN - THE FIRST EVIL TRAIT

An exceptionally evil trait that is common among women is that they never seem to forget the smallest excuses to refresh an argument. When the opportunity arises, they will recall little details and carry out laborious nitpicking exercises to prove their point. Although their argument may not be strong, they tend to prolong the matter indefinitely. There is scarcely a home that is free from this malady.

Almost every quarrel between mother and daughter, between mother-in-law and daughter-in-law and between sisters-in-law are a result of suspicion and unverified information. They hear stories about their in-laws from other women who spice up the details by adding hundreds of lies, misleading adjectives, adverbs and expressions. In her foolishness, the woman records all of this in her memory bank and, adding a host of other details to it, she concludes that the information is correct and that she well understands the intentions of every speaker mentioned in the stories.

A typical scenario is as follows: The housekeeper approaches the elder daughter-in-law living with her in-laws and says, "Dear, I must tell you about the rice you cooked today. Well, your sister-in-law (your husband's younger brother's wife) said that her husband was outraged about the food and said, 'Doesn't my brother's wife know how to make rice after all these years? She disgraced us in front of all the guests.' And that's not all..." She then proceeds to convey a series of other tales about the younger daughter-in-law, which the elder daughter-in-law believes without question.

Thereafter, adding some spice to the incident, the elder daughter-in-law relates the incident to the mother-in-law.

With a few tears added to it, the mother-in-law is convinced about the story. The mother-in-law then begins formulating schemes to "fix" the younger daughter-in-law because her mind has already called for witnesses from her past memories and it has already acted as judge to condemn the innocent lady. The housekeeper was sufficient as a prosecutor and the elder daughter-in-law was the plaintiff lodging the case. The case is then lodged before the younger sister-in-law who represents the High Court. The final judgement is then given by the elder sister-in-law.

When it is the younger daughter-in-law's turn to cook, fate has it that a little extra water fell into the rice or a little extra salt fell into the gravy. According to plan, the other women in the house launch their attack at the table.

> "Look at how you cook!" someone calls out.
> "You think that we are little girls!" another shouts.
> "And you dare to insult us!" commented a third.

Surprised at the outburst, the younger daughter-in-law denies that she said anything, adding that even her two recording angels knew nothing about it. When she asks to be informed about the source of the information, the others say, "We will not betray our informant. She is an extremely honest and pious woman who will never say anything she never heard." The fact that the housekeeper has worked for the family for many years is now suddenly used a mark of her piety whereas it has nothing to do with this. After this, insults and accusation are freely exchanged and the house becomes a battlefield where even parties remotely related have their names smeared.

The entire scene described above and so many other similar incidents are based entirely on hearsay and unconfirmed reports. It is best not to listen to gossip and if one does hear about a complaint about oneself, the truth of the matter has to be confirmed directly from the source. This is the prescribed method of handling such matters according to the *Shari'ah.* Whenever one has a complaint against another, the matter should be addressed to the person himself without revealing it to others. Once the sprouts of ill-feelings are allowed to take root in the heart, they swiftly develop into deep-rooted trees that cannot be uprooted without much difficulty and damage to the heart.

Therefore, if any one has a complaint against another someone, the matter should be resolved as quickly as possible and there should be no ill-feelings between the two. If the cause of the complaint is found to be unauthentic, then this will be clarified for life and unnecessary rancour will be eliminated. By clarifying matters, tale carriers will be exposed and they will stop their evil practice.

## An Interesting Incident

It has been narrated that a wolf was on the prowl one morning, searching for food to feed himself and his family. He happened to overhear a woman saying to her son, "If you do not learn your lessons, I shall feed your goats to a wolf." The wolf was ecstatic and waited there so that the goats could be fed to him. However, he waited until the evening without getting anything. That evening, he heard the mother saying, "Son, Mashaa Allah, you are a very good child. You must have learnt your lessons. Now if a wolf comes to eat your goats, we shall kill it." Hearing this, the wolf wasted no time to run away. When he returned to his family without food, his wife asked him what had happened. After relating the incident to her, he added, "This happened to me because I took the word of a woman."

("*Zahraat min Rowdhil Mar'atil Muslima*" Pg. 126)

This incident tells every Muslim male and female not to trust the word of any woman without verification. It is best to disregard what they say.

## A Du'a that Every Woman should Make

One should always bear in mind that malice is not merely a sin but it opens the doors to many other sin as well. It is form of sweetened anger. It gradually contaminates the entire heart as it fills every part of the heart with grief and unrest. Because it more commonly affects women, every woman should make the following *Du'a* after every *Salaah*:

{Translation: "**O our Rabb! Do not place in my heart any malice for the Mu'mineen. O our Rabb! Indeed You are the Most Forgiving, Most Merciful.**" } (*Surah Hashar*, Surah 59, verse 10)

If Allah purges one's heart from malice, it is an extremely great favour from Him. One should always wish the best for others and never wish evil to befall anyone. One should endeavour to conceal the faults of everyone else and to look for only their good qualities. The bounty of cleansing the heart from malice and animosity is such a great favour that it is counted as being among the bounties of *Jannah*. In *Surah Hijr*, Allah says about the people of *Jannah*,

> **"We shall remove any animosity that may be in their chests (before they enter *Jannah*). As brothers they will be seated on couches, facing each other."** (*Surah* 15, verse 47)

## The Second Evil Trait

Although this trait is also found in some men, it is especially common among women. The trait is that when an argument arises, they dig out past incidents which have already been resolved and forgiven. As a result, even though the incident at hand is trivial, the reminder of a past incident generates a fresh argument leading, to an extremely combustible situation. The situation becomes graver when the reminder is phrased insensitively - a skill of expression that many women have perfected to an art.

Therefore, women should try to forget such matters as soon as possible. Whenever someone brings any gossip to you, rebuke them and refuse to listen. Tell them that he are causing friction between Muslims and should stop visiting your home if they persist in carrying tales. At the same time, you should warn other women about such a tale-carrier so that they do not fall prey to her deception.

Hakeemul Ummah Maulana Ashraf Ali Thanwi (A.R) has mentioned that it is tragic that women nowadays actually wait for women to come from other towns so that they may ask them what other women are speaking. The embellished information that these women carry lay the foundation to suspicion and very soon, an entire building of malice and ill-feelings is constructed. The finishing touches to the building are added when the women begin using the telephone to spread the word around. The entire network of women then spice up the stories even further so that the house of mistrust and malice becomes properly furnished. Eventually, two Muslim homes are irreconcilably divided and Allah's wrath is directed against everyone concerned.

Remember! Causing disunity between two Muslims is a grave sin. When Rasulullah ﷺ was about to inform the Sahabah رضي الله عنهم about the date of "*Laylatul Qadr*", the ill effect of a dispute between two Muslims caused this knowledge to be lifted from the heart of Rasulullah ﷺ. Rasulullah ﷺ said on hat occasion, "I came to inform you about the exact night on which "*Laylatul Qadr*" will take place but the argument between such and such persons caused this information to be lifted from me. Perhaps this is better in Allah's knowledge."

*(Bukhari)*

Rasulullah ﷺ once said to the *Sahabah* رضي الله عنهم, "Should I not show you an act better than *Salaah*, fasting and *Sadaqa*?" When the *Sahabah* رضي الله عنهم requested to be informed, Rasulullah ﷺ said, "Maintaining good relations between yourselves is the best deed. Fighting between yourselves shaves off your *Deen* i.e. just as a razor instantly removes hair, in-fighting instantly removes *Deen* from people's lives."

Every woman should therefore take heed not to engage in gossip and not to listen to gossip. Nothing should be spoken about which is not necessary because one will suffer the penalty for gossiping in this world as well as in the Hereafter. The Qur'ãn explicitly condemns backbiting and entertaining evil thoughts of others.

("*Huququz Zowjayn*" Pg. 324; "*Islaah Khawateen*" Pg. 219)

## ANIMOSITY BETWEEN WOMEN CAUSES ANIMOSITY BETWEEN MEN

It often occurs that a woman complains to her husband about everything that his mother and sisters tell her in addition to the fights that the children of the family had with her children. She dramatises the situation and tells him that he should do something about it. Although the husband is tired and weary after a hard day at work, he suddenly becomes rejuvenated when hearing this because of the shallowness of his perception. In his rage, he may even hurt someone and cases have been reported where people were killed because of such insensitiveness. Eventually, the relationship between blood brothers is eternally severed all because of one woman.

Every woman should bear in mind that if she does not desist from causing dissention between two brothers and between mother and son, the time is not far off when someone like her may cause the same disunity between herself and her sons or between her sons. The adage is famous that states that one will be treated as one treats others. A famous Urdu saying states: "You will receive what you dish out. If you do not believe this, try it and find out. *Jannah* is a reality and *Jahannam* is also a reality. If you do not believe this, then die and find out."

## An Appeal to Men

Husbands are urged not to listen to such complaints of their wives. Affectionately place your hand on her mouth when she starts speaking about such things. When a woman can lie about something she sees, she can certainly do so concerning the things she hears from others. History testifies to the fact that women have deceived countless men who were reputed to be great intellectuals, professors and philosophers. A poet says:

"Akbar was not killed by any army of the enemy
Akbar was martyred by the pinch of a woman."
(Translated from an Urdu Poem)

It is therefore imperative that men do not listen to the complaints and charges that women level against other. If something of this sort is overheard, one should pay no heed to it. Instead, one should encourage one's wife to forgive by explaining the virtues of forgiveness. Explain to her that if she will exercise patience and tolerate the difficulties, Insha Allah her progeny will also be tolerant towards her. Make her understand that all the arguments boil down to petty squabbles that are not worth the fuss being made about them. Tell her that this world is a place of trials and difficulties which will all pass by. True peace and contentment is reserved for the *Aakhirah*, where the fruits of one's patience will be realised. The sign of a courageous person is that she/he tolerates the difficulties that others present without fussing about them.

If there have been problems among the children, explain to her that the family's children are all like your own. If any of your children are involved in a fight, it will be cruel for someone else to exact revenge from the child. The same should apply to all the children of the family. Just as one would explain to one's own children what is right, so too should one explain the right to one's nephews, nieces and other children of the family. Give them some sweets or chocolates and tell them what to do and what not to do. Recite "Bismillaahir Rahmaan nir Raheem" seven times and blow on their food or drink as explained earlier in this book. This is an extremely effective prescription to calm children who are aggressive and who frequently throw tantrums. One may also recite "Yaa Lateef" seven times, blow on some water and give the child to drink. When children misbehave, adults should not imitate their behaviour by becoming abusive and violent. Instead, one should adopt an attitude of understanding and ingenuity.

It is also necessary to explain to one's wife that if she is the eldest sister-in-law, she should show more concern and behave like a mother towards the other sisters-in-law. Just as a mother does not abandon her child for misbehaviour, she should also not severe ties with the others when they do something wrong. If your wife is a younger sister-in-law, tell her that she should regard the other sisters-in-law as her real sisters. Just as she would not consider the scolding of her real sister to be a sign of enmity, she should believe the same to be true in the case of her elder sisters-in-law. Not only Islãm, but all religions teach their followers to respect elders. Therefore, when one's elders treat one shabbily, the best recourse is to exercise patience and continue living together with love. In this manner, Allah will give respect to one and grant one obedient children.

A husband should advise his wife in this manner instead of becoming angry with everyone else. Hakeemul Ummah Maulana Ashraf Ali Thanwi (A.R) said, "In my opinion, husbands should tell their wives that even though they may be truthful in their reports about others, they (the husbands) will not believe them. Of course, I am not saying that all husbands are like this (i.e. spineless and affected by whatever their wives tell them). There are many husbands who behave like real men by using their intelligence when such situations arise." ("*Tuhfa Zowjayn*" Pg. 82)

A husband should not start fighting with one's little brothers (especially if they are without a father or mother) or with one's parents and sisters merely because one's wife complained about them. If you are unable to explain matters to your wife, never scold your mother even though it may be her fault. Rather arrange separate quarters for your wife or if this is not possible, arrange a separate kitchen for her. Never rebuke your mother for anything because she is your mother and deserves the highest respect. Of course, you should never oppress your wife because of your mother. To fulfil the rights of both mother and wife, the best course of action is to arrange for them to live or cook separately.

When there is friction between mother-in-law and daughter-in-law, it is senseless to force them to live together, thereby destroying the lives of the innocent children who will have to see their mother and grandmother always at loggerheads. When living separately, each of the two will be at ease and the friction will disappear. This is the instruction of the *Shari'ah* and it holds immense benefit for one's well being in this world as well as in the *Aakhirah*.

## Caring for Orphaned Brothers and Sisters-in-Law

When one is charged with caring for one's orphaned brothers and sisters, one should deal with them kindly when one's wife complains about them. This is because orphaned children are really not among the living since their spirit died with their parents. It is therefore inappropriate to hit a dead spirit. In fact, even showering excessive love on an orphan cannot revive his/her spirit. There is always a sense of gloominess about them and they can always sense death. In fact, Maulana Ashraf Ali Thanwi (A.R) has mentioned that when an orphan and another child are seated together and something is placed before them with the instruction that the one who grabs it first shall keep it, the orphan will not even attempt to take it. This is because the orphan's heart is dead. ("*Islaah Khawateen*" Pg. 224)

It is therefore necessary that women caring for their orphaned brothers or sisters-in-law should give them extra attention and be gentle with them. Men who are charged with this duty should also be gentle and loving and should take care never to overreact to their wives exaggerated complaints. May Allah grant everyone the ability to practise accordingly.

## TWO PRINCIPLES FOR AVOIDING DOMESTIC DISPUTES

If women adhere to the two principles mentioned hereunder, I am certain that all her disputes with her husband will be effectively terminated. Failure to implement these two principles has led to many unnecessary arguments and divorces as well as unnecessary scolding and abuse of children because of the great tension within the household. Insha Allah, when these two principles are implemented, the qualities of love, understanding, self-sacrifice, gentleness and service-above-self will be created and consolidated.

### The First Principle

This principle entails learning to frequently use the word "Alright". To avoid arguments, one should agree and say "Alright" even if one's husband says that day is night. If he says that you should cook something, say "Alright" and if he says that you need to go somewhere today, say, "Alright". In other words, agree to whatever he says. Even if he does not want you to mix with certain people, do not argue with him. For example, if he tells you not to attend a wedding hosted by your brother, tell him that you accept what he says and will not attend because he is more important to you than your brother. Thereafter, make *Du'a* to Allah saying, "O Allah! The hearts of all livings are in Your control. O Allah! Fulfil my desire if it is good for me because none can repeal Your decision. However, if there is harm for me in what I desire, remove the desire from my heart."

When your husband is in a good mood, tell him sweetly that the occasion a your brother's house is one of happiness and joy and their happiness will be incomplete without your presence. Explain to him why you should attend without offending him in any way. Also tell him that you would appreciate his generous gesture if he permitted you to attend. If you are a good wife, there is scarcely a man in this world who would still refuse permission. This approach should be adopted for any other purpose as well. If after this he still refuses, exercise patience and accept what he says. It will not be long thereafter that he will have perfect reliance and confidence in you. He will then accede to all your requests and will even consult you in all matters.

Because Allah has made men leaders of women[1], every man expects his wife to listen to him. A wife should therefore abide by whatever her husband decides. Of course, she may present her opinion on any matter and he will certainly consider it. However, the final decision is his. If a woman wants her word to be binding on her husband and effuses to acknowledge that he is her leader, she is opposing Allah's natural system as well as the *Shari'ah.* In fact, she is also opposing logic and will therefore be the cause of dissention in the home. A husband will never be able to

1. *Surah Nisa,* Surah 4, verse 34.

point a finger at his wife if she accepts him as her leader and does everything that pleases him.

Whenever a woman is leaving her father's home as a bride, she should always remember that following advices that a father gave to his daughter. He said:

"O my beloved daughter, the light of my eyes
O the radiance of my home, the delight of my life
Remember this advice of your father, but my daughter
Bear in mind that since time began, the nature of every daughter has been one of patience and contentment
Never let every little thing cause tears of blood to flow
Tolerate everything that life presents
Keep the pleasure of your lifelong companion ahead of everything and everyone for as long as you live, and please
Never allow a blemish to taint your father's name
The *Du'as* of your parents are ever with you, so
May this journey of your life be ever so blessed."

(Translated from an Urdu poem)

## The Second Principle

Acquaint yourself with asking forgiveness. Accept responsibility for your actions, admit your faults and add that you will do your best never to repeat what you did wrong. Remember that a couple are both mature and sane adults who will be living with each other for 365 days a year, 24 hours a day. Disputes and disagreements are therefore bound to happen. Many stages of life will pass when there will be happiness as well as joy, illness as well as good health, hope as well as despondency. There may be times when the couple will have to contend with their children having problems at school or coming home with pains and injuries due to either their own negligence or negligence on the part of the school staff. There may be times when the husband may become unemployed or his business may suffer a loss. There may also be times when the food may burn or may not be according to taste. In addition to all of this, there may be problems with in-laws or with one's temperamental husband. The solution to all of these problems is fear for Allah, commonly referred to as *Taqwa*.

When a couple are imbued with the quality of *Taqwa*, they will be cautious not to hurt each other's feelings. They will be apprehensive of standing before Allah on the Day of *Qiyaamah* because they will have to answer for every deed they carried out and for every word they spoke. If the couple are pious and imbued with *Taqwa*, they will be united and will brave rough waters side-by-side. However, if any disputes arise, the wife should always remember that she should seek pardon and assure her husband that she would not repeat herself. Instead of proving her innocence during the heat of the moment and prolonging the argument, she should concede that the fault was hers and that she will not repeat what she had done or said.

The act of seeking forgiveness is so effective that it even melted the heart of the notorious Hajjaaj bin Yusuf. While on a journey, Hajjaaj once passed by a villager and asked him what he thought about his governor. The villager complained about the governor and said that he was a tyrant. Hajjaaj then asked him, "Do you know who I am?" When the villager declared that he did not know, Hajjaaj said that he was the governor Hajjaaj. The villager then asked, "Do you know who I am?" When Hajjaaj declared that he did not know, the villager said, "I am a slave and I become insane for three days every month. Today happens to be the first of the three days so please forgive me." Hajjaaj laughed and let the man go free.

There are so many little squabbles between husband and wife which eventually lead to grave consequences. All of these can be avoided if the wife takes the initiative to apologise and seek forgiveness. If every woman takes a lesson from the villager in the above story, many problems will be solved. By calling himself a madman and seeking pardon, he managed to save himself from grievous harm. Similarly, if the wife has to admit that the fault is hers and that she would never repeat her mistake, she would also be saving herself from great harm. Every person is prone to err. However, the punishment of the criminal who confesses is lighter than that of the criminal who is found guilty after insisting that he is innocent.

"Why did you do that!" "How did it happen while you were standing there watching?" "You and your family are all the same!" "How did the food burn? Were you not checking on it?" "How could you speak to my mother like that!" "My sister came here and you could not even greet her properly!" "I did you a favour by marrying you. Otherwise no one would have taken you!"

These are but a few examples of what many uncaring men tell their wives. However, the reply of an intelligent wife to all of these and thousands of other allegations is simply to say, "Sorry, I made a mistake. Please forgive me. I shall not do it again." Once she says this, a threatening inferno will be reduced to nothing. This is the standard answer to every situation and it will disarm *Shaitaan* completely. Only a foolish wife will contest what her husband says by counter questioning him and denying everything she did. Instead of excusing herself by saying "Sorry, I made a mistake. Please forgive me", she will tell him that he raves on about nothing or that he should do the work himself. The argument then develops into a raging war, often ending in divorce. May Allah save all Muslim couples from such disputes. *Aameen.*

## An Excellent Method of Softening One's Husband

Here is an excellent elixir that will save women from many a difficulty. It will turn a tyrannical husband into a lamb, a foolish husband into a sensible human being and an irreligious husband into a pious man. The formula for this is that whenever there is an altercation between your husband and yourself, never immediately try to justify what has happened. Even if the fault is his, admit that it was yours and ask for forgiveness. This will save you from the consequences of his anger and will allow him to cool down.

When his temper has subsided, speak to him nicely and explain to him that it is wrong for him to continuously scold you without verifying the matter. Then clarify the contentious matter with him. He will then feel ashamed of himself and will always think before doing or saying anything in future.

Admitting one's fault and seeking forgiveness can soften the hardest hearts and extinguish the severest flames of wrath and fury. It can also turn an arch enemy into a bosom friend. In the words of the Creator of man,

> **"Good and evil cannot be equal. Resist with that which is best, and the one between yourself and whom there was enmity will instantly become like your bosom friend."**
>
> (*Surah Haa Meem Sajdah, Surah* 41, verse 34)

When one fights evil with good such as replying to someone's swearing by using sweet words, the person will soften. In fact, a wise man once claimed that if one eats something sweet when in anger, one will begin saying sweet words. Try this for yourself and see the results. When a woman regards her husband to be her pride and honour, her leader, her means of entering *Jannah* and her true friend, his little hut will be like a palace for her. Even though she may not be able to have the best of foods, clothing and furniture, she will count her home as being among the dwellings of *Jannah*. In the words of Sheikh Saadi, "A good and obedient wife can turn a pauper into a prince." If a man gets a good wife who is also pretty, he will be extremely fortunate. However, if she is only beautiful without a good character and without piety, she will be a bane for him instead. May Allah save all Muslim men from such women. *Aameen*

## A Miracle Cure

Hakeemul Ummah Maulana Ashraf Ali Thanwi (A.R) has reported the incident of a woman whose tongue was extremely malicious. Because of her insolence, her husband often hit her. However, her tongue could not be silenced even while hitting her. Annoyed and frustrated with all the hiding, she eventually approached a saint for advice. She requested him to give her a *Ta'weez* (an amulet) that would tame her husband and make him subservient to her and to make him love her. The saint somehow realised that she was being beaten because of her malicious tongue. He therefore asked her to bring him some water so that he could recite something and blow into the water. When she did this, he told her that whenever her husband was angry, she should take a handful of the water into her mouth and sit down. If she did this, he said, her husband would stop hitting her.

When she started doing this every time her husband became angry, she was too occupied to tell him anything and he gradually became angry less often until he finally stopped getting angry with her. Allah has granted women the ability to do get away with many things by merely speaking sweetly with their husbands. When a woman kindly asks her husband to forgive her, he has no option but to forgive. It is probably for this reason that the evidence of only women in many court proceedings is not accepted. By shedding a few tears, a woman can turn the heart of a judge into wax and easily have judgement passed in her favour. Even the brothers of Hazrat Yusuf عليه السلام used their tears to convince their father of their innocence.

A malicious tongue is a common disease among women and stems from pride. They continue arguing their case so that they never have to bow their head in submission. May Allah grant all women the ability to admit their faults and ask for forgiveness. May Allah also grant all men the ability to run their homes efficiently and the ability to resolve disputes amicably after hearing all sides. *Aameen*

## A Woman's ability to Tame a Man

A story is narrated about a woman who was constantly at loggerheads with her husband. She was concerned about the fact that not a day would pass without an argument between the two. A friend of hers advised her to consult a certain renowned Hakeem (practitioner in alternative medicine) in the area. When she consulted the learned man, she expressed her concern that the problem between her and her husband may be the result of black magic or an evil spirit. She said to him that her husband constantly became angry with her at the slightest provocation, after which she would also fly into a towering rage, making the situation worse. The Hakeem told her that he would be able to cure her quite easily on condition that she brought him three hairs from a lion's nape.

Leaving his premises, she immediately started formulating a plan to acquire the hairs from a lion. Taking a piece of meat, she proceeded to the local zoo. She threw the meat to the lion who readily ate it up. She then made it a ritual to take a piece of meat to the lion each day at the same time so that the lion would become familiar with her. Each day she threw the meat closer to the bars of the cage so the lion came closer to her. Eventually, the lion became so comfortable with her that was able to stroke it on its neck as it ate the meat. When this situation prevailed, she seized the opportunity to quickly pluck three hairs from its nape.

When the Hakeem learned how she was able to get the hairs from the lion, he smote his forehead and said, "Alas! You managed to tame a lion and get it eating from your hand. You can then very well win your husband over because he is definitely not as wild as a lion. Just as you were able to tame the lion by feeding it regularly, you can certainly win your husband's confidence in some way. Take care of him and you will soon have him eating from your hand. This will solve all your problems." The woman happily left the Hakeem with a resolution that she would do her utmost to please her husband.

If every Muslim wife abstains from backchat and admits her mistakes without trying to justify them, she will soon win the confidence of her husband and her in-laws. This approach will be even more effective if she accepts responsibility for wrongs that she did not do.

## WOMEN CANNOT BE EQUAL TO MEN

Hakeemul Ummah Hazrat Maulana Ashraf Ali Thanwi (A.R) explains that distinction between man and woman is so irreconcilable that Rasulullah ﷺ said, "If I were to command anyone to prostrate before a being besides Allah, I would have commanded women to prostrate before their husbands." (*Tirmidhi* Vol. 1, Pg. 219)

This *Hadith* makes it clear that the position of a husband in the *Shari'ah* is so great that his wife ought to prostrate before him if this were permissible. Women should bear in mind that they should never become angry with their husbands because one may become angry only with those people who are inferior than or equal to oneself. Becoming angry with one's husband and justifying one's wrongs are wrongs themselves. There is a common adage in Urdu which states that making excuses for one's wrongs is worse than the wrong itself. If a woman truly believes that she is subservient to her husband, she will find it impossible to become angry with him irrespective of how angry he makes her.

Every wife should therefore accept her status and realise that Allah has made men the leaders of women and they should therefore remain silent when their husbands are angry. Women should purge their minds of the misconception that they are superior to or equal to men. It is only when the husband's anger has subsided that she may tell him, "I had admitted that I was wrong that time. I now wish to explain why you were wrong on that account. Because you did not give me the chance to clarify the situation and because you did not enquire about the facts, you unnecessarily became angry with me." When the affair is clarified in an amicable manner like this, it will be easily resolved and the husband's confidence in his wife will keep growing. ("*Tuhfa Zowjayn*" Pg. 51)

## AN EFFECTIVE MANNER OF CREATING LOVE IN YOUR HUSBAND'S HEART

When your husband returns home in the evenings or when he returns from a journey, spare some time to welcome him and to be with him irrespective of the work you still have pending. It should never occur that you are so indifferent towards him that you have no idea when he arrives and when he leaves. Remember that a friendly greeting, a smiling face and a caring attitude are more effective in sweetening the mouth and heart of a husband than all the sweets, chocolates and sweetmeats of the world. It is therefore noticed that sweets and chocolates are used more in homes that are without the sweet tongue of a good wife and without her sweet attitude to alter the bitterness of worries and grief.

## WHEN ALLAH LOOKS AT A COUPLE WITH LOVE AND MERCY

In his book "*Showhar ke Huqooq*", Hazrat Mufti Taqi Usmani (Daamat Barakaatuh) quotes a *Hadith* that he has not personally read in any compilation of *Ahadith*, but which he read in the advices of Maulana Ashraf Ali Thanwi

(A.R) and which Maulana Ashraf Ali Thanwi (A.R) has quoted in several books. The *Hadith* states that when a man arrives home and looks at his wife with love and she in turn looks at him with love, Allah looks at the two of them with mercy. A loving relationship between husband and wife therefore benefits the couple in the *Aakhirah* just as it does in this world.

Every wife should therefore do everything to please her husband and should realise that the success of her life in this world as well as in the Hereafter depends on how she treats her husband. Unfortunate indeed is the wife who does not care to meet her tired husband at the door. In fact, a wife ought to do everything that pleases her husband before he can even ask her for it. Even if it means giving him a glass of plain water, when this is done with love and concern, the gesture would even melt a heart of stone. Although the glass of water may not have any vitamin supplement or tonic, it will provide every type of vitamin to his exhausted body. Try it and see.

If a wife realises her value in society, she will come to know that she performs the vital function of injecting life and vigour into her husband, thereby adding vitality to the entire society. When your husband returns home, do not immediately begin relating the problems of the day. Allow him time to first rest, to regain his composure and to complete any necessities he may need to attend to first. Thereafter, you may tell him whatever is necessary without adding the things that are not absolutely necessary. Present a rose to him when greeting him because the scent will raise his spirits. Get the children washed and dressed before he arrives and teach them the proper etiquette of greeting. When your husband returns, he will find their sweet voices more relieving than any pain-killing medication on the market.

If only women would learn all of this, dress presentably when their husbands arrive home and wash off their fatigue with the soap of a gleaming smile. By recalling the immense rewards that a mother will receive when tolerating the crying and disturbances of the children and the irritation presented by others, one will be able to overcome every difficulty. In addition to this, one's husband will behave more compassionately towards one and will sympathise with your pains and problems. Decorate your tablecloth with the best of whatever your husband can afford and have the food ready on time. When this is done diligently, even the most ordinary food will be a sumptuous meal for him. If the food is delayed for some reason, request him to excuse you for the inconvenience.

## A SMILE REVIVES THE HEART

A smile opens the doors of the soul. Because the soul affects the mind and the mind affects the heart, a mere smile will instantly rejuvenate a strained heart. A beautiful wife is not necessarily one who has attractive physical features. A beautiful wife is one who brings happiness to her husband's heart. Seeing a smiling face automatically prompts one to smile. A person who is always smiling attracts others and they enjoy being with such a person. On the contrary, no one enjoys being with a person whose face is always sour and whose constant frowning has caused deep creases on his/her forehead. People avoid such persons and they tend to dampen the spirits of others as well.

A French writer has mentioned that the heart is made most happy when a happy and smiling person is with one. The saying has been quoted from a book dating more than 1800 years. It reads: "Hapiness in the heart is as beneficial as any excellent medicine." A certain Doctor Hugh Lang has written that smiling and laughing is an excellent exercise which also aids in digestion. A Doctor Marshall said, "If you are an intelligent person, you will smile often." Another prominent doctor has mentioned that the most destructive day of one's life is the day in which one did not smile.

It is therefore extremely necessary for every wife to do her best wear a smiling face whenever she meets her husband. She should also teach her children the importance of this. The husband and children should also ensure that they wear a smiling face when entering the home. Every member of the family should bear in mind that a smiling face places smiles on others. An effective manner of creating love between husband and wife is to keep smiling to each other and to refrain from speaking about things that make one unhappy. A smiling face is truly a great bounty of Allah.

# A PIOUS LADY CALLED HAZRAT UMMU SALEEM

Hazrat Ummu Saleem was one of those fortunate women of the *Sahabiyaat* about whom Rasulullah said that they would enter *Jannah*. Her real name was Rumaysa. Hazrat Jaabir narrates that Rasulullah said, "I saw myself walking in the gardens of *Jannah* when I suddenly beheld Abu Talha's wife Rumaysa." There are several incidents in her life that make her one of the most distinguished *Sahabiyaat*. Haafidh Abu Nu'aym Isfahaani (A.R) has narrated several incidents about her in his book "*Hilyatul Awliya*" (Vol. 2 Pgs. 57-61). The following are a few of these incidents with some explanatory notes.

## As a Preacher

Hazrat Ummu Saleem had received a marriage proposal from Hazrat Abu Talha before he accepted Islãm. She said to him, "Abu Talha, do you realise that you are worshipping a tree that grows from the ground and that an Abyssinian man from a certain tribe had placed it where it is?" When he admitted that he did realise this, she said, "Are you not ashamed at worshipping a tree. I would not have declined your proposal if I had not already accepted Islãm. However, if you accept Islãm, I shall not ask you for a dowry to marry me." Abu Talha said, "But my accepting Islãm is not sufficient dowry for a woman like yourself." "What do you consider as sufficient dowry?" "Gold and silver," he replied. She said, "I have no need for gold and silver. All need is for you to accept Islãm."

Abu Talha then left to meet Rasulullah ﷺ. Rasulullah ﷺ was in the company of some other *Sahabah* ﷺ when he noticed Abu Talha approach. Rasulullah ﷺ said to them, "I see the light of Islãm shining between the eyes of Abu Talha." Hazrat Abu Talha ﷺ accepted Islãm and married Hazrat Ummu Saleem ﷺ.

## As a Warrior

Hazrat Anas ﷺ narrates that during the Battle of Uhud he saw Hazrat A'isha ﷺ and Hazrat Ummu Saleem ﷺ carrying filled water bags on their backs to the *Mujaahi Deen* on the battlefield. Whenever the water finished, they would return to refill it. The laws of *Hijaab* were not yet revealed at that time.

During the Battle of Hunayn, Hazrat Abu Talha ﷺ saw Hazrat Ummu Sulaym ﷺ standing with a dagger in her hand. When he asked her what the matter was, she replied, "I am holding this dagger because I intend to plunge it into the belly of any *Kaafir* who comes close to me." When Hazrat Abu Talha ﷺ related this to Rasulullah ﷺ, Rasulullah ﷺ appreciated her spirit and he told Hazrat Ummu Saleem ﷺ that she would not need the dagger because Allah was sufficient for her.

## As a Pillar of Fortitude and Wisdom

A child of Hazrat Abu Talha ﷺ was very ill when he left home to tend to his affairs. While he was away, the child passed away. Hazrat Ummu Saleem ﷺ wrapped the child in a sheet, left him in the room where he passed away and began preparing food for her husband. Because Hazrat Abu Talha ﷛ was fasting that day, she did not want to upset him by revealing the news to him immediately. When he arrived, he asked about the child and proceeded to the room to see him. Hazrat Ummu Saleem ﷛ told him that the child was at peace and that there was no need to see him. Satisfied that his child was well, Hazrat Abu Talha ﷛ did not enter the room.

He then ate comfortably and Hazrat Ummu Saleem ﷛ gave no hint to darken his spirits. The couple spent the night as any happy couple would. When the two awoke for the *Tahajjud Salaah,* she said to him, "The people of a certain tribe are strange. Another tribe lent them something but they refuse to part with it, thinking that it belongs to them. When asked to return the thing they borrowed, they now become angry instead of returning it." Hazrat Abu Talha ﷛ said, "Their behaviour is very bad and extremely unjust." Hazrat Ummu Saleem ﷛ then told her husband, "Allah has loaned you your child and has now asked for him back. Allah is his Master and all we can do is to exercise patience."

Shocked at his wife's behaviour, Hazrat Abu Talha ﷛ complained to Rasulullah ﷺ. Commending the behaviour of Hazrat Ummu Saleem ﷛, Rasulullah ﷺ prayed, "O Abu Talha! May Allah bless your night." As a result of this *Du'a,* a son called Abdullaah was born to the couple as a result of their night's relationship. This son Abdullaah had nine sons all of whom were learned scholars of the Qur'ãn.

## Rasulullah ﷺ's Concern for her

Hazrat Anas رضي الله عنه (who was the son of Hazrat Ummu Saleem رضي الله عنها narrates that besides the homes of his wives, the only home in Madinah that Rasulullah ﷺ frequented was the home of Hazrat Ummu Saleem رضي الله عنها. When someone asked Rasulullah ﷺ for the reason, he replied, "I feel sorry for her because her brother was killed before my eyes."

Hazrat Anas رضي الله عنه also narrates that Rasulullah ﷺ was sleeping at their house one afternoon. Because of the heat, his body began to perspire excessively. Being a Mahram to Rasulullah ﷺ, Hazrat Ummu Saleem رضي الله عنها began collecting the perspiration in a piece of glass. Rasulullah ﷺ awoke when he felt her doing this. When he asked her what she was doing, she replied that she was collecting his perspiration to add to her perfumes because his perspiration was more fragrant than perfumes.

## Her Sacrifices for the Propagation of *Deen* and the Glad Tidings of Rasulullah ﷺ

When Hazrat Ummu Saleem رضي الله عنها fell pregnant after the *Du'a* of Rasulullah ﷺ and was in the final stages of pregnancy, her husband Hazrat Abu Talha رضي الله عنه was preparing to leave on a *Jihaad* expedition. She insisted that she would accompany the expedition so that she should not be deprived of the honour of accompanying a *Jihaad* expedition led by Rasulullah ﷺ. Because the journey was going to be a tedious one, which would prove difficult for a pregnant woman Hazrat Abu Talha رضي الله عنه sought permission from

Rasulullah ﷺ for her to accompany them. She therefore accompanied the expedition.

She was also with the Muslim army when the Muslims conquered Makkah as well as when the marched to Hunayn. Here were occasions when even healthy men would be reluctant to participate. However, Hazrat Ummu Saleem رضي الله عنها's fervour to serve *Deen* was so great that she even participated when she was in a weakened condition of the final stages of her pregnancy. Determined to purify Allah's earth from the filth of *Kufr*, she marched with the Muslim army. Allah made the Muslims victorious and she returned with them to Madinah. On the last leg of the journey, before entering Madinah, she began experiencing labour pains.

Anxious that they should not lag behind the rest and not enter Madinah with Rasulullah ﷺ, Hazrat Abu Talha رضي الله عنه made the following *Du'a*: "O my Rabb! You know well that I love to leave Madinah with Rasulullah ﷺ and that I love to enter Madinah with Rasulullah ﷺ. I am now delayed by that matter that You see." Allah always responds to the *Du'as* of His beloved who are prepared to sacrifice everything for Him." As soon as he completed his *Du'a*, Hazrat Ummu Saleem رضي الله عنها told him that the labour pains had vanished and that they may proceed with the rest. The pains returned once they reached Madinah and she delivered a bouncing baby boy.

As soon as the child was born, she called for her son Hazrat Anas رضي الله عنه and sent the baby with him to Rasulullah ﷺ saying that none should feed the child until the child was taken to Rasulullah ﷺ. When Hazrat Anas رضي الله عنه brought the child, Rasulullah ﷺ said, "It seems as if Ummu Saleem has delivered." When Hazrat Anas رضي الله عنه confirmed this, Rasulullah ﷺ asked for an Ajwa date, chewed it until it was soft and placed a part of it into the baby's mouth. When the baby gleefully sucked the date, Rasulullah ﷺ said, "Just look at the love that the Ansaar have for dates." Rasulullah ﷺ then passed his hand over the baby's face and named him Abdullaah.

Because of her sacrifices for *Deen*, Allah had accorded her a position in *Jannah*. Rasulullah ﷺ once mentioned that he had heard footsteps in *Jannah*. When he asked the angels whose footsteps they were, he was informed that these were the footsteps of Hazrat Ummu Saleem رضي الله عنها the mother of Hazrat Anas رضي الله عنه. (*Muslim* Vol. 2 Pg. 292)

After reading these incidents, we should make this *Du'a* to Allah: "O Allah! Allow me to make sacrifices for Your *Deen* alongside my husband and allow me to be of assistance to him in the effort of *Deen* throughout the world just as You accepted Hazrat Ummu Saleem رضي الله عنها to participate in the expeditions of *Jihaad*, in the conquest of Makkah and the Battle of Hunayn. Guide us, assist us, grant us understanding and accept us for the propagation of Your *Deen* just as You accepted the *Sahabiyaat* رضي الله عنهن for the same. Remove the love of the world from our hearts together with the desire of amassing the commodities of the world. Replace these inclinations with the love for You, the love for Your *Deen* and the love to see You. Turn our days into an effort to propagate the *Deen* to the *Kuffaar* of the world and effort to make the Muslims of the world proper practising Muslims. Also turn our nights into an effort of weeping before You and begging from You. I am making this *Du'a* for myself as well as for all Muslim men and women throughout the world. Use me as a vehicle for the guidance of every person on earth. *Aameen.*"

Commenting on the *Hadith* which mentions the death of Hazrat Ummu Saleem ﷺ's child, Hazrat Maulana Muhammad Zakariyya (A.R) writes, "It took great patience and courage to endure the death of her child in a manner that her husband knew nothing about it. Because her husband was fasting, she feared that it would become difficult for him to eat if he learned about the child's death."

Every woman should learn a lesson from this incident. It is inappropriate to begin recounting every problem in detail as soon as one's husband steps through the door. Such an approach will have an adverse effect on any man's psychological well-being. The incident clearly highlights that extent to which the *Sahabiyaat* ﷺ understood human psychology. Whereas people in today's times claim that they have mastered psychology, their practical lives indicate that they are children in the field when compared with the Sahabah ﷺ. When a husband enters the home, the burden of the day's problems should not be immediately dumped on his shoulders that are already sagging beneath the pressures of his occupation.

One should strictly abstain from telling one's husband about anything that would cause him to harbour ill-feelings towards another person. Always remember that if you create ill-feelings between him and his mother or sisters, the day will soon dawn when your beloved son's wife or your beloved brother's wife will cause a rift between you and your son or brother. This is the way in which fate takes its course. It should not be that you ever have to say: "As a daughter-in-law, I could not find a good mother-in-law. Now as a mother-in-law, I cannot find a good daughter-in-law."

If a daughter-in-law adopts the life of people like Hazrat Khadija, Hazrat Faatima (A.R) and other pious women, Insha Allah she will not have to suffer the trouble of a difficult daughter-in-law. She should learn to be tolerant, loving and able to use flowers to repel thorns.

Another important principle that a Muslim wife should never forget is that she must not burden her husband with the day's problems as soon as he walks into the house because he could be even more stressed than her. A wife should first ask him about his day. If her husband is shocked because he has just narrowly escaped an accident or if he has just had some terrible experience, it will not only be inconsiderate for her to burden him with her problems, but it will be absolutely cruel. Therefore, if she needs to tell him something, she should tell him only after she is certain that he is composed and willing to listen. May Allah grant this understanding to all Muslim men and women. *Aameen.*

## WOMEN WERE ALSO MUFTIS

An eminent scholar by the name of Imaam Abu Bakr bin Mas'ood Kaasani (A.R) has written a renowned masterpiece called "Badaai'us Sanaa'i", which is a commentary of his teacher's book titled "*Tuhfatul Fuqaha*". According to Allaama Shaami (A.R), "Badaai'us Sanaa'i" is a masterpiece that cannot be matched by any other book of Fiqh (Islãmic jurisprudence). When he presented this book to his teacher Sheikh Ala'ud *Deen* Samarqandi (A.R), the Sheikh was so happy that he gave his daughter Faatima's hand over in marriage to Imaam Abu Bakr Kaasaani (A.R). By then she had already received many proposals from several kings and princes.

The lady was extremely well versed in *Fiqh* and had mastered the subject to the extent that she was authorised to issue *Fatwas.* Therefore, the situation was not uncommon that when someone required a *Fatwa,* part of the *Fatwa* was written by her, a part by her father and another part by her husband.

## FIVE QUALITIES OF A PIOUS WIFE

The mentor and guide of mankind Rasulullah ﷺ has condensed the qualities of a pious wife into four sentences in one *Hadith.* Another *Hadith* has mentioned a fifth quality. Before reading what these five qualities are, one should make an intention that one will do one's best to practise these qualities. At the same time, one should also make *Du'a* that Allah should grant oneself as well as all other Muslim women the ability to do this.

Rasulullah ﷺ said that a pious wife "obeys her husband when he instructs her, she pleases him when he looks at her, she fulfils his oath when he swears an oath (that she should do something within the bounds of *Shari'ah*) and when he is out, she safeguards her chastity and his wealth."

## The First Quality

The most important quality of a good wife is that she obeys every instruction of her husband that does not violate the commands of Allah. It is of course not permissible for a wife to obey any instruction that is against the *Shari'ah*, such as attending mixed gatherings and going to places of sin. When a wife obeys all her husband's lawful instructions for the pleasure of Allah, she will win his love and trust. He will become her best friend and will do anything for her. Needless to say, this will happen only when the wife does everything to obey him. She should be prepared to sacrifice her rest and pleasures for him and always remember that any humiliation suffered in serving one's husband is actually an honour. When a bride adopts this attitude and remains steadfast, she will soon win over her husband's affection. The couple will then be like two hearts in one soul or like two minds in one body, doing everything together as a united body. They will plan and think as one person and work together to dispel any difficulty.

Whenever a wife senses grief in her husband's face, she should immediately share his feelings and sympathise with him. When he is happy, she should also share his happiness and not do anything to spoil it.

## Hazrat Abu Dardaa ﷺ advises his Wife

With great love and affection, Hazrat Abu Dardaa ﷺ once said to his wife, "When you see me angry, (affectionately) make me understand and I shall do the same when I see you angry. If we do not do this, we can never make any progress together."

A wife should wear what her husband wants her to wear, cook as he wants her to cook and do everything as he instructs on condition that his instructions do not violate the injunctions of the *Shari'ah.*

Every new bride should understand that things are going to be different after marriage. Before marriage, her sleep was sleep without worries, as were her moments of eating, drinking and playing. Her life after marriage will be one of responsibilities, a life in which she will be living under a new government. It is for this reason that the first lesson that girls of good upbringing receive when they marry is the lesson of being obedient. She is taught to sacrifice her own pleasures for the pleasure of her husband and to do everything as he wants it done. Married life, though enjoyable, has its own set of rules and restrictions. Whereas life was lived for oneself before marriage, life after marriage is lived for others. After marriage, a woman's dressing will not be for herself, her sleeping will not be when she wants and she will not be waking up when she wants. Everything will be subject to the needs of her husband.

A bride should therefore proceed step-by-step into her new life, acclimatising to the changes as they occur. She will have to curb her desires as she goes along and she may have to eat after others have eaten, placing herself last. Her dressing and beautification will have to be to please her husband and when she has children, they will also demand her attention. As a result, she will again have to give precedence to their needs over her own because she will be directly responsible for the upbringing of this new generation.

Every wife should therefore not forget that the first requirement of a good wife in the words of Rasulullah ﷺ is that she obeys her husband. Although the feat is not an easy one, she should remember that the rewards are tremendous. Hazrat Ummu Salma رضي الله عنها narrates that she heard Rasulullah ﷺ saying, "The woman who passes every stage of her life and finally reaches the final stage while her husband is pleased with her, she will surely enter *Jannah*. It is as if there is no barrier between *Jannah* and her." The wife who keeps her husband happy and is always concerned about his feelings will therefore attain the ultimate goal of every person.

In fact, every Muslim woman understands that th *Shari'ah* has made it obligatory for her to obey ... commands of her husband because of the great honou that Allah has granted the husband. The *Hadith* has already been quoted in which Rasulullah ﷺ says, "If I was to command anyone to prostrate to another, I would have commanded wives to prostrate to their husbands. If a husband commands his wife to move a rock from a red mountain to a black mountain and then from the black mountain back to the red mountain, she is obliged to do as he says." (*Ibn Majah* Pg. 133)

## Uniting Two Hearts

Allah has appointed men as leaders of women in the couple's journey through life. Every post of leadership in this world is temporary. A leader today is soon an ordinary citizen. On the converse, a prisoner today may well be president of his country tomorrow. However, the leadership that Allah has granted a husband will last as long as he is married, which is often as long as he lives. In addition to this, his relationship with his wife is an intimate relationship by which their hearts are united, much unlike political leadership which is merely official. Because the husband remains her leader throughout the wife's life Rasulullah ﷺ has emphasised his position by stating that she would be commanded to prostrate before him if this was permissible for anyone besides Allah.

The worst difficulties of this world are temporary. Keep the final stages of your life in mind together with the bounties that Allah shall bestow on you for being an obedient wife. In this manner, every thorn will seem like a rose and nothing will be too difficult. Never make your husband angry and you will have no worries when Allah asks you on the Day of *Qiyaamah* whether you had fulfilled the rights of your husband. You will be able to say that by pleasing your husband you sought Allah's pleasure, which you will have on that day.

May Allah make you the ruler of your husband's heart and include you in the ranks of people like Hazrat Faatima ﵂ who shall be the leader of the women in *Jannah* and in the ranks of people like Hazrat A'isha ﵂ in whose lap Allah's beloved Rasul ﷺ passed away despite the presence of thousands of *Sahabah* ﵁ who would give their lives for him. *Aameen.*

## The Jihaad of Women

Hazrat Asmaa bint Yazeed Ansaari ﵂ once said, "O Rasulullah ﷺ! The other women have sent me to ask you something. Indeed Allah has sent you as a messenger to both men and women. We women have therefore believed in you and in Allah. However, we have to remain indoors, tend to our domestic chores, fulfil the desires of our husbands and bear their children. Despite all of this, men excel us in earning great rewards for things that we are unable to do. They perform their daily *Salaah* and *Jumu'ah Salaah* in the *Masjid*, they visit the ill, attend funerals, perform *Hajj* after *Hajj* and above all, they fight in *Jihaad*. When they go for *Hajj*, *Umrah* or *Jihaad*, we look after their property, raise their children and weave cloth for them. Do we not share their rewards?"

After hearing this question, Rasulullah ﷺ turned to the *Sahabah* ﵁ and said, "Did you ever hear a woman asking a better question?" "We never thought that a woman would ask such an excellent question," replied the *Sahabah* ﵁.

Addressing Hazrat Asmaa ﵂, Rasulullah ﷺ then said, "Listen attentively and tell the ladies who have sent you that when a woman seeks the pleasure of her husband and carries out all her domestic chores to his satisfaction, she receives the same rewards that men receive for all their deeds." Hazrat Asmaa ﷺ returned very happily with this reply.

Obedience to and kind treatment of one's husband is an extremely great virtue which many wives are negligent in performing.

## The Second Quality

The second quality of a pious wife is that "she pleases him (her husband) when he looks at her". Such a wife employs lawful means to look after her beauty and cleanliness so that she remains attractive for her husband. She also dresses lawfully in a manner that pleases him.

## A Grave Error of Many Women

Hakeemul Ummah Maulana Ashraf Ali Thanwi (A.R) has mentioned that it is indeed strange that many women look like street-sweepers and servants when at home with their husbands but dress up smartly when going out of the house. Is she dressing up only for others to see? She does not dress up for the husband for whose pleasure the clothes were made and for whom she made herself a bride, but she does this for others. She dresses shabbily before her husband and does not speak politely to him, yet she dresses exquisitely before others and speaks most sweetly with them. Others are therefore thrilled at the husband's expense. While demanding her rights and maintenance from the husband, she spends the same to please others. Is this justice? ("*At Tableegh wa Dawaa'ul Uyoob*" Pg. 91)

It is indeed improper for a woman to reserve her good clothes only for going out and to look shabby and untidy in the house with her husband. It is for this reason that Rasulullah ﷺ described a good wife as one who pleases her husband when he looks at her. If a wife takes pride in her appearance and beautifies herself, she will be the most beautiful woman to her husband.

## The Third Quality

The third quality of a pious wife that Rasulullah ﷺ described is that she fulfils her husband's oath when he swears an oath (that she should do something within the bounds of *Shari'ah*) e.g. he says on oath that she should visit his mother or that she should perform *Tahajjud Salaah* on a certain day. When this happens, she should do her best to ensure that she does exactly as he swore that she should. Of course, she should do this only when the act is permissible.

Such a situation usually arises because of the husband's love for his wife or because he takes pride in something she does. He will therefore take an oath that she does it so that he may see it happen or so that another may see it. It may also occur that he makes the wife take an oath that she will do as he says. When a wife has true feelings for her husband, she will do anything he wants her to do especially when an oath is involved.

**Ruling:** According to the *Shari'ah*, it is normally not binding on someone to fulfil an oath that another person takes.

## The Fourth Quality

Whenever the husband leaves the home for some reason (as most men do), it is the duty of the wife to safeguard her chastity and his wealth just as she would do when he is present with her. No honourable man would want his wife to be in the company of a non-Mahram man or that she should even make eye-contact with such a man. He wants his wife exclusively for himself.

When a woman marries, she becomes the focal point of his life and it is with her that he will satisfy himself and find solace. She holds this fundamental position in his life when he is with her as well as when he is not.

In addition to this, he also entrusts her with his wealth and possessions when he leaves the home. She should therefore safeguard his possessions when he is not at home. She should never waste his money or spend on others without his permission. Should she fail to take care of her chastity or his wealth, she will be guilty of breaching a trust. She should ask her husband for only those things without which some harm may come to them. Never should a wife insist that her husband buys her something merely because someone else has it. Irrespective of how attractive something may be, she should not ask for it if it is not necessary. By unnecessarily burdening the husband with such demands, she is guilty of extravagance as well as misappropriation of trust. Allah also describes a pious woman in the Qur'ãn when He says,

> **"So the pious women are obedient and, in the absence of their husbands, are protective because of that which Allah has protected."**
>
> (*Surah Nisaa Surah* 4, verse 34)

Protecting her husband's home means that a woman should first ensure that she does not commit any sins. Thereafter, she should ensure that his wealth and other possessions do not fall into the wrong hands. In another *Hadith*[1], Rasulullah ﷺ makes it clear that "a woman is a guardian over her husband's home." It is therefore clear that safeguarding her husband's wealth and possessions is not only a necessary quality of a good wife, but it is actually her duty.

## A Wife Should be Genuinely Concerned about her Husband's Wealth

Hakeemul Ummah Maulana Ashraf Ali Thanwi (A.R) has mentioned in his advices that a wife's heart should pain when her husband's wealth is spent wastefully. It is her responsibility to be concerned about his wealth. She must never be liberal with his money or allow the servants to do as they please with it.

Whenever the desire creeps into one's heart to have something that another has, one should think about the following:

---

1. *Bukhari.*

1. Death and the thought of what the less fortunate one has in this world, the less will one be accountable in the Hereafter. The more one has in one's home, the more will one have to account for.
2. The simplicity of the homes of Hazrat Faatima رضي الله عنها, Hazrat Khadija رضي الله عنها, Hazrat Zainab رضي الله عنها and Hazrat A'isha رضي الله عنها. The more one's home resembles the homes of these illustrious ladies, the closer will one be to them in the Hereafter.

By keeping these thoughts in one's mind, one will welcome death because the love for the material things of this world will not have permeated one's heart. Seeing the simplicity of one's home, others will also follow suit and the money saved can be invested for the *Aakhirah.*

We have not come into this world to amass wealth and possessions. We have come to carry out deeds that please Allah. The simpler we keep our homes, the more Allah shall love us. If we donate our excess possessions to the poor, they will benefit tremendously while we will lose nothing. In fact, nearly every household has things in almost every room that are in excess of their needs.

**Lavish Weddings**

Women are inclined to waste a great deal of money in weddings. On such occasions, all matters are referred to women, almost as if men know nothing about spending. As a result of wastefulness on such occasions, many homes have been destroyed. Many people have remained indebted all their lives because of such lavish wedding ceremonies, causing them to age before their time.

**Hosting Simple Marriage Ceremonies**

If people really want blessings in their marriages and desire that the marriages should be filled with love and pious offspring, they should follow the advice of Rasulullah ﷺ, who said, "The marriage with the most blessings is the one in which the least expenses are incurred."

Rasulullah ﷺ has also mentioned, "The best of women are those who ask for the least dowry." (*Ibn Hibbaan*)

According to another *Hadith*, Rasulullah ﷺ said, "The signs of a blessed woman is that her proposal comes soon, her dowry is small and her child is born soon."

(*Kanzul Ummaal*)

One can well imagine that if the *Shari'ah* encourages the least expense for the dowry, which is a prerequisite of marriage, it will certainly encourage even less expenditure for the wedding ceremony and trousseau, which have no status at all in the *Shari'ah.*

Hazrat Sufyaan Thowri (A.R) has mentioned that when a bridegroom asks his bride what she brought with her, he is a thief. His wicked nature is indicated by the fact that instead of asking for mundane commodities from his in-laws, he should be grateful to them for giving him the light of their lives whom they painstakingly raised for so many years. By this token, it is also improper for a son-in-law to send a gift to his parents-in-law with the desire that they should also send him a gift.

Every woman will naturally say that she wants to incur the least expenses for her parents and will therefore not mind if her parents gave her little or even nothing when she marries. "However," she will concede, "I have no choice in the matter because my mother-in-law and sisters-in-law will ridicule me and people will look down on my family." It is the custom in many countries that the bridegroom's parents prepare a list of items that they want from the bride's parents. They even request what should be given to the bridegroom himself, what should be given to his father, to his mother and to each of his brothers and sisters. If this is not given in writing, it is made clear to the bride's parents in some other manner. This practice is unjust and violates the injunctions of the *Shari'ah.*

It is therefore imperative for every woman to bear in mind that she will soon be a sister-in-law or a mother-in-law when her brother or son marries. When the occasion arises, she should ensure that she or her mother do not impose on the parents of her son's or brother's in-laws. If her mother demands anything from her brother's in-laws, she should explain to her mother that the practice is unjust and that if she imposes on them, the time may come when her daughter's in-laws may impose on her. Favours should be sought only from Allah. Causing people unnecessary expenditure will invite Allah's wrath.

## The Fifth Quality

The *Sahabah* ﷡ once said to Rasulullah ﷺ that they would like to know what form of wealth is best to have.

Rasulullah ﷺ replied, "The best wealth is a tongue that engages in *Zikr*, the heart that is grateful and a *Mu'min* wife who assists her husband in his *Imaan*."

("*At Targheeb wat Tarheeb*" Vol. 2 Pg. 198 & Vol. 3 Pg. 41)

Wealth is generally referred to as something that is helpful to one and fulfils one's necessities. Whereas people generally regard money, businesses and property as wealth, Rasulullah ﷺ described three things as true wealth because of their immense benefits to man. Commenting on the above *Hadith*, Mullaa Ali Qaari (A.R) writes in his commentary of "Mishkaat" that a wife who assists her husband in his *Imaan* refers to a wife who is concerned about her husband's religiousness and reminds him when it is time to perform *Salaah* or fast, etc. In addition to this, she also ensures that he refrains from fornication and all other sins.

In our fast corrupting environment, we desperately need women who are concerned about the religiousness of their husbands and children. However, it is tragic to note that we are faced with a worsening situation because instead of encouraging their husbands to practise the injunctions of *Deen*, many women nowadays actually prevent their husbands from religious practices. Instead of encouraging them to be practical Muslims, such women tease their husbands and call them names because they wish to grow a beard or dress according to the *Shari'ah*.

The above *Hadith* speaks about having a grateful heart. When a woman is blessed with such a heart, her life becomes one of contentment and happiness because she is grateful for whatever her husband provides. Ulama have therefore mentioned that when a wife is grateful for her lot, she will be blessed with a life that is almost free of arguments. In fact, religious thinkers maintain that ingratitude is the worst trait that anyone can possess. On the other hand, there can be no greater blessing than gratefulness. Allah asserts with great emphasis,

> **"If you show gratitude, then I will definitely give you more, and if you are ungrateful, then indeed My punishment is severe."**
>
> (*Surah Ibraheem* 14, verse 7)

## A FORMULA THAT WILL ELIMINATE DISPUTES BETWEEN COUPLES

Women should inculcate the quality of thankfulness within themselves so that they could be grateful for everything that their husbands provide. Even if their husbands can afford only simple foods, they should regard this as the most exquisite delicacy, bearing in mind that millions of people do not even have this privilege. Unfortunately, there are many women who are never satisfied with what they get. Whenever they are asked about their clothing, utensils, food, etc, they complain that they hardly have anything even though they have these things in excessive quantities.

A wife should express her gratitude for everything that her husband provides, irrespective of how little it is. When she views everything through the lenses of gratitude, she will see only the good in every item and no faults. A person once said that he cried for lack of shoes but when he saw someone without feet, he thanked Allah for blessing him with feet.

When a woman expresses her gratitude to her husband and to her in-laws, she will be expressing gratitude to Allah at the same time. One should accustom one's tongue to constantly say, "Al Hamdu Lillaah (all praises are for Allah). O Allah, I thank You." When looking at every big and small item in the house, one should say, "*Al Hamdu Lillaah.* O Allah, I thank You." In fact, even when experiencing difficulty, one should say, "*Al Hamdu Lillaah.* O Allah, I thank You." For example, if one has a headache, one should think, "*Al Hamdu Lillaah.* O Allah, I thank You. At least my arms, my legs, my back, my stomach and the rest of my body is well." In this way, one's difficulties will also be alleviated. Always bear in mind that Allah promises to increase one's bounties when one is grateful. May Allah grant us all the ability to be grateful for everything. Aameen.

Rasulullah ﷺ once addressed a congregation of ladies and said to them that majority of the inmates of *Jahannam* were women. When they enquired about the reason, he said that this was on account of women being ungrateful to their husbands. This *Hadith* makes it clear that showing ingratitude towards one's husband is a cause of landing a woman in *Jahannam*.

The wives of Rasulullah ﷺ are referred to as the mothers of the Mu'mineen and every Muslim is proud to be known as their children in Islãm. Despite living lives of poverty and hardship, they never complained to Rasulullah ﷺ. They neither had good clothing, exquisite jewellery, expensive furniture nor delicious food and never demanded these things even when the Muslims began conquering territories and wealth was streaming to Madinah.

After the demise of Rasulullah ﷺ, Hazrat A'isha ؓ was once eating some food when she said, "Whenever I eat to my fill, I cannot help weeping." When one of her students asked the reason, she replied, "I recall the time when Rasulullah ﷺ departed from this world. By Allah! He never ate bread and meat to his fill twice in a day." Such was the life of the illustrious soul whom we claim to follow. Unlike us, he never regarded this world as his permanent abode. He understood that this world is a temporary place through which people pass as travellers.

The person who attaches herself to this world is like a foolish traveller who begins to furnish and decorate the waiting room of a platform while waiting for a train. Eventually, when the train (the angel of death) arrives and she has to leave the station, she begins to regret what she did. It will then be too late for one to make excuses and to say that one will no longer be extravagant and will no longer incur Allah's wrath by parading the streets in un-Islãmic dress. When death comes to one, it will be too late for regrets. Therefore, one should not waste one's precious wealth on new curtains, expensive furniture and items for one's display units. Rather save the money to spend it for the propagation of *Deen* throughout the world. Give the money to your husband so that he can travel to spread *Deen* and also use it to support a needy relative or someone else who is poor. Endeavour to give charity in a manner that the left hand does not know what the right hand gives.

Ponder awhile about the home of the beloved wife of the most beloved creation ﷺ. All that she had in her room was a bed, a straw mat, bedding, a pillow stuffed with the bark of a date palm, one or two utensils to store dates and flour, a utensil for water and a cup to drink water with. She mentioned that months would go by without a lamp being lit in her room.

## The Story of Hazrat Isma'eel (عليه السلام)'s First Wife

We will presently relate the stories of two wives of Hazrat Isma'eel عليه السلام, the son of Hazrat Ibraheem عليه السلام. These two incidents make it clear that a grateful wife and an ungrateful wife cannot be compared. Whereas the first wife complained about poverty instead of being grateful for her lot, the second wife expressed thanks to Allah despite their poverty. As a result of her attitude, Hazrat Ibraheem عليه السلام made *Du'a* to Allah to grant the couple blessings in their food and drink. As a result of this *Du'a*, the couple and their progeny (the Arabs) have enjoyed tremendous blessings. Gratitude therefore brought great blessings while ingratitude caused the first wife to lose her status as the wife of a Nabi عليه السلام. This makes it clear that ingratitude was never tolerated in the pure homes of the Ambiyaa (A.S).

After Hazrat Isma'eel عليه السلام got married, his father Hazrat Ibraheem عليه السلام came to Makkah to visit him. Not finding his son at home, Hazrat Ibraheem ﷺ asked his daughter-in-law where her husband was. Unable to recognise Hazrat Ibraheem ﷺ, she said that her husband Hazrat Isma'eel ﷺ was out hunting. Hazrat Ibraheem ﷺ then asked her about their condition. She complained to him that they were very poor and were experiencing great difficulty. After hearing her complaints, Hazrat Ibraheem ﷺ told her to convey his regards to Hazrat Isma'eel ﷺ and to tell him to change the threshold of his door.

When Hazrat Isma'eel ﷺ returned, he asked his wife whether anyone had visited that day. She described Hazrat Ibraheem ﷺ, saying that he had come to look for Hazrat Isma'eel ﷺ. She also told him that the old man had asked about their condition, to which she replied that they were experiencing great difficulty. When Hazrat Isma'eel ﷺ asked her if the man had left a message, she replied that he had instructed her to convey his regards to Hazrat Isma'eel ﷺ and to tell him that he should change the threshold of his door. Hazrat Isma'eel ﷺ then told his wife that the man was his father Hazrat Ibraheem ﷺ and that the instruction meant that he should divorce her. The couple were subsequently divorced.

## The Story of Hazrat Isma'eel (ﷺ)'s Second Wife

Hazrat Isma'eel ﷺ later married another woman. When Hazrat Ibraheem ﷺ visited the home after a long time, his son was out hunting again. Hazrat Ibraheem ﷺ also asked this wife about their condition, to which she said that they were happy. When she offered him some food, he declined and asked her what they usually ate and drank. When she told him that they ate meat and drank water, he made *Du'a* to Allah to bless their food and drink. Relating the story to the Sahabah رضي الله عنهم, Rasulullah ﷺ said that the blessings in food they saw was the result of this *Du'a* of Hazrat Ibraheem عليه السلام. Hazrat Ibraheem عليه السلام then told his daughter-in-law to convey his regards to her husband and to tell him that he should keep the threshold of his door firmly in place.

When Hazrat Isma'eel عليه السلام returned, he asked his wife whether someone had visited them that day. She told him that an extremely kind and handsome old man had visited and enquired about their condition. She praised Hazrat Ibraheem عليه السلام and told her husband what reply she gave. When Hazrat Isma'eel عليه السلام asked her what message the man left, she told him that the man had left his regards and instructed that he should keep the threshold of his door firmly in place. Hazrat Isma'eel عليه السلام told her that the man was his father and that she was being referred to as the threshold. His father had instructed him to keep her in his marriage.

Although the second wife had meat only occasionally, she mentioned Allah's bounties to Hazrat Ibraheem عليه السلام without speaking about the many difficulties that came with it. Such an attitude was greatly appreciated by both husband and father-in-law. When a wife praises her parents-in-law as Hazrat Isma'eel (عليه السلام)'s wife did, the husband is instantly impressed, his confidence in her is strengthened and he regards her as his own. If women could only understand this! When a daughter-in-law speaks only good of her in-laws, they will be very happy with her and even make *Du'a* for her and for her parents because they had raised her properly. They will feel that she has honoured them and is loyal to them. May Allah cast the shadow of Hazrat Isma'eel (عليه السلام)'s grateful wife on the wives of the *Ummah* and grant them her excellent character. *Aameen*

Every wife should therefore make an effort to express gratitude to Allah in every situation, favourable or not. One should constantly say, "*Al Hamdu Lillaahi Alaa Kulli Haal*" (I praise Allah in every condition).

Rasulullah ﷺ has mentioned that whoever does not thank people has not thanked Allah. One should therefore thank every person for the good they do to one. The best method of thanking people is to tell them: "*Jazaakallahu Khayran*" (May Allah grant you the best reward). Mothers should also teach their children to say "*Jazaakallahu Khayran*" whenever they are given something. Parents should also thank their children in this manner whenever their children do something for them.

## BOTH HUSBAND AND WIFE SHOULD EXERCISE PATIENCE

Scholars throughout the ages are unanimous that Hazrat Luqmaan was an extremely wise man. In fact, some are of the opinion that he was a prophet. He was once working in an orchard when the owner of the orchard asked him to bring a cucumber. After peeling the cucumber, the owner sliced it and gave Hazrat Luqmaan slice by slice to eat. Hazrat Luqmaan ate every slice with relish. Seeing the enjoyment on Hazrat Luqmaan's face the owner decided to eat the last slice himself. However, the taste was so bitter that he instantly spat it out.

"This tastes worse than poison, yet you were eating it with so much relish!" exclaimed the owner. "That's true," replied Hazrat Luqmaan. "Why did you not tell me that it is so bitter?" queried the owner. "Why should I complain," replied Hazrat Luqmaan "when the same hand that always feeds me delicious food once gives me something bitter to eat?"

After relating this incident, Maulana Ashraf Ali Thanwi (A.R) comments that there will be no disputes between husband and wife if both remember the above rule. If the wife thinks that since her husband is always good to her, it matters little if he once behaves harshly towards her. At the same time, she should bear in mind that there are many times when he had to overlook things that she did. It is foolish to forget a lifetime of favours merely because of a single annoyance or scolding. Because of a single error on the husband's part, the wife should not blurt whatever she pleases by saying that she has only known hardship after marriage and would be better off dead. Such statements are unfortunately very common and should be avoided at all costs.

By the same token, husbands should remember that their wives do everything to serve them and should not be scolded merely because she once slipped up or did not do as desired. It is therefore imperative for both husband and wife to remember this principle that Hazrat Luqmaan demonstrated.

## When Something Goes Wrong

Whenever one is faced with hardship, the best recourse is what Allah has Himself advised in the Qur'ãn. By practising what Allah advises will earn Allah's pleasure and mercy. Once this is secured every difficulty will become easy and every problem solved. Allah declares,

> **"O you who believe! Seek help by means of patience and *Salaah*. Verily Allah is with the patient ones."** [*Surah Baqara, Surah* 2, verse 153]

In this verse, Allah tells every Muslim male and female that whenever they face any difficulty, they should take support from the pillars of patience and salaah. When this is done, Allah shall alleviate the difficulty because He always remains with the patient ones. It is understood that if Allah is in attendance of those who exercise patience, He will surely be with those who perform *Salaah* because *Salaah* is the greatest of all forms of *Ibaadah*.

A few verses later in the same *Surah*, Allah says,

> **"So give glad tidings to the patient ones."**
> (*Surah Baqarah,* verse 155)

Describing the patient ones, Allah says further,

> **"(They are) those who, when any adversity befalls them, say, 'Verily to Allah do we**

**(together with out wealth and children) belong, and to Him is our return.' These are the ones upon whom the collective and special mercies of Allah descend and who are rightly guided."** (*Surah Baqarah*, verses 156—157)

These verses make it clear that the truly patient people are those who are convinced that everything belongs to Allah. They know that if the Owner of something wants his property back, it is foolish to object. They also know that they will soon be returned to Allah where they will receive the rewards for exercising patience. Such people will be showered with Allah's special mercies reserved only for them. At the same time, they will not be deprived of the collective mercies that others will receive. Praising these people further, Allah says that they have truly been guided because they realise that everything is in control of Allah and that benefit and harm all proceed from Him.

One cannot imagine the great position of people who receive Allah's collective and special mercies, concerning whom Allah Himself has declared that they are rightly guided. Whenever one is faced with any difficulty, one should think that it is happening because Allah wants it to happen. None can avert the decree of Allah or protect one against Allah. Allah's system is unique and there is always a good reason for everything that happens.

One should always remember that life would not be so cherished had there been no death. Similarly, the day would not be appreciated had there been no night just as happiness would be a dull experience without grief and difficulty. This world is a blend of happiness and sadness and one will inevitably face both favourable and unfavourable conditions. The vigour and carefree nature of youth is dampened by the feebleness of old age and the joy of affluence is always threatened by the gloom of poverty. Such are the vicissitudes of this temporary life.

Those Muslim men or women are truly fortunate and wise who realises that every condition is from Allah and should turn to Allah at all times. Allah says in the Qur'ãn,

> **"It is certainly Him (Allah) Who makes (people) laugh and cry."** (*Surah Najm, Surah* 53, verse 43)

If Allah wills, He can make a crying person laugh in an instant and vice versa. Allah is constantly testing His bondsmen to assess their *Imãn*. One should therefore accept every hardship with a smile and seek Allah's assistance by exercising patience and by turning to Him in *Salaah* and *Du'a*.

When faced with a problem, no portion of one's heart and no drop of one's blood should turn to anyone besides Allah or have the inclination to solicit assistance from someone else. Assistance should be sought only from Allah because only He has the power to assist one and He is Most Kind and Most Merciful. Every person wishes to be Allah's friend like Hazrat Ibraheem عليه السلام was without realising that Allah makes only such a person his friend who is prepared to dive into the raging fire of Namrood upon Allah's instruction. Such a person cleanses his heart of all inclinations except his inclination towards Allah. He is convinced that everything that has happened, everything that is happening and everything that will happen in future takes place only by Allah's decree.

## ADVICE TO WOMEN

In his famous work "*Behishti Zewar*", Hakeemul Ummah Maulana Ashraf Ali Thanwi (A.R) says that although it is seldom necessary for women to be told what is right from what is wrong, reminders are always beneficial. By understanding the following principle, many matters will become clearer. The husband and wife relationship is a lifetime relationship. If the couple's hearts are united, they can have no greater bounty. On the contrary, if their hearts are divided, they can suffer no greater calamity.

A woman should therefore win over her husband's heart and should be ready to respond to his slightest indication. Her success in both worlds lies in her readiness to do anything that he wishes. She will have the eternal bounties of the Hereafter in exchange for the temporary hardship of this world. She should do her best never to upset him. Even if he tells her that day is night, she should accept his word without hesitation. Difficult as this may be, it will make the couple inseparable.

## KEEPING THE HUSBAND'S FEELINGS IN MIND

A wife should be vigilant over her husband's feelings and moods. She should joke and laugh with him only when his mood allows. The husband-wife relationship is not a hollow relationship. It is therefore necessary for the wife to realise that she should always maintain a high level of respect for her husband's feelings. It is incorrect for a wife to think that her husband is her equal.

A wife should refrain from asking her husband to do anything for her and if he affectionately wants to massage her arms or head, she should not shrug him off. Such behaviour is disrespectful towards one's father and is even worse towards one's husband because the husband's position is greater than that of one's father. A wife should always respect him in their conversations and should never overstep the limits of respect. ["*Behishti Zewar*"]

## AN UNPARALLELED RELATIONSHIP

Despite taunts of being a "wife-worshipper", a man could not be deterred from his devoted affection for his wife. When she was asked about this, the intelligent lady replied, "I regard my husband as my *Jannah*. The truth is that we are so much in love that we cannot bear separation for even a few moments. Although I am speaking to you presently, my heart is with him. Our love for each other is solely for Allah's pleasure. You may call me a besotted woman but I truly love him because he responds to my love with his own love. He is just as besotted about me and will do anything lawful for me. He takes me to *Deeni* lectures for ladies, from which I benefit tremendously. He rectifies my faults most affectionately and I do not feel offended in any way.

When there is so much love between us, how can we not be besotted with each other?"

Such a relationship is not exclusive to the couple mentioned above. Every woman can harness her husband's love by submitting to him and doing everything he instructs. The proof of the pudding is in the tasting.

## HOW I CONQUERED MY HUSBAND

The following is an account of a Muslim sister. She says:

> The hardships and difficulties I experienced during the years of my marriage are too many to discuss here. All I wish to express is the manner in which I became the darling of my husband.
>
> At the beginning, my husband wanted nothing to do with me and was even prepared to divorce me. However, he changed his mind when some good people managed to persuade him not to do so. I bitterly regretted my decision to marry him and my heart would burn to ashes when I used to see happily married couples. My husband never spoke to me and refused to even drink the water I served. However, my parents-in-law possessed angelic qualities and were always trying to reason with my husband. Their efforts regrettably fell on deaf ears. They nevertheless sympathised with me and treated me well.
>
> During a spare moment one day, I happened to read a book by Hazrat Maulana Ahmad Muhammad Hatorni

Saheb concerning Muslim husbands and wives. Together with this, I perused through some other books containing advices to brides and women a large. I found many factors in these books that applied to me and my life. My heart skipped a beat when I read the discussion about keeping one's husband happy. It occurred to me that I was also capable of conquering my husband as the book discussed.

I studied my behaviour and habits and focussed all my attention on my husband. I convinced myself that I could inculcate in myself all the qualities that my husband admired in women. I thought that if I am successful in this, my husband would certainly pay more attention to me. I therefore gave attention to the following three factors:

1) Determining the temperament of my husband.
2) Determining what qualities he admires in a woman.
3) Determining what he dislikes.

I then exerted all my faculties in studying his temperament, his likes and his dislikes. I managed to determine exactly what he admired in other women and I beautified myself accordingly. I also inculcated in myself the behaviour that he liked and cooked everything he liked. One day, he said to me, "You are becoming more beautiful each day." I gave no reply and thought to myself that by Allah's grace the arrow had struck its target. I could not stop thanking Allah as my heart swelled with joy. He then said, "Why are you looking so stunning?" I now thought that I would lose the opportunity if I did not reply.

I smiled and said, "When was I not attractive? I always looked like this but you took no interest." While saying this, I chanced to look him in the eye. I hit the mark and the prey had been ensnared in the trap. He affectionately responded, "No. You are extremely beautiful. I have behaved unjustly towards you and have hurt you unnecessarily. I shall mend my ways and will not allow you to leave my sight."

I have now become my husband's darling. In fact, he refuses to even eat another woman's food. He does whatever I ask and always confers with me before doing anything. My parents-in-law cannot believe what has happened and have congratulated me on my success. My advice to every woman who cannot make an impression on her husband is that she tries what I did. Insha Allah she will certainly succeed. Initially when my husband used to ignore my beauty, my youth and my enthusiasm, it seemed as if I was a widow living with my husband.

## DO NOT DIVORCE ME

A married man struck up a relationship with a widow and wanted to marry her. However, she made it clear to him that she would marry him only if he divorced his wife. When he seemed determined to divorce her, she started making *Du'a* to Allah in earnestness. A friend of hers who was a pious lady gave her some advice. She told her to keep certain factors in mind so that she could win back her husband's love. She also wrote a touching poem for the lady to read to her husband which accurately portrayed her feelings. Al Hamdu Lillaah, this poem had a miraculous effect. The husband changed his mind about marrying the other woman and was saved from her lure. Hereunder follows a translation of the poem:

"I used to be proud of the one who is no longer in my fortune
What wrong did I do? Why was I no longer worthy of his love?
I am no longer the decoration of my own home
I am now a worthless object
Without reason, people have now made me a target of abuse
Today I swear on oath that I have always been loyal
A bud in season, I had been a lovely flower in my youth
Alas! Now a bird without wings
The house that we just built is now too small
Oh the grief! Who has become less accommodating?
The one who once regarded me as his thornless rose
The one who for years has been calling me the queen of bouquets

The one who has given me radiance and sunshine
Today he makes me cry, makes me appear like a mere wall
Oh! Was my beauty not an elation for you?
Were you not my king and crown?
If you become annoyed, let it be with me for I shall calm you
As far as you may be from me, I shall call you closer
Do not stagger. Come forward and I shall accommodate you
I shall seat you in my eyes and in my heart
The wealth and assets of this world are trivial and can easily be lost
This entire world is trivial - but not my husband
Please tell me if I have erred
What crime can deserve such severe punishment?
Or are you hurting me for no reason? Then continue
My head is suspended in a noose, hit it as you please
I implore you in the name of the Magnanimous Rabb,
Keep me as your wife even if it be as a servant to your other wife
Why should I express what is in my heart?

I am happy with whatever pleases you
I am busy praying for you, my beloved
You have come to me and left me for carnal pleasures
The day will soon arrive when you will long for true love
Should I be a candle for the privacy of others?
Alas! To die for a woman!
Why did Zulaikha come out alive from Yusuf عليه السلام's room,
When she would have wished to emerge as a corpse (for shame)?
Others may see your familiar appearance
But my self-respect will never allow that
I see this calamity without tears flowing from my eyes
All I require is the drape of chastity (marriage)
It may be said that I will live taking your name
I swear by the Rabb of honour and grace,
I shall give my life serving you
I shall remain loyal to you even though you are not
I shall remain in attendance as a sweeper
If I am unfit for the home, I shall be a wall
Keep me even if I have to be a servant
I shall at least have some support to dispel my grief

I remember how you used to sometimes decorate these plaits,
But never saw the tears (of joy) welling in these eyes
You would sometimes twirl these plaits over your arms
And this lap was often your pillow
I remember when you used to split my path
When you were a gardener, I was your flourishing garden
My bridal garland has not even withered away yet
Sitting here for you, from where has this calamity come?
Who will now see this dejected face of mine
If I exercise patience, my heart will burn to cinders
Separation from you would make me weep forever
Nevertheless, my head is bowed and I submit to the one who issues the divorce."

[Translated from an Urdu poem]

## NEVER ASK FOR ANYTHING ABOVE YOUR HUSBAND'S MEANS

A wife should be content with whatever her husband can afford to provide for her. If she desires something that he is unable to afford, she should not ask for it.

Should she ask for such a thing, the husband will automatically think that she is inconsiderate. Of course, if the husband asks her what she would like to have, she may express her desire. She should not ask for it without his request because asking people for things lowers one in their sight. Ask only from Allah. Allah loves those who ask from Him and is displeased with those who do not ask of Him. On the other hand, people become displeased when asked for something. Remember that Allah has given people whatever they have and He can easily give you the same.

Dear sister! It is unfortunate that nowadays we tend to live beyond our means. Apart from the fact that the cost of living has soared, people tend to turn a blind eye to their necessities and keep buying things that they do not need. A man who is not in debt should be very grateful to Allah. One should remember that besides Allah, no one will be there for one if one is in a financial crisis. Never buy anything that one can do without and never spend beyond one's means.

It is extremely imprudent of many "fashionable" women to waste their husbands' hard-earned money on unnecessary clothing and fashion accessories. Every wife ought to economise and save something every month for rainy days. Economising does not mean that one should be miserly. It simply means that one should not spend on things that are not necessary and that one should not pay more for something that can be bought for less.

## How an Intelligent Woman Runs her Home

"The first element of sound home management is dexterity

Worry about others before yourself

Timeless practice dictates that the man shall earn and provide

The wife's task is to use the money prudently

For peace of mind, the bedding should be only as large as the material

How can a woman lacking this skill ever enjoy prosperity?

The woman deficient in wisdom can only be called a poor housewife

She can achieve nothing with the task of service entrusted to her

She will waste all their money in so many things

Her mother-and-sisters-in-law will then be antagonistic towards her

Not one, but hundreds of calamities will strike because of this

Her husband will regret his marriage with every breath

He will kill himself working without having anything at home

She squanders everything that he brings home

Such behaviour is wrong, refrain from it dear sister

Spend in a avenues where spending is required

Your father-in-law will be happy, your husband will be happy and you will still remain as you are." [Translated from an Urdu poem]

## THE ETIQUETTE OF MEETING ONE'S HUSBAND WHEN HE RETURNS FROM A JOURNEY

Before leaving on a journey, a husband asked his wife what he should bring for her. She said, "May Allah bring you back safely because you are my greatest blessing in this world and the Hereafter. I need nothing but that you return to me safely." Any husband would be glad to hear such a reply because it indicates that she loves him more than material things.

When the husband returns, the wife should ask him how he is feeling and whether everything went well. She should show concern about what he ate and what he did. She should express gratitude to Allah for returning him home safely and should also tell the children to express gratitude to Allah. When her husband returns, the wife should never bombard him with all the problems she experienced in his absence and then follow this up with a barrage of questions like "What did you bring for me?", "What did you bring for the children?" and "Did you spend all our money?" Such questions will cause a wife to fall from the sight of her husband.

Of course, once he has settled at home, she may ask him everything about the journey. She should also show happiness with whatever he brings for her even though it may not be exactly what she wants. She should never tell him that he should have brought something in a different style, a different colour, etc. Saying such things will hurt his feelings and discourage him from bringing gifts in future. She should praise everything he brings and thank him profusely

## TAKE GOOD CARE OF YOUR HUSBAND'S POSSESSIONS

A wife should be particular about caring for her husband's possessions and keeping them in an orderly fashion. The room should always be neat, the bed should always made and the bedding always clean. It is useless if the husband has to tell the wife to keep the house tidy because things are more appreciated when they get done without a bidding. The wife should be even more particular about the tidiness of those things that her husband is fussy about. If he gives her something to put away, she should ensure that she keeps it safely. His clothes should be folded or hung neatly and not left strewn around.

There are women who will be found beating the children when the husband steps into the house. Whereas the man may be returning tired and frustrated, yearning for peace and quiet at home, he is confronted by wailing children and an irritated wife. The result: He cannot bear being at home and seeks an outlet in parks, clubs, restaurants and other company. He gradually begins to hate his family, regarding them as punishment for his sins. The incompetence of the wife therefore deprives the innocent children of their father's love and attention. A woman who is constantly screaming at the children and hitting them falls from her husband's eyes and he will soon begin to admire women who are calmer.

Picture this scene. The husband returns home tired. As he enters the door, his wife is chatting to her neighbour over the fence or talking to someone on the phone. Her dressing is shabby and her hair dishevelled. The house is in a mess, with flies buzzing about the dirty dishes scattered about the kitchen. Opening the refrigerator for some water, he finds it dirty, with no water in the water bottle. Picking up a glass to take water from the tap, he finds it sticky and greasy. Such a man is justly warranted to weep over his situation. Who can blame him for looking for another wife?

Women should also refrain from making excuses for things they do not do and from lying because this will reduce their husbands' confidence in them. It should not be that their husbands stop believing even the truths they say.

## WHAT A WIFE SHOULD DO WHEN HER HUSBAND BECOMES ANGRY

When a woman's husband becomes angry or annoyed with something, she should not reciprocate his anger. She should rather hold his hand and apologise even though the fault is not hers. She should regard this apology and asking forgiveness as an honour because gestures like this save marriages. When the fault is hers, she would be foolish to become angry and to sit apart from him because this will drive them further from each other.

When one's husband is angry, one should never say anything that will aggravate him further. If he says anything unpleasant, she should exercise patience and not say anything in return. She should remain silent and ask for forgiveness. Once his anger has subsided, he will regret his behaviour and realise that his wife's conduct was excellent. In this manner, he will not become angry so frequently. If the wife says something during his moment of anger, the situation may erupt and reach dramatic proportions.

## The Approach of a Wise Wife

A man by the name of Waleed had to face a disciplinary hearing at work after being falsely accused of doing something. He was not even given the chance to defend himself. When he returned home, he was obviously upset and irritated. Despite his efforts to suppress his anger, he failed and he burst into a rage merely because he could not find his socks where they usually were. His wife was an intelligent woman and she immediately realised that her husband was not himself that day. She therefore did not interrogate him or rebuke him. She thought it inappropriate to discuss the mater until the couple has eaten and had time to themselves. She then gradually raised the subject and lovingly consoled him. As he spoke to her, the burden on his shoulders began to lighten and her felt much better. By the time he went to bed, he was completely at ease and felt pleased that his lifetime companion was so understanding and comforting.

## WHEN A HUSBAND STRIKES UP AN EXTRA MARITAL RELATIONSHIP

A wife should never accuse her husband of having a relationship with another woman merely because of suspicion. If he is innocent of this, he will be deeply hurt by the accusation. If he is guilty of such a relationship, it will be useless for the wife to vent her anger on him or to make life difficult for him. Such behaviour will sink the wedge between them even deeper and obliterate the last vestiges of feelings he may have for her.

To make one's husband abandon such relationships and to win his complete attention, one should first stand up in *Salaah* during the late hours of the night and make sincere *Du'a* to Allah that one's husband should desist from such practices. At the same time, one should also tell him about the harms of such practices without offending him. Insha Allah, he will soon mend his ways and become one's slave when Allah guides him. If this approach does not bear the desired effect, one should exercise patience and consult pious and learned people.

One should never expose him to others and disgrace him. Neither should one impose on him to stop him because this may make him more adamant. When a wife makes life more difficult for her husband and disgraces him by exposing his faults to others, she will be deprived of even the little attention he used to pay to her.

## HOW TO LIVE AMICABLY WITH IN-LAWS

Together with blood relatives, Allah also speaks about the importance of in-laws.[1] This makes it clear that there are rights due to one's parents-in-law just as there are rights due to one's own parents. It is the right of one's parents-in-law that one should serve them as long as they are alive. If one has to live with one's parents-in-law, one should regard it as one's honour to serve them. Constantly thinking about living by oneself will spoil one's relationship with one's parents-in-law.

Think awhile. A mother carried her son with immense difficulty and endured untold sacrifices and hardships in rearing him. The father also invested his efforts and money in raising his son. After all the effort in raising their son and getting him married, his parents entertained the hope that they will be able to live peacefully with their son and daughter-in-law in their old age and enjoy their grandchildren. How inconsiderate will that daughter-in-law be whose first concern when getting married is to separate this son from his parents? When the mother-in-law learns that the daughter-in-law is planning to separate them from their beloved son, matters begin to deteriorate and life becomes unbearable for all concerned.

A daughter-in-law should live amicable with all her in-laws. She should respect the elders among them, show

1. Allah says:
"It is He Who has created man from water and has appointd for him relatives by blood and relatives by marriage. Your Rabb is Ever Powerful." (*Surah Naml* 24:54)

compassion towards the children of their families and should not feel embarrassed to do what her mother-in-law or sisters-in-law tell her to do. She should never inform her mother about the wrongs that her mother-in-law does because this will lead to unnecessary disputes and will do no good whatsoever.

## SOME ADVICES

1. It should not upset you if your husband gives all his money to his parents and gives you nothing. In fact, if he hands the money over to you, you should decline the offer and suggest that he give it to them. In this manner, your parents-in-law will be impressed and will regard you as one of their own. Always obey your parents-in-law and never occupy your thought with leaving their house because this leads to a strained relationship.
2. Never look down at or feel embarrassed about the work that your in-laws do. By assisting them in their work, they will have great love and admiration for you.
3. Never listen to gossip. Keep away from women who gossip and never add to their gossip.
4. Treat every instruction of your mother-in-law like an instruction from your own beloved mother. Give her pleasure precedence over everything else even though she may not treat one very well. Never contradict her instructions and never backchat when speaking to her. Speak to her with great respect and

never address her as you would address an equal. Never say anything if she scolds you and always remember that your mother-in-law is more important than your husband's mother-in-law. Never speak harshly to her and sip her harshness like a sweet drink. If she delegates a task to someone else, try to do it yourself.

5. Behave respectfully towards all elders like the wives of your husband's elder brothers. Always keep their ages in mind and do not speak to them as you would speak to women of your age. Treat them like your own sisters and you will soon notice that others will treat you likewise. If they are younger than you, be loving and kind towards them and if you cannot do their work for them, assist them as far as possible. Adopt the same attitude towards your husband's sisters. However, you should adopt moderation in your approach because matters may become difficult once the limits of social relations are overstepped. Friendly relations with other women should never lead you to speak about others because anything said about another person which s/he does not like is regarded as backbiting. Backbiting is a major sin.

6. In addition to this, you should also show love and affection towards the children of the family, such as the children of your brothers-and-sisters-in-law. Rasulullah ﷺ has mentioned that the person who does not respect elders and does not show mercy towards youngsters is not from among his followers.

Our beloved Rasulullah ﷺ had great love for children. He once took a child in his lap and took no exception when the child wet him. In fact, he had so much love for children that he did not even approve of deceiving them. A woman once called for a child, telling the child that she would give him something if he came to her. Unlike many people who tell children this as a ruse, she had a date to give him. When Rasulullah ﷺ learnt that she actually had something to give the child and had not intended to deceive him, Rasulullah ﷺ told her that she would have been a liar if she had nothing to give him.

7. Never burden your servant with more work than she can manage. If additional work has to be given, you should assist her. Never behave harshly towards her and be sympathetic towards her if she is ill or experiencing some difficulty. Assist her in her work if she is not well. However, do not spoil her and make her lazy because she will then have to face the wrath of every employee she works for after you. If you have some delicacy to eat or drink, keep aside a share for her, even though it may be only a little.

**Note:** Hakeemul Ummah Maulana Ashraf Ali Thanwi (A.R) has written[1] that although a woman should do her best to abide by the above, these are all moral teachings and she is not obliged to live with her in-laws. If she demands to live separately, her husband

1. "*Islaah Inqilaab*", vol. 2, Page 188.

is obliged to provide separate quarters for her. In fact, moral conduct demands that if the parents-in-law do not need anyone to care for them, the husband should provide separate accommodation for his wife if he possibility is strong that she would not be able to live comfortably with his parents (as is the general case nowadays).

## Ponder Awhile!

In many cases where a daughter-in-law wants to live separately, it is the sisters-in-law (husband's sisters) who oppose the idea. However, the same sisters-in-law seem to forget that when they married, they made *Du'a*, asked others make *Du'a* and even had *Ta'weezaat* (amulets) made so that they could live separately. Despite the fact that they may have some difficulty in running their own home, women prefer to live on their own because they realise that living by themselves is the key to happiness. It is rather strange that when women become mothers-in-law and sisters-in-law, they forget the benefits of living separately and can suddenly prove to anyone that there is more harm in living separately.

Our *Daarul Ifta*[1] regularly receives complaints from parents whose daughters are unhappy living with their in-laws. Many of them are even prepared to provide alternate accommodation because they realise the harms of living together. Regrettably, these are the same people who insist

1. A faculty of a Darul Uloom (Islamic University) staffed by Muftis who respond to queries from the public.

that their daughters-in-law live with them when their sons marry. One ought to realise that just as one's daughter finds it difficult to live with her in-laws, one's daughter-in-law is also someone's daughter and may also experience the same difficulty. One will be unjust to demand separate accommodation for one's daughter and insist on sharing accommodation with one's daughter-in-law.

If a man cannot afford to provide separate accommodation for his wife, the least he should do is provide her a kitchen of her own or allow her to cook by herself.

**Four Things are Required from a Woman**

Piety in her Heart.
Modesty on her Face.
Sweetness on her Tongue.
Diligent work on her Hands.

May Allah abundantly reward every Muslim sister who reads this book and encourages others to do the same.

## HOW A WOMAN CAN BECOME HER HUSBAND'S DARLING

Women often have to bear the brunt of their husband's ill-treatment as well as ill-treatment from their mothers-in-law. If they follow the advices that Rasulullah ﷺ outlined, Allah will soon place compassion for her into the hearts of her husband and her mother-in-law. As a result of this, she will be able to live happily and the entire family will also be able to live with happiness. May Allah grant every Muslim woman the ability to practise these advices. *Aameen*

Here are four factors that will certainly create compassion in any husband's heart irrespective of his wife's level of intelligence. By employing these, the couple will be able to live with love and happiness. The four factors are:

i) The husband and wife should be pious.

ii) The wife should understand the husband's temperament.

iii) The wife should praise the husband and have true love for him.

iv) She should cook good food for him.

### (1) The Couple Should be Pious and United

Unless and until the husband and wife both become pious, they cannot hope to be united. Allah says in the Qur'ãn,

**"So the pious women are obedient and, in the absence of their husbands, are protective**

**because of that which Allah has protected."**

(*Surah Nisaa, Surah* 4, verse 34)

This verse of the Qur'ãn describes the pious wife as one who accepts her husband as her leader, who obeys him and who safeguards her chastity and his wealth in his absence. Her behaviour should be chaste both in his presence and absence. She should also ensure that she manages the domestic affairs efficiently. "*Saalihaat*" (pious women) as described in the above verse also refers to women who are particular about their *Salaah*, fasting and all their other religious duties. Together with fulfilling Allah's rights, she also fulfils the rights of her husband. A person who disobeys Allah cannot be expected to obey anyone else.

A woman should neither miss any *Salaah* nor delay it. She should begin preparing for *Salaah* as soon as the time for the *Salaah* sets in. In addition to the *Faraa'idh*, she should also be particular about the *Sunnah* and *Mustahab* acts. She should perform *Salaah* with so much concentration as if she is looking at Allah. If this is not possible, she should bear in mind that Allah's watching her. One will be able to perform *Salaah* with perfect concentration when one does not lose sight of the fact that one is standing in Allah's court.

Every wife should also make time to recite the Qur'ãn and to engage in *Zikr*. Special attention should be given to abstaining from sin. One should ensure that no non-*Mahram* man sees any part of your body. Allah has granted every limb and every hair of the body as a trust. Every person is therefore obliged to safeguard this trust. A woman should undertake to screen her body from every person whom Allah has commanded that she veil herself, even from her cousins and brothers-in-law. She should guard against every sin and should she inadvertently commit a sin, she should repent immediately.

If you need to leave your house for some necessity, ensure that you are covered properly and that no non-*Mahram* can see any part of your body. Should he see any part of your body, he will be sinful for looking just as you will be sinful for exposing that part. You will therefore be guilty of sinning as well as for being a cause of another person sinning. If a woman emerges from her house without covering herself as she should and a hundred men look at her, she will be the cause of two hundred eyes becoming the prey of Allah's wrath. If she has been the cause of Allah's wrath, how can she possibly earn her husband's pleasure? How will her children be obedient to her? Because she has incurred the wrath of the *Rabb* of the universe, she can expect hardship to come her way. Of course, Allah's wrath can be averted from her if she sincerely repents to Allah and resolves to abstain from all major and minor sins.

The woman who carries out the injunctions of the *Shari'ah* and who adopts the pure character taught by Rasulullah ﷺ will become worthy of being called a human being. Such a woman will be regarded as a cultured person and will be an embodiment of love and compassion. She will then be able to endure difficulty for the sake of others and tolerate others. The man who marries such a woman will remain a happy man. If a woman becomes pious, she can attain ranks higher than those of many men and will enter *Jannah* before them.

**Women Entering Jannah before their Husbands**

Addressing some women, Rasulullah ﷺ once mentioned that a pious woman shall enter *Jannah* before her husband. When her husband arrives in *Jannah*, she will have already taken a bath and applied perfume. She will be transported in red and yellow carriages and youngsters resembling scattered pearls will accompany her. Commenting on this *Hadith*, Hakeemul Ummah Maulana Ashraf Ali Thanwi (A.R) has mentioned that the only requirement needed for this honourable position is for a woman to become pious, which is not a difficult task at all. A poet says,

> "Bow in submission to the *Shari'ah* of Muhammad ﷺ
> By his mere indication, be prepared to kill yourself
> The head that does not bow to Allah's commands
> Will have to bow to powerless idols
> Kiss the Qur'ãn with respect as you place it on your forehead
> Contentment is the capital of the heart, so place it in your bosom." (Translated from an Urdu poem)

**The Person Who Refuses to be a Servant of One will be the Slave of Thousands**

One should never think that the woman who roams the streets without dressing according to the *Shari'ah* is a free woman. Remember that the person who is not subservient to Allah has in fact chosen to be subservient to thousands of others. The person with the most freedom is the one who opts to pay servitude to One Allah. Allah will fill the heart of such a person with peace and contentment.

Ask any woman not dressed according to the *Shari'ah* what prevents her from dressing like a proper Muslim should. She will tell you that her relatives, her society or something else is preventing her. This reveals that she has opted to serve these people instead of the Wisest of the wise. Instead of serving Allah, she prefers serving her relatives, her manager, her director, her principal, her company's rules, her friends, the customers at the shop or restaurant where she works, the passengers of the airline that employs her, her boss for whom she plays the role of a private secretary or the clients who see her at the reception desk where she works.

In his book concerning the hoax of women's liberation, Hazrat Mufti Taqi Usmani (A.R) has mentioned that the slogans of women's liberation have been used as a subterfuge to remove women from their homes and to parade them on the streets. To achieve this aim, women have been given posts as clerks, secretaries and typists. To boost sales in businesses, they have been made salesladies and models and every part of their bodies has been made an advertisement to promote products. The woman whom Islãm has crowned with honour and chastity has been reduced to a lowly showpiece to sell cheap commodities and a toy to dispel man's boredom.

If one looks at the occidental countries of the world, one will notice that lowly jobs have been assigned to women. One will scarcely find a waiter in a restaurant, only waitresses. Hotel staff who clean rooms, people serving customers at businesses and receptionists are predominantly women. It is appropriate to quote a stanza from the above poem a second time:

> "The head that does not bow to Allah's commands
> Will have to bow to powerless idols."

## The Strange Psychology of a New Culture

It is indeed strange that when a woman prepares food and serves it to her husband and children, enjoying their loving gazes and conversation, she is labelled as a backward and oppressed person. On the other hand, when she serves food to thousands of strange people as an air-hostess, becoming the target of countless lustful gazes, she is regarded as being a liberated and progressive woman. This is the warped philosophy of today's culture. The mentality of people has retrogressed to such an ebb a woman thinks that she is respectable when she uses her charms to attract customers as a saleslady or a model or when she charms her boss into thinking that she is a good secretary.

In the sight of Allah, a truly respectable woman worthy of immense rewards is that woman who remains indoors to diligently serve her family and manage their domestic affairs. Man's psychology has reversed. Instead of serving her family, each of whom will give their lives for hers, today's woman prefers to rather serve people she does not know, many of whom would not bat an eyelid to ravage her honour and chastity. Instead of serving people who look at her with respect as their mother, she would rather serve people who look at her as a servant ready to jump at their bidding. This is really the disfigured psychology of people who dare to call themselves civilised.

**To Summarise:**

To summarise what has been mentioned above, it may be said that no one is free in this world. A person is either subservient to Allah or to *Shaitaan.* While some choose to submit to the *Shari'ah,* others submit to their carnal desires or to social pressures. Every person therefore has the choice to choose which type of bondage s/he wants for herself/ himself. Addressing faithful wives, a poet says:

"When the dark night enshrouds the woman's world
Your braided hair puts the morning to shame
Dancing on the stage with their harps, many women are selling
The charm of their eyes and the colour of their cheeks
Before them every new opportunity is a showcase
While your stage is the gaze of your husband."

(Translated from an Urdu poem)

**Progress or Destruction?**

No one denies that bread can be eaten in a restaurant just as it can be eaten at home. Similarly, the night will pass whether it is spent in a nightclub or at home. A sick person can be cared for in a hospital as well as in his own home. By the same token, women can be bribed with money and other rewards to bear children for the state, who will be reared and cared for by paid nurses in state institutions (as is reportedly being done in Russia). However, one should remember that living in restaurants and dying in hospitals can never replace family life just as children raised by the state cannot make a nation.

There is a world of difference between rearing children and manufacturing shoes. If rearing children is treated like manufacturing commercial products, the end result will resemble a human being in looks but will be devoid of human qualities. Although a clone looks like the real thing, it can never be like the original.

Irrespective of how "free" women deem themselves, they will always be subservient to man in some respect or another. From the beginning of time up to the present day, women have never succeeded in overshadowing men. This proves that fate has already determined that women should exist under the leadership of men. This is because Allah has declared

> **"Men are the leaders of women because of the virtue, Allah has bestowed some of you over others."** (*Surah Nisa*, 4:34)

None can alter this decree of Allah and whoever attempts to do so shall meet humiliation and destruction.

## (2) Recognising the Husband's Temperament

The second factor by which the wife can win her husband's heart is by always taking his feelings and sentiments into consideration. She should take to heart everything he says and comply with his lawful desires. Pay attention to what he says and do not speak while he is speaking because this is disrespectful by any standard. If you need to say something, do so after he has spoken. It often happens that a person interrupts the speaker with a question before he has completed his piece whereas the question would have been answered during the course of the speech if the listener had been patient. Matters tend to become complicated and confusing with interruptions. Repeated questions also aggravate the speaker, leading to unnecessary problems. When your husband has said his piece, his instructions should be duly carried out.

Hazrat Qaari Tayyab (A.R) has mentioned that it is compulsory for a wife to do as her husband says. A wife should obey her husband even if he instructs her to do something that she dislikes. In such an event she should not behave arrogantly and backchat. The home will run smoothly when the wife obeys the husband and when he takes her feelings into consideration. However, she cannot win over his heart unless she obeys everything he says and regards him above herself. Obedience breeds obedience whereas disobedience will create dislike for her in his heart.

The wife who wants her husband to be her slave should first become his slave. As she obeys him, so too will be begin to obey her. Every wife should therefore always take cognisant of the things that her husband dislikes so that she may refrain from them. She should not do what he dislikes, should not cook what he dislikes, should not wear what he dislikes and should not go to places he disapproves of. In doing this, she will be doing the things that he likes and gaining his pleasure all the time.

It is also necessary for the husband to take his wife's feelings and desires into consideration. She has come to his home with a set of likes and inclinations. He should determine what these are and set out to satisfy them as best as he can. Besides him, there is none who can do this for her. When both partners play their role well, the show will run smoothly and all will be happy.

## (3) Praising the Husband and Having True Love for Him

The third factor effective in harnessing the affection of one's husband is to have true love for him and his family and to praise them in front of others. Many women have the bad habit of always trying to find out whether relations are good or tense between a woman and her in-laws. They will make every attempt to "fish out" the situation from an unsuspecting daughter-in-law. It is appalling that mothers actually train their daughters to backbite and find faults by asking them on the second day of marriage about their mothers-in-law.

It is unfortunate that when they return to their parents' home, women grossly exaggerate the faults of their in-laws and the hardships they experience. Hearing this, other women spice interpretation the stories and narrate them with great relish to everyone else. Eventually, an extremely ugly picture of the mother-in-law and her daughters is painted. When the story eventually reaches the mother-in-law, she is naturally upset beyond proportions.

The mother-in-law then tells her son what his wife is informing people about them. She also makes others witness to what has been said and often tells him that the narrator is truthful beyond doubt. The husband then begins to drift away from his wife, often without her even realising that she was the cause. The disputes and arguments between the couple then become uncontrollable and divorce or a lifetime of marital problems are often the end result.

It is therefore necessary for a wife to praise her husband, his parents and his relatives when speaking about them. She should not speak ill of them even when asked. This attitude will foster good relations between husband and wife and when her mother-in-law and sisters-in-law find out that she praises them in front of others, their love for her will grow and they will treat her well. They will even praise her in front of her husband, causing his admiration for her to increase. When the couple are happy, they will be able to prepare for their *Aakhirah* and concentrate on raising their children as good Muslims who will be a great asset to Islãm.

In addition to being a major sin, speaking ill of one's husband and in-laws violates the sanctity of the home and does not behove a good wife.

If a husband's love for his wife is lacking for some reason, praising him will increase this love substantially. She should also tell him how much she loves him, emphasising that she loves him more than anything else in this world and that she cannot live without him. Hazrat A'isha ﵂ used to recite the following couplets when Rasulullah ﷺ used to return home:

"I have a sun and the horizon has a sun
But my sun is better than the sun in the sky
Because that sun rises after dawn
While my sun rises after Isha."

When a man hears words like this from his wife, not only will his love for her increase, but his health, his youth and every other faculty will gleam ever so brightly. Such sweet words are sufficient to cure any physical or mental ailment and to dispel any anxiety. There will definitely be a large place reserved for such a wife in her husband's heart. In fact, this was one of the reasons why Rasulullah ﷺ loved Hazrat A'isha ﵂ the most. Every wife should attempt to study a biography of Hazrat A'isha ﵂ to learn what the factors were that made her so beloved to Rasulullah ﷺ. A comprehensive biography of this nature has been written by Hazrat Maulana Sayyad Sulaymaan Nadwi (A.R). By emulating her pure lifestyle, every wife can become the focus of her husband's attention. He will then see to her every need and will not do anything without her.

The words of Hazrat A'isha ﵂ were not mere words but true expressions of her feelings for Rasulullah ﷺ. She also said, "If the women who taunted Zulaikha had seen Rasulullah ﷺ, they would have cut their hearts instead of just their hands." These can only be the words of someone truly in love. They do not have to be taught to such a person, but will flow spontaneously.

Another sign of love for one's husband is that the wife does everything to increase his happiness when he is happy. When he speaks to her with love and kindness, she should respond in a like manner. When the husband is distressed and worried, the wife should do what she can to relieve his grief.

Hazrat Ali رضي الله عنه once light-heartedly said the following couplet:

"Women are certainly *Shayaateen* created for (misleading) us
We seek Allah's protection for the evil of the *Shayaateen*."
In response to this, his wife Hazrat Faatima رضي الله عنها replied using the same Arabic style of poetry:
"Women are certainly fragrant flowers created for you
And each of you draws close to them, hoping to get a whiff."

After a tiring day at work, every man will be refreshed by the sweet and inspiring words of his wife.

Hazrat Aatika رضي الله عنها was married to Hazrat Abdullaah رضي الله عنه the son of Hazrat Abu Bakr رضي الله عنه. When he was martyred at

Taa'if, she was extremely grieved and said, "I swear that grief shall never part from my eyes nor will dust leave my body." These words truly express the intense love that she had for her husband. In fact, the *Sahabiyaat* رضي الله عنهن possessed such extreme love for their husbands that the nations of the world fail to match.

Loving one's husband plays a vital role in *Deen* because it is a means of securing Allah's pleasure. It is a means of safeguarding the chastity of society and ensuring the stability and happiness of future generations. It is an extremely effective solution to marital problems. The story of Hazrat Ibraheem (عليه السلام)'s daughter-in-law portrays an example of how a wife ought to be grateful and praise the good in her home without mentioning the difficulties. Her behaviour pleased her father-in-law and pleased Allah as well. In fact, this lady was so blessed that together with earning the *Du'a* of Hazrat Ibraheem عليه السلام, Allah made his most beloved Rasulullah صلى الله عليه وسلم a scion of her progeny.

Every bride should therefore express gratitude to her husband from the very first day of her marriage, irrespective of how little she gets. She should never find fault with anything in her new home and should rather praise whatever he gives her and be thankful to Allah. Through the blessings of such an attitude, her husband will be more compassionate towards her and pious people will be born in her progeny, who will be of great service to the *Deen*. It is not farfetched to expect that today's women can also raise children the likes of Hazrat Khaalid bin Waleed رضي الله عنه, Amr bin Al Aas رضي الله عنه, Umar bin Abdul Azeez, Aalamgeer, Salaahud *Deen*

Ayoobi, Shah Isma'eel Shaheed, Maulana Muhammad Ilyaas and Maulana Ashraf Ali Thanwi (A.R). However, it is necessary that women become exemplary role models for their children.

A lady once wrote:

"If you count yourself among the daughters of this *Deen* of guidance
If you have value for the narrations of your predecessors
What are we, what is our veiling, our abstinence and our piety?
Do not ask what the Mu'min women of the first century have done
It was their love for their husbands and service to their children
It was their smooth running of the home and obedience to Allah
It was their donning the *Hijaab*, their modesty, their chastity and their loyalty
It was their chaste behaviour in adhering to Allah's command when He says
'Do not speak in lowered tones'
And it was their preparation for *Jihaad*."

(Translated from an Urdu poem)

## A Principle to Follow for a Sound Relationship Between Husband and Wife

A woman once came to Hazrat Umar ﷺ and made it clear to him that she had no instinctive love for her husband.

Hazrat Umar ﷺ explained, "Never make this known to your husband. Tell him that you love him very much (even though you have to pretend) because there are very few homes built on instinctive love. People live with each other on the basis of their status and Islãm (i.e. people respect and obey each other because of their regard for each other's status and their being Muslims). The couple should accept and fulfil the responsibilities that Islãm has detailed for each of them. This is the only way by which their relationship will become pleasant."

There are few couples blessed with perfect compatibility which enables them to have strong instinctive love for each other. The love of such people keeps growing despite numerous obstacles. Because everyone is not blessed with such a relationship, the *Shari'ah* has chalked out principles by which others can also develop their love. If a couple respect each other, are prepared to overlook each other's faults, keep expressing their love for each other, forget past mishaps and proceed with clear hearts, they will soon find themselves deeply in love. They will then become a united body, sharing everything, including each other's heartache. No obstacle will be insurmountable because they will be doing things together.

Another principle that Hazrat Umar ﷺ mentioned as recorded in another narration is that the couple should always express more love than their hearts contain. In this manner, their love will steadily grow and they will both be at peace with each other. They will then be able to carry out all their functions for this world as well as for the next.

## A Sign of True Love

Another manner of securing the attention and compassion of one's husband is to always apologise and ask for forgiveness after an altercation. This will remove any anger and dislike that may creep into his heart. A good wife cannot get any rest until her husband is happy with her. When people have rancour and enmity in their hearts, they are deprived of Allah's mercy and are vulnerable to calamities and hardships. People whose hearts are contaminated with such impurities can expect problems that are beyond their expectations. One should therefore cleanse one's heart from any ill-feelings towards others.

Allah has taught man the following *Du'a* in the Qur'ãn:

> {Translation: "**And do not place any impurity in our hearts against those who believe. O our Rabb! Indeed You are the Most Forgiving, Most Merciful.**"} (*Surah* 59, verse 10)

One of the bounties of *Jannah* will be that people's hearts will be cleansed of malice and hatred for each other. Allah says in *Surah Hijr*,

> "**We shall remove any animosity that may be in their breasts. As brothers they (the people of *Jannah*) will be seated on couches, facing each other.**" (*Surah* 15, verse 47)

The hearts of husband and wife should be as clear as mirrors for each other. Their hearts should exude love for each other at all times, whether in health or illness;

happiness or sadness; youth or old age. They should always bear in mind that their disputes are not merely disputes between the two of them, but will affect perhaps hundreds of people when both families get involved. Their ripple effects of their disputes could run down to many generations.

It is therefore necessary that the couple always patch up their relationship after every dispute. They should immediately dispel any malice that may have crept into their hearts. Because the wife's heart is softer, she should be the first to ask for forgiveness even though the fault is the husband's. If she does not apologise, the husband should do so. They should then forget the entire episode. When such a situation arises, she should remember the following *Hadith.*

**The Woman who will Enter Jannah**

Imaam Tabraani (A.R) has narrated from Hazrat Anas رضي الله عنه that Rasulullah ﷺ once asked the *Sahabah* رضي الله عنهم, "Should I inform you which of your men shall enter *Jannah*?" "Certainly," responded the Sahabah رضي الله عنهم. Rasulullah ﷺ said, "Every prophet shall be in *Jannah,* every *Siddeeq* will be in *Jannah,* every martyr shall be in *Jannah* as well as every person who visits his brother in the far end of the city only for Allah's pleasure." Rasulullah ﷺ then asked, "Should I inform you which of your women shall enter *Jannah.*" When the *Sahabah* رضي الله عنهم requested to be informed, Rasulullah ﷺ said, "The women who has tremendous love for her husband, who bears many children and when she gets angry or is ill-treated or when her husband becomes angry, she (takes his hand in hers and) tells him, 'My hand is in yours. I shall not line my eyes with sleep (I shall not have any rest) until you are pleased.'"

("*At Targheeb wat Tarheeb*" Vol. 4 Pg. 125)

This *Hadith* makes it clear that a woman can earn her entry into *Jannah* by merely becoming uneasy when a rift is created between herself and her husband. If only women could understand this!

When a wife has true love for her husband, she will be unable to rest, eat or sleep after an argument. She will not find pleasure in anything until they make up have forgiven each other.

## (4) Cooking Good Food for Him

The fourth method by which a woman can capture her husband's attention is by learning how to cook well for her husband and being able to place a wonderful meal before him. This skill is exceptionally important for a good wife because it is a well-known fact that the way to a man's heart is through his stomach. The meals that a wife prepares affects the husband's heart as well as every limb of his body. The method and hygiene the wife employs to prepare his meals has a profound effect on the husband's love for her as well as on his opinion about her intelligence and skill.

Although serving bread, butter and jam for breakfast and simple dishes for lunch and supper will fill his belly, preparing sumptuous dishes is healthier and will increase the love he has for his wife. Every woman should master her culinary skills at her mother's home. She should learn to prepare tasty dishes from whatever means her husband is able to provide. She should also learn how to prepare the same meals in various ways so that it may taste different on various occasions. When a woman does this, her husband will fulfil her desires without her having to ask and will give her a choice in all matters. He will also ask her what *Du'as* she would like him to make for her.

When a wife cooks to please her husband for Allah's pleasure, she will earn the following three rewards:

1. She will be rewarded for pleasing Allah.
2. She will be rewarded for pleasing her husband.
3. She will be rewarded for the gratitude to Allah that every person who eats the food expresses. Therefore, if her husband, her in-laws and her children enjoy the food, they express their gratitude to Allah for the good food. Because she was the cause of them being grateful to Allah, she will be rewarded for the gratitude that each of them expresses to Allah.

Laying out the table-cloth[1] is also something that every wife should learn. Whether she has only a plastic sheet to

1. The word tablecloth is used here and in other places instead of the word table. This is to emphasise the *Sunnah* method of eating on a table-cloth spread on the floor. As proven by many *Ahadith*, Rasulullah ﷺ never ate from a table as is common today. Every Muslim home should therefore acquaint themselves with sitting on the floor when eating.

spread or whether she has a lace cloth, she should ensure that it is clean. If she has only plastic dishes instead of fine porcelain crockery, the most important factor is that it must be clean so that one is tempted to drink the water poured in because of its remarkable clarity. The person drinking will then be compelled to say:

> {Translation: "All praise be to Allah who has provided cool, palatable and quenching water for us to drink without making it salty and bitter because of our sins."}

Together with all the dishes and cutlery being gleaming, the fruit and vegetables should also be clean. Even if you are making salad, arrange it in a tempting manner. According to your means, serve some sweet drink whenever possible to add extra flavour to the food. Hukamaa (plural of Hakeem - practitioner in alternative medicine) are of the opinion that looking at a fresh and green plan or tree early in the morning strengthens and soothes the eyes. This being the case, one cannot imagine how much more soothing to the eyes and comforting to the mind and body is the sight of a smiling wife with sweet words pouring from her lips at this time of the day.

Hukamaa also mention that when the tablecloth and eating area is spacious and clean, digestion is aided and the food supplies all the necessary nutrition by Allah's command. It is therefore beneficial to have a vase with roses or other flowers on the tablecloth. In addition to this, the dining area should be spacious and well ventilated. Of course, there is really no need for flowers when Allah has granted a couple real flowers in the form of wonderful and cheerful children who add a special ambience to the meal. The sparkling company that these flowers provide with their beaming faces are more conducive to good digestion than any medication.

It is unfortunate that lack of understanding and short-sightedness has led parents to feel that their children are a burden. They fail to realise that these children are the cure their illnesses and difficulties. Many women feel that they cannot do any constructive work with their children in the way, little realising that caring for their children is itself a great and noble work. They fail to realise that rearing their children and serving their husbands as great a virtue as reciting Qur'ãn and making *Zikr.*

Girls should therefore be trained to cook from a young age. If, for example, a woman can prepare chicken in ten different manners, she will be able to serve ten different dishes. A simple dish prepared and served with flair is often much more enjoyable than an expensive dish. Similarly, serving a dessert, salad, sauce or drink lends opulence to even a simple meal.

However, one should remember that all one's time should not be used for cooking, leaving no time for *Ibaadah,* rest or tending to the children. It does not behove a Muslim woman to spend all her time in the kitchen. Every woman should therefore bear the following three factors in mind so that all her time is not squandered in the kitchen:

1. She should make *Wuzu* and perform her *Ishraaq*[1] *Salaah.* She should also perform *Salaatul Haajah* [2] and ask Allah to grant her needs, especially on the days when she is expecting visitors. On such days, she should make *Du'a* to Allah saying, "O Allah! Only You can give taste to food, so add taste to my food. Create light in the hearts of everyone who eats this food so that they may become pious and beloved to You. You be pleased with me for preparing this meal for my husband's pleasure."
2. Be particular about cooking early in the morning immediately after the *Ishraaq Salaah* because Allah has blessed the mornings for the *Ummah* of Rasulullah ﷺ. During this time, one can achieve in a single hour what would take three or four hours during any other part of the day. Women who do not begin early in the morning find no blessings in their time and often have to work late to complete their work. One should therefore engage oneself in *Zikr* and recitation of the Qur'ãn after *Fajr Salaah* and then begin one's work immediately after *Ishraaq.* Everything will then get done easily and in the shortest time.
3. Continuously make *Du'a* and *Zikr* while doing your work. If one knows *Surah Yaaseen* or any other

---

1. This comprises of two to four *Rakaahs Salaah* performed once the sun has risen to the equivalent of a spear's length above the horizon.
2. Two *Rakaahs Salaah* that may be performed at any time with the express intention that Allah should assist one with something.

*Surahs* of the Qur'ãn, these should also be read if one is not in the state of impurity. However, the various forms of *Zikr*, *Durood* and *Istighfaar* may be recited in any condition. This will also help in making the food tasty and getting the work done easily and quickly. By preparing the food in the state of *Wudhu* and making *Zikr* while cooking, Allah will fill the hearts of those eating the food with *Noor* (celestial light). The result of this will be that the person eating will receive spiritual nutrition together with physical nutrition. She/he will then be able to carry out more good deeds and stay away from sin.

May Allah grant every woman the guidance to carry out what has been mentioned. *Aameen*

## IMAAM GHAZAALI (A.R)'S ADVICE TO THE BRIDE

In his masterpiece "*Ihyaa'ul Uloom*", Imaam Ghazaali (A.R) has given the following advices to brides:

- A pious woman should stay indoors. It is unbecoming of a respectable woman to climb on to the roof of her home (in areas where people use the roofs of their homes as another storey) and to gaze out of the windows.
- Speak less to your neighbours and visit only when necessary. In fact, you should go out of the house only when necessary.

- Whether your husband is home or not, you should be concerned about his welfare.
- Make his pleasure the object of everything you do.
- Never be unfaithful to him.
- Always safeguard his property.
- Never go out of the house without his permission and if he does permit you, wear the simplest clothing and fulfil all the requirements of *Hijaab.* Use roads that have the least traffic.
- Do not become familiar with any non-*Mahram* and make yourself as least conspicuous as possible.
- Keep yourself occupied with the affairs of your home and caring for your property.
- Always be particular about your *Salaah.*
- If any friend of your husband visits while he is out, inform him of your husband's absence using the least amount of words.

## A SPECIAL PRACTICE

One of the sterling practices of a pious wife is that she does everything she can for the home. The management of the affairs of the house rests on her shoulders and she should not neglect any of these duties.

Hazrat Asmaa رضي الله عنها narrates that when she married Hazrat Zubayr رضي الله عنه, he possessed no land, no wealth and no slaves. All he had was a horse and a camel to carry water. She used to feed the horse, water it, and do everything to care for it. She also used to crush date stones for the camel to eat, fill the buckets of water, mend the bucket, knead dough, bake bread and carry date stones from a distance. It was only afterwards that her father Hazrat Abu Bakr رضي الله عنه gave her a slave. After receiving the slave, she felt as if she had been released from bondage. (*Bukhari*)

## THE REWARDS FOR CARRYING OUT ONE'S DOMESTIC CHORES

People are often given to thinking that the husband-wife relationship is a association confined to one's worldly affairs. They regard marriage as a mere medium of fulfilling one's passions. This notion could not be further from the truth. The husband-wife relationship is a union that is replete with religious benefits. If a woman gets married with the intention of fulfilling an injunction of the *Shari'ah*, understanding that her function is to please her husband - a function which will secure Allah's pleasure. Whatever a wife does with this intention in mind will earn her tremendous rewards. Her every act from morning to evening every day of the year will earn Allah's pleasure and will be regarded as a form of *Ibaadah.* Each of these deeds shall be invaluable investments for the *Aakhirah*, even though it means cooking, cleaning the house, rearing the children or seeing to the comfort of her husband. These will be rewarded on condition that the intention is correct.

## DOING THE HOUSEWORK

Allah has assigned the task of working and earning to men. The task of doing the housework, caring for the children and seeing to other domestic affairs has been assigned to women. This has been the practice of mankind since time immemorial.

Whether a woman is rich or poor, she will feel a sense of achievement and elation when she does her housework by herself. In fact, she will do better than a servant. Doing the housework is also an excellent form of exercise and every educated and uneducated person will agree that exercise is vital to the health of every person. Of course, a woman may employ the services of a servant if she needs to. However, the smooth running of the home will be jeopardised when everything is left to the servant. While servants may be able to carry out the menial tasks, the more important tasks should be done by the wife herself.

It is unfortunate that many women nowadays feel ashamed to do their housework and entrust their servants with doing everything. There are also many Muslim women who insist that they should have a maidservant to shirk their responsibilities even though their husbands find it difficult to employ one. Every woman should bear in mind that by doing no work besides issuing instruction, they will become inactive and lazy. Their health will be adversely affected and they may eventually reach a stage where they will be unable to do anything.

Just as men require exercise to maintain their health, women also require the same. Every woman has so much to do at home that she will get the required exercise merely by completing her tasks. Experience has proven that women who do their housework themselves are much healthier than those who have hired help. Women who are accustomed to having servants rapidly succumb to obesity and ill-health.

The *Sahabiyaat* ﷺ did their own housework, as did Rasulullah ﷺ himself. Hazrat Aswad ﷺ once asked Hazrat A'isha ﷺ what Rasulullah ﷺ used to do at home. She replied, "He used to assist his wife in her duties and then leave when it was time for *Salaah*." In another narration, Hazrat A'isha ﷺ narrated that Rasulullah ﷺ would himself mend his shoes, patch his clothing and assist with the housework.

## THE DOMESTIC LIFE OF HAZRAT FAATIMA ﷺ

"In poverty, her condition was such,
she had neither a maidservant nor a slave
Calloused both her palms had become
for daily the grindstone she turned
Carrying the waterbag across her chest again and again
she had become pale even though from her face the light still radiated
Dusty did her clothing remain
on account of her daily sweeping strain
She eventually approached the messenger of Allah ﷺ her father

but fate had it that he was then swamped by
another and another
Because they were not Mahram, she could not
say her part
Since modesty did not allow her there, hastily
did she depart
When Rasulullah ﷺ visited her after a day
he asked, 'What was it that brought you
yesterday?'
Her bashfulness prevented words from reaching
her tongue
So her message did Hazrat Ali رضي الله عنه convey
The pure lady stood there silent
Boldness deserted her because it was an occasion
of respect
Such were the lives of the *Ahlul Bayt*
such was a scene from the life of the daughter of
the best of creation." (Translated from an Urdu poem)

## ACQUIRING SKILLS

Intelligent women do not waste their valuable time in play and entertainment. They invest their time learning new skills such as sewing, knitting, weaving and other crafts. A skill acquired as a child remains useful throughout one's life. People who have learnt a craft need never be dependent on others. A craft that one acquires is a companion in solitude and extremely useful when faced with financial difficulty. One will then not have to stretch out one's hands to others.

The *Sahabiyaat* ﷺ also acquired skills. Hazrat Sauda ﷺ mastered the craft of curing and dying hides that she received from Taa'if. For this reason, she was always more financially independent that the other wives of Rasulullah ﷺ. Hazrat Faatima bint Shayba ﷺ mastered the art of sewing, weaving and stringing beads. Hazrat Safiyya ﷺ mastered the art of cooking. There were many other *Sahabiyaat* ﷺ who spent their time weaving cloth. Hazrat Ummu Ziyaad, Ummu Shahjiyyah ﷺ and a few other *Sahabiyaat* ﷺ were skilled in spinning cloth and were of great assistance to the Muslim army that marched to Khaybar.

## THE ROUTINE OF A PIOUS WIFE

"Early in the born does the loyal wife rise
Beginning the day with the *Fajr Salaah*, no surprise

Here we have the servant lighting the stove
There we have the wife comforting the children

While one is on her lap, the other is tugging at her skirt
These stars are there roaming the garden

The one cries for a biscuit
Another cries to be dressed

She washes each one of them
She feeds something to all

When the husband washes and arrives
The food is before him to choose

With a smile and gleam he is out and away
She completes her meal, content to know that she shall stay

Bringing the baskets, bringing the clothes
Sorting them out by herself

Grabbing the chance between her *Salaah* and *Ibaadah*
She reads avidly from '*Fadhaa'il A'maal*' and '*Behishti Zewar*'

When a friend without *Hijaab* passes by
She is grieved and almost begins to cry

Make *Jannah* your home if you wish
Increase the contents of *Jahannam* if you wish

Elevate our honour if you wish
Or plunge us into disgrace if you wish

Be a disgrace to your era if you wish
Or transcend the limits of honour if you wish

The progression of time makes it clear
The call is coming from everywhere, my dear

'Educating women about Islãm is the door to progress'
'Educating women about Islãm is the pride of progress.'" (Translated from an Urdu Poem)

## LEARNING A LESSON FROM THE LIFE OF HAZRAT FAATIMA رضي الله عنها

When Hazrat Faatima رضي الله عنها married Hazrat Ali رضي الله عنه, the couple decided that he would work outdoors while she tended to all domestic affairs. She therefore fulfilled her tasks and served her husband with great enthusiasm and devotion. However, unlike today's times, the time in which they lived was a period of difficulty. Just to have bread, a woman of those times had to grind the wheat into flour by herself, gather wood to light the oven, kindle the fire and then bake the bread. Despite the hardship involved in this single task, she dutifully continued with all her chores without a word of complaint.

When the Muslims conquered Khaybar and a great deal of booty including many slaves fell to their lot, someone suggested to Hazrat Faatima رضي الله عنها that she request her father ﷺ for a slave to assist her in her work. Consequently, she went to the room of Hazrat A'isha رضي الله عنها and requested her to ask Rasulullah ﷺ for a slave on her behalf because her hands had become calloused as a result of grinding flour and her chest had developed blue lines because of the strain of carrying the water bag to and from the well. When Hazrat A'isha رضي الله عنها related what Hazrat Faatima رضي الله عنها had told her, Rasulullah ﷺ sent for Hazrat Faatima رضي الله عنها. According to another narration, she approached Rasulullah ﷺ directly but returned without placing her request because there were many people with him at the time. According to this narration, Rasulullah ﷺ came to her house afterwards and asked her what she had come for. Because she found it hard to relate her sufferings to Rasulullah ﷺ, Hazrat Ali رضي الله عنه explained the situation to Rasulullah ﷺ. One can well imagine the grief that Rasulullah ﷺ felt when he heard about his daughter's hardship.

Addressing Hazrat Faatima رضي الله عنها, Rasulullah ﷺ said, "I deem it inappropriate that the daughter of Muhammad ﷺ should be given a slave until every person in Madinah has one. However, I shall prescribe for you something that is better than a slave. When you lay down to sleep at night, say '*Subhaa Nallah*' 33 times, '*Al Hamdu Lillaah*' 33 times and '*Allahu Akbar*' 34 times. This is better for you than any slave." She was after all the daughter of the best of creation. Therefore, without saying a word, she felt contented with what her father told her. This prescription is therefore called *Tasbeeh Faatimi.* (*Jaami'ul Usool* Vol.6 Pg. 501)

In this episode, Rasulullah ﷺ used his own beloved daughter to teach Muslims that irrespective of the rights that her husband owes to her from a technical perspective, a Muslim wife ought to care for her husband's home and regard this task as her own. (Mufti Taqi Usmani in his book concerning the rights of husbands)

## RIGHTS PERTAINING TO WEALTH

❖ The wife owes three rights to her husband with regard to his wealth. These are:

1. She should safeguard his wealth.
2. She should not ask for more than she needs.

3. She should be concerned that he does earn unlawful wealth.

- It was therefore the practice of women of the past to remind their husbands every morning to stay away from unlawful earnings. They would reassure their husbands that although they did not fear poverty and were able to bear hunger, they dreaded *Jahannam* and would be unable to bear its punishment. They were therefore contented with anything they received even though little, on condition that it was earned lawfully.
- Every wife should bear in mind that the rights she owes to her husband take precedence over the rights she owes to even herself and over the rights she owes to all her relatives.
- It is also among his rights that she keeps herself clean and neat at all times because he may need to fulfil his conjugal rights at any time.
- Every wife should also treat her children well and display great love and mercy towards them. She should refrain from scolding them too often and should conceal their faults from others.
- One of the most important responsibilities of a wife is that she should not waste her husband's wealth. In fact, it is not at all appropriate for a Muslim wife to waste money on unnecessary clothing, shoes, jewellery, etc. Money is often wasted on these things when extravagant functions like weddings, parties,

etc. are hosted. The object is then merely to show off.

❖ She should spend only on those things that are absolutely necessary for personal self. Whatever is extra should be spend for the propagation of *Deen*, on pious people and the poor. We will now narrate a few incidents about some pious Muslim wives who spent generously in Allah's path.

## Hazrat A'isha ﵂ Spends on Others

Hazrat Muhammad bin Munkadir (A.R) once asked Hazrat A'isha ﵂ for some money which he desperately needed. She said, "I have nothing to give to you presently. If I had ten thousand, I would have given it all to you. However, I have nothing at the moment." A short while after he left, Hazrat Khaalid bin Asad ﵁ sent ten thousand as a gift for Hazrat A'isha ﵂. When the money arrived, she said, "It seems as if my word is already being put to test." She then sent for Hazrat Muhammad bin Munkadir (A.R) and gave him the entire amount. With the money, Hazrat Muhammad bin Munkadir (A.R) bought a slave girl for a thousand. From her, he fathered three sons whom he named Muhammad, Abu Bakr and Umar. All three were among the pious saints of Madinah. (*Tahdheeb*)

Being one of the causes for the birth of these three men, Hazrat A'isha ﵂ will certainly share in the rewards that they all earned for their *Ibaadah*. It is not surprising that Hazrat A'isha ﵂ was so magnanimous because she was after all the daughter of Hazrat Abu Bakr ﵁.

In his book "*Stories of Sahabah* ﷺ", Sheikhul *Hadith* Maulana Muhammad Zakariyya (A.R), has quoted an incident in which Hazrat A'isha ﷺ distributed two bags full of *Dirhams.* Although the bags contained more than a hundred thousand *Dirhams,* she forgot to keep aside even a single *Dirham* to buy meat with which she could break her fast that evening. Another narration is reported in which a similar incident took place with her while she was distributing a thousand *Dirhams.*

Hazrat Tameem bin Urwa (A.R) narrated that he saw his father's aunt viz. Hazrat A'isha ﷺ distribute seventy thousand *Dirhams* to the poor while she wore patched clothing. (*It'haaf*)

## A Wife who Used to Spend on Allah's Pious Bondsmen

A pious lady by the name of Raabi'ah bint Isma'eel (A.R) sent a marriage proposal to a pious saint by the name of Ahmad Ibn Abil Hawaariy (A.R). He was an extremely pious person who was reluctant to marry. When he received the proposal, he declined saying that he did not want to get married because he was too engrossed in his *Ibaadah* and *Zikr.* She sent him a reply stating that she was more engrossed in acts of devotion than him and herself did not need to get married. However, she wished to marry him so that his pious friends could benefit from a great fortune that her late husband had left for her. In spending on them, she felt that she would have a share in their efforts and be able to tread easily on the path to salvation.

Hazrat Ahmad Hawaariy (A.R) took leave to consul with his teacher Abu Sulaymaan Daarani (A.R), saying that he would marry her only if his teacher permitted. Although, Abu Sulaymaan (A.R) had already prohibited Hazrat Ahmad (A.R) from marriage, he permitted him to marry Hazrat Raabi'ah (A.R) saying, "Marry her for she is Allah's friend and her speech resembles that of the *Siddiqeen*." After marrying her, he mentioned that she hosted so many people for meals that they had a pond built in which the guests washed their hands. This pond was only for those who needed to rush and could not take the time to wash their hands properly. Despite this, the pond soon became damaged because many people who used it.

Hazrat Ahmad Hawaariy (A.R) narrated that he married three other wives after her but instead of getting angry, she was glad and would send him off to these wives after feeding him well. She was to Shaam what Hazrat Raabi'ah Adawiyya (A.R) was to Basrah. (Ihya)

## A Woman who Entertained Guests

Hazrat Abur Rabee (A.R) narrates that he was once visiting a village when he heard that the goat of a certain woman called Fiddah gave milk as well as honey. Surprised at this, he bought a cup and proceeded to the lady's house. He told her what he had heard and said that he had come to witness this blessing for himself. When she made the goat over to him and he milked it, he found that it really did give milk and honey.

When he asked her how she came to own such an animal, she narrated her story to him. She and her husband were poor people who possessed nothing but one goat which produced the milk that they subsisted on. When the occasion of Eidul Adhaa arrived, her husband told her that he would have to sacrifice the animal. However, he changed his mind when she explained to him that the goat was their only livelihood and that it was not compulsory for them to sacrifice an animal because of their poverty. As it would be, they received a guest that very day. She said to her husband, "We have been commanded to entertain guests. Since we have nothing but this goat, you may as well slaughter it to feed the guest. When he set out to slaughter it, she thought that her children would be grieved to see it being slaughtered. She therefore told her husband to take the goat outside and slaughter it behind their wall. When he slaughtered the goat, another goat appeared on the wall and climbed down into their yard.

Thinking that the goat had escaped from her husband, the lady went out to see, but found her husband already skinning the slaughtered goat. When she told him about the other goat in their yard, he told her that Allah must have already replaced the goat for them. This goat was the very one that gave milk and honey. This was all because of the blessings of entertaining one guest. The woman then addressed her children saying, "This goat feeds on (what is in) your hearts. As long as your hearts remain pious and clean, the milk will continue being good. As soon as your hearts become tainted, the milk will also become the same.

Keep you hearts good and everything else will also be good for you."

## The Queen Zubayda (A.R)

Zubayda was the wife of the Khalifa Haaroon Ar-Rasheed. The famous lady was the daughter of Khalifa Mansoor's son Ja'far. It was because of this son that Mansoor was called Abu Ja'far (the father of Ja'far). Zubayda was born in Mousil while her father was the governor of the city. However, she was only two or three years old when her father passed away. She was then brought up by her grandfather the Khalifa Mansoor. Her grandfather loved her very much and although her name was Amatul Azeez, he affectionately called her Zubayda. This name stuck so well that people eventually forgot her real name. She married Haaroon Ar Rasheed when she was only fifteen or sixteen years old. No one expected Haaroon Ar Rasheed to become Khalifa because his elder brother Haadi was heir apparent to the throne. However, Haadi passed away before ascending to the throne and Haaroon Ar Rasheed became Khalifa with Zubayda as his queen.

The loving relationship of Haaroon Ar Rasheed and Zubayda is proverbial. Allah blessed her with piety, compassion and the rare ability to put things in order. She orchestrated the affairs of the royal palace like none other had ever done. Her generosity is also proverbial and no beggar left her door without receiving something. There were a hundred slave women in her palace, all of who had memorised the Qur'ãn. Each of them recited ten parts of the Qur'ãn daily, completing the Qur'ãn every three days. Whoever passed the palace could hear the Qur'ãn being recited.

She was very concerned with charitable community projects. In the year 208 A.H. (824), she left for *Hajj* and took a large contingent of engineers with her. Wherever she found people having difficulty with water or roads, she immediately arranged the means for addressing the difficulty. While travelling towards *Baytul Muqaddas*, she passed an area that experienced water shortages. She dispatched people to search for a suitable water source in the mountains to irrigate the area. Through this effort, water was channelled from a source which developed into a strong source of irrigation for the area as well as for many other areas.

She had hundreds of dams, *Masjids* and roads built for the benefit of the public. However, her most famous achievement was the engineering masterpiece known as "*Nahr Zubayda*" (the "Canal of Zubayda"), which for centuries provided water for the people of Makkah and for the millions of pilgrims arriving for *Hajj*. The source of the canal was a spring in a mountainous area approximately 25 to 30 km east of Makkah. Later on, another spring was joined to the canal. The canal passed by Arafat, Muzdalifa and Mina en route to Makkah. A major portion of this canal lies beneath the ground and it fills reservoirs built at appropriate places. The water used to supply hundreds of thousands of *Hujjaj* who stayed for many days at Mina and for a day at Arafat and Muzdalifa.

When the cost for constructing the canal was estimated, she was told that it would be extremely expensive. She responded by saying, "Even if I have to pay a single labourer a gold coin for every strike of his spade, I shall happily do so but I shall never abandon the project." Zubayda spend no less than seven hundred thousand gold coins on community projects during this *Hajj* journey.

These were people who truly appreciated the Allah's bounties and spend as much as they could on Allah's creation. They understood that wealth is useless when squandered on the luxuries of just a few people. Zubayda passed away at the age of seventy and although centuries have passed since her demise, her name still lives on because of her noble deeds. The hand of death cannot erase the good works that people do.

It is the responsibility of every wife to utilise her husband's wealth for good causes. At the same time, she should be concerned about safeguarding his Imaan. These are important rights that she owes to him and she should never be negligent of these.

## An Important Right of the Husband that Women are Heedless About

Hazrat Jaabir ﷺ narrates that Rasulullah ﷺ's gaze once inadvertently fell on a woman. He immediately proceeded to his wife Hazrat Zainab ﷺ and satisfied his need. He then addressed the *Sahabah* ﷺ saying, "A woman appears as a *Shaitaan*. When any of you sees a woman who attracts him, he should immediately go to his wife because she has exactly what the other woman has." (*Tirmizi*)

Rasulullah ﷺ has likened women to *Shaitaan* because the natural attraction they possess presents the ideal opportunity for *Shaitaan* to deviate man. Their emergence from their homes is like the emergence of *Shaitaan* himself. This fact makes it clear that women should not roam about and Muslims should make every effort to stay away from mixed gatherings.

Muslims men should guard their gazes because when their eyes meet those of a non-*Mahram* woman, *Shaitaan* exploits the opportunity to destroy their lives in this world as well as in the *Aakhirah*. One should always guard one's gazes because *Shaitaan* will develop sexual inclinations in people when they mix freely.

When a man satisfies himself with his lawful wife, his inclination to develop illicit relationships will be killed and he will be saved from the clutches of *Shaitaan*. It is therefore necessary for every wife to respond to her husband's need for intercourse, whether he asks directly or indirectly. Of course, she may excuse herself if she has a valid excuse to do so, such as menstruation. When a woman implements this attitude, she will be benefiting her husband from a physical, religious, mental, medical and spiritual perspective.

It is instinctive for the average man to look up at a passing woman, thereby creating an impression in his mind. It often happens that he may then become sexually aroused, plunging him into a state of uneasiness. When such as situation arises, Rasulullah ﷺ has instructed that the man should satisfy himself with his wife so that *Shaitaan* may not exploit the situation and cause him to sin. The solution is therefore simple and effective.

However, there may be rare cases when one wife may not satisfy a man's needs. In such cases, he may take up to three other wives on condition that he is absolutely certain that he can treat them all justly and provide adequately for them all. The *Shari'ah* has permitted these avenues because adultery is an intolerable sin. The chastity and moral fibre of society is highly coveted in Islãm. Implementing the injunctions of the *Shari'ah* will safeguard these objectives and save society from the many illicit relations already existing such as affairs between brothers-and-sisters-in-law, cousins, etc. Women should therefore be particular about satisfying their husbands and should stop making excuses like saying that they will be unable to complete their tasks if they are delayed by taking a bath after intercourse. Muslim wives who make frivolous excuses of this nature should remember that if their husbands satisfy themselves in *Haraam* avenues, they (the wives) will also be liable for the sin because they had been the cause of it.

## A Woman Should Respond Immediately

Hazrat Talq bin Ali رضي الله عنه narrates that Rasulullah ﷺ said, "When a husband calls his wife to satisfy his sexual need, she should respond even if she is busy at the oven." (*Tirmizi*)

This *Hadith* makes it clear that she should not refuse his call irrespective of how occupied she may be.

## Nikaah is the Means of Securing Chastity

Allah has instilled passionate instincts in every man and woman. Allah has also prescribed the means by which man can fulfil these instincts. This means is Nikaah. The primary objective of Nikaah is to satisfy these instinctive passions in men and women. The husband should therefore do his best to satisfy the wife and she should do the same so that none of them has to resort to illicit means of sexual gratification.

## Reward for Satisfying One's Desire Lawfully

Rasulullah ﷺ once told the *Sahabah* رضي الله عنهم that a person is rewarded for satisfying his sexual desire with his wife. When the *Sahabah* رضي الله عنهم expressed surprise that a person could be rewarded for satisfying a carnal passion, Rasulullah ﷺ asked them, "Will a person be sinful if he satisfies his desire unlawfully?" "Certainly," responded the *Sahabah* رضي الله عنهم. Rasulullah ﷺ said, "Therefore, if a couple refrains from unlawful relations and fulfil their needs within the command of Allah, they will be rewarded." (Ahmad)

## The Woman Whom the Angels Curse

Hazrat Abu Hurairah رضي الله عنه narrated that Rasulullah ﷺ said, "When a man calls his wife to bed (for conjugal relations) and she refuses to respond (or does something by which his desire is left unfulfilled and he becomes angry with her), the angels continue cursing her until the next morning." (*Bukhari* Vol. 2 Pg. 782)

In the Arabic context, the meaning of a person being cursed is that the person is distanced from Allah's mercy. The husband sees to the needs of his wife and provides for her from his hard-earned wealth. In addition to this, he fulfils her many other rights as well. In return for all of this, she is expected to at least fulfil his sexual needs so that he may be saved from sin. She should bear in mind that the fundamental object of Nikaah is to protect the man's chastity and to save his eyes from roving. She should therefore not fail in this vital task because her failure would be disastrous for both of them. In addition to this, she would then also be subjecting herself to the curses of the angels.

Commenting on this *Hadith*, Maulana Aashiq Ilaahi (Daamat Barakaatuh) says that because a mere indication is sufficient for an intelligent person, further elucidation is not necessary for this *Hadith*. It is simple to understand and every woman who sees her failings in this regard should take heed.

Women who disregard this *Hadith* find their husbands marrying other wives or (even worse) forsaking their chastity. The husband-wife relationship is extremely special because they can fulfil their needs with none other but themselves. It is therefore of paramount importance that their relationship should be one of love and understanding.

Rasulullah ﷺ understood human psychology very well and identified all man's needs. His advices were therefore pertinent and effective. However, when one acts contrary to these advices, one will experience bitterness and conditions will worsen.

It is only by way of example that Rasulullah ﷺ mentioned that the angels will curse such a woman until the morning. This does not mean that she will be exempt from these curses if she refuses during the day. It is necessary for her to respond to him at any time unless she has a valid reason like menstruation, etc.

Hazrat Abu Hurairah رضي الله عنه narrates that Rasulullah ﷺ said, "A woman who spends the night away from her husband's bed (to avoid cohabiting with him) shall dwell under the curses of the angels until she returns."

(*Bukhari* Vol. 2 Pg. 782)

The above *Ahadith* make it clear that refusing to cohabit with one's husband is a grave sin that warrants the curses of the angels. Similarly, if a woman leaves her husband's bed against his wishes, she will also be subjected to the curses of the angels until she returns. Rasulullah ﷺ had specifically mentioned all these things because these are factors that ruin families.

## The Opinion of Experts in the Field of Psychology

Based on their vast knowledge and experience, experts in human psychology assert that the best wife is she who actively participates in love-making. It should be borne in mind that when one pan of the scale of love in empty, the other pan will empty by itself. When enthusiasm is lacking, the couple's sexual life begins to die. If the wife's attitude towards sex is cold, if she expresses reluctance towards it or if she oversteps the limits of bashfulness, the couple's relationship will be stifled and eventually killed.

On the other hand, when the couple enjoy a healthy sex life with both partners as eager participants, their love for each other will grow as well as their mutual trust. Such a couple will even have children who are active and intelligent. Such a couple will experience happiness and peace of mind.

A woman will be guilty of extreme laziness and insolence when she responds coldly to her husband's warmth, kind words and favours as he makes advanced towards her. This causes him to dislike her and to develop negative feelings towards her. In essence, the benefits of sexual relations are attained only when both partners are equally stimulated and when both enjoy their relationship.

By employing her intelligence, gentle nature, beauty and other methods of attraction, a bright woman can maintain hers and her husband's youth and their period of sexual activity without resorting to extreme measures. When couple's sexual activity contains receptiveness, attraction towards each other and fulfilment coupled with the intentions of pleasing Allah, fulfilling their duties towards each other and being parents of pious children, they will experience unparalleled pleasure.

Allaama Ibn Qayyim (A.R) writes that the sign of such pleasure will be that every limb of the body will be at ease and the mere sight of one's spouse will delight one's eyes. In addition to this, his words will be a song to the ears, his fragrance will the most precious in the world, his kiss will sweeten the mouth and the touch of his hand will generate a powerful emotion, giving contentment to the entire body.

However, if anything is lacking in the relationship, the contentment will be incomplete and wanting.

(*Rowdhatul Muhibbeen* Pg. 216, 217)

When a person enjoys doing something permissible, he will be rewarded for it on condition that he does the act to please Allah because it is a command of Allah and a practice of Rasulullah ﷺ.

Rasulullah ﷺ also said, "May Allah's curse be on the woman who says, 'I'm coming, I'm coming.' When her husband calls her to bed, she keeps saying, 'I'm coming, I'm coming,' until he falls asleep." (*Tabraani*)

Muslim narrates a *Hadith* from Hazrat Abu Hurairah رضي الله عنه in which Rasulullah ﷺ says, "By the Being in whose control is my life! When a husband calls his wife to bed and she refuses, He in the heavens becomes angry with her until her husband is happy with her."

The reason for this is that *Shaitaan* becomes extremely pleased when he separates the couple and they become enemies instead of benefiting from each other's love and company. Another *Hadith* of Muslim mentions that *Shaitaan* sets up his throne on water and then disperses his disciples to cause mischief. The closest to him is the one who causes the most evil and strife. When the disciples gather afterwards, one of them says, "I worked on so-and-so until he committed adultery." Another says, "I did not rest until separated a couple." Hearing this, *Shaitaan* congratulates the disciple and seats him closest to him, telling him, "You are the one! You are the one!"

This narration makes it clear that Allah's enemy is most pleased when a rift is created between two hearts containing the love of Allah and His Rasul ﷺ. Therefore, when a husband calls his wife to bed and she thinks that he thinks only of sex or that she will have to take a bath in such cold weather, she should immediately tell herself that these thoughts are from *Shaitaan*. She should then recite thrice "*A'oodhu Billaahi Minash Shaitaanir Rajeem*" and thrice "*Laa Howla wa Laa Quwwata Illa Billaah*". She should then go immediately to her husband. *Insha Allah*, this will disgrace *Shaitaan* and he will leave the house. Allah will then make such a wife beloved to her husband.

## Nafl Fasts may be Observed Only With the Husband's Permission

Hazrat Abu Hurairah رضي الله عنه reports that Rasulullah ﷺ said, "It is not permissible for a woman to fast (an optional fast) in the presence of her husband unless he permits her. She may not also allow anyone into his house without his permission." (*Bukhari*)

Although the *Ahadith* have mentioned many virtues of observing optional fasts, a woman may not observe them without her husband's permission because fasting would deny him his conjugal rights. Of course, a good husband would never prevent his wife without good reason. He should not deny her the virtues merely because he is upset with her on some other account. However, should he refuse her permission, it is not permissible for her to fast because obeying him takes precedence over *Nafl* fasts.

## Obeying One's Husband is more Important than Nafl Acts of Worship

The above *Hadith* makes it clear that obeying one's husband takes precedence over all *Nafl* (optional) acts of worship. Therefore, when a woman obeys her husband, she will receive rewards greater than what she would receive for *Nafl* acts of worship. For this reason, a woman should never feel that her husband has deprived her of rewards if he refuses her permission to observe *Nafl* fasts. She should reflect on her reasons for fasting. It is obvious that she is fasting to be rewarded and to attain Allah's pleasure. These being the reasons, she should bear in mind that by obeying her husband's instruction not to fast, she will receive greater rewards and in pleasing her husband she will attain Allah's pleasure because Allah will not be pleased with her until her husband is pleased with her. The obedient wife will therefore receive a greater reward for eating and drinking than she would receive for fasting.

## A MOTHER'S ADVICE TO HER DAUGHTER

Parents should give their children a proper upbringing by adorning them with the jewels of sound Islãmic education, the gems of managing a household, the garments of fear for Allah, the bangles of *Taqwa* and the trousseau of obedience to Allah and engaging in His *Zikr*. These are real gifts.

It is especially important for mothers to display respect for their husband in front of their daughters because their daughters will treat their husbands exactly how they see their mothers treating their fathers. There are many good mothers who raise their daughters so well that their sons-in-law and their families consider it their good fortune that these fine ladies have married into their families. Men marrying such women have attained kingship even though they may be living in shacks. They are wealthy with the sweet words she speaks and her ever-endearing smiles. The children born to such a couple will also be righteous servants of Allah, blessed with intelligence and keen aptitudes because they have been brought up in the lap of an excellent mother.

Among the ranks of such mothers was Hazrat Asma bint Khajta Fazaariya (A.R) who gave the following golden words of advice to her daughter. These words are an inspiration to every bride.

"Beloved daughter! You are now departing from this home where you spent the days of your childhood and where you first set your foot upon the threshold of adolescence. You will now be the decoration of a bed that exudes a fragrance which will be unfamiliar to you. You will be treading step-by-step with a lifelong companion who is still a stranger to you."

"Dear daughter! Become the ground for your companion so that he may become your heaven. Become his cradle and he will become your supporting pillar. Become his slave and he will become yours. Never nag or force him into anything because he will then despise you. Never stay away from him because he will then forget you. If he draws close to you, draw even closer to him. Show concern for even his nose, ears and eyes (i.e. never cause him even the slightest harm). Be particular about using perfume because it comforts his mind via his nose. Keep watch over your tongue because your sweet words gives him comfort via his ears. Keep your appearance attractive because so that you may be the delight of his eyes and his source of contentment. Let him always see you in a good condition with your hair combed, with kohl in your eyes, with neat clothes and a scarf on your head."

"My precious daughter! If you are particular about practising these advices, your home will be reminiscent of *Jannah* no matter how small it may be."

May Allah grant every Muslim wife the ability to practise the advices given above. It should never be that a bride dresses well and beautifies herself only while her marriage is new and then begins to resemble a maidservant after a few months, dressing up only when going out. A wife should never appear shabby in front of her husband because this will destroy his love for her.

## A GROOM'S GIFT TO HIS BRIDE

An Arab groom lovingly presented to his bride four golden lines of poetry when they met the first night. We shall quote this as advice for the benefit of every new bride as well as for every married woman because it is never too late to practise. May Allah grant every woman the ability to practise. *Aameen.*

"Overlook my errors and my love for you will be eternal
Never backchat when I'm angry for this will be infernal

You should never beat me like a drum you beat
For you know not what sound you will meet

Never complain incessantly because this destroys affection
My heart should then never reject you because hearts are quick to change with every new attraction

I have seen that when love and annoyance unite in one heart
Love does not stay but has to depart."

In the second couplet of the poem, the poet tells his wife that she should never chance to backchat and retaliate when he is angry because this could produce a reaction that both of them will regret. In the final couplet, he warns her that by backchat, complaining and annoying him in any other way, his love for her may soon depart.

**A Brief Analysis of the Poem**

1) If a woman wants the love of her husband, she should forgive and forget his faults and errors.

2) She should remain silent when he is angry. She should rather admit her fault and ask for forgiveness instead of defending her wrong. In fact, she should ask for forgiveness even if the fault is his. In addition to this, she should do whatever he asks.

3) Never complain. Rather be grateful to Allah for whatever you have. Patiently bear the difficulties that come your way from your sisters-and-mother-in-law. Of course, there is no harm in telling your husband your difficulties, but never chose to do so at a time when he is tired and unwilling to listen.

4) Incessant complaining irritates the husband and this will diminish the love he has for his wife in his heart.

## SOME GOLDEN PRINCIPLES FOR EVERY BRIDE TO FOLLOW

We will now present some extremely precious principles for every wife to follow so that she may live happily with her husband and her mother-in-law. These principles appear in the book "*Tuhfatul Khawaateen*" (A Gift to Women), which was written by Maulana Muhammad Ahmad Surti Saheb in the Gujarati language and has been translated into Urdu by Maulana Sulaymaan Saheb. May Allah grant us all the ability practise these principles and to make *Du'a* for the author of this book and the translator.

Beloved daughters! Remember that you have not been made to live forever in your parent's home. Their home was merely an inn for you. Allah had intended that you will soon leave this home. Has any visitor stayed forever at your house? Just as every visitor has left after a short while, you will also soon be leaving. Your parents will have to see you off when you have come of age and groomed for marriage. You will then have to leave to be with your in-laws. This is why a daughter is often referred to as a fleeting treasure. Your parents are doing nothing wrong because this is the command of Allah and the practice of our beloved Rasulullah ﷺ. Such is the practice of people throughout the world, whether they are princes or paupers.

Precious daughters! Today you live with your parents and have shade beneath the roofs of their homes which are filled with love and affection. You are being reared here without experiencing any difficulties and without worrying about preparing food and sewing clothes. Here you have only peace and contentment. Whatever harm you do is quickly forgotten and your parents gently correct your mistakes. Your parents want only comfort for you and do not want to burden you with any worries.

However, dear daughters! Have you ever thought that you will one day be living with your in-laws? Will they also turn a blind eye to your iniquities? Never! They do not have the accommodating nature of your parents. There you will have to work to establish your self-respect and your honour. You will have to prove that you are competent and resolute. Without this, you cannot expect to have peace and happiness.

I shall first tell how to live with your parents, much of which you may have already experienced. Thereafter, I shall tell you how to live with your in-laws and you will become aware of everything. If you practise what you are about to read, you will be able to transform any home into a garden of paradise. Everyone will then embrace you with open arms and congratulate your every trait. People will congratulate your parents and no one will dare to do you any harm. The entire family will be compassionate towards you and your husband will boast about you. Young and old will respect you.

It is commonly understood that a woman's ability to cope with her housework is the first test she is put through when she starts living with her in-laws. It will also be seen whether you can run a home, whether you can keep your home clean, whether you can entertain guests and whether you behave well with relatives. If you are found lacking in any of these fields, it will be said that you know nothing. Today there is someone to correct you, afterwards there will be none to advise you. Then you will have to do things by yourself. If you do nothing today, how will you be able to cope then? Even if you do manage to cope then, it will be extremely difficult without today's training. If you are accustomed to being lazy, others will look down on you. How then can you expect respect? How can you then be happy?

I therefore have the desire that today you acquire the skills and expertise that will be a shield against future difficulties and which will navigate you through troubled waters. You will be mistaken to behave proudly and say that you know everything and will be able to manage by yourself. You should not rest assured merely because you can cook a few dishes, can stitch on a button, can decorate a few things, can recite the Qur'ãn or have read a few books. You will then be no better than a person who spent the entire night reading the story of Yusuf and Zulaikha and cannot even say the following morning whether Yusuf was a man or a woman.

It is therefore necessary that notwithstanding the tediousness of any task, you should never leave it incomplete. You also have to develop the ability to complete your tasks without any assistance. You should be independent of your mother-or-sisters-in-law as well as of any other helper. You should do things with such rapture and competence that the men of the house are left gaping. Continue your housework together with tending to the children and bringing them up properly. It should never be that a single problem should cause you a hundred other problems or that a single need should cause you to forget a hundred others. Be cognisant of everything and never sway to extremes. Be moderate in all that you do. When you keep these things in mind, you will be able to correct matters whether they are done mistakenly or purposely.

Regard you friends as friends and enemies as enemies. Think before doing anything and you will save yourself and others from harm and inconvenience. This will also avert squabbles and disputes. If you behave in this manner, people will overlook your errors because when a sensible and careful person slips up, people are forgiving. On the other hand, people mock a fool even when he makes sense. Remember that all the good of this world and the Hereafter can be acquired by utilising one's intelligence correctly. Intelligence and modesty are two invaluable gems because modesty saves people from evil. I shall begin with mentioning those factors that will prove to be guiding lights for the future.

## How to Live in your Parent's Home

Serve your parents with heart and soul and never cause them any grief. Have their meals ready on time as they prefer it. Listen attentively to what they says and dutifully carry out their instructions. Never disturb them when they busy and have things done as they are accustomed to doing it. Never nag and never demand. Arrange their clothing in an orderly fashion and always put soap, towels, etc. in their place. Keep their home clean.

Wake up early in the mornings, quickly fulfil your needs and perform your *Fajr Salaah*. Recite the Qur'ãn, perform *Ishraaq Salaah* and then begin your work, bearing in mind that you should be ready to serve them at any time. Apologise and seek forgiveness when they become angry with you and never try to confuse them. Never even say, 'Oof!' to them in protest. Never be ungrateful to them and always remember their favours to you. If you do them a good turn, never remind them about it. Do everything by yourself and always put your stationery, clothing and other things away. If you all of this, I can truly say that you know something. If not, you should never think that you are capable.

Dear daughters! Remember that if your faults are not ironed out early, they will soon show their colours. Bad character, insolence, immoral behaviour, stinginess, pride and stubbornness are such evils that you may be unaware of and which your parents may brush aside, attributing them to your young age. They may turn a blind eye to these traits thinking that they will disappear by themselves. However, these traits will only thrive with age and prove to be your downfall. They will then only be identified and corrected when they cause one to stumble and fall.

An intelligent person is one who employs evasive measures long before the floods come. In time, your intelligence will show you the road, modesty will save you from evil and Allah will ease the difficulties that are headed your way. This world is fuelled by intelligence and the person whom Allah has blessed with the most intelligence shall be able to manage affairs most wisely. The stability of every structure pivots on the amount of intelligence employed.

## The Manner of Living with One's Husband

Dear daughters! I will now explain to you the manner in which you should live when you move in with your in-laws. Always remember that the relationship between husband and wife is not like loose threads that can be separated whenever one wishes. Marriage is a lifelong commitment. It takes nothing less than death to sever this union. If the couple's hearts are united, they can share no greater bounty and it is as if *Jannah* has come down to earth for them. On the other hand, if their hearts are not united, they can experience no worse tragedy and will not be blamed for thinking that *Jahannam* has come to earth.

Every woman has the ability to make her marriage work. It is imperative for a wife to win over her husband's heart by dying herself in his colours and doing everything he wants her to do. She should convince herself that if he commands her to fold her hands and stand all night long, her success lies in doing as he says. Success in the Hereafter should be sought even if it means enduring some hardship in this world.

## Capturing Your Husband's Heart

A marriage can be successful when the couple are compatible and united. Without this, their lives will be incomplete and troubled. It is therefore imperative that every wife does her level best to learn the method of capturing her husband's heart. Without learning this method she can never be successful irrespective of how educated, attractive or wealthy she may be.

Wise people have mentioned many methods of harnessing one's husband's love. A woman who regards serving her husband and loving him as an important aspect of her *Imaan* has no option but to practise the guidelines which will be mentioned hereunder.

- ❖ Regard your husband as a wealthy man even though he may be poor.
- ❖ Consult with him in all matters and do as he advises.
- ❖ Never do anything against his wishes and always give precedence to the things that please him.
- ❖ Always be concerned about his peace of mind and

never do anything that will cause him grief.

- Accept whatever he gives you with a happy heart.
- Do whatever he asks you to do in a manner that he is left without a worry.
- Always be happy and smiling so that all his worries can disappear merely by looking at you.
- Fulfil his needs before your own.
- Feed him as best as you can.
- If he cannot afford to buy clothes, sew them yourself.
- Try to do everything by yourself.
- Never ask him for something that he cannot afford otherwise he will be saddened if he cannot give it to you. If you are destined to have it, you will surely get it without asking.
- Do not ask him to do anything that you can do by yourself.
- Never tell him all your problems as soon as he arrives because his mind may already be inundated with other problems.
- Speak of good things while eating because when a person is happy, even the simplest meal is as tasty as the best delicacy. On the other hand, a delicious meal will seem dull to a troubled mind. When a woman begins telling her husband all her day's problems as soon as he walks in, his eating, sitting and resting will become difficult. In fact, he may even lose his appetite. Together with upsetting him, such behaviour is also displeasing to Allah.

- If Allah grants you the ability, assist him in his work.
- Share his problems and console him whenever he has a problem so that the burden may be raised from his shoulders.
- When he is in debt, assist him to settle it by earning some money without violating the laws of the *Shari'ah*. If you have some money of your own or some jewellery that can be sold, give this to him if he needs it so that he may appreciate the fact that he is more valuable to you than these things. Never remind him about such favours afterwards and do not even make an effort to remember such things.
- Never neglect your duties to him and always do things that are in his best interests.
- Try to do all your housework by yourself. Insha Allah, Allah will soon show you easier days.
- Spend as little as possible and try to save as much as you can. If your savings are meagre, never stop saving with the thought that it is too little. Whatever you save will come in handy during rainy days because when days are dark, friends are always few. You will then be saved from the humiliation of stretching your hands out in front of others. Your husband will then be amazed at your prudence and farsightedness.
- Sew your clothing by yourself, cook by yourself and look after the children by yourself.
- Reply gently when he asks a question.
- Be gentle when he is angry.

- Continue fulfilling his rights even if he is unhappy with the way you do things. This will please Allah.
- Do your share even though it may be difficult.
- Be content with whatever he is content with.
- Spend his wealth with care and with a conscience.
- Whatever your husband brings home is in your care. You may either apply your inventiveness and capabilities to make your home valuable or you could behave like a slovenly and lazy wife by laying everything to waste. Your poor husband will have no say in the matter. Your home is what you make of it. A skilled and capable wife is never distressed.
- Everyone seeks refuge from a disorderly and chaotic home. Although difficulties will arise from time to time, sometimes depriving you of food and rest, you must make an effort to keep the house in order because a man will not be able to bear a chaotic home for long. When he cannot find peace and rest at home, he will be forced to find it elsewhere. He may then begin to regard his home and his children as calamities.
- A good wife is always making an effort for her home to be an example of *Jannah*. Together with herself being at ease in her home, she does her best to make every occupant of the house comfortable as well.
- Men appreciate women who are competent and who are able to organise affairs well. It is unfortunate that many beautiful women lack these qualities and

have thus become worthless in the eyes of their husbands. It should be borne in mind that most men appreciate inner beauty more than outer beauty. Irrespective of how unattractive or imprudent a woman may be, she will certainly win over her husband's affections if she is obedient.

It is not difficult for every wife to apply all the above principles in her life, thereby earning the devoted love of her husband. However, it is tragic that most women fail to understand this and wrongly think that they will be able to force their husbands into submission by behaving harshly and temperamentally. It is really the women who strive to please Allah and who serve their husbands with love and gentleness who become the beloved of their husbands and whose husbands would give their lives for them. The husbands of such women will do anything to please them and are proud of them. Such couples are the ones who live happily ever after. Intelligent women avail themselves of such behaviour while foolish women are deprived of it.

As an intelligent woman you should always bear the following in mind:

- ❖ Forsake your egotism and your temperamental behaviour.
- ❖ Do not allow pride and selfishness to approach you.
- ❖ Do not speak to a strange man in private.
- ❖ Do not speak ill of your husband in front of another.
- ❖ Do not breathe a word against him.
- ❖ Do not eat before him.

- Do not discuss matters that do not appeal to him.
- You can even win over a temperamental husband by diligently serving him.
- Be as he wants you to be and do what pleases him.
- Keep his secrets safe within your heart.
- Beautify yourself as he prefers.
- Stay away from the company of evil and ill-mannered women.

By keeping all the above in mind and practising accordingly, you will enjoy good fortune and your husband will be yours forever.

## EVERY WOMAN'S WISH

It is the natural desire of every woman to have a husband who does what she wants, who consults with her before doing anything and who hands all his money over to her so that she may run the home as she desires. Despite having this desire, many women fail to make any efforts to realise this desire. Without having any respect for their husbands, they become furious about the littlest thing and storm out of the house at the slightest provocation. They are constantly arguing with their husbands about clothing and jewellery and still expect their husbands to do as they say. Not only are such women disrupting the homes of their husbands, but they are destroying the lives of both their families.

## Learn to Love Your Husband

Every woman should learn to love her husband. Irrespective of how evil, ill-mannered or dim-witted her husband may be, the wife holds in her hand the keys to set her husband straight. There are numerous examples of women who have successfully changed their husbands for the better. There are no obstacles for the patient woman. To purge her husband of bad habits and to make him receptive and sympathetic towards her, she should narrate to him anecdotes from the lives of the pious, she should encourage him to participate in religious gatherings and she should also read good books of *Ahadith* at home so that he may hear. In addition to this, she must also do what pleases him and serve him with sincere devotion. When a woman sincerely loves and serves her husband, it is impossible for him to stray away from her.

## Conquer His Heart

Your husband's heart will be conquered by the resounding throb of love emanating from the deepest recesses of your heart. Always keep your home clean and ensure that everything of beauty in your home is well arranged. Keep your loving gazes fixed on him and always meet him with a smile. Obey whatever he tells you instead of arguing. Insha Allah, this will ensure a happy marriage.

## "You Mind Your Own Business and I'll Mind Mine"

When there is enmity and dissention between a couple and they lack love for each other, the words "You mind your own business and I'll mind mine" will be commonly heard. Happiness will rue visiting such a home and the buds of joy will wilt. Eventually, every hope the couple entertained will be rubbed into the dust.

## Secure Fasten the Bond of Love

Allah has created the bond of love between people and this bond can only be secured with the injunctions of the *Shari'ah.* This bond is not a loose one and will not break with a slight jostle. When a couple get married, they have pledged their loyalty to each other and the wife is always in a position to fasten the bond more securely. By doing everything to please him and by sharing his joys and problems, the bond will be cemented. In this transaction, profits are accrued when everything is given without anything taken in return.

## Identify his Preferences

To conquer her husband's heart, a wife should ensure that she introduces into herself everything that her husband likes. It is imperative for her to know exactly what to do to please him. She should therefore cook what he likes and wear what he likes. In fact, she should bring her pleasures to coincide with his.

Sadly, there are many men whose wives are extremely attractive, yet they will be found in the company of women much less beautiful. Beauty, wealth and a good education are not sufficient to keep one's husband for oneself. What is required is the art of knowing what pleases the husband.

A wife should know how to capture her husband's interest. She should know what he likes so that she could keep his gazes fixed on her.

## What Do Men Like?

Because every man is different, it is not possible to specify exactly what every man likes. While some men prefer women with make-up, others prefer women without it. While some men prefer fashionable women, others prefer simple women. While some prefer extroverts, others do not. In this manner, tastes vary from man to man. It is therefore necessary for women to inculcate such qualities within themselves which their husbands would value and appreciate. Some of the qualities that men adore are as follows:

1. One of the primary features men love is beauty. Even though a woman may not be naturally beautiful, she can make herself look beautiful by dressing well and making themselves up. Of course, she may adopt only those means of beautification that the *Shari'ah* permits, and these are more than sufficient.
2. Men also look for innocence and an appreciative nature in women. They would dare not approach women who harbour malice in their hearts, who deceive and whose hearts bear ill-feelings against others. Women should therefore make every effort to make innocence and gratitude of paramount importance in their lives. In fact, these qualities develop modesty and inner beauty. When a woman's

heart is filled with malice and ill-feelings against others, her husband loses confidence in her and other people also lose their respect for her.

3. Men do not want their wives to be more intelligent than themselves. When an ordinary man marries a graduate, he remains uneasy because he feels weaker and inferior than her, causing him a considerable degree of embarrassment. A wife should therefore not extol her academic achievements when these would make her husband feel inferior.

   In addition to this, she should not make him feel less intelligent in any other way. A man may stand in awe of a highly educated woman, but he can seldom love her. By the same token, women also do not like men who assert their authority and who want their wives to dance at the snap of their fingers.

4. The most effective manner of harnessing the undivided attention of one's husband is to be humble before him and to serve him diligently. Men feel content when their wives are obedient and their love for them grows tremendously. Men detest women who are impudent, immoral and stubborn.

5. Men also like women who are forgiving and who love them despite their faults.

6. Men love women who are compassionate towards others; women who are naturally tender and who would take orphans into their laps because they feel them sorry. Men do not like women who are selfish and who feel nothing to insult and abuse others.

They also do not like women who withdraw into spells of silence because they feel dejected and without hope.

7. Men adore women who are lively and happy because such an attitude makes others also feel happy. Such a woman lifts her husband's spirits when he is feeling under the weather and also dispels his tiredness, providing him with peace and contentment. She should therefore always make an effort to do and speak about things that make him happy. The proverb is famous that says: Laughter is the best medicine. Women should always bear this proverb in mind and she will be her husband's best doctor.

8. The most cherished quality in a woman is her chastity. A woman's beauty sparkles with added radiance when she is chaste. Only such a woman can remain loyal to her husband. A woman lacking chastity will be worthless to her husband even if she is bestowed with immense physical beauty.

When a woman does as she pleases without caring how others feel, she will fall from her husband's esteem. Obey your husband and the world will obey you. Secure his confidence and you will earn the confidence of the entire family. Conquer your husband's heart and your home will be reminiscent of *Jannah*.

# A DIALOGUE BETWEEN MOTHER AND DAUGHTER

"Look, the carriage has come
    Let me weep till my heart is done
If I cannot weep as much as I would like
    Just allow my heart to become light
I suppose I will have to leave
    Leave the ties of love that seem impossible to retrieve
What shall my abode be?
    When I have to leave the affection and love showered on me
Leave the doting, attention and affection
    Leave my parents, sisters, brothers and their attraction
I am breaking away and leaving them all
    I am taking leave from them all
I was the little chirping bird of the garden
    Oh has it really passed by, I beg your pardon
I was a little doll to play with as I went
    Oh how blissful was the adolescence I spent
Every one of my friends I could meet
    With a heart wide open, clean, with nothing discreet
Though I shall be leaving you all
    Never shall I forget you at all
In my heart here shall always dwell
    Until *Qiyaamah* something to tell
Never shall I forget you, O mother

For the fondness you showed me with no bother
Nor the generosity and compassion
With which you raised me in your unique fashion
You let me play gleefully on swings
This I shall never forget, the treatment given to kings
Never shall I forget
All that you did for me without regret
What now is this final deed
Merely for show, that the world may heed?
To see what you have done for me
Out of your home you have cast me
A disgrace of fate
What banishment of late!
Your generosity for me seems a thing of the past
Out of your home have I been cast."

## The Mother's Reply

"Listen well, O my broken-hearted one
All that has happened is your turn has come
This period dawns on every child
This bridge has to be crossed by everyone meek and mild
This time of separation does arrive
For all people in the world alive
Such is the custom of the world in which we have mirth
Such are the practices of our earth
The one whom you call mother with such love
Was also someone's daughter, their turtledove

She was also the beloved child of her mother
Showered with the affection of her sister and brother
Those who have raised you, with whom you have grown
Never shall you be separated from them to be on your own
Theirs you shall always be and they yours
Then whatfor do you grieve, always open are their doors
On a throne they always gave you a seat
Showed you happiness most complete
Despite hardship, they gave you comfort and ease
They never held anything against you, so should you, please
Never speak against them an ill word
Not even 'Oof!' or something unheard
The reputation of your family you now hold in your hand
Honour it, do not rub it in the sand
You are the product of my efforts and toil
You are the fruit of my love, from my very soil
You will find everything with us here
So leave with happiness, have no fear
There shall be difficulty and strain
There shall be effort and pain
There will be heartache, but every tunnel ends with light
You will also have love, happiness and delight
By no behaviour, by no manner, not at all
Should you ever allow this to topple and fall
Those who have nurtured and raised you so

Still love you and are letting you go
This enjoyment, this pleasure
This blissful life, this leisure
This carefree life without sorrow
Are all fleeting by, not there tomorrow
May Allah grant you happiness where you are headed
Even more than you had here where your roots are embedded
May Allah grant you everything you want and need
Love, contentment, happiness and all on which your heart can feed
Not by error or by something you earn
For the home of your parents should your heart never yearn
From every mother comes this advice so sincere
Never forget it, never disregard it my treasured dear
Always serve your husband well
Fulfil his wishes before he can tell
You will flower and bear fruit too
If you remember what I have just said to you
What my mother used to say was true
Her advice was good I always knew
In certain ways the husband is unto his wife
Like her Rabb, the Giver of her life
He will always keep her happy and content
If she devotedly remains his, doing nothing without his consent

Her world will be like *Jannah* so near
Her *Aakhirah* will be *Jannah* without fear
True were the words of my mother dear."

(Translated from an Urdu poem)

## DISPUTES BETWEEN MOTHERS AND DAUGHTERS-IN-LAW

It has become common among many people to keep their sons with them after marriage because their sons are too young to earn or to run a home by themselves. The daughter-in-law therefore has no option but to live with her parents-in-law. This practice has become so popular that a man is frowned upon when he decides to live by himself. People then start labelling him, calling him a naïve and stupid person. In fact, his parents feel hurt to think that they raised him for so many years and now he suddenly wants to leave them. They feel that once their son has married, they will be able to enjoy their grandchildren growing up in front of them.

As a result, the entire family lives together and the mother-and-daughter-in-law are separated from each other only when one of them leaves this world. When the two live together, it is impossible for harmony to prevail. An Urdu proverb rightly says that when two dishes are put together, they are bound to clatter. There is scarcely a bride who is spared this route.

The disputes and problems between mothers-and-daughters-in-law will continue until the custom of living together is abolished. Until this happens, it will be futile to even write about creating harmony between them.

## The Evil of Disputes and Arguments

Nobody needs to be told that an argument between two persons is unpleasant irrespective of who the persons are. It destroys any peace and harmony that exists between them and the two will always be apprehensive of each other. This is especially serious when the argument is between mother-in-law and daughter-in-law. Living in such a home eventually becomes unbearable for everyone. Everything one of them says or does will be a thorn in the other's side and each will search for the other's faults.

The husband then becomes caught in an impossible situation. If he sides with his mother keeping her rights in mind, his wife becomes upset. Of course, he does not want this because he has still the rest of his life to spend with her. On the other hand, if he sides with his wife, his mother becomes upset, calling him an ungrateful traitor. The husband is now torn apart. Whereas upsetting his wife will ruin the relationship for the rest of his life, his mother is his ticket to *Jannah* and it was she who raised him with great difficulty and who spent many sleepless nights for him.

To save a man from such a situation, it is necessary to search for a solution that would eradicate disputes between mothers-in-law and daughters-in-law altogether. It is necessary to identify the factors leading to such disputes so that their hearts are cleansed from hatred, jealousy and other ill-feelings towards each other. If a woman does this, she will be saving herself from much grief and heartache. To achieve this, it is also important for the husband and the father-in-law to read books like "A gift to the husband and wife" by Maulana Ashraf Ali Thanwi (A.R) and "The rights of wives" by Maulana Muhammad Taqi Usmani (Daamat Barakaatuh).

## Disputes Caused by the Mother-in-Law

One of the greatest causes of disputes between mothers-and-daughters-in-law is the absence of religiousness in the home. When the consciousness of *Deen* dominates a household, it will be purged of problems and arguments. As for the disputes generally caused by mothers-in-law, seven of the most common ones are discussed below.

**I$^{st}$ Cause:** The natural jealousy in the heart of the mother-in-law who thinks that someone new has taken control of her beloved son whom she reared and cared for with great pain and difficulty.

**II$^{nd}$ Cause:** The mother-in-law plays the role of a ruler. She asserts her authority to ensure that everything happens only as she wants. When her daughter-in-law enters the house, she feels that her domination will be threatened and that she will be overthrown.

**III$^{rd}$ Cause:** The mother-in-law demands control of not only her husband's money, but also wants to control her son's money. Problems arise between her and her daughter-in-law when the daughter-in-law also expects her share of the money.

**IV$^{th}$ Cause:** Some mothers-in-law become suspicious that their daughters-in-law are sending things from their husbands' homes to their mothers.

**V$^{th}$ Cause:** Mothers-in-law seem to forget that they were also daughters-in-law at some stage of their lives. When they keep this in mind, they will realise that their daughters-in-law are also women with desires and feelings.

**VI$^{th}$ Cause:** When a single suspicion is created, a chain of unwarranted suspicions crowd the mother-in-law's mind, eventually forcing all good thoughts of her daughter-in-law to vanish from her mind.

**VII$^{th}$ Cause:** Because many women have a harsh and uncompromising nature, they treat their daughter-in-law very cruelly. They assassinate the character of their daughters-in-law for every little reason, giving them no peace to do anything properly. When the poor scapegoat has become frustrated, she eventually retaliates and all hell breaks lose.

## Disputes Caused by Sisters-in-Law

When a man marries, his sister begins to find life difficult because she is not as free as she always was in her home. She dreads touching or doing anything for fear that it should upset her sister-in-law. As a result, she begins to abhor the new bride, making things difficult for the poor woman. She then leaves no stone unturned to search for her sister-in-law's faults and to stir trouble between her brother and his wife and between her mother and her sister-in-law.

## Disputes Caused by the Daughter-in-Law

A daughter-in-law is generally naïve and inexperienced. She fails to realise how trivial matters can spiral into a furore and fails to value the benefits of remaining silent. She wants her husband to instantly become her slave and cannot tolerate taking instructions from her mother-and-sisters-in-law. She had been indoctrinated with the belief that her mother-in-law will be policing her every action and monitoring her every move. She feels that just as she has entered the home as a daughter-in-law, her mother-in-law was also in the same situation some day. She therefore regards herself equal to her mother-in-law and believes that she can wield as much authority in the house as her mother-in-law can. She tells herself that she is not a slave and that she will tell her mother-in-law a mouthful if the lady tells her anything. Her friends have by then brainwashed her into thinking that if she once bows to the sway of her mother-in-law, she will always be oppressed. "The first impression is the lasting impression", they told her. She will therefore never tolerate being an underling.

Of course, there may be several other causes and these may vary from situation to situation, but I am convinced that the causes mentioned above are really responsible for creating baseless suspicions and ill-feelings between daughter-and-mother-in-law. These well up within their hearts and when they become impossible to contain, they burst forth like a raging volcano. Mother-and-daughter-in-law are then at loggerheads and are continuously fighting, providing free entertainment for neighbours and relatives.

If both the mother-in-law and daughter-in-law realise their positions and reflect upon these causes which are really fuelled by being naïve, selfish and intolerant, they will be able to overcome the situation. They should educate themselves in Islãm and develop a sound understanding of *Deen*, which will go a long way to eradicate all problems.

## How Every Mother-in-Law Should Think

A mother-in-law should always bear in mind that her daughter-in-law is also a human being with aspirations and feelings. She has made the sacrifice of leaving her parents home to be with her husband forever. The mother-in-law should therefore treat her daughter-in-law like her very own daughter. She should be gentle with her and think that if she behaves harshly towards her, the poor girl will have no one to turn to because she has left her family behind. She is not a slave and her husband owes her many rights, which have been ordained by Allah and His Rasul ﷺ. Just as the mother-in-law was once also a daughter-in-law, she should not forget that her daughter-in-law also enjoys the things that she once enjoyed. She should treat her daughter-in-law as she wanted her mother-in-law to treat her. While the mother-in-law has already enjoyed good times in her life, he should now give her daughter-in-law the chance.

When the mother-in-law harasses her daughter-in-law and behaves sternly with her, she should bear in mind that this behaviour is futile because the daughter-in-law cannot run away and will continue living there. All that will be achieved is that others will have free entertainment and will have ample gossip to keep them busy. In addition to this, the honour of the family will be dragged through the mud.

Every mother-in-law should therefore be as accommodating as possible. She should forgive and forget her daughter-in-law's errors knowing that she is not doing them purposely but because she is still inexperienced and naïve. In all probability, the mother-in-law also made the same mistakes when she was a young daughter-in-law. When she adopts this attitude, life will become pleasant for both mother-and-daughter-in-law.

A mother-in-law should bear in mind that she may not expect her daughter-in-law to do everything in the house. The daughter-in-law should never think that when her mother-in-law first met her to chose her as a wife for her son, she was extremely sweet and pleasant. However, her charms seem to have disappeared after her son's marriage.

I personally feel that it is best for the mother-in-law to hand over all the affairs of the home to her daughter-in-law and occupy herself with *Ibaadah*, taking care not to heed the instigations of her other daughters-in-law. If her daughter-in-law makes serious mistakes, she should be corrected with affection and forbearance. She should not be reprimanded for every little error as is done with one's own children. With all these factors considered, the home will be like *Jannah* for all.

## How the Daughter-in-Law Should Think

Every daughter-in-law should bear in mind that if her mother-in-law is really her enemy, she would never have allowed her son to marry her and would have never allowed her to live in her home. All mothers-in-law are not bad. It has often occurred that the foolishness of the daughter-in-law has led to problems in the family, causing a rift between mother and son. Many daughters-in-law cause tremendous difficulty for their mothers-in-law, especially in situations where the mother-in-law is dependent on her son and daughter-in-law. Such daughters-in-law often behave most insolently towards their mothers-in-law, shunting them around the house and not allowing them any say in even their own affairs. Some of them even extract services from their mothers-in-law. The poor old lady is then stricken with grief and often curses her daughter-in-law.

There is many daughter-in-law who makes mountains out of little molehills and elaborates these to her husband so that the man should be antagonistic towards his parents and sympathetic towards her. Unaware of the truth, the man falls for her ploy and argues with his parents and sisters while his wife watches from a distance. There have been many oppressive daughters-in-law who have suffered terrible diseases because of their tyranny.

Every daughter-in-law should remember that although she is not a slave, Allah has made it compulsory for her to serve her husband. She should also not forget that there should be none more honoured in her husband's sight than his mother because his *Jannah* lies beneath her feet, as Rasulullah ﷺ has explicitly mentioned in the *Ahadith*. If a husband becomes blinded by his love for his inconsiderate wife and behaves disrespectfully towards his mother, how will he ever enter *Jannah*? Being the cause of his entry into *Jahannam*, how will his wife stay alone in *Jannah*? It is therefore imperative for every wife to keep in mind the fact that her husband's entry into *Jannah* hinges on his behaviour towards his mother.

A woman will be doing a great service to her husband if she cares for his mother. She should not lose sight of the fact that her mother-in-law is much older than her and may soon be leaving this world. Thereafter, the daughter-in-law will assume control over household affairs. There is therefore no reason to hasten the situation. If her mother-in-law has ill-feelings against her, she should overlook these and bear in mind that she will soon be a mother-in-law herself and may be exposed to the same feelings.

Every daughter-in-law should also remember that her mother-in-law has always been the queen of her home and expects everyone young and old in the household to respect her authority, to do as she expects and to consult with her before doing anything. She is therefore unable to tolerate rebellion and impertinence from her daughter-in-law. The daughter-in-law should respect her mother-in-law and bear in mind the difference in their ages.

If Muslim women were religious and if they possessed sound Islãmic knowledge, we would not experience the problems we have today. Even if these problems did arise, it would neither be as widespread nor as serious as it is presently. It is therefore necessary for women to daily read books like "*Fadhaa'il-e-A'maal*", "*Fadhaa'il-e-Sadaqaat*" at home and accompany their male *Mahram* relatives on Tableegh visits. With Islãmic knowledge, a person will be able to differentiate between right and wrong and both mothers-in-law and daughters-in-law will respect each other and live amicably.

A daughter-in-law should treat her mother-in-law like her own mother. In fact, she should respect her even more because while her mother is her mother, her mother-in-law is her husband's mother and she should regard her husband higher than herself. When a daughter-in-law treats her mother-in-law well, the old lady will make *Du'a* for her and it is with *Du'as* like this that people are saved from calamities and tragedies in their lives. The patience that the daughter-in-law has to exercise with her mother-in-law will save her from having to exercise patience in much more trying times. She should remember that the *Du'as* of her mother-in-law shall prove to be an impregnable fortress for her children. Serving her mother-in-law on a cold winter's night will earn her such rewards that she will treasure once she leaves this world.

If a woman wants to bear luminaries like Rabia Basriyyah (A.R) and Rasheed Ahmad Gangohi (A.R), she should exercise patience with her irritable mother-in-law and her instigating sisters-in-law and forgive them. She should refrain from backbiting them, she should make *Du'a* for them during her *Tahajjud Salaah* and ask her mother-in-law for forgiveness even if the fault is not hers. By doing this, her offspring will become great people who will be the cause for the guidance of many others.

A daughter-in-law must never speak ill of her in-laws when visiting her parents. Just as she is loved and respected in her parents home because of her sterling attributes, she should employ the same attributes to win the respect of her in-laws. A truly respectable woman is one who is respected by both her parents and her parents-in-law.

If a daughter-in-law employs the approaches mentioned above, her mother-in-law will have no reason to harass her irrespective of how harsh and uncompromising her mother-in-law may be. By the same token, if a mother-in-law practises the advices given above, her daughter-in-law will not clash with her even though her daughter-in-law may be impertinent and stubborn. All the members of the family will then be able to live in peace and harmony.

## A House Burned Down By Its Own Lantern

We will now present to you a drama which depicts the state of affairs when a man lives with his mother, his wife, his sister/s and sister/s-in-law. You will notice that many characters in the drama are people who are not conscious about the obligations they owe to Islām and do not have a sound knowledge of Islām. It is hoped that this drama will assist the reader to understand many things. If you are a daughter-in-law, you will learn that it is important to respect your mother-in-law and to abstain from behaving insubordinately with her.

If you are a mother-in-law, you will learn that it is unwise to have two daughters-in-law living with you. If you are forced to even keep one daughter-in-law with you, you will realise that you should not interfere in her matters, that you should not persistently go to the kitchen when she's busy and should not ask too many questions. If your daughter-in-law is prepared to cook for you, you will be doing yourself and her a favour by leaving the kitchen in her capable hands. You may then keep yourself busy in *Ibaadah* and in assisting people in Allah's path. You will then be served three good meals with respect and honour.

If you are a sister with married brothers, you should be very diplomatic and tactful in ensuring that you do not have to live with your brothers' wives. If you are the elder sister-in-law and your husband's younger brother's wife insists that she wants to live on her own, you should not oppose her decision. May Allah guide us all to practise *Deen* properly.

The cast of the drama is as follows:

| | |
|---|---|
| Afdhal Ahmad | A wealthy bridegroom |
| Maryam | Afdhal Ahmad's bride |
| Muhammad Waseem | Afdhal Ahmad's friend |

| | |
|---|---|
| Zubayda | Afdhal Ahmad's young sister |
| Aamina Bibi | Afdhal Ahmad's mother |
| Bhai Sulaymaan | Afdhal Ahmad's father |
| Maasi | The maidservant |
| Unays | The servant |

It is evening and Afdhal Ahmad is returning home from his shop when he meets his friend Muhammad Waseem. After greeting each other, Muhammad Waseem asks how his friend is keeping.

**Afdhal Ahmad:** What can I say? I have such a backlog of work that I can hardly being to explain. I have to cancel a few orders because the strikes seem endless.

**Muhammad Waseem:** The workload nowadays is becoming overwhelming and we can barely meet our payments. In fact, I was just about to leave today when my boss called me back for more work at the office.

**Afdhal Ahmad:** The strange thing is that even after overcoming the work at the business, you have to face a series of other problems at home.

**Muhammad Waseem:** Oh yes! I have no fear for the complications at work, but those at home! May Allah protect us! Those things can reduce a man to dust.

**Afdhal Ahmad:** You have hit the nail on the head. Since I got married I have a new crisis staring me in the face every time I reach home. I have my mother relating one story to me and my wife relating another story altogether different.

**Muhammad Waseem:** Your situation is not unique. Everyone is having this problem nowadays. I feel that we should all engage in *Taubah* and *Istighfaar*.

**Afdhal Ahmad:** I don't think so. In fact, I don't think that anyone's situation can be as pitiable as mine. I have lost every desire for life. Before marriage I used to hear about disputes between mothers-and-daughters-in-law who are at loggerheads every day. I now have first-hand experience. The constant bickering between daughter-and-mother-in-law causes friction between husband and wife. I blame the mothers-in-law for all these problems. Too many times have I seen my mother admonish my wife for every little thing. It seems as if my mother's full-time occupation is to watch the poor lady like a hawk and haul her over the coals for everything she does wrong.

**Muhammad Waseem:** I am having the same problem. Every day my wife begs me to either get her a house of her own or to send her back to her parents. I have no idea what to do any more!

**Afdhal Ahmad:** What can the poor wife do? I am most surprised to see that it is the mother-in-law who looks for a daughter-in-law and then suddenly becomes the lady's arch enemy. She doesn't seem to realise that the woman is after all her son's wife. When the daughter-in-law does anything commendable, she gets no praise, very unlike the scolding she gets when she does anything wrong. Irrespective of who does something wrong in the house, a mother-in-law thinks of no one else's name but that of her daughter-in-law.

**Muhammad Waseem:** Dear friend, we seem to be in the same boat.

**Afdhal Ahmad:** We are not the only ones suffering. Today, there is scarcely a Muslim home that is free from such problems. Wherever, a mother-and-daughter-in-law share a house, they turn it into a pit of *Jahannam*. Among the primary causes for the suffering new brides experience are jealous and evil sisters-in-law.

**Muhammad Waseem:** What can be the solution?

**Afdhal Ahmad:** The only visible solution is to live separately from our parents. Of course, the difficulty will be that people will point fingers at us and call us sinners. In addition to this, our parents will regard us as unfaithful and disobedient sons. However, I have now made up my mind to get myself a house of my own. Although my wife and I do not watch television and videos, these are still present in my father's house. As my wife says, we are also affected by its evil presence because Allah's curse falls on the house. Besides this, it is practically impossible to stop our children from watching. Everyone knows that today's movies are a major cause of promiscuity, leading our children to fornication. They also contribute substantially to crime and all other sorts of evil. Especially for the sake of the children, I have therefore decided to live by myself even if I have to rent a house somewhere.

It is unfortunate that nowadays an obedient and good person is said to be the one who allows matters to proceed as they are. In doing this, he is destroying his life and dragging his defenceless wife through hell, whereas Allah has placed her in your mercy and protection. Perseverant as the two may, the attitude of the mother-and-sisters-in-law will never change. As a result, the upcoming generation will suffer falling prey to negative emotions like fear, mistrust and cowardice.

**Muhammad Waseem**: Anyway, are you attending the Maulana's lecture at the *Jaamia Masjid* tonight?

**Afdhal Ahmad**: Of course. In any case, I will have to go to the *Jaamia Masjid* tonight to make arrangements for some people going out in the path of Allah. You carry on home, I'll meet you later.

(Afdhal Ahmad goes home where he hears the following):

**Aamina Bibi**: Maryam! Maryam! What are you doing? Is the tea not ready yet? I've told you a hundred times to work quickly!

(Maryam arrives with the tea).

**Aamina Bibi**: Where have you left the cake?

**Maryam**: Zubayda is coming with it, mother.

**Aamina Bibi**: Couldn't you do it yourself? Did your hand break? If this is the case, why didn't your parents send a servant with you so that you wouldn't have to do anything?

**Afdhal Ahmad:** Who baked this cake?

**Zubayda:** Maryam did.

**Aamina Bibi:** Will she never learn anything?

**Afdhal Ahmad:** Zubayda, take this tea away, I shall rather have some at the restaurant.

**Aamina Bibi:** Why Afdhal Ahmad? What is wrong with the tea?

**Afdhal Ahmad:** There is no difference between drinking this tea and drinking hot water.

**Aamina Bibi:** What can I do son? I am at my wits end with this woman.

**Unays:** Mister Muhammad Waseem is at the door.

**Afdhal Ahmad:** It is already eight 'o clock. I'm late. I will have my tea at the restaurant. (He then leaves the house).

**Aamina Bibi:** I have not seen a woman as stupid as you. Did your parents not teach you anything? You cannot even make tea. My poor son had to leave without having his tea.

**Maryam:** But mother, it's not my fault. Zubayda told me that the tea was done and you were rushing me.

**Aamina Bibi:** Oh dear! Are you not ashamed to put the blame on others?

**Maryam:** No mother. I never pass on the buck.

**Aamina Bibi:** Be quiet! You talk too much!

(A cough is heard as Bhai Sulaymaan enters the house. Maryam and Zubayda disappear into their rooms.)

**Bhai Sulaymaan:** Where is Afdhal Ahmad's mother? (He sees her sitting.) What are you doing sitting here?

**Aamina Bibi:** I am lamenting over my ill fortune.

**Bhai Sulaymaan:** What is there to lament about? Allah has granted you sons, daughters and daughters-in-law. What more can one ask for?

**Aamina Bibi:** What else? Our precious daughter-in-law gives me endless grief. Her tea tastes like hot water and my beloved Afdhal Ahmad had to go without tea.

**Bhai Sulaymaan:** What was wrong with the tea?

**Aamina Bibi:** She threw the tea leaves in before the water could boil.

**Bhai Sulaymaan:** You must have been rushing her again. You are none the better. You fuss about every little thing. You want to be in charge of everything that happens in the house and blame everything on our daughter-in-law. I do not at all approve of your behaviour!

**Aamina Bibi:** Oh! So your daughter-in-law is faultless, is she?

**Bhai Sulaymaan:** You have finished with her and it seems like its now my turn to suffer the brunt of your anger. See how you become angry at the slightest provocation. Nobody says that daughters-in-law are perfect. Is it her fault that she has become your daughter-in-law?

**Aamina Bibi:** Get away please! She will never have a mother-in-law like me even if she has to have another life.

**Bhai Sulaymaan:** After this life I do not think that she would want another.

**Aamina Bibi:** Oh dear! You are adding fuel to the fire by siding with that useless woman. My entire body is alight. How sad that my precious son had to go without tea!

**Bhai Sulaymaan:** You must try to control your tongue. You have no idea how many pots of tea Afdhal Ahmad empties with his friends in restaurants. You have no need to worry about him not having a cup of tea here.

**Aamina Bibi:** You have no love for your son.

**Bhai Sulaymaan:** How can you say such a thing? Why would I be standing here defending his wife if I had no love for him?

**Aamina Bibi:** Now you are presenting evidence like a lawyer. This is all your fault. I was always reluctant to propose for Khadija Aapa's daughter.

**Bhai Sulaymaan:** What wrong did Khadija Aapa do to? She did us a favour by bringing to our home a bride who dons Islãmic Hijaab and is well educated in Islãmic knowledge.

**Aamina Bibi:** In that case, I would rather have an illiterate daughter-in-law!

**Bhai Sulaymaan**: Please tell me why you do nothing else all day besides following the poor lady like a shadow?

**Aamina Bibi**: You would like to say that I am doing this because I am insane.

**Bhai Sulaymaan**: I cannot understand why you have changed so much.

**Aamina Bibi**: How have I changed?

**Bhai Sulaymaan**: Do you not remember the time when my mother was alive? Do you not remember how many times you asked me to either get us a house of our own or send me back to your parents? Remember how you used to complain about the things that my mother used to tell you and how you used to get tired of serving her? Did you not feel that my mother used to scold you even though you were capable of doing everything? Was this not hurtful?

**Aamina Bibi**: Not at all.

**Bhai Sulaymaan**: Alright. If it was not hurtful, why were you always complaining to me? You know well that you were hurt, but you do not want to admit it because you have now become a mother-in-law instead of a daughter-in-law. Think awhile. Does your constant nagging and scolding not hurt your daughter-in-law as well? Will she not be complaining to Afdhal Ahmad about your harshness? Do you not think that she also must be wanting to have a house of her own? Why do you behave like this when you have experienced the same situation?

A surprised that women forget that they were daughters-in-law once they become mothers-in-law. Imagine what your reaction would be if your Zubayda was in this situation.

**Aamina Bibi:** I would never marry my Zubayda in a family where the mother-in-law behaves like an executioner.

**Bhai Sulaymaan:** While you would not tolerate the harshness of a mother-in-law for your daughter, you see nothing wrong in ruining the life of someone else's daughter.

**Aamina Bibi:** Who is ruining her life?

**Bhai Sulaymaan:** You are doing worse than ruining her life because you are practically enslaving her. You rebuke her at every step and keep insulting her. This is worse than a slow lingering death. There are too many vibrant young brides who have withered away and entered their graves as demoralised souls because of the bitter remarks and insults of their mothers-in-law.

**Aamina Bibi:** You seem to be intent on lecturing today. Leave all this for now and let us eat. Zubayda is coming with the food.

**Bhai Sulaymaan:** I shall not eat until you promise that you will not tell our daughter-in-law anything in future.

**Aamina Bibi:** Alright! Alright! Let's eat. In future I shall say nothing to Afdhal Ahmad's wife. Are you happy?

**Bhai Sulaymaan:** I shall be happy only when you keep your word. Otherwise, you two will have to live separately.

**Note:** You should read this drama as a sister-in-law so that you would refrain from causing harm to your brother's wife or the wives of your husband's brothers. As a mother-in-law, you should ensure that your daughter-in-law is comfortable if she has to live with you and never listen to what others have to gossip about her. If your mother has daughters-in-law, you should ensure that you restrain her from behaving unjustly towards them. May Allah guide us all to the right path. *Aameen*

## PARTING ADVICE

When a young woman leaves her home as a bride
It is as if *Qiyaamah* has arrived
Giving some parting advice to her departing daughter, the mother said
Greet your mother-in-law with Salaam when you arrive
Show respect to your father-in-law so that none may say
This is a girl without respect
Always honour your husband

And your life will be one of distinction and merit
Be happy and friendly to everyone in your house
You will then be their illuminating lantern
Never speak in high and harsh tones
And live with simplicity and good character
Take care not to walk about bare-headed
Keep your hair always covered and concealed
You are most fortunate to have your marriage made
Remember that you should now remain chaste forever
Sleep the earliest and be the first to wake up
Keeping your attention fixed on your heart
I understand well your uncertainties and fears
These are part of heat of your spark of love
When the sharp rays of the sun extend from you
Remember to show the glow and serenity of the moon as well
Do not hesitate to do the housework
Because this is the practise in the world throughout
When you apply yourself to the housework
You will gain respect and honour from all at home
Do the work of everyone young and old
And, our daughter, you will make a name for yourself
Never backchat with your husband
So that you may never be disgraced in the Hereafter

I have rendered my parting advice
I have taught you everything you need to know
I would sacrifice gold, silver, anything for you
Now marriage has come, waiting for you
May Allah bless this hour
Now that our parting has come so beautifully.

(Translated from an Urdu poem)

## THE PRECIOUS PARTING GIFT OF A FATHER TO HIS DAUGHTER HAFSA

The time has finally arrived when hearts are embellished and hurt
This hour of helplessness was waiting you for a long time
Now you will be leaving your sisters and brothers
Leaving your father, your home, your family and your town
I have accepted this and have imagined the heartbreak
It bores a hole in the heart and breaks it to pieces
This is Allah's command, the practice of the world
A girl will leave for her husband's home, leaving this temporary one
That is your real home, so proceed there
From this day on, your living and dying shall be there

This is not the time to weep, take it from me
Hear well what I say and make no mistake
You are going only to your real home
Do what is honourable and the respect will be immense
Fulfil the rights of one and all
Serve your husband through every pitfall
You understand well the status of your husband
Should he be displeased, *Jahannam* shall be your end
Be steadfast on the *Shari'ah*, O my beloved
And be aware of the rights of all
The life of a happy couple is itself *Jannah*
So always bear in mind the prophetic life the *Sunnah*
Higher than your mother is your mother-in-law
And higher than your father, your father-in-law
Serve and respect them at all times
As long as you live, for always
Hold fast to the *Shari'ah* of *Deen*
Even if you have to give your life and be killed
I have much to say, but what can I do
I have no control of my heart, no strength to contain
I am restraining my emotions, what about you?
Dear daughter, you have exhausted an ocean of tears
You do not weep so when someone leaves on a journey
Things will remain as they are, nothing will change

Exercise patience, for the status of the patient one is high
With the patient one is his Rabb, what more can he want?
Enough now, my beloved, everyone is making *Du'a*
Stand up and express gratitude to Allah
Ask whatever you need from Allah
Your father is also asking Him for you
O Allah, O Merciful and Kind
Wherever Hafsa goes, let happiness not be far behind. (Translated from an Urdu poem)

## THE ETIQUETTE OF LEAVING HOME

A good wife prepares herself to leave long before the time that her husband fixes for leaving so that they may leave in time. With a bit of extra effort from the wife, she will be able to assist her husband so that he should not forget anything in the rush. If often occurs that the husband may forget something and remember it only long afterwards, because of which he has to turn back or make alternate arrangements. This causes undue difficulty for both husband and wife.

When rushing to leave home in the mornings, the husband may forget something that he was to take with him or he may forget something in the pocket of the trousers he changed out of. Before her husband leaves in the morning, a good wife will ensure that all his things are kept together and that his breakfast is prepared on time. In this manner, her husband can leave without worries. He will then leave every day making *Du'a* for her and will even be able to perform two *Rakaahs Salaah* before leaving. With peace of mind, he will also be able to recite the *Sunnah Du'a* for leaving the home. The *Du'a* is:

> {Translation: I leave with the name of Allah and I trust only in Allah because there is no power to do good and no might to resist evil except from Allah}

In response to this *Du'a*, the wife should say:

> {Translation: I entrust your *Deen*, your safety and your final deeds in the care of Allah}

*Shaitaan* will be unable to cause a rift between such a couple who are in the care and protection of Allah. Insha Allah, *Shaitaan* will be unable to even enter their home.

A woman can therefore earn her husband's *Du'as* and pleasure by carrying out simple deeds like this. By doing this, she will also attain Allah's pleasure and she will be able to bring up her children under the shade of Allah's mercy and benevolence. May Allah grant all women the ability to carry out such rewarding deeds. *Aameen*

### The *Du'as* that Women Make for their Husbands Every Morning

An Arabic newspaper once interviewed several women and asked them what they do every morning when their husbands leave for work and what *Du'as* they make for them. The following were some of the replies:

*A.* "I look towards the heavens and say:

{Translation: O Allah! Return him to me quickly and return him safely."}

*B.* "I greet him warmly and say:

{Translation: O my Rabb! Protect him for he is an excellent husband and an irreplaceable father to my children."}

*C.* "I always make the following *Du'a*:

{Translation: O Allah! When will you make us wealthy enough so that this ageing husband of mine will not have to work eight hours a day."}

*D.* "When he leaves, I always say to myself:

{Translation: Will he return to me safely or will an ambulance bring him back home like it brought back the corpse of my neighbour's husband."}

*E.* "I look at the clock after he leaves thinking to myself:

{Translation: When will the clock reach 6 PM so that I may see my husband again."}

*F.* "I get busy cleaning the house and preparing food for my husband and my children because men do not return to dirty homes and unpalatable food."

*G.* "When he leaves, I tell myself, 'Should I not perhaps give him another kiss so that the feeling remains on his lips until he returns?'"

*H.* "I try to forget about him because if I think about him, I will be unable to wash clothes or cook food."

*I.* "I look towards the heavens and say, 'O Rabb! Why did You throw me to this man when there are millions of men better than him.'"

The last woman mentioned won the prize.

You have read all the above replies and may have liked some of them. If you were the tenth woman in this competition, you would do well to give the following reply:

"I first greet him with *Salaam*, adding '*Fi Amaanillaah.*' When he leaves reciting the *Du'a*:

I say to him:

{Translation: Fear Allah concerning us and feed us nothing that is unlawful."}

This is a reminder for the husband not to employ any means of earning that violates the injunctions of the *Shari'ah*. A pious husband ensures that he does not indulge in transactions involving interest, lying, bribery, etc. He is particular about performing his *Salaah* with *Jamaa'at* in the *Masjid* and encourages others to do the same. If he employs other Muslims, he allows them also to perform *Salaah* with *Jamaa'at* in the *Masjid*.

A good wife also reminds her husband that man has been sent to this world not only to earn a living. He should therefore spend some time in the *Masjid* with others to make an effort that everyone practises total *Deen.* She should tell him that he must not invest all his valuable time to earn this temporary world but he must invest time to secure salvation in the Hereafter.

We shall now relate the incident of an Arab Baduwian woman so that every reader my glean something from it. By inculcating the same devotion she possessed, a woman can transform her home into a garden of Jannah.

The Baduwian lady relates, "When my husband goes out in the woods to gather firewood, I feel the fatigue he feels while earning for us. I feel the blazing heat beating down on him as he works on the mountain and it seems as if the thirst he feels will soon scorch my throat even though I am sitting in my hut. I therefore ensure that the house is clean, change into clean clothing and wait for his return with cold water in my hand. When he enters the door after collecting the firewood, I welcome him as a bride deeply in love welcomes her bridegroom. I give him all my attention and make him most comfortable. If he wants my company, I make myself available to him just as a little child plays and frolics with her father."

## THE ETIQUETTE OF CONVERSING WITH ONE'S HUSBAND

Whenever the youngest wife of Hazrat Abu Dardaa رضي الله عنه related any *Hadith* from her husband, she would begin by saying, "My master narrated to me..." The Arabic word

"*Sayyad*" (translated as "master") is used to denote extreme respect. When the speaker attaches the word to himself/herself such as saying "*Sayyadi*" ("my master") or "*Sayyadina*" ("our master"), the phrase denotes love and admiration as well.

When speaking with her husband, a wife should bear the following in mind:

1. She should listen attentively to what he says without speaking between his sentences. After he has spoken his piece, she may ask him something only to clarify what she does not understand. She should be silent when he is speaking because any doubts she has will most probably be explained during the course of his talk. By interrupting his speech, she may cause him to omit some important detail or to dwell on some unimportant subject.

   If a wife needs to tell her husband to do something, she may tell him to do so without referring to what other men do. For example, instead of saying, "Why don't you take us out once a week like how my sister's husband does?" she should rather say, "We would really appreciate it if you could take us out once a week."

2. When referring to her husband in conversations with others, a wife should not use the pronoun "he". She should refer to her husband as "my husband" or by a title people use for him. She may also refer to him as someone's father e.g. "Muhammad's father", "Saabera's father", etc.

3. A wife should always speak softly with her husband. She should never allow anger to make her raise her voice when speaking to him.

4. She should refrain from interrogating him with words like "Why?" "What?" "When?" "What for?" etc. For example, she should never question him disrespectfully by saying, "Why have you come late?" or "Why do you beat the children like an animal?" or "What on earth did you do that for?" or "We never know where you are. Why don't you ever tell us where you are off to?"

   Instead of phrasing her questions like this, she should adorn them with sweet words and gentle tones so that his heart is softened and he will respond kindly to the questions. She will then have the answers she requires without hurting her husband. For example, instead of saying, "Why have you come late?", she should say, "We waited very long for you to return. I cannot rest until you return. Neither the kids nor I could eat without you."

   Similarly, instead of saying, "Why do you beat the children like an animal?" she should say, "You hit Rasheed very hard last night on his ear. Children sometimes lose their hearing when struck so hard. We should then not fall prey to Allah's wrath." She may also say, "When children are beaten, they begin to regard their parents as oppressors. They start forming the idea in their minds that their parents hit them merely to vent their anger and have no feelings for them. They convince themselves that they will be hit whether they do right or wrong. Such children then become stubborn and disobedient. We should therefore exercise patience when the children misbehave. In this way, we will be greatly rewarded. It is things like this that make parenthood a most rewarding experience. Instead of beating them, we should try to reform them in other ways. They will soon realise the error of their ways and change their habits."

In a like manner, instead of rebuking him for coming late, she should say, "I would be so happy if you could inform me exactly when you expect to return so that I could prepare myself beforehand and have things ready for you." Instead of ranting and raving about being unaware of his whereabouts, she should merely express her concern for his safety, telling him that she would feel at ease if he kept her informed about where he was.

Whereas interrogating the husband would have only negative effects and create animosity, phasing her questions with wisdom and love will win his respect and love together with addressing the problem at hand. The incorrect approach will make matters worse and if the husband is not a considerate man, he may purposely do things to aggravate the situation. He may start returning home even later or start beating the children more brutally.

When the wife phrases her questions more wisely, her husband's heart will soften and he will regret his ways.

He will always take heed not to repeat his mistakes and will be proud of his wife's intelligence and diplomacy.

Irrespective of the situation, the wife should maintain her composure and take care never to raise her voice when speaking to her husband. She should respect him at all times and never allow herself to fall prey to backchat. By behaving respectfully and courteously, even the most tyrannical husbands can be moulded like wax.

**Remember** that the slip of a tongue at an inopportune moment may have implications that can plague one for a lifetime. Always adopt a soft tone when speaking so that no feelings are hurt. If this world fails to rewards you for this approach, do not forget that the Hereafter will not be so miserly to reward.

A harsh approach will definitely cause harm at some stage. If one has been harsh towards one's husband, one should lose no time in apologising and doing one's best to make him happy by serving him diligently.

**Remember** also that regardless of how wealthy your parents may be, you should never be fooled to think that you may leave your husband at any time to live with your parents. Although it may seem easy to call your father or brother to fetch you, it will be most difficult to return when the time comes. Leaving your husband is to leave him in the hands of other women. If he ever returns to you after sharing the company of others, he will never be the same person who was exclusively yours; he can never be. Although your mother and younger brothers will support you in your separation, you will rue your decision as time passes, especially once your brothers marry and you have sisters-in-law to contend with. The occasion should never arise when they tell you, "You could not live in harmony with your own husband and mother-in-law, it is no surprise that you cannot live with us as well!" Such a tacit remark is sufficient to instantly wilt the most blooming flower. Whereas a woman can bear a thousand insults from her husband, she cannot withstand a single insult from her sister-in-law. Dry bread and water in your husband's home is much better than eating *Biryani* in your brother's home.

Ladies of the past were often heard saying, "The sedan came as a wedding procession and left as a funeral bier." A couplet from a poem quoted earlier reads:

"Others may see your familiar appearance
But my self-respect will never allow that
I see this calamity (of separation) without tears
flowing from my eyes."

Her husband's home is the only home for a woman and she should make every effort to ensure that life therein remains pleasant for all. She should accept every hardship with a smile because these will all pass by with her still living in the same home. She should turn her attention to Allah whenever she encounters any difficulties and cry before Him to alleviate them. However, she should never think that she will be better off somewhere else. *Insha Allah*, the time will soon arrive when Allah will make her home reminiscent of a garden of *Jannah*.

5. Another important factor that every woman should consider when addressing her husband is that she should not phrase any sentence as a command. Human nature dislikes being commanded, especially when a harsh tone is used. A person commanded in such a manner will either flatly refuse or grudgingly comply. Jurists have even mentioned that a father should not use a commanding tone when instructing his child to do something because if the child refuses to do as told because of the tone, he will be sinful. The father should rather say, "Son, I think that it would be best if you did that."

   (**"Khulaasatul Fataawaa"** Vol. 4 Pg. 340)

   Therefore, instead of telling her husband, "Bring this", "Do that" or "Tell him this", a wife should rather say, "It will be best if you did this" or "I would like you to do that" or "I would really appreciate it if you could bring that."

If every wife could act on these pieces of advice, they will certainly see the positive difference it brings to their lives. May Allah guide all Muslims women to act accordingly. *Aameen.*

## WHAT A WIFE SHOULD NEVER DO

1. A wife should never force her husband to do things that he simply cannot manage to do, e.g. she should not pressurise him to spend more than he can afford. Women often compare what their husbands give

them to what their husband's brother/s give their wives so that their husbands may spend more on them. They also compare what their children get to what other fathers give their children. In doing so, they pressurise their husbands to spend beyond their means, often causing their husbands to fall deeply into debt. Even if the husband is wealthy, they deprive the poor and needy of his charity because they are interested in serving only their own desires.

The eminent *Sahabi* Hazrat Mu'aadh bin Jabal رضي الله عنه counted such women as one of the greatest tests for men. May Allah save every man from such women and every woman from becoming such. Hazrat Rajaa bin Hayaa (A.R) has narrated that Hazrat Mu'aadh bin Jabal رضي الله عنه said, "You people exercised patience when you were tried with the test of hardship. However, I fear for you the test of prosperity, which is the test of women who beautify themselves with gold, who wear the fine garments of Shaam and the crowns of Yemen. They make wealthy husbands tired of spending on them and burden poor husbands with more than they can bear."

It is with reference to such a woman that an Arab poet wrote:

> "If you burden me with more than what I can bear
> Remember that you will suffer more difficulties than the ease I gave you thus far."

2. A wife never should repeatedly complain to her husband about his mother. If a person is displeased with his mother, there is no way that he can ever change her for another. A good wife should regard her mother-in-law as a guest who will soon be leaving. By exercising patience and treating her mother-in-law well, a woman can attain the valuable *Du'as* of the old lady, which will prove beneficial in this world as well as in the next.

Every woman should also bear in mind that her mother is also ageing and it should never occur that her sister/s-in-law ill-treat her mother if she ill-treats her mother-in-law. The principle is clear that one will be treated as one treats others. By the same token she should also bear in mind that she will herself become an ageing mother-in-law one day. It should not be that her daughter-in-law ill-treats her because she did the same to her mother-in-law.

At the same time, she should also remember that people become more like children as approach the age of senility. Therefore, just as one would not abandon one's two-year old child who is impossible to live with, one may also not abandon an old person.

Therefore, if your husband is the only son or if he has other brothers who refuse to care for their mother, do not deprive yourself of the tremendous reward of caring for an old lady. Never pester your husband to provide separate accommodation for you unless the relationship between yourself and your mother-in-law is so strained that it jeopardises your mental and spiritual welfare in this world and in the Hereafter. Under such circumstances, it is best for you to live by yourself. However, even then you should ensure that you serve your mother-in-law so well that she does not even have to get a glass of water by herself.

Whether you are living with your mother-in-law or not, you should make it clear to your husband that when he is with his mother, he should give her more attention. In this way, his mother will not feel that he has forsaken her for his wife.

3. When travelling by car, allow your mother-in-law to occupy the front seat with your husband. Whereas you always have the opportunity to sit in the front seat, you will make her happy by sharing the privilege with her. By pleasing her, you will also be pleasing Allah and when Allah is pleased with you, you will be short of nothing in both worlds.
4. Always give your mother-in-law the first choice whenever the two of you have to choose between two things. For example, if there is a choice to make between two types of materials, give both in her hand so that she may choose which one she likes best. When she has made her choice, take the other one happily. If there is a fear that the mother-in-law will deprive the daughter-in-law of her share and give it to her own daughter instead, the husband should give his wife her share in private. If the mother-in-law has to object, she may be told that her daughter-in-law's mother or another relative had sent the item as a gift for her.

5. Especially if your mother-in-law is a widow, never leave her alone at home when you go out with your husband unless she is happy to stay behind. By refusing to take her along with you, unnecessary ill-feelings may develop in her heart towards you.
6. When a mutual relative phones, allow your mother-in-law to speak to the person as well. Because some mothers-in-law are anxious to know who phoned and what is being discussed, it is best to call them to the phone to speak whenever possible. Of course, if the husband can afford to do so, it will be best if he could arrange a separate phone for his wife in her room and another for his mother so that each could have her privacy.

**Remember** that the sign of a good wife is that she is able to tolerate every difficulty that her in-laws give her. Fire will never extinguish fire. It is water that will do this. Whenever an act is done with gentleness and composure, the act is beautified and multiplied in value.

Another right that the wife owes to her husband is that whenever he brings a gift for her, she should tell him to get the same for his mother. If he cannot afford to do so, she should tell him to give it to his mother and give her the same whenever Allah gives him the means. She should remind him that he is deeply indebted to his parents and that even his hardest efforts cannot repay this debt. The wife who turns her husband against his parents should bear in mind that she is merely littering her relationship with her husband with thorns.

There are many women who refuse to forget even a slight altercation with their mothers-in-law. While their husbands are at work, they compound the matter in their minds, inflating it beyond proportions. Eventually, when the husband returns tired from work, the wife bursts into tears. When the concerned husband tries to pacify her and enquires the reason for the outburst, she brushes off the issue by saying that he should not worry. This she does purposely to stimulate his concern further. After begging her to express her feelings, she eventually tells him that she would be better off dead because she cannot tolerate the misery of living with his mother. Accentuating the episode with false tears, she reports the incident to make her mother-in-law seem like an ogre. If the husband is a shallow-thinking person, he may scold his mother and speak to her harshly, thereby attracting Allah's wrath to his home.

Women should therefore try to forget the little arguments that ensue with their mothers-in-law and face the night with new vigour when their husbands return so that the men do not have to return home with the dread that all hell is soon to break lose.

Again, we should not overlook the fact that if arguments between a mother-in-law and daughter-in-law are a daily occurrence, making life miserable for all at home, the only solution is to arrange separate quarters for the two. If this is not possible, the least that can be done is that separate kitchens be arranged for the two because most arguments erupt over the stove. Of course, arrangements could also be made that the kitchen be the exclusive domain of the daughter-in-law, who would be free to do as she pleases with the mother-in-law coming in only to eat meals.

One should always remember that the status of parents is indeed extremely high. An excellent wife is the wife who encourages her husband to maintain good relations with his parents, brothers, sisters and other relatives. We shall now quote a letter from the book "*Tuhfatul Uroos*" that a new mother wrote to her mother after giving birth to her first child. She wrote:

**To my mother, my beloved mother.**

I love you very much and I need you today more that I have ever needed you in my life. Everything around me is causing this love for you to burst forth from my heart like it has never done before. I have never before realised the great intensity of this love. Although I have always loved you, but I have never before felt the depth of this love as I do now. It is indeed strange that I feel like this now whereas I have never experienced this feeling when I was a little girl on your lap.

I have always noticed your intense love for me and the attention you showered on me. I sensed your love for me as I grew from a little infant, to a young girl and then a young lady. When I eventually became a bride, I started living a new life, a life that was strange from the life I was used to with my parents, and family. When I noticed the favours and attention you showered on my brothers and myself, I was astonished to discover that there could actually exist a being as magnanimous as yourself who would be prepared to sacrifice her life for the comfort and happiness of her children. I then began to wonder exactly who is this great person whom I call mother. I wonder which mine has produced such a gem and what kind of heart you had to be able to exude only love and gentleness.

Dear mother! The first scream of my newborn daughter has exposed the secret to me. Her innocent gurgling has taught me volumes and a discovered a great deal when I took her in my lap and wiped away her warm tears. I then had the answers to every question that had plagued my mind for so long. Today I can appreciate your feelings and see through your eyes. Your graces are being showered upon me even to this day without ever desiring repayment. Today I have realised what it means to be a mother because I have just become one. I can see your radiance in this little child and I can see my entire life in her, my infancy, my blossoming, my marriage and my becoming a mother.

Dear mother! The moments of labour were extremely severe. During those moments that every mother experiences, I wished that you had been near. However, I have now forgotten the pain and only have memories of the little pounding heart that has now occupied my world. From a distance I recognised my child as the nurse carried her to my bed to lay her down. I had been carrying her in my belly for nine months as she grew and was nourished with my blood. I had been eating and sleeping as normal and carrying out my tasks while carrying the world's greatest treasure.

Dear mother! She is now my life. She is everything to me. She is my cherished bud. She is my daughter. For a long time I had been cherishing the kiss of your affection. Now I feel your presence with us whenever I kiss your little granddaughter.

**Your loving daughter**

This touching letter clearly expresses the deep love that every mother has for her child and the love that every child has for his/her mother. It is therefore imperative for a wife not to complain to her husband about his mother. Even though your mother-in-law may insult you, rebuke you or even hit you, you should always remember that she is after all the mother of your husband. She is the mother of your lifelong companion, the mother of your beloved. She is the same woman who carried your husband with difficulty for nine long months. It was she who cared for him as an infant, who used to sacrifice her rest and sleep to nurse him when he was little and who had to endure countless difficulties when raising him. Is it just to get him to fight with her merely on account of a little altercation she had with you?

May Allah never show me nor anyone else the day when a woman makes a man fight with the one who bore him, making him forget the difficulties and hardships she endured for him. Even the Qur'ãn pays tribute to the hardship that mothers endure for their children. When delivering her child, every mother puts her life at risk. Every wife should picture this supreme sacrifice that her mother-in-law made for the life of her husband. It does not behove a Muslim to forget the sacrifices that his mother made for him by scolding her or by speaking to her harshly, especially when siding with his wife. Similarly, it does not behove a Muslim wife to pitch a son against his mother merely because of a little injustice done to her.

The life of this world is but a life of a few days. Just as day follows the night, difficult conditions will soon give way to good times. People spend many decades in prisons with hard labour and still emerge alive. A few years with one's mother-in-law will then surely not kill a person.

If you are not living with your mother-in-law, do try to send some cooking or baking to her regularly. Always phone her to enquire about her welfare and keep sending your children to visit her. It is tragic that association with the *Kuffaar* has made our Muslim women disassociate their children from their children's paternal grandparents and paternal aunts. As a result, the children have little regard for their paternal relatives and associate only with their maternal grandparents and maternal uncles and aunts. Whereas children will readily take to their maternal relatives, they are afraid of their paternal relatives, almost as if they are a different creation. Remember that just as you have sisters-in-law from whom you turn your children away, you may also be a sister-in-law to some woman who may do the same to you.

You should therefore repent for your shortcomings and abstain from destroying your good deeds by backbiting your sisters-in-law. By doing this, you will be giving them all your good deeds and burdening yourself with their sins. May Allah save all women from conniving sisters-in-law who will leave no stone unturned to cause trouble for their brother's wife. *Aameen*

## THE FORMULA FOR AVOIDING ALL TYPES OF TROUBLES

One should always bear in mind that the bond between husband and wife is among the signs of Allah's immense power. A man is closer to his wife than he is to any other person. In a like manner, a woman is closest to her husband. When another person steps between this relationship, no good can be expected from it. Problems between couples are caused mostly by the interference of relatives. To achieve his sinister end of separating husband and wife, *Shaitaan* sometimes uses the wife's relatives and sometimes the husband's relatives.

It is therefore important for a woman not to complain to her husband about her mother-in-law or sister-in-law. She should also conceal such matters from her mother as well and always speak favourably of her in-laws. However, she may reveal the reality of the situation if circumstances are so grave that the couple's relationship is at stake. Always remember that you should never reveal the faults of your in-laws to your family because this will only cause harm.

Rasulullah ﷺ said that on the Day of Qiyaamah Allah will conceal the sins of the person who conceals the shortcoming of others. On the other hand, when a person discloses the faults of another, Allah will expose his faults to the extent that he will be disgraced sitting in his own home. Rasulullah ﷺ has also mentioned that the worst form of usury is to embarrass a Muslim.

It therefore does not behove a Muslim woman to disclose every fault of her in-laws to her family. Many women have the evil habit of telling their family and friends everything that the husbands say and do as well as whatever his family does at home. Muslim women have to refrain from such practices to safeguard their years of *Ibaadah* from being registered in the accounts of the people whom they backbite or slander.

An intelligent wife should excuse herself to tend to some activity when an argument is brewing between her husband and herself. She should interrupt the altercation to pretend to see to the food cooking on the stove or she may excuse herself to put a child to sleep. In this way, she will be leaving the place of dispute. She should also try to get her husband away from the place because this is an extremely effective manner of cooling tempers. Doing this will also conform with the *Sunnah* practices of Rasulullah ﷺ, each of which holds tremendous benefits and mercy for the *Ummah*. Practising the *Sunnah* of Rasulullah ﷺ is a great source of creating love, blessings and harmony between people. It is because Muslims today have neglected the *Sunnah* practices of Rasulullah ﷺ that they are tasting the punishment of disputes and discord.

Bukhari and Muslim narrate a *Hadith* from Hazrat Sahl bin Sa'd رضي الله عنه in which he says that Rasulullah ﷺ once visited his daughter Faatima رضي الله عنها. Upon arriving at her home, he did not see her husband Hazrat Ali رضي الله عنه. When Rasulullah ﷺ asked where Hazrat Ali رضي الله عنه was, Hazrat Faatima رضي الله عنها informed him that she and Hazrat Ali رضي الله عنه had an argument because of which he left the house. When Rasulullah ﷺ sent someone to look for Hazrat Ali رضي الله عنه, he was informed that Hazrat Ali رضي الله عنه was sleeping in the *Masjid*. When Rasulullah ﷺ came to the *Masjid*, he found Hazrat Ali رضي الله عنه lying on the ground with some sand on his exposed shoulder. Rasulullah ﷺ said to him, "Rise, O Abu Turaab (Father of Sand)! Rise, O Abu Turaab!" Hazrat Sahl رضي الله عنه says that the title of Abu Turaab became Hazrat Ali رضي الله عنه's favourite title.

The behaviour of Rasulullah ﷺ with his son-in-law teaches a lesson to the relatives of all women, making it clear to them that they should never overreact and side with the woman when a problem arises. Many people take their daughters/sisters away to their homes after she has had an argument with her husband, forcing the husband to go there and beg for his wife.

The other important lesson that the incident teaches us is that a person should leave the place of an argument and lie down somewhere else until his anger abates. This is imperative because a person is likely to say or do something regrettable when he is angry. Once one has regained one's composure, *Shaitaan* will not be able to manipulate the situation. This *Hadith* therefore contains the following three important lessons:

a. When tempers flare, the couple should leave the place where the dispute is taking place.

b. The couple should not elaborate on the details of their dispute in front of relatives. They should be especially cautious not to make mountains out of molehills. Domestic problem should be confined to the home where they should be resolved internally with the help of *Du'a* to Allah.

c. The person resolving the dispute should try to lighten the atmosphere and not dwell on the dispute, as Rasulullah ﷺ did when he raised Hazrat Ali ؓ's spirits by telling him, "Rise, O Abu Turaab (Father of Sand)! Rise, O Abu Turaab!" In a like manner, when Rasulullah ﷺ separated himself from his wives for a month, Hazrat Umar ؓ lifted Rasulullah ﷺ's spirits by jesting, "O Rasulullah ﷺ! We men of the Quraish were always dominant over our women. Since we arrived in Madinah it seems as if our women have been influenced by the Ansaar women who dominate their men." This remark made Rasulullah ﷺ smile.

These incidents teach us that the person attempting to reconcile disputing parties should begin by lightening the atmosphere so that anxiety and anger are dispelled before proceedings commence.

## EVERY WOMAN SHOULD THINK FOR HERSELF

There are many brides who are reluctant to apply their minds and who prefer to behave like children who do only what they are indoctrinated to do and say. You will find that they cannot do anything without first consulting their mothers or friends. As a result of this, even their marital lives are governed by others. Although it is wise to seek advice from one's pious mother, she may fail to understand the complete situation at home and the temperament of the husband. As a result, her advice may be detrimental to the couple.

In addition to this, every husband expects his wife to be his confidante and close companion without having an intermediary. He cannot tolerate it if even his blood relatives interference in this relationship. It is therefore imperative for a wise wife to tread carefully every step of the way, taking assistance from *Du'a* without repeatedly referring to her mother for advice. She should use the natural intelligence that Allah has granted her and not become dependent on the advice of others.

## A WOMAN SHOULD NOT DISCLOSE HER FAMILY'S SECRETS TO HER HUSBAND

A secret remains a secret as long as it is not disclosed. Although parents may not specifically tell their children that certain matters are confidential, they expect their children not to disclose them. It is therefore expected that a person should not disclose family secrets to his/her spouse after marriage. The first harm of disclosing family secrets is that it is tantamount to betraying one's parents. This is a grave matter because one's parents have always showered one with countless favours and one cannot ever repay them for what they did. They will be extremely grieved to know that the child whom they painstakingly raised for twenty years is now disclosing their secrets to a stranger.

The second harm of this is that a person's feelings and attitudes are susceptible to change. In fact, the heart is called "*Qalb*" in Arabic because it is so prone to changes. Therefore, if the couple have to separate at some stage, these secrets may be made public, causing untold embarrassment to the entire family.

The third harm of disclosing family secrets is that your spouse may use it to tease you if ever the opportunity arises. These secrets are dormant weapons that can be used against you at any time. When you could not stop these secrets from escaping your one mouth, how will you stop it from escaping your husband's mouth as well? He will soon disclose the secret to his parents, brothers and sisters, who will in turn reveal the same to their in-laws and relatives. When the news spreads as a secret, it travels faster and will not reach the ears of the people who form the subject matter.

## An Incident to Illustrate How Molehills become Mountains

Khaalid's company is sending him to Australia for a week. He calls his wife from work to tell her to pack their bags because she could stay with her parents for the week while he is away. She immediately phones her sister to tell her to come over to their parent's home for a few days so that the sisters could spend some time together. The sister secures permission from her husband Ahmad and also starts packing. When Ahmad meets Khaalid at *Asr* time, he asks, "When do you intend leaving for Australia?" Khaalid is stunned to know that his brother-in-law already knows about his journey whereas hardly two or three hours had passed since his company told him about it. He returns home angry with his wife for telling "the whole world" about his trip and a storm erupts. That night, his wife again calls her sister and scolds her for informing her husband, who in turn received a tongue-lashing from his wife for "opening his mouth when he knows how sensitive his brother-in-law is". As a result, two homes are alight and Ahmad has to beg Khaalid for forgiveness.

Situations like this cause many men to lament about their wives, just as an Arab poet once wrote:

> "Stay far from me! Stay away! May Allah protect the world from you
> Are you like a sieve that sifts secrets only to pass them on to others?
> In my opinion, your life is one of sin and your death a relief to the righteous ones."
>
> (Translated from an Arabic Poem)

May Allah save all Muslim men and women from developing such habits. *Aameen*

We shall now relate a true incident from an article written by Sheikh Muhammad Rasheed Al Aweed, entitled "*Risaalah ila Hawa*", which appeared Arabic journal called "*Jareedatul Qabs*". The article reports an incident related by a Dr. Lancaster who served for many years as a marriage counsellor in New York. In support of her opinion that couples should not disclose all their family secrets to each other, she reports a case where a couple experienced serious marital problems after being happily married for ten years.

When the cause was investigated, it was discovered that the wife disclosed to her husband that her father always loved in fear of her mother because she was an extremely ill-tempered person. However, he patiently tolerated her behaviour until she mellowed as the children grew. He was then relieved of his anxiety. She revealed this secret to her husband in confidence little realising that whenever the two were embroiled in an argument, her husband taunted her by saying that she followed in her mother's footsteps. He would also tell her that if he had known that her family was like that, he would have never landed himself into the snare. Another one of his statements was that she should never think that he is a softie like her father. In this manner, their relationship deteriorated very drastically.

The same advice is given by Dr. Kenneth, a leading psychologist. She says, "The harms of being explicit to one's spouse about one's feelings are greater than its benefits. A typical example of something you should never tell your spouse is: 'I cannot understand why I can't seem to love you.' In a single year, I have witnessed 184 cases in which the harms of being explicit and candid with one's spouse are manifest. A wife should therefore never disclose her secrets to her husband and if her husband discloses his secrets to her, she should place her hand over his mouth, making it clear to him that her should tell her anything of the sort. Similarly, they should also not disclose their deepest feelings to each other."

Instead of being frank about the absence of love between them, the couple should make it seem to each other that their love is undying and strong, even though this may require sheer flattery. Therefore, instead of candidly stating that you did not miss him in his absence, you should say, "I could not sleep without you" or "My food would not digest until you returned."

Just as you should not disclose your secrets and the secrets of your parents to your husband, you should also not disclose the secrets of your brothers and sisters to him. For example, you should not inform him about the problems that your sister is having with her in-laws or about the reasons for your brother's broken engagement, etc. You should rather take these secrets with you to your grave and never disclose them to anyone whether you are asked about them or not. As a faithful slave of Allah and follower of Rasulullah ﷺ, you should bear the principles of the *Shari'ah* in mind and protect the honour of you family by keeping such secrets a secret. May Allah guide all Muslim women to do what is right and to remain steadfast on the truth. *Aameen*

## THE COUPLE SHOULD NEVER REVEAL THEIR PRIVATE LIVES TO OTHERS

Rasulullah ﷺ has strongly prohibited Muslims from revealing the details of their private lives to others. It is extremely shameless of a bridegroom or a bride to tell his/her friends about their meeting with each other on their first night of marriage. When Rasulullah ﷺ was informed that people revealed such matters to others, he said, "Never do this! It is like a male and female devil having intercourse on the road with everyone watching." (*Musnad Ahmad*)

Describing the pristine traits of righteous women in the Qur'ãn, Allah mentions,

> **"So the pious women are obedient and they safeguard the private affairs (that take place between them and their husbands)..."**
>
> (*Surah Nisa, Surah* 4, verse 34)

It is also important for women not to describe the beauty of other women to their husbands because this may cause their husbands to be attracted to the women described. The incidents of hurt caused by unfaithful husbands are too numerous and well known and therefore do not need elaboration. It is also improper for women to tell their husbands about intimate details relating to non-Mahram women, such as their pregnancies, etc.

Rasulullah ﷺ said, "A woman should not associate with another woman and then describe her to her husband as if he is looking at her." (*Bukhari & Abu Dawood*)

You may have heard several incidents of men divorcing their wives to marry the associates or family members of their wives. Such relationships have often started when the man's wife introduced him to the other woman or when she spoke about her to him. It is primarily because of the absence of *Shari Hijaab* that such illicit relationships have destroyed many marriages. More devastating are the cases where men foster illicit relationships with their domestic servants and other employees. It is therefore vital for women to observe the *Shari* injunctions concerning *Hijaab* whether their families approve of it or not. Among the men they should conceal themselves from are all their cousins and brothers-in-law.

Many women make the mistake of regarding their cousins (especially the sons of their maternal aunts) as their brothers whereas such men are definitely not *Mahram*. Women should ensure that they conceal themselves from such men at all times. In addition to this, every woman should ensure that her husband is not exposed to non-*Mahram* women such as her sisters, her sisters' mature daughters and his cousins.

It is not futile to reiterate that women should not praise the beauty of any non-*Mahram* woman to her husband. She should not make statements like "she was looking stunning in that red dress" or "she does not even 'show' even though she is in her sixth month". It is *Haraam* to reveal such details to one's husband or to one's brother.

## GUARDING THE HUSBAND'S SECRETS

A wife should not disclose any of her husband's secrets. Among his most confidential secrets are the details of their love-life. Not only is it *Haraam* to disclose these details, it is also *Haraam* to ask another woman about it. Rasulullah ﷺ has classified people who reveal these details as the worst of people. He said, "Verily the person in the worst condition on the Day of *Qiyaamah* shall be person who engaged in sexual relations with his/her spouse and then revealed these secrets to others." A wife may not reveal these details at any stage of her life.

Although there may be many other secrets that are not as confidential as the above category, it is still unbecoming of a good wife to reveal these even to her adult children. She ought to guard his secrets up to her grave and not become the target of statements like that of an irate husband who once said, "No secret remains safe in a woman's custody except her age."

The incident leading to the revelation of *Surah Tahreem* (Surah 66) is well documented and you must have read it somewhere. If not, you should refer to an authentic commentary of the Qur'ãn and try to acquire one to read at home. Among such commentaries are Hazrat Mufti Shafi (A.R)'s "*Ma'aariful Qur'ãn*" and Hazrat Mufti Aashiq Ilaahi (Daamat Barakaatuh)'s "*Anwaarul Bayaan*", both of which have been translated into English. The incident tells us about a secret of Rasulullah ﷺ that Hazrat Hafsa رضي الله عنها knew about and which she disclosed to Hazrat A'isha رضي الله عنها. This angered Allah and He revealed the following verses of Surah Tahreem to chide them:

> **"If the two of you repent to Allah, then your hearts have surely turned. However, if you two assist each other against him (Rasulullah ﷺ), then his protecting friends are Allah, Jibra'eel and the pious believers. Besides these, the angels are also aides to him."** (*Surah* 66, verse 4)

## HARMONISING ONE'S SENTIMENTS AND PREFERENCES WITH THOSE OF ONE'S HUSBAND

Every person has his own set of likes and dislikes. A good wife makes every effort to harmonise her likes and dislikes with those of her husband. Of course, she should not subscribe to those inclinations and sentiments of his that oppose the laws propounded by Allah and His Rasul ﷺ. In fact, she should be so closely associated with him that she can fulfil his wish even before he can mention it to her. She should do things as he wants them to be done and should also conduct herself as he wants her to conduct herself. This is one of the most important ingredients to ensure that the couple's love for each other remains sturdy and everlasting. Whereas beauty and wealth are fleeting commodities, inculcating valuable qualities can never bore one's husband and cannot be lost overnight.

The souls and thoughts of the couple should be united and they should do things in unison. Each one should like what the other likes and dislike what the other dislikes. Such a relationship will ensure that the couple live happily together and together see to the healthy upbringing of their children. When a couple live in this manner, their children will have a happy life which will lead to the sound development of their capabilities and character traits. Such children will prove to be confident and capable, making excellent leaders for humanity.

Made-up beauty is false and even real beauty is contentious and temporary. However, a wife who is in harmony with her husband remains praiseworthy even after her death.

Hazrat A'isha رضي الله عنها reports that she was once drinking water during her menstrual cycle when Rasulullah ﷺ took the cup from her and drank the left-over water, placing his mouth on the same place where hers had been. When a husband and wife drink each other's left-over water from the same utensil, they will be practising a *Sunnah* of Rasulullah ﷺ. You should remember that when you are candid and free with your husband, your relationship with him will be more lasting, your love will be deeper and your honour maintained.

If even the most foolish man on earth gets a wife who is pleasant and eager to please him, he can easily join the ranks of the wisest of men. On the other hand, if a wise man has the ill-fortune of marrying a disobedient and foolish wife, it is only a matter of time before he is relegated to the ranks of the foolish. One of the fortunate men to be blessed with an excellent wife was the famous Chief

Justice Qaadhi Shurayh (A.R). When Imaam Sha'bi (A.R) once asked him about matters at home, he replied, "My wife has not displeased me for the past twenty years." When Imaam Sha'bi (A.R) asked the reason for this, Qaadhi Shurayh (A.R) replied, "From the first night of our marriage, our personalities united and up to this day we are like one soul in two bodies. When I met her the first night and saw how beautiful she was, I performed two *Rakaahs Salaah* to express gratitude to Allah. When I turned my head to end the *Salaah* with *Salaam*, I saw her also ending her *Salaah* with *Salaam* beside me. When I stretched my hand towards her after completing my *Du'a*, she said, 'Be patient, O Abu Umayyah.'"

"She then said, 'All praise is due to Allah. I praise Allah, I seek His assistance and invoke His choicest mercies on Rasulullah ﷺ and his family. I am a simple lady who is unaware of your personality. Do tell me what you like so that I may carry it out and tell me what displeases you so that I may forsake it. There are many women from your people whom you could have married. Similarly, there are many men from my people to whom I could have been married. However, when Allah decrees a matter, it comes to pass. You have now become my master, so do as Allah has commanded every Muslim husband, i.e. that his wife should either be

**"Retained in good faith or released in kindness."** (*Surah Baqarah*, Verse 229)

Thus do I terminate my speech. I seek forgiveness from Allah for myself and for you.'"

Qaadhi Shurayh (A.R) continued, "When I heard this speech, I was compelled to reply. I therefore said to her, 'I praise Allah, seek His assistance and invoke Allah's choicest mercies and peace on Rasulullah ﷺ and his family. You have indeed spoken such words that will be a source of good fortune to you if you remain steadfast by them. However, if you have to detract from them, they will be held against you.' I then proceeded to mention everything I liked and everything I disliked. I then said to her, 'Whenever you see anything good, spread the word around and whenever you see anything evil, conceal it.'"

"She then asked, 'What love do you have for my family?' I replied, 'I do not want to visit them so frequently that they get tired of me.' She proceeded to ask, 'Which of your relatives do you approve of so that I may allow them into the house and which of them do you disapprove of so that I may make some excuse.' I then informed her of my those relatives who are pious and those who required *Du'a* for guidance so that she may avoid them."

Qaadhi Shurayh (A.R) then said to Imaam Sha'bi (A.R), "She has lived with me for twenty years and I have never needed to reprimand her for anything. I only once reprimanded her for something, but was wrong to do so."

(Extracted from "*Al-Mar'atul Mithaaliyya fi A'yunir Rijaal*" Pg. 34)

It is therefore necessary for a wife to act and think according to her husband tastes. It is in the marriage of such women that people as great as Qaadhi Shurayh (A.R) can be of service to humanity. Despite being a pauper, a person with a wife like this will have a life better than that of a king. May Allah make all women icons of compatibility for their husbands. Aameen.

The above incident makes it clear that the couple should ask each other about their likes and dislikes from the beginning so that they may adopt what the other likes and abstain from whatever the other dislikes. If the adage is true that there is a woman behind every successful man, then the life of Qaadhi Shurayh (A.R) is an excellent example of its accuracy.

## A GOOD WIFE IS CONTENT WITH WHAT ALLAH DECIDES

Another sterling attribute of a good wife is that she is pleased with whatever Allah decides, whether the decision is in her favour or against it. Whatever her condition, she is always grateful to Allah.

Imaam Isma'ee (A.R) reports that he once visited a town where he saw an extremely beautiful woman in the marriage of a very unattractive man. When he asked her how she could be pleased top be married to him, she replied, "Be silent! You have uttered a very unpleasant statement. In his relationship with his Creator, my husband may have pleased Allah so much that He has made me his reward. On the other hand, in my relationship with my Creator, I must have displeased Allah so much that He has made him my punishment. I am pleased with Allah's decision for me." So saying, she silenced Imaam Isma'ee (A.R).

("*Al Mar'atul Mithaaliyya*" Pg. 37)

A similar incident is narrated in the book "Aqdul Fareed". An extremely unattractive man by the name of Imraan bin Hittaan was married to a very beautiful woman. She once said to him, "We are both definitely destined for *Jannah.*" When he asked her the reason for this, she said, "You were given a wife like myself and you were grateful to Allah while I have been granted a husband like yourself and I have exercised patience. The patient ones and grateful ones are certainly destined for *Jannah.*"

## HOW AN INTELLIGENT WIFE SHOULD DEAL WITH A FOOLISH HUSBAND

It often happens that when a foolish man's mother or sisters instigate him against his wife, he starts insulting her parents or other relatives, telling her that they are bad people. Because a woman has natural love for her relatives and especially for her parents, she is bound to retaliate by insulting his family. When she retaliates in this manner, matters get out of control and *Shaitaan* has a field day and ravages the marriage which may have been a happy one for many years.

An intelligent wife does not retaliate in this way. When her husband insults her brother for example, she should say, "I seek forgiveness on my brother's behalf. If my parents or any of my relatives have hurt you in any way, I seek forgiveness on their behalf and I shall tell them not to hurt you in this manner again. Please do forgive them. I feel that if they have caused hurt to you or to anyone else, we should not allow their wrong to disrupt our home. The wrong they did will not be corrected by us arguing. Instead, two wrongs will be perpetrated and two relationships will be destroyed. We should therefore first resolve one problem before creating another."

We shall now narrate an incident from every reader will learn invaluable lessons, *Insha Allah.* Addressing a relative of his, Khaalid bin Yazeed once spoke ill of his wife's brother Hazrat Abdullaah bin Zubayr رضي الله عنه. Khaalid's wife Ramla bint Zubayr رضي الله عنها was sitting nearby and overheard what was being said. However, she said nothing and kept her head bowed. After saying whatever he wanted to say, Khaalid's anger had not yet abated. He then turned to his wife and said, "You have said nothing. Did you remain silent because you agree with whatever I have said about your brother or was your silence due to your disagreement?"

She replied by saying, "It is neither this not that. A woman has not been created to interfere in the dealings men have between themselves. We are merely fragrant flowers who have to be admired and smelt. We have no reason to interfere in your matters." Hearing this remarkable reply made Khaalid stand up and kiss his wife's forehead. Every trace of anger and malice that dominated him a while ago was forgotten.

It is because of women like this that Hazrat Sulaymaan عليه السلام remarked in one of his judgements, "An intelligent woman builds a ruined home while a foolish woman ruins a built home." ("*Al Mar'atul Mithaaliyya*" Pg. 26)

Such a woman mends tattered hearts with her intelligence and *Du'as.* She irrigates dead hearts with the water of her love and heals burnt hearts with the balm of her sincere affection. If Hazrat Ramla ﷺ had defended her brother or agreed with her husband, matters would have worsened considerably. Instead, the intelligent lady extinguished the flames of her husband's anger in an instant without hurting anyone. Neither did she blot her brother's image by siding with her husband nor did she infuriate her husband by defending her brother. It is sincerely hoped that every Muslim woman will learn from this incident and adopt the ways of their pious predecessors.

By employing her natural intelligence and sweet tongue, a woman can conquer the hardest man. All she needs to do is to comfort him when he is grieved, be devoted to him and win a place in his heart. It is because of the magic in her voice that the Qur'ãn has forbidden women from speaking to non-*Mahram* men in sweet tones. Her voice is sufficient to entice a man to commit sins. A woman should therefore treat her husband's foolishness with a dose of love, gentleness and kind words. This will effectively stem the tide of his anger and calm his fury. We shall now quote some Arabic verses which eloquently described the manners of speech. By employing these manners of speech, many wives will Insha Allah solve many of their domestic difficulties.

Praising his wife's manner if speech, the famous Arab poet Bashaar bin Bard says:

"When with her, Salma's words fall like pearls
off a necklace, each one dispelling my every
concern and deepest worry
Her speech is so warm that if people left meat
with her, they would find it roasted when they
returned
The echoes of her words are like sections of a
garden filled with fragrant flowers."

Every bride should emulate the excellent manner of speech that Bashaar's wife employed. Her manner was always cordial and friendly, instantly dispelling his every worry and concern.

It has been reported that when a slave girl was brought to the Khalifa Haaroon Ar Rasheed, he commented, "If it were not for the blemishes on her face and pigmentation on her nose, I would have purchased her." Hearing this, the lady requested permission to speak. When she was permitted to speak, she recited the following couplets:

"Despite its good looks, the beauty of the deer is
not perfect, never!
Neither is the beauty of the full moon that people
laud
The deer has blemishes on its nose
And the full moon has blemishes that all are
aware of."

Hearing the eloquence of her words, the Khalifa purchased her and she became one of his most favoured slave girls. Even though she lacked physical beauty, this woman won the Khalifa's favour purely on account of her intelligence. She taught the Khalifa and all those present that although the moon has obvious blemishes, these do not affect its radiance and overall beauty. She indicated that although Allah had not blessed her with physical beauty, Allah had blessed her with the gem of intelligence by which she could be of sterling service to her master.

It is praiseworthy of a woman to beautify her physical self without the use of jewellery and to beautify her inner self with attributes such as:

- Intelligence coupled with diplomacy
- Maintaining a clean and tidy home
- Obedience to her husband
- The concern to beautify herself for her husband so that he could be attracted to her without burdening him with expenses.

The Khalifa Mu'tadid once fell asleep while resting his head on his wife's thigh. She gently placed a pillow beneath his head and left. When he awoke, he was upset to see that she had left. He asked her what was the reason for her behaviour because he felt that her action stemmed from pride. She denied this and said, "We were taught never to sit near a sleeping person and never to sleep near someone who is sitting." Mu'tadid was satisfied with this reply.

Every woman should be grateful to Allah for every quality that Allah has blessed her with, whether the quality be related to her inner self or her physical appearance. By being ungrateful for these blessings, they will gradually diminish and she will begin to lose confidence in herself. She will then doubt her abilities and the value that others attach to her.

A woman should do everything with foresight and a conscious mind. In this manner, she will be respected and admired. It will not be redundant to again quote the statement of Hazrat Sulaymaan عليه السلام who said, "An intelligent woman builds a ruined home while a foolish woman ruins a built home." Whereas an intelligent woman will introduce orderliness to a chaotic home and will be able to understand the personality of her husband, a foolish woman will disrupt an orderly home, replace its love with enmity and its tranquillity with agitation. May Allah save every home from such a woman. *Aameen.*

A poet once said:

"O beautiful lady! Harness your loose tongue!
Do not taint your beauty with your words.
O unattractive one! Be righteous!
Do not join two negative traits within yourself
(i.e. unattractiveness as well as impiety)."

Whereas a man can tolerate unattractiveness, he will not be able to tolerate a woman who does not control her tongue.

## A GOOD WIFE IS ALWAYS LOYAL TO HER HUSBAND

A good wife always stands by her husband's side regardless of circumstances. Whether he is experiencing prosperity or whether he is suffering hardship, she never leaves his side. A man is most unfortunate when he has a wife who is actually married to his wealth. Such a woman will remain loyal to her husband only while he is wealthy.

A true wife loves her husband only for Allah's pleasure. She has no obsession for the things of this world and her only obsession is pleasing her husband. She ensures that he is never displeased with her and treats him equally well whether he is healthy or ill. True love dictates that even once a woman's husband has passed away, she still adheres to the lifestyle she lived while he was alive. Just as she did nothing to displease him during his lifetime, she will do no such thing after his death. Such was the behaviour of Hazrat Umar bin Abdul Aziz (A.R)'s wife. After he passed away, her brother asked her whether she wanted back her jewellery which her late husband had deposited in the state treasury. She replied, "How can I be happy with it now when I was not happy with it during my husband's lifetime?"

It is in praise of his loyal wife that a Baduwian suffering starvation once recited the following couplets:

"O my Rabb! I am sitting here as You see
Sitting with me here is my wife as You see
My belly is empty as You see

What is Your opinion about what You see?"

(Translated from an Arabic poem)

If a woman refuses to stand by her husband's side when he is in difficulty, his grief will be doubled. When a man suffers a setback like loss of employment, a good wife will wipe away the perspiration of anxiety from his forehead. She should comfort him by telling him that wealth comes from Allah and that He takes it away only for good reasons. She should advise him to regularly perform his *Salaah* and to constantly recite "*Yaa Mughni*" (يامغني) and "*Yaa Ghani*" (ياغني). In addition to this, he should also recite the following *Du'a*:

> (Translation: "O Allah! Grant me sufficient *Halaal* sustenance so that I may save myself from Haraam and, by Your grace, make me independent of everyone besides You.")

She should tell him that she does not mind living, eating and dressing simply for as long as they need to so that he may not have any financial burden. With such support from his wife, no difficulty is insurmountable for a man. Her inspiring attitude can lift him out of any gloom and convert any illness to glowing health.

On the other hand, when a woman regards her husband only as a means of fulfilling her needs, she will rebuke him in his difficulties instead of comforting him. She will tell him things like, "Did I not tell you not to do business with so-and-so?" or "I warned you against investing there! Now you have lost everything just as I told you!" or "Now how will we pay the children's fees, the lights and water? How will I do without our domestic servant? I will now have to bear the brunt of your foolish dealings!"

It is with reference to such women that the famous Arab poet Abu Amr Ibn Alaa wrote:

> "If you ask me about women, I have profound knowledge of their behaviour and am also a physician to treat them
> When a man's hair whitens or when his wealth diminishes, he will have no place in her heart."
>
> (Translated from an Arabic poem)

## A GOOD WIFE HAS EYES ONLY FOR HER HUSBAND

Another outstanding feature of a good wife is that she loves only her husband and this love is solely for the pleasure of Allah. She has no ulterior motives for this love. Rasulullah ﷺ has mentioned that a woman will enter *Jannah* if she passes away when her husband is pleased with her. (*Tirmidhi* Vol. 1 Pg. 219)

When a woman's love for her husband is not related to his wealth, his beauty, his position, his qualifications or anything else, she will win a prized position in his heart which none can wrest from her.

One of the traits of the women of *Jannah* is that they will be

**"Maidens with lowered gazes".**

(Surah Rahman, *Surah* 55, verse 56)

This means that these women have eyes for none besides their husbands. Another of their qualities is that they are

**"Damsels sheltered in tents".**

(Surah Rahmaan, Surah 55, verse 56)

This verse means that they are women who do not beautify themselves and roam about for others to admire. They reserve their beauty exclusively for their husbands. A good wife should therefore have eyes only for her husband and she should not look at non-*Mahram* men. At the same time, she should go out of her house only when absolutely necessary so that she does not become the admiration of every other man.

The famous king Haaroon Ar-Rasheed had a black slave girl whom he loved very much and who also loved him very much. She was his favourite slave girl. Because of his attachment to her, the other slave girls became extremely jealous of her and they were always scheming against her so that the king may devote less attention to her. As a lesson to them all, the king once spread out a tablecloth filled with jewels, gold and silver. He then made an announcement that every person can take whatever she/he can lay his/her hands on. When they heard this, all the king's servants and courtiers started taking whatever they could. However, his favourite slave girl stood where she was, intently looking at the king. When the king asked her why she was not taking the jewels and treasures, she asked, "Is the announcement true that a person can keep whatever she lays her hands on?" When he confirmed this, she calmly stood up and, placing her hand on the king's shoulder, said, "I desire the master of this gold and silver. If I have him, I shall have all of this and if he is not mine, I shall have nothing." The king presented this as an example to the rest, making it clear to them that although she did not possess the beauty they had, she more than made up for it with her love for the king.

The lesson that every Muslim should learn from this incident is that we should seek to please Allah at all times regardless of what people say. When we have secured Allah's pleasure and have won Him over, the contents of the heavens and the earth shall be at out disposal. However, if He is displeased with us, we shall be perpetually worried and depressed even though we may possess the riches of the world. May Allah make every Muslim His sincere bondsmen and bondswomen who follow in the footsteps of His beloved Prophet ﷺ. *Aameen*

## A MOTHER'S ADVICE TO HER DAUGHTER ON THE NIGHT OF HER MARRIAGE

When the leader of Kindah Amr bin Hajar was married to Ummu Iyaas bint Awf bin Muslim Shaybaani, her mother *Umamah* bint Haarith (A.R) called her aside on the night of their marriage and gave her the following pieces of advice. Every new bride should heed these valuable pieces of advice, which outline the rights that every wife owes to her husband.

She said, "Dearest daughter! You are now leaving the environment in which you grew up and you are turning your sights onto a horizon which you are unfamiliar with. Your companion there will be someone with whom you are not acquainted. Today, all of you shall be under his authority. You should therefore become his slave girl and he will become your conscientious slave. Adopt ten attributes which will cause your husband and other people to speak favourably of you and which will be a treasure for you in the Hereafter. These attributes are:

**The first and second** are that together with being content with whatever he gives you, you should humble yourself before him. Listen attentively to whatever he says and obey his instructions.

**The third and fourth** are that you should always be conscious about how your husband likes to see you and smell you. Whenever he sees you, his opinion of you should not be tainted and whenever he smells you, he should never smell anything besides a pleasant fragrance. Kohl is the best, easiest and least expensive form of beautification while water is the best fragrance because taking a bath regularly and making wudhu often ensures that the body remains clean and does not exude an unpleasant odour.

**The fifth and sixth** attributes are that you should always take his times of eating and sleeping into consideration because the sparks of anger are usually ignited by hunger and lack of sleep. Have his meals prepared before time and if you get delayed, feed him something light while the meal is being prepared. If he gets angry when the meal is delayed, apologise and present your excuse. However, you should never use anger to reply to anger.

**The seventh and eighth** attributes are that you should always safeguard his wealth as well as his family and his status. His wealth is best safeguarded by sound financial management and his family is best safeguarded by good supervision.

**The ninth and tenth** attributes are that you should never disobey his instructions and never disclose any of his secrets. Disobedience will fill him with rage and disclosing his secrets will make you vulnerable to any plot he may scheme against you. He will then have no confidence in you and will never regard you as his own. Never express joy when he is grieved but rather share his grief and comfort him. On the other hand, you should also take care never to express grief when he is happy.

**Remember**, my daughter dear! You will never be able to conquer his heart until you give preference to his pleasure over your own and until you like what he likes and dislike what he dislikes. We now leave you in Allah's care. May He grant you every good and save you from every evil."

("*Silsilatul Usratil Muslimatis Sa'eeda*" Vol. 1 Pg. 45)

May Allah grant every Muslim wife the guidance and ability to implement all of the above in their lives. *Aameen*

## A FATHER'S ADVICE TO HIS DAUGHTER

It is *Mustahab* (commendable) for a father to advise his daughter on the occasion of her marriage. Hazrat Anas ﷺ narrates that whenever the *Sahabah* ﷺ sent their daughters as brides to their husbands, they would emphasise the importance of serving the husband and fulfilling his rights. ("*Tuhfatul Uroos*" Pg. 77)

Hazrat Abdullaah bin Ja'far bin Abi Taalib ﷺ gave the following advice to his daughter:

> "Avoid jealousy and pride because these are the keys to divorce. Avoid rebuking because this creates enmity and resentment. Use kohl because this is the best means of beautification and the best perfume is water."

When Hazrat Farafasa bin Ahwas gave his daughter Naa'ila in marriage to Hazrat Usman ﷺ, he advised her in the following words:

> "Dearest daughter! You are going to be in the company of women of the Quraish who have better access to perfumes than you have. Therefore, remember these two pieces of advice that I am giving to you. Use kohl and apply the perfume of water (i.e. bath regularly) so that you may smell as fresh and fragrant as rain water." ("*Tuhfatul Uroos*" Pg. 122)

In addition to the advice given above, Abul Aswad advised his daughter thus:

> "Pay attention to your physical appearance and remember that kohl is the best means of beautification. Always apply perfume and remember that the best perfume is to perform wudhu properly."

In fact, even many non-Muslims have identified that washing the face several times with cold water is an excellent manner of maintaining one's beauty.

The above quotations make it clear that Islãm strongly recommends women to beautify themselves for their husbands. Whether a woman is rich or poor, young or old, at home or travelling, she should bath at least once daily. During summer, she may even bath twice a day. Of course, this depends on her health. Otherwise, she will be making wudhu several times for her five daily *Salaah*. Besides these times, she should wash her hands and face after completing her work in the kitchen.

Women should also ensure that they use kohl, which is inexpensive means of beautification that does not require much time to apply. In addition to this, it does not have to be removed when making wudhu or when taking a bath. If women could adopt these simple but highly effective means of beautification, the Muslim *Ummah* will save millions which could be utilised for more worthy causes.

It is commonly said that women are men's dolls. It is therefore necessary for every husband to provide the means of beautification for his wife so that her added beauty may attract him to her and increase their love for each other.

Hazrat Abul Faraj Isfahaani (A.R) has mentioned that even beautiful women need to beautify themselves and keep themselves clean to win a place in the hearts of their husbands. These factors enhance her beauty. In addition to this, she should also dress attractively. Of course, a woman may only use those types of clothing and means of beautification that the *Shari'ah* permits. She should be cautious that her husband should not see her in an unkempt condition and that he should not get an unpleasant odour from her.

A wife should remember that she will suffer the consequences of her failings in this regard. If she does not take care of herself and allows herself to fall prey to shabbiness and obesity, her husband will detect her indifference and he may be attracted to other women.

Women should also be cautious not to allow their clothing to get soiled. They should immediately remove any stain that falls on their clothing. It is commonly mentioned that when a person keeps his/her clothing free from stains and dirt, Allah will keep his/her heart free from the stains of sin.

The importance of personal hygiene cannot be overemphasised. One's teeth and mouth should always be clean and nails always neatly pared. Although this is especially important for a wife, the husband should never neglect the same for himself. The details of this will Insha

Allah be mentioned in the book "Gift to a husband". When the men of the Bani Israa'eel neglected personal hygiene, their women resorted to adultery.

## THE ADVICE OF HAZRAT MAULANA MUHAMMAD AHMAD SURTI (A.R) TO HIS DAUGHTER

Dearest daughter! You are now leaving for your husband's home. Leave happily. May Allah bless your new home. May you spread light wherever you go and may Allah grant you the understanding and foresight to brighten your future. May you find happiness with your husband. May Allah grant both of you such great love for each other that lights the way ahead and which provides comfort for your in-laws as well.

Dearest daughter! May Allah guide you to uphold the honour of your parent's home when you live with your in-laws. Never allow disgrace to come to your parents or your parents-in-law. Our honour is now in your hands. Never allow anyone to criticise the careful and loving upbringing that your mother gave you.

Dearest daughter! May Allah grant you the ability to tackle every difficulty with courage and determination. May He also grant you the ability to cross every intricate and delicate situation with dexterity and skill. Keep away from arguments and disputes and Allah will grant you the traits of a respectable woman.

Dearest daughter! From the day you were born, we realised that you were not meant to stay with us always but would be leaving us for another. You were destined to live as a guest in our home and we raised you until you developed the ability to run your own home. We are now handing you over in the safe custody of your in-laws.

Dearest daughter! You are now leaving your parents, your brothers and your sisters. What a painful moment indeed! Women have come from near and far to attend the wedding and children are all dressed in excellent Islãmic dress, all beaming with excitement. All your father's friends are here as well as friends and relatives from our families and associates. Some are weeping openly, others are sobbing silently while the eyes of so many are welling up with tears, each one of them trying to lighten the grief burdening their hearts. Looking across the spectrum of people young and old, a strange form of gloom seems to have enveloped them all.

Dearest daughter! Look at your mother! Her grief is inexplicable. She bore you in her womb for nine long months, feeding you with her own blood. She would sleep on the wet portion of the bed, keeping you snug on the dry part. She then kept her gazes fixed on you for eighteen years. How will her tears every dry? She sacrifices her rest for you and forfeited many nights of sleep during her youthful days for your sake. When it came to you, she neither knew day as day or night as night. How will her days and nights now pass without you?

You cannot imagine the difficulties she endured for your education and for raising you. A slight frown on your face would eliminate all her happiness and your single tear would ignite a thousand sparks in her heart. You are now leaving this warm lap of your mother. She fed you the best food without desiring it for herself and dressed you in the best clothing without wishing that the money had been spent on her. Her heart always told said, "When my daughter eats well, it is as if I am eating and when she dresses well, it is as if I am dressed."

To alleviate your single worry, she would take a thousand worries upon her head. Can you remember how many good nights your mother passed in anxiety for you? She would sit at your bedside for hours when you were ill and would pay no heed to her own health because of her concern for your health. Alas! What must be passing through her heart at this moment? She will now have to bear this separation. Only Allah can grant her the ability to bear it.

Dearest daughter! You are leaving your beloved sisters behind as well. Together with being your sisters, they were also your close companions. You were always together and did nothing without each other. You played and enjoyed yourselves together and were so close that you even thought the same thoughts. They love you dearly and were always ready to do what you told them. Your happiness was their happiness and your grief was theirs. They laughed when you did and trembled when you showed the slightest sign of displeasure. You played together on the swings and sat together through long nights listening to the stories of the pious. You slept together and woke up together.

How depressed are they today? Although they will continue their activities, their tearful eyes will always be searching for you. They simply cannot forget you.

If only you could see your friends today! One stands in the corner weeping while another is sobbing silently somewhere else. If they did not see you for two consecutive days, they would become restless and find an excuse to come looking for you. They would attend and host Islãmic programmes for ladies to be with you. Now they will be unable to meet you for weeks. Perhaps only you know the grief that they will experience during these times.

Dearest daughter! Today you will also be leaving me. I always desired that you should be an educated and knowledgeable young lady with refined manners and donning Islãmic dress with *Hijaab.* Together with ensuring that you have the best food and clothing, I always wanted you to be blessed with excellent morals and a noble character. You are now the sterling example I always envisaged. I also entertained the hope that you would become a wife from whom good wives learn to better themselves and from whose behaviour bad wives correct themselves.

You will recall that I was never harsh with you in your upbringing, yet I never ignored any bad habit. I always prohibited you from reading books and novels that promoted immorality and I always brought home for you such books to read that taught good morals and valuable lessons. I also protected you from the filth of television, video and cinema because it is these things that have destroyed many noble homes and brought disgrace to honourable families.

Dearest daughter! You know well that I have always given preference to your comfort over my own. I have always chosen the best teachers for you and safeguarded you from the corrupted secular syllabus. I have always been taking you and your mother to Islãmic programmes and have always devoted special attention to your education. I have always regarded my home and children as a trust which Allah has placed in my care so that I may teach you good manners and conduct. I realise that I will be answerable to Allah if I were to fail in teaching you Islãmic morals and conduct After having done all of this, I now place you in the custody of another good family.

Light of your father's eyes! You are really leaving us today. Separation from you is truly heartbreaking. However, this day is an extremely momentous day for you. Although it appears as if you are merely moving from one home to another, this move is really an enormously significant one. To this day you were free to do as you pleased in your parent's home. However, from today you will have to do things with dexterity and skill. To this day, you were free to desire whatever you pleased. From this day onwards, you will have to foresee the consequences of your aspirations before setting your sights on them. Whereas you could previously ask others for the things you desire, you will now have to play a role in fulfilling the hopes of others.

Up to this day, you were issuing instructions for others to follow. Now you will have to take instructions from others. Without first being a slave, you cannot become a queen.

Dearest daughter! Today your entire world will be changed. The ways and procedures you were accustomed to will have to be altered. You will even have to change your ways of speaking. Every facet of your life will take a new meaning and new angle.

I remember well how you used to behave stubbornly and throw tantrums until we were all forced to give in to you. I accept that these occasions were rare, but remember that you should think carefully before you express your desires in future. You should first try to ascertain what the reaction of your husband and his family will be. Remember that you will be unable to control the hearts of others until you are able to control your own.

Your life has now taken such a momentous turn that it resembles a vehicle turning into a different road. Your thoughts and tendencies are sure to change, just as your hopes and aspirations will. You will experience such a personal revolution that you will begin to forget the past. Your attitudes, outlook, pace of life and pattern of life will change so dramatically that even you will be surprised.

Dearest daughter! My sense of duty urges me to tell you certain things today that will be of use to you and which will save you from many difficulties and complications in future. Failure to adhere to these guidelines has already destroyed many marriages.

The first factor to understand is the meaning of marriage. Marriage is not a contract to enter into slavery. Marriage is a contract of mutual assistance. Marriage is a contract whereby a couple agree to spend their lives together according to the principles stipulated by the *Shari'ah*. A couple therefore have to share a mutual bond of love and concern for each other. They need to be loyal to each other and have to regard each other as their own. Marriage is the shackle that binds the couple so that they may lead their lives together in harmony and solidarity. To make this relationship work, either party has to make sacrifices.

There is no doubt about the fact that Allah has given men superiority over women and has allowed men to lead women. This does not allow men to dictate to women, but is intended to entrust men with the responsibility of protecting and providing for women. If this were not the case, men would not have been enjoined to fulfil the innumerable rights they owe to women. To maintain harmony between the couple, women have also been commanded to fulfil numerous rights that they owe to men. When the two fulfil the rights due from them, they will enjoy a pleasant and harmonious life.

Since marriage is a relationship of mutual support and assistance, the couple are dutibound to formulate principles and blueprints by which they will be able to provide maximum comfort to each other. Each of you should understand what duties you have to fulfil. The definition of these duties will depend on your existing circumstances. However, I would like to point out some factors in this regard.

Dearest daughter! We are seeing you off from our home with flood of tears. On the contrary, when you arrive at your in-laws, you will be received with smiles, laughter and happiness. There it will be different world. The atmosphere will be filled with joy and every person's face will be lit with glee. Everyone will be speaking fascinating words and they will embrace you happily. You will be the star attraction and everyone's attention will be focussed on you. Every lady will be waiting anxiously to see you and a thousand praises will be expressed at your every step. This attention and adoration will last only a few weeks but you must be cautious and alert during this while because your every movement will be scrutinised. A slight error will be magnified and inspected. However, you are intelligent enough because you have seen many women become brides. I am confident that you will pass this period of scrutiny carefully without giving anyone the opportunity to smear your name.

Dearest daughter! The first person to acquaint yourself with is your husband. He is the person on whom the prosperity or damnation of your future depends. Therefore, your most important duty is to understand him and to harmonise your thoughts and desires with him. In this manner you will be able to avoid clashes. When a couple's desires and thoughts are incompatible, they are prone to disputes, which eventually ruin their lives. I shall not discuss the duties of the husband because I am presently concerned with addressing you. I am sure that your husband's parents have fulfilled their responsibilities by informing their son about his duties. Since they will be living with him, they will certainly advise him from time to time.

Remember that Allah has described the husband as clothing for his wife and the wife as clothing for her husband. If a person is wearing no upper garment and has a wound on his shoulder from which puss is flowing, people will certainly be repulsed. Similarly, they will also be revolted to see filth on his body when he is wearing no clothes to conceal it. However, if a person has such a wound or filth on his body but covers it with clothing, none will have the opportunity to speak ill of him. In this manner, each partner will conceal the defects of the other.

A poet once said, "I have become you and you me. If I am the body, then you are the soul."

Just as clothing protect people from the elements, the wife protects the husband and vice versa. Regard your husband as your own self and guard him likewise. The one who serves is really the master. You can only win people over by regarding them above yourself.

Always pray to Allah saying, "O Allah! Forgive my sins, allow me to die in a good condition, allow me entry into *Jannah* and accept my progeny to spread *Deen* throughout the world." People are prepared to give their lives for *Jannah*. However, I am convinced that you will be able to achieve this great prize by fulfilling the requirement stipulated by Rasulullah ﷺ. Hazrat Ummu Salma رضي الله عنها has narrated that she heard Rasulullah ﷺ say that a woman will enter *Jannah* if she passes away when her husband is pleased with her. In another *Hadith*, Rasulullah ﷺ told women that their husbands are their *Jannah* or *Jahannam*. The lofty gardens of *Jaanatul Firdous* are waiting for every woman and the maidens and servant of Jannah are anxious to welcome them. However, the condition is that she has a certificate to certify that her husband is pleased with her.

Dearest daughter! Remember that diligently serving your husband is as easy as it sounds because you will have to reduce yourself to nothing. However, Allah has made it easy for woman to earn *Jannah*. While He has commanded men to remain pleased with their wives, He has also made the husband's pleasure a means for every wife to enter *Jannah*. Every woman should therefore grab the opportunity and leave no stone unturned to keep her husband pleased. Even if a woman has a husband who is foolish, he will still be the most important person in her life because most of her time will be spent with him. Because the couple will almost always be doing things together, you should remain loyal to your husband and bind yourselves together.

Remember that you will only be able to win a place in the hearts of others once you have won a place in his heart. The woman who has fallen from the sight of her husband has really lost this world as well as the Hereafter. A woman can rule her husband's heart only once she has won his love and affection. If a husband has no love for his wife, her status in his home will be simply like that of a maid servant.

Every husband is but a human and desires love and doting. He expects to find love and comfort after marriage and if his wife provides these blessings for him, he will have to be a fool to seek them elsewhere. When a husband steps into his home, he will be delighted to find his wife at the door to welcome him home. Her gleaming face and her happiness to receive him is enough to dispel his every worry. When she follows this reception up with a sincere desire to fulfil his every need, there will be none more beloved to him in the entire world.

A person employing servants will be most pleased with the servant who serves her the best and who is most concerned about her comfort. If such a servant has to leave, she will be sad and will miss her all the time. However, if a lazy and uncooperative servant leaves one's employment, one will be more relieved than sad. Similarly, when a wife wins her husband's heart with diligent service and after making many sacrifices, her husband will be unable to bear separating from her for even a minute. On the other hand, if a wife does nothing to please and comfort her husband, her presence in the home is as good as her absence. Such a woman cannot expect her husband to have any love for her and cannot expect him to miss her when she leaves. Whereas a lazy servant can be changed at any time, the marriage contract which is entered into after much deliberation cannot be dissolved as easily. Marriage is a union that is made to last a lifetime.

It is therefore only a foolish woman who will forfeit entry into *Jannah* merely because she does not want to serve her husband to please him. It can only be such a woman who would sell the everlasting bliss of the Hereafter for a few day's rest in this world. It is indeed unfortunate that there are so many women who are so short-sighted that they cannot appreciate the love of their husbands. It is for this reason that they remain adamant and refuse to do what their husbands tell them. As a result, they have not only destroyed their lives in this world and the Hereafter, but they have also destroyed the lives of their posterity.

Dearest daughter! Do you remember a time five years ago when a respectable man became our neighbour. Although his parents lived with him, they were always happy with their daughter-in-law and there were no disputes between her and his parents. He was earning well and they always lived comfortably. However, it always appeared that the couple were perpetually ill. Although they were physically well, their health was always poor. The only reason for this was that the two could not get along together. They lacked love and devotion to each other. Their opinions always conflicted and they fought endlessly. He was adamant about his views while she refused to give in to his standpoint. Little realising how this was ruining their lives, neither would allow the other's opinion to dominate.

Such disputes are devastating indeed. If one has to analyse such disputes, one will find no tangible reason for them. However, disputes require no important matter to hinge upon. They will readily spring from the most insignificant differences and they are bound to happen in the lives of every couple. It is therefore necessary to adopt humility and give in when necessary. This will resolve all disputes and ensure harmony between the couple.

Dearest daughter! You may have seen that couples fight for hours only because someone moved the husband's chair slightly forward or simply because a little extra salt fell into the food by mistake. Such rows sometimes last the entire night, forbidding sleep for the neighbours. Word soon spreads throughout the town that the couple's marriage is on the rocks, giving every person the opportunity to add delightful titbits to the story. The town is then flooded with rumours like, "Did you hear that she has been by her mother's place for the last six months and her husband does not even bother to call her back? When he is forced to call her back, he does so reluctantly." The wife's name is eventually smeared and she is disgraced.

An example of this was the marriage of your cousin. You know how much she suffered when her husband separated from her without divorcing her and without giving her any maintenance. Even she admits that she failed to appreciate the love he showered on her when they married. Instead, she never did what he instructed her. Matters were not too serious at the beginning because he exercised a great deal of patience then. However, when she refused to mend her ways, the couple were forced to separate. She always opposed his views and contested everything he said. The couple did not understand each other's disposition and did not even make an effort to do so. Eventually, they contested everything and she was soon off to her parent's home. Although his brother is presently supporting her and her children, signs of friction are already starting to surface between her and her brother's wife. After all, a woman who has no concern for what her husband says cannot be expected to have concern for what her sister-in-law says.

Every man gets married for happiness and comfort. No sensible person marries a woman merely to plague her life with difficulties. Even a person with a little sense will not want to make life miserable for himself and his wife by arguing with her for every trivial matter. He will not want the life of his children to be ruined by parents who are always at loggerheads.

Remember that a man is at liberty to marry another woman whenever he pleases. Even if he does not remarry, he is not forced to tolerate an impudent wife. It is the woman and the children who suffer the worst effects of a broken home.

You also have the example of your aunt's son. While he is a man brought up in a modern society, he married a girl who hailed from a simple, but noble background. While he adored modernism, she hated every bit of it. She refused to do anything different and would even get a headache when he asked her to cook something new. Although he did not insist that she becomes an icon of modern fashion, he wanted her to forsake the *Shari'ee* way of dressing. To his dismay, she refused to yield. Eventually, matters deteriorated and she started taking exception to everything he said. Life became intolerable for both and, as you know, the only way out was divorce.

He was wrong to expect her to forsake the *Shari'ee* injunction of *Hijaab* to parade the streets like the shameless *Kuffaar*. He also tried to force her to forsake her salaah. His attitude is not a modernist approach, but insanity. He failed to realise that he was inviting Allah's wrath to himself. He failed to realise that in the words of Rasulullah ﷺ, a wife who practises the injunctions of the *Shari'ah* is the greatest bounty a man could possess.

An intelligent wife will realise that no man will undertake the many responsibilities of marriage merely to cause problems for himself and his wife. She should therefore convince herself of his love for her and she should not be stubborn. Therefore if a woman does not want her marriage to break, she should not oppose him openly. She will never succeed in contesting an issue as soon as he proposes it, especially if he is in a bad mood. She should seek the perfect opportunity to discuss every matter with him in an amicable manner, stating her point of view without offending him.

When a couple differ about any matter, you should discuss your differences with love and concern for each other. You should both present your motivation and a final decision should be taken at the end to decide which course you will be following. Remember that you will both have to alter your opinions a little before a decision is reached. In this manner, each will be making some sacrifice for amicability to prevail. Although you will both suffer some difficulty in altering your opinions, remember that this is much better than being embroiled in a vicious circle of ego-trips and endless bickering.

If you ever feel that your husband is treading a path that may lead to harm for your family or relatives, you should explain the danger of the situation to him with love and sincerity. If you approach the matter with love and if you make sincere *Du'a* to Allah to make your husband understand, I am certain that Allah will reconcile his views with yours and conflict will be avoided. You should make *Du'a* to Allah for this after every *Farz Salaah* and at the time of *Tahajjud.* If he fails to understand your opinion at once, *Insha Allah* he will understand it at a later stage. When a woman adopts humility, wisdom and diplomacy, she will be able to avert disastrous consequences."

## THE IMPORTANCE OF KEEPING THE CHILDREN CLEAN AND TIDY

We often receive mail from men who complain that after their children were born, their wives have become extremely slovenly in their dressing and personal hygiene. In addition to this, they also neglect their children. As a result, staying in the house becomes unbearable for these men. Every woman should avoid such a situation because it should never occur that a father's heart is divorced from his children. By depriving her children of their father's love, a woman is harming only herself. She will be destroying the morale and courage of these innocent souls who will soon be tomorrow's leaders. She will be the cause of her children growing up with an inferiority complex which will certainly stunt their confidence and ultimately their progress. What chance will such children have of becoming valuable sons and daughters of Islãm like Hazrat Umar bin Abdul Azeez (A.R), Salaahud Deen Ayoobi (A.R) and Raabiya Basriyya (A.R)?

A mother should therefore never destroy their children in this manner. She should always keep them clean and neat so that any person in the house will readily pick them up and love them dearly. These people will also be pleased to make sincere *Du'a* for such children. One will then see that when the child's grandmother sees the child, she will be saying,

> (Translation: "O Allah! I beseech You to protect this child as well as her progeny from the accursed *Shaitaan*.")

Seeing such a child, she will also pray to Allah saying:

> (Translation: "O Allah! Make her pious and righteous.")

Picking up such a child, the grandfather will say:

> (Translation: "O Allah! Accept her (for all good) in a most beautiful manner and raise her in all safety and prosperity.")

Seeing the child smiling and laughing, he will also say:

> (Translation: "May Allah always keep you smiling.")

When taking such a child in his arms, words of *Du'a* will automatically emerge from the father's lips:

(Translation: "O Allah! Make her the coolness of my eyes.")

Even the mother will be inspired to pray for the child saying:

(Translation: "O Allah! Illuminate her heart and make her one who establishes *Salaah*.")

Instead of scolding the child when she cries, the mother will say:

(Translation: "May Allah save you from crying (out of grief and regret) and may He bless you with good fortune in both worlds.")

Hugging the child with love, the uncle will say:

(Translation: "O Allah! Make her one who will serve Your *Deen* and one who will always be calling people towards Your *Deen*.")

Kissing the child affectionately, the aunt will say:

(Translation: "O Allah! Grant her the understanding of Your *Deen*.")

When the child is ill in bed, the mother will say:

(Translation: "Do not worry (Allah shall soon cure you). This illness is a means of purification, *Insha Allah*.")

She will also add:

(Translation: "May Allah cure you from every illness that may affect you.")

It goes without saying that a child who receives so many *Du'as* from family and relatives is truly fortunate and will certainly be protected from *Shaitaan*, Jinn, black magic, etc. Allah will also make such a child a good Muslim and servant of the *Deen*.

**Note:** All the above *Du'as* apply to females. When they are made for males, the Arabic pronoun "*haa*" (ها) should be changed to "*hoo*" (هُ). Therefore, the phrase: should be read as:

Whereas the clean and tidy will receive all these and more *Du'as*, a dirty and unkempt child will only hear comments like, "What an unfortunate child you are to have such a neglectful and slipshod mother!" May Allah guide all mothers who have this terrible attitude. *Aameen*

Every mother should adhere to the following guidelines:

1. Bath the children at least twice daily during the summer months.
2. Change the children when their clothing becomes soiled.
3. Never allow the children to get used to being dirty or shabby.
4. Do not delay in washing the children's soiled linen. Never allow any soiled linen of garments to stay in the house because these things allow the *Shayaateen* an opportunity to occupy the house and cause dissent

and problems. One should therefore not suffice by merely allowing linen or garments to dry after a child has urinated on them. One must ensure that these are thoroughly washed. For further details on this subject, one should refer to books dealing with the Islãmic upbringing of children.

Every mother should devote all her attention to the upbringing of her children. If she has the means, she should hire a servant to attend to the domestic chores while she gives her undivided attention to the children. Mothers should also ensure that every child is not born too soon after another so that each child can be given due attention. Together with ensuring that there is no deficiency in the child's physical and educational instruction, care should be taken that the child's spiritual instruction also received special attention. By having several children in rapid succession, the mother becomes weak and the children are also born physically weak. In addition to this, the children are deprived of their mother's attention and their father's affection. Such children usually suffer from an inferiority complex and lack self-confidence and courage. As a result of receiving inadequate attention, they are prone to bad company.

It is advisable for a woman to conceive a child only after the previous child has been weaned off breast milk at the age prescribed by the Shari'ah. By this time, the mother would have regained her strength and the child will be healthy and confident enough to pass through the various stages of his life. By this time, the mother may start preparing for another child if she has no *Shari'ee* excuse preventing her from this. Experienced Muftis are of the opinion that the spacing of a few years between children is permissible on condition that the intention of the parents is not wrong. For example, family planning is not permissible when the parents are doing it out of fear for poverty. Of course, permanent methods of contraception are permissible only under special circumstances.

We shall now present some poems of Ibraheem bin Saalih concerning the upbringing of children. May Allah instil in the heart of every mother the importance of raising her children well so that they can serve the *Deen* brought by Rasulullah ﷺ. It will be beneficial for anyone who understands Arabic to memorise these poems.

> "Acquaint your children with good manners from young
> So that they may be a delight to your eyes when they grow up
> Educating them in childhood is like an inscription upon a rock."

The poet emphasises the fact that when children are taught good habits from a young age, these habits remain with them permanently.

Hereunder are a few verses from Sheikh Qattaan, taken from his book.

> "Delighted are the eyes of her husband when he sees his obedient wife

The modest little child is hail and healthy
She keeps the room clean so that he feels comfortable
He eats a delectable morsel prepared by a most precious woman
His simple home is better than hours in lofty palaces
Better than these places which sinning has exposed to a flaming punishment."

**Note:** Although keeping the children and the home clean is extremely important, a woman should not spend so much time cleaning that she has no time to prepare meals or to do anything else.

## USING PERFUME FOR THE HUSBAND

A woman should regularly apply a perfume that her husband likes because perfume makes her more attractive and enhances their love. It is effective in dispelling any animosity that may exist between the couple. Perfume creates a sense of vigour and it is also pleasing to the angels. Just as the eyes are messengers of the heart, which have direct access to the heart, the nose also shares the same privilege. Therefore, when a person sees or smells something pleasant, he takes an immediately liking to it. On the other hand, when he sees something unpleasant, like the sight of his shabby wife, he develops an immediate feeling of aversion. It is for this reason that wise women are always cautious that their husbands should never see them unkempt and that their husbands should never smell an unpleasant odour from them.

Perfume has such an attraction that Rasulullah ﷺ prohibited women from leaving the home after applying perfume. This is because the perfume will attract men. While men's perfume has a strong smell, women's perfume ought to have a light fragrance. Rasulullah ﷺ mentioned that the things of this world that he liked most were his wives, perfume and *Salaah*, which was the coolness of his eyes.

(*Haakim, Nasa'ee, Bayhaqi*)

Women should not apply perfume at all when leaving their homes for any purpose whatsoever because the fragrance of their perfume may attract non-*Mahram* men. She may apply perfume only at home for the pleasure of her husband. As mentioned earlier, the best perfume is water because regular washing, making *Wudhu*, bathing and paying attention to one's oral hygiene will ensure that no foul odours leave the body. Women should be especially particular about applying perfume during their periods of menstruation.

Hazrat A'isha رضي الله عنها narrates that a woman once asked Rasulullah ﷺ about the method of taking a *Farz Ghusl* (bath). After explaining the procedure to her, Rasulullah ﷺ added, "Then purify yourself with a swab of musk." When the woman asked how would she be purified with a swab of musk, Rasulullah ﷺ told her that she would be purified with swab of musk unable to understand the hint, she repeated her question. Rasulullah ﷺ said, "*Subhaan Allah*! Purify yourself with it." At this stage, Hazrat A'isha drew the woman aside and explained to her that she should use the swab of musk to apply some musk to her pubic area so that the smell of menstrual blood may be eliminated.

By applying perfume regularly, a woman can strengthen the love between her and her husband. May Allah make the use of perfume a common feature in every Muslim home and free every home from physical and spiritual filth. *Aameen*

It is also important for the wife to ensure that their bedroom always has a pleasant fragrance. A wife should also apply perfume on her husband because this was one of the *Sunnah* practices. By doing this, their love will grow and they will earn the rewards of practising the *Sunnah.* Hazrat A'isha says, "I applied the best perfume I could find to Rasulullah when he entered into the state of *Ihraam* (i.e. just before forming the *Niyyah* for *Ihraam*) and after emerging from the state of *Ihraam* (i.e. after he had completed all the rites of *Hajj* besides the *Tawaaf Ziyaarah*)." (*Muslim* Vol. 1 Pg. 378)

According to another narration, she said, "I personally applied perfume to Rasulullah when he entered into *Ihraam.*"

When Hazrat A'isha was experiencing her menstrual cycle and could not enter the *Masjid* when Rasulullah was in *I'tikaaf,* he would lean his head into her room (which was adjacent to the *Masjid*) so that she could wash and comb his hair.

These *Ahadith* teach us how a woman can express her affection for her husband. It is therefore wise for a woman to sometimes apply perfume to her husband's body and clothing, especially before the *Jumu'ah Salaah* or even before other *Farz Salaahs.* She will also be rewarded for practising a *Sunnah* if she combs him. At least once in her lifetime, she should practise the *Sunnah* of washing her husband's hair. By doing these things, *Insha Allah,* the couple will also share the strong bond of love that existed between Hazrat A'isha رضي الله عنها and Rasulullah ﷺ.

## HONEYMOONS

I appeal to all readers to imagine themselves as sisters-in-law (i.e. sisters of a married man) when reading this chapter instead of regarding themselves as wives. In this manner, they will employ the advices here to benefit their sisters-in-law (brothers' wives) instead of using it as an excuse to burden their husbands with the expense of an exotic holiday.

Here is no harm done if a newly married couple spend some time by themselves after their marriage, especially if they are to share a home with the husband's family afterwards. In fact, it is necessary for them to spend time together so that they may acquaint themselves with each other. By learning each other's disposition and preferences, they will develop trust and love for each other. In this way, they will be able to fulfil their purpose of being comforts and supports for each other. This time to develop their mutual love and concern is their vehicle for attaining the good of both worlds. As a result, they will be able to earn great rewards by carrying out good deeds and by refraining from evil.

By understanding each other, the couple will be saved from harbouring ill-feelings against each other and they will behave mercifully towards each other. By doing this, they will be earning Allah's pleasure because as they look at each other with love, Allah will look at them with love and mercy.

Allaama Ibn Qayyim (A.R) wrote, "When two hearts are united in their love for Allah and His Rasul ﷺ, they become the favourite target for Allah's enemy, who will everything to create discord between them. It is therefore extremely important to be on guard for *Shaitaan's* plotting to disunite married couples."

Newly married couples should therefore take some time to journey somewhere by themselves. If possible, they should spend the major portion of their honeymoon spreading the *Deen* of Allah so that the beginning of their new lives together can commence with a beginning that is in Allah's obedience coupled with the concern of Rasulullah ﷺ. They should share Rasulullah ﷺ's concern for every individual to be saved from *Jahannam* and become a worthy resident of *Jannah.* When a relationship germinates from the seed of this concern, its branches can only yield blossoms of the likes of Hazrat Hasan رضي الله عنه and Hazrat Husayn رضي الله عنه, with fruit the likes of Salaahu Deen Ayoobi (A.R), Hazrat Umar bin Abdul Azeez (A.R), his wife Hazrat Faatima bint Abdil

Malik (A.R) and Zubayda the wife of the Khalifa Haaroon Ar-Rasheed.

If the couple have the means to view some scenery, they should do so. However, my personal opinion is that minimum expenses be incurred during the honeymoon, as well as during the *Walima* and other marriage expenses so that the couple may rather spend the money on *Hajj, Umrah* or on things that they require. If the couple have the means, they may also use the time to perform *Umrah* so that they can make *Du'a* for themselves and their progeny in Makkah and Madinah. They may make the following *Du'a*:

> (Translation: "O Allah! Create between us the love that You created between Hazrat Muhammad ﷺ and Hazrat Khadija رضي الله عنها. O Allah! Create between us the love that You created between Hazrat Muhammad ﷺ and Hazrat A'isha رضي الله عنها.")

They should also make *Du'a* to Allah to bless them with pious children.

We will presently quote a letter that a Kuwaiti bride wrote to her mother after her honeymoon. May Allah bless every couple with the happiness that He blessed this couple with and may every couple heed the lessons taught in this letter. *Aameen*

My dearest Mother

*As Salaamu Alaykum wa Rahmatullaahi wa Barakaatuh*

After spending a wonderful honeymoon, I have returned to my little home that my husband had built. I wish that you were nearby so that I could tell you all the new experiences I have had with my husband.

My husband is a wonderful man who loves me as dearly as I love him. Of course, I am still unaware of many of his habits. I sometimes feel as if I have known him for years, while the feeling also returns often that he is a complete stranger. Although I had no contact with him at all in the little world where I was brought up, yet I wish to do my utmost to please him because this is what you have taught me. Because you had always emphasised these teachings, I am convinced that I am able to remember every piece of advice that you gave me. I am also practising everything you taught me. I remember especially well the advices you gave me with tears in your eyes and with a smile that betrayed shuddering lips. Today I recall every word that emerged from your lips. They are still ringing in my ears as I think of how you said them to me as I sat on your loving lap clinging by your heaving chest. With your words in my mind, today as a daughter-in-law, I see every situation you described then.

Dear mother! Today I have your sterling example to look up to. I have before me the exemplary manner in which you treated my beloved father and your children, myself included. I shall do as you did. You taught us the meaning of love through your life of sacrifice and planted the seed of love in our hearts with your own caring hand. You even taught us how to walk.

I received your sweet letter in yesterday's post. Mom, as I read your letter filled with love, every line was ringing with your wonderful voice, opening every sinew in my ears. I searched through every word but was unable to find your warm kiss that you have addicted me to.

I have just finished preparing a meal for my husband who must be on his way home by now. Dearest Mom! Rest assured, I am now very capable of perform preparing delicious meals. I am exceptionally pleased with myself because my husband thoroughly enjoys the food I cook and he never forgets to thank me for a wonderful meal afterwards.

I am performing my five *Farz Salaahs* regularly and do not delay in taking a *Ghusl* immediately after my monthly period. In addition to this, I observe my *Qadhaa* fasts as quickly as possible after Ramzaan. I am paying the full *Zakah* due on my jewellery and we daily read the books "*Riyaadus Saaliheen*" and "*Fadhaa'il A'maal*" at home. I am also doing my best to encourage my servant at home, my neighbours and my acquaintances to be particular about their *Salaah* and about observing the *Hijaab*.

I can now hear the keys in the door. It must be my husband. He would also like to read this letter. He ought to know what we are communicating about. He also wishes to share the moments when my soul is lost in thinking about you. He now wants the pen from me and wants me to leave space on the paper so that he could also write something.

I am blowing kisses to you, to father and to all my brothers. I leave you all in Allah's care.

*Was Salaamu Alaykum wa Rahmatullaahi*
*wa Barakaatuh*

Your daughter

XYZ

# YOUR HUSBAND IS EITHER YOUR JANNAH OR YOUR JAHANNAM

Hazrat Husayn bin Mohsin ﷺ narrates that his aunt once came to Rasulullah ﷺ to address some need. When her need was addressed, Rasulullah ﷺ asked her whether she was married. When she replied in the affirmative, Rasulullah ﷺ asked her about her relationship with her husband. She told Rasulullah ﷺ that she did everything her husband asked from her except those things that she was incapable of doing. Rasulullah ﷺ said to her, "Consider well your relationship with him because he is either your *Jannah* or your *Jahannam*."

(*Ahmad* Vol. 6 Pg. 419 & *Haakim* Vol. 2 Pg. 189)

When a woman fulfils the rights of her husband, she will become worthy of entering *Jannah*. On the other hand, when she neglects her duties towards him, her negligence could be a cause of her entering *Jahannam*. May Allah save all women from such misfortune. *Aameen*

What are the rights that a wife owes to her husband? We have prepared a list of these rights at the end of this book. Read these well and ensure that you are not found lacking in any of them. If you have neglected any of them, ask your husband for forgiveness and make up for the hurt you have caused to him. Seek forgiveness from Allah as well.

One of the greatest rights that a wife owes to her husband has been outlined in the following *Hadith*. Rasulullah ﷺ said, "Take heed! You have rights over your wives and they have rights over you. Among the rights your wives owe to you is that they never allow on your bed anyone whom you dislike and that they never allow into your homes anyone whom you dislike." (*Tirmidhi* Pg. 220)

It is not permissible for any Muslim woman to talk with any non-*Mahram* man without concealing herself. They should never speak openly to even the sons of their neighbours when these sons come of age. When a woman's husband is not at home, she should never allow any non-*Mahram* into her house irrespective of who he is. A woman should avoid the company of non-*Mahram* men just as desperately as she would avoid snakes and other dangerous creatures. There have been many chaste women who have been divorced because they had neglected these important injunctions of the *Shari'ah*.

If a husband comes home to find his wife with a non-*Mahram* man, he will be plagued with suspicion throughout his life even though she was completely innocent. A woman who practises the teachings of Rasulullah ﷺ will have honour in this world as well as in the Hereafter.

## A COMPARISON BETWEEN TWO WOMEN

During my years as a *Mufti*, I have dealt with thousands of marital problems. To solve the crisis in their marriages, people have asked questions and many have requested for *Ta'weezaat* (amulets). We shall present the causes of these problems as examples of two women, so that every woman can do her best to emulate the example of the first woman and avoid being like the second woman. If every woman adopts the practices of the first woman, she will save her marriage from problems in the future. May Allah guide all Muslims wives to do what is right. Aameen.

**The First Woman:** She wakes up early to perform her *Fajr Salaah.* If her husband has fallen asleep after *Tahajjud,* she gently wakes him up. After briefly reciting Qur'ãn and making *Zikr,* she starts preparing breakfast for her husband and children.

**The Second Woman:** After a great effort, her husband manages to wake her up and she performs her Fajr *Salaah* with great difficulty just as the sun is about to rise. She then goes straight back to bed.

**The First Woman:** She wakes up her little children, ensuring that they recite all the morning *Du'as.* She uses a Miswaak or something else to brush the children's teeth and then feeds the family with love and affection. With every morsel of food she feeds the children, she gives them valuable advices such as observing the etiquette of attending school and *Madrasah,* obeying the instructions of their teachers, not being mischievous, etc. She then dresses according to the *Sunnah,* reciting the relevant *Du'as* and putting on each garment from the right. She then sends them off to school and greets her husband with a beaming face.

**The Second Woman:** She wakes up late and rushes because it is almost time for the children to start school. From the kitchen, she shouts at the eldest child to wake up. When the child does not wake up after many shouts, she hits the child shouting, "It's almost seven and you're still not up!" Then turning to the smaller child, she screams, "Get up! Your transport will arrive at any moment!" Distressed by her temperament, the entire family starts conversing with the heavens. However, her bellowing voice and their fear for her does not allow them to procrastinate. With broken hearts, the stumble out of bed, getting no inspiration from their father's gloomy face. They eventually find their way out of the house without even eating properly. Leaving the door, the youngest child shouts, "Mom, I've forgotten my lunchbox." The reply comes, "You idiot! That is why I tell you to wake up early!" She then rushes out of the door to give him his lunchbox without bothering about her unkempt appearance. Seeing her shove the lunchbox in her child's hand and looking most bedraggled, the neighbour takes pity on the husband and children. He thinks to himself, "How did this poor man get saddled with such a shrew?"

**The First Woman**: After seeing everyone off, she makes *Wuzu* and perform four *Rakaahs* of *Ishraaq Salaah*. Thereafter, she recites Qur'ãn and *Wazeefah* books like "*Munaajaat Maqbool*", "*Hizbul A'zam*" or "*Dharee'atul Wusool*". She makes sincere *Du'a* to Allah and then engages in *Zikr*. Hearing her littlest daughter cry, she hurries to see what has happened. She sees that the child has fallen. Taking the baby in her arms, she says:

(Translation: "May Allah Illuminate your face, O Faatima.")

She then sees to the child. When the domestic servant arrives, she gives her the dishes and clothing to wash. She then cleans their bedroom herself. Noticing that her husband has forgotten to take his wallet with him, she immediately phones him to tell him that she has it with her and has put it away safely. She then perform her *Chaast Salaah* (*Salaatut Duha*) and busies herself with the cooking.

It is not long before the children start arriving from classes. She therefore prepares a light but wholesome meal for them. She thinks to herself that when they arrive, she will warmly greet them with *Salaam* and serve the food to them with water to quench their thirst.

**The Second Woman**: After everyone has left the house, she sits down to drink her tea without bothering to clear the kitchen. Hearing the baby cry, she shouts from the kitchen, "Now what? Am I supposed to die for you lot? You children extract every drop of blood from me. And I have no rest at all?" She then gulps down her tea and proceeds to the child's room. She scolds the child for waking up so early and playfully slaps the child's bottom. However, the child howls even more. She changes and washes the child, but the crying does not cease. She then grabs the bottle that was used the previous night and fills it with milk without washing it. The child drinks the milk happily and stops crying. Although the child is satisfied, only Allah knows what germs and bacteria may have entered his stomach with the milk.

She then hurries to clear the kitchen. When she takes the tablecloth[1] out to dry, she meets her neighbour who is also outside. "I heard the baby crying a lot today," the neighbour asks. "I cannot understand these children," she replies, "The one has to be at school early and this one wakes up so early in the morning. Then instead of helping me by calming the child or preparing the breakfast, my husband demands that everything should be done quickly." In this manner, she spends half-an-hour chatting to her neighbour.

She then starts cleaning the bedroom and cooking. By then the servant arrives, late as usual. She spends ten minutes scolding the servant for arriving late; "Is this the time to come? It is almost time for the children to return from school! Hurry with your work!" She then hurries to prepare food, not caring whether it is cooked well or not. She then dumps the food in a lunchbox and leaves the kitchen. When the children arrive home and ask the servant where their mother is, they receive the reply, "She is in the room," or "She is at the neighbour's place."

---

1. The word tablecloth is used here and in other places instead of the word table. This is to emphasise the *Sunnah* method of eating on a tablecloth spread on the floor. As proven by many *Ahadith,* Rasulullah ﷺ never ate from a table as in common today. Every Muslim home should therefore acquaint themselves with sitting on the floor when eating.

**The First Woman:** She greets the children with *Salaam* as they arrive and kisses each one of them. At the same time, she reminds them to recite the *Du'a* for entering the home, viz.

Giving the child a biscuit to eat, she tells him to bath, to change out of his school uniform and to get ready for *Madrasah.* When the child tells her that he received a star in school for his work, she expresses her pleasure and reminds him that he should thank Allah for granting him the ability to complete his homework the previous night and for making him get a star as a reward for his efforts.

When her husband arrives from work for *Zuhr Salaah,* she greets him with a wide smile as he enters the door and cheerfully says, "*As Salaamu Alaykum wa Rahmatullaahi wa Barakaatuh.*" The tablecloth was already laid for his meal, but he has to perform his *Salaah* first. She has his sandals ready for him to make *Wudhu* and a fresh towel as well. After returning from the *Masjid,* he eats a hearty meal and rests for a while before returning to work.

**The Second Woman:** After hastily dressing the children for *Madrasah,* the scene at her house is as follows: "I do not want to go to *Madrasah* because the *Ustaad* hits me too much!" cries the young son. "He hits you only because you never learn your work," comments the elder sister. "Not true!" the little rascal retorts, "He hits me for nothing!" "I shall tell your father about this and he will give you a hiding," the mother threatens. "You may tell him. I am not afraid of him."

Eventually, after a great deal of scolding and shouting, one child attends *Madrasah* while the other does not.

**The First Woman**: After neatening the bedroom and spraying some fragrance, she closes the door. Because the family will be visiting the father's parents that evening, she busies herself with ironing the children's clothing for the evening. When the children arrive from *Madrasah*, she washes them, gives them some juice and biscuits to eat and prepares to perform her Asr *Salaah*. Giving the baby some toys to amuse herself, she tells her eldest daughter to look after the baby while she performs her *Salaah*. The daughter happily agrees and asks, "Are we visiting grandmother and grandfather today?" "Yes my dear," she replies, "Insha Allah we will all be visiting them this evening."

**The Second Woman**: The eldest daughter returns from *Madrasah*. Because she neither took a bath in the morning nor in the evening, her body is dirty and her hair dishevelled. As soon as she returns, she starts playing. As the mother is busy speaking to her neighbour, the son starts crying for money to buy something. Swinging around, she slaps the child and says, "Can't you see that I'm speaking?"

Eventually, she manages to hastily perform her Asr *Salaah*, make tea and give milk to the baby. She hardly completes preparing the children's clothes for the next day, when it is time for *Maghrib*. Her husband is returning home and dreading making an appearance because he expects to meet a wife who is screaming at the kids. He therefore returns home only after performing his *Maghrib Salaah* in the *Masjid.*

When he returns home and enters his room, he smells something awful. The child was drinking milk and spilled it all over the bed. Here are also biscuit crumbs all over the room and toys scattered about. The kitchen is its usual mess and as soon as his wife arrives, she starts her usual verbal assaults; "Just look at our opposite neighbour's husband! He takes the family out every day. They are visiting the children's grandparents today. When will you ever take us out?"

Exhausted, the husband falls on the bed asking, "When will supper be ready?" "You will get your supper just now," she replies and heads for the kitchen. Twenty-five minutes pass without a call to the table and he again calls out, "When do we suppper?" The husband is now irritates and, seeing the children fighting, he seizes the opportunity to vent his anger. Hitting both of them, he shouts, "Can't you see that I'm tired? Can't I have even a few moments of rest?" When the family is eventually called to eat, they have to consume a meal that was too hastily prepared to be tasty. Forcing the food down his throat, the husband laments his ill-fortune.

The First Woman: After performing her *Maghrib* and *Awwaabeen Salaah,* she tells her eldest daughter to show her what homework she has for the night. She then supervises what her daughter is doing and assists her where necessary. She then proceeds to make the rotis before her husband arrives home. When she is about to begin with the rotis, she hears the doorbell ring. As the children run to the door, she fills a jug of water to place on the tablecloth. As the husband walks through the door, one child holds his hand while the other takes the basket of fruit from his hand and gives it to their mother. Seeing his beautiful and clean children, the husband is forced to kiss them both.

Taking her father to her room, the elder daughter shows him what lessons she has learnt for the day. As he is sitting to revise some work with her, they hear the mother's sweet voice calling them to eat. Engrossed with the children, he fails to sit down immediately for the meal. When she comes to room saying, "Come on now, the rotis are getting cold," he apologises for not coming immediately and they all sit down to eat. After reciting the *Du'as* for eating, the family start enjoying a delectable meal, observing all the etiquette of eating. "We are going to my mother's today, have you made anything?" he asks. "Yes," she replies, "I have made the custard you brought because she enjoys it. I have also cooked some knuckles which your father loves." "Excellent," he smiles, "we shall leave after *Salaah Insha Allah*." Although he is bust eating, he thanks Allah for the excellent wife and children that Allah has granted him. Sincere *Du'as* in her favour pour forth from his heart with every morsel he eats.

Every reader is a liberty to decide which of the two women is the better one. Of course, the decision is not a difficult one. May Allah grant every woman the guidance to emulate the example of the first woman. Aameen.

(Adapted from "*Silsilatul Mar'atil Muslimatis Sa'eeda*" Vol. 1 Pg. 45)

A man who is hard at work all day and who has to bear the strain of travelling home afterwards needs a wife who has completed all her daily chores and is waiting for him at home. He needs her to be looking good for him, with fragrance decorating the air about her. His fatigue and the frustration he suffered with his employers, customers or clients will all vanish when he sees her cheerful smile and warm welcome. However, his fatigue and frustration will only be increased when he returns to a wife who is angry with the children and who fills his ears with stories of the arguments she had with neighbours and tales about her sisters-in-law.

## HOW CAN ONE TIRED PERSON COMFORT ANOTHER TIRED PERSON?

If both the husband and the wife are tired and frustrated, neither can offer any comfort to the other. Neither will be able to smile with the other to ease the fatigue. If the parents cannot laugh and brighten life for the children, their lives will be merely an unfortunate existence. This scenario is common in the lives of couples who are both employed. Such people become like machines, whose lives are reduced to programmed drudgery. How can contentment and happiness ever find their way into the lives of these people? Their lives revolve around their work and their homes lack contentment and peace. Such an automated existence defies nature, defies logic, defies *Deen* and defies civility.

Allah has created couples so that they provide love, comfort and compassion for each other, thus leading to the survival of humanity on earth in a manner that is promising for all concerned. When a woman provides for her husband the necessary love and compassion, she will not only be a his toy in bed, but his valued advisor and trusted confidante as well. By assisting each other through life, the couple will be able to easily fulfil their worldly duties as well as the responsibilities they owe to the *Deen.*

An Urdu book dealing with the status of family life in Islām[1] mentions that when love exists between a couple, they will be able to taste the flavour of *Ibaadah* and find pleasure in obeying Allah and remembering Him. They will be sources of comfort for each other when they have concern for each other. Therefore, a good wife should ensure that she keeps herself neat and clean before her husband arrives from work so that she may alleviate his fatigue and so that he may feel comfortable and relaxed. The secret formula for making children good and obedient is for the mother to have a light meal ready for the children when hey return from school. The mother who starts scolding and shouting at the children as soon as they return home is indeed extremely foolish. She should never welcome them with remarks like, "Why is your clothing so dirty?" or "Why do you throw your books around?", etc.

The mother should not think that the child has been away from home for six hours, but she should think that the child has been deprived of motherly compassion for six hours. She should think that for the past six hours, they have been deprived of feeling their mother's delicate touch on their cheeks and from having their mother's warm gaze

1. The title of the book is "*Islām Main Khandaan ka Muqaam*"

on their faces. She should therefore shower her love on them because their fatigue and hunger cannot bear the burden of a scolding. After feeding them their meal, she may advise them against certain untoward behaviour and encourage them to do good. The advice taught in childhood remains with a child throughout his/her life.

## THE PERFECT WIFE

Arabic is such a beautiful language that no other language can match it. Its beauty is magnified when expressed in the words of an eloquent Arab Badwee. We shall now present the reply of one such Bedouin who was asked to describe the perfect wife. With wisdom and in an advising manner, he points out that the most important trait of a perfect wife is humility. If you understand Arabic, you should analyse his words and derive direct benefit from them. You should also not deprive your children and younger sisters and brothers from the opportunity to learn Arabic.

The Badwee says:

> Translation: "The best of women is she who appears to be the tallest when she stands, the most outstanding when seated and is certainly the most truthful when she speaks.
>
> When she becomes angry, she subdues her anger, she smiles instead of laughing and whenever she does something, she does it well.
>
> She obeys her husband and prefers to remain indoors. She is honourable in the eyes of her

people while remaining unassuming without any pride.

She loves her husband dearly, expresses her love and is very fertile. In fact, everything about her is praiseworthy."

In his book "*Al-Mar'atul Mithaliyya*", Sheikh Usman narrates from Abu Ma'shar that a person once took an oath that he will not marry until he had conferred with a hundred people. After conferring with ninety-nine people, he decided that the hundredth person will be the first person he sees coming up the road. It so happened that the first person he saw was someone who appeared to be a madman. After greeting the person, he said to him, "I have experienced many problems with women and have taken an oath not to marry until I have conferred with a hundred people. You are the hundredth person. What do you advise me to do?"

The man replied, "Women are of three types. The one is exclusively yours, the other has been appointed over you and the third is neither yours nor appointed over you. You should marry the one who is exclusively yours. She is the one who is young and friendly, whom no man has ever touched. If she sees any good in you, she is grateful and praises you. On the other hand, if she sees anything bad in you, she merely says, 'All men are like that.'"

Such a woman never complains about her husband and never laments her fortune by comparing her husband's faults to the strengths of other men. She should think that everything is from Allah and if her *Shari'ah* has any shortcomings, other men also have shortcomings of their own. We will not describe the other two types of women because their description is of no use to you. All we wish to do is to present to you this wonderful trait; whenever you experience anything good, praise and thank Allah and your husband and whenever you experience anything bad, console yourself by thinking that every home has its problems.

## TRUE LOVE BETWEEN HUSBAND AND WIFE

A woman can have her husband eating out of her hand by expressing her love for him and obeying him. By being his servant, he will become her servant, will love her tremendously and make her his confidante. To attain this status, a bride will have to make some sacrifices during the early part of her marriage. You are already familiar with an example of such sacrifice which was displayed by the daughter of Rasulullah ﷺ Hazrat Zainab رضي الله عنها. Her mother taught her how to serve her husband diligently, thereby making him loyal to her.

When the Quraish told him that if he divorced her, they would allow him to marry any woman of the Quraish he desired, he said to them, "By Allah! I shall never leave my wife. I would not like any other woman of the Quraish in exchange of my wife." Although he was not yet a Muslim then, his love for Hazrat Zainab رضي الله عنها had sunk so deep in his heart that he could not leave her despite having the choice to marry any other woman. There is a lesson in his words for every Muslim woman. The lesson is that even though a man was not a Muslim, he appreciated the loyalty and service that his wife showed. He realised that although he had the choice of marrying any beautiful woman, he would never find someone as loyal and diligent as she.

An Arab Badwee from the Bani Udhra tribe once married a beautiful woman. When he suffered poverty, the woman's father forcibly kept her in his home, refusing her permission to return to her husband. When the husband approached the governor Marwaan about the matter, Marwaan summoned the woman and her father. When Marwaan saw the woman, he fell in love with her and forced the husband to divorce her. After her *Iddah*, Marwaan bribed her father and he married the woman.

However, the Badwee was still very much in love with his wife and he travelled to Syria to plead his case before the *Ameer.* The *Qaadhi* (judge) summoned the woman and sternly reprimanded Marwaan after the facts were made clear to him, Marwaan begged for pardon and pleaded that when he saw her, he fell helplessly in love with her and could not help himself.

When the Ameer summoned the husband and wife to appear before him, he also fell in love with her and wanted to marry her. He therefore asked the husband, "What do you say if I marry her?" The Badwee refused to permit the marriage and recited the following couplets:

"By Allah! By Allah! I cannot forget my love for
her until I disappear
in my grave and decompose
How will I ever console myself after leaving her
when every my love
for her has permeated my every sinew?
If I ever have to leave her, I shall never be able
to repay the good she
has done for me."

The *Ameer* then asked the wife what she thought about the proposal. He asked her, "Which of us do you love most? Do you love the *Ameer* so that you may live with respect, with honour, with jewels and in palaces? Or do you love Marwaan who acquired your hand oppressively? Or do you prefer your Badwee husband with his poverty and little shack?"

The lady replied in eloquent Arabic verse. If only every reader could understand Arabic! Although her words are being translated, no language can justly express the depth and effect of Arabic. Every Muslim should have the enthusiasm to learn Arabic. If you cannot learn Arabic, you should at least encourage your children or little brothers and sisters to do so. Her reply was as follows:

Translation: "Despite his poverty and his little shack, he have given me so much love and affection, that he is more noble to me than all my family and relatives. As for the ruler (the *Ameer*) and his governor Marwaan, they merely have silver coins and gold coins i.e. all they can give me are gold and silver coins without true love and affection."

May Allah bless every Muslim couple with the love and loyalty he blessed this couple. May he bless them all with selfless devotion for each other and with the fervour to assist each other in carrying out good deeds such as performing *Tahajjud Salaah* and making an effort for the *Deen* to spread throughout the world. Aameen.

## WHO IS A BEAUTIFUL WOMAN?

In the words of an Arab poet, a beautiful woman is not one with whom a man falls in love at first sight, only to find out later that her character is not as beautiful. However, a truly beautiful woman is one whose beauty increases each time a man looks at her and each time he observes her various attributes. Such a woman will be found smiling whether she is experiencing good conditions or whether circumstances are trying for her. She is a comfort for her husband during prosperity and during poverty. Her husband is unable to detect any difference in her attitude when the children are crying, when he is away on a journey or when she is ill. Regardless of the circumstances the couple face, she is always pleased with Allah's decision for them. During prosperity, she is always grateful and during difficult times, she exercises patience.

When a young woman asked beautiful old lady what she used to preserve her radiant beauty, she replied, "For my lips I use the lipstick of truth, for my voice I use the Zikr of Allah, for my eyes I use the kohl of lowering my gazes (thereby refraining from looking at things that are forbidden), for my body I use the training programme of doing good deeds, for my posture I use dedication, for my heart I use the love of Allah, for my intelligence I use wisdom and foresight, for my soul I use obedience and to control my desires I use the conviction that Allah is watching."

Read the above statement once again and make *Du'a* to Allah that He should bless you and every Muslim with the same excellent qualities.

Remember that the true beauty of a woman lies in her obedience to her husband. In gratitude for the effort that he makes to support her, she should at least serve him diligently and fulfil the many rights she owes to him. Advising women about the rights of their husbands, Hazrat A'isha ﵂ once said, "O gathering of ladies! If you knew the rights that you owe to your husbands, you would use your cheeks to wipe the sand off their feet."

(*Ibn Hibbaan & Bazzaar*)

The beauty of obedience attracts love. When a home is filled with love and affection, a woman will enjoy true happiness because it is impossible for her not to enjoy the fruits of the devotion and dedication she showers on her family. Women are the fountains of love and compassion and their mere presence exudes radiance and affection, bringing warmth, blessings and prosperity to the entire family. A husband will be overjoyed when he merely looks at his obedient wife and his love for her will increase all the time. It is the duty of every woman to create an atmosphere of love in her home so that her husband may never have to use the option of divorce which lies exclusively in his hands.

The foundation of every happy family has always been built on mutual love, compassion and loyalty. With such a foundation, every member of the family can carry out his/her functions effectively without anyone getting frustrated and bored and without feeling uneasy.

The more obedient a wife is, the more beautiful she will appear to her husband. Despite her abilities to manipulate situations and her powers to attract men, a woman still remains weaker than a man. She will therefore have to submit to her husband's superiority at some stage and desist from opposing him. A husband cannot value his wife's beauty and attractiveness when she is disobedient. It is therefore wise for every wife to remain obedient to her husband and walk the path of their life with him instead of against him.

Rasulullah ﷺ has sternly warned women against disobeying their husband when he said that the *Salaah* of two types of persons will not even pass their heads. The first person is the slave who runs away from his master. His *Salaah* will not accepted until he returns to his master. The second is a wife who disobeys her husband. Her *Ibaadah* will also not be accepted until she starts obeying her husband. (*Tabraani* & *Haakim*)

## OPENING THE LOCKS TO YOUR HUSBAND'S HEART

Irrespective of how indifferent a man may be towards his wife, every woman has been blessed with faculties that will force him to turn all his attention towards her. She has been blessed with natural looks, a melodious voice, a charming smile, graceful manners, a sweet tongue, delicate lips, smouldering eyes and a soft touch. Using these qualities, she will easily be able to conquer her husband's heart. These traits are such that they are more effective than any magic potion available. It is therefore surprising when any woman asks for a *Ta'weez* (amulet) to build her husband's love for her.

A man may still be excused for asking for a *Ta'weez* so that his wife's love for him may increase. He may even be advised to try some formulas. However, in her natural physique, her appearance, her voice and, above all, in her obedience to her husband, a woman has the most effective love potion. With these things, she will be able to conquer her husband's heart very easily.

It is commonly said that if a woman is standing on top of a 130 storey building, a man passing beneath will naturally look up to see her. The attraction that a woman has on a man is stronger than the attraction a magnet has on a piece of iron. In fact, psychologists state that if a man's bone and a woman's bone were thrown on an open field, there will be a force of attraction between them.

("*Tuhfatul Uroos*")

It is for this reason that jurists state that it is not permissible for even an extremely old woman to travel without a *Mahram*. Regardless of her old age, there is bound to be an old man who will be interested in her. A woman's body and her movements find their way into a man's heart very quickly and she can easily make him fall for her.

Not even a picturesque island or a breath taking scenery will capture a man's heart as effectively his good and obedient wife when she smiles at him and speaks to him sweetly. When she does this, he will readily respond to anything she says. A woman therefore has no need to resort to radical means of winning over her husband unless she happens to be married to a man whose heart is locked away from charm or if she needs something extra. For such drastic situations, we shall present five keys to the locks of a man's heart. By using these keys, a wife will be able create an atmosphere of true love in her home, thereby her happiness in both worlds. The five keys are:

## (1) Sight

Among the most important factors that conquer a man's mind and heart are the things that he sees. One something appeals to the eyes, the heart readily takes a liking to it. On the contrary, once the eyes dislike what they see, the heart confirms the dislike. Therefore, when a woman's appearance appeals to her husband, his love for her settles deep within his heart. She should therefore ensure that he never sees her in a condition that may repulse him.

Together with her personal hygiene and beauty a woman should also ensure that she maintains a high degree of cleanliness when tending to her children and home. In this manner, her husband's opinion of her will not be tainted.

A survey conducted by psychological researchers has revealed that in the opinion of most men, a clean and tidy bedroom with flowers, with pictures of scenery and with clean linen all tastefully arranged is extremely effective in creating a restful and peaceful environment. These factors create such an idyllic atmosphere even though the bedroom is small. Irrespective of how insignificant something may seem, its importance is increased significantly when cleanliness and tidiness are added.

## (2) Hearing

A woman's sweet voice is sufficient to melt a man's heart. When a woman uses her naturally endowed voice to tug at the chords of her husband's heart, she will never complain about her husband beating her, about him neglected her, about him not listening to her, etc. By addressing him sweetly, he will be ready to fulfil her every desire. Her voice will be a source of comfort and jubilation for him, even reviving his dead spirits.

A woman should therefore develop her understanding to be able to realise what to say on which occasion. She should know when to be silent and when to speak softly. She should also remember that whatever enters the heart through the doors of the ears very seldom leave the heart. May Allah bless the poet who said:

Translation: "The injuries of swords and spears can heal but the injuries caused by the tongue cannot."

It is therefore imperative for a couple not to hurt each other by the things they say. A husband should never hear statements like, "You never take us anywhere!" or "Look at our house! We have nothing here. You should see the curtains and furniture in the neighbour's home!" or "You spend so much on others (your parents) while your own wife and children are living in poverty!" By making statements like this, the wife will drive her husband further away from her instead of drawing him closer. After statements like this, she will not even have the curtains and furniture she desires because he will have no love for her. However, once she wins his love, she will have whatever she desires and he will be happy to give it to her. He will then ask her what she desires so that he could fulfil her wishes.

### (3) Smell

Many people do not realise the powerful effect that smell has on a person. Philosophers have always maintained that the effect that the sense of smell has on personal relationships is profound indeed. They say that a woman's sweat glands produce an extremely subtle fragrance which can drive a man emotional. The more fragrant a woman is, the stronger attraction she has on men. Of course, Allah only knows the truth of this theory.

Because the sense of smell strongly influences a person, every woman should ensure that she always applies perfumes that her husband likes. However, she should take care not to apply perfumes that have a strong smell. Because women have a keener sense of smell and know which perfume should be used for which occasion, a wife should apply her husband's perfume to his body. As was previously mentioned, Hazrat A'isha ﵂ applied perfume to Rasulullah ﷺ's body.

Many people think that staying away from women is an act of *Ibaadah* and sacrifice. This notion is erroneous because while performing *I'tikaaf* in the *Masjid*, Rasulullah ﷺ used to allow Hazrat A'isha ﵂ to wash and comb his hair. This *Hadith* has been quoted earlier. Since Rasulullah ﷺ is the best example for mankind, his exemplary behaviour teaches us that staying away from one's wife is not an act of piety. If it were, Rasulullah ﷺ would have been the first to do it. May Allah grant every Muslim the guidance to practise every *Sunnah* of Rasulullah ﷺ. *Aameen*

Every wife should ensure that her husband never smells an unpleasant odour on her. She should therefore keep her body and mouth clean and smelling good at all times. She should see to it that toilet is never dirty and foul-smelling. For this, the use of an air-freshener is extremely useful. In short, she should make sure that her husband does not smell anything unpleasant at home. In this way, their love will grow and *Shaitaan* will have much less opportunity to create animosity between the couple.

In this regard, every wife should remember the words of Umamah bint Haarith, who said to her daughter, "whenever he (your husband) smells you, he should never smell anything besides a pleasant fragrance. Kohl is the best, easiest and least expensive form of beautification while water is the best fragrance because taking a bath regularly and making *Wudhu* often ensures that the body remains clean and does not exude an unpleasant odour."

## The Importance of Oral Hygiene

Islãm has placed great emphasis on hygiene. A Muslim should always bear in mind that the cleaner and purer she is, the closer she will be to Allah. The angels will then also remain in her constant attendance. On the other hand, when she is dirty and unclean, *Shaitaan* and his companions keep in her company.

If a woman performs *Salaah* while her mouth is dirty and foul-smelling, the angels are revolted and stay far away. It is appalling for a person's mouth to be foul-smelling when the same mouth is used for Allah's Zikr and for the recitation of the Qur'ãn. The true measure of a person's cleanliness is not her fragrance or make-up. A person will be said to be an icon of cleanliness when her mouth does not emit a foul smell, when her teeth are clean, when the unwanted hair on her body is removed, when her nose is clean, when her nails are short, when her hair is neatly combed and when her fingertips and soles of her feet are clean and sparkling. If a woman claims to be clean, it is by scrutinising these aspects that she can be given the title. In addition to these determining factors, it will also be seen whether her kitchen, her refrigerator and her bathroom is clean. When a woman is particular about maintaining the cleanliness of all the above, she can truly say that she has love for cleanliness. A woman would also be doing herself a favour by asking another woman to tell her of her shortcomings in this regard so that she may correct herself.

It will not be redundant to repeat that the woman who is particular about all the above can truly be called a clean woman. Perfume and make-up alone do not constitute cleanliness.

Islãm has emphasised the importance of oral hygiene. It is unfortunate that many women regularly eat sweets, chocolates or "*Paan*"[1] and then sleep without first brushing their teeth. Let alone neglecting their own teeth, they also allow their children to sleep without brushing. It is indeed tragic that we have lost the teachings of our *Deen*. In a *Hadith* of Bukhari, Hazrat Urwa رضي الله عنه states that he would hear his aunt Hazrat A'isha رضي الله عنها brushing her teeth with the *Miswaak* while he was in another room. A narration of Muslim also mentions that she could be heard using the *Miswaak*.

Hazrat A'isha رضي الله عنها narrates that whenever Rasulullah ﷺ woke up from his sleep during the day or during the night, he would brush his teeth with a Miswaak before making *Wudhu*. (*Ahmad & Abu Dawood*)

1. Betel leaves eaten with various types of flavouring, often with Tobacco.

Rasulullah ﷺ was extremely particular about oral hygiene. When someone asked Hazrat A'isha رضي الله عنها what was the first thing that Rasulullah ﷺ did whenever he entered the house, she replied that he first used the *Miswaak*.

(*Muslim*)

Every person should ponder whether she makes any effort to revive the *Sunnah* of Rasulullah ﷺ. Did you ever encourage your husband, brothers or sons to use the Miswaak as soon as they enter the home? By encouraging others, you will be receiving their rewards as well as the reward of enjoining a righteous act. You should also ensure that you are as particular about brushing your teeth as Hazrat A'isha رضي الله عنها was. The following points should always be kept in mind:

1) According to your preference, get yourself a thin or a thick Miswaak. Keep your Miswaak clean and trim the bristles often. If possible, change your Miswaak regularly, just as you would change your toothbrush when necessary.
2) Brush your teeth thoroughly after every meal, especially after eating foods that leave an odour. In fact, after eating or cutting such foods, you should wash your hands thoroughly as well.
3) Use dental floss in front of a mirror so that all traces of food remaining between the teeth are effectively removed. It is such pieces of food that often cause diseases and bad breath.
4) Try to brush your teeth while looking at a mirror.

5) Abstain from eating "paan" and prevent your children as well because it is harmful and has very few benefits.

6) Ensure that you brush and floss before going to bed because germs breed easily on the food particles in a sleeping person's mouth, giving rise to plaque, tartar and various oral diseases. This is especially important after eating sweet things. Remember: "sweets eat teeth".

7) At least once a year you should visit a female dentist or a doctor who could examine the condition of your teeth. The healthier your teeth, the healthier will the rest of your body should be. When one's teeth are healthy, one will be able to chew one's food well, thereby facilitating easier digestion and a healthier stomach. A healthy stomach is the foundation of better overall health.

The importance of oral hygiene cannot be overemphasised especially because it goes a long way in strengthening the love between husband and wife. Its importance can be gauged from the following two directives that Rasulullah ﷺ gave Hazrat Ummu Saleem رضي الله عنها when he sent her to assess another woman for marriage. He told her to smell the woman's mouth to gauge whether she is particular about oral hygiene and to observe the area around her Achilles tendon to see whether it is clean or not.

(*Ahmad* Vol. 3 Pg. 231, *Haakim* Vol. 2 Pg. 122 & *Bayhaqi* Vol. 7 Pg. 87)

This *Hadith* makes it clear that Rasulullah ﷺ attached great importance to oral hygiene and would first have this assessed before taking a woman into his marriage. Cleanliness of the mouth is necessary because even a woman is beautiful, all her beauty will fade when she opens her to reveal an incomplete set of decayed teeth. When her mouth is foul-smelling because of neglecting her teeth, no one will want to be near her.

In fact, Islãm so much discourages women from appearing unkempt and unattractive before their husbands that Rasulullah ﷺ told the *Sahabah* ﷺ never to return home from a journey at night without first informing their wives of their return. He emphasised that if they should return suddenly, they should first inform their wives of their return "so that a woman with dishevelled hair may comb her hair and remove unwanted hair." (*Bukhari*)

Islãm disapproves of a wife allowing her husband to see her in a condition that will make him dislike her because their love for each other is the foundation of their relationship. It is after all the strength of this relationship that will assist them to attain success in both worlds. The relationship of a couple can be likened to a little kingdom with the husband as king and the wife as queen. The stronger their love and compassion for each other, the more good and blessings spread in their kingdom. It is therefore necessary for a wife to ensure that she does nothing to taint her husband's love for her. This is the reason why the *Shari'ah* instructs men to give their wives time to prepare themselves before returning home from a journey.

This principle also teaches us that if a wife expects her husband home by a certain time and he happens to return sooner than expected (even if it be from his workplace), he should try to inform her beforehand.

## (4) Touch

After marriage, every couple realises that the greatest factor which joins their hearts is when their bodies touch. The heat of each other's body is sufficient to quell their fears, comfort their hearts and cure their illnesses. A wife should therefore assist her husband in taking pleasure from touching her. Instead of drawing back when he touches her, she should advance towards him and encourage him to touch her. Doing so, she should make the intention that he will be reminded of the pleasures of the Hereafter when he experiences this pleasure. In this way, he will be encouraged to prepare for the Hereafter. He may then also realise that just as the pleasures of this world are temporary, the nature of his life is the same. He will realise that he will soon be leaving for the Hereafter where the bounties are eternal. To attain those bounties, it is necessary to repent and to make a concerted effort.

## (5) Taste

The first medium with which a person tastes is his mouth. Because the mouth is the most sensitive part of a person's head, its response is extremely quick. The first avenue to this mouth is a kiss. Without the need for proof and substantiation, a kiss effectively expresses the love that a couple share. Although a kiss is without words, it speaks volumes about the depth of a couple's love. It reveals the innermost contents of the heart in the sincerest and most convincing manner. There is scarcely anything more effective then a kiss to consolidate a couple's love.

A kiss is more effective than a thousand advocates in convincing a man that his wife loves him. When a wife kisses her husband affectionately, he truly believes that she is exclusively his.

There is no specific time for kissing, neither does it require a special occasion. When one's love is overwhelming, one is forced to express it with a kiss or a few kisses so that the flood of emotion subsides. It is extremely unfortunate that many women neglect this important factor and kiss their husbands only when they engage in sexual relations. The *Sahabiyaat* ﷺ used to kiss their husbands often. Among the many occasions when they kissed them was whenever they left home. To express their love and respect for their husbands on this occasion, they kissed them on the forehead.

One should also make a point of kissing one's husband when he leaves the home and whenever he returns. When one's husband kisses one on one cheek, one should offer the other cheek as well so that a second kiss would cement their love for each other. Unfortunate is the wife who deprives herself and her husband of this extremely sweet and enjoyable expression of love. An intelligent wife showers kisses on her husband because she knows that this is a most effective key to the locks of her husband's heart.

When a woman employs all these means of conquering her husband's heart, she will have no need to pay exorbitant fees for *Ta'weezes* and love potions. A study of cases where husbands have either divorced their wives, separated from them or married a second wife against their wishes will reveal that most of the women involved were negligent of using the above five keys to find their way into the hearts of their husbands. They lacked the ability to express their love for their husbands.

The less couples kiss, the less will their love for each other grow. If the couple kiss each other for Allah's pleasure, they will also be rewarded in the Hereafter. Of course, attaining the pleasure of Allah is the greatest reward.

## THE ETIQUETTE OF WRITING A LETTER TO YOUR HUSBAND

Writing a letter is half as good as meeting a person. However, when a wife is writing a letter to her husband, the matter receives added importance. A husband greatly values a letter from his wife when he is out on a long journey and his children are small. Such a letter is a great comfort and companion. We will therefore present some guidelines to observe when writing to your husband.

1. Begin the letter with "*Bismillaahir Rahmaan nir Raheem*".
2. Thereafter, write your name, followed by the name of the person to whom the letter is addressed. Next

comes "*As-Salaamu Alaykum wa Rahmatullaahi wa Barakaatuh*" and then the Islãmic date.

3. Thereafter, you should praise Allah, convey Durood and *Salaams* to Rasulullah ﷺ. However, if you are writing to someone about whom you fear that she will disrespect the name of Allah and Rasulullah ﷺ, you may recite the *Bismilla* verbally as you write.

4. Instead of taking your husband's name, address him with terms such as "My beloved husband", "The joy of my life", "Sweetheart", etc.

An example of such a letter is as follows:

*"Bismillaahir Rahmaan-nir-Raheem"*

To my most beloved husband and most honoured companion ....................................

From your loving wife ....................................

*As Salaamu Alaykum wa Rahmatullaahi wa Barakaatuh*

6 *Rabi-ul-Awwal* 1422

I praise that Allah besides whom there is none worthy of worship, Who is our Creator and Sustainer. May Allah shower His special mercies, blessings and peace on Hazrat Muhammad ﷺ, after whom there shall be no Prophet.

> I hope that this letter finds you in the best of health. I have just received your letter. It lit up my day and was a comfort and blessing for me. It saw me through my daily chores and was a companion in my loneliness. However, my joy cannot be perfected until I see you and speak to you directly. I wish that I had wings so that I may fly to meet you. Whenever our little one hears a car, he runs to the door expecting you to arrive.

5. Try not to give him any bad news in the letter. If you feel that you have to tell him something of this nature, first think to yourself how you would feel if someone conveyed such news to you while you were on a journey.

6. Always express your love in your letter and tell him how much you are missing him. You may say things like:

   - "Although our bodies are far apart, our souls and thoughts are always together."
   - "There has not been anyone who missed their travelling companion as much as I am missing you. May Allah make the hours of our separation pass by quickly."
   - "I shall bear this separation from you for the pleasure of Allah because you are making an effort for His *Deen* to spread. Otherwise, no soul will be able to bear being separated from a person as kind and beloved as you."

- "I hope that our time apart passes by quickly and that we are soon reunited with good health and happiness."

7. Always ask your husband to make *Du'a* for you and your family. You may say, "I make *Du'a* for you after every *Salaah* and the children also make *Du'a* for you. Please do not forget us in your valuable *Du'as.*"
8. Do not ask him to bring gifts for you and the children if you fear that he may not have enough money. Tell him that all you require from his trip are his *Du'as* because according to the *Ahadith*, the *Du'as* of a *Musaafir* are readily accepted.
9. Ask him for forgiveness in your letter. You may say, "We have been married for ten years and I have made many mistakes. I beseech you for forgiveness for everything that I may have done which has offended you or hurt you in any way. I shall do my best never to repeat these mistakes again."
10. If your husband is away on business, remind him about his obligations to the *Deen*. You may say, "I read an interesting *Hadith* last night and though that is should it with you. The *Hadith* states that ... I also hope that you are taking your friends along with you to the *Masjid* for you five *Salaah*s and that you are encouraging them to also participate in the *Deeni* gatherings taking place at the *Masajid.*"
11. If your husband has left to spread *Deen*, give him encouragement to remain steadfast.

You may conclude the letter as follows:

I am now reluctantly taking leave from you. Please lower your forehead that is always prostrating before your Rabb in the *Masjid* and at home so that I may place a kiss on it. I shall extent my sinful hands to you so that you may kiss them as well even though they do not serve you as well as they should. The children also wish to kiss you because they are missing their father's loving shadow over them.

May Allah keep you safe wherever you are and may He return you safely home very soon.

Yours and only yours truly,

Was *Salaam*u Alaykum wa Rahmatullaahi wa Barakaatuh

Your loving wife

............................

## A LETTER TO A BELOVED

I am sitting her all by myself, in silence and with heartache
My heart is grieved and my eyes are wet
It seems as if the world's anguish has enveloped me
I am therefore writing this sorrowful poem
O my beloved, my most loved one!

Thoughts of you keep coming to me
Wreaking havoc in my heart and soul
I am shaking and shuddering
In the downpour of distress showering on me
O my beloved, my most loved one!

My heart has lost hope and my home is lifeless
Where is the spirit that once occupied it?
Everything has become rudderless
And the pain of bereavement has overtaken me
O my beloved, my most loved one!

I am now weary of loneliness,
Frightened to be swamped by heartache
However, my heart consoles me by saying
That we shall soon be reunited one day
O my beloved, my most loved one!

Our day of meeting shall be one of great jubilation
Every pleasure will be up and dancing
Every evening will be colourful and every morning cheerful
It shall be a grand day, the day we will be reunited
O my beloved, my most loved one!

You steadily made me exclusively yours
By being vibrant, by winning my heart

Have you now forgotten me since you went to
South Africa?
Has your love for me been lost?
O my beloved, my most loved one!

No letter of yours has yet reached us
By which we could have taken some support
For Allah's sake, do not be so forgetful
Otherwise my life will be destroyed
O my beloved, my most loved one!

Please explain to me the reason
For depriving me of your communication
Are you upset about something, dear love
Do give me a reply, tell me something
O my beloved, my most loved one!

(Translated from an Urdu poem)

## PINNING ONE'S HOPES ONLY IN ALLAH

A Muslim should not pin any hopes in people. It is especially important for a good Muslim wife not to pin her hopes in her husband, her father, her brothers, her mother-in-law, her sisters-in-law or anyone else. She should not expect anything from them. Remember that no one can give anything without Allah's command. Allah's the only One Who gives and He is the only One in Whom a person may pin her hopes.

Everything that any person possesses is from Allah. People are merely the temporary custodians of the wealth they possess. Their possessions are a test for them and while they may have it today, tomorrow it will be with someone else. The basis of almost every domestic dispute is that the husband or the wife expects something from the other and when this expectation is not met, an argument erupts.

It often happens that a woman marries a wealthy husband and expects to receive many things from him. However, it is often the case that people seem wealthy but are really not so. It is therefore wrong to pin hopes in the wealthy just as it is incorrect to lose hope in the poor.

Even worse than pinning hopes in people is to ask them either directly or indirectly. One should ask all one's needs only from Allah. If Allah grants something, none can withhold it and if Allah withholds something, none can grant it. If one does not receive something after asking Allah for it, one should rest assured that not having it is better for one.

Hazrat Imaam Ahmad (A.R) used to make the following *Du'a*:

> (Translation: "O Allah! Save my tongue (from asking from others) just as You have saved my face (from turning to others in worship).")

A poor man once came to the Khalifa Haaroon Ar-Rasheed to ask for something. However, he found the Khalifa engaged in *Salaah*. After completing his *Salaah*, the Khalifa made *Du'a* to Allah before turning to the poor man. When he asked the poor man what he wanted, the person said, "My need has been seen to. I have received what I came here for." When the Khalifa asked him to explain what he meant, the man said, "I came to ask you for some money for my daughter's wedding. However, I have seen you extend your hands to ask from someone else. I then decided that I should rather ask my needs from the One whom you ask. You are a beggar just like me and also have to stretch your hand to someone. What can one beggar give another? I shall therefore ask directly from the Independent One whom you ask and Who gives you."

When a wife constantly asks from her husband, she falls from his esteem. A wife should abstain from asking her husband for things and should tell him that his *Du'as* are sufficient for her. She should tell him that his smile alone is priceless for her because it makes Allah pleased with her, and when Allah is pleased with her, her *Du'as* will be answered very quickly. When she refrains from asking from her husband and from expecting things from him, Allah will inspire him to ask her what she needs. When he sincerely asks her what she wants, she should not disappoint him by denying that she wants something. She may then inform him of her needs.

A wife should also bear in mind that if her husband brings her something she dislikes, she should not ask him why he brought it or that he should not have wasted money on something she does not need. Whatever the gift, she should take it happily and say, "*Jazaa Kumullaahu Khayran*"

("May Allah reward you virtues"). She should thank him profusely and praise the choice of gift.

If it does occur that a wife desperately needs something which the husband is not providing, she may suggest to him saying, "I feel that this is needed in our house. What do you think?" or "Do you also feel that we need this?"

Rasulullah ﷺ has mentioned, "When you need to ask for something, ask from Allah and when you ask for help, ask only from Allah."

Imaam Raazi (A.R) has written the following, which are worth their weight in gold. Every Muslim should read them often until the message they contain penetrate the innermost recesses of the heart. He says that it appears as if Allah is addressing man saying:

> Translation: "Your heart is Mine so do not enter the love of another into it
> Your tongue is Mine so do not make the Zikr of anyone but Me
> Your body is Mine so do not use it to serve anyone but Me
> When you require something, do not ask it from anyone but Me."

If one does not immediately get what one wants, one should not be disappointed and should neither ask nor desire that someone should give it to one. Allah provides for everyone and will certainly provide for someone who begs from Him. Even if one's need is something small, one should ask it only from Allah. Allah gives and never tires of giving.

## A GOOD TURN IS NEVER FORGOTTEN

It is commonly said that someone who does a good turn to another may forget the good that he did, but the one to whom the good turn was done never forgets it. It is also understood that a person becomes the slave of someone who does him a favour. These two statements should encourage every wife to serve her husband diligently. A wife should think that when she leaves this world, her husband will not forget the service she gave him and will always make *Du'a* for her. He will remember her sterling service throughout his day and night and the *Du'as* he will make for her could well be the cause for her salvation.

Hazrat A'isha رضي الله عنها would say that from all the wives of Rasulullah ﷺ, she envied Hazrat Khadija رضي الله عنها the most even though she had never seen her. The reason for this was that Rasulullah ﷺ always spoke fondly of Hazrat Khadija رضي الله عنها and whenever he slaughtered a goat, he would search for her friends to give them a piece of the meat. When Hazrat A'isha رضي الله عنها told Rasulullah ﷺ that he speaks of Hazrat Khadija رضي الله عنها as if there is no other woman like her, he extolled her virtues and added, "My children were also from her. The best woman of previous times was Maryam bint Imraan and the best woman of our period is Khadija bint Khuwaylid." Saying this, Rasulullah ﷺ pointed towards the heavens and the earth. (*Bukhari, Muslim & Tirmidhi*)

Hazrat A'isha also narrated that she envied Hazrat Khadija more than any other wife of Rasulullah because he thought of her so often. Once, when Rasulullah spoke of Hazrat Khadija, Hazrat A'isha asked him why he thought so often of her when Allah had given him better wives. Rasulullah replied, "By Allah! The wives Allah gave me after her are not better than her. She brought Imaan when others were Kuffaar. She believed me when others refused to believe. She sacrificed her wealth for me when people denied me theirs. Allah has given me children through her and not through any other wife."

(*Bukhari, Ahmad & Tabraani*)

The life of Rasulullah clearly displays the saying that a good turn is never forgotten. Rasulullah remembered her very fondly, which is clear proof of her loyalty, noble character and sound intellect. Although Hazrat Khadija was fifteen years elder than Rasulullah, he did not marry another woman during her lifetime even though it was customary among the Arabs then to do so. This is also ample testimony of the value that Rasulullah had for her. His loyalty to her and her devotion to him are perfect examples for every Muslim couple. May Allah grant these sterling qualities to every Muslim couple in this period of time when disobedience has become the order of the day and people no longer seem to value the good that others do for them.

Without doubt, the lives of any couple will be truly blissful when the husband and wife behave compassionately towards each other, when they value each other's company and when they provide comfort for each other. Such a relationship will change the lives of many for the better in our current environment where people are living like animals, without any direction whatsoever. It is to every couple that we present as a gift the beautiful example of Hazrat Khadija ﷺ's relationship with Rasulullah ﷺ. It is for every wife to emulate the love, service, obedience, respect, gentle speech, self-sacrifice, patience and gratitude that she displayed.

We plead to every woman to string the pearls of these qualities into a necklace which should never be taken off her neck. She should apply all of these qualities to her relationship with her husband so that she could become worthy of the highest echelons of *Jannah.* May Allah assist every woman to abstain from every sin and to hasten towards good deeds. *Aameen*

## THERE IS A GREAT WOMAN BEHIND EVERY SUCCESSFUL MAN

You may have heard this cliche many times already. However, you should apply yourself to be such a great woman. You should be the driving force behind the success of your husband, your brother/s and son/s. Of course, you should also motivate your daughter/s and sister/s equally. You should empower all these people around you with firm Imaan, unshakeable conviction in Allah, resoluteness, courage, the best of morals and noble character. However, you will be unable to imbue them with noble character if you have not acquired it already.

If you shout at the children whenever they make a mistake, calling them all sorts of names and being harsh with them, all they will learn is harshness. One should rather be gentle and compassionate with them so that these qualities penetrate their hearts.

When dealing with her husband, a wife should be loving, gentle, patient, vibrant, methodical, resolute and smiling. This will give him courage and confidence to face any hardship with ease. It will also give him peace and comfort whenever he enters the home. These qualities will also assist in the upbringing of the children, will bring honour and respect to the home, and will prepare the husband and children to accomplish great feats in future. They will thus become worthy of leading the *Ummah* successfully and become worthy sons of Islãm. At the same time, a woman should make every effort to remove the love of this world from the hearts of all those around her. Such women are themselves great leaders.

If we analyse the accomplishments of Rasulullah ﷺ, we will definitely find the input of Hazrat Khadija رضي الله عنها and his other pure wives. Similarly, the women of the Ansaar played a significant role in the spread of Islãm just as the women of the *Muhaajireen* were an indispensable ally in the *Hijrah* and efforts of their men. Faatima bint Abdul Malik was a shareholder in the achievements of Hazrat Umar bin Abdul Azeez just as Zubayda played a key role in the empire of Haaroon Ar-Rasheed. In the same fashion, the wife of the eminent Chief Justice Qaadhi Shurayh must also receive credit for his accomplishments.

Just as the expression in the heading holds true, it is also true to say that behind every lazy and ill-tempered man there is a woman just like him or one who is an immoral and corrupt "intellectual". Whereas many women of the past were a calamity because of their ignorance, today's college and university graduates are egotistical, self-centred and arrogant. It is tragic that they are consumed by the desire to amass the pleasures and comforts of this world. The Western culture that they have imported into their lives has removed them from the safety and chaste environment of their homes and made them parade the streets and catwalks only to attract customers. They have thus forsaken their families and children, who suffer the worst repercussions of such an immoral society.

Because mothers are too busy in offices and businesses, they are depriving their children of breast milk and raising them on powdered and tinned milk. In doing this, they are not only depriving the children of the nutrition they need, but they are also misappropriating a valuable trust that Allah has placed in their custody. Whereas Allah has granted breasts to women for the purpose of suckling their children, today's women have corrupted its role by using them as showpieces in night-clubs and on the streets.

Remember that the benefits of breast feeding are not only restricted to filling the child's stomach, but it is via this means that Allah transfers the character traits of the mother and her family to the child. It is also by this means that the child absorbs the mother's love, which cannot be found anywhere else. It is also possible that a child could develop animalistic instincts when fed the milk of animals. However, the details of this are lengthy. Those who wish to read about this may refer to books concerning the Islãmic upbringing of children.

A great mother is required to raise a great child. A great mother is one who gives the child her own milk, who showers the child with her love and whose children have complete confidence in her and complete reliance on Allah.

A wife should run her home so well that the husband does not have to worry about anything pertaining to these affairs. In this way, he will be able to use his time to serve Allah's *Deen*. She should also encourage her children to learn the Qur'ãn, the various aspects of *Deen* and Arabic. At the same time, she should create within them the urge to spread the *Deen* throughout the world. Equipped with the knowledge of *Deen*, the Qur'ãn and the *Ahadith* of Rasulullah ﷺ, they will be tremendous assets to the *Ummah* and whatever good they do will accrue to the account of their parents even after the parents have left the world. In addition to this, if they are a means of guiding others to do good, the parents will even attain the rewards that these other people do throughout their lives. It is with regard to such women that a poet said:

> "If our women were like those women who passed, women would have been better than men."

## THE DESCRIPTION OF A PERFECT WIFE

We shall now present the description of a perfect wife in the words of Ulama and wise men with vast experience who have studied various times and aspects of life. We appeal to all women to add the qualities described here to their practical lives instead of just adding them to their registry of general knowledge. To bring something into one's life, it is necessary to first make an intention. When a person resolves to lead a pious life, Allah makes it easy for her. You should therefore make an intention now to implement everything you are about to read. If possible, perform two Rakaahs *Salaah* before continuing so that Allah may make it easy for you. Make *Du'a* to Allah saying, "O Allah! Grant me the ability to adopt all the good qualities of an excellent wife that are pleasing to you and your beloved Rasul ﷺ. Allow me to practise these so that I may please my husband and my family and become a source of comfort for them all. *Aameen.*"

**The perfect wife** is she who provides encouragement for her husband, she who behaves intelligently, she who turns her husband's attention towards her, who wins his heart and who showers her love and compassion on him.

It is said that *Shaitaan* addresses women saying, "You are half my army and are my arrow which never misses its target." This makes it clear that half of *Shaitaan's* armament is in the form of carnal desires. The remaining half is in the form of anger and frustration. When a husband does not find comfort with his wife, *Shaitaan* will turn his attention towards other women.

Whereas women can be extremely simple and unpretentious, they can also be very difficult and hard to handle. While they have the qualities of purity and virtue, they are also capable of causing enmity and corruption. If they chose, they can bind a broken family just as easily as they can divide a united family. An irreligious woman is a scourge to her family and to her progeny to come. No one can give happiness to her family and they will always remain deprived of comfort. On the contrary, a good and pious woman is the light of her home and enjoys the status of a queen in her home.

**The perfect wife** is resolute and follows the path that Islãm has chalked for her. She refrains from adopting the practices and modes of dressing of the *Kuffaar*. In fact, she even abstains from buying perfumes and other articles that the *Kuffaar* manufacture so that her wealth is rather spent on articles that Muslims manufacture. This she does so that her money can benefit the Muslims instead of their enemies.

She neither apes the West in their fashion, their domestic lifestyles or in their ways of living. She realises that the blessings of life and the blessings of the home are derived from the love and understanding that a couple develops between themselves. She knows that these blessings are neither acquired by wearing expensive clothing nor by decorating the house with exclusive furniture, appliances and curtains. These things are after all merely for show.

**The perfect wife** is she who encourages her husband to carry out good deeds. Addressing all men, a woman once said, "The true hero among you is the one whom us women cannot entice towards sin." In fact, it was because of a woman that the son of Hazrat Adam عليه السلام committed the first murder on earth when he killed his brother.

**The perfect wife** has the deep-rooted fervour within her to assist her husband and to cooperate with him. In fact, the husband and wife should both share this commitment and should be prepared to make sacrifices for each other. They should both have the inclination to give rather than to take.

**The perfect wife** is prepared to dedicate her life to her husband. She has made up her mind to live for her husband's pleasure instead of for her own pleasure. Whatever she does should be according to her husband's liking. When she does this, the time will not be long before her husband will do the same for her. However, she will have to make many sacrifices during the early years of marriage.

**The perfect wife** is one who detests pandering to the desires of her *Nafs* (carnal self). She does not allow her *Nafs* to beguile her, thereby causing her to either barter her family's honour, to compromise on the children's proper upbringing or to neglect her husband's rights. This quality of a woman is sufficient to win her husband's heart and to give him peace of mind. Such a wife advises her husband to abstain from earning money via *Haraam* means, assuring him that the family are prepared to tolerate hunger rather than the fire of *Jahannam.* She constantly reminds him that he should not usurp the rights of others, he should not lie or cheat in business, he should not infringe on the rights of his employees, he should not miss his *Salaah* with *Jamaa'at* and should do nothing else by which his earnings become tainted, thereby exposing the entire family to fire of *Jahannam.*

## ADVICES FOR A BRIDE

Allah has passed a decree that the person who disobeys Him shall never have a life of contentment even though she/he seems to be living a life of affluence and luxury. Despite these pleasures, his/her heart is filled with worries and anxiety. Such a person cannot really enjoy any of the pleasures available to him/her. As for the life of the Hereafter, only worst can be expected. May Allah save us all from such damnation. *Aameen*

It is therefore necessary for every bride to make up her mind to lead her life in harmony with the injunctions of the *Shari'ah.* She should resolve that she will not earn the wrath of Allah regardless of the pressures that others apply on her. We shall therefore present the following valuable advices for every bride to practise.

## *Salaah*

Steadfastly perform every *Salaah* as soon as the *Azaan* is called out. Prolong your *Salaah* and ensure that the limbs of your body are at rest during your *Salaah* so that you resemble a tree or a pillar. Pause after every verse of *Surah Faatiha* and others.

## Hijaab

Every Muslim woman should be particular about keeping her body concealed from non-*Mahram* men. She should ensure that no part of her body and no hair is exposed to them. In fact, she should even ensure that no non-*Mahram* man hears her voice.

If ten non-*Mahram* men look at a woman walking about without covering her hair, twenty eyes have been subjected to Allah's wrath. The woman has thus become a cause of attracting Allah's wrath her way. A bride should therefore ensure that she dresses properly when visiting her in-laws. It is unfortunate that many Muslims actively attract Allah's wrath by encouraging the custom where women are expected to shake hands with their brothers-in-law, the uncles of their husbands and other non-*Mahram* members of the family. A new bride should refuse to shake the hands of any non-*Mahram*, making it clear to all that the act is *Haraam*. It is therefore best for a woman to clarify such matters with the person proposing. She should tell them that she should not be asked to do anything contrary to the *Shari'ah*.

The wife of Dr. Muhammad Ridhaa has written an article in an Arabic magazine about the harms of disregarding the *Shar'ee Hijaab*. In it she writes, "When a bride walks out of her house in attractive clothing, she is actually inviting every young and old, cultured and uncultured man to have a good look at her. She is actually saying to them, "Will you not look at this stunning lady? Are you not tempted to get close to me?" Walking in the streets and commercial centres, she is really like a hawker peddling her wares. She is just like the sweetmeat merchant who decorates his sweetmeats with various colours, wraps them in attractive silver foil and places them in appealing containers so that passers-by may ogle at them and get tempted to buy them. By doing this, there is soon a string of customers waiting to have their share."

Rasulullah ﷺ has mentioned that among the inmates of *Jahannam* shall be women that are naked despite being dressed. In addition to attracting men to themselves they are also attracted to men. They parade the streets with their heads swollen (with pride) like the humps of camels. Rasulullah ﷺ made it clear that let alone entering *Jannah*, such women will not even smell the fragrance of *Jannah* even though the fragrance of *Jannah* can be smelt from a very great distance. (*Muslim*)

It is *Haraam* for any Muslim woman to wear clothes that are thin enough to reveal the limbs of her body, her complexion or even her hair. Similarly, it is *Haraam* for her to wear clothing that is so tight-fitting that it reveals the shape of her body. Such clothing attracts men and rouses their desires. Of course, she is permitted to wear this and any other type of clothing in front of her husband because he is the person she ought to entice. Such clothing will cause him to focus all his attention on her, excluding all other women.

When women do observe *Hijaab,* it is necessary for them not to wear clothing that attracts the gazes of men. Their garments should therefore not be colourful or made attractive in any way. It should be as least attractive as possible. Every woman walking the streets without *Hijaab* is perpetrating a grave injustice to every other woman because even if a man looks at such a woman by mistake, the thought of her being his wife may enter his heart. These types of thoughts are very common when sisters-in-law and brothers-in-law mix. The consequences of this are, needless to say, disastrous because when the thought enters the mind as a seed, *Shaitaan* ensures that he nurtures and cultivates the seed until it develops into a large tree.

When this thought takes root in a man's mind and he happens to see his wife in a dishevelled state, his heart becomes more detached from her. This is an excellent catalyst to such an explosive situation because he soon starts reprimanding her for even the littlest fault. If she makes the mistake of behaving insolently, the situation may become violent. Eventually, he may lose all hope in her and decide to end the marriage, thinking that he should have married the other woman who is always attractive when he sees her. However, he fails to realise that the other woman looks much worse than his wife when she removes her elaborate make-up. It is only a heartless and cruel woman who would parade in front of another woman's husband to attract him.

When a wife allows her husband to mix freely with other women, she is exposing the family to ruin. It could seem as innocent a situation as his uncle's daughter-in-law congratulating him on the opening of his new business, but the thought lingers long in his mind, "She spoke so sweetly. I wonder if..." The tongue is one of *Shaitaan's* most efficient agents and a woman speaking in alluring tones can easily seduce a man. *Shaitaan's* efforts are concentrated on the eyes, hearts and genitals. It is therefore necessary for every Muslim to be on guard when these organs are involved.

One can well imagine a situation where a young woman is entertaining non-*Mahram* family men such as her brothers-in-law, her cousins and others, causing them to become attracted to her ways and talks. By doing this, she is actually ruining the marriages of her sisters, her sisters-in-law and other relatives. She will be inciting arguments and problems in all these homes when these men return to their wives still thinking of her. Women like this should bear in mind that people who cause disputes in the homes of others will be unable to save their own homes from disputes. Such a woman should beware that her husband does not become attracted to another woman, leaving her as a divorcee. May Allah save all Muslim homes from such problems and may He grant every Muslim woman the guidance to don the *Shar'ee Hijaab. Aameen*

The harms of men looking at women are too numerous to mention. A poet writes about a woman who beautified herself and stepped into a shop. Seeing her just once caused the shopkeeper to instantly hate his wife, it destroyed the spirituality of his *Salaah*s and fasts, and soon led him to sin. An Arabic couplet reads:

> Translation: A look, a smile, a greeting, a word, a promise and ultimately the meeting.

One will be horrified to hear about the incidents reported to our *Daarul Ifta*.[1] There are incidents about men married to young and pretty women who blacken their faces by having relationships with their servants, with beggars and with middle-aged divorcees who have already been divorced twice. As mentioned earlier, a person who earns Allah's wrath cannot expect contentment in her life.

It is unfortunate that when people get their daughters married, they are advised not to indulge in *Haraam* activities such as videoing the function, hosting functions where sexes intermingle and being extravagant. However, they disregard these advices, saying that the Ulama merely want to put dampers on their fun. They also say that they will do as they please because such functions take place only once in a lifetime. It is not long after the marriage that things start going wrong. They then learn that the man is interested in someone else and had no concern for his wife. Otherwise, the bride is experiencing great

1. A faculty of a *Darul Uloom* (Islamic University) staffed by *Muftis* who respond to queries from the public.

difficulty with her in-laws. The same people who then wanted to do as they please, rush to some Ulama, asking for a *Ta'weez* to make up the marriage.

It should be borne in mind that no *Ta'weez* and no *Du'a* can remove Allah's punishment. It is only *Taubah* that will benefit a person then. A woman has to repent for her sins, especially for the sin of discarding the *Hijaab* and the sin of being extravagant. *Insha Allah*, Allah will alleviate her difficulty.

## Abstaining from Photographing and Videoing

The third advice to every bride is that before the marriage she should make the condition that she will not tolerate photographing and videoing at her marriage. She should make it clear that she will not attend any function where these two activities take place because such a function is sure to attract Allah's wrath. In act, it has happened that a person taking a video of a function kept a copy of the video with him and managed to alter the footage. He then blackmailed the family to pay him a large sum of money to prevent him publicising the video.

Apart from such an occurrence, the harms of photographing and videoing are numerous. If a woman decides to change her life and don the *Hijaab*, her days of flaunting her assets and flouting Allah's commands will be preserved on paper or on film. In fact, this will still be there for all to see long after she has left this world. Any man who then sees this will take pleasure in doing so. Although she may be dead, her sins will still live on.

Because a woman was filmed, she will become the cause of thousands of men sinning during her lifetime as well as long afterwards.

Every bride should therefore do herself a favour and avoid taking videos and photographs. She should also refrain from using make-up that prevents her *Wuzu* and *Salaah* from being valid.

**Remember** that love and peace in a home can be attained only by pleasing Allah because every person's heart is in Allah's control. By attending a beauty parlour, a woman will be breaking Allah's commands because the parts of her body that ought to remain concealed are then exposed to others. Although a woman may think that she is pleasing her husband in this way, the ill-effects of such places will soon drive the couple apart at some stage of their lives if not sooner.

A woman should not go to beauty parlours or private beauticians but should rather do what they can for themselves at home. The hearts of mankind are completely in Allah's control. When a woman adopts the permissible means of beautification, Allah will cement the love for her in her husband's heart from the very first night. However, when she exposes the most private areas of her body to others (even though the others may be Muslim women), she will be committing a major sin and earning Allah's wrath.

May Allah grant all Muslim women the guidance to practise the teachings of *Deen* by carrying out every deed they ought to carry out and by abstaining from everything what the *Shari'ah* forbids. *Aameen*

## Beauty Salons

The desire to be beautiful is a natural instinct within every woman and it is the right of every to be given the opportunity to beautify herself. Islãm does not dispute this instinct. In fact, Islãm encourages this instinct on condition that it is carried out only for one man viz., the husband. A woman is at liberty to use all types of perfumes and make-up for her husband as long as the ingredients are permissible.

Rasulullah ﷺ has mentioned that a woman is akin to an adulterer when she applies perfume and leaves her home, passing by people who can smell her fragrance.[1]

Islãm does not permit a woman to walk about out of her home applying perfume, especially when she has to pass by men. This is so because perfume is a subtle but exceptionally effective invitation to men. Whereas physical beauty can be concealed, a sweet fragrance cannot be hidden. It moves ahead of a woman and lingers in the air long after she has passed by, stirring desire within the men who smell it.

Neglecting the advice given above will certainly cause many marital problems and could eventually lead the couple to divorce. A woman should therefore be very cautious about her behaviour. Although she must maintain

1. *Ahmad* Vol. 4, Page 414, *Ibn Khuzayma*, Vol. 3, Page 91, *Nisai* Vol 8, Page 53, *A'wan-ul-Ma'bood* Vol. 11, Page 230.

her beauty, she should not overspend. She must always be mindful of her husband's budget and should avoid burdening her husband with expenses such as unnecessary jewellery and fashionable clothing.

It is unfortunate that many women are fanatical about clothing. A man in Bangladesh distributes free saris to women every year. It so happened that 19 women once died in a stampede as others were rushing to grab hold of a sari. The poor women left their homes to get saris but returned only in their *Kafans* (burial shrouds). It is necessary that every woman realises that she has to be conscious about her husband's financial situation when spending on clothing and jewellery. Even if a woman's husband is wealthy, she should spend as little as possible on herself and use the rest for the causes of *Deen*.

Another harm of visiting beauty salons has been mentioned in an article written by Dr. Abdul Mun'im, who is the dean of the Faculty of Medicine at the Cairo University. He writes, "To have the hair set, cut, dyed, uprooted and implanted according to western fashions requires the use of many unnatural methods which cause hair loss. The many instruments, machines and chemicals used are extremely harmful to the hair. It is therefore not advisable for any Muslim woman to visit such places."

When a woman has her styled, undue pressure is exerted on the hair roots, causing the roots to be deprived of their required blood supply. As a result, they become brittle and start falling off. When women become accustomed to visiting beauty parlours for their facials, hairdos, threading, waxing, bleaching, etc., they appear very beautiful for a while. However, the toll is soon taken on their skin and bodies when a 25-year old woman starts looking like a 40-year old.

Women who visit beauticians and salons are generally women who are not conscious about their *Deeni* obligations. They are heedless of their *Salaah* and engage in various deeds that earn Allah's wrath. Eventually, the effect of their sins causes their husbands to lose interest in them. They then become like the many *Kaafir* women who attend to them at such salons, who neither have any interest in their husbands and whose husbands have no interest in them. They lead separate lives and share only the same home. How can such women make a new bride attractive for her husband when they have not succeeded in winning their own husbands? Muslim women should not allow such women to lay a hand on them.

If the salon is staffed by men or if men visit as well, there can be no doubt that the Muslim woman visiting there is causing Allah's wrath and curses to shower down on herself.

A Muslim woman should care for her beauty by herself at home. She should remember that it is not only the accessories and make-up that attract her husband to her, but it is her piety. As already mentioned, Allah creates the attraction within the husband's heart and it is He who unites their hearts. This He will not do if the woman is disobedient to Him.

We will now quote some Arabic poetry which was translated from Persian by Sheikh Basheer Al Ghazzi (A.R). It is extracted from the book "*Tarbiyatul Banaat*" by Sheikh Ali Fikri. Every woman should try to memorise these couplets. She should avoid the company of evil women and women who are extravagant. She should also not allow beauticians and women at beauty salons to touch her body. The poet says:

"I said to the sand:[1] 'Are you musk or ambergris? Your fragrance has certainly made me fall madly in love with you.'

The sand replied by saying, 'I was just ordinary sand (being trampled upon) but my association with a rose has made me fragrant and honoured (so that I am now applied to the head).'

In this manner, I have associated with many pious and knowledgeable ladies and have had my knowledge increased.

Such will be the condition of any woman who associates with such women; she will also have status and honour (and be the pride of her parents and husband)."

Remember that any "friend" who pressurises you into visiting salons and beauticians is destroying the hard-earned money of your father or husband in a single sweep.

---

1. A type of sand iun Syria which is mixed with the rose fragrance to produce a long-lasting perfume. Women apply this to their hair after taking a bath.

This money could have been better used on your little brother/sister or little children. Even if they do not need anything, keep in mind that every Muslim in the world is your brother or sister and there are millions who could have used the money for more important things. You should never let your love for luxuries blind you from the more important aspects of life. In fact, it was recently reported that a boy from Lahore committed suicide recently because his parents did not buy him new clothing for Eid. His desire for new clothes was so intense that it blinded him from seeing his parent's poverty.

There are millions of people whose money finishes before even spending half the month. They can barely afford food, let alone school and *Madrasah* fees for their children. Therefore, if any woman forces her "friend" to spend a few hundreds if not thousands in vanities, she is not worth having as a friend. She is obviously unsympathetic to the plight of others. When the money spent at a beauty parlour in a few hours could provide food for a family for an entire month, it would be foolish to even consider going there, especially when one will be incurring Allah's wrath as well. When a woman is pressurised into such a situation, she should remember that she is not just an ordinary woman. She is the daughter of illustrious souls like Hazrat Khadija رضي الله عنها and Hazrat A'isha رضي الله عنها. She is cast in the same mould as people like Hazrat Zainab رضي الله عنها and Zubayda (A.R). She is also the mother of people who will follow in the footsteps of Hazrat Umar رضي الله عنه and Hazrat Khaalid bin Waleed رضي الله عنه. She cannot lower herself to emulate people who have no regard for Allah and His Rasul ﷺ.

Remember that just as fragrant flowers cannot flourish in barren ground and just as beautiful song-birds do not perch on thorny bushes, someone as great as a future Salaahud Deen Ayoobi (A.R) will not be found cradles in the arms of some beauty salon product who is flaunting her charms for public approval and flouting the commands of Allah. No child as great as Hazrat Khansa رضي الله عنها or Hazrat Zainab bint Jahash رضي الله عنها will suckle from the breasts that have had their size and shape exhibited to every passer-by. Children of worth, who will be assets to the *Ummah* cannot emerge from the homes of such women. Such women cannot be mothers to the illustrious souls of the past, whose names Muslims are proud to take and to use for their own children.

Of course, it is not far-fetched to expect such people from today's Muslim *Ummah.* All that is needed is that Muslims apply themselves diligently to Islãm and do their utmost to ensure that the *Deen* reaches every person on earth. Every Muslim mother should have reliance only in Allah and devote herself to her husband. She will then be a cause of happiness and joy for every member of her family, encouraging them to emulate the examples of Islãm's great heroes and heroines.

May Allah grant every Muslim adult and child the ability to practise *Deen* in its totality and spread it throughout the world. *Aameen*

## AVOIDING *TA'WEEZAAT* THAT DO NOT CONFORM WITH THE SHARI'AH

Every Muslim woman should take care not to ever consult any astrologer, fortune-teller, palm-reader, exorcist, witch doctor, faith healer or others of the type. They should also not advise other women to consult such people. The *Ahadith* have strongly condemned visiting fortune-tellers and believing them. Also included in the ambit of this *Hadith* is consulting any of the other persons mentioned above. People who visit them will also be deprived of Rasulullah ﷺ's intercession in the Hereafter.

One should remember that all conditions come from Allah and Allah sends conditions to people according His wills. Therefore, when one faces any difficulties, one should immediately mend one's ways and make an attempt to please Allah. Instead of seeking help from these people and looking for amulets to wear and incantations to read, the best cure is attaining the pleasure of Allah. Rather than solve problems, such people only create dissention in families and contribute to a person's anxiety. In fact, many men have divorced their wives because their wives were secretly having *Ta'weezaat* (amulets) made for them.

Of course, if the need truly arises for a person to receive treatment, she may consult a reliable *Aalim* with her husband's consent. If he does permit her, she should have the treatment done through the means of her *Mahram*. However, it must be stated that a *Ta'weez* is a *Du'a*. Therefore, more important and more effective than a *Ta'weez* is for a person to make *Du'a* to Allah. The most effective prescription to ward off evil is to recite the "*Manzil*". One should keep a copy and also make one's children and little brothers/sisters memorise it. It should be recited regularly every morning and evening.

## AVOIDING JEALOUSY

A woman should never be jealous of her sisters-in-law, be they her husband's sisters, her brothers' wives or her husband's brothers' wives. Jealousy is a malady that harms the jealous person more than the victim because the jealous person's heart is always on fire.

*Shaitaan* always assaults a woman's mind with thoughts about the good fortune of her sisters-in-law, making her forget what she has or what she had. He makes a woman believe that her sister-in-law (husband's brother's wife) receives more from her in-laws than she does and that her in-laws listen to her sister-in-law more than they listen to her. *Shaitaan* also makes her jealous of the way that her sisters-in-law are treated by their husbands. In this manner, he plagues her mind with hundreds of thoughts so that an inferno of jealousy eventually consumes her.

To be safeguarded from such deception, a woman should console herself with the thought that whatever people have comes from Allah. She should think that if she needs something that others have, she should ask Allah for it instead of burning her heart. Allah will soon grant her what she wants. In this manner, she will not be causing difficulty to herself and to her family and she will not be guilty of showing ingratitude for Allah's bounties to her. Her success in this world and the Hereafter will therefore not be jeopardised.

If one must envy another, it should be because the other person is actively engaged in acts of virtue such as *Tahajjud Salaah,* recitation of the Qur'ãn, etc. May Allah save every Muslim from jealousy and from every other spiritual diseases. Aameen.

## WHEN A WOMAN HAS THE ILL-FORTUNE OF BEING MARRIED TO A CONSTANTLY WARRING INGRATE

There are many women who have the misfortune of being married to men who have no love for them, who do not appreciate anything they do for them and are constantly at loggerheads with their wives. To solve a problem like this, it is necessary to pinpoint the cause of his behaviour, a feat which requires a great deal of skill and experience.

It is often the case that besides the apparent cause, the source of the couple's differences is a factor that deeply embedded within the lives of the couple and which only the couple themselves will be able to identify through mutual understanding and mutual trust. The root of the disputes may be that they did not acquaint themselves with each other's habits from the beginning or that a mother-in-law, sister-in-law or someone else is creating the division between them. It may therefore be necessary to refer the matter to a trustworthy Aalim who has experience in marriage counselling. However, one should never be despondent. If one person's advice does not solve the problem, other people should be consulted, even if they are family members.

There are times when the couple realises from the outset that their marriage may be short-lived. This often occurs when the husband is displeased with his wife's looks. The reason for this is often that the husband does not see his wife before marriage and the proposal for marriage is extended on the basis of what his mother, sister or another relative tells him. It is therefore necessary that the man is taken to see the woman he intends marrying so that both are satisfied with each other's looks. In addition to this, each one should make enquiries about the other, consult with reliable Ulama and make *Istikhaara*.

However, if one is already married, there is no need to lose hope. The thought of separating should never enter your mind. If from the beginning the couple strongly feel that they will be unable to make up their marriage, the woman should be cautious to avoid falling pregnant. This is necessary because if the couple are divorced, it is the innocent child who will suffer the consequences of their divorce. Such a child will be emotionally scarred.

There have been many couples who detected problems from the beginning but continued along the rocky path until several children were born. When they were eventually forced to separate, the children began to develop many psychological and emotional problems. It is such children who grow up into adults with low self-esteem, lack of confidence, weak-heartedness and a range of other emotional problems in addition to many physical illnesses as well. Those couples who unsuccessfully force themselves to stay together pass years of daily arguments making life a hell for themselves as well as for their innocent children.

However, the period of birth control should be brief. It is therefore best to consult with reliable Ulama after a while to decide what course to take because it also happens that the birth of a child bonds the couple and transforms their disparities into pure love.

The problem is not uncommon where a couple have been married for a long time and may even have children. However, they are always arguing and love seems to be lacking between them. In a situation like this, the wife should analyse the problem by asking herself questions like, "During which times does he get most angry?" "Concerning which matters does he get most angry?" "What reduces his anger?" "Why were there no arguments today?" By asking such questions, the couple will be able to solve their own problems without external intervention. Of course it is necessary for both to be committed to resolving their differences. It should not be that one is doing everything to resolve the differences while the other has no interest in the matter.

It is a fact that most married couples are capable of leading peaceful and amicable lives, happily navigating through the rough tides of life and enjoying the blessings, strength and fortunes of married life. When there is a problem, the responsibility rests more heavily on the wife's shoulders to identify the root of the problem. She should then employ her feminine subtlety and ingenuity to amicable solve the problem. In doing this, she may have to make a few concessions, but she should never regard this to be a difficulty because every hardship and difficulty that she endures will be amply rewarded. The great extent of this reward can be gauged from the fact that obedience to one's husband is second only to obedience to Allah and obedience to Rasulullah ﷺ.

The most important priority is to identify and eradicate the root of the problem without the intervention of close family members because when close family members intervene, they are prone to take sides and further complicate the problem. In such situations, every wife should implement the following:

1. Always speak in soft and gentle tones.
2. Remember that man is a slave to favours i.e. people adore those who do them favours and are morally indebted to them. The best favour a wife can do for her husband is to do what he pleases.
3. Endure his reprimands and constantly make *Du'a* to Allah to cement the love between you and your husband. You may also recite "*Bismillaahir Rahmaan nir Raheem*" thrice followed by *Surah* Faatiha once (before) blowing on his food and drink. Make *Du'a* to Allah to improve his character as well as your own so that you two may live in harmony.

We will now narrate a true-life account from which every heart-broken wife may take comfort, knowing that the dark night will soon give way to a bright morning. This incident is narrated by Sheikh Mahmood Istanbuli and the central figure of the story is a friend of his. He says that his friend was a short-tempered but simple man. He had hardly completed his studies when he got married. As a result, he was totally unaware of the etiquette and conduct of treating women. Therefore, the day soon came when he behaved in a harsh and impolite manner.

His wife complained to her mother about his behaviour. Fortunately, her mother was a wise and pious woman. She said to her daughter, "Dear, your husband is still young and very inexperienced. However, the signs of piety and amiability are apparent on his face. You should therefore bear with him and gradually lead him aright. Gently explain things to him and he will soon treat you as he should." The daughter took her mother's advice and she did not have to wait long before her mother's prediction was realised.

A Muslim wife should therefore never lose hope in Allah's mercy. All she has to do is fulfil her duties and make *Du'a* to Allah to mend their relationship. Allah has so often bonded people who were arch enemies, making them bosom friends. It is therefore easy for Allah to bond a couple who have committed themselves to living with each other.

Many disputes between husband and wife arise when one of them does not respond immediately to the other's call. Therefore, when one of the couple calls for the other or asks for something, the other should respond immediately. Among the people who Rasulullah ﷺ cursed are the "*Musawwifaat*". These are those women who say "*Sowfa*" ("soon") when their husbands call them to bed i.e. instead of responding immediately, they say, "I am coming soon." Eventually, when they do arrive, their husbands are already fast asleep. (*Ibn Hibbaan*)

Of course, it is necessary to bear in mind that whereas men are quickly aroused, women need time and foreplay before she is ready for intercourse. Every couple should understand this natural difference. It is therefore necessary for every newly-wed man to study books like "*Tuhfatul Uroos*" or "A Gift to a Husband".

When a couple are sincerely committed to pleasing each other, it will be very easy for them to respond immediately to each other's call. They will be prepared to make sacrifices for each other, thereby solving countless potential problems in their lives. This commitment will transform grief into happiness and selfishness into self-sacrifice.

It often happens that although the couple are happy and compatible, financial or other difficulties cause their relationship to be strained. As a result, they drift apart and have little time for each other. They will lie on the bed facing opposite directions, showing little or no interest in each other. Such a situation should not be misinterpreted as personal dislike or enmity. It is merely the stress and tension of the situation which creates this temporary rift. During such periods, the wife should treat the situation with caution and make every attempt to understand the problem. She should say and do nothing that may aggravate the problem. She should remember that even sweet things taste bitter to a sick person.

She must try her best to put him at ease and make things comfortable for him. For example, if he is tired and worried and goes straight to his room to lie down when he returns home, she should ensure that the children are quiet so that he may rest in peace. She should not allow her children to suffer the brunt of the problems he encountered while at work. The food should also be prepared on time so that he is not further disturbed and the situation not further inflamed. Although the husband realises that he will be wrong to make his wife or children suffer for his anxiety, he may still scold them because of the strain he is suffering. The wife should ignore this outburst and remain silent because any response from her will transform a spark into an inferno that may be extinguished only by divorce.

Here are a few guidelines to alleviate your husband's worries. Of course, every woman understands her situation better and may use any other method that she deems appropriate.

1) Ask Allah to forgive your and your husband's short comings every morning and evening. Also encourage your husband to do the same.
2) Recite the various *Du'as* and *Aayats* prescribed for alleviating worries. Encourage your husband to do the same.
3) Besides the five *Farz Salaahs*, you should perform two Rakaahs of *Salaatut Taubah* often and make *Du'a*

to Allah begging Him for assistance.

4) Give whatever *Sadaqah* (charity) you can afford and urge your husband to do the same. This *Sadaqah* should be given secretly.

Dissention between a couple is commonly caused by mothers-in-law and sisters-in-law. From the numerous cases of divorce, separation and disputes between couples that have been reported to the *Daarul Ifta*, it has been noticed that most of them have been caused by interferences from a woman's mother-in-law or sisters-in-law viz. her husband's brothers' wives or her husband's sisters.

In my humble opinion, the most effective solution for this problem is for a couple to live by themselves, even though in a rented apartment. In this manner, their lives and the lives of their innocent children will be saved from ruin. In fact, breaking a marriage is the most loved act in the sight of *Shaitaan*. The *Shayaateen* make tireless efforts to separate husbands from their wives and they have a remarkable level of success. However, they are unable to influence the lives of those couples whom Allah showers with His mercy.

If a daughter-in-law is having problems with her mother-in-law who is dependant on her, arrangements should be made so that the daughter-in-law is able to cook by herself and provide three meals for her mother-in-law. Of course, if the mother-in-law is happy to live with another daughter-in-law, she may do so if the other daughter-in-law is also happy with the arrangement. However, even in this case, every other daughter-in-law should at least send some dish regularly for the mother-in-law. In this manner, every daughter-in-law will receive the *Du'as* of their mother-in-law and their relationships will remain cordial.

May Allah grant happiness to every couple and transform every strained situation in their homes into joy and pleasure. *Aameen*

## A VALUABLE LESSON FOR EVERY GOOD WIFE

A man bought a slave and, after bringing her home, the following conversation ensued:

"What is your name?"

"A slave has no name. Whatever name my master prefers, that shall be my name."

"What food do you like?"

"I like whatever my master likes for me."

"What clothing would you like me to buy for you?"

"I am pleased with whatever clothing you buy for me."

"What work can you do?"

"I shall do whatever work you need me to do."

"Tell me what you enjoy."

"Of what significance are the pleasures of a slave compared to the pleasures of her master. I enjoy whatever you enjoy."

Hearing these replies of the slave, the master began to weep because it made him realise that his relationship with Allah ought to be the same. He said to her, "You have taught me what my attitude with Allah should be." The slave then focussed her attention to Allah and said, "O Allah! What bounty can I have that is better than the ability to diligently serve one of Your bondsmen. So by Your infinite grace, forgive my sins and shortcomings for I know that You are the Most Kind and the Most Merciful."

It is the duty of every Muslim to behave like the slave in the above incident and to have no desire that is opposed to what Allah and Rasulullah ﷺ want. Just as the slave woman expressed loyalty and obedience to her master, so too should every wife do everything to please her husband, even though she may have to sacrifice her own pleasures in doing so. She should do everything with the thought in mind that pleasing her husband pleases Allah. When Allah is pleased with a person, no difficulty is insurmountable.

## COURTING AFTER THE ENGAGEMENT

It is our plea to every Muslim sister that she should not allow her fiancé to court her after the engagement because he is still regarded as a non-*Mahram*. It is therefore *Haraam* for the two to see or speak to each other. Allowing this will lead to ruin in this world as well as in the Hereafter.

The disastrous consequences of courting that have been reported to our *Daarul Ifta* are too painful to mention here. The harms of courting are sufficiently illustrated by the opinion of expert psychologists who state that if a man's bone and a woman's bone were thrown on an open field, there will be a force of attraction between them. Shaitaan's claim is famous. He said, "If Rabia Basriyya and Hasan Basri were alone together, I will be able to lead them to sin." If he can lead these two great saints astray, what chance do others stand?

Allowing a strange boy to accompany a girl to a place where there is none to watch them is like placing fresh meat in front of a hungry wolf. In such a situation, there is little if no chance at all that the girl will ever be able to protect her chastity. Eventually, the family is embarrassed when the girl falls pregnant. They can then not find anywhere to hide their faces and many parents even subject their daughters to the trauma of an abortion.

It is unfortunate that many foolish girls fail to realise that such behaviour will taint their family's name and smear their honour for generations to come. In addition to this, the ill-effect of their sins remain with the couple well into their marriage. There have been many cases where a boy and girl have been dating for a very long time, sometimes even for years. They would be seen together everywhere and would spend hours on the phone speaking to each other. However, their marriage does not last. People are astonished to learn this and no one can make sense of it. The girl's name is then spoilt for life and no one wants to marry her because they know that her husband has divorced her. We therefore plead to all women not to incur Allah's wrath by courting and dating. They should avoid such relationships like they would avoid snakes and scorpions. If the couple feel that they have to be together, they should be married as quickly as possible. May Allah save every Muslim from perpetrating *Haraam. Aameen*

One should also remember that the engaged couple should not even communicate by telephone because this always goes further. They will eventually meet and become intimate. The couplet has already been quoted earlier where a poet says:

> "A look, a smile, a greeting, a word, a promise
> and ultimately the meeting."

After the couple meet alone it is only a matter of time before they perpetrate the ultimate sin. When one makes a resolution to refrain from sin, Allah assists one all the way.

## NEVER SHAKE HANDS WITH NON-MAHRAM MEN

The intrinsic quality of a good woman is that she never raises her gaze to look at non-*Mahram* men, never greets them and certainly never shakes their hand. It is only when absolutely necessary that she will have to say few words, and then too, the barest minimum. It is most unfortunate that in many parts of the world, Muslim women are forced to shake hands with their husbands' family on the day of Eid. She is also compelled to kiss the hands of these non-*Mahram* men even though she opposes the custom. They are also required to shake and kiss the hands of their cousins and brothers-in-law. Such acts serve only to attract Allah's displeasure and curse.

Women should always bear in mind that a perfect lifestyle can be ruined when Allah is displeased with one just as a ruined lifestyle can be made perfect when Allah is pleased with one.

The situation will arise that when a sensible woman refuses to shake the hands of non-*Mahram* men or when she refuses to speak with them, other members of the family will mock her. However, she should ignore their mockery and make *Du'a* to Allah that He should guide them. She should encourage such women to attend Islãmic programmes for ladies so that they may be inspired to practise the injunctions of the *Shari'ah.* Remember that when Allah's commands are violated, the home will be deprived of love and blessings.

A woman should only try to explain her reasons to women who are willing to understand. If they are not willing, she should rather maintain silence. She should explain to these women that the least harm of shaking hands with non-*Mahram* men is that they will find her hands softer than those of their wives. In addition to this, they may also find her more attractive than their wives, especially when she is dressed up and beautified on the day of Eid and on other occasions. As a result, they will lose interest in their wives and start wishing that they had married her instead. Displeased with their wives, they will start arguments at home and ruin the entire family's life. Therefore, by shaking the hands of non-*Mahram* men, a woman will be doing a great injustice to the wives of these men. Although the act seems good, the consequences are disastrous.

On the other hand, when a woman shakes the hands of these men, she may find them more attractive than her own husband. She may fall for his smile, his perfume or his looks, thereby becoming discontented with her husband. She should also explain to them that such acts incur Allah's wrath and when Allah is displeased with anyone, they can expect only difficulty and hardship. When a woman explains this to those who are mocking her, they will also realise the harms and see the truth.

*Insha* Allah, when a woman convinces others about this and they begin implementing all the injunctions of the *Shari'ah*, she will receive the rewards of all their deeds even after she passes away.

## RASULULLAH ﷺ'S ADVICE TO WOMEN

Addressing a gathering of women, Rasulullah ﷺ said, "O group of women! Spend abundantly in charity (*Sadaqah*) because I have seen that a large number of women are in *Jahannam*." When the women enquired the reason for so many women entering *Jahannam*, Rasulullah ﷺ replied, "Because women curse often and are ungrateful to their husbands." (Muslim)

In this *Hadith*, Rasulullah ﷺ advised women to avoid falling into *Jahannam* by spending abundantly in charity. In another *Hadith*, Rasulullah ﷺ mentioned that *Sadaqah* cools Allah's anger just as water extinguishes fire.

Hazrat A'isha ﷺ narrates that Rasulullah ﷺ once delivered a sermon for the women. He said, "O believing women! Give gifts to each other, even though it may be the hoof of a goat because giving gifts develops love and eliminates enmity." (*Muslim* Vol. 2 Pg. 714)

A Muslim woman should therefore give gifts to the women of her husband's family, even if it means preparing a dish for them. However, her intention should be to please Allah.

## HE EARNS BUT SHE REAPS THE REWARD

Hazrat A'isha ﷺ reports that Rasulullah ﷺ said, "When a woman gives the food in her home as charity without spoiling her act (by ostentation, extravagance, etc), she will receive the rewards of what she spent while her husband will receive the reward for earning it and the treasurer shall have the same reward. The rewards of each of the three shall not diminish because of the rewards of each other." (*Mishkaat* Pg. 72)

According to another *Hadith*, Allah will enter three persons into *Jannah* because of a morsel of food or a handful of dates. The first is the owner of the house (i.e. the husband), the second is the wife who cooked the food and the third is the servant who took the food to the beggar.

Hazrat A'isha ﷺ's sister Hazrat Asma ﷺ asked, "O Rasulullah ﷺ! I have nothing to give in charity except that which my husband Hazrat Zubayr gives me. Rasulullah ﷺ replied, "Spend generously and do not hold back, otherwise provisions will be held back from you."

Ulama have written that giving *Sadaqah* will safeguard a person from *Shaitaan* when he is on his deathbed. It also saves him from uttering words of ingratitude when suffering severe illness and from dying a sudden death. In brief, giving *Sadaqah* ensures a good death. Another *Hadith* states that *Sadaqah* saves one from heat in the grave and that a person will rise on the Day of *Qiyaamah* beneath the shade of his *Sadaqah.*

It has been reported that once, while leading the *Salaatul Kusoof* , Rasulullah ﷺ was shown *Jannah* and *Jahannam.* He noticed that most of the inmates of *Jahannam* were women. When the *Sahabah* رضي الله عنهم asked the reason for this, Rasulullah ﷺ told them that it was because women forget the good done to them and are ungrateful to their husbands. Rasulullah ﷺ also said to them, "If you are good to them (women) all your life and there comes a time when she is upset with you, she will say, 'I have not seen a single good day with you!'" (*Bukhari* and *Muslim*)

This trait that Rasulullah ﷺ described is commonly seen among women. Despite the good treatment many of them enjoy, they are often heard telling their husbands, "I have only experienced hardship since I arrived in this house!" Although this phrase and statements of this nature have become clichés in the female world, they should be avoided.

Because Rasulullah ﷺ saw so many women in *Jahannam,* he did prescribed a solution for the women of his *Ummah.* The solution is to spend generously in charity. It is for this reason that when Rasulullah ﷺ informed the *Sahabiyaat* about this, he took Hazrat Bilaal with him to the place where the women were seated to collect their *Sadaqah* from them. After hearing what Rasulullah ﷺ had to say, the women generously gave away their earrings, necklaces and other jewellery in *Sadaqah.*

It is unfortunate that today's women do not heed the stern warnings mentioned in this *Hadith.* Even if they do, they make their husbands spend on their behalf. It is therefore their husbands who have to give *Zakah* and *Sadaqah* for them. If a woman does spend herself, she often takes the money from her husband rather than use her own wealth. A woman's jewellery may get lost or stolen or she may sell or pawn it to pay for an unnecessary function, but it is very unlikely that she will ever donate it as *Sadaqah* for Allah's pleasure. If nothing of the above occurs, they leave their jewellery behind as inheritance without it being of use to her in the Hereafter. They keep changing their jewellery, having them always remodelled until the value is scarcely what it was because of labour costs. In this manner, they are wasting a great deal of money that could be used in better avenues.

## The Virtues of Sadaqah

The *Hadith* of Rasulullah ﷺ is famous in which he stated, "Save yourselves from *Jahannam* even though it is by means of half a date." Nabi ﷺ has mentioned that *Sadaqah* extinguishes sins just as water extinguishes fire and that every person will rise in the shade of his *Sadaqah* on the Day of *Qiyaamah*. (*Ithaaf*)

According to the amount of *Sadaqah* that a person gives in this life, his shade on the Day of *Qiyaamah* will be correspondingly greater. On the Day of *Qiyaamah*, every person will require shade because the heat will be so intense that many people will be drowning in their own perspiration.

A *Hadith* of "*Mishkaat*" states that *Sadaqah* extinguishes Allah's anger and saves one from a sudden death. A narration in Ihyaa mentions that Hazrat Luqmaan advised his son to give *Sadaqah* whenever he committed a sin. The incident is famous about an immoral woman who was forgiven because she did the charitable act of giving water to a thirsty dog.

Hazrat Abbaad bin Umar (A.R) has mentioned that people will be extremely hungry, thirsty and naked on the Plains of Resurrection. However, Allah will feed those who fed the hungry in this world, He will give drink to those who gave a drink to the thirsty in this world and He will clothe those who gave clothing to the poor in this world. (*Ihyaa*)

According to another narration, the people destined for *Jahannam* will be standing in a row when a pious Muslim destined for *Jannah* will pass by them. Seeing him pass, one of the people headed for *Jahannam* will ask him to intercede on his behalf. Turning to him the pious

Muslim will ask, "Who are you?" "Do you not recognise me?" the person heading for *Jahannam* will ask, "I am the one who gave you water to drink on a certain day." The pious person will then take this person by the hand and plead to Allah saying, "O Allah! I owe this person a favour." Allah will then forgive the person and enter him into *Jannah* as well.

According to another *Hadith*, the people destined for *Jannah* will form rows and the people destined for *Jahannam* will also form rows on the Plains of Resurrection. A person from the row of people headed for *Jahannam* will recognise someone from the row of people headed for Jannah and will call to him, reminding him of a favour he did to him. as a result, the person headed for *Jannah* will take this person by his hand and secure forgiveness for him from Allah.

Rasulullah ﷺ has also mentioned that the following announcement will be made on the Day of *Qiyaamah*: "Where are the poor people from among the *Ummah* of Muhammad ﷺ? Let them rise and search the Plains of Resurrection for anyone who for My sake has given them a morsel of food to eat, a sip of water to drink or a garment to wear. Let them take such people by the hand and lead them to *Jannah*." Consequently, the poor people will identify all such persons and take them along to *Jannah*.

It is therefore necessary for Muslim women to open their hearts and to stop refilling their refrigerators all the time. The least they should do is to give away everything that they do not require, while the best will (of course) be to give to others what one needs for oneself. One should remember that although the food that one selfishly keeps away from the poor will not rot in the refrigerator, it may rot in one's stomach and harm one's health.

## The Harms of Hoarding

When someone once sent a piece of cooked meat as a gift to Hazrat Ummu Salma ﷺ, she kept it aside on a niche in the wall because she knew that Rasulullah ﷺ liked meat. A while later, a beggar came to her door saying, "Give something for Allah's sake. May Allah bless you." The beggar received the reply, "May Allah bless you too," indicating that there was nothing to give him. The beggar therefore left. When Rasulullah ﷺ arrived and asked if there was something to eat, Hazrat Ummu Salma ﷺ sent her servant to get the meat from the niche. However, instead of finding the meat, the servant found only a white stone. When Rasulullah ﷺ was informed about this, he told them that Allah had transformed the meat into a stone because the beggar was denied it.

Commenting on this *Hadith*, Hazrat Sheikhul Hadith (A.R) writes, "This incident teaches us that the food that is not given to the needy and which one refuses to give to them is actually like a stone because instead of giving one the benefit it should, it creates hard-heartedness. Therefore, despite having the food, a person is deprived of its benefits and virtue. This is why we enjoy the many bounties of Allah without receiving their benefits."

People nowadays say that things no longer have the effect and benefits they used to have. This is not because of any fault in the things themselves but because our intentions are no longer sincere.

Every woman should therefore develop the habit of spending generously in charity. This should be done in a manner that the left hand does not know what the right hand gives. Instead of keeping leftover food in the refrigerator, they should give them to the poor. Similarly, it is fruitless to amass wealth in banks when it can benefit others much more. One should remember that anything given to others for Allah's pleasure is regarded as *Sadaqah*, irrespective of how little it is. Whatever one gives to relatives, friends and neighbours are regarded as gifts rather than *Sadaqah*.

Whenever Allah blesses someone with a bounty, the manner of expressing gratitude is to give the old bounty away. For example, when someone gets new clothing, he should give his old clothing away either as a gift or as *Sadaqah* if he will not be needed them any longer. Similarly, if Allah grants one a motorcycle when he has only a bicycle, he should give the bicycle away if he can afford to do so. The same applies if one has a motorcycle and Allah grants him a car.

It is sad that when a person buys a new refrigerator for a few thousands, he prefers selling the old one for a few hundreds or even less instead of giving it away to someone deserving. By giving it away, one will attain tremendous rewards each time someone uses it. One will also attain their invaluable *Du'a*, which could be a means of one's salvation in the Hereafter.

Even more distressing is the fact that many women sell their old clothing and old dishes when they receive something new. Some even go to the extent of selling the empty paint tins they used when painting their homes. Such behaviour is not necessary when Allah has granted these people in abundance. They would earn much more by giving things away to others for Allah's pleasure.

The best way to spend in *Sadaqah* is to clear out your cupboards every week or at least every month. You should then give away everything that you do not need so that whatever Allah has in store for you is not delayed in reaching you because you are retaining what you do not need. When you give something away for Allah's pleasure, Allah replaces it by at least ten fold. Therefore, spending one coin for His pleasure will earn you ten coins and if these ten are also spent for his pleasure, you will earn a minimum of a hundred. In this manner, your wealth will continue increasing.

Think of it like this. Allah has granted you what you have so that you may distribute it. You should keep what you need of it and give the rest to others. If you keep the extras without having any use for it, what reply will you give Allah when you die?

Another excellent manner of earning rewards is to send a bit of what you cook to your neighbour. By doing this, mutual love will grow and you will be rewarded for practising the advice of the *Ahadith*. Rasulullah ﷺ said that a woman should throw extra water into her food so that the gravy is increased and some food can be sent to her neighbours.

According to another *Hadith*, the benefit of this gesture is that love will grow between the neighbours and ill-feelings and malice will be removed from their hearts.

It is not necessary for you to cook a special dish to send to your neighbour. You should send whatever you are cooking for the day, even though it is not a rarity. Of course your intention should be to please Allah, to carry out the advice of Rasulullah ﷺ and to make such a practice common among the *Ummah*. A friend of mine living in Makkah Mukarramah told me that by Allah's grace, he eats meals from three countries every day. Because his one neighbour is Syrian and the other is Indian, he eats what they prepare together with what his wife prepares as an Egyptian. Whatever he eats he sends to his neighbours and they sent to him whatever they are eating. As a result, they all have at least three dishes every day.

Islãm desires that the Muslim society functions like a single family unit. When there is a strong sense of brotherhood among all Muslims in a society and they all have sincere feelings for each other, they will enjoy peace, prosperity, safety and justice. When non-Muslims see such an environment, they will naturally be captivated and this will be a cause for them to accept Islãm.

## THE RIGHTS OF NEIGHBOURS

Giving due regard to the rights of neighbours is exceptionally important for anyone wishing to give their children a sound upbringing. Who are your neighbours?

Your neighbours are everyone living in the forty houses to your right, your left and about your house. Because all these people are you neighbours, there are certain rights that you owe to all of them. This definition of a neighbour is established from a *Hadith* narrated by Hazrat Ka'b bin Maalik t, which Imaam Tabraani (A.R) has reported in his book. Hazrat Ka'b bin Maalik ﷺ says that a person once complained to Rasulullah ﷺ that the people closest to him in his neighbourhood are the ones who cause him the most difficulty. Rasulullah ﷺ immediately instructed Hazrat Abu Bakr ﷺ and Hazrat Umar ﷺ to stand at the doors of the *Masjid* and announce that a neighbour extends up to forty houses away and that a person will not enter *Jannah* if his neighbours are not safe from his evil.

There are four basic principles concerning the rights of neighbours are as follows:

1) One should not cause any harm or difficulty to one's neighbour.
2) One should protect one's neighbour from people who may harm him.
3) One should be friendly towards one's neighbour.
4) One should repay his rudeness and bad manners with tolerance and good conduct.

## Behaviour with One's Neighbours

The ground rules governing one's behaviour with one's neighbours have been outlined in a *Hadith* which Khir'ati and Tabraani have reported from Hazrat Abdullaah bin Umar ﷺ. He says that Rasulullah ﷺ said, "That person is not a proper Mu'min who closes the doors of his home to his neighbours and the one whose neighbours are not safe from his evil is also not a true Mu'min. Do you know what the rights of your neighbours are?

- You should help him when he requests your help.
- You should grant him a loan if he asks you for one.
- You should visit him when he is ill.
- You should grant him what he needs.
- You should console him in his grief.
- You should attend his funeral when he passes away.
- You should not build your house higher than his without his permission.
- You should not cause difficulty for him with the steam of your cooking unless you intend giving him a share of it.
- You should give him a share in the fruit you buy. If you cannot afford this, take the fruit secretly into your house and do not allow your child to eat the fruit outside where the neighbour's child may see.

Rasulullah ﷺ has also counted good behaviour towards one's neighbours as one of the traits of Imaan. Rasulullah ﷺ said, "A one who believes in Allah and the Last Day ought to honour his neighbour." (*Bukhari* & *Muslim*)

## A Good Neighbour

Hazrat Abdullaah bin Mubaarak (A.R) had a Jewish neighbour whom he treated so well that when the Jew put his house up for sale, he fixed a price of two thousand Dinaars (gold coins). When people complained that his house was only worth a thousand Dinaars, he told them that while a thousand Dinaars were for the house, the other thousand were for the honour of having a wonderful neighbour like Hazrat Abdullaah bin Mubaarak (A.R).

A good neighbour is a great treasure. To create a good neighbourhood, we should present an excellent example. If our neighbour is a non-Muslim, we should display the proper Islãmic character so that the neighbour will be encouraged to accept Islãm. On the other hand, if we are fortunate enough to have a Muslim neighbour, we should make an effort to ensure that the neighbour's entire family becomes pious and righteous Muslims. We should therefore never allow our neighbour to leave our house without hearing some story or lesson in Islãm. In fact, as Muslims our concern should be that every person throughout the world become righteous and practising Muslims.

## Observing Hijaab in Front of Neighbours

There are two important factors to always bear in mind when associating with one's neighbours. Failure to observe these will lead to disastrous consequences for either family. These are as follows:

1. Ensure that there is no contact between the females of your home and the males of your neighbour's home and vice versa. Even your neighbour's twelve-year old son should not enter your home without permission. In fact, children of the opposite gender should not be allowed to play together. When neighbours get friendly and discard the laws of *Hijaab*, *Shaitaan* quickly manipulates the situation and involves them in sin.
2. Take every precaution to ensure that your children do not involve themselves in *Haraam* activities while visiting the neighbours. One such evil is the television. Explain to your children that they should avoid this evil which pollutes society with the immorality of the west that it vomits out. The television is one of the primary causes for the cancer of licentious and indecency that is contaminating society. You should neither have a television in your own home nor should you allow your children to watch television at the homes of others. If your neighbour is the cause of corroding the moral and religious fibre of your family, you will then have to restrict your interaction with her and make *Du'a* to Allah to guide her.

## A WIFE WITH SALAAH

Hazrat Abu Hurairah ﷺ narrates that Rasulullah ﷺ said, "If a woman performs her five daily *Salaah*, fasts during Ramzaan, safeguards her chastity and obeys her husband, she will have a choice of entering *Jannah* from whichever door she pleases." ("*Mishkaat*" Pg. 281)

Among the qualities that take a woman to *Jannah*, Rasulullah ﷺ has listed *Salaah* as the first priority. When a woman hears the *Mu'azzin* calling, "*Hayya Alas Salaah*" ("Come to *Salaah*") and "*Hayya Alal Falaah*" ("Come to success"), she should immediately convince herself that her success lies in performing *Salaah* and in nothing else. She should therefore terminate every activity and prepare for *Salaah*. Delaying the *Salaah* to complete what she is doing will make the task more difficult and cause it to be prolonged. Experience has proven this. When a woman tells herself that she will perform her *Salaah* as soon as she completes the task, she ends up delaying the *Salaah* for a long time until she eventually performs it during the Makrooh times. She is therefore deprived of the blessings of her *Salaah* and also becomes guilty of a sin.

Every woman should therefore make a resolution to perform her *Salaah* as soon as the *Azaan* is called out so that she can perform it with proper composure and concentration. She should remember that the *Du'as* made after such a *Salaah* is readily accepted and that the *Salaah* performed on time is most beloved to Allah. The *Ahadith* tell us that a *Du'a* is accepted with every *Farz Salaah* that a person performs. It is really strange that Muslims should have problems when Allah has granted them *Salaah* as a solution to all their problems. When a Muslim performs her *Salaah* properly, she will need no *Ta'weez* or special holy waters. If a woman is experiences with her husband or her in-laws, she should make *Du'a* to Allah to soften their hearts and to mend their relations.

It should also be remembered that neglecting one's *Salaah* is a tremendous loss and the Muslim who neglects her *Salaah* will be raised with the *Kuffaar* on the Day of *Qiyaamah.*

## Stealing From One's *Salaah*

Rasulullah ﷺ said, "The worst thief is the one who steals from his *Salaah.*" Astonished, the *Sahabah* رضي الله عنهم asked, "O Rasulullah ﷺ! How can a person steal from his *Salaah?*" Rasulullah ﷺ replied, "By not performing *Ruku* and *Sajdah* properly." (*Daarmi*)

There are several *Ahadith* concerning this matter. Stealing is a dishonourable act and people look down on someone who steals. Apart from this, Rasulullah ﷺ added that the person who steals from his *Salaah* is not merely a thief like other thieves, but he is the worst of all thieves. One can therefore imagine the gravity of sin.

According to another *Hadith,* Allah does not even pay any attention to the *Salaah* in which *Ruku* and *Sajdah* are not performed properly. Yet another *Hadith* states, "A person can be performing *Salaah* for sixty years without a single *Salaah* being accepted because when he sometimes perform *Ruku* properly, his *Sajdah* is not proper and when he performs *Sajdah* properly, his *Ruku* is improper."

The great reformer, Hazrat Mujaddid Alf Thaani (A.R) had written many letters emphasising the importance of

*Salaah*. In one of these letters, he writes, "It is extremely important to ensure that the fingers of each hand are kept together in *Sajdah* and that they are apart during *Ruku*. The injunctions of the *Shari'ah* to keep the fingers together and apart are not without good reason. It is therefore very necessary to observe them even though they seem insignificant." He states further, "When standing in *Salaah*, the gaze should be fixed to the place of *Sajdah*; when performing *Ruku*, it should be fixed on the feet; in *Sajdah*, it should be focussed to the nose and when sitting, it should be directed to the hands. By doing this, humility and concentration will be developed in *Salaah*. When even these seemingly minor etiquette hold such great importance, one can well imagine how much benefit there is in the more major etiquette and the *Sunnah* of *Salaah*."

## Other Deficiencies in Our *Salaah*

It is sad to note that while many sisters are performing their *Salaah*, they rush with the *Ruku* and *Sajdah*. They therefore fail to maintain composure during these two postures whereas composure during all postures of *Salaah* is *Waajib*. In fact, according to certain *Ulama*, this composure is *Farz* and *Salaah* will be nullified without it. It is therefore necessary to keep the following factors in mind when performing *Salaah* so that your *Salaah* can be counted perfect one:

1. Recite *Surah Faatiha* slowly, ensuring that you pause after every verse. The other *Surahs* should also be recited slowly.

2. Recite the *Tasbeeh* of *Ruku* ("*Subhaana Rabbiyal Azeem*") slowly at least three times. If possible, it is advisable to recite it five, nine, eleven or twenty-one times. The more you recite, the better it is.
3. After getting up from *Ruku*, slowly recite:

سَمِعَ اللهُ لِمَنْ حَمِدَهُ رَبَّنَا لَكَ الْحَمْدُ

Thereafter, recite:

رَبَّنَا وَلَكَ الْحَمْدُ حَمْدًا كَثِيْرًا طَيِّبًا مُبَارَكًا فِيْهِ

One may also recite:

— اَللّٰهُمَّ رَبَّنَا لَكَ الْحَمْدُ مِلأَ السَّمٰوٰتِ وَمِلأَ الْأَرْضِ وَمِلْأَ مَا شِئْتَ مِنْ شَيْءٍ بَعْدَ

By reciting any of these *Du'as*, the requirement of composure will be met.

4. In *Sajdah*, recite the *Tasbeeh* of *Sajdah* ("*Subhaana Rabbiyal A'la*") at least thrice. Of course, it is best to recite it several times in odd numbers.
5. When sitting in the posture between the two *Sajdahs* (called *Jalsa*), you should at least recite:

اَللّٰهُمَّ اغْفِرْلِىْ

However, it is best to recite:

اَللّٰهُمَّ اغْفِرْلِىْ وَارْحَمْنِىْ وَاجْبُرْنِىْ وَاهْدِنِىْ وَارْزُقْنِىْ

By reciting these *Du'as*, composure will be achieved in the Jalsa posture as well. You should try to learn these *Du'as*, which appear in the book "*Hisnul Haseen*".

6. It often occurs that while many women regularly perform their *Salaah*, they delay its performance. *Shaitaan* deludes them into thinking that they can perform their *Salaah* at leisure after first finishing what they are doing. However, they become engrossed in their activity and manage to perform their *Salaah* when the time has almost expired. Many women end up perform *Zuhr* during the time of *Asr* and Asr during the time of *Maghrib*. A woman should perform all her *Salaah*s as soon as the *Azaan* is called out.

You should therefore ensure that you do not deprive yourself of the full reward of your *Salaah*. Perform your *Salaah* on time and at a leisurely pace. Performing *Salaah* properly and on time will earn Allah's pleasure and *Du'as* after such *Salaah* is more likely to be accepted. This is therefore the best manner to have all your problems solved.

Many new brides are shy to perform their *Salaah* during the early days of their marriage. However this is the time when she should be especially particular about her *Salaah* because this is the beginning of a new life for her. It is rather those women who do not perform their *Salaah* who should be ashamed.

7. Many women fail to perform their *Salaah* immediately after completing their menstruation cycle, thereby missing a few *Salaah*s in the process. It is necessary that a woman begins to perform her *Salaah* as soon as she discovers that her menses are complete. However, if the bleeding stops before three

days, it is preferable for her to wait until the final hours of the *Salaah* time before taking a bath and performing her *Salaah.* If three days are over but she has not yet completed her habitual cycle, it is also *Mustahab* (preferable) for her to wait until the closing hours of the *Salaah* before taking a bath and performing the *Salaah.* However, the ruling regarding the permissibility of intercourse during this period is a different question. Nevertheless, it is not permissible for a woman to miss any *Salaah* after discovering that her menstruation cycle has ended. Every woman should refer to the books of Islãmic *Fiqh* for the details of the rulings pertaining to menstruation.

8. Many women wrongly wait for forty days after childbirth before performing *Salaah* even though they have stopped bleeding after three days. This practice is incorrect because as soon as a woman stops bleeding after childbirth, she should take a bath and start performing *Salaah* immediately, even though she has bled for a period less than forty days. If a woman missed any *Salaah*s in this manner, she has to perform the *Qadhaa* for all of them.

9. Every woman should do her best to learn to recite the Qur'ãn correctly. Even though a woman may not be able to perfect her recitation until she dies, she will Insha Allah be resurrected with those who recited the Qur'ãn properly if she sustained the effort to learn proper recitation throughout her life. She

should be able to distinguish between the letters ḥ (ح) and h (ه), s (س) and th (ث), q (ق) and k (ك) etc. It is necessary to practise the pronunciation of these letters with some learned *Mahram* or lady. This is absolutely important because if the letters are not pronounced correctly, the meaning of the Qur'ãn will be distorted.

One should also demonstrate one's *Salaah* to a knowledgeable lady or a Mahram so that one's *Salaah* can be corrected if there are any failings. One should also read books concerning the *Salaah* of a female so that one's *Salaah* becomes like the *Salaah* that Rasulullah ﷺ taught the *Ummah*.

10. It is unfortunate that many women fail to perform the *Qadhaa Salaah* of the many *Salaah*s that they miss after their menstrual period by their delay in taking a bath. If a woman is conscious about the ruling pertaining to menstruation and if she is careful, she will not have to miss any *Salaah*. If she still does miss any of her *Salaah*, she should ensure that she performs the *Qazaa* immediately.

In addition to performing one's own *Salaah*, one should ensure that one's daughters who are more than seven years of age also perform their *Salaah* regularly. If one has sons of this age, one should send them to the *Masjid* to perform their *Salaah*s with *Jamaa'at*. One should also have a deep concern that one's servants and employees perform their *Salaah* regularly. There should not be a soul in one's home who neglects his/her *Salaah*. At the same time, one should make sincere *Du'a* to Allah that He should guide every Muslim on earth to perform *Salaah* regularly and correctly.

One should not neglect reciting books of *Ahadith* like "*Fadhaa'il-e-A'maal*", "*Riyaadh-us-Saaliheen*" , etc to the entire family. This should be done on a daily basis so that their family can be encouraged to carry out good deeds and to adhere to all the practices of *Deen*. Of course, non-Mahram men and women should be allowed to sit together.

The guidelines pertaining to *Salaah* mentioned above have been extracted from the book "*Islaahul Khawateen*" by Hakeemul Ummah Maulana Ashraf Ali Thanwi (A.R). Every woman should make an attempt to read this valuable book.

We shall now quote two incidents from the book "*Fadhaa'il-e-Sadaqaat*" to illustrate the attachment that women of the past had with *Salaah*.

*A.* It has been reported that after performing her Isha *Salaah*, Hazrat Habeeba Adawiyya (A.R) would wrap herself properly and stand on the roof of her home to make *Du'a*. She would say, "O Allah! The stars have hidden themselves and people have gone to bed. The kings have all closed their doors and people are in solitude with their loved ones. I am now standing before You." She would then perform *Salaah* the entire night until dawn.

When dawn broke, she would make *Du'a* to Allah saying, "O Allah! The night has departed and the day has arrived. I wish I knew whether You have accepted my night's worship so that I may congratulate myself, or whether You have rejected it so that I may sympathise with myself. I swear by Your honour that if You have to shove me away from Your door, I would never leave it because I am well aware of Your extreme munificence."

*B.* Hazrat Ujra (A.R) was a blind woman who used to spend the entire night awake in *Ibaadah*. She would be extremely grieved when the night drew to a close and would say, "O Allah! Your group of worshippers have spent the hours of darkness running towards You. They have been racing with each other to acquire Your mercy and forgiveness. O Allah! I am begging from You only and have none but You to ask. I beseech You to admit me to the ranks of earliest stalwarts of Islãm, to include my record of deeds among those of the highest status and to join me with those who are extremely close to You. You are truly the Most Merciful of those who show mercy, the Highest of all those who have position and the most generous of all those who show generosity. O the Most Kind, shower Your kindness on me." She would then fall into prostration, weep profusely and make *Du'a* until dawn broke.

## THE SALAAH OF A WOMAN

You must keep the following guidelines in mind when performing *Salaah.*

1. You must ensure that you face the Qibla.
2. stand up straight and keep your gazes fixed on the place of *Sajdah.* It is *Makrooh* to stand with the head bent forward in a manner that the chin rests on the chest. It is also incorrect to unnecessarily bend the back.
3. Your toes should also face towards the Qibla. Facing the toes of the right foot towards the right and those of the left foot towards the left is contrary to the *Sunnah.*
4. Maintain a space of approximately four fingers (breadth-wise) between the feet.
5. Wear a large shawl which covers the entire body from head to feet. Of course, the shawl should not be made of thin material. It is permissible for the face, feet and hands (up to the wrist) to remain uncovered because *Salaah* will be correct whether they remain covered or uncovered.
6. *Salaah* will be invalid if you perform *Salaah* wearing garments through which the body is visible or which do not conceal the entire body.
7. If during the course of your *Salaah* a quarter of any part of your body (besides the face, hands and feet) becomes exposed for the duration in which "*Subhaana Rabbiyal Azeem*" can be recited thrice,

your *Salaah* will be invalid. If it is exposed for a duration less than this, the *Salaah* will be valid but you will be guilty of a sin.

8. It is *Makrooh* to perform *Salaah* wearing clothes that one will not wear in front of people because it is extremely disrespectful for one to appear before the King of all kings wearing clothing that one is ashamed to wear in front of ordinary mortals.

## When Commencing Salaah

1. Have the intention within your heart that you are performing the *Salaah* in question. There will be no harm done if the intention is not recited verbally.
2. Facing the palms towards the Qibla and the fingers up to the sky, raise the hands to the shoulders without taking them out of your head covering. A woman does not raise the hands up to the earlobes as men do.
3. While raising the hands in the above manner, say "Allahu *Akbar*" and then place the left hand on your chest with the right palm on top of the back of your left hand. Unlike men, a woman will not grasp the wrist of the left hand with the thumb and little finger of the right hand, neither will she fold her hands beneath the navel as men do. This action of saying "Allahu *Akbar*" while raising the hands is called *Takbeer Tahreema*.

## When Standing Upright

1. The standing posture after the *Takbeer Tahreema* is called *Qiyaam*. When performing *Salaah* by yourself,[1] first recite the *Sana* followed by "*A'oodhu Billaahi Minash* Shaitaanir Rajeem" and "*Bismillaahir Rahmaan nir Raheem*". Thereafter recite *Surah* Faatiha, adding the word "Aameen" immediately after saying "*Wa Lad Daaleen.*" Then recite "*Bismillaahir Rahmaan nir Raheem*" and any *Surah* of the Qur'ãn or at least three verses of any *Surah*.
2. If you happen to be following an *Imaam* in *Salaah*, you should recite only the *Sana* and then listen to his recitation of the Qur'ãn. If the Imaam is not reciting loudly, then concentrate on the meaning of *Surah* Faatiha without reciting it.
3. When reciting *Surah Faatiha*, pause after reciting every verse instead of reciting many verses with a single breath. However, when reciting the *Surah*s after *Surah* Faatiha, there is no harm in reciting many verses with a single breath. A woman should recite silently in all *Salaah*s.
4. Do not move any limb of the body unnecessarily. Remain as still as possible during *Salaah*. You may only scratch a part of your body when the itch is unbearable and when only one hand is used.

---

1. It is *Makrooh* for a group of women to perform *Salaah* together in congregation. However, there is no harm if the women of a household perform *Salaah* behind a man who is their *Mahram*. In such a case, the women should all stand behind him and not beside him.

5. It is wrong to rest the weight of the body on one leg while the other bends. You may either apply your weight equally to both legs or if you need to take weight off one leg, do so in a manner that the other leg does not bend.
6. Do your best to suppress a yawn. If this is not possible, cover your mouth with your hand.
7. To avoid looking about while standing, you should fix your gaze to the place of *Sajdah*.

## When in *Ruku*

1. After completing the recitation of a *Surah* in *Qiyaam*, say "*Allahu Akbar*" and proceed to bow in *Ruku*. Commence saying "*Allahu Akbar*" as soon as you start bowing down and complete it once you have settled into the *Ruku* position.
2. A woman should bow down only until her hands reach her knees and not completely as men do.
3. While in *Ruku*, a woman should keep her fingers tightly together and not spread them out widely as men do. She should also bend her knees slightly forward and keep her elbows against her sides.
4. Remain in *Ruku* for as long as it takes to recite the Tasbeeh of *Ruku* (viz. "*Subhaana Rabbiyal Azeem*") slowly at least three times. If possible, it is advisable to recite it five times, seven times, nine times, eleven times, etc in odd numbers. The more you recite, the better it is.

5. Fix your gaze on your feet while in *Ruku.*
6. Balance your weight equally on both legs without leaning on one side.

## Getting Up from *Ruku*

1. After *Ruku,* stand up completely straight with each joint in place. This posture is called *Qaumah.*
2. Keep your gaze still fixed on the place of *Sajdah.*
3. It is noticed that when rising from *Ruku,* many people do not stand upright and keep their backs bent forward before proceeding into *Sajdah.* When one does this, the *Salaah* has to be repeated. It is therefore imperative that a person exercises composure during the *Qaumah* posture.
4. You should at least stand for the duration in which you can comfortably recite

رَبَّنَا لَكَ الْحَمْدُ ـ

However, it is best to recite:

رَبَّنَآ وَلَكَ الْحَمْدُ حَمْدًا كَثِيْرًا طَيِّبًا مُبَارَكًا فِيْهِ

You may also recite:

اَللّٰهُمَّ رَبَّنَا لَكَ الْحَمْدُ مِلأَ السَّمٰوَاتِ وَمِلأَ الْأَرْضِ وَمِلْأَ مَا شِئْتَ مِنْ شَيْءٍ بَعْدَ

By reciting any of these *Du'as,* the requirement of composure will be met and you will be amply rewarded.

## When in Sajdah

1. When proceeding from *Qaumah* into *Sajdah*, bend the chest forward and first place the knees on the ground. Thereafter, place the hands on the ground, followed by the nose and finally the forehead.
2. A woman in *Sajdah* should keep her body compressed in a manner that her thighs are against her stomach and her arms are against her sides. Instead of keeping her feet upright in *Sajdah* as men do, a woman should extend her feet towards her right, keeping them horizontally on the ground. If possible, she should try to face her toes towards the *Qibla*.
3. In *Sajdah*, recite the Tasbeeh of *Sajdah* ("*Subhaana Rabbiyal A'la*") at least thrice. Of course, it is best to recite it several times in odd numbers. It is not permissible to raise the head out of *Sajdah* immediately after putting the forehead on the ground. During *Nafl Salaah*, you may recite the longer *Du'as* of *Sajdah* that have been reported in the *Ahadith*. These can be learnt from the book Hisnul Haseen. The easiest of these is "*Rabbigh Firli*" ("O my Rabb, forgive me"), which should be recited thrice.

## Sitting between Sajood

1. After completing one *Sajdah*, one should sit upright for a while before proceeding into the next *Sajdah*. This sitting posture between the two *Sajdah*s is called

*Jalsa*. It is sinful to hasten this posture by not sitting upright. Your *Salaah* will have to be repeated if you do not sit up straight in the *Jalsa* position.

2. After getting up from *Sajdah*, a woman should sit on her left buttock and extend both feet towards her right, keeping the right calf on top of the left calf. The feet should be spread horizontally on the ground. The hands should be on the thighs with the fingers kept tightly together.
3. Your gaze should be on your lap while sitting.
4. You should sit in the *Jalsa* posture for the duration of at least one *Tasbeeh* (i.e. for as long as it takes to recite "*Subhaa Nallah*" once). However, it is best to recite:

{Translation: "O Allah! Forgive me, have mercy on me, grant me safety and good health, guide me, provide for me, compensate for my shortcomings and elevate my status."}

## The Second Sajdah

1. Just as the first *Sajdah*, in the second *Sajdah*, you should also first place the knees on the ground, followed by the hands, the nose and finally the forehead.
2. The second *Sajdah* should be performed just like the first.
3. When rising from *Sajdah*, first lift the forehead off the ground, followed by the nose, the hands and then the knees.

4. One should not use the hands to lift oneself from *Sajdah* into a standing position unless one is overweight or ill.
5. Recite "*Bismillaahir Rahmaan nir Raheem*" before *Surah Faatiha* during every Rakaah.

## In Qa'edah

1. Every sitting posture in *Salaah* besides the *Jalsa* is called *Qa'dah.* The method of sitting in the *Qa'dah* posture is the same as the method of sitting in *Jalsa.*
2. While reciting the *Tashahhud*, raise the index finger of the right hand when you reach the part "*Ash Hadu An la Ilaha*" and then drop it when saying "*Illallaahu*".
3. When raising the index finger, the middle finger and thumb should form a ring while the little finger and the one next to it remain curled. When raising the index finger, do not point it towards the sky, but towards the Qibla.
4. When dropping the index finger as you say "*Illallaahu*", keep the other fingers in the position mentioned above. This position should be maintained up to the end of the *Salaah.*

## When ending the Salaah with Salaam

1. When saying "*As Salaamu Alaykum wa Rahmat-ullaah*" and turning the face to either side, you should turn your face so that someone behind you, can see your cheeks.

2. Fix your gaze on your shoulders when turning your head and make the intention that you are greeting all the angels on your right as you turn right and all those on your left as you turn left.

The above is merely a brief discussion of a woman's *Salaah.* Refer to books like *Behishti Zewar* and others for the detailed method of performing *Salaah* and the various *Du'as* to be recited during *Salaah.*

## MAKING *Du'a*

### The Method of Making *Du'a*

1. When making *Du'a,* raise the hands to the level of your breast. There should be a small space between your hands so that the hands are neither touching each other nor very far apart.
2. While making *Du'a,* you should be looking at your palms.

### *Du'a* After the Farz Salaah

1. Be particular about making *Du'a* after every *Farz Salaah* because *Du'as* are readily accepted after the Farz *Salaah.*
2. Begin the *Du'a* by first praising Allah profusely. Thereafter, recite Durcod followed by *Du'a* for yourself, your family, the people of your community and for all the Muslims in the world. Make *Du'a* that Allah guides the non-Muslims to Islãm and that

Allah grants safety and comfort to all suffering Muslims.

3. You should spend at least twenty minutes daily making *Du'a*. If you are unable to make *Du'a* for twenty consecutive minutes, distribute this time throughout the day. For example, you may make *Du'a* for five minutes after *Fajr*, five minutes after *Asr* and for ten minutes after *Isha*. If Allah grants you the ability to perform *Tahajjud Salaah*, do not pass up this opportunity to engage in *Du'a*. It is indeed tragic that people have hours to spend in idle chatter and hours to spend in preparing for wedding receptions and other functions, yet they cannot spare twenty minutes to beg from their Most Merciful *Rabb*. They fail to realise that even if they get tired of asking from Allah, He is so Generous that He never tires of giving. Whereas people become angry when you keep asking from them, Allah gets pleased as you ask more from Him. You should therefore force yourself to make *Du'a* for at least twenty minutes until you form a habit of making lengthy *Du'as*.

4. Make a firm resolution that you will not ask from none besides Allah, not even from your husband, brothers or father. Remember that everyone is dependent on Allah and whatever people have with them has given by Allah. In fact, even if you are thirsty, first ask Allah to quench your thirst before drinking water because the water will be able to slake

thirst only by Allah's command. Ask your every desire from Allah, even while walking about.

## An Excellent Du'a For Every Woman

{Translation: "O Allah! Bless me with splendid character, excellent deeds and fantastic speech because none but You can guide anyone to the best of this. Keep me distant from the evil of all this (i.e. from evil character, evil deeds and evil speech) because none but You can safeguard me from the evil of these things."}

If one is unable to memorise the Arabic *Du'a*, it can be made in any language as well.

## Du'a for a Good Partner

When a boy or girl comes of age, the parents, elder brothers and sisters and other family members should encourage him/her to make *Du'a* for a good partner so that life will be pleasant and comfortable. Allah has mentioned this *Du'a* in the Qur'ãn to convey the message to people that this is the *Du'a* that they should present in His court. This *Du'a* is therefore very likely to be accepted. The *Du'a* is:

(Translation: **"O our Rabb! Accord to us the coolness of our eyes from our spouses and children, and make us leaders of the pious (i.e. make our families pious)."**

(*Surah Furqan, Surah* 25, verse74)

This *Du'a* should be made throughout one's life, even after marriage. In addition to this, a woman may make other specific *Du'as.* For example, she may say, "O Allah! Grant me a husband who practises *Deen* completely and who will assist me to do the same. Make him a soft-hearted person who will appreciate and honour me. Grant us pious children and make us among Your chosen slaves who have a fervour for *Jihaad* and who are a means of spreading Your *Deen* throughout the world. Make him a person whose love for You is deeply entrenched in his heart, whose *Imaan* is unshakeable and who places the love for Your Rasul ﷺ and the *Sahabah* رضي الله عنهم before his love for all other mortals. He should be a person who is averse to the pleasures of this world and whose attention is focussed on the life of the *Aakhirah.* O Allah! Make him a source of delight, comfort and support for me. Aameen."

Another effective *Du'a* is to recite *Durood* followed by the following *Du'a* and again *Durood* afterwards. The *Du'a* is:

> (Translation: "O the Greatest Giver! Grant me a pious husband.")

Because association with other women is often the cause of problems, it is also necessary for a woman to make *Du'a* to Allah to save her from such problems. For example, she may say, "O Allah! Grant me a comfortable home from my husband's *Halaal* earnings where I will be able to eat in peace and happily express my gratitude to You. Save me from homes where I shall have to face disputes with my in-laws every day. O Allah! If I have to serve my in-laws, ease the task for me and create the means for me to be able to cook by myself without anyone interfering in my affairs. Make me a good daughter-in-law and grant me a mother-in-law who will appreciate my services and who will ignore the backbiting and slander that others direct at me. O Allah! Grant me a home where I shall be able to easily observe *Hijaab* from all brothers-in-law and other non-*Mahram* men. Save me from homes that you have cursed because of the presence of a television or pictures of animate beings. Grant me a home in which I will be able to avoid all major and minor sins and in which I will be instrumental in spreading the *Deen*. Also grant me the wisdom and diplomacy to be able to save others and myself from sin."

## The *Du'a* after Marriage

Together with the *Du'as* already mentioned, every bride and to be bride should recite the following *Du'as*:

1) {Translation: "O Allah! Create between me and him the love that You created between Hazrat Muhammad ﷺ and Hazrat Khadija رضي الله عنها. O Allah! Create between us the love that You created between Hazrat Muhammad ﷺ and Hazrat A'isha رضي الله عنها."}

2. {Translation: "O Allah! Join my husband and me in *Jannah* as You have joined us in this world."}

3. {Translation: O Allah! Make me a delight to my husband's eyes in this world as well as in the *Aakhirah*."}

4. {Translation: O Allah! Make me a wife who assists her husband in his faith."}

5. {Translation: O Allah! Make me a wife who obeys You as well as my husband. Make me a pious wife, one who pleases her husband when he looks her and one who safeguards her chastity as well as his possessions and children in his absence."}

Recite the above *Du'as* after every *Farz Salaah* as well as at the time of *Tahajjud.* Make these and other *Du'as* at all times, especially when terminating your fast during the month of *Ramzaan* and at the sanctified places when performing *Hajj* or *Umrah.* If Allah grants these bounties to a woman, she and her family will enjoy blissful lives in this world as well as in the *Aakhirah.*

## Du'as for Protection From an Evil Husband and an Cruel Mother-in-law

Every girl and her parents should always make *Du'a* to Allah to safeguard her from an unkind husband, a cruel mother-in-law and an unpleasant family of in-laws. They should also make *Du'a* to Allah to grant her steadfastness in *Deen, Halaal* sustenance and everything she requires. The following *Du'as* are also very beneficial:

{Translation: "O Allah! I seek Your protection from every plotting friend whose eyes are always watching me and whose heart is always occupied with thinking of me (in search of my faults); who buries any good he sees in me and publicises any evil he sees in me."}

{Translation: "O Allah! I seek Your protection from a husband who may cause harm to befall me."}

{Translation: "O Allah! I seek Your protection from every woman (mother-in-law, sister-in-law) who may cause harm to befall me."}

{Translation: "O Allah! Because of my sins do not allow any such person (husband) to govern me who will have no fear for You in matters concerning me and who will not have mercy on me."}

Besides the above *Du'as*, the *Ahadith* have reported many other *Du'as* that are effective to secure a good and pious husband as well as good children. There is no good *Du'a* that Rasulullah ﷺ has not taught the *Ummah* and there is nothing harmful from which he has not taught us a *Du'a* to secure protection. May Allah grant him the highest positions and may He grant us the ability to make all these *Du'as. Aameen.*

These *Du'as* are extremely valuable because they are like a formatted request that a king's chief minister gives to the subjects of a country, the approval of which is guaranteed. Every woman should also include the recitation of a part of "*Munaajaate Maqbool*" or "*Hizbul A'zam*" into her daily routine because the *Du'as* mentioned in these books are extremely beneficial. Also very useful are the books "*Dharee'atul Wusool ilaa Janaabir Rasul* ﷺ" and "*Sattar Istighfaar ki Du'ae*", which one should try to read daily as well. If Muslim women read a part of these books daily and sincerely make the *Du'as* mentioned in them, Muslim homes will be enveloped in Allah's mercy and the children of these homes will Insha Allah become shining stars of Islãm.

## Waking Up at Night to Make *Du'a*

The best formula for creating love between a couple is that each of them should constantly make *Du'a* to Allah to strengthen their love. By doing this, they will soon notice that their bond will cement in a short while. Just as mortar is needed to join two bricks and glue is required to attach two pieces of paper, Allah's special grace is needed to join two hearts. The external factor needed to acquire this grace is the wife's obedience. She should do whatever her husband asks her to do (provided that his requests do not contradict the *Shari'ah*) and should apologise for anything that she does against his wishes. This should be done even though it appears to her that he is at fault. In addition to this external factor, the internal factor is also required. The internal factor is the fundamental aspect of *Du'a* both the husband and the wife should make with open and sincere hearts.

When making *Du'a* for your husband, think that he is after all the servant of Allah and a member of Rasulullah ﷺ's *Ummah*. If he is an ill-tempered man, he will only make life miserable for another woman if you leave him. However, if you makes *Du'a* to Allah, Allah will transform him into a gentle and loving man. Make *Du'a* to Allah after every *Farz*

*Salaah* and also wake up to make *Du'a* during the late hours of the night when others are asleep. After performing at least two *Rakaahs Tahajjud Salaah*, cry to Allah to guide your husband and the husband of every Muslim woman. We shall now quote the *Du'a* that a saint used to make to Allah during the still hours of the night.

{Translation: "O My Allah! The kings and sovereigns have all locked their doors, but Yours are still open for beggars.

O My Allah! The stars have disappeared and people are fast asleep. You are the Living One, the One Who Maintains everything. Neither does slumber nor sleep touch You.

O My Allah! Beds have been laid out and every lover is alone with his beloved. However, You are the beloved of those who exert themselves in *Ibaadah* and You are the companion of those in fear.

O My Allah! If You choose to punish me, I certainly deserve the punishment and if You forgive me then You are undoubtedly Munificent and Forgiving.

O My Allah! If You chase me away from Your door, at whose door shall I find refuge and if You do not accept me for Your service, of what use shall I be? O the Most Forgiving, allow me to taste the coolness of Your clemency and the sweetness of Your mercy even though I am not worthy of it. You are the only One who can rightfully be feared and the Only One from Whom forgiveness can be sought."}

After making this *Du'a*, make *Du'a* for your husband, your children, your family and for all the Muslims in the world. Experience has shown that *Du'as* are quickly accepted when one has conviction that they will be accepted. Another excellent *Du'a* to make is:

> {Translation: O Allah! Make us both (husband and wife) people who hearken to Your commands and who obey You. Make us sincere friends to each other and close companions."}

## TEN PRACTICES OF RASULULLAH ﷺ

Rasulullah ﷺ was a mercy to both men and women. By implementing the *Sunnah* practices of Rasulullah ﷺ, a person's home will be filled with Allah's mercy. As a result of this mercy, love will grow between the members of the household and each person will also develop the love for Allah and His Rasul ﷺ. Once the love for Allah and His Rasul ﷺ has permeated a person's heart, he will give precedence to the *Deen* over everyone else. Their hearts will harbour no malice for others because all they will concern themselves with will be pleasing Allah. They will do anything and everything in their power to ensure that Allah is pleased with them regardless of what people say or think.

It is therefore necessary for every woman to learn about the *Sunnah* practices of Rasulullah ﷺ and apply these to her life. Before doing anything, she should ponder how Rasulullah ﷺ did the same thing and emulate his manner of doing it. Every deed and every statement of Rasulullah ﷺ should be more valuable to a Muslim than that of any other person or nation. Regardless of what a Muslim has to lose in the process, he will be prepared for the loss rather than compromise on the *Sunnah* of Rasulullah ﷺ.

We shall now present some Sunnah practices of Rasulullah ﷺ so that every reader can introduce them to her life. By doing this, she will also attain the pleasure of Allah.

1. Brush your teeth regularly with a *Miswaak*, especially when making *Wudhu* for every *Salaah*, before and after eating, at the time of *Tahajjud*, before reciting Qur'ãn and on every other occasion. If possible, change your *Miswaak* every week, otherwise cut the bristles regularly so that spoilt bristles is not used all the time.

2. Learn and recite the *Du'as* for all occasions e.g. the *Du'as* for eating, the *Du'as* for sleeping, the *Du'as* for the morning and evening, for wearing clothes, for making *Wudhu*, for seeing the new moon, for entering and leaving the house, etc. You should also teach these *Du'as* to your children and younger brothers and sisters. Insha Allah by reciting all these *Du'as*, theirs and your tongues will remain pure because they are uttering the same words that the tongue of Rasulullah ﷺ spoke. These *Du'as* will also earn you great rewards in the *Aakhirah*.

   An important *Du'a* from among the many *Du'as* is the *Du'a* after sneezing viz. "*Al Hamdu Lillaahi*

*Rabbil Aalameen Alaa Kulli Haal*". When you hear another woman sneezing, recite "*Yar Hamu Kallaah.* If a *Mahram* sneezes, recite "*Yar Hamu Kallah*". Whenever anyone gives you anything, ensure that you thank him/her by saying "*Jazaa Kallahu Khayran.*"

In addition to this, you should give and take things with the right hand, recite "*Bismillaahir Rahmaan nir Raheem*" when locking the doors at night and cover all open utensils containing food.

3. Whenever anything breaks, any difficulty occurs or any loss whatsoever takes place, immediately recite, "Innaa Lillaahi wa Innaa Ilayhi Raaji'oon" ("To Allah we belong and to Him shall we return"). By reciting this, a Muslim acknowledges that nothing belongs to her and that everything she possesses comes from Allah, Who is at liberty to take it back whenever He pleases. Nothing will last forever and we should be prepared to lose things during our lives.

4. When taking your children to the toilet, ensure that they neither face towards the *Qibla* nor face their backs towards the *Qibla.* If the toilet faces towards the *Qibla*, teach them to face somewhat towards the right or the left. Remember that facing towards the *Qibla* or facing the back towards the *Qibla* is a grave sin and you should take every precaution to avoid it.

5. It was the practice of Rasulullah ﷺ to resort to *Salaah* whenever he experienced any difficulty. You should also inculcate the same practice. Therefore, if any of

your children fall ill, you should perform two Rakaahs *Salaah* and make *Du'a* to Allah to cure the child. You may say, "O Allah! This illness has come by your command and the cure for all diseases also comes by Your command. I beseech You to cure my child." You should take the child to a doctor for treatment if necessary and also give some *Sadaqah*.

In the same manner, if there is a shortage of anything in the home, first perform two *Rakaahs Salaah* and make *Du'a* to Allah before asking your husband. If it is the time of the month when you are unable to perform *Salaah*, make *Wuzu* and engage in the *Zikr* of "*Al Hamdu Lillaah*", the third *Kalimah, Durood* or you may even recite *Surah Faatiha*. Then recite:

A hundred times or even more if you can. Thereafter, make *Du'a* to Allah and ask Him for whatever you need. By always doing this, your relationship with Allah will be greatly strengthened.

6. Always greet other women with "*As Salaamu Alaykum wa Rahmatullaahi wa Barakaatuh*" before starting a conversation. It is unfortunate that many women start a conversation with statements like, "How are you?" or "How are the children?" or "I haven't seen for you for such a long time!", etc. All this and more can be said as long as *Salaam* is made first. This important *Sunnah* should also be taught to your children.

## The Method of Greeting

Commenting on verse 86 of *Surah Nisaa* (*Surah* 4), Hazrat Mufti Muhammad Shafi (A.R) states, "The verse makes it clear that when someone is greeted, he should reply to the greeting using better words or at least the same words used to greet him. Rasulullah ﷺ explained this verse by his actions when someone greeted him with the words, '*As Salaamu Alayka*, O Rasulullah ﷺ.' Rasulullah ﷺ replied by saying, '*Wa Alaykumus Salaam wa Rahmatullaah*'. Thereafter, another person arrived and greeted saying, '*As Salaamu Alaykum wa Rahmatullaah*, O Rasulullah ﷺ.' Rasulullah ﷺ added to his reply when he said, '*Wa Alaykumus Salaam wa Rahmatullaahi wa Barakaatuh*.' Another *Sahabi* ؓ then greeted Rasulullah ﷺ using all the words of *Salaam* when he said, '*As Salaamu Alaykum wa Rahmatullaahi wa Barakaatuh*, O Rasulullah ﷺ.' To this, Rasulullah ﷺ merely said, '*Wa Alayk*' (i.e. 'The same to you'). Surprised, this *Sahabi* ؓ asked Rasulullah ﷺ why the others received lengthier replies (thus more *Du'as* from him), whereas he received the briefest reply despite his complete greeting. Rasulullah ﷺ told him, 'You had left nothing for me to add. Because you included all the words of *Salaam* in your greeting, I acted according to the Qur'ãnic verse and gave you a reply equal to your own greeting.' Ibn Jareer (A.R) and Ibn Abi Haatim (A.R) have both narrated this *Hadith* from various narrators."

The above verse and *Hadith* teach us that our reply to a greeting should include words that are better than those of the person greeting us. We should therefore add extra words of *Du'a* to our greeting as Rasulullah ﷺ did.

## The Benefits of Greeting

A saint mentioned that if every Muslim from every town and country has to merely make *Salaam* to other Muslims of their own towns as well as Muslims from other towns and countries daily, there will be peace and safety throughout the world. One of the main causes for the enmity and strife existing throughout the world is the lack of greeting with the words of *Salaam*.

One of the most effective ways to create love between couples and families is for them to regularly greet each other with "*As Salaamu Alaykum wa Rahmatullaahi wa Barakaatuh*". The couple and the members of the family should greet each other when they enter the room, when they start conversations, when they meet each other after waking up in the morning and before going to bed. In fact, they should not pass up any opportunity to greet each other.

The status of *Salaam* is so great that even in *Jannah* people will greet each other with *Salaam*, the angels will greet them with *Salaam* and Allah will Himself greet the people of *Jannah* with the words of *Salaam*. Allah says in verse 58 of *Surah Yaaseen* (*Surah* 36),

> **"They will have a greeting of peace from the Most Merciful Rabb."**

Hazrat Abdullaah bin Umar رضي الله عنه used to frequent the marketplaces for the express purpose of greeting everyone there, irrespective of who they were or what their purposes were. Remember that you will be greatly rewarded every time you greet a Muslim sister, so the more often you greet, the more you will gain.

## The Meaning of the *Salaam*

The *Salaam* is a *Du'a* that one Muslim makes for another Muslim. The Muslims greeting is really telling the other that she wants her to live in peace and safety and that she wants Allah to shower His mercy and blessings on her. You can well imagine that if a mother greets her children with these words several times, daily the children will be enveloped in Allah's mercy and *Shaitaan* will have no avenue to them.

## Another Meaning of *Salaam*

When one Muslim sister greets another with the words "*As Salaamu Alaykum wa Rahmatullaahi wa Barakaatuh*", she is actually reminding the other that she should not forget that Allah is Omnipresent and is watching her at all times. When the other replies with the same words, the first woman is also reminded of the same. In this manner, every person will be cognisant of Allah's presence and they will all avoid sin.

Adults should greet children first so that children may learn the habit of greeting. By doing this, they will also be practising the *Sunnah* of Rasulullah ﷺ, who always greeted children before they could greet him.

## The Islãmic Greeting is Better Than any Other Form of Greeting

It is common place with every nation and creed that they greet each other in a particular manner to express their love and concern for one another. A study of all forms of greeting will reveal that Islãm's manner of greeting is the most comprehensive. In addition to merely expressing love, the *Salaam* is a *Du'a* for the person, invoking Allah's safety from all calamities and difficulties. In addition to this, it is a reminder for the person that we are all in need of Allah and that He is Ever Present and All Powerful. Because of this factor, the *Salaam* becomes a form of *Ibaadah* as well.

When the person greeting is desirous for the safety of the one she is greeting (as indicated by the words of *Salaam*), it is obvious that the one greeting will not want to harm the one she is greeting. By this token, the *Salaam* is also a surety to the one being greeted that s/he need not fear any harm from the one who is greeting. It is for this reason that Hazrat Ibn Uyayna (A.R) said, "Do you know what is *Salaam*? The person making *Salaam* is really saying, 'You have nothing to fear from me.'"

## In a Nutshell

The greeting of Islãm viz. "*As Salaamu Alaykum wa Rahmatullaahi wa Barakaatuh*" includes all of the following:

- It is the Zikr of Allah.
- It reminds other of Allah.
- Is it an expression of love and concern.

- It is an excellent *Du'a.*
- It is a surety for the person being greeted that s/he has nothing to fear from the one who is greeting. In fact, Rasulullah ﷺ mentioned that a Muslim is one from whose tongue and hands other Muslims have nothing to fear. (*Bukhari* Vol. 1 Pg. 6)

If Muslims use the greeting of *Salaam* with awareness and appreciation instead of using it as a mere customary salutation, the *Salaam* would be sufficient to transform their lives. It is perhaps for this reason that Rasulullah ﷺ emphasised that the *Salaam* should be popularised among the Muslims. Rasulullah ﷺ has also counted making *Salaam* among the best of deeds. Besides this, he has enumerated many virtues and benefits of *Salaam.*

In a *Hadith* of Muslim, Hazrat Abu Hurairah رضي الله عنه narrates that Rasulullah ﷺ said, "You will not be able to enter *Jannah* until you have *Imaan* and your *Imaan* will not be complete until you have love for each other. Shall I not inform you of something that will create love between you? Popularise *Salaam* among you."

Hazrat Abdullaah bin Umar رضي الله عنه reports that a person once asked Rasulullah ﷺ what the best of all deeds were. Rasulullah ﷺ replied, "Feed people and make *Salaam* to everyone, whether you know a person or not."

(*Bukhari & Muslim*)

Hazrat Abu Umaamah رضي الله عنه narrates that Rasulullah ﷺ said, "Indeed, the nearest people to Allah are they who are the first to greet." (*Ahmad, Tirmidhi & Abu Dawood*)

Hazrat Abdullaah bin Mas'ood ﷺ reports from Rasulullah ﷺ that the word "*Salaam*" is one of Allah's names, which He has sent to earth. Therefore, people should popularise it among themselves. Whenever a person comes to a gathering and greets the people there with *Salaam*, his status is extremely exalted in Allah's estimation because he has reminded them of Allah. If the people do not reply to his greeting, those of a higher calibre than them (viz. the angels) reply to him. (*Bazzaar, Tabraani*)

In another *Hadith*, Rasulullah ﷺ stated that the most miserly person is one who is miserly with greeting. (*Bazzaar*)

It is because of these and the numerous other virtues of *Salaam* that made Hazrat Abdullaah bin Umar ﷺ frequent the marketplace only to greet people with "*As Salaamu Alaykum wa Rahmatullaahi wa Barakaatuh*".

(*Ma'aariful Qur'ān*, Vol. 2 Pg. 503)

## An Important Ruling

It is not permissible for a woman to shake hands with or to speak directly with any non-*Mahram* man even though he is her brother-in-law or her cousin. Doing this will certainly incur Allah's wrath and lead to difficulties in this world as well as in the next.

We shall now continue with the seventh *Sunnah* in our discussion of ten important *Sunnah* practices of Rasulullah ﷺ.

7. Attribute every occurrence to Allah, saying that it happened by the will of Allah. If a person falls ill,

say that the illness is from Allah without attributing it to the heat, cold, food, etc. Similarly, when a person is cured of an illness, say that it was Allah who cured him/her and not that it was some medicine or doctor that provided the cure. One may say that Allah used the cold as a means for one to become ill and that He placed the cure in the treatment of a certain doctor.

If someone's husband suffered a loss in any way, she should not rebuke him by telling him that he suffered the loss because he did not listen to her. A woman who has trust in Allah would rather console him by saying that everything happens by Allah's command and that they should be patient and hope for reward from Allah.

People are generally accustomed to using the phrase "by chance" and the word "coincidentally" e.g. "I got it quite by chance" or "Coincidentally, my sister happened to visit at the same time that you did". It is incorrect to use these words because nothing happens by chance. Everything that happens, happens by the command of Allah and for good reason. Every leaf falling off a tree will fall only with Allah's command just as every drop of rain falls with His command. Everything happening presently and everything that will happen in future is by His command. Therefore, everything you speak about should be attributed to Allah.

Hazrat Bayazeed Bistaami (A.R) was a great saint. After he had passed away, someone saw him in a dream and asked him how he fared in the next life. He said that when Allah asked him what he had brought, he replied that he had brought nothing besides his belief in *Tauheed*. He did not mention all his many good deeds because he feared that they may be rejected on account of deficiencies found in them. However, Allah reminded him of a particular morning when he suffered pain in his stomach and said, "This is because of the milk I had drunk last night." Allah therefore asked him where his belief in *Tauheed* had disappeared that morning and whether the stomach pain was result of the milk or Allah's command.

There is of course no harm in saying that the milk had caused stomach pains as long as one believes that the true cause is Allah. However, he was reprimanded for this because of his high status as a saint. This incident is an eye-opener for us all.

We should also guard ourselves against attributing things to ourselves e.g. "The meal that I cooked was very tasty." You should rather say, "*Al-Hamdu Lillaah*! Allah added great taste to the food I cooked." Everything that happens should be attributed to Allah and to none else.

This lesson should be emphasised to your children as well. When your child asks for something, do not tell him to ask his father to buy it for him. Encourage him to first make *Wudhu*, to perform two *Rakaahs Salaah* with devotion and then to make *Du'a* to Allah. Thereafter, he should ask his father so that his father may attain the reward of fulfilling his desire. Tell the child that his father will then get him what he wants when Allah grants his father the means and the inspiration to do so. In this manner, the child will develop trust in Allah and will not resort to asking from others when s/he grows up. Such a child will not entertain hopes in others and will ask from Allah only. The child will remain pleased with whatever Allah decides and will be able to exercise patience whenever a difficulty arrives.

8. Just as you conceal yourself from strangers, you should also observe *Hijaab* when associating with your non-*Mahram* relatives, whether they are your cousins or your brothers-in-law. Failure to do so is a major sin even though there may not be any fear of falling into sin with such as person. If a person truly loves Allah and His Rasul ﷺ, she will practise every injunction of the *Shari'ah* and steer clear of incurring their wrath, which will ultimately destroy her life in this world as well as her life in the *Aakhirah*.

9. You should be particular about replying to the *Azaan*. Rasulullah ﷺ has mentioned that the person who replies to the *Azaan* with conviction in the heart will certainly enter *Jannah*.[1] In addition to this, Rasulullah ﷺ has also stated that such a person will be forgiven and that he will definitely intercede on behalf of the person who recites the *Du'a* after the *Azaan*. (*Muslim*)

You should therefore ensure that you maintain complete silence when the *Azaan* is being called out and that you

1. *Hisn-ul-Haseen.*

repeat everything the *Mu'azzin* says. Of course, when the *Mu'azzin* calls out "*Hayya alas Salaah*" and "*Hayya alal Falaah*", you should say, "*Laa Howla wa Laa Quwwata Illa Billaah*". The *Du'a* to recite after the *Azaan* is:

{Translation: "O Allah, the Rabb of this perfect call and the Rabb of the forthcoming *Salaah*! Grant Hazrat Muhammad ﷺ the station of '*Waseela*' (an exalted station in the *Aakhirah*), grant him eminence and the position of '*Maqaam Mahmood*' which You have promised him. Verily, You never breach Your promise."}

("*Mishkaat*" Pg. 65)

Hazrat Ummu Salma رضي الله عنها narrates that (in addition to the above *Du'a*) Rasulullah ﷺ taught her to recite the following *Du'a* after the Maghrib *Azaan*:

(Translation: "O Allah! This sounds the arrival of Your night, the departure of Your day and the cries of those making *Du'a* to You. Please forgive me.") ("*Mishkaat*" Pg. 66)

Although this verbal reply to the *Azaan* is *Mustahab*, the physical reply to the *Azaan* is *Waajib* (compulsory). For men, this physical reply to the *Azaan* entails proceeding to the *Masjid* for *Salaah* and for women, it entails performing *Salaah* after the *Azaan*. Even if you are at the stove when the *Azaan* is called out, switch off the stove and start preparing for *Salaah*, thinking that your *Rabb* has summoned you to prayer and that your success lies in performing your *Salaah*. Never allow your *Nafs* and *Shaitaan* to deceive you into thinking that you should first complete the work before performing *Salaah*. By falling for this guile, your *Salaah* will be delayed (maybe even missed) and your work will take more time than it should.

When the *Azaan* is called out, you should ensure that all mature males in you household as well as those approaching the age of ten proceed to the *Masjid* for *Salaah*. Use wisdom and diplomacy to encourage them instead of being brusque and harsh. Those children in the house who are between seven and ten years of age should be trained at home to perform their *Salaah*.

## Simplicity

10. Simplicity is an extremely important *Sunnah* of Rasulullah ﷺ. A *Hadith* mentions that the person who revives a *Sunnah* of Rasulullah ﷺ after people have discarded it shall earn the reward of a hundred martyrs. You will therefore earn this great reward if you inculcate simplicity in your life. You should therefore resolve to introduce simplicity in your life and make an effort to bring simplicity into the lives of all Muslims. By introducing the *Sunnah* practices of Rasulullah ﷺ into your life, you will have tremendous blessings and mercy in everything you do. When a woman resolves to lead a life of simplicity, the rest of the family will quickly follow suit. There are three specific areas in which simplicity ought to be introduced. These areas are (i) in

marriages, (ii) in the building of a house and (iii) in the finishing and furnishing of a house. When this is done, love will develop in the family and many sins will be avoided. In addition to this, wastage, ostentation, boasting and unnecessary amassing of wealth will be avoided.

Hakeemul Ummah Maulana Ashraf Ali Thanwi (A.R) has mentioned, "Women are experts in training men and in confounding their intelligence. When a man asks a woman what he is expected to do after marriage, all she utters is a brief statement i.e. 'Not much. Just do as much as you can.' When a man really decides to do as she says and asks for an explanation of this statement, his ears are filled with thousands of demands which spell disaster for him in both worlds." ("*Islaah Khawateen*" Pg. 130)

Many men have their heads permanently bowed with the weight of the debts they owe others while others have even committed major sins to satisfy the demands of their wives. It is therefore necessary for women to adopt simplicity in their lives to alleviate the burden on their husbands. By adopting simplicity in especially the three areas mentioned above, the entire family will be relived of unnecessary stress and anxiety.

When building your home, ensure that the design is not elaborate so that additional expenses are not incurred. Think awhile about the homes of the Sahabah ﷺ. The roofs of their homes were made of the fronds of date palms, while the walls were made of mud. There were neither any carpets, nor any expensive beds, cupboards or a large variety of crockery. Despite the absence of these luxuries, their homes were filled with comfort, peace, love, good health and mutual compassion. Neither did a Muslim have fear for a *Kaafir* nor did a *Kaafir* fear that a Muslim would harm him.

A wealthy Arab friend of mine has resolved to adopt simplicity in his home for the sole purpose of emulating the *Sunnah* of Rasulullah ﷺ. With the assistance of his wife he has achieved this goal and is enjoying the tranquillity that the *Sunnah* of Rasulullah ﷺ brings to one's life. When a person truly has love for Rasulullah ﷺ, his every action is more valuable than all the riches and kingdoms of the world.

The second very important matter in which we should endeavour to adopt simplicity is in the finishing and furnishing of our homes. We should have in our homes only what is necessary. What is really a necessity? The true meaning of a necessity can be clearly understood from the nature of the Arabic word for necessity, which is "Dharoorah". This word is derived from the root word "Dharar", which means 'to harm' or 'to cause difficulty'. Necessities have been termed "Dharoorah" because without them, a person will experience great difficulty.

Therefore, if you need to carpet you house, choose the carpet that is the simplest. Similarly, when choosing curtains, choose curtains that are the simplest. In this manner, everything else that is necessary should be simple. Whatever you spend on your house should be well within your husband's budget. Your excess wealth should be spent in charity so that this wealth will be of benefit to you in the Hereafter. Whenever you do something, always stop to think whether Allah will be pleased instead of thinking whether your friends or other people will be pleased. Remember that Allah's pleasure should have precedence over the pleasure of everyone else.

It is also extremely important to adopt simplicity when hosting functions. Whether it is your brother, your sister or any of your children getting married, ensure that the function is as simple as possible. Never ask the opposite party for anything and make it clear to them as well as to everyone else that the *Shari'ah* has only prescribed the *Waleema* function, which is hosted by the bridegroom. This function should also be extremely simple. In addition to this, the trousseau should also be simple. Instead of squandering money on elaborate wedding ceremonies and trousseaus, the money should rather be given to the bride to use for her home and future.

Remember that the more simplicity you adopt, the closer you will get to Allah. As a mother, brother, sister or family member you should also exert your influence over others who intend hosting such functions so that they also receive the benefits of the *Sunnah* and are saved from unnecessary problems in their lives.

A narration of Ahmad reports that Rasulullah ﷺ said, "The marriage with the most blessings is the one that has the least expense." This means that a couple will experience tremendous blessings in their marriage when the expenses from the period of the proposal until the bride's departure to her husband are reduced to a bare minimum. Such a marriage will be a source of contentment and bliss for not only the couple, but for both their families as well. In addition to this, the relationship will also ensure their success in the *Aakhirah.* The first visible results of these blessings will already become manifest before the marriage when the parties will not be plagued by sleepless nights and the burden of taking debts upon their heads. By adhering to colloquial customs and traditions (such as "Mehndi nights", bridal showers, etc), people will be unnecessarily burdening themselves with anxiety, in addition to suffering the repercussions in the *Aakhirah* for imitating the lives of the *Kuffaar.*

In trying to impress people by hosting large functions, families only earn insults and abuse instead. After many a large function, people will be heard complaining about the food being too strong, too mild or too oily. Further fuelling disputes, the bride's sister-in-law will be heard grumbling, "She couldn't even show me her wedding outfit at the bridal shower!" Another sister-in-law will say, "She didn't even greet me on the night of the wedding!" In this manner, a barrage of problems will assault the marriage even before the couple can live together.

Rasulullah ﷺ himself married and he also got his daughters married. Every Muslim should learn from the pure examples that he set in this regard.

### Rasulullah ﷺ Marries and Hosts a Waleema Function While on Journey

During one of his journeys, Rasulullah ﷺ married Hazrat Safiyya رضي الله عنها. To celebrate the occasion, Rasulullah

ﷺ hosted a *Waleema.* The *Waleema* meal comprised of some dates, butter and a few pieces of cheese which were scattered on a tablecloth for the people present to eat. Neither does Islãm encourage elaborate feasts nor pompous ceremonies; least of all, the printing of wedding invitations.

If we imitate the practises of Rasulullah ﷺ and marry our sons and daughters in this manner, there is every hope that this deed alone will guarantee our salvation in the *Aakhirah.* When marriages are conducted in the manner that the *Shari'ah* prescribes, it is not at all farfetched that such marriages will produce gems like Salaahud *Deen* Ayyubi (A.R) and Raabiya Basriyya (A.R) who will be responsible for saving thousands of souls from *Jahannam.* However, these types of delectable fruit will be borne only from trees that can bear the heat of people's insults when assiduously adhering to the *Sunnah* practices of Rasulullah ﷺ. A poet says:

"The first condition for following the true *Deen* is love for Muhammad ﷺ

Compared to him, everything else is imperfect

When you are loyal to Muhammad ﷺ, everyone is yours

The things of this world are yours, as are the *Lowhul Mahfoodh* and the pen

Do not be disturbed if the world is upset with you

You do not really need everyone to be pleased with you

When you look at things, decide for yourself

What you ought to do and what you need not do (in conformance with the *Shari'ah*)

If You are not mine (O Allah) then nothing is mine

When You are mine, everything is mine including the stars and the earth

*Tauheed* is that on the Plain of Resurrection, Allah should say

'It was for My sake that this slave of Mine was angry with the world.'"

(Translated from an Urdu Poem)

## OPPRESSIVE MOTHERS-IN-LAW

If every woman resolved that she would be kind and gentle when dealing with the innocent lady who will soon be living in her home as her daughter-in-law, life would become pleasant and comfortable for many people. Not only will it be easier for women to marry, but hundreds of parents will not have to lose sleep over the troubled lives of their married daughters. Among the deeper effects that such behaviour will lead to is that immodesty and nudity will be considerably lessened because people will be encouraged to marry.

It is not incorrect to assert that an oppressive mother-in-law together with her daughters who serve as accomplices are among the greatest elements that discourage men and women from marrying. They actively destroy marriages and cause many men to perpetrate major sins. A catalyst in their efforts is the wife of their elder brother who is well-versed in all colloquial customs and traditions. Such women make unnecessary demands from the family of a bride coming to their family. The father of the bride-to-be is then forced to accede to their demands because he fears that they will make his daughter's life a misery if he does not comply. Consequently, he has to bear the burden of incurring debts to pay for the exorbitant expenses.

It is unfortunate that if a man does not host an elaborate wedding function for his daughter, she will have to hear taunts and insults from her mother-in-law for the rest of her life. This will make life unbearable for her and will place undue pressure on her marriage. To avoid this situation, the bride's father has to lower himself to take loans from others. The blistering singe of being refused a loan only aggravates the embarrassment of asking from others. In many cases, the customs of the area demand so much from the father of the bride that he cannot afford them even though he is wealthy. Such burdensome customs include giving elaborate gifts to the groom's family and hosting several functions before the wedding itself. Despite being unable to afford all of this, the bride's father is forced to find the money for it because he knows that after the marriage, his daughter will be unable to bear the stigma that her mother-in-law will attach to her and the insults that will be heaped on her throughout her life. The father is eventually forced to accept any money he can find, whether it is interest, *Sadaqah* or ill-gotten money.

Mothers-in-law who behave in this manner should beware of Allah's punishment. It has often been noticed that mothers-in-law who have oppressed their daughters-in-law suffer debilitating diseases in the lives. May Allah save us all from such diseases. Problems between mothers-in-law and daughters-in-law are extremely common nowadays because mothers-in-law do not treat their daughters-in-law like their own daughters and daughters-in-law do not treat their mothers-in-law like their own mothers. It is therefore best for a mother-in-law and a daughter-in-law to live separately. If this is not possible, she should at least have her own kitchen.

According to the explicit instruction of Rasulullah ﷺ, the bride is not obliged to bring anything to her husband's home, but it the duty of the husband to provide dowry and, of course, the other household necessities. Unfortunately, many of today's mothers-in-law will terrorise their daughters-in-law if they fail to provide something for the house. It is therefore necessary for Muslims to erase these customs from their lives and to make each other understand that they have no right to pressurise the bride's party into providing anything.

## The "Jaheaz"

Although the custom of demanding "*Jaheaz*" from the bride's family is disappearing from the lives of many Muslims, there are still many ignorant homes that have failed to see the light. While the groom requires only a wife who is obedient, understanding, loving, attractive and compassionate, his mother, sisters and sisters-in-law also want something from the marriage. It is for this reason that they force the groom to deliver a list to his fiancé's parents with all their demands. These demands are referred to as the "*Jaheaz*". Unfortunately, many people have taken this custom so far that they actually specify the make and model of the appliance or furniture they ask for. Such demands are sheer oppression and contrary to the *Shari'ah*. In fact, when dissecting the Urdu word "*Jaheaz*" *Ulama* have mentioned that each letter is represented as follows:

- The first letter "Jeem" (ج) stands for "*Jurm*" i.e. injustice.
- The second letter "Haa" (ہ) stands for "*Hawas*" i.e. carnal desires.
- The third letter "Yaa" (ی) stands for "*Yalghaar*" i.e. assault.
- The last letter "Zaa" (ز) stands for "*Zaher*" i.e. poison.

The "*Jaheaz*" is really an injustice against the bride's father, a result of the carnal desires of the groom's family, an assault from their side and a poison in the hearts of the bride's parents because it will soon affect their health when they have to bear the disgrace of begging from others.

Whereas people should accept a woman into their homes on the basis of her credentials as a good wife, it has now sadly become the norm in many areas that she is accepted merely on the basis of the quality of the "*Jaheaz*" she can bring along. It is therefore not uncommon in such that an excellent woman is looked down upon merely because the "*Jaheaz*" she brought for her in-laws was not up to standard. On the other hand, a shrew is regarded as a good woman only because she was able to bring a handsome "*Jaheaz*" for her in-laws. Instead of the people of neighbourhood coming to see and congratulate the bride, they now ask whether the washing-machine arrived or whether any other item of the "*Jaheaz*" came as requested. When the groom receives everything that was requested as "*Jaheaz*", people say that he has been very fortunate.

However, people fail to realise that the most valuable "*Jaheaz*" that a groom can hope for is a capable wife who manages the home with dexterity and who has received a sound Islãmic education and upbringing. An excellent wife is one who can ably serve her husband and her in-laws and who can raise her children as good Muslims. The best clothing that a woman can bring with her as "*Jaheaz*" is the clothing of Islãm and obedience. The best jewellery that she can bring are the jewels of *Ibaadah*, the best perfume she can bring is the perfume of the *Sunnah*, her best make-up is trust in and fear for Allah. Better than the brand-named appliances and furniture that she can bring as "*Jaheaz*" is good character, a smiling face, the knowledge of *Deen*, modesty and the excellent attributes of the *Sahabiyaat* رضي الله عنهن.

In the past, people were embarrassed to ask others for anything because this entailed begging. However, with customs like "*Jaheaz*" and bridal showers, the rich have devised sophisticated methods of begging from people because they asking people to bring them the gifts they want. It seems that the richer people become, the greedier they get. Taking advantage of functions like these, they ask others to bring the most expensive gifts merely to save their own money. This has become an excellent method of dipping one's hands into the pockets of others. It is unfortunate that material possessions are more precious to people than a good wife for their son. It appears that people are auctioning their sons and marrying them to the highest bidder. May Allah guide all Muslims and make them realise the error of their ways before they ruin the lives of others together with their own lives in the *Aakhirah*.

In sensitive customs such as demanding a "*Jaheaz*" will stop only when the wealthy class decide to put an end to it. At least some members of this class should marry their children according to the simple Sunnah method that Rasulullah ﷺ taught us. In this manner, they will be unshackling the yoke that is suffocating so many poor people. Whereas it is the responsibility of the husband to provide for the wife, the tables have turned to such an extent that nowadays fathers have to part with their most precious daughters as well as thousands of their hard-earned wealth. If this is not oppression on the father, it can be nothing less.

The curse of such customs will not come to an end until the members of a community take decisive action to put an end to it. May Allah assist those who will take the initiative to promote the *Sunnah* of Rasulullah ﷺ so that people can breathe more easily. *Aameen*

## The "Jaheaz" is a Hindu Custom

Allah has given men superiority over women because they have the honour of spending the wealth on women. In addition to this, the *Shari'ah* has explicitly specified that it is the man's responsibility to ensure that he provides everything necessary in the home. When a marriage takes place, the woman has no financial responsibility whatsoever. The *Shari'ah* makes it clear that it is the husband who has to spend on his wife and not the other way around. It is only in the upside down world of certain communities that the woman is obliged to make a contribution.

Allah says in the Qur'ãn,

> **"Men are the guardians of women because of the virtue Allah has bestowed some of you over others and because of the wealth that men spend (on women)."** *(Surah Nisaa, Surah 4, verse 34)*

The great commentator of the Qur'ãn Imaam Raazi (A.R) has mentioned that this verse refers to the dowry that the husband pays to the wife as well as the maintenance that he spends on her.[1] Because the words of this verse are general, it refers to every expense that the husband incurs during the course of his marriage and in preparation for his marriage. Together with providing food and accommodation for his wife, the husband is obliged to provide all the

1. *Tafseer Kabeer*, Vol. 10, Page 88.

necessities that his wife requires. The Qur'ān and *Ahadith* do not even make vague reference to the fact that the bride has to contribute the household expenses. Therefore, none of this may be demanded from the bride's parents.

Because Hindu custom dictates that daughters should receive nothing from the estate of their fathers, Hindu fathers spend as much as they can on the "*Jaheaz*" of their daughters. The separation from their daughters on the occasion of marriage therefore signifies a permanent separation for them because her share of his estate is given then. With this in mind, Muslims should completely leave off themselves from this Hindu custom and make a concerted effort to prevent other Muslims from it as well.

## A Misconception

Many Muslims dwell under the misconception that the few items that Rasulullah ﷺ gave his beloved daughter Hazrat Faatima رضي الله عنها when she married was "*Jaheaz*". The reply to this misconception will benefit only those Muslims who really wish to know the truth and who are willing to heed advice. As for those who are bent on exploiting others and who take pleasure in embarrassing others, reading this reply will be an exercise in futility.

The reply is that the things that Rasulullah ﷺ gave for his daughter were actually bought with the dowry that Hazrat Ali رضي الله عنه had given prior to the marriage. Allaama Zurqaani (A.R) writes in "*Sharh Mawaahib*" that Hazrat

---

1. Vol. 2, Page 3 as quoted in *Ahsan-ul-Fatawa*, Vol. 5, Page 31.

Ali ﷺ had a coat of armour which he presented to Rasulullah ﷺ as dowry. Rasulullah ﷺ sold the armour for 480 *Dirhams* and used the money to buy a few household items which he sent with Hazrat Faatima ﷺ after the marriage. Among the items that Rasulullah ﷺ asked Hazrat Bilaal ﷺ to buy with the money was perfume, some clothing, bedding and a pillow. It is therefore clear that the things which Rasulullah ﷺ gave Hazrat Faatima ﷺ was not really a "*Jaheaz*" as people would call it. If it one insists on calling it "*Jaheaz*", it should be borne in mind that it was not paid for by the father but by the son-in-law.

Another factor that disproves the misconception that Rasulullah ﷺ paid for the "*Jaheaz*" of Hazrat Faatima ﷺ is the fact that he did not do the same for his other daughters. It is not possible for Rasulullah ﷺ to do something for one daughter which he did not do for the others because he has emphasised that parents deal justly with their children. This reinforces the fact that the so-called "*Jaheaz*" was paid for by Hazrat Ali ﷺ and not by Rasulullah ﷺ.

If the "*Jaheaz*" was something important in the *Shari'ah*, Rasulullah ﷺ would have certainly given it to all his four daughters. However, the *Ahadith* do not mention any "*Jaheaz*" being given to all his daughters. It is therefore evident that the *Shari'ah* attaches no significance to the concept of giving "*Jaheaz*".

It should also be borne in mind that Hazrat Ali ﷺ was in the care of Rasulullah ﷺ and it was therefore Rasulullah ﷺ's duty to see to the marriage and the home of his ward.

Another lesson that we should learn from this incident is that Rasulullah ﷺ neither gave anything for his son-in-law nor did Hazrat Ali رضي الله عنه ask Rasulullah ﷺ for anything. This was the *Sunnah* practice of Rasulullah ﷺ. It is this practice rather than the oppressive practice of "*Jaheaz*" that should be implemented. However, it is tragic to note that many Muslims are still adamant to follow the ways of the Hindus. It will not be redundant to reiterate that asking the bride's family for anything is Haraam, whether the asking is done verbally or by hinting.

In his book condemning the custom of "*Jaheaz*", Maulana Muhammad Shihaabud *Deen* Nadwi has mentioned that people who make demands from the bride's party to augment their own luxuries are really stealing from them. They is like thieving parasites, sucking the blood of their relatives.

People who do this and who taunt their daughters-in-law if they did not receive enough "*Jaheaz*" should remember that they will have to account for this in the *Aakhirah*. A woman who asks her son's future in-law to get things for her daughters, for her other sons, for her daughters-in-law and for other members of the family really does not deserve the honourable title of mother which forms part of her description as a mother-in-law. Such people can only be those whose hearts are bereft of fear for Allah. It is indeed unfortunate that they fail to perceive the sin involved in begging. In fact, asking for "*Jaheaz*" does not only entail begging, but is also a type of unjust tax.

Rasulullah ﷺ said, "The person who asks for something despite having what he requires is only accumulating the smouldering stones of *Jahannam*." When the *Sahabah* ﷺ asked Rasulullah ﷺ what the meaning of "having what he requires" was, he replied, "That he has enough to feed himself for a night." (*Daar Qutni* Vol. 2 Pg. 121)

There are many other such *Ahadith* that make it clear that begging from people is a despised and condemned act in the *Shari'ah*. What makes matters even worse is that the beggars in this situation actually force people to give them. Those being begged from have no option to refuse because refusal spells either a lifetime of torment for their daughter or her divorce. In fact, there are many people who actually threaten the bride's family in this manner, reminding them that once the fact is publicised that they do not want to pay sufficient "*Jaheaz*", no one will propose for any of their daughters in future.

## Giving a Gold Necklace to the Groom's Mother

Another Hindu custom that has crept into Muslim ranks is the attitude that the groom's mother has done a favour to the bride's mother by accepting her daughter into her home. To return the "favour", the bride's mother is expected to buy a gold necklace for the groom's mother. As a result, the poor woman had to beg, borrow or steal the money for this, otherwise she is warned that her name will be spoilt and she will be unable to find husbands for her other daughters. On the other hand, if she obliges, she is assured that her daughter will receive fine treatment and that her other daughters will find matches almost immediately.

Such behaviour is reminiscent of the dark days of ignorance in which the pagan Arabs wallowed in degradation and absurdity. They dreaded having female children and regarded this as a form of disgrace. This is exactly how matters have reverted because many Muslims have adopted the ways of the Hindus who honour sons and look down on daughters.

If you are in an area where this custom is rife, you should remember that your son's mother-in-law will not be happy to part with a gold necklace regardless of how rich she may be. You should therefore never think that it is fine to accept it as a gift because she is happily giving it to you. If you really want to test whether she is giving it happily, tell her that if she does not give you the necklace, you will not retaliate in any manner. Tell her that you will neither harass her daughter nor smear her or her family's name in any way. Add also that if she really feels that she wants to give the necklace, she should give it to her daughter instead. Rest assured that after telling her this, the thankful lady will immediately return home to perform salaah as a thanksgiving to Allah and she will also make special *Du'a* for you for not imposing the tax on her. If her situation is such that she feels obliged to give you the necklace because of social pressure, tell her that if she has so much extra money with her, she may give the necklace privately some months after the wedding without anyone knowing about it. Only time will now tell whether you receive the necklace or not.

If one thinks carefully, one would realise that if anyone deserves a gold necklace as a form of thanks, it is actually the bride's mother who deserves it the most. It was she who invested her money and her priceless time, effort and love to ensure that her daughter one day becomes capable of being the gem of another person's home. She bore the girl in her womb with great difficulty and then fed and cared for her for many long years. She taught her daughter everything she needed to know to care for her husband and children. After marriage, she has entrusted her precious daughter with her new family and has to bear the pains of separation after so many years of close association. For her sacrifices, she more than deserves even the most jewels on earth.

When it is not permissible for the groom to demand things from his in-laws, how can it be permissible for his mother to do so?

Quoting from canonical books like "Bahrur Raa'iq" and "Shaami", the famous book "*Fataawaa Aalamgeeri*" has mentioned that if the bride's parents take any money from the groom when he takes their daughter home as his wife, he is at liberty to take the money back because this is a form of bribery. Such money is *Haraam* even though it is given with a smiling face. This practice has become common in certain area of the Muslim world. However, if it is *Haraam* for the bride's party to take anything from the groom, it will be even worse if the groom's party take from the bride's family. Demanding the "*Jaheaz*" entails oppressive taxation as well as blackmail because the girl is threatened with divorce or unending taunts.

Another important factor to consider is that if the *Shari'ah* attached importance to giving something to the groom's mother, Rasulullah ﷺ would have certainly given something to Hazrat Ali رضي الله عنه's mother, whose name was Faatima bint Asad رضي الله عنها. Neither did she ask for anything, nor was anything given to her. Despite this, she bore no ill-feelings towards her daughter-in-law.

May Allah guide all mothers-in-law to understand the true nature of the *Shari'ah.* To rid society of this evil, it is also necessary to wage *Jihaad* against this practice so that women can breath a sigh of relief when they have to get their daughters married.

## Feeding the Bride's In-laws

No *Hadith* mentions anything about Rasulullah ﷺ feeding the families of any of his sons-in-law. The *Ahadith* also do not mention that the responsibility of hosting a *Waleema* is that of the bride's father. However, the *Ahadith* do make it clear that the expense of the *Waleema* celebration has to be borne by the groom.

It is therefore necessary forms to break away from the un-Islãmic custom of hosting wedding ceremonies at the expense of the bride's father. You should not host such ceremonies and you should also encourage others to do the same especially if you have an influence over them. Encourage people to rather spend the money on the poor and needy or to at least give it to their daughter in the form of cash, jewellery, property, etc.

Although Rasulullah ﷺ got four of his daughter married and the *Sahabah* ؓ also got their daughters married, there is no proof in any hadith that they hosted functions where the groom's family were fed. Neither did the groom's family ask for such a function nor did the bride's family attach any significance to the act. If this was the practice of Rasulullah ﷺ and his illustrious *Sahabah* ؓ, why should today's Muslims demand to do things as the *Kuffaar* do? Not only do people insist that the groom and his immediately family should be invited to a wedding, but they also go to the extreme of demanding that an additional five hundred to a thousand people should also be invited. Is this not a sophisticated way of begging for food? Is this not a wastage of someone's life savings? Is this not opening the door to years of financial struggle for a mere day's entertainment?

One will wonder why there is not a single person from among the five hundred or thousand guests who will oppose the function when they know well that their host is unable to afford the celebration. If the host is a wealthy person, he should realise that by hosting an extravagant feast, he is making life difficult for the poor because they will be forced to either follow his example or to beat it. In this manner, he will be a cause of delaying many marriages, if not preventing them altogether. If there was any significance in hosting a wedding, Rasulullah ﷺ and the *Sahabah* ؓ would have certainly set the example. However, it appears as if Muslims prefer following the ways of others and destroying the *Sunnah* of our beloved Rasulullah ﷺ.

# THE MARRIAGE AND WALEEMA ACCORDING TO THE SUNNAH

When the groom is hosting a *Waleema*, it is not necessary for him to serve meat dishes. Even something as simple as dates and juice will suffice because the purpose of the *Waleema* is to express one's gratitude to Allah. The *Ahadith* make it clear that a marriage should be as simple as possible and according to what a person can afford. This is necessary because marriage signifies the building of a home and not the destruction of a home (which is the case when people are forced to cater beyond their means).

The manner in which Rasulullah ﷺ married the queen of *Jannah* Hazrat Faatima رضي الله عنها is a lesson for the world. Hazrat Ummu Salma رضي الله عنها and Hazrat A'isha رضي الله عنها both report that Rasulullah ﷺ asked the two of them to prepare Hazrat Faatima رضي الله عنها and take her to her husband Hazrat Ali رضي الله عنه. Consequently, the two of them went to the house where Hazrat Faatima رضي الله عنها was to reside and spread the soft sand of "Bat'haa" on the ground so that their bedding may be spread on soft ground. They also placed two pillows there, which they personally filled with the bark of a date palm. For the *Waleema*, they served dates, water and a sweet drink prepared from dates to the people present. When this was over, they placed a stick in the couple's room so that they could hang their clothing or a water bag on it. After narrating this, they added that they never saw a marriage better than that of Hazrat Faatima رضي الله عنها. (*Ibn Majah* Pg. 616)

This was the home and marriage of the woman whom Rasulullah ﷺ described as the queen of *Jannah.* It was strikingly simple and without stress. However, we have burdened ourselves with the difficulty of hosting elaborate functions, making life difficult for everyone else. Because marriage is one of the necessities of life, it ought to be kept extremely simple so that every person may find it easy.

It is therefore quite obvious that the marriage of Hazrat Faatima رضي الله عنها did not feature any elaborate feasts coupled with an expensive bridal suite in silk and velvet. The food and the preparation was most simple so that every member of the *Ummah* until *Qiyaamah* may find it easy to emulate. However, one will scarcely find people today who are prepared to emulate the simplicity of Rasulullah ﷺ's life. Instead of being proud to emulate his lifestyle, many wretched people actually feel ashamed to do so. One should bear in mind that if Rasulullah ﷺ wanted to host an elaborate wedding ceremony for his youngest daughter, he could have easily done so. However, he chose the simplest route for the convenience of his *Ummah*; so that they do not have to tire themselves in this effort and rather concentrate their wealth and efforts in the propagation of the *Deen.* It is rather foolish of Muslims to opt for the difficult ways of the *Kuffaar* instead of the easy way of life that Rasulullah ﷺ lived.

It is obvious that the pomp and extravagance with which many Muslims host wedding functions is all done for name and show. Allah and His Rasul ﷺ despise any action done for the purpose of show. Concerning those who behave extravagantly (obviously for show), Allah says in the Qur'ãn,

> "Without doubt, the extravagant ones are the brothers of the *Shayaateen*."
>
> (*Surah Bani Isaraa'eel*, verse 27)

When Allah grants a person wealth, this wealth is a test for him and on the Day of *Qiyaamah*, Allah will question him about the avenues in which he spent this wealth. One's wealth should be spend only as the *Shari'ah* prescribes.

Squandering money on elaborate wedding ceremonies is not condemned only in the eyes of the *Shari'ah*, but even common society realises that this is an evil and a great wastage. Muslims should realise that it is futile to destroy the lives of people merely for a day's frolicking. It is like someone burning the home of another to ashes merely to build a house of his own. He may enjoy the house very much, but will soon have to wake up to reality and find that someone else is burning down his house to build one of his own.

It is therefore the responsibility of every Muslim to follow the lifestyle of Rasulullah ﷺ and to encourage the world to do the same so that he rot and evils invading society are quickly weeded out. In fact, it has always been the Muslims who have been responsible for bringing the world out of darkness and into the light. The purpose of a Muslim in this world is not to frolic in its pleasures and vanities. What the world needs is for the Muslim *Ummah* to rise to the occasion and wage *Jihaad* against the foolish customs and traditions that are plaguing people and making their lives a misery.

## To Summarise

The blessed lifestyle of Rasulullah ﷺ is long calling to the Muslims, telling them to forsake their false vanities and to adopt the pure practices of Rasulullah ﷺ because this will ensure their success in both worlds. However, if they insist on following the customs of others, they should understand that nothing will be able to check their downfall. One can either be the slave of Allah or the slave of ignorant customs. If women take the initiative of eradicating these customs from their lives, they can do so quite effectively and will earn tremendous rewards from Allah.

## WIVES OWE THE RIGHTS TO THEIR HUSBANDS

1. Obey all his instructions as long as they do not contravene the injunctions of the *Shari'ah*. Never neglect serving him and always do things that please him if these do not violate the laws of the *Shari'ah*.
2. Never ask him for more than he can afford.
3. Never allow anyone to enter the house without your husband's permission.
4. Never spend any of his wealth without his permission.
5. Do not leave the house without his permission.

6. Do not observe *Nafl* (optional) fasts without his permission.
7. When he calls you to bed for intercourse, do not refuse without a valid *Shar'ee* excuse.
8. Never look down on your husband because of his poverty, nationality, looks, lack of knowledge or for any other reason.
9. Respectfully correct him if you notice him doing anything contrary to the *Shari'ah*.
10. Never call him by his name because this entails disrespect.
11. Never complain about him to anyone.
12. Never speak to him disrespectfully.
13. Never behave harshly with his relatives because this will hurt him. This applies especially to his parents. Treat them respectfully and kindly.

## PARTING ADVICE FOR THE BRIDE

Remember that marriage is the natural and most honourable course for every woman to take. If there was any better course to follow, then the pure daughter of Hazrat Abu Bakr رضي الله عنه would have followed it. In fact, the daughter of the best of mankind would have also followed that better course. However, they all took the route of marriage, thereby setting an example for the rest of mankind. Their submission and obedience to their husbands is a source of pride for every Muslim woman and whoever follows their example will surely be treading the path to salvation.

Therefore, the tears you shed upon departure should be tears of joy instead of tears of grief. Blessed are the women who follow the sterling examples of Hazrat A'isha ﷺ and Hazrat Faatima ﷺ. Blessed also are their husband and their fathers. Marriage is no calamity or punishment but it is a great form of *Ibaadah* by which a person can attain the pleasure of Allah. Rasulullah ﷺ said that marriage was the practice of all the Ambiyaa (*Alaihimus Salãm*). Because the Ambiyaa (*Alaihimus Salãm*) were the beloved of Allah, whoever follows in their footsteps must also become Allah's beloved.

Hazrat Abdullaah bin Abbaas ﷺ has narrated that Rasulullah ﷺ said, "You will not see anything better for two lovers than marriage."[1] There are various reasons for love to exist between people just as there are various reasons for enmity. This *Hadith* tells us that the factor which best causes hearts to bond is marriage. When a couple marry and devote themselves to each other, the bond of love that is created between them becomes so great that the two become inseparable even though they may be from different nationalities and different cultures.

There are many people who claim to be lovers and who live together. Their association is maintained for ulterior motives even though they claim that it is love that had united them. Once the ulterior motives are removed, they drift very far apart and separate from each other. In fact, their reluctance to marry proves the insincerity of their love.

1. "*Mishkaat*", Page 268.

The objective of marriage is not merely the satiation of carnal passions. It is a commitment to live your life with your spouse and it multiplies a person's status as a man or a woman. After marriage, a man earns the respectable status of being a husband and a father, while his wife is the queen of her home. Each partner becomes a source of comfort and happiness for each other, something that would never have been achieved without marriage. In addition to this, the marriage bonds the families of each partner leading to many social benefits for all concerned. Together with her commitment to make her marriage work, a woman's sacrifice by leaving her home and family is incentive enough for her to devote herself to the marriage, thereby ensuring the sound and healthy upbringing of her children.

## THE DU'A FOR A MARRIED COUPLE

> {Translation: "May Allah destine a blessed life for you, may He bless you and unite you two with good health and prosperity."}[1]

In addition to the above *Du'a*, the following *Du'as* should also be made for the couple:

> "O Allah! This man and woman have united in marriage and have accepted the responsibility that has been placed on the shoulders of so many before them. This they have undertaken for Your pleasure and following the practice of Your beloved slaves. O Allah! Unite their

1. *Hisnul Haseen*, Page 328, from *Ibn Majah, Abu Dawud, Nasai, Tirmizi, Ibn Hibban* & *Haakim*.

hearts with true love as You had united the hearts of their ancestors Hazrat Adam ﷺ and Hazrat Hawwa .

O Allah! Through the blessings of all Your pious servants who have treaded the same path, allow this couple to pass through the trials of life and keep them steadfast through all the adversities that may afflict them. Safeguard them from all evils that may stealthily creep into their souls. Pave the way for them in this world and grant them the best in the *Aakhirah.* Guide them to emulate the examples that Rasulullah ﷺ, Hazrat Khadija ﷺ and Hazrat A'isha ﷺ set and protect them from the evils of colloquial customs, sins and *Bid'ah.*

O Allah! Entrench the love for Your *Deen* deep within their hearts and allow them to serve Your *Deen* in their youth and even when they are passing the various stages of old-age. When they have married their children as You desire and have started growing white hairs, keep the flame of love burning brightly within their hearts. Even then, keep them steadfast as ambassadors of Your *Deen* so that they can be instrumental in bringing Your *Deen* alive in the lives of mankind.

O Allah! Safeguard them as well as their progeny from present and future evils and deceptions regardless of how innocent these may appear to people. Keep their feet from slipping even during the terrible times that Your Rasul ﷺ predicted; when people will openly ridicule Your Book and Your *Deen* and when people will lose their *Imaan* overnight. Keep the armour of

Islãm on their bodies as long as they remain alive and allow them to pass on from this world wearing the crown of *Imaan.* Fill their hearts with love for You and make them among those who eagerly await their meeting with You. When they are presented for reckoning on the Plains of Resurrection, do not allow them to be disgraced in front of humanity.

O Allah! Even if the world turns traitor, allow us all to remain loyal to Your *Deen* until our deaths and allow us all to enter *Jannah.* O Allah! Accept this *Du'a* of ours." *Aameen*

## REPLY CLEARLY

Many domestic disputes will be effectively averted if women learnt to express themselves clearly and convincingly. They should explicitly say whatever is in their hearts so that misunderstandings are avoided. We shall present a few guidelines for your benefit that will Insha Allah assist you in a great deal when conversing with your husband and others as well.

1. When your husband asks you a question, do your best to understand what he intends knowing from you before replying.
2. Reply only to the question he asks without adding anything extra. The harm of adding to your reply is that arguments may spring from the additional information and that you may unintentionally disclose a fault of yours, leading to him losing

confidence in you. A wise person once said, "Every human errs. However, the wise person is he who successfully conceals his errors while the fool is he who discloses his own errors." It is therefore necessary for you to neither leave an important detail unspoken nor to add more to what has already answered the question.

For example, your husband tells you to make some custard for the night because he is expecting guests in the evening. However, you discover that you have no custard and are unable to get it from anywhere else. Because you understood that your husband's intention was to entertain his guests, you will make something else to serve the purpose. This may be some pudding, cake, etc. Therefore, when the evening arrives and he asks if the custard is ready, you will say, "I could not make the custard but made some pudding instead." He will thank you heartily and feel relieved. However, the incorrect approach will be to not to make anything, thinking that he asked for custard and you were unable to comply because you did not have the means. This will obviously lead to an argument with disastrous consequences.

Another approach to such a situation is to at least inform your husband well before time about your inability to comply with his request. In this manner, he will suggest an alternative or he may buy something like ice-cream to serve to his guests. Whatever the case, you should never wait for your husband to ask you about developments before addressing the problem. Remember that insignificant matters often spark the most serious disputes. If you wait until he arrives home before informing him of the situation, he will find it extremely difficult to go out of the house again to buy something that you need and this will ignite further problems.

If matters are so bad that you were unable to comply with his request until he returned and were unable to inform him earlier, you should perform two Rakaahs salaah and ask Allah to mend the situation. When he arrives, gently apologise for not doing as he asked. May Allah guide all Muslim women to always do what is correct. Aameen.

## HAVE MERCY ON YOUR CHILDREN

A common failing among many women is that they do not respond immediately when their husbands call for them. If a woman wants to earn the pleasure and *Du'as* of her husband, she should respond as soon as he calls for her. She should not delay in answering with the intention that he will do the work himself. For example, if the husband returns tired from work, immediately lies down to rest and then calls for his wife, she will immediately realise that he wants her to do something minor such as adjusting the speed of the fan, bringing him a glass of water or something else that he can do by himself. She therefore remains silent when he calls with the intention that he should realise that she is busy doing something else and cannot hear him. As a result, he will be forced to do the work himself.

It is such behaviour that often leads to arguments. What ggravates such situations is when the wife responds to the ill with an insolent remark such as "I am busy ironing our clothing, you know!" or "Don't you realise that I am usy preparing your supper!"

If you wish to attain your husband's undying love, you vill have to ensure that your husband's heart is never tainted vith any ill-feelings towards you. You should never give im the opportunity to say that your mother had not taught ou well enough or that you cannot compare with the wives f his friends or other women. It is therefore best for you to ither stop your work immediately when he calls or you hould inform him that you are busy before you start so hat he may know that you are busy. For example, you may sk him whether he wants his meals immediately or a little ater because you need to perform your *Isha Salaah*. Employing a bit of diplomacy is always helpful and will ensure a happy marriage. Among the benefits of deliberated uch diplomacy are:

1. Unnecessary disputes will be avoided.
2. He will not burn your heart by comparing you with other women but he will appreciate everything you do for him.
3. You will have no fear that your neighbours or in-laws will hear his shouting and then make a meal of their gossip about you.
4. You will always benefit from the *Du'as* of your husband both in your lifetime as well as after your death. Your children will also grow up to be pious,

capable and resourceful, thereby enabling them to lead their lives successfully.

5. The greatest benefit of such behaviour is that your children will be saved from suffering complexes as a result of the incessant arguments in their home. Enjoying a life of peace and goodwill, they will develop many sterling qualities such as good self-esteem, courage and determination. When a child lives in a home where arguments are common, she will grow up either feeling that her mother is incapable or that her father is a tyrant. She will be plagued with the idea that if her father is always making her mother cry, how will he be able to listen to her? The child's capabilities will also be stifled because she will be living with a mother who is constantly scared of her mother-in-law or sisters-in-law.

By the grace of Allah, I have had the opportunity to teach in both state and private schools and Madaris. I have encountered children of all types and I have dealt with them both as an educationalist and a counsellor. In my experiences with children whose homes are the battlefield of their parents, I have noticed the following:

- They fail their grades very often.
- They are often absent from classes.
- They are extremely silent and unreceptive in class.
- They are reluctant to participate in games and other activities with other children.

- They are unable to answer questions despite knowing the answers.

Such children are the victims of quarrelling couples. The vision of the father slapping the mother and the sound of the mother's sobbing are always in the child's mind. Such a child can never match the confident and happy children in her class.

You should therefore take pity on your innocent children and spare them the grief of your disputes with your husband. Do not give your husband the opportunity to get angry with you. If he does get angry on some account, remain silent and do not provoke a further argument. For the sake of the children you should rather apologise even if he is at fault and make an attempt to change the subject.

May Allah guide all Muslim women to be able to run their homes efficiently without giving anyone an excuse to point a finger at them. *Aameen*

## AN ESTRANGED WIFE'S LETTER TO HER HUSBAND

It was a Friday night and father and brother were gone out to the weekly Friday night gathering at the *Masjid.* The only man in the house was my brother Bilaal because of his studies at the Daarul Uloom. There was no end to my uneasiness and anxiety that night as I lay down to sleep with a disturbed mind. As I fell asleep, I dreamt that *Qiyaamah* had taken place and everyone was being raised from the ground. Everyone was taken to the Plain of Resurrection and they were all concerned with the accounts of their deeds that were due from them.

When I looked to my right, I saw many people entering splendid palaces without any reckoning. They entered beautiful gardens that were filled with the most colourful and exquisite flowers. There was every conceivable pleasure to be found there and a cool breeze blew for them. the men and women entering there were exuberant and carefree. I also hastened to follow them.

As I was about to enter the gate, the gatekeeper stopped me and asked for my entry permit. Surprised, I asked him what ticket he meant. He told me that if I had no permit, I would have to return to the queue of people awaiting their reckoning. Throwing my hands up in the air, I asked him how much the permit would cost. He said, "Respected lady! This permit cannot be bought with money." When I asked him how I could get one, he replied, "For Muslim men, their permit is the pleasure of their parents and for Muslim women it is the pleasure of their husbands. Without this permit, none can enter this *Jannah*."

"Will the pleasure of my parents not suffice?" I asked him with hope brimming in my heart as I looked at him. Breathing a sigh, he replied, "I am sorry. A married woman has to carry the permit of her husband's pleasure." Despondent, I stared with envy at all the women entering without reckoning. Among them were women whom I recognised, such as my cousins and friends, all of them entering happily with their little children. I felt so embarrassed that I wished that the ground would swallow me up.

Standing there ashamed of myself, some of my friends took pity on me and called me to enter with them. When I did not respond to their call, they came to fetch me. However, when they saw that I did not have the permit of my husband's pleasure, they turned away from me in disappointment. My friend Salma was always a straightforward person. When she saw me like this, she said, "Did we not tell you that the life of the world is very short and that you should keep your husband happy so that you would not have any regrets after death? You did not listen to your husband when he told you not to walk about without *Hijaab* and not to take videos at weddings. You took no heed when he told you that you should stop missing your *Salaahs* and that you should stop preventing him from going out in Allah's path without an excuse."

I bitterly regretted my deeds and wished that I also had the permit of my husband's pleasure so that could enjoy the bounties of *Jannah* with the others. My thoughts were interrupted by voices shouting, "Make way! Move out of the way!" I turned to see that a woman was arriving on a conveyance and that her entourage and escort were clearing the way ahead for her. As she arrived at the gate of *Jannah*, even the gatekeeper greeted her with great respect and honour. When she has dismounted and entered, I asked the gatekeeper who the lady was. He replied, "This lady loved her husband very much and was so obedient to him that he always made *Du'a* for her. She has attained this high status even though she lived with her husband for only eight years."

Upon hearing this reply of the gatekeeper, I began to reflect over my married life. I was at loggerheads with my husband for even the most insignificant matters. I had even left him to come to my parents home, thinking that I am not his slave and that if he does not care me, I will not care for him either. I always thought that I do not need him when my parents can ably look after me. Whereas other women preferred living under their husband's authority, I could not even bear the thought of it. My soul would emerge from my body if I ever heard talk of a woman being subservient to her husband. The times when women served men have passed by. However, although the snake has slithered away, the tracks are still present. I felt that men ought to open their eyes and ears to take a lesson from Europe and America. These were all my misguided thoughts, which I seriously put to question when the gatekeeper told me about the woman who had received such great honour. I was suddenly overcome with envy for her and my emotions were beyond control. I wished that I had also dutifully served my husband as she did so that I could also share her honour. I could bear this no longer and gave a loud scream.

Hearing my scream, my mother and our little sons woke up with a shock. Mother was flustered and asked me what the matter was. Seeing me sit up erect and shivering, mother rushed to my bed and took my head to her chest to comfort me. What could I tell her? As I looked around the room, I saw neither the Day of *Qiyaamah*, nor the beautiful spectacle of *Jannah* or the gatekeeper. My mother comforted me by telling me that nightmares are from *Shaitaan* and that I should not worry about them because they will have no effect on my life. I complied as she bade me to sleep, but my mind was now in a frenzy. It was not long before I had returned to the realm of dreams.

In another dream, I saw that the scene was set for a wedding to take place. There I saw you looking quite happy as the bridegroom. I ran to you and angrily grabbed hold of your hand asking, "What is happening here?" However, without even looking at me, you coldly shoved me aside. With tears in my eyes and a shattered heart, I returned to my parents home with your words ringing in my ears as you said, "You have caused me tremendous grief and heartache, forcing me to consider remarrying. Before marrying you I was actively serving the *Deen*, reciting Qur'ãn regularly, making *Zikr*, etc. However, since you entered my life I have been unable to do this properly." Unable to bear this, I again gave a loud scream and sat upright in my bed.

Although mother consoled me by telling that matters between you and I were not so bad that you would leave me to marry another woman, I was still not convinced. She again bade me to sleep, but the two dreams had forbidden sleep for me. They had changed the course of my life. I resolved not to disobey you in future. As I seriously considered your complaints against me, I begged Allah for forgiveness. Whereas I was under the impression that you were always pandering to the wishes of your mother and sisters, you maintained that it was I who was causing you grief. After doing some introspection, I realised that I am at fault.

I regretted that you often had to eat take-away foods because I rarely cooked a good meal for you. Whenever you invited people home for meals, you always had to suffer the embarrassment of serving them sloppy dishes. Whereas I always blamed you and your family for having extravagant tastes, I failed to realise that I was at fault for not even making an effort to learn good cooking skills. Although I now became angry with my mother and sisters for not pointing these things out to me, I have also realised that I cannot really blame them because whenever there was a problem, I always put the blame on you without telling them the reason for your anger.

It then occurred to me that your hints about me not maintaining my beauty were spot-on target. I now realised that I have been neglecting myself and rarely beautify myself for you. In addition to this, I also neglect our two children, failing to keep them clean and presentable. They therefore look shabby and unkempt when their father sees them, so you cannot appreciate their appearance either.

I also admit that the times are too often when I behave coldly towards you. I beg your forgiveness for not responding to your sexual advances at times and then waking the children up to throw a spanner in the works. With my mind entangled in such thoughts, I hastily got up to make *Wudhu* and perform *Tahajjud Salaah,* begging Allah for forgiveness. The *Ahadith* of Rasulullah ﷺ began flooding my mind at that point.

"If I were to command anyone to prostrate to another (human), I would have certainly commanded a wife to prostrate to her husband."

"The angels curse the wife who does not respond when her husband calls her to bed and he spends the night angry with her.

"There are three categories of people whose *Salaah* and every good deed is not accepted. The three are: (1) The slave who escapes from his/her master, (2) the woman whose husband is displeased with her and (3) the person who is drunk until he becomes sober."

Because the time of *Tahajjud* is a time when *Du'as* are accepted, I prayed to Allah to forgive me.

O my beloved husband! Think of all the problems I have given you thusfar as a bad dream and forget it all. Reality is what I have written I this letter. I am now your devoted slave and regret all my previous mistakes. Just as Allah forgives His slaves, you also forgive me and do not deprive me of your large heartedness. Forgive me for coming to my parents home against your wishes. I am prepared to return home as soon as you would permit me to. Remember that I am always yours.

The children are also missing you terribly and cannot wait to see you again. In conclusion I would like to add that Insha Allah you will never again have cause to be displeased with me in future.

Yours truly,

Your loving wife

XYZ

## THE HUSBAND'S REPLY

No sooner had the husband read his wife's letter wher he replied:

My beloved wife

Your letter reached me after a while. All I can say is that your changed attitude can only be the results of your father's or my father's sincere *Du'as*. I am pleasantly surprised by what you have written and can only thank Allah for it.

Although some time has passed, you have now realised your errors. I was not upset only because you were disobedient to me, but you were also disobedient to Allah and His Rasul ﷺ. The hurt I felt because of your behaviour is already healing and the future will only do it good. Allah is witness to the fact that my heart is filled with love for you. With the grace of Allah, you have a pious father who will assure you that I have no other woman besides you in my heart. I love you deeply and have definitely forgiven you for your errors.

If the past was a bad dream, then your sweet words and new resolve have dispelled all thoughts of past dreams. I am prepared to forget the past and work for our future. You obviously need no permission to return home because you had none to leave in the first place. This is your home and you are the queen. You may return whenever you please.

It is only Allah Who has made you realise that without pleasing Him, you cannot hope to please anyone else. By performing all your salaahs, Allah will be pleased with you and He will ensure that I am also pleased. To keep Allah pleased, we should also avoid weddings and other functions where the laws of Allah are violated.

Convey my love and kisses to the children.

Yours truly,

XYZ

## The Story Afterwards

Relating her story afterwards, the lady says, "When I returned to my husband, I resolved to be the first to wake up every morning and the last to sleep at night to ensure that my kingdom is in order. The same house that was once a battlefield transformed into a garden of bliss and contentment. Our home now generates an atmosphere of righteousness and is a model for others to emulate. My husband finds happiness whenever he enters the door and has no need to tell me what to do. Everything gets done on time and he is always making *Du'a* for me, his loyal servant. By Allah's grace, we have an abundance of everything we need and people are always praying that our relationship goes from strength to strength. The past has been forgotten.

The two dreams have really transformed my life and people are now full of praises for me instead of insults. The women of the neighbourhood now ask me to give them advice. It is a fact that when a woman practises Islām and treats her husband well, she will become a shining beacon for others to follow. Not only will she have success in this world, but in the *Aakhirah* as well."

**My Advice to My Sisters**

"You have read my story. Based on my experiences, I would like to advise my Muslim sisters that she controls the character, the health and the happiness of not only her husband, but her children as well. Every woman should treat her husband as a new bride would and she should always be prepared to make sacrifices for him. She should be his comforting companion and his heroine who rescues him from all worries and anxiety. Like a kind teacher, she should also be there to lovingly protect him from sin.

Remember that a man is not the slave of a beautiful face, but easily becomes the slave of an obedient wife who strives to please him. An obedient wife will capture her husband's heart, thereby having her wishes addressed without even asking. This is the key to her happiness as well.

Another piece of advice to my sisters is that they should always bear in mind the *Hadith* of Rasulullah ﷺ that states: "Exchange gifts with each other, you will love each other." Every wife should therefore buy gifts for her husband. If she is unable to do this, she should get her father or brother to buy it and give it to him as a gift from them. Exchanging gifts develops love and removes malice from the heart.

My final advice is that a wife should ensure that all her domestic chores are complete before her husband returns home from work. This will impress him and win his heart. It is because many women are negligent of this that they have problems with their husbands."

## AN EXAMINATION PAPER

Read each question carefully at least three times. If your answer is yes, give yourself five points. Thereafter, add them up to see whether you are a good wife or not. The sum of your points will give you a percentage so that you can gauge your position on a scale of a hundred.

1. Are you awake before your husband and children every morning, encouraging the boys to proceed to the *Masjid* for the *Fajr Salaah*?
2. Do you ensure that your husband's clothes for the next day are ready for him and that everything else

he needs for the day are kept together to save him the inconvenience of searching for them?

3. Do you ensure that everything is in order for your husband when he proceeds on a journey; that his bags are packed and that he has all the necessary travel documents, etc?

4. Do you ensure that your children are attending their school and *Madrasah* classes regularly and that they are completing their homework daily?

5. Do you prepare dishes that your husband likes even though you do not like it or you find it difficult to prepare?

6. Do you encourage your husband to bring his guests home for meals so that he does not feel difficult to ask you to prepare meals for them?

7. Do you ensure that you beautify yourself when he is at home?

8. When he returns from work, do you have something pleasant waiting for him such as some juice or even plain water so that his frustration can be calmed? By doing this, he will feel that there is someone for him after all the trouble he may have experienced at work.

9. If your husband has to tell you that he is inviting his mother or his sisters over for meals and that he is going to give them Idara Ishaa'at-E-Diniyat Publishers latest book releases as a gift, will you welcome the idea with a happy face?

10. When he is sleeping during the day or busy doing something important, do you keep the children occupied so that they do not disturb him?
11. When the children do something dangerous or foolish, do you shout and scream at them or do you rather place your hand lovingly on their heads and explain the wrong to them so that the impression lasts with them that you are concerned about them and not only interested in venting your anger?
12. When your husband is angry, do you apologise and seek forgiveness even though the fault is not yours?
13. When your husband calls for you once, do you ensure that he does not have to repeat himself?
14. When you are unable to comply with a request he makes, do you inform him beforehand so that he does not learn about it only after asking? For example, if he wants a certain dish prepared and you were unable to prepare it for some good reason, will you tell him this only after he asks for it when sitting down to eat or well before time?
15. Do you place your hand on your children's heads and make *Du'as* for them such as "Abdullaah! May Allah make you a Haafidh and an Aalim" or "O Faatima! May Allah use you for the service of His *Deen*", etc? (Remember that you should never curse your children because this will deprive them of honour and status in people's eyes).
16. When you notice a fault in your husband (such as his failure to tend to the nurturing of the children),

do you speak to him kindly instead of rebuking him and do you choose the correct times to speak to him?

17. When you are expecting, do you ensure that you avoid all sins (such as watching television) so that the unborn child is not adversely affected by the spiritual ill effects of sins? (Remember that the good deeds you carry out during this period will have a positive effect on the child by making him/her a good Muslim who will be a valuable asset to the *Ummah*).

18. When buying toys for your children, do you ensure that the toys are also educational and that they are free of pictures of animate objects? (Remember that the angels of mercy do not enter homes in which pictures of animate objects are displayed).

19. Do you abstain from backbiting and lying about your sisters-in-law (husband's brothers' wives) to earn nearness to your mother-in-law and your other sisters-in-law (your husband's sisters)? (Remember that a person with whom Allah is displeased will not have contentment even though she has all the luxuries of life. Jealousy, carrying tales, lying and making others jealous of one are sins that attract Allah's wrath).

20. (A) Do you respond to your husband's sexual advances?

(B) Do you know who curses the woman who refuses to fulfil her husband's sexual desires without good reason? (Each question here carries 2.5 points).

You now have an idea of where you stand in relation to the ideal wife. If you have done well, make *Du'a* to Allah to keep you steadfast and always improving. Also make *Du'a* to Allah to create such sterling qualities in all Muslim wives. If you have faired miserably in this examination, remember that men actually seek protection from the likes of yourself because you cause them to age before their time. You should therefore resolve to mend your ways and to inculcate the qualities of a good wife. Also make sincere *Du'a* to Allah to assist you with this and to make you among the fortunate women about whom Rasulullah ﷺ gave the glad tidings of entering *Jannah*.

## THE LAST WILL AND TESTAMENT OF A MUSLIM

The *Ahadith* have emphasised the necessity of having one's will written especially if a person has missed *Salaahs* in her lifetime, has missed her *Hajj* when it was *Farz* on her or when she owes *Zakah*. When a Muslim fails to write a will under these circumstances, she will be guilty of a sin. The evil of this sin will prevail as long as she does no write the will. You should consult the more detailed books of Islãmic jurisprudence to learn the method of writing your last will and testament.

## A GOOD HUSBAND'S PARTING WORDS TO HIS WIFE

One of Islãm's leading warriors was the Turkish general Anwar Pasha. He devoted his entire life to fighting the enemies of Islãm and was blessed with martyrdom while fighting the Bolshevik Russians. A day before his martyrdom, he wrote an affectionate letter to his wife the princess Bakhiyya. The letter was published in Turkish newspapers and was first translated in Indian newspapers on 22 April 1923. The letter contains many lessons and advices for every Muslim. It reads as follows:

To Bakhiyya, my lifelong companion and my source of happiness

Allah is your most Honoured and Esteemed Protector. Your last letter to me is now in front of me. Rest assured, this letter will always remain close to my heart. Although I cannot see you, I can visualise your delicate fingers writing every word; the same fingers that so gently caressed my head when we were together. My eyes are often filled with a vision of your beautiful face in the haze of my tent.

Sadly, your letter suggests that I have forgotten you and have no affection for you anymore. You say that I have broken your heart which is brimming with love merely to play with fire and blood in this far-off land. You say that I have forsaken a lonesome woman who has to spend the nights counting the stars while yearning for my companionship. You say that I love war and swords. However, when writing these words which were obviously motivated by true love, you had no idea of the deep wound it would inflict on my heart. How will I ever be able to convince you that I love nothing in the world more than I love you. You are the goal of all my love. I have loved none besides you because it was you who stole my heart. Then why did I leave you? You may certainly ask this question, my love.

Listen with care! I have not left you in search of wealth and property. Contrary to what my enemies claim, I have also not left you to consolidate my throne. I have left you only because my duty to Allah has brought me here. There is nothing superior to fighting *Jihaad* in the path of Allah. *Jihaad* is that great deed the intention of which makes one worthy of *Jannatul Firdous.* With the grace of Allah, I have not only made the intention of fighting in *Jihaad*, but I am currently engaged in the same.

My separation from you is the single greatest barrier to my resolve, but this makes me extremely happy because my love for you is proving to be the greatest test of my resolve. I am grateful to Allah for granting me the ability to successfully pass this test by giving precedence to His command and to my love for Him over my personal desires. You should be happy and thankful to Allah that your husband has sacrificed his love for you for the love of Allah.

Although *Jihaad* with the sword is not compulsory for you, you are still not exempt from *Jihaad*. In fact, no Muslim male or female is exempt from *Jihaad*. Your *Jihaad* is to give precedence to your love for Allah over other desires and over your love for everything else. Together with your love for your husband, you should also develop your love for Him.

Remember that you should never make *Du'a* for your husband to return from *Jihaad* safely to your lap because this would be selfish. Allah will not be pleased with this. Rather make *Du'a* that Allah should accept your husband's efforts in *Jihaad*. Make *Du'a* that Allah should either allow him to return victorious or allow the cup of martyrdom to be taken to his lips; the lips that were never polluted with alcohol but always remain moist with the recitation of the Qur'ãn and the *Zikr* of Allah.

My beloved Bakhiyya! How dear will the moment be when this head which you praised will be separated from the neck. Anwar's greatest desire is to be martyred and raised with Hazrat Khaalid bin Waleed رضي الله عنه on the Day of *Qiyaamah*. This life is one of a few days and death is inevitable. How can one then fear death? If death is a certainly, why should a person die lying on his bed? Martyrdom is not death but life, an everlasting life!

Dearest Bakhiyya! Listen to my last bequest. After I am martyred I want you to marry your brother-in-law

Noori Pasha because he is the closest person to me after you. I desire that after my departure to the Hereafter, he should be the one to loyally serve you.

My second bequest is that you inform all your children about my life and send them all out in *Jihaad* to defend Islãm and their country. I shall be very offended with you in *Jannah* if you fail to do this.

My third bequest is that you should always treat Mustafa Kamal Pasha well. Assist him in every possible manner because Allah has placed the salvation of the nation in his hands.

I now bid you farewell, my beloved Bakhiyya. I do not know why my heart tells me that I shall not be writing another letter to you after this one. How strange will it be if I am martyred tomorrow. I exhort you to be patient. Instead of being grieved, rejoice over the fact that I was of service to the cause of my Allah.

Bakhiyya, I shall have to go now. In my mind, I am embracing you now. Insha Allah, we shall meet in *Jannah* and shall never be again separated.

Your Anwar

This letter has been extracted from pages 127 to 130 of the book "*Turkaan Ahraar*", printed in Lahore. It should be borne in mind that at the time when the letter was written, Mustafa Kamal Pasha was only a soldier in the Turkish army. This was long before he took antagonistic steps against Islãm as president of Turkey.

## A GOOD WIFE'S PARTING WORDS TO HER HUSBAND

When writing her final bequest to her husband, a wife should add the following:

1. She should request him to forgive all her short-comings and everything that she may have done which has hurt him in any way. She should remember the words of Rasulullah ﷺ who said, "A woman will enter *Jannah* if she passes away while her husband is pleased with her."[1] She should therefore do her best to obey everything lawful that he asks her to do.
2. If she has the bad habit of applying nail polish, she should remind him in her bequest that this should be removed before her corpse is bathed because the bath will be invalid with the nail polish on.[2]
3. She should advise her sons and grandsons to become *Huffaaz* of the Qur'ān and *Ulama*. At the same time, she should also advise her daughters and granddaughters to be righteous Muslims and to learn Arabic. If her sons have grown up and she was unable to make the *Huffaaz* and *Ulama*, she should apologise to them and emphasise that they should ensure that their sons become *Huffaaz*, *Ulama* and sincere callers to Islām.

---

1. *Tirmizi*, Vol. 1, Page 219.
2. "*Ahsan-ul-Fataawaa*", Vol. 4, Page 237.

If her children are still growing, she should advise them ɔ study *Deen* and to apply themselves to the service of ılām at all levels. She should stress that they make every ffort to ensure that the *Deen* of Allah dominates all other eligions, as will happen before the Day of *Qiyaamah.*

4. She should encourage her husband to remarry after her death so that his home will continue running smoothly and so that he may be saved from sin. She should also caution him against allowing another woman to abuse her children.
5. She should remind him to recite *Du'as* and to do good deeds on her behalf so that she could benefit from the rewards of these deeds.
6. She should instruct him to destroy the photographs of her that appear on her identity document, on her passport or anywhere else so that no photographs of her remain. In this way, her sin of having her photographs taken will not live after her.
7. She should also direct him to look for pious partners for her children once they are ready for marriage. She should issue explicit instructions that the marriage should be simple and contracted only after consultation with elders, *Istikhaara* and the consent of the couple. In addition to this, she must stipulate that her daughter-in-law should be given her own quarters as soon as she marries.

## SOME BENEFICIAL BOOKS FOR WOMEN TO READ

The books mentioned below are extremely beneficial for all women. We urge all women to study them carefully and to encourage other women to read them as well.

1. **Ma'aariful Qur'ãn:** Hazrat Mufti Muhammad Shafi (A.R) has written this dynamic commentary of the Qur'ãn. One should try to read a few Aayaat daily with their commentary. In this manner, one will understand Allah's message to mankind. Wherever one is in doubt about anything or has difficulty understanding something, one should mark the spot and ask one's *Mahram* to query the difficulty from a reliable *Aalim*. To date, the English translation of this commentary is incomplete and only a few volumes have been released.
2. **Behishti Zewar (*Heavenly Ornaments*)**: This book is truly a gift from heaven for women on earth. By studying this book, a woman will be able to master many injunctions of *Deen* and will be able to lead her life correctly in a manner pleasing to Allah. The book is extremely comprehensive and encompasses a wide variety of subjects pertinent to every woman.
3. **A Gift to (Muslim) Women**: This comprehensive book is worth reading several times over. Every woman is advised to recite at least a part daily and to read it to others as well. Two English translations of the original Urdu version of this book are currently

available, one is titled "A Gift to Women" and the other is titled "A Gift to Muslim Women".

4. **Fadhaa'il A'maal:** This book should be read for at least ten minutes to the entire household every day. *Insha Allah,* it will lead to a spiritual transformation in the household within a short while. The effects of evil will leave the house and sins will be much more infrequent. Love will develop among the household members and ill-feelings will disappear.

5. **Fadhaa'il Sadaqaat (*The Virtues of Charity*):** This book should also be read to the entire household on a daily basis. Regular recitation of this book will quickly expel love for this world from a person's heart. One will be convinced about the temporal status of this world and one's love for the *Aakhirah* will grow. Difficulties will seem insignificant and one will look forward to the Hereafter.

6. **The Upbringing of Children/*The Bringing up of Children*:** These books are a must for every parent. These books and books of this nature should be studied carefully so that our children can be raised to be valuable assets of Islãm.

7. **One Minute Madrasah:** This valuable book compiled by Hazrat Hakeem Akhtar (Daamat Barakaatuh) is a collection of the advices given by his spiritual mentor Hazrat Shah Maulana Abraarul Haqq (Daamat Barakaatuh). It is unfortunate that after years of performing *Salaah,* we neither know what we are reciting nor do we perform the *Salaah*

correctly. We are also involved in many sins tha destroy our deeds and we deprive ourselves of grea rewards because we do not know the virtues of thes deeds. This book sheds light on all these factors in simple manner. It is beneficial for mothers to read t their children as well as for *Imaams* of *Masaajid* t read to the congregation after *Salaah*.

# IN CONCLUSION

We request every reader to remember us in their pious *Du'as* for whatever benefit you may have derived from this book. Do not forget to make *Du'a* for all Muslim sisters. Pray to Allah to guide them all to lead their lives as Allah and His Rasul ﷺ have instructed. It is now your responsibility to raise your children as mentioned in this book and to imbibe the qualities of a good woman in their friends and family. You should also allow other women to read this book so that they can also benefit from it. It should not be allowed to rot in the shelves. After reading this book, recite the following *Du'a*. This *Du'a* should be recited after terminating any gathering so that Allah may forgive any shortcomings.

{Translation: O Allah! You are Pure from all defects and all praise belongs to You Alone. We testify that there is none worthy of worship but You. We seek Your pardon, O Allah and turn to You (in repentance)."}

{Translation: May Allah bestow His choicest blessings and mercy on the best of His creation Muhammad ﷺ, as well as on his family, his companions, his wives and all his progeny."}

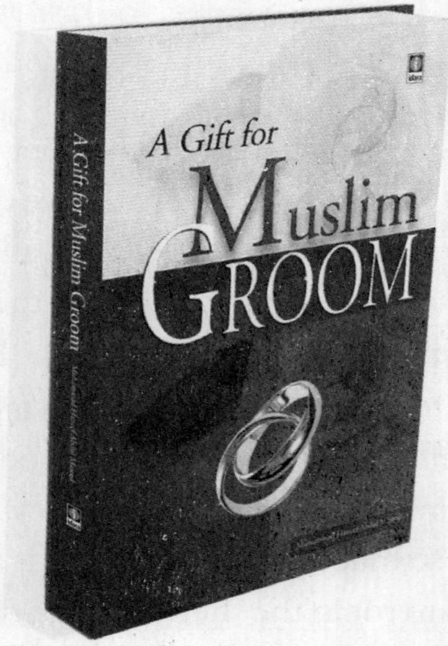


ISBN 81-7101-642-1 Hard Back
Size 14.5 x 22.25 cm Pages 316

The book deals with; identifying the Islamic responsibilities o husband towards his wife, persuading him to pay heed to h rights, loving and respecting her, pleasant ways of ignoring h mistakes and saving his wife from the disobedience of Allah, t topic assigning her thoughts for all the relatives and women of t area to act upon the complete religion. Likewise laying dow Muslim psychological principles to escape all the tensions, worri and confusions between the husband, wife, mother, daughter ar sister-in-law in such a way so as to create prosperous and satisfie society.

A Muslim groom, after praying, should read this book b the intention to act upon it, so that Allah the Almighty with H grace may create true and hearty love, affection and intimacy i between the married couples, Amen!

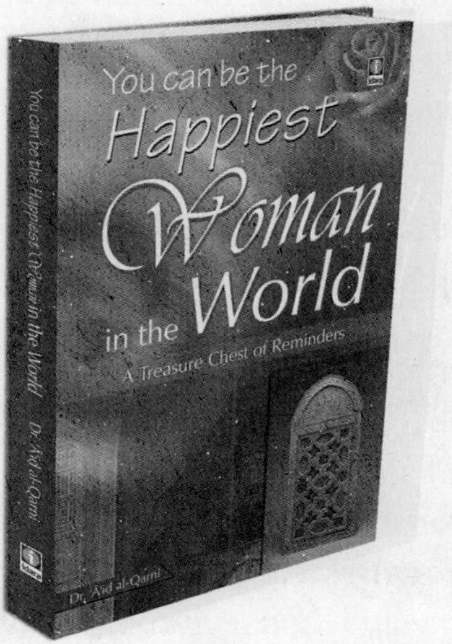


ISBN 81-7101-630-8 Hard Back
Size 14.5 x 22.25 cm Pages 272

Do you want to be happy? We are all looking for an escape from worry, stress and depression, and for ways to find happiness. This book presents the route to happiness in a nutshell, drawing on Islamic teachings and the voices of "experts" both western and eastern. So sit back, relax and read it from cover to cover, or dip into it a page or two at a time in between other activities in a busy life as a wife, mother, student or worker.

You are holding in your hands a treasure chest of reminders that will help you learn important lessons and set you on the path to happiness in this world and in the Hereafter, *Insha'Allah*

ISBN 81-7101-375-9 Hard Back
Size 14.5 x 22.25 cm Pages 932

It would be redundant to state that Women make a priceless contribution towards the construction and development of a nation. A mother's lap is the child's first school as well as fostering institution: and the lessons leant from this institution are more indelible than a line carved on a rock. That is why the importance attached to women in Islam is no less than that of men.

This book covers almost all the aspects of life in detail, particularly the problems faced by women with their solutions in the light of Holy *Qur'an* and *Ahadeeth*. Utmost efforts have been taken to compile the traditions and problems reported by women. For the easiness and benefits of the readers, different aspects of life have been divided into several chapters i.e Prayers, Supplications, Nikah, Education, Divorce, Social moral, Etiquettes, veil, Dress & Adornment, Purification etc.

# A Gift for Muslim Groom

**A Guide for Joyous and Successful Married Life**

(A Complete English Translation of the Famous Book ***"Tohfa-e-Dulha"***)

*Rendered into English by:* **Mohammad Saleem**

MUHAMMED HANEEF ABDUL MAJEED

idara

www.idaraimpex.com

A Gift for Muslim Groom

**Compiled by: M. Haneef Abdul Majeed**

*Rendered into English by:* **Mohammad Saleem**

9788171016426 00000

Edition 2019

ISBN: 81-7101-642-1

TP-809-19

*Published by Mohammad Yunus for*

**IDARA IMPEX**

D-80, Abul Fazal Enclave-I, Jamia Nagar
New Delhi-110 025 (India)
Tel.: +91-11-2695 6832 & 085888 33786
Email: **info@idara.in | www.idarastore.com**

Retail Shop: **IDARA IMPEX**
Shop #6, Nizamia Complex, Gali Gadrian, Near Karim's Hotel
Hazrat Nizamuddin, New Delhi-110013 (India) Tel.: 085888 44786

بسم الله الرحمٰن الرحيم

In the light of the Prophet's (Peace be upon him) saying, it is proven, that in the relation between husband and wife there are some specific obligatory rights for both of them, if these are taken care of, then the house may become a sample of the Paradise. All the same, if these rights are ignored, then this mutual relation becomes a curse inspite of comfort. Besides these obligatory rights, there are some desirable & fitting points also, if taken into consideration this relation becomes more powerful and everlasting.

It is the perfection of *Shari'at-e-Islamia*, that it does not compel anyone to obey it, rather its virtues and merits are told, that is if you perform accordingly what will you get in the Hereafter?

Thus, by obeying *Shari'ah* one gets dual benefits, i.e. worldly benefits and afterlife benefits in the form of Paradise and Blessings of Allah the Almighty. By studying the traditions of the Prophet (Peace be upon him), we can guess how much stress is given to family affairs. The Prophet Muhammed (Peace be upon him) has said خیر کم خیر کم لا هله وانا خیر کم لاهلی *(Best of you is one who is the best for his family and I am the best of you for my family)*. Just guess from this tradition how much significance is given to family's happiness in Islam.

This book, "**A Gift for Muslim Groom**" is written by our friend Maulvi Mohd. Haneef and his some companions, before this they have written a very useful book "**A Gift for Bride**". Both these two books, deal with the orders and decencies, in detail, regarding mutual relations of bride and groom alongwith some beneficial advices.

May Allah accept these books and guide the *Ummat-e-Muslimah* to work accordingly and may He favour Maulvi Sb. to serve the Islam and Muslims likewise. In my opinion these two books should be in each and every house.

**Hazrat Maulvi Mufti Nizamuddin Shamizi**
Professor of Hadees
Jami'at-ul-Uloom-il-Islamia
Allama Binaury Town, Karachi-5

# Contents

# INTRODUCTION

This book *"A GIFT FOR MUSLIM GROOM"* deals with; identifying Islamic responsibilities of a husband towards his wife, persuading him to give wife her rights, principles of being faithful to wife always, love for wife, respecting wife, showing good behavior towards her, pleasant ways of ignoring her mistakes and saving his wife from the disobedience of Allah and the topics assigning her thoughts for all the relatives and women of the area, to act upon the complete religion, likewise laying down Muslim psychological principles to escape all the tensions, worries, confusions in between husband and wife, mother-in-law, daughter-in-law and sister in-law in such a way so as to create a prosperous and satisfied society. Thus creating love, affection, intimacy and good relation between husband and wife. If the groom acts upon the mentioned principles, then the house may become a sample of Paradise and the family members will get success & honour in the world and the after-life. A Muslim groom, after praying, should read this book by the intention to act upon it, so that Allah the Exalted with His grace may create true and hearty love, affection and intimacy in between the married couples, Amen!

# Foreword

نَحْمَدُهٗ وَ نُصَلِّی عَلٰی رَسُوْلِهِ الْكَرِيْمِ حَامِداً وَّ مُصَلِّياً وَمُسْلِماً۔

By the grace of Allah and well wishes of friends a new book came into being by just arranging; the *Shari'ah* rules and orders which I have presented in my previous book "A Gift for Bride", the articles of some eminent scholars, which were very important and to the point, are included exactly as they were. In this book we have gathered reformatory articles from different books with the sole intention of inviting the Muslim community to contribute in the reformation of our social status.

We have dealt with, how to avoid fighting and straining of relations in the family members, we have given some advices to be saved from these circumstances. May Allah guide us to the right path, direct us to work accordingly, Amen!

*Was-Salamu 'Alaikum Wa Rahmat-Ullah*

## How would you read this book?

Since, this book has a great importance for the family life and if the family affairs are normal then only reformation in society occurs; that's why it is our request to pay full consideration and seriousness, towards its reformatory topics and righteous articles, to be extra careful of the shortcomings towards which this book has withdrawn our attention. These shortcomings are such that generally people do not care for them and bear losses because of their ignorance. We hope that the study of this book will be done, keeping in mind our these requests:-

(1) Before reading the book pray Allah to make it the means of your righteousness, to make your wife and your child a solace for you, make you one who fulfil their rights and one who treat the wife kindly.

(2) One important request is that you should read the book from the beginning to the end, no matter, how much time it takes, but should be read completely. Best way is to divide its pages for daily reading.

(3) Another request is to keep a pen with you and mark the points you feel you are erring in, read it repeatedly and pray Allah for your reformation . The second benefit of the pen will be, that while reading the book, if you feel something necessary and beneficial, either for the book or for the readers or for being a Muslim husband or father etc. please tell us we will be very thankful to you. While reading the book pray Allah to create love and affection in between husbands and wives, to give them righteous and pious siblings.

(4) Take a free time to read this book so that it may not create any tension.

In the end please pray for the writer of the book, all those preceptors whose work or saying had helped us in preparing this book. May Allah the Exalted bless you for that, Amen!

# First step of Nuptial Affinity

## Selection of a pious wife

Selecting a spouse or life-partner is a very hard and painstaking stage, whilst making haste is very harmful, likewise cowardliness, despair are just deadly poison. After visiting some places, and getting rejected, one becomes so dejected, that his elders begin to say, that we have seen the whole family none is ready to give his daughter, so, we have to marry him however to an unsuitable girl.

In this way a well to do man is married to such a women, who in any way was not suitable for him, then the whole life becomes a battlefield for the husband, wife and their parents which sometimes lead to *Talaaq & Khula*'.

So, the groom must be courageous enough and must not allow his family members to be frustrated, hoping for a good affinity, Pray Allah and after scrutiny and due consideration proceed on and search a suitable match.

(1) First of all pray either (2) two Raka't or as much you can *Salaat-ul-Haajat*, then ask, Allah the Exalted humbly and repeatedly, His Blessings in getting a good match for you. Pray in *Sajda* (Prostration) of *Nafil* obligatory prayers,

رَبَّنَا هَبْ لَنَا مِنْ اَزْوَاجِنَا وَ ذُرِّيّٰتِنَا قُرَّةَ اَعْيُنٍ وَّاجْعَلْنَا
لِلْمُتَّقِيْنَ اِمَامًا

*Our Lord! Vouchsafe us comfort of our wives and of our offspring, and make us patterns for (all) those who ward off (evil)* (Furqan :74)

Keep reciting this supplication.

يَاوَهَّابُ هَبْ لِىْ زَوْجَةً صَالِحَةً

*"O The Provider! Provide me a pious wife."*

Recite this after optional and obligatory Prayers.

اَللّٰهُمَّ اِنِّيْ اَعُوْذُبِكَ مِنَ اِمْرَاَةٍ تُشَيِّبُنِى قَبْلَ الْمَشِيْبِ

*O Allah! I take your refuge from the women who could make me old before the old-age.*

This is also an important prayer one should give importance to it. The Prophet Muhammed (Peace be upon him) also had taken refuge with Allah from such a woman, this type of women is a hoop of neck.

The preceptors has said only of such a woman;

اَلْمَرْأَةُ السَّوْءِ غِلٌّ يُّلْقِيهِ اللّٰهُ تَعَالٰى فِىْ عُنُقِ مَنْ يَشَاءُ مِنْ عِبَادِهٖ

*The bad woman is a hoop of neck, Allah, the Exalted put it in anyone's neck He wants.*

May Allah, save each and every faithful (Mu'min) Amen!

(2) Attach importance of good thought with Allah as a Hadees says.

اناعندظن عبدى بى

*"I am with the thought of my slave."*

(Bukhari, Kitabut-Tawheed H.No. 6951)

If we have good thought with Allah, then He will do accordingly for us, so with courage one must believe that he will get a good and pious wife who will make this small house of the world a replica of paradise.

(3) One must do counselling as its important and stress is there in Islamic *Shari'at*. Allah has said in the Qur'an;

وَاَمْرُهُمْ شُوْرٰى بَيْنَهُمْ

*And whose affairs are by mutual consultation* (Shoora:38)

وَشَاوِرْهُمْ فِى الْاَمْرِ

*And consult with them upon the conduct of affairs.*

(Aal-e-Imran:159)

Therefore counselling is more important then *Istikhara*, but counselling should be done with those who are experienced and capable of counselling, moreover some other things also should be taken care of; these people should be (1) religious (2) intelligent (3) experienced (4) confident. That is because such people will give you best of advices through their experience and intelligence and will take care of your secrets. Likewise one has to consult the elders of his family and the in-laws of the would-be-wife's brothers and sisters, that he is going to be married with so and so what is your opinion.

There was a person, in whom, the feeling of well-wishing gained up, he thought to get the Pleiades and Canopus married, but he was aware of the importance of counselling, not just like us, that, "whatever occurs in my mind is the best". He went to someone and consulted him, he told him:

ايها المنكح الثريا سهيلا　　عمرك الله كيف يلقيان

هى شامية اذما استقلت　　وسهيل اذا ما استقل يمان

*"O the one! Going to marry the Pleiades and Canopus, may Allah give you a long life to do these good works, but, think how they will meet. As when the Pleiades raises it become visible on Syria and when Canopus rises, it raises on Yemen".*

One should care for the suitability of husband and wife also, is she suitable for our family or not, a great difference matters but little difference or diversity does not. Such as the would-be-groom is very rich while the would-be-bride is very poor or conversely to this, she is highly qualified while he is not or conversely to this, she is a religious scholar while he cannot even read the Qur'an by seeing or conversely to this, both the families must consider these points. The parents of the groom should also look for the family where she is brought up, how is her mother and sister....?

When you have different views, consult the intelligent and sensible persons of your family also, then pray Allah so that He may add His Help and Blessings in decision making. Recite the supplication of counselling which is:

اَللّٰهُمَّ اَلْهِمْنِىْ رُشْدِىْ وَاَعِذْنِىْ مِنْ شَرِّ نَفْسِىْ

*O Allah! Inspire me with the best for me I seek (your) refuge by the evil of my soul.*

(4) Taking care of *Istikhara* and must remember what the religious preceptors and godly scholars have described about it;

(a) There is no time restriction in offering the *Istikhara* prayer, that it must be read either in night or after *Isha*, according to *Ahaadees*. Thus one can offer this during the whole day, but should care for the prohibited time.

(b) Do *Istikhara* yourself, most of the people say that we are sinful, let us get *Istikhara* done by someone else. So, first repent of your small and big sins, seek Allah's forgiveness and then do *Istikhara*, Allah will accede to us much more.

(c) It is not necessary that the reply of *Istikhara* would come in dream only, rather keep an eye on the prevailing conditions whether they are favorable or not and there is any obstruction. If the conditions are favourable it means there are blessings in it for you, otherwise it is not good for you. Remember that counselling is better then *Istikhara*, consult the elders of your family and if you are still not satisfied then either repeat the method of *Istikhara* for seven days or offer 14 *Raka't* in two's and pray. These are the *Sunnat* methods, be content with it and keep yourself aloof from the customary methods. May Allah guide us to do *Istikhara* according to *Sunnat*, Amen!

# One should look for these qualities in the would-be-wife

## (1) FAITH:

The first or foremost quality in the women should be her faith, religion and piety. If the women is faithful, religious, fulfilling all the decrees of Allah and the Prophet (pbuh) then the marital life will be durable, pleasant, dignified, full of mutual affection and pleasure.

The coming generation can be a great blessing for the *Ummat-e-Muslima*, after being brought up by an intelligent, pious and veiled lady. This quality should be sought in the beginning by each and every Muslim.

The Prophet (pbuh) once said:

تنکح المرأة لاربع لما لها ولحسبها ولجمالها ولدينها
فاظفر بذات الدين تربت يداک

*The woman is married due to four (of her qualities); (a) Wealth (b) Lineage (c) Comeliness (d) Faith. So get the faithful one, though your hands becomes dirty (it will take some time)*

(Bukhari, Muslim, Mishkaat H. No. 2941)

So, every Muslim should make the faith and piety of his would-be-wife, his standard acting on this advice of the Prophet (pbuh), he should tell his family members that he will marry only a religious, a veiled, and a girl having knowledge of the Holy Qur'an and *Hadees*. Allah will definitely bestow him a faithful wife, *In-Sha'Allah*.

The muslim men should understand that Islam is the only religion that teaches a women her duties towards her husband, parents-in-law, sisters-in-law, the whole family, the human being and also the animals. Religion will only save her from backbiting, falsehood, rudeness, betrayal, immodesty treachery. Only religion will restrain her from obeying the sensual wills and the Satan and to work according to him.

Only the religion will help in the children's reformation, bringing up, teaching them good manners, dignity, politeness, and modesty.

The sole purpose of marriage is mutual agreement, love, peace and true friendship. This is also a reality that as much as the mutual love and affection have access on the religion, nothing have on it because sometimes all the relations and connexions except religion are finished in the world itself otherwise these will be finished on Doomsday. There is a Prophet's (PBUH) saying narrated by Hazrat Ayesha (may Allah be agree with her) and quoted by Ibn-e-Maja, Dar Qutni and Hakim;

تخيروا لنطفكم وانكحو الاكفاء

*"Select the best (women) for your sperm and marry among the equals".* (Ibne-Maja, Kitabun-Nikah H.No. 1958)

Ibn-e-Maja & Dailami narrates the Prophet (PBUH) as saying:

تخيروا لنطفتكم فان العرق دساس

*"Select the women of good family for your children as blood will tell".* (Ibne-Maja & Dailami)

Ibn-e-Adi narrates the Prophet (pbuh) in his book "Kamil"

تزوجوا في الحجر الصالح فإن العرق دساس

*"Marry in the good family as the blood will tell".*

(Ibne-Maja & Dailami)

These *Ahaadees* guide the aspirants of marriage that they should select such wives who are; brought up in the righteous and pious families, brought up in the cradle of chastity and nobility and who are the daughters of such parents who are of noble and respected forefathers. The secret of this, when a men gets married his children gets respect, nobility good nature, Islamic high morale, graciousness and perfection as if they have become their second nature.

In the light of this principle Hazrat Usman bin Abi-al-'Aas al-Thaqafy drew up his will telling his sons that, the man who wants to marry is like one, who sows seed so the man must see where he is sowing the seed, a women of bad caste and lineage really can't give birth to a noble and honorable child, so we have to chose the women of noble lineage though it may take some time.

Once Hazrat Umar (mabawh) said replying a querry: what right a child has over his father? He should give due consideration in selecting his mother, name and teach him the Qur'anic sciences.

Our Prophet Hazrat Mohammad (pbuh) has asked the *Ummat-e-Muslima* to select a faithful wife. This very recommendation has a specific significance in today's life. That's why hereditary science has proved that the child carries his parents morale, physical and mental epithets by birth. Therefore if the selection of boy/girl is done on the basis of ancestral nobility, piety and sanctity then the children by birth will be having these qualities.

If the persons, intending to get married, want their children to be noble, pious, chaste, and faithful, they should consider and scrutinize their selection of spouse.

## (2) LINEAGE:

After faith one should see; the family and the ancestors of the woman to whom he wants to marry, her etiquette, intellect and sagacity. That's why some older people have said: “Don't enquire about the school she attended but enquire about the family in which she is brought up”.

One should marry a girl whose mother is noble and pious moreover if she is obedient, a true-loving and respecting one to her husband, then ultimately the girl will also be having the same qualities, therefore the instantaneous marriages do not succeed and one must avoid it. The criteria for perfect selection is to consider; her habits rather her wealth, her bringing up rather the dowry, her modesty and nobility rather the price of her clothes or the mode of life. Enquire the relatives and neighbors about the girl's politeness, tenderness and compassion. Look for the family's behaviour, their religiousness and not the cleanliness of their air conditions, washing machines, handicraft items, decoration pieces and beautiful furnitures. See how dexterous, neat and clean are the residents of the house. See the prayer and veil not the beautiful house, see the delicacy and elegance in them rather their B.A & M.A degrees.

Evaluate and assess the virtue and honor of one another and its best way is to send the women of your family to their neighbour in order to enquire about the girl and her family, as you are going to make her mother of your children, her brother will be their maternal uncle, her parents will be their maternal grand father/mother and, her sisters will be their maternal aunt. All these relations leave great impact on the moral and mental development of children and leave great effects on them.

Due to these the lineage must be checked.

## (3) <u>COMELINESS:</u>

After faith and lineage, the comeliness of the would-be-wife should be seen. One should decide his life partner with confidence, surety, insight and wisdom. Most of the boys, their parents and sisters etc. fascinated by the made-up faces, finalized the affinity but alas! When the make-up is washed .....................

It is better to see the girl in her house than in any of the functions, therefore it is better for the boy to see the girl as usual (without make-up etc.) before the marriage and the *Shari'at* has allowed this. One of the *Hadees* says: Hazrat Abu Huraira (mabawh) says: he was with the Prophet (pbuh), one man came and told "I had married an Ansari women". The Prophet (pbuh) asked, have you seen her? He says no, the Prophet (pbuh) said, "Go and see there is something in the Ansari women, their eyes are small."

(Muslim, Nisai)

The reason given in another *Hadees*: see that women! It will be more suitable to keep love in between you.

(Tirmizi, Nisai)

It means, if one wants to keep the love, intimacy, friendship and confidence safe and secure, seeing the girl by the boy is more important.

If going to be engaged and strong enough in his plan and ready for marriage, family members have checked her manners, character and lineage etc. each member of his family had approved her and decided in her favor after complete enquiry. The boy after consulting his mother/sister about her features, characters and manners, has decided that she will be suitable for him, I have to cast a look on her just to satisfy the mind. Now by taking the advantage of the permission given by the Prophet (pbuh) the boy should see the girl, there are many benefits and philosophy hidden in it, though photos must be avoided neither ask for hers nor give her yours. Its worst evil is that to get one benefit, we have to pull down a number of religious restrictions and orders therefore it is not allowed. The other evil is that there is no reality in the photos and one can't guess correctly from the photos so it must be avoided. There are many more methods of seeing but taking her parent's permission is compulsory, if granted then proper method must be used. Many youths are heard saying when asked, have you seen your would-be-wife? Their simple reply will be "We have seen the religion and nothing".

Some say "My mother and sisters are very intelligent, they have seen and this is enough". Some say "We hardly have got one if we ask to see, it will be a problem". Some say "Why we should do it, it is not a custom in us".

Remember! We shall succeed only by returning to our real nobility and honor and by fully obeying the Prophet Mohammad (pbuh). According to the decrease in obeying the Prophet (pbuh) the honor, nobility prosperity and blessings of the religion, and the world will decrease like wise. Don't depend merely on hearsays i.e. we have seen the faith only or the education, but the standard of faith is different in each person and the safety of the husband and wife's religion is in their living with love, regard, intimacy and confidence, to fulfil each other's rights, honor and safeguard each other's souls. Allah the Almighty has pointed to this when He says:

هُنَّ لِبَاسٌ لَّكُمْ وَاَنْتُمْ لِبَاسٌ لَّهُنَّ

*"they are raiment for you and you are raiment for them"* (Baqra-187)

It will be, when comeliness and lineage are also seen with faith. To say that my aunt, mother etc. has seen her, then O my brother! Are you going to marry or............? You have to spend the life with wife or...........? That's why seeing and checking yourself is better also. May be your parents have seen her according to themselves; she is very simple and will serve us very much or she will increase the dignity of the house.

Our friends who are entangled in customs and usages they are mistaken because after the saying of the Prophet (pbuh) no room is left. The real cause of flaws in customs and usages is that the life becomes narrow and the people can't obey the *Shari'ah* so it is better to discontinue all these customs and usages.

As far as hopelessness is concerned we have already said that one must have good thought with Allah so keeping good hope and thought he must see the would-be-wife if possible. Thus, it will not create any problem in the future.

Pay attention to one very important thing, in the above lines we have persuaded you to see the girl, but it is when you are fully ready either for marriage or for engagement, and all the formalities have been completed; faith, lineage, nobility, family and education all are up to your satisfaction and you have consulted your mother and sisters about her features which are also up to your taste. Then only one is supposed to see the girl and remember that one should not reject the girl due to a common or minor defect, it is mere selfishness and narrow-mindedness while the girl and her parents become heartbroken.

Remember, that the permission and persuasion to see the girl was just to satisfy you in order to gain peace of mind that she is just as described by your mother and sisters, to remove your anxiety created by the discussion of the girl by your family's women, and not to reject the girl due to a common or minor defect which she cannot avert.

If you dislike her at first sight, as she is not such as

described by the family members than you must decline and refuse the girl without any hesitation, it would be better for you and would-be-wife in order to live a happy married life.

## A USEFUL ADVICE

One useful advice is to collect the details of the girl, chosen by the sisters and mother of the would-be-groom, such as her age, her education, her religiousness, her physique, her parents' family, her father's occupation, religiousness, and politeness, nobility, regularity in prayers of her brothers and sisters etc. After collecting all the details, the sensible members of the family should sit together after offering and invoking the prayer, by making the father or any other suitable person the *Emir* of the meeting. Then either any of the parents or the would-be-groom himself may consult each member, for example there are details of three different girls. Which of these three girls will be suitable for our family or which will be suitable for our brother. The *Emir* considering the opinions would decide where to send affinity, if needed another meeting may also be held. The *Emir*, while taking the decision should honor the groom's opinion.

The greatest and foremost benefit of this consultation will be that one of Mohammad's (pbuh) *Sunnah* will be revived and where *Sunnah* is revived Allah's mercy is there.

The second benefit of it is that mutual love and affection is established in between the family members, all the brothers and sisters will feel that the parents have given us importance and value, especially the elder married brothers will be happy that the parents have consulted them for the marriage of their younger ones.

Its third benefit will be that this will be a collective decision rather than a single person's decision, no one can say that you have not asked and consulted me.

Nevertheless, the etiquettes of counselling should be described, which are:

(1) Each member of the counselling team should give his opinion one by one, if a person who already had given his opinion, wants to give another he should give such in the end after taking the permission of the *Emir*.

(2) One should not interfere in someone's opinion, rather he can give the benefits and ingenuities in his opinion.

(3) Opinion should be given as a mere opinion not just as decision. If one's opinion is not granted he should neither quarrel nor taunt nor say that I was saying this earlier if anything wrong happens. If you had accepted my opinion it would not have happened etc. All members of the counselling team should agree with what the *Emir* or head of the family has decided.

If counselling, by the sensible and confidential family members, is done keeping these etiquettes in mind then *Insha'Allah* many virtues will come.

If it is not possible then the groom after collecting all the informations should contact and consult a religious scholar, who is aware of the local people's mood and their mode of life. If mind accepts, send the affinity or see the girl and this seeing will help in decision-making.

May Allah create true love between husband and would-be-wife, accept them in the service of the religion and make each of our pleasure, as well as our grief, the means for the spreading of the religion (Islam).

# THE RITUAL OF BETROTHAL

It means that the affinity for a son or daughter is send to a home after due consideration and *Istikhara*, while a date is fixed to finalise the marriage by the elders of the family and a treat is given. It is neither necessary nor unlawful, if a gift is given as memento to show pleasure or as a sign of confirmation of affinity, but it should be within the *Shari'ah* limitations. (Neither men and women should be mingled nor boy and girl should come face to face nor they put rings in each other's fingers. "Only the women of the boys' family would give the gift to the girl after congratulating her". Without thinking of exchange while every thing should be done simply). It is not necessary that the girl's family should also give a watch etc. to the boy, this very exchange system transforms these into customs and rituals that is prohibited. There should not be photography in the function. The prayer's time should be taken care of. An elderly woman should consult the women of girl's family for the dower and the date of marriage while the men should settle in men. At the same time, invocations must be continued so that there be the Blessings of Allah.

This was the simplest way–It is not sagacity to be in debt either in order to comply with customs or as a mere show in the kith and kin or to become famous. At present, the gathering and expenditure in this function is such that a person has said seeing these "Bring a Qazi to perform matrimonial rites". Why so much of complications in betrothal.

There is another important point, that is do not delay the marriage unnecessarily after the betrothal, as this leads to certain rituals and customs such as loads of fruits and sweats in addition to suits on both the Eides, all these are prohibited in Islam but they are the integral part of our society. There are some lawful actions which has become customary part of the betrothal, if one does not do that he is ashamed of, all these are prohibited and sinful. Then, this exchange itself is a burden for both, sometimes due to this, the relation are so strained that the affinity is broken. Is there any wisdom in creating a tense situation by complicating it (betrothal) – the prelusion of the marriage.

Therefore we request humbly and especially to the would-be-groom to convince his parents that there is no use of so much expenses and botherations, inspite of all these some will be pleased and other might be displeased, while pleasing the Creator is easy, as His pleasure is in abiding by the *Shari'ah.*

We are marrying in accordance with the order of Allah the Almighty and the Prophet (pbuh), that's too, to be saved from the sins. How is this saving from the sins for which we have to do hundreds of sins while betrothal is only its prelusion. It is better to do any business in the name of would be husband and wife with the money we are expending in these, or to give this very amount as a deposit/ advance to the landlord of the house where they (bride & groom) may live on rental or if there is only one son and the mother will become alone while the groom and bride live separately, then one may buy a house or a flat and give it on rent to secure extra money for them. So that, they live a life of their choice, free of altercations between mother and daughter-in-law, free of differences between different sisters-in-law, they keep visiting the elders, serving and consoling them as much as possible.

So, don't let the betrothal become a custom. We have written a short essay on "the betrothal", hoping by the grace of Allah, that after reading it you will try to be saved from wrong and irreligious customs at the time of betrothal, moreover, you will pray and toil in saving the Muslims from the customs.

But Alas! Today the wealth of Muslim and his ability are being spent on such rituals which neither have the benefits of this world nor of the after-life. Would that these Muslim men and women had spent their lives and ability in diverting the infidels to Islam and in inciting the Muslims to abide by the *Shari'ah*. Many would have entered in Islam, become faithful, thus ignorance would have ended and knowledge and practice would have prevailed. If the wealth spent by the Muslims in marriages and betrothals is collected many madarsas, hospitals and schools might have been run by it and many mosques might have been built by it.

## PRECAUTIONS AFTER BETROTHAL

After betrothal but before *Nikaah* there is an evil in our society, that is, the boy meets his fiancée, call her on phone, goes with her for entertainment without feeling it wrong, he enjoys by thinking about her mere "nearness" when she is not his lawful wife, all these things make Allah the

Almighty unhappy and avert His mercy, Muslim bride and groom must avoid and protect themselves from these evils.

Now we are copying two questions from one of the renowned scholars, Maulvi Mohd. Yousuf Ludhianvi's (may Allah bless him in age) famous book *"Aap ke Masai'l aur inka hal"*, read them carefully and understand, so that you may consider its contempt of being wrong, and be saved from these evils and try to save others also.

**Question No.1**

One person was saying " meeting, calling on phone and strolling with the fiancée is not good". I told him, "this is what prevailing in our society and no one feel it wrong". Then he could not clarify my querry, because of this I am confused. Is it really not good?

**Answer**

The fiance before *Nikah* is non-*Mehram* (marriageable) as he is like a general man and mingling of the girl with him is prohibited. Your saying "it is preavailing in our society, no one feel it wrong" is not correct as in good and noble societies it is felt very bad. Moreover, if any thing becomes a custom in any society, this is not a proof of it being allowed. A wrong custom which is against the *Shari'at* is itself reformable. In our colleges and universities the girls stroll about freely with unrelated boys, will this be lawful?

**Question No.2**

How should be the relations between boy and girl loving each other before marriage–meeting, talking with each other, without being guilty of any immoral posture–In this way, is there meeting religious?

**Answer**

Seeing the girl once, either himself or by any confidant woman, with whom he is planning to marry is lawful, but before marriage neither "relations" more than this between boy and girl, nor chatting nor meeting is permitted. Their meeting before marriage is in itself an "immoral act".

# MESSAGE OF THE SERMON OF NIKAH

Now we are copying an article, of Mufti Taqui Usmani "Message of the Sermon of Nikah" published in daily Jung. Karachi, to clarify the aim and importance of marriage.

Possibly, there may not be a person who has not attended any marriage function. Almost marriage celebrations are held daily and are attended by hundreds of people. You would have seen in these functions that before proposal and consent, the master of (marriage) ceremony reads a sermon though this is not an inevitable condition for the validity of *Nikah*. Without this also, if in the presence of two witnesses, the proposal and consent is done, the marriage will be valid. But the Prophet (pbuh) used to read the small sermon before marriage ceremony, and he had taught its first words to Abdullah-b-Masood (mabawh).

These are the same words which we hear from the master of the marriage ceremonies *(Qazi-e-Nikah)* in almost each marriage function. Generally the words of sermon, their aim and meaningfulness are lost in the comic disturbances of the marriage. They are heard inattentively and if the gathering is huge and there is no loudspeaker then most of the people, could not listen these words, the people are seen talking each other at the very time of this sermon.

It is also the dilemma of this very inattentiveness that people, who spend lacs of rupees on the function, do not take care to spend a little more on loudspeaker so that, the sermon, the proposal and the consent, the real essence of the function could be preformed in a peaceful and dignified way and the people could listen these auspicious words peacefully without any uproar.

However! If the sermon is heard, generally it is thought as a mere benediction, while its aim in the mind of general people is to get blessings only, nothing more.

Therefore, there may possibly be a men who would have tried to understand the meaning of these words, why these are read on this occasion and how these are related with the marriage? Since these words are approved and taught by the Prophet (pbuh) himself, hence we must understand its meaning, aim and background, so that we could really know the meaningfullness of this blessed *Sunnah*.

These words begin with the praise of Allah, while we being Muslims, are advised to begin our every important work with the praise of Allah as no work in this world could be done without His help. Marriage is the most important turning for the two lives who are starting a new chapter of their lives.

We are specially taught to begin this journey (new life after marriage) by the praise of Allah and supplications. How beautiful and comprehensive are the words of praise and supplications taught to us by the Prophet (pbuh), we can guess this by their translation. The Arabic words are:

الحمد للّٰہ نحمدہ و نستعینہ ونستغفرہ ونومن بہ و نتوکل علیہ،
ونعوذ باللّٰہ من شرور انفسنا ومن سیئات اعمالنا من یھدہ اللّٰہ فلا
مضل لہ ومن یضللہ فلا ھادی لہ و نشھد ان لا الہ الا اللّٰہ وحدہ لا
شریک لہ و نشھد ان محمدا عبدہ ورسولہ (صلی اللّٰہ علیہ وسلم)
وعلی آلہ واصحابہ اجمعین اوکما قال علیہ الصلوۃ والسلام

*All the praises are for Allah, we praise Him, we seek help from Him, we seek pardon of Him, we believe in Him, we rely on Him, we take refuge with Him from the evils of our souls and our deeds. No one can seduce anyone if He wants him to be guided while no one can guide anyone if He wants him to be seduced. We witness that there is no God except Allah, He is alone, He don't have any partner, we witness that Muhammad is His servant and His Messenger. May Allah pour His mercy and peace on him, his progeny and companions.*

(Muslim Babul-Jumu'ah H.No. 1436)

At the time of Nikah not only the bride and groom, but their family also are on tender edge of their life–if they find themselves congenial then the house may become a sample of heaven otherwise it (marriage) becomes a headache for both the families.

Therefore, we have been persuaded to "seek His help" by praising Him. Since, generally the discords in marital life are created by our own malice and misdeeds, hence, relying on Allah, His refuge is sought from the evils of our own misdeeds. His help is sought in guiding us to right path and saving us from seduction. Since, all these praises and supplications are useless without having full faith in the unity of Allah and His Messenger therefore, witness of His unity and the Prophet (pbuh) are being renewed. In the end, Allah's blessings on the Prophet (pbuh) are invoked as he only brought us the guidance.

These are the introductory words of the sermon of *Nikah*, after these words generally four verses of the Holy *Qur'an* are recited. The first verse is from *Surah Aal-e-Imran* verse No. 102.

يٰاَيُّهَا الَّذِيْنَ اٰمَنُوا اتَّقُوا اللّٰهَ حَقَّ تُقٰتِهٖ وَلَا تَمُوْتُنَّ اِلَّا وَاَنْتُمْ مُّسْلِمُوْنَ ○

*"O ye who believe! Fear Allah as He should be feared, and die not except in a state of Islam."*

The second verse is the first verse of the *Surah Nisa*;

يٰاَيُّهَا النَّاسُ اتَّقُوْا رَبَّكُمُ الَّذِىْ خَلَقَكُمْ مِّنْ نَّفْسٍ وَّاحِدَةٍ وَّخَلَقَ مِنْهَا
زَوْجَهَا وَبَثَّ مِنْهُمَا رِجَالاً كَثِيْرًا وَّنِسَآءً ۚ وَاتَّقُوا اللّٰهَ الَّذِىْ تَسَآءَلُوْنَ
بِهٖ وَالْاَرْحَامَ ؕ اِنَّ اللّٰهَ كَانَ عَلَيْكُمْ رَقِيْبًا ○

*"O mankind! Fear your Guardian Lord, Who created you from the single soul, created, out of it, his mate, and from that twain scattered (like seeds) countless men and women; fear Allah, through whom ye demand your mutual (rights), and be heedful of the wombs(that bore you); for Allah ever watches over you."*

While the third and forth are from *Surah Ahzaab* verse 70-71

يٰاَيُّهَا الَّذِيْنَ اٰمَنُوْا اتَّقُوا اللّٰهَ وَقُوْلُوْا قَوْلاً سَدِيْدًا۝ يُّصْلِحْ لَكُمْ اَعْمَالَكُمْ وَيَغْفِرْ لَكُمْ ذُنُوْبَكُمْ ط وَمَنْ يُّطِعِ اللّٰهَ وَ رَسُوْلَهٗ فَقَدْ فَا زَ فَوْزًا عَظِيْمًا۝

*"O ye who believe! Fear Allah, and make your utterance straight forward; that He make your conduct whole and sound and forgive you your sins; he that obeys Allah and His Messenger, has already attained his great victory."*

The Prophet (pbuh) has selected specially the above mentioned verses from amongst the countless verses of the Holy Qur'an, there must be some great expediency. If considered, one will find that the main topic of these verses is "fearing Allah", all these verses are starting with the word "fear Allah". An ignorant person can say, what is the link between fearing Allah and marriage?

But a person, who knows the ups and downs of the life, delicateness in the husband and wife relations and the intricacies of marital life, can say that "fearing Allah" is mandatory in order to fulfil each other's rights. The relation of husband and wife is very delicate, their emotions and real natures are so much opened before them that can't be opened before anyone.

A man can conceal his maliciousness in the veil of external grin, can cover his interior with beautiful words and gilt of politeness before others, but before wife he can't. Anyhow, he has to come out of this sheath of plausibility, if this interior of the man is not having "fear of Allah" he will ruin the life of his partner.

The sufferings received by a wife from her husband, could not always be compensated by a court, as most of these sufferings are such that she can't tell these before any of her close relatives rather in a court.

Likewise, a husband could have some complaints against his wife to which neither he has any solution nor anyone else, its only solution is that both of them should have "fear of Allah" in their hearts.

It means they should have the feeling of being entrusted to each other and they are supposed to defend this before Allah. They could be saved from the wordly defence if they harass their life partner, but one day while standing before Allah, they would have to pay the penalty of their each and every usurpation. This feeling is called the "fear of Allah" and this is what impose restriction on the soul in the solitude, where no one is to see him.

The Prophet Mohammad (pbuh) wants when a man and women are being made life partner, they should have the invisible guard in their heart, so that their friendship be durable and mutual love in their heart should not be the result of timely carnality which ends as the time passes. Rather that should be a durable affection under the shadow of "fear Allah" free of selfishness and adorned with the feelings of selflessness, faithfulness and well-wishing. That's why the Prophet (pbuh) has chosen these verses, in the *Nikah* sermon, starting with an order of "fearing Allah" and this is its basic message. (JUNG)

## SUMMRAY

(1) The sermon of Nikah and the proposal and consent are the real essence of the marriage function, one should hear these with respect.The organizers of the function should try to arrange the loudspeakers.

(2) We are advised, after Allah's praises in the sermon, to fear Allah which means that, when a man and women are being made life partner, they should have this invisible guard in their heart, so that their friendship be durable and the mutual love in their heart should not be the result of timely carnality which ends as the time passes.

Dear readers! If you have got this book after being married then also it is useful. Modify your conduct according to the guidance given in this book because "the prodigal deserves no reproach after his return"

# THE DOWER

The first incumbent right of the wives upon husband is the dower, although, without it no one can be married but there are certain deficiencies and imprudences in it. We are mentioning these here, may Allah help us to be saved from the deficiencies and imprudences and act according to the luminous and auspicious traditions of the Prophet (pbuh).

When a Muslim decides that he will live by conciliating Allah. He will prefer only the commands of Allah, will neither prefer the customs nor the society nor the kith and kin, and he will abide by the traditions of the Prophet (pbuh). He will try his best for the revival of the *Sunnah* in the marriages and in all the stages of Muslim's life. Allah will help such a Muslim, make him medium of guidance while *Sunnahs* are revived by each of his actions. May Allah keep us alive, while obeying the traditions of the Prophet (pbuh) and give us death on these.

**General deficiencies in the dower:-**

(1) While settling the dower, the parents and relatives of the bride do not pay attention to the capacity of the groom, rather they only want to settle for the maximum, which sometimes lead to disputes and in some cases the marriage is withheld due to this very dispute. They take pride in settling for a higher dower, while it is a pride of pre-Islamic days and it should be condemned. If higher dower would have been an honor or supremacy, then the dower of the

wives and daughters of Muhammad (pbuh) would have been higher. The Prophet Muhammad (pbuh) had not settled the dower of his wives or daughters more than 500 *Dirhams*, which equals to 131.25 *Tolas* of silver. Suppose the rate of silver is Rs.50/- per *Tola* then the value of 131.25 *Tolas* of silver would be Rs.6563/-, (this figure may very according to the fluctuation in the price of silver, anyhow the weight should be 131.25 *Tolas*), this is called *"Mahr-e-Fatimi"*. Some eminent scholars, when requested to perform matrimonial rites, used to say "Settle for *"Mahr-e-Fatimi"* then only we will perform otherwise arrange for another".

Briefly, the Muslims should take pride in the good examples (*Uswa-e-Hasana*) set by the Prophet (pbuh) and should settle for such dower as the Prophet (pbuh) had for his wives and daughters, whosoever is more honorable then him (pbuh). Even though settling for a higher dower than this, is not a sin but taking pride in higher dower, instigating dispute and making it a base for mutual strained relations should be avoided as they are the works of pre-Islamic period.

(2) The people in some rural areas consider that the dower of Rs.32/25 is "*Shara'-e-Muhammadi*" though this amount does not equal to even the least limit of dower, but people consider that this is according to *"Shara'-e-Muhammadi"* which is completely wrong. Allah knows from where this all

begun, but alas! for the *"Miyan Jee"* (teacher in mosque school) they also do not tell this theorem to the people. The least limit of the dower according to Imam Abu Haneefa is 10 *Dirham* (2 *Tolas* and 7.5 *Mashas* of silver) settling the dower lesser than this is not lawful. If someone has fixed lesser than this then dower of 10 *Dirham* is obligatory.

(3) Paying dower is not considered necessary. It is in vogue that wives forgive the dower. It is worth consideration that the dower is just like other payable debts for the husband. Though the wife can forgive the whole dower or a part of it, but considering it unpayable from the beginning is a huge mistake. It is quoted in a *Hadees* that "a man who marries and has no intention to pay the dower is an adulterer."

(4) There are many flaws in our society, one of these is that taking dower or part in the legacy by women is considered improper. Therefore they consider forgiving necessary though inevitably otherwise they are disgraced in the society. It is a duty of the religious class to efface this social vice, cause to be given the dower and the part in the legacy to the women. If they want to forgive, then they should be told to take their right, keep in their possession for sometime then they may return if willing and they should not be compelled for this.

(5) Another flaw in the dower is that, if the wife died before her dower is paid then it is embezzled. However, according to *Sharia't-e-Islamia* if wife

dies before being together in one place or intercourse, she should be paid half the dower otherwise full dower should be paid. This dower must be included in her legacy and distributed among her legal heirs while this must be asked from Ulema.

What prevails in our society is that, if the woman dies in her in-laws' house, they get hold of all her legacy and don't give any thing to her heirs, while if she dies in her paternal home they get hold of her legacy and don't feel necessary to give the husband's share whereas taking unlawful possession of the dead's wealth is a cheap act and unlawful wealth not only causes misfortune and inauspiciousness but also ruins other wealth. May Allah bestow us the faith and wisdom and save us from erroneous customs and rituals of pre-Islamic period.

The Prophet (pbuh) has said about dower; Hazrat Abu Salma (mabawh) says, I asked the mother of faithfuls, Hazrat Ayesha Siddiqa (mabawh) what was the dower of the Prophet (pbuh) for his purified wives. She said 12.5 Okas which corresponds to 500 *Dirhams*. (Muslim, Mishkaat 277)

Hazrat Umar bin al-Khattab (mabawh) said, See! Don't increase the dower of the women, if it would have been the cause of honor in the world or a thing of abstinence near Allah then the Prophet (pbuh) was more deserving of this. It is not in my knowledge that the Prophet (pbuh) would have married any of her wives or daughters for more dower than 12 Okas.

(Ahmed, Tirmizi, Abu Daud, Nisai, Ibn-e-Maja, Darimi, and Mishkaat- 277)

Now we are copying an article *"Mahr ki Shara'i Haisiyat"* (religious status of the dower) by Mufti Muhammad Taqui Usamni, published in the daily Jung dated 12-11-1995. Before reading it pray Allah, so that He may guide us to the right path and make our pleasure and mourning as well as our illness and health in full accordance with the *Sunnah*, Amen!

## RELIGIOUS STATUS OF THE DOWER

A few days earlier I saw a matrimonial deed, the passage "Rs.32/- *Mahr-e-Sharai*" was written in its *'Mahr'* column. During conversation with people before this also, it was felt that only God knows, how people started considering Rs.32/- as *"Mahr-e-Sharai"*. The impression, "it is commendable in the *Sharia't* to settle the dower as low as possible", is quite common. Inspite of this there are certain misconceptions among people regarding the dower which should be abolished.

"*Mahr*" is basically an "honorarium" which is given by a husband to his wife, while its purpose is to honor the women. It is neither the price of the woman, so as to consider her as sold to the husband after paying it and now she is just like a bond-maid, nor a mere fictitious action which is not supposed to be paid. *Sharia't's* motive by making the dower of wife incumbent on the husband is that when a man brings his wife to his home he should defer her suitably and give her a gift in accordance with her esteem and deference.

Therefore, the *Sharia't's* dun is neither to settle the dower so less that the sense of deference and esteem would vanish completely nor so excessive that the husband could not pay it and at last either he bid farewell to the world (die) without paying it or be compelled to get it forgiven by the wife. By the *Sharia't's* point of view each women's real right is that she be paid the "*Mahr-e-Misl*" (customary dower). "*Mahr-e-Misl*" means such an amount which is being settled generally for the women of bride's family and if there is no woman in her family then the amount being settled generally for other women of the same status as of her, that is her "*Mahr-e-Misl*". And according to *Sharia't* , wife is entitled to receive "*Mahr-e-Misl*".

Due to this, if at the time of marriage neither *Mahr* is fixed nor settled through mutual consent, then "*Mahr-e-Misl*" would be considered incumbent automatically and it becomes necessary for the husband to pay her "*Mahr-e-Misl*". However if a wife is agreed happily on a lesser amount or the husband settles happily a higher amount then the "*Mahr-e-Misl*", this also is lawful.

## AMOUNT OF THE DOWER *(MAHR)*

The maximum limit of *Mahr* had not been fixed in *Sharia't* but the minimum is fixed and that is 10 *Dirhams* (2 *Tolas* and 7.5 *Mashas* of silver) according to *Fiqh-e-Hanafi*.

10 *Dirhams* or 2 *Tolas* and 7.5 *Mashas* of silver is equal to about Rs.700/- according to current rate, it doesn't mean that so much *"Mahr"* is chosen by *Sharia't*, rather it means that if a women herself is agree for a lesser *Mahr* than this, *Sharia't* does not agree for this, because the aim

of *Mahr* (deference and esteem of women) is not fulfilled. This minimum limit is prescribed keeping in mind the financially weaker section, so that, they also can marry if a women is agree.

It doesn't mean that the *Sharia't* wants *Mahr* to be Rs.700/- and this amount would be called as "*Mahr-e-Shara'i*". The people who settled for Rs.32/- as *Mahr* and called it "*Mahr-e-Shara'i*" have made two mistakes;

(1) The value of 10 *Dirhams* might have been Rs.32/- at any given time and they had considered it to be Rs.32/- forever.

(2) The minimum amount of *Mahr* fixed by the *Sharia't* was thought to be chosen one by *Sharia't*, and any higher amount could not be settled, though this conception is absolutely baseless.

This could be guessed by the Prophet's (pbuh) action when he himself fixed *Mahr* of his daughter Hazrat Fatima (mabawh) at 500 *Dirhams* which equals to 131 *Tolas* and 3 *Mashas* of silver, while its value according to current rate is about Rs.35000/- (thirty five thousands Rupees). The Prophet (pbuh) himself also has settled the *Mahr* of most of his wives almost the same, which is in accordance with the middle class. Some people has given the name *"Mahr-e-Sharai"* to this very *"Mahr-e-Fatimi"*, and in all probability they mean that settling for a lesser or more *Mahr* than this is not chosen by *Sharia't* this conception is also not right. There is no doubt, if both the parties would settle for "*Mahr-e-Fatimi*", while their intention should be that the amount fixed by the Prophet (pbuh) would be moderate, blessed and they would be rewarded for following the *Sunnat* also. Then this feeling is much blessed and commendable, but to consider it as *"Mahr-e-Shara'i"*, in the sense settling for a lesser or more amount then this is unlawful, is not correct. Whereas there is no harm, according to the *Sharia't* in settling for more or lesser than this amount.

One should keep in mind the deference and esteem of the women as well as the capacity (financial position) of the husband while settling for *Mahr*. The preceptors who have prohibited people from settling more *Mahr*, their main intention was that if *Mahr* is settled beyond the capacity then it becomes a mere red-tapism, which is never paid in reality and the sin of not paying *Mahr* remains on the husband.

Secondly, sometimes there is the intention of ostentation in keeping a higher *Mahr* and people settle for unusual *Mahr* just to show there pomp. Both these two issues are against the disposition of Islam. That's why the preceptors have prohibited people from settling unusual *Mahr*, while there is one incidene of Hazrat Umar (mabawh) about it, to be remembered;

Once Hazrat Umar (mabawh) in a speech during his caliphate said not to settle for more *Mahr*. A women objected and said that the *Holy Qur'an* has used the word "*Qintaar*" meaning a heap of gold or silver for *Mahr*, which means that the *Mahr* could be a heap of gold or silver, then why are you prohibiting from settling more *Mahr*? Hazrat

Umar (mabawh) after listening to the women said in fact the argument of the women is correct and to prohibit from settling more *Mahr* in general is not correct.

Which means if ostentation is not intended, while intention and capacity to pay is also there, then settling more *Mahr* is lawful if any of these is intended it (more *Mahr*) is unlawful. While *Mahr* is being mentioned, one more point be clarified and that is, kinds of *Mahr*.

## TWO KINDS OF *MAHR*

Two kinds of *Mahr* are famous: ***Mahr-e-Mu'ajjal*** (Prompt Dower) and ***Mahr-e-Mu-ajjal*** (Defferred Dower). Since these words are heard in the marriage functions only, that's why most of the people don't know their meaning. Prompt Dower ( *Mahr-e- Mu 'ajjal* ) is that which becomes necessary for husband just after marriage and now it is his duty either to pay at the time of *Nikah* itself or whenever she would ask for it, but generally the woman in our society do not ask for it, it does not mean that it is not necessary to pay rather it is a duty of the husband to be relieved of his responsibility as soon as possible without waiting for the demand by the woman. Whereas, Deferred Dower (*Mahr-e-Mu-ajjal*) is that for which the two parties have fixed a date. The payment of this kind of *Mahr* is neither incumbent for the husband nor can the wife ask for it before the fixed date.

Thus, dower being deferred means that at the time of marriage some date is fixed for its payment, but in our society the date is not fixed rather it is said that so much dower is deferred. While according to our society it means that this much amount of dower will be payable when the marriage will come to an end i.e. if divorce happens or any of man or woman dies.

One more notable point is that, in our society, the ornaments given to the bride by the husband had no link with *Mahr*, it is not the property of the bride, and rather it is given to her for temporary use. The wives neither can sold it nor can present it to anyone nor can use it in anyway without the permission of husband and if Allah forbid, the divorce happens then the husband takes back these ornaments. Therefore the dower is not paid by these ornaments, however, if the husband tells his wife clearly that I had given these ornaments in your possession as *Mahr* then only one can consider it a *Mahr*. In this case, the wife being the owner can use it as she like and it can't be taken back from her in anyway. Besides this, if the husband clarifies that it is your property and do not consider it in the dower, then it will be the property of the wife and the dower should be paid separately.

> However! It should be clear that determination of *Mahr* is not merely a customary or insubstantial procedure done without consideration rather it is a religious obligation which needs complete seriousness. It is a serious matter which should be clear and evident legally (according to *Sharia't*) and should be paid accordingly. It is very much unjustice that one did not think of paying it his whole life and when he is on the death-bed, seeks forgiveness from the wife, when there is no way for her except to forgive due to the pressure of the situation. (With thanks from Jung)

## EASY WAY OF PAYING *MAHR*

Now we are giving some easy ways for those husbands whose dowers were fixed beyond their capacity and now they want to pay the dower. Whether they thought of its payment after reading this book or getting knowledge from any other source.

(1) Generally the ornament given to the wife at the time of marriage is the property of husband and he only pays its *Zakaat*. Give her ornaments equal to the quantity of *Mahr* and make her the owner of that much quantity clarifying her that it is your *Mahr*, now you have to pay its *Zakaat*.

(2) To pay a certain amount monthly and tell her that I will pay your *Mahr* in instalements.

(3) While giving pocket-money to the wife, intend that you are paying her *Mahr* and tell her about this.

(4) While giving a costly gift either at any auspicious occasion or at the time of any Islamic festival, intend of *Mahr* and tell her.

# THE REALITY OF THE DOWRY

We came to know by studying the Hindu laws, that there is no share of a Hindu woman in the legacy, that's why, she is sent out as a bride after decorating her well and giving her a lot of things at the time of marriage. The best way of Hindu marriage is called "Brahma" in which there is a conception of presenting the girl, it means that the father has gifted the girl. Now she has no connection with the family, due to this she is sent out as a bride with a lot of ornaments and other things according to the capacity of the father, just to win over her. Now she can't come back to his father's house, could not live without her father and mother-in-law, can't get share in father's legacy, can't marry again after the death of her husband, she is either supposed to die by burning or have to spent the life as a widow .

The author of the book 'The position of woman in Hindu civilisation' has written, "The bride should be given in marriage alongwith suitable oruaments, but their number and price is left entirely to the discretion and ability of the bride's father"

In the earlier days this law of dowry was for the upper-class Hindus,later on, it became so common and remained increasing day by day, that the Indian Govt. had to pass the Dowry Prohibition Act in 1961, in which there was a provision of six months' jail and a fine of Rs 500/- for the person giving or asking for dowry .

Due to the ignominy of dowry, in India many newly weds are being punished by burning for uncommitted sins while the rule of nature and providence is being laughed at.

According to a report of 1975 only in Delhi, 350 brides were given death either by burning alive or by strangulating or by hanging till death. Between June 1980& 1985, only in one area of Maharashtra 200 women were killed likewise. In Lucknow, one newly wed bride is being sacrificed for dowry on every 5th day.

(Deccan Herald Bangalore 3/1/1989)

In our country though they are not burnt alive rather a live and helpless bride is being jeered and taunted by mother and sister-in-law (husband's mother and sister). In addition to this, to guess the number of innocent girls, who are sacrificed for dowry by the in-laws' family, is very difficult .i.e the brides whose life had became a curse due to the demands of mother-in-law and husband's sister, some of these demands are;

Give something at the birth of a child to husband's sister and mother-in-law..........

Give something in the marriage of husband's younger brother..................

Give something on the festivity of Eid.............

Give any golden thing in the marriage of husband's younger sister.............

Give in greeting to the husband's sister on the birth of a son..................

Give something as (we are) going for Haj...........

Give gifts to all by name after retuning from Haj......

Give as the father has come back from a journey...

Give as the brother of the bride is married...........

Give dry fruit as winter has come ....................

Give summer fruit in summer..........................

The brides can neither fulfill the demands of begging husbands and the in-laws nor can increase the helplessness and destituteness of their poor parents by pressing to fulfil these illegal and unlawful demands.

Therefore, either they will prefer to suffer all these with chagrin or by taking poison or by putting a noose round their neck to save themselves from this embrassment forever. Due to this, the incident of suicides by the brides are increasing day by day.

So, a wise groom and his family members must try to abolish this faulty custom from the society, as it is ruining the society, is a revolt against the law of nature , is a social cruelty , is the gateway of greed and avidity while there is no proof of these in the Qur'an and Islamic jurisprudence. If it would have any importance in the *Sharia't* it would not have been neglected.

The Prophet Mohammed (pbuh) had married his four daughters and had not given the dowry to anyone. The things given to Hazrat Fatima (mabawh) were bought out of the *'Mahr-e-Mu 'jjal'* (Prompt Dower) given by Hazrat Ali (mabawh). The Prophet (pbuh) had only arranged one coverlet, one water-skin and a pillow. (Nisai-Hadees No.1356) While in some books one bedding is also mentioned. Were these things real dowry?

Then what is its link with today's requested dowry?

There is no proof, in the time of the companions (mabawt), that they would have asked the dowry from the girls' family, have accepted it (requested dowry)considering it as their assumed right or have considered it necessary. Therefore the groom and his family should not ask for the dowry and should raise voice against it. If the father of the girl wants to give her anything willingly, he should give it quietly, though after marriage. The groom's family should not insist on feast by the girls' family rather they should convince them that it is a practice of Hindus and in Islam it has no proof even though it is not unlawful, you can do , but we will be pleased if you don't, as the Prophet (pbuh) has neither fed his son-in-law in the marriage of his four daughters nor his relatives. If you have excess money then, inspite of spending it on feast either buy a property or ornaments and gift it to her… these will be beneficial for her.

The groom should have the courage to convince his mother and sister not to taunt the coming bride, otherwise they will be punished in the world itself for this, not to compel the girls' family for the feast or gift against the laws of Allah the Almighty and to taunt for going against their wishes. The end of such mothers and sisters-in-law is supposed to be very pitiable. Most of them are afflicted with hemiplegia, cancer and T.B etc. in the final stages of their lives only due to the lamentations of this innocent girl, some of these taunts are:

Why your father has not given a feast?

Why I was not given a necklace?

Why my son did not get a costly watch and suit?

Why the dowry is not given?

Why you came empty handed from father's house?

Why so and so is not given a suit?

When I went to your home with my relatives, why they were not given an envelope of Rs 101/-each?

These types of taunting don't suit to the mother of a noble family's Muslim son. May Allah give us courage and His divine help in reforming this bad custom, in making the marriage easy in order to save the society from these evils, Amen!

Now, we are narrating an article of Mufti Taqi Usmani which was published in the series *"Zikr-O- Fikr"* of Jung daily.

## SOMETHING ABOUT DOWRY

Before some years one preceptor of Syria, Sheik Abdul-Fattah came to our house, by chance a local friend also came. When he saw an Arab sitting, he asked him to pray saying "I have two marriagable daughters, pray Allah so that He may provide me the means to marry them", the Sheik asked him, "Are you not getting any appropriate affinity for them?" He replied that, "the affinity of both has been settled, but I don't have as much financial resources to marry them". The Sheik asked perplexedly," Are they your daughters or sons?"

He said, "Daughters", the Sheik said perplexedly, "what is the use of financial means in the marriage of the daughters?" He said, " I don't have any thing to give in their dowry." The Sheik asked, "what is dowry?" The audience told him that there is a custom in our country according to this the father of the bride at the time of marriage has to give his daughter ornaments, clothes, furniture and many other things, it is called "Dowry", while it is considered to be the responsibility of the father, without this no one can thought of marrying his daughters, as the in-laws of the girl ask for it . Sheik became more perplexed after listening this and said "Is marrying daughter a sin that the father is being punished like this?"

Then he told that there is no such ritual in our country. In most cases, it is considered to be the responsibility of the groom to arrange the furniture and the necessities of the bride before bringing his bride to his home. The father of the bride is not supposed to expend anything. In some rare cases, the father of the bride buys the furniture and other things keeping in mind the necessities of the bride but the groom pays for these things. Although if father wants to give some gift at the time of sending his daughter as a bride, he can, but it is not compulsory.

One can guess by this incident that in our society the dowry is considered to be the inevitable part of the daughter's marriage and what is the view of dowry in other Islamic circles?

As told with reference to the Sheik that the reality of the dowry in the *Sharia't* is just, that one can give a gift at the time of sending his daughter out as a bride within his capacity. And it is better to take the future necessities of the bride in consideration while giving the gift.

It is neither a necessary condition for marriage nor the in-laws have any right to ask for it. If a girl is not given the dowry or given a little, one should neither feel offended nor taunt the girl as it is not a thing of ostentation that one can show him off by displaying it.

## THE FLAWS OF THE DOWRY

The wrong conceptions, regarding the dowry and prevailing in our society, in short are as follows;

(1) The dowry is considered to be the necessary condition of the marriage therefore the girl is not married unless one has enough money to give dowry. So many girls in our society remained unmarried as their fathers have nothing for the dowry. If the marriage is settled then the father has to adopt unlawful means of getting wealth, so that he can fulfil the condition of the dowry, if he doesn't want to use the crimes such as bribe, forgery, fraud, cheating and embezzlement then he is compelled to bind himself in the clamps of loan and debt.

(2) The quantity of the dowry and the list of its necessary items is also increasing day by day. Now the dowry

is not merely a gift of father for his daughter which he is giving happily within his capacity but a social compulsion as it not only contain the necessities of the daughter but also that of groom, while decorating her house is also a necessary part of it whether the father of the girl wishes or not, he has to fulfil all these.

(3) It is not merely fulfilling the necessities of girl or pleasing her, rather the display of the dowry has compelled, that it should please every onlooker and get their praise.

(4) The worst about the dowry is that the husband and his family keep an eye on it. Some people ask for the splendid dowry with full audacity, while some do not ask it openly but they hope that the bride will bring a good dowry and when their hopes are not fulfilled, they harrass her by taunting.

The intellectuals of our society have the feeling of the flaws created by these conceptions and rituals of the dowry, they have written much about it and many proposals have been made. The government has also enacted some laws. *Alhamdulillah*, now people's conception of the dowry has changed, its display has become rare and international marriages have also controlled its compulsion. But it is still there.

Some people say that it should be prohibited completely by law. However, it is a social issue which neither could be solved through law only nor it is possible to act accordingly rather it is necessary to prepare the people mentally through education and media for this. There is no moral or legal (*Shara'i*) flaw, if a father gives her daughter anything useful to her for her future life while sending her out as a bride. The Prophet (pbuh) himself has given his daughter a little of the dowry, while in *Sharia't*, no such quantity is fixed. If other evils are not there, father can give as much as he wants.

Evil starts from here only as it is made a means of show and the boys' family consider it their right–hoping for more and more dowry. The worst thing is that if it fell short than the girl and her family is taunted. All the classes of society will have to work together against these conceptions to abolish the flaws of the dowry. It is necessary to describe regularly the evils of these conceptions through media, education and sermonizing.

So that, these cheap things would become such a blemish for all and sundry to be ashamed of. Wrong conceptions in any society are to be removed by the authorities, intellectuals and influential people of that society but for this compassionate and endeavouring persons are needed. Alas! Most of the people of these classes are so busy somewhere else, that they do not pay heed to the reformation of society which is necessary for building a nation.

One who invites towards virtue must not be weary of saying virtues, he should do so with out getting bored. At last a time comes when truth and virtue attracts others also and revolutionize not only the thinking but also the working of nations. (Taken from "Jung")

EXPLANATION

Muslim of Indian sub-continent has taken this custom from the Hindus as giving dowry is a custom among Hindus. Its reason is that in Hindus, the danghters have no share in the legacy, so after giving them dowry they become free. Whereas the concept of the dowry among Muslims, in most parts of the world except the Indian sub-continent, is not found. Therefore, it is not better to say that the status of the dowry according to *Sharia't* is just like a gift given happily. Generally, the people feel that the Prophet (pbuh) had given some dowry to his daughter Hazrat Fatima (mabawh). The people who defend the dowry, first of all, gave this very proof but it is not correct.

Correct is that the Prophet (pbuh) at the time of the marriage of his daughter Fatima (mabawh) with Hazrat Ali (mabawh) had given her a handmill, a pillow of palm leaves, an earthen jar for water, however the most important thing in it is that he had not given these as dowry. The Prophet (pbuh) being the guardian of Ali (mabawh) after his father's death, arranged these things to help Ali (mabawh) in marrying his daughter Fatima (mabawh) it was not a dowry. While its proof is that these things were bought in reality from the money Ali (mabawh) got after selling his chain-armour. The money spent on the purchases was that of Ali (mabawh) and not of the Prophet (pbuh). One may consult either the books of *Ahadees* or *Ulema* (religious scholar) for more details of this incident. So we should not convert this Hindu ritual into an Islamic one. If this would have been a part of Islam then the Prophet (pbuh) would have given to all his daughters (mabawt). I would say with utmost politeness, that this is a loathsome act which has corrupted the society. We have adopted this Hindu ritual by living with them for centuries and we have tried to bring the dowry into Islam like many other rituals. We must call upon Allah to help us in marrying with simplicity and to accept us for any ordinary service of His religion.

(Taken from the Daily "Jung" a review by Daud Azeez, London)

## MARRIAGE OR BUSINESS?

In short, in today's avaricious society, all these flaws and principles of religion and good manners have become a symbol of obsoleteness while today's generally accepted principle is how much wealth and dowry the girl will bring? Moreover, nowadays the boys' family make formal demands and haggle as if they are doing business inspite of marriage. Every person is selling himself in this market and whosoever gives a higher price, he will sell himself to him. It looks that the boys have become "VENAL" now, whosoever needs them can purchase from the market. While in reality it is the worst social offence which is the reason of ruining the civilization and this is not a conduct of the slave of Rehman but of the slaves of Satan. Briefly, a person who cannot respect a good-natured wife, can't be the slave of Rehman. Whereas if in any society the importance is not given to character and conduct, and due to this only, the helpless and sinless girls are compelled to live in their parents' house then, this will be the sign of its downfall and decline, while a society like this should wait for its perdition.

## PERDITION OF THE DOWRY

Today, the wrong and unreasonable customs and rituals of the demanded dowry has been harrassing the society–covetous demand is prevailing very much while neither any religion nor any law can approve these as legal or just. Not only before and at the time of marriage but after marriage also these Satanic demands are being made, these were not thought of previously, all these are the produce of modern time and are derogatory and these covetous people are the enemies of humanity. Actually due to this mean and vile custom only every year thousands of woman are sacrificed to the abominable deity "dowry" while the society has been entangled in it fully.

The poor, helpless and sinless girls have no option, in such society, but to take the extreme step i.e suicide either by strangulating themselves or by poisoning or by lying under a moving train.

## ANANXIOUS MOMENT FOR THE CONSCIENCED MEN

Suicide is forbidden in *Sharia't*, but the one instigating for this forbidden act is that cruel society which after becoming extremely covetous and greedy, is committed to the massacre of humanity. In short whether you consider intellectually, rationally or religiously you will find the dowry ritual to be vile, mean and terrible while the well-wishers of the humanity especially the Muslims who are the rescurer of humanity must keep themselves away from it.

## USURPATION OF WOMAN

Nowadays a wrong custom is in vogue that is the people do not pay dower of their wives, which is their religious right, rather they gave much more preference to an irreligious demand–the dowry–over *Sharia't* and law, under its dismal influence families are breaking and the society is being ruined. The demanded dowry has now become an oozing ulcer and a sign of ruin. So as soon as possible after abolishing it, we should concentrate on naturalism and rule of Allah (*Sharia't-e-Islami*) after avoiding all types of prodigality, we should held the marriage function simply as the prodigals in the eyes of *Sharia't* are like Satans (in accordance with the Qura'nic verse No. 27 from Bani Israel ). The wealth is also given by Allah and the man will be asked about it in the Hereafter. This mere showy business of the wealthy persons had made the life of poor miserable, therefore this prodigality and showy business should be stopped.

## REFORMATION OF SOCIETY AND RESPONSIBITY OF THE YOUTH

In this field our youth must come forward to take reformal initiative and to vow that neither they will ask any for dowry nor they will let another ask it. They should convince the people seeking dowry, that it is irreligious and forbidden, inspite of this if they do not agree, then they should be boycotted socially so that their mentality be settled. Muslim youth after constituting Anti-Dowry Committees in each locality and cities, can take such initiatives in this matter, these will bear good results and be good to many poor families, which are waiting for well-behaved boy for years due to lack of financial resourcess.

This type of reformal initiative will not only bring the pleasure of Allah and the Prophet (pbuh) but will also be helpful in rebuilding an exemplary society. As long as the youth will not come forward, any reformal movement can't succeed, therefore some righteous and influential youths should come forward. Allah willing–these some words may effect the hearts of the sympathizers of Muslims.

# NUPITALS

Under this we want to give one clarification, that is the new grooms should neither feel uneasiness nor be embarrased nor talk to any inexperienced friend and unaware scholar nor to pay attention to their sayings, rather do these two things .

(1) Consult any reliable Jurist (*Mufti*)and note down some traditional and religious ways of living with wife, and read a book by elderly and reliable scholar before marriage on this topic.

(2) Supplicate Allah for easiness in every matters and ask any of your serious thinking, married and reliable friend or any of your close relative for some 'experience'.

Don't go to them often and never consult more than one person in this matter, as everyone will give his reason and ideas while you will get yourself confused by them. There is an English proverb corresponding to it "Too many cook spoil the dish."

Another harm in consulting more persons is that they all will be waiting for the main moment, in order to probe what happened. They will try to do same joking and probing, saying that he was so much confused before marriage, let us ask of his well-being. Thus by going to so many people you have disturbed yourself.

Best way is what we have told you earlier, that is to read some important books and keep it with you out of necessity, mark the ambiguous part and consult a reliable jurist to understand it. Consult only a serious and mannered friend to ask any needful.

By doing this, the uneasiness of your heart, the unknown perplexity or the strange embarrassment will be quashed up completely. Supplicate to Allah for your wife, this will crop up your love in her.

In reality, the groom suffer because he thinks that if something wrong happened on the very first day and he could not do the "satisfying job" properly, then the wife will tell her friends and thus his secret will be opened. This self-imposed embarrassment is useless, as she is not coming for one day only and thats' too just for checking, rather she will be forever with you, moreover, *Sharia't* has not made (doing that satisfying job) copulation obligatory for the first night.It could be delayed due to tiredness and a lot of other excuses, therefore nothing is to worry. This is such an easy and natural job that as much one will be free of tension regarding this one can do it easily.

# THE CUSTOMS OF MARRIAGE

Hazrat Abbul-Rahman bin 'Auf (mabawh) is one of the ten companions of the Prophet (pbuh) to whom he (pbuh) had conveyed of being the heavenly ones. Once the Prophet (pbuh) saw a yellowish mark on his clothes and asked him about it. He said that he had married a woman (it means that he had put some scent on his clothes at the time of marriage, and it has left its mark) the Prophet gave him blessings and said *Waleema* should be done though of a goat.

Just imagine, that Hazrat Abdul-Rahman bin 'Auf is so near to the Prophet (pbuh) as he had counted him in the blessed ten, when he got married, he did not invited even the Prophet (pbuh) rather when the Prophet (pbuh) saw the mark of scent on his clothes then only he (pbuh) asked him and he told that he had got married. The Prophet (pbuh) too had not complained rather he blessed him and persuaded him for *Waleema*.

In reality Islam has made the marriage so simple and easy, if the two parties are agree they could do it (without any improper obstructions) freely.

*Sharia't* has not put this condition that only a scholar or *Qazi* should perform the matrimonial rites rather the condition is that there should be two witnesses at the time of the marriage ceremony. If the bride and groom both are sensible and adult, and one of them tells other that I want to marry you while the other accepts it, the marriage is done. There is neither any need to go to a court nor to arrange a function nor a feast and dowry is compulsory only the dower to honor the bride is compulsory.

It is better to settle the dower at the time of marriage and if by chance it is not mentioned at the time of marriage then also marriage becomes legal and the customary dower is considered necessary. Giving sermon at the time of the marriage is traditional and one should get its blessings but validity of marriage did not depend on it therefore, if without sermon the proposal and consent is done, marriage will be valid.

*Waleema* for which the Prophet (pbuh) has persuaded in the above mentioned *Hadees* is also a mere tradition of him (pbuh), it is neither an Islamic duty nor obligatory that without this marriage could not be completed. The *Sharia't* has neither fixed the quantity of guests nor the quality of food necessary for *Waleema*, rather it depends on the financial capacity of the groom without taking any loan. Moreover, if one can't do *Waleema* it won't bring any defect in the marriage.

Islam had made "the marriage" much more easy as it is the best way of fulfilling legally the most important demand of human nature. If this legal way is being made hard or obstacles are being put in its way, then its inevitable result will be debauchery, because when a man will find the legal ways of fulfilling his natural needs closed, then ultimately he will incline towards illegal ways and the whole society will get effected.

Islam had made "the marriage" very easy but our today's mode of life has made it very hard. We have made the marriage so complicated with lots of unnecessary customs, rituals and prodigality that neither a poor nor middle-class person could marry his ward easily. No one can think of marriage unless he has at least 2 lac Rupees, this amount is needed to observe different customs and not for the different real duties of the marriage which do not help in fulfilling the real life necessities.

At the time of marriage only one feast ( *Waleema*) is traditional in *Sharia't* and that's too according to the capacity of each individual, but today the feast and functions are increasing day by day. The function of engagement has almost become a marriage function and at the very time of marriage the ritual of Henna, Ubtan etc. all have become necessary and the feast thereafter, moreover without these false and un-Islamic rituals, marriage is not thought of. Then with the advancement of time new expenses are adding, new demands are being made and new rituals are being generated. In short the marriage has become a heap of prodigality, which the poor people in general cannot fulfil with his legal earnings and he has to take support of some illegal means. In this way the marriage inspite of being a good deed has become a heap of so many sins and misdeeds. And how the marriage, which began wih sins and misdeeds, could be a blessed one? *Sharia't* has not restricted enjoyment moderately.

Whereas, in the name of enjoyment we have brought ourselves under the influence of so many rituals, consequently the happiness has become a bygone thing and the rituals have surpasses it. When these rituals are violated, there starts complaints, accusations and taunting remarks. Thus the marriage functions have become a perfunctory place for these rituals which need a lot of money, give tiredness to the organisers and nothing else.

Although all of us consider this very situation reformable orally, but when the time of action comes we forget everything and surrender to all these rituals one by one.

There is no way out except that the influential and prosperous persons must come forward in order to hold their marriage functions with as much simplicity as possible and reduce the rituals, which has made the marriage a curse.

If wealthy persons are not leaving these rituals, then at least the middle class should avoid copying them, should live within their means and should not exceed their capacity.

If we take care of the following points then *Insha Allah* these flaws will decrease.

(1) The functions other than *Waleema & Nikah* ceremony; such as engagement, *Henna*, *Ubtan* and *Chauthi* etc. should be abolished completely and one should resolve that these functions will not be held in his marriage. If the two parties want to exchange gifts due to happiness, they can, but without arranging any funtions.

(2) One should not deem any specific way of showing happiness as necessary but he should select the way

in accordance with his capacity and financial means so that he may not become ritual bound or a prey of greed to be taunted.

(3) One should held the *Waleema* and *Nikah* ceremonies too simply and within his capacity. While no one should complain him if he is not invited to these function as the organizers are holding these within their limits.

(4) We should keep the saying of the Prophet (pbuh) in our mind, as he has said, "The most blessed *Nikah* is one which has minimum over-burdening" in other words, we can say, in which one is neither over-burdened financially nor would suffer from unreasonable hard work.

Taken from M. Taqi Usmani (The daily Jung )

## *NIKAH* AND *WALEEMA*

### Some questions & their answers

In the previous articles, while giving some advices about certain rituals of marriage, the readers sent me many questions and suggestios which reveal;

(1) How much the people are embarrassed of these silly rituals and they want its solution.

(2) How much ignorant, the people are of religious teachings regarding marriage and today even well educated people don't know the common issues, what the earlier general Muslims were knowing.

(3) That the people now want to know the religious status of these issues.

I am not quoting all these letters, as the following paras will cover the answers to all these question *Insha-Allah.*

In marriage, only *Waleema* is a function which is formally a tradition of the Prophet (pbuh) and he had urged the Muslims to do it, explicitly.

While doing *Waleema*, one should remember that;

(1) *Waleema* is a tradition of the Prophet (pbuh)which should be followed.

(2) There is neither a fixed number of guests nor a fixed criteria of food, but these two are fully dependent on the capacity of each individual.

There is a *Hadees* in *Saheeh Bukhari* according to this the Prophet (pbuh) spent only 2 *Ser* (about 1.864kg) of barley in one of his *Waleema*. *Waleema* of Hazrat Safia (mabawh) was held during a journey by laying the table and putting some dates, cheese and ghee, while in the marriage of Hazrat Zainab (mabawh) mutton and bread were served. Therefore it is not right to consider a large number of guests and quality food as necessary and if one is financially weak he must do it within his capacity without taking any loan. Whereas, there is no harm in arranging a bigger feast if one can and that's too without any intention of ostentation.

Within these limits *Waleema* is traditional and a virtuous deed,while ruining its sanctity by different sins is its disgrace. Showing glory…., initiatives of ostentation …., loss of prayers due to busyness in the function……., intermingling of well adorned men and woman ……and video coverage of these things etc. have undone the blessings of this function, we should save this blessed function from these evils.

Another misconception about *Waleema*, which is prevailing in our society and confusing many people as one man has sought the clarification citing this confusion, that is, *Waleema* is not valid? If intercourse has not taken place.

While in reality, *Waleema* could be done anytime either at the time of *Nikah* or after the departure of bride from her parental home, but after the departure it is *Mustahab* (desirable) while departure means only departure and nothing else–bride had come to the house of groom and they had met in seclusion–so , if due to any reason, the intercourse has not taken place, it doesn't effect the validity of *Waleema*. In this way, the *Waleema* neither become unlawful nor supererogatory (*Nafil*) nor one should understand that *Sunnat* is not obeyed rather it is not done in its desirable time. (If some one wants to know more, he can consult "Fath-ul-Bari" by Ibn-e-Hajr Vol. 9 page 231 and Hadees No. 5166 of al-*Waleema* Chapter)

## TAKING PERMISSION OF THE GIRL

One man has asked, that at the time of *Nikah*, when a member of bride's family seeks her consent, is it necessary for her to speak or only her signature will suffice?

In our society, generally the brides are not supposed to be among the marriage gathering, but a member of her family acts as her agent after taking her permission by saying, "I want to marry you with such and such against so much dower, Do you agree? If the bride is maiden then her speaking is not necessary but preferable. If she does not refuse or signs the *Nikah* document, these will be deemed as her permission. Whereas, if the bride was married earlier and it is her second marriage, then she must speak otherwise *Nikah* can't happen.

The person who has taken the bride's consent , being her agent allows *Qazi-e-Nikah* to recite the sermon, and the words which *Qazi-e-Nikah* utters after the sermon is "PROPOSAL" and what the groom utters is "CONSENT" after this the *Nikah* ceremony is completed.

(Taken from Zikr-o-Fikr by M.Taqi Usmani)

## FEAST AND PROCESSION OF MARRIAGE

Mufti Taqi Usmani writes, in another column, about the feast and procession of marriage, that he received a letter of a British Muslim, he had written in it "I want to draw your attention towards dowry, which is prevailing in India and Pakistan. When the Muslims of India and Pakistan settled here (in Britannia) they brought this custom with them and now this custom is prevailing in the west also. You are requested to explain its *Shara'i* status, so that the new generation of European Muslims would know it and perhaps it might change the luck of thousands of girls who are not being married due to non availability of dowry. Is dowry necessary? If yes what is its quantity? Is it not necessary to give her share in the legacy after giving the dowry? Generally women withdrew themselves from the share of legacy as they have got dowry, they hope for the help of their parents in their pleasures and afflictions and a huge amount had been spent on their marriage. All these things are applicable for a son also, so how he becomes eligible for a share in the legacy? What is the *Shara'i* status of the feast given by the bride's family to the marriage procession? In the Arab countries, the expenses done by the bride's family are paid by the groom then why these expenses are borne by the father of the bride in our society? Whereas, in some places the father of the bride asks the groom for more money than what he has spent in the marriage , what is its *Shara'i* status?"

Answers of some of these questions have already been given. For example, it has been said that neither dowry is a part of the marriage nor it is legal to keep the girl's marriage in abeyance for long due to its non-availability and if one wants to give his daughter a gift within his capacity happily, while sending her as a bride, he can. One should neither consider it an inevitable condition of the marriage nor one should take a view of ostentation in it nor it is lawful for the groom and his family either to ask or hope for it.

## RIGHT OF LEGACY DOES NOT CEASE WITH DOWRY

Now the question is, “Whether is it necessary to give her share in the father’s legacy after giving dowry or not?”

This misconception is prevailing in our society but infact it is not connected with it in any way. If a father has given his entire wealth as dowry then also her right of legacy does not cease. It will never be lawful for her brothers to embezzle all the legacy of their father after his death, on the basis of dowry given to their sisters. They must get their share in the father's legacy. If the father has given anything, in his life, either to his son or daughter, it also has no impact on their share in the legacy. Whereas, the father should take care of equality while giving anything to his children so that, no one might be disappointed. Anyhow, there is no bitch of hindrance in it legally (*Shara'i*) that neither the girl's share ceases by giving her dowry nor this much will be deducted from her share in the legacy, rather she must get her full share.

Another question, "what is the *Shara'i* status of the feast given by the bride's father to the marriage precession?" General people's thinking is that, organizing a feast by the girl's father on the occasion of *Nikah* is either traditional (*Sunnat*) just like *Waleema* or desirable in *Sharia't* this thought is completely baseless. If the girl's family is organising a feast, it is neither traditional nor desirable rather it is merely lawful if there is no other flaws. The same thing applies to the marriage procession also, neither *Sharia't* has made *Nikah* dependent on the marriage procession nor it is traditional whereas, there is no evil in it, if it is free of flaws. The general people's thinking, that taking out marriage procession and feast given to them by the girl's family, is a sin and prohibited by the Qur'an or *Sunnat* is also not appropriate. In reality, if a few people are going to the bride's home for marriage and the guardian of the bride is giving them a feast alongwith some of his friends and relatives as a gesture of happiness on the completion of his duty, then there is no sin in it. Whereas, the evil starts by considering these an integral part of the marriage, rather one is compelled to perform all these things though by taking loan and if one can't perform these he is taunted. Whereas he should be praised because he is going by the tradition of simplicity.

For example, some people give feast to celebrate the children's success either in their exams or in getting a better employment–there is no harm in it–while some others don't. The society don't taunt them, why they have not given feast, in the same way we should not taunt a person who is not organising a feast in the marriage.

## One Bad Ritual

The last question in the letter is, 'What is the *Shara'i* status of the excess money asked by the bride's father from the groom at the time of marriage otherwise he does not marry his daughter'. Certainly this baseless ritual is quite prevalent in our society, it is completely unlawful in *Sharia't*. Muslim jurists have called it bribe and it is just like selling one's daughter. Due to this very reason, the groom treat her (the bride) as a self-purchased maid, so this is the worst custom according to *Sharia't* and morality, which should be avoided.

Taken from "Zikr-o-Fikr' by M.Taqi Usmani

## UNTRADITIONAL METHOD OF TRADITIONAL *WALEEMA*

Certainly marrying a suitable girl is in itself a blessing of Allah the Almighty, a thing of happiness for man, while he is supposed to thank Allah for this. Whereas, *Waleema* is the way of showing hearty happiness and its philosophy is not only to pronounce marriage but also showing their happiness and thanking Allah the Almighty. By which the family of newly wed girl is satisfied, moreover mutual relation and affection is multiplied. The Prophet (pbuh) has given its importance through his sayings and actions.

It is narrated by Hazrat Anas (mabawh) that the Prophet (pbuh) asked Abdur-Rehman bin 'Auf (mabawh) seeing a yellow sign (on his clothes and body) what is this? He replied that he had married a woman against Gold which equals to a stone of date (this is her dower). The Prophet (pbuh) said may Allah bless you, do *Waleema* though by a goat.

The words of the Prophet (pbuh) اَوْلِمْ وَلَوْ بِشَاةٍ means one should do *Waleema*, though only a goat is available with him, he should slaughter it. (Mishkaat page 277)

Moreover the Prophet (pbuh) has himself done *Waleema* after his each marriage. Hazrat Anas (mabawh) has said;

"The Prophet (pbuh)has not done *Waleema* in his marriage as he has done after marrying Zainab bint Jahesh (mabawh), by slaughtering a goat."

This *Hadees* tells us that the Prophet (pbuh) has done his *Waleema* by slaughtering a goat, only in his marriage with Hazrat Zainab (mabawh), which in itself is very simple. Whereas in his other marriages it was more simple and short. As is told in the coming *Ahadees*.

Hazrat Anas (mabawh) narrates, We were on the way back from Khayber that the Phophet (pbuh) married Hazrat Safiya (mabawh), while still in journey and spent the night with her, then I invited the Muslims for his *Waleema* as he has told me to do so. There was no meat and no bread rather he asked to lay the table, then we put some dates, cheese and butter etc. (only this was his *Waleema*).

(Mishkaat page 278)

The Prophet (pbuh) himself had not arranged anything but whatever we had, we brought on the table and we ate collectively.

Hazrat Anas (mabawh).......... narrates that the Prophet did his *Waleema* after marrying Hazrat Safiya bint Hayi (mabawh) with only dates and *Sattu*.

Hazrat Safiya bint Shaiba (mabawh) narrates that the Prophet (pbuh) has done *Waleema* of some of his wives with some barley. (Mishkaat page- 278)

Another Hadees, Hazrat Yahya bin Saeed narrates that he has been informed that the Prophet (pbuh) sometimes used to do *Waleema* without meat and bread.

In the light of these *Ahadees* we came to know, though, *Waleema* is the tradition of the Prophet (pbuh) adopting simplicity in it is also his tradition. If anyone doing *Waleema* with so much of formalities while leaving simplicity then he is not acting on the tradition of the Prophet (pbuh).

**Let us look ourselves now:-**

Let us have a look on the marriage in our families, what importance do we give to the traditions of the Prophet (pbuh)? Do we marry according to the chosen way of the Prophet (pbuh)? Or we make fun of this tradition (*Nikah*) by marrying according to our own wishes and committing so many sins in the name of a tradition.

## CARING MORE OF *SUNNAT* THAN *FARZ*

The persons who arrange *Waleema-e-masnoona* either in their marriage or in their children's marriage, just check their day to day life, whether they are obeying the obligatories (*Fara'iz*) and essentials (*Wajibat*) as imposed by the *Sharia't* or not?

Are they discharging the obligations of *Namaz, Roza Zakat* and *Haj*?

Are they fulfilling the essential rights of their children, relatives, wives, parents and neighbours?

If they are not discharging these obligatories (*Fara'iz*) and essentials (*Wajibat*), they must take care of these first, because the men will not be asked of discharging *Sunnat* but he will be asked of discharging obligatories and essentials in the Hereafter. Hence, if a man is not doing

*Waleema-e-Masnoona*, as he can't do it properly. Whereas if he is discharging all the obligatories and essentials he won't be asked in the Hereafter why had he not done the *Waleema*?

Through our practice, it looks as if the obligatories and essentials imposed on us by the *Sharia't* had become unnecessary and *Sunnat* has become very much necessary and it should be done in any way. One must avoid changing the *Shara'i* status of anything.

## DOING *WALEEMA* BY TAKING LOAN.

Doing *Waleema* is *Sunnat*,while one is capable of it and had the means for for it otherwise he should not do it. Nowadays doing *Waleema*, though by taking loan, has become a matter of status. If someone is not doing *Waleema*, he is disgusted, abused and taunted in his kith and kin, his in-laws taunt by saying, had he married a widow, that he is not doing *Waleema*?

Whereas, the married one thinks that marriage is done once in the life, let me vent my spleen on it, by taking heavy expenses for *Waleema* upon himself with other expenses and if it is out of his capacity then he takes loan. by doing *Waleema* in this way he wins fame and ovation for sometime, *Maashaa'Allah* what a feast of *Waleema* he has given, but the loan remains biting him and money-lenders run after him. All the tranquillities and peace of life ends with this.

All this happened, as he has not performed the

*Sunnat* of the Prophet (pbuh) according to his simple method. Had the Prophet (pbuh) ever done the Waleema by taking loan?

He had never done–then, why we are doing *Waleema* by taking loan? Is this to discharge the *Sunnat* of our Prophet (pbuh)? Never we do just to vent our spleen on it, to please the kith and kin and to get ostentation. When we will keep, our interests instead of obeying the Prophet (pbuh) in our mind, then this *Waleema* naturally will create problems for us. Nowadays, the aim of only few people is to get the reward of following the Prophet (pbuh), whereas most of the people do it to save them from taunting and to gain fame in their kith and kin.

## SHORT *WALEEMA*

Nowadays, when invitation are given for *Waleema*, generally one tries to invite all the relatives, friends, neighbours, acquainted persons and even the distant relatives, while this is just to get ostentation and fame. The people will discuss his wealth, whereas they do not know the reality, that is, this feast is being organised by taking loan, rather nowadays all the people know the reality. Secondly, one thinks that if he does not invite all his relatives and acquainted persons, then they will taunt him, that such and such has not invited them, one wants to be saved from this type of taunting.

In this regard, we even don't consider, that how the Prophet (pbuh) has done *Waleema* and how many people he had invited in the feast, rather he used to feed as much companions (mabawt) as were present on the occasion. There was neither the formality of inviting each and every person nor one used to be angry if not invited.

If by acting on this very tradition of the Prophet (pbuh), we do not gather a crowd, rather discharge it (*Sunnat* of *Waleema*) shortly and with simplicity, then *Inshaa' Allah* we will get the reward of discharging *Sunnat* and be saved from many inconveniencies and hardships.

By doing *Waleema* in this way you may face the taunting and reviling of your kith and kin, the best way is not to heed their taunting and reviling, rather you should consider that you are discharging only the tradition of the Prophet (pbuh) and if some one is taunting or talking unpalatable, it will not harm you.

In reality, if you want to live peacefully , then you should do whatever you feel better for yourself, taking in view the *Sharia't,* do not care for the people's taunting but you must be bold enough to hear them without this you cannot live happily and peacefully. If you are not bold, then as soon as, you wish to do anything, people will start taunting you and as a consequence you will leave that thing.

It means, that you do not have the courage and boldness to act youself but you are fulfilling other's wishes. Remember! Such person neither can stand on his own nor can get a bigger rank or post. A bold person in worldly affairs also is one who compels others to fulfil his wishes rather fulfilling their wishes, similarly you must show courage to guide people in religious matters rather following them in religious ways.

Show this very courage and boldness in the *Waleema* feast also–if according to your capacity, you can invite all your relatives and friends without taking loan, you can–feast of *Waleema* is *Sunnat*, but there is no need to take loan for this feast as it will keep you choked. Therefore, it is better to do *Waleema* within capacity and with simplicity rather to do by taking loan and remain thinking of repaying it. *Inshaa'Allah* in this way you will get full reward of *Waleema-e-Masnoona*, and blessings of discharging *Sunnat*.

## VARIETIES OF FOOD IN THE *WALEEMA* FEAST

An extravagance done in the *Waleema* feast is that inspite of preparing a single variety of food, various varieties are prepared. Suppose, if *Biryani* and *Zarda* are there, then not only *Qormah*, *Shir-maal* is added but either *Kheer* or Egg's *Halwa* or custard is also added, moreover chicken *Qormah* is considered more preferable then mutton or beef *Qormah* though it may create the finanacial problems. While its sole purpose is self-boasting and showing wealth, however one can't be superior to others merely by showing these things. Whereas by such sumptuous food people will become jealous and enemy of you as they will talk about your copious wealth.

Let us leave all these formalities and do *Waleema* with simplicity by acting upon the *Sunnat* of the Prophet (pbuh). If Allah the Almighty has given you ample wealth, then there is no harm in preparing various varieties of food but there should neither be ostentation nor self-boasting nor showing of wealth. Remember that simplicity and diligence are the two quintessences of Islam, one should adopt these two and persuade others also to adopt these.

## CARDS FOR *WALEEMA* FEAST

Another extravagance done in the *Waleema* is that costly and exquisite cards are printed. Thousand of rupees are spent only on cards as one wants that his card should be a unique one, whereas its only purpose is to communicate the time of *Waleema* which could also be done orally.

The card start with "Bismillaahir-Rahmaanir-Rahiim" and under it "*Waleema-e-Masnoona*" is printed in bold letters. Whereas in today's *Waleema* the word *Masnoona* is mocked at by doing different silly and anti-*Shari'at* activities in it.

When these cards are received by the relatives and friends, they get information of the feast by reading once only, and its purpose is achieved. What is its further use?

There is no futher use of the card, so it is thrown in the dust-bin and Bismillaahir-Rahmaanir-Rahiim and the blessed names are disgraced whereas due to this disgrace all the inviters and invitees become entitled to sin and anger of Allah. One can give invitations orally also, then why should we spend money on printing the cards and if we give this very money to the poor and needy then we will be eligible for the reward and mercy of Allah.

Whereas today–a machine age–people are busy in their work like a machine and they do not have time to go to each and every person to invite orally. Invitation by card is an easy substitute as it should reach the invitee by any means. If under any circunstances, printing the card becomes inevitable, use ordinary paper and simple language, get it eletrostated or printed if a large quantity is required and neither use costly cards nor write "Bismillaahir-Rahmaanir-Rahiim" on the card rather write only "786".

## *WALEEMA-E-MASNOONA* AND VIDEO COVERAGE

The flaws mentioned above are performed before the *Waleema-e-Masnoona*. Now we will discuss the flaws, which are done at the time of *Waleema* and at the top these flaws is video-coverage.

Nowadays, Video-coverage has become an integral part of our each and every feasts. Whether it is on the occasion of *Waleema*, *Aqueeua* or marriage etc. no feast is free of this curse whether it is in a rich, a poor or a labour family. Let's discuss its flaws.

You would have seen that generally a film-maker, is called to make the film of the whole function, alongwith two or three helpers to carry the search-light and wire etc. and all these men are unknown and non-*Mahram*. They are not only allowed to go anywhere in the function rather they are guided in order to make the film of the whole gathering whether they are men or women, they are told that this place and these persons are remaining, till there remains not a single person or a corner which is not covered in the film and that's too through different angles.

Outwardly, this walking around of strange men between women is a matter of immodesty and shamelessness; moreover it will anger Allah and avert His Blessings and Mercies. In these circumstances fear of mischief and vice increases as young ladies come in full make-up and adornment, whereas every lady wants to outstrip others in make-up and adornment. This immodesty and shamelessness reach its perfection, when the young ladies ask the video-maker that their different and clear poses should come in the film, so that their beauty, dress, ornaments and make-up should prevail in the whole film.

The sole purpose of all these is just self-exposition, so that when people see the film afterward, they should see us only and ask , who this lady is? Who is looking like a heavenly Hourie. Now as the whole film is saved in a cassette, it goes to each and every friend, relative and neighbours where it is fully exposed without caring that the persons seeing it are *Mahram* or non-*Mahram*, everyone enjoys it.

Sometime a human commits an indecent action ignorantly and feels that none has seen him,but this video-cassette saves each and every actions whether decent or indecent and hundreds of people will see what a certain man is doing.

Nowadays, it has become very difficult for an

honorable woman to attend the functions as before the video-coverage usage there used to be separate arrangement for ladies. But its usage has rendered this privacy and secrecy useless. The film-makers not only pursue the younger ladies but also the older-ones sitting in the farthest corner and chewing betel-leaf quietly, while these old women do not know that they are being filmed and hundreds of non-*Mahram* men will see them later.

## MIXED GATHERING AND UNVEILING

Earlier there used not to be mixed gathering in the functions rather there used to be separate partitions for men and women. Whilst nowadays, there is no such arrangement which is absolutely forbidden and unlawful, rather it is a clear mockery of the Prophet's (pbuh) tradition and human will be punished either in the world or in the Hereafter for this violation.

## EATING WHILE STANDING

Today, we have westernized ourselves very much and we have entered into brutality–May Allah have mercy on us and guide us to the righteousness, its biggest demonstration is done at the time of *Waleema-e-Masnoona*–As we make fun of this tradition of the Prophet (pbuh) by eating while walking and scrambling rather we are above brutality as there is no scrambling among animals, everyone of us wants to reach the table first.

When there is an announment–food is ready–we pounce upon the dining table like animals and show our complete brutality, ignorance of the etiquettes of taking food and boorishness, as if we don't know how to go to the dining table and we are getting food after certain days' gap. Most of us even don't think to wash hands before eating another tradition of the Prophet (pbuh), whereas some of us think that there is no harm in leaving this small tradition, if we engaged ourselves in washing our hands then either we will have to wait for the second shift or the food may be finished.

Perhaps, the organizers of the standing feast arrange it, thinking that they will save the rent of chairs; they should note that it is not sagacity to leave a tradition of the Prophet (pbuh) in order to save a scanty amount while you are spending lacs of Rupees in the marriage or *Waleema*.

Some people say, a standing feast takes lesser time, when we are wasting our precious time in so many silly things why can't we give some more time to discharge a tradition of the Prophet (pbuh).

In reality these are mere excuses under westernization and whosoever organizes standing feast, tries to expose himself as modern and civilized but these people, due to their conduct, are disgraced by those Muslims who follow the religion (Islam) strictly. Whereas, the westernized Muslims though dignify this but in fact they also call it "invitation of brutality."

Some people say that our friends and relatives are asking for standing feast, this is also not true because only some westernized peoples want this,while most of the invitees want sitting arrangement. This very desire is seen in a feast where some sitting arrangement is done for older people, these seats are quickly occupied while the older people remain standing. To see the desire of general people, just arrange both, you will see that the chairs are occupied quickly and the persons who could not find chairs, unwillingly eat while standing.

However! If due to friendship or relationship you are attending such feast, there are many ways to be saved of this curse, if you want, such as you can find a chair lying nearby take it, sit on it and start eating, if you don't find a chair put some food in a plate and go to the hall where chairs are there, use a chair like a table, sit on another and start eating.

In some cases, it is seen that sitting arrangement is there but the guests are supposed to bring food themselves, whereas to supply every thing to the guests is one of the etiquettes of hospitality but sometimes it is not possible due to the number of guests. In this type of feasts, guests are set free to bring, as much food as they can eat, to their seats. Another benefit in it is that food is saved from being wasted and ruined.

There is a flaw in this system also, that is old peoples who could not move are seen waiting to take food in their plates, if they want to take some more food then it is difficult for them to move while the younger people are busy in filling their own bellies. There should be a way in this system also so that the guests need not to stand from their seats again and again to take their food peacefully.

Whereas, the best is to lay the table, and let every

guests to take his food sitting, in this way a *Sunnat* will also be revived. May Allah help us to act upon the traditions of the Prophet (pbuh) Amen!

## THE PRECEPT OF EATING WHILE STANDING IN FUNCTIONS

Following are the sayings of the Prophet (pbuh) about taking food while standing in the functions.

عن انس رضی اللّٰہ تعالیٰ عنہ: نھی رسول اللّٰہ صلی اللّٰہ علیہ وسلم
عن الشرب قائما وعن الاکل قائما

*Hazrat Anas (mabawh) narrates that the messenger of Allah (pbuh) has prevented from drinking and eating while standing.* (Kanzul-Ummal Vol. 20p. 134)

عن انس رضی اللّٰہ تعالیٰ عنہ عن النبی صلی اللّٰہ علیہ وسلم انہ نھی
ان یشرب الرجل قائما قال قتادۃ فالاکل قال ذالک اشر واخبث.

*Hazrat Anas (mabawh) narrates that the messenger of Allah (pbuh) has prevented to drink while standing, Hazrat Qatada (mabawh) asked what about eating? He said it is more mischevous and worst.*

(Muslim Vol.2 P. 172)

In the light of these traditions it is clear, that eating or drinking while standing is anti-Islamic and against the teachings of the Prophet (pbuh). It is a custom of the enemies of Islam, infidels and westernized people we should save ourselves from these. The best way of eating according to Islamic culture, humanity and the traditions of the Prophet (pbuh) is to eat by laying a table cloth on the floor and sitting by its side with humility and meekness.

# SOME GUIDANCE FOR THE GROOM

Each Muslim should enquire about Islamic guidance, instructions and precepts regarding marriage, when either he himself or his brother or his son is going to marry, what Allah and His messanger (pbuh) has given to us. For this we are giving the names of some books, every Muslim groom, his father or guardian should read before marriage:

1) A Gift for Muslim Couple by M.Ashraf Ali Thanvi (Ra)

2) Guidance for a Muslim Wife by M.Majaz Azmi (Ra)

3) A Gift for Muslim Women by M. Ashiq Elahi (Ra)

4) A Gift for Muslim Bride by M. Haneef Abdul Majeed

5) Islami Shaadi by M. Ashraf Ali Thanvi (Ra)

6) Islaami Dulhan by Naseer Hussain Naqshbandi Ghafoori

The most important guidance is that the groom should try to marry with simplicity because as much simplicity and less expenses will be in the marriage it will be having as much blessings in accordance with the saying of the Prophet (pbuh), as he has said;

عن عائشه رضى الله عنها قا لت قال النبى صلى الله عليه وسلم
ان اعظم النكاح بركة ايسره مونة

*Hazrat Ayesha (mabawh) narrates that the Prophet (pbuh)has said, verily the most blessed marriage is that in which expenses are the least.* (Mishkaat)

Therefore, if the groom wants blessings in his marriage, and wants it to be a mean of prosperity in the world and in the Hereafter, a cause of peace and tranquility, to get the pleasure of Allah and His messenger (pbuh) he should expend as less as possible.

In the time of the Prophet (pbuh) the marriage used to be held secretly and sometimes these were held all of a sudden (without any prior arrangement) for example; Hazrat Abdur Rahman bin 'Auf (mabawh), the richest man of Madeena Munawarah, marries without even informing the Prophet (pbuh) or seeking his presence in the marriage ceremony as a blessing. When he came to the Prophet (pbuh) he asks him about the yellow colour on his clothes. Then only he tells that he has got married, the Prophet (pbuh) gives him the blessing and asked him to do *Waleema*. You can find this very incident in all the six authenticated *Hadeeth* books. Just like this the Prophet (pbuh) had performed the marriage of many of his companions (mabawt) all of a sudden.

(Tirmidhi 3/421-422)

According to *Islami Shari'at* there are two essentials in the marriage to be followed;

1) Presence of two witnesses

2) Proposal and consent, moreover the dower of the bride and announcement of the marriage are also the necessary parameters of the marriage.

It means though the marriage becomes legal if only

two witnesses are present, but announcing is better socially in order to dispel doubt– As for *Waleema* it is a tradition of the Prophet (pbuh), neither it is compulsory nor obligatory– *Qormah & Roti / Biryani & Zarda* or several varieties of food are not a part of *Waleema*, if someone gives any edibles or gives *Sharbat* only to some of his nears and dears, it will also suffice. Therefore doing *Waleema* out of one's capacity or by taking loan is un-Islamic and unlawful whereas prodigality and extravagance for ostentation is entirely prohibited.According to the Holy Qur'an (*Suarah:Isra-27*), the prodigals are the brothers of the Satans. Giving sermon at the time of *Nikaah* is also a tradition of the Prophet (pbuh)– only these things are necessary in the marriage, all other things are un-Islamic and man-oriented which should be deemed as innovations in religion and nonsense. Islamic jurisprudence is a blessing for us as it is the simplest and easiest one, which can be practiced by both–poor and rich–without any difficulty. But we ourselves have made it complicated by our stupidity.

A Muslim should avoid un-Islamic customs and copying non-Muslims as how can we expect the blessings of Allah by disobeying and revolting against His laws? How can we expect His favours by violating His orders? Allah has said in the Holy Qur'an addressing the Bani Israel;

وَاَوْفُوْابِعَهْدِیْ اُوْفِ بِعَهْدِكُمْ.

*And fulfil your Covenant with Me and I shall fulfil My covenant with you.* (Baqra : 40)

This very saying of Allah is now applicable to us also.

If you are capable of spending extravagantly, then you are creating problems for the poors by doing so, as they will deem it as the standard of doing *Waleema* and will entangle themselves arranging for this.

People will never be happy, how ceremonious and splendid *Waleema* you are doing. While reviewing among them after the feast someone will say "chilly was more", "oil was more", "the rice has become soft", "fried items were cold" and "the other party has done better than him".

Just imagine, you have faced so much of trouble in arranging the *Waleema* but people have hurt your feelings through taunting, if you would have done it simply, the people would have said only that inspite of being a wealthy man you had not done the *Waleema* in accordance with your capacity. This sentence is better than severe taunting, if you spend the money, saved by doing *Waleema* simply, on orphans, widows and spreading of religion, this would give you much reward in this world as well as in the Hereafter and Allah the Almighty will be pleased with you as you have saved yourselves from prodigality and ostentation.

## SECOND ADIVICE

The groom and his family should understand well that according to nature and Islamic jurispudence, it is upto man to arrange home with all its essentials, money for marriage and *Waleema* and the maintenance allowance of the bride. Whereas, house-essentials include the kitchenware and bed etc, to spend on bride is obligatory for men whether she is rich or poor.

Allah has said in the Holy Qur'an clearly that the

man spends his money on the bride, hence, Allah has given the men superiority over women in Surah; Nisa-34

اَلرِّجَالُ قَوّٰمُوْنَ عَلَى النِّسَاءِ بِمَا فَضَّلَ اللّٰهُ بَعْضَهُمْ عَلٰى بَعْضٍ وَّبِمَآ اَنْفَقُوْا مِنْ اَمْوَالِهِمْ

*Men are the protectors and maintainers of women, because Allah has given the one more (strength) than the other, and because they support them from their means.*

This verse has thrown light in an eloquent and significant way on the limitations and obligations of men and women towards each other. The men have been asked to arrange money, in order to spend on his family's fooding, lodging, dressing and house-wares.

That's why, they are appointed as the protectors and maintainers of the house. Now it is upto women to obey their husbands, to look after their wealth in their absence and their other rights. Hence, in the second part of this very verse, Allah has called the obedient woman as "the righteous woman".

The same thing has been depicted in Hidayah Awwalain on Page No: 417, a famous book of Islamic Jurisprudence;

النفقة واجبة للزوجة على زوجها مسلمة كانت او كافرة اذا اسلمت نفسها الى منزله، فعليه نفقتها وكسوتها وسكناها

*All the expenses of a wife are obligatory on her husband whether she is a muslim or an infidel, when she, after surrendering herself to her husband, comes to his house. Now he is supposed*

*to arrange for her dressing, lodging and other expenses.*

One can't compel his bride or her family to arrange for these things. Whereas its demand, whether orally or through customs prevailing in the society is a shameful and reproachable act.

Therefore burdening a bride by asking to bring bedding, kitchen-ware, fridge and washing machine etc. to give necklace to the groom's mother, hold a feast for 500 odd men, give a ring to the groom's sisters, suits, watch and perfume to the groom is just like changing the system of nature and metamorphosing the human nature.

It is not only an open violation of the rules made by Allah but also a revolt against Him, which is the cause of corruption in the society, while one who is revolting against the rules of Allah and nature will have a bad end. As Allah the Almighty neither endures ruining the human rights nor social injustice, moreover it is a custom of Non-muslims and against the manliness and nobility of a man as Allah has asked him to spend while he is begging each and everything from his father-in-law. (Taken from Jahez, Aik Ghair Islami Tasawwur p.n.42)

## ADVICE OF THE GROOM TO HIS BRIDE IN THE FIRST NIGHT

Generally, there comes a wedding night once in every men's life , while it effects clearly the coming life, so one should spend this night in a way that it may leave good effects on the coming life, in accordance with an idiom "first impression is the last impression". One must give such an impression that the wife may be convinced of his piety, affection and ability.

We are giving you an important advice, with a hope from Allah that if you act accordingly then *Insha Allah* all the disputes of mothers and daughters-in-law will never occur and you will know how to keep them together. While seeing your bride for the first time, either you will praise her dress or ornaments or you will try to please her, at the same time you must tell her that you will be pleased if you keep my advice with you and will act accordingly.

That important advice is ......................

If my mother or sisters or brothers' wives are misbehaving with you then have patience by keeping quiet, in order to please Allah the Almighty and get better reward in the Hereafter and you must not tell me I don't want to listen that your mother has misbehaved with me or your sister has called me so and or your brother's wife don't talk to me politely or your nephew and neice have ruined my such and such things while neither your sister nor your brother's wives forbad them, or your mother and sisters found faults in the food cooked by me.

Remember if after listening your irrelevant talks, I accepted it to be 100 percent correct and behaved impudently with my mother then both of us will fall in the estimation of Allah and He will be displeased with us, as a result we will not be trauquilized inspite of having all the worldly resources.

Remember that the men come to their house in search of peace after getting tired while working and the wives give them the details of their disputes with mother and sister-in-law, it is harmful for both of them. So just keep this very mine advice in your mind and you will see its benefits later on.

Dear groom! We request you also that when your wife starts giving you details of her disputes with mother and sister-in-law, just ask her to solve these herself, as you yourself have told your mother not to tell anything about the disputes with your wife to you. As, the wife sometimes feel that the mother-in-law may poison the ears of her husband while the mother wants the son to come to her directly from the work, as the daughter-in-law may do the same...... therefore it is better to tell them not to implicate you in their disputes rather solve them mutually.

Most often it so happens, that after listening to the mother or the sister or the wife, the man tells some improper words to his wife and all the family had to regret, whereas if he speaks to his mother improperly she starts with a sigh, I had this very support after my husband's death and it is also lost and curses both. This curse may spoil their lives and influence the coming generation badly.

Therefore, Mr. groom! Let it be settled in your mind that you are not going to listen to the disputes of women, as it may spoil your married life. Tell your wife the benefits and virtues of forgiveness, if you will live happily with mother and sisters-in-law now, then only you will be happy with your children in future, you are supposed to face all these in the world whereas the real peace is in the Hereafter.

## A SIMPLE WAY TO CREATE LOVE BETWEEN MOTHER AND DAUGHTER-IN-LAW

The simplest way is that you ask your wife to give your mother such gifts which she likes most, though you yourself have brought those gifts. Whenever your wife goes to her parents' home ask her to bring some gifts for the mother, sisters-in-law and brothers' wives as well as for children also, while she herself should distribute these among them. This will increase mutual affection and you will get their wishes.

If, inspite of all these, you feel that the dispute is still there then arrange a separate house for your wife and if you can't then separate the kitchen so that there would be no room for disputes.

## IS HUSBAND A METAPHORICAL GOD

**Question**: If woman says that she dislikes her husband as he is ugly, if she lives with him then she could take false steps and she wants *Khula*' (divorce at the instance of wife) whereas her parent's view is that, "pointing to a husband's ugliness is a sin". She was told that "Hindu women consider their husbands as God, whereas in Islam the marriage happens through mutual happiness, and if woman wants, she can take *Khula'* to be saved from false steps, as the main aim of the marriage is "to be saved from social evil". Now the question arises; is considering husband a metaphorical God, a custom of Hindus in reality?

If it is like this then I had oppressed my obedient wife by considering myself a metaphorical God and a supreme commander, am I sinful or not due to my ignorance or am I supposed to seek her forgiveness? so that, Allah also forgave me or I am right and it is wrong that considering husband a metaphorical God is the custom of Hindus.

**Answer**: Allah has made the man commander over the woman but he is neither a real God nor a metaphorical God being a commander, neither he can oppress her nor he can scorn or humiliate her– the husbands who oppress their wives are the worst oppressors. You should behave your wives kindly and let bygones be bygones.

Giving husband the status of God may be a Hindu custom but Islam does not allow this. Whereas it is desirable from the wives to respect their husbands, not to call them by their name and not to refuse their legal orders. She can take *Khula'* if they don't have mutual love either due to husband's ugliness or rudeness or irreligiousness or any other reason.

## DONOT FORBID WIFE FROM PRACTICING *SHARI'AT*

Now we are giving some advices to such people who are not fully religious. May Allah make all of us fully religious and one who takes care of lawful and unlawful, right and wrong, tradition and heresy (*Bid' at*)

(1) With the blessings of Allah, if you have got a wife who is fully commited to Islam, don't compel her to obey different heresies being a husband. Such as making *Halwa* on *Shab-e-Baraa't* or *Kheer* on 10th of *Muharram* or filling *Koondas* (dough trough) in the month of *Rajab* etc. The things which are not approved by the Prophet (pbuh) or his companions (mabawt),are the additions in Islam and should be avoided. You should feel yourself lucky as you have got a pious wife who is keeping you and herself aloof from useless complications and imperfect rituals.

(2) If she is keeping herself in complete hiding, and is very careful about it , she is not opening even her hair or wrist either in front of Christian Nurses or Hindu she-sweepers (this is Islamic way) then why you are getting angry over her. If she does not want to go to such gatherings, where there is no

religiousness and she does not want to meet such ladies who are far from religion, do not compel her to attend these gatherings and to meet such ladies.

It is not sagacity to weaken your faith just to save others from being heart-broken.

(3) If she is hiding herself completely from your brothers (whether elder or younger to you), all of hers and your cousin-brothers, all of hers and your maternal or paternal uncles and your friends, moreover, if she does not want to go to such gatherings where there is a chance of intermingling with them, why you are making her a show piece. Is this because they bring in their wives in front of you. Remember! They are bringing their wives infront of you just to see your wife.

Remember! The end of all these mean and unlawful actions is the anger of Allah the Almighty, being afflicted by different embarrassments and misfortunes in the world and the Hell after death. May Allah save all of us! While she came as a bride fully veiled, as required by the *Shari'at* from her father's house then why you are compelling her to remove the veil.

O ignorant men! Why you are not hiding your wives they are an adornment for your houses only, why are you taking her out unveiled, she is for your pleasure alone. Just think! When you are taking your wife out unveiled, hundreds of eyes will see her and will receive Allah's anger and you became the reason of this unveiling, so you also will get affected of Allah's anger. That's why keep her hidden.

(4) If she is not attending parties due to photography, video-coverage and other unlawfuls happening there, don't compel her saying the organizers will be displeased or get angry. Once Hazrat Thanvi (Ra) said, " sometimes, you also get angry and displeased with your kith and kin saying you will not attend such functions, where so many unlawfuls are happening, as Allah and His messenger (pbuh)will also be displeased if we came.

## DON'T GIVE UP PIETY TO MAKE WIFE PIOUS

A righteous person should always try to make others especially his dependents righteous. In other words, guiding other to the righteous path is a part of self-righteousness, but he should not give up his righteousness. A person can never succeed either by taunting or by bantering and vexing or by concealing the details in making some one righteous. If you are seeing any deficiency in your wife or she is sticking to any vice, neither be angry nor abuse rather try to convince her patiently and that's too after sometime, when you are not irritated as you will not accept any of her excuses. We request you not to leave the religious path while convincing your wife. The clerics have said that it is a sin for the judges and *Muftis* (expounders of Islamic code of law) to decide the cases while they are angry. If you are consulting a *Mufti* or cleric regarding any *Shar'ai* issue or you got any important and worth following thing in any book then you must ask the preceptors in whose touch you are, the way to impose these on your family. First of all you have to prepare, your family members, mentally to act according to your wishes.

**Three golden principles for living happily with wife:**

If one is married, he has to live happily with his wife whether he likes her or not, as the case may be. To live happily he has to abide by these three advices.

(1) Save your eyes completely. Most of the time it so happen, when a man does not save his eyes he can't remain chaste, however may his wife be beautiful, Satan keeps him entrapped in his trap. While he himself remain restless by considering every made-up woman more beautiful than his own wife. One must pray Allah to be saved from this, as this spoils the spirituality and disgraces him in the eyes of Allah the Almighty.

One should save his eyes from his cousins and brother's wives as after seeing these woman of one's own family, he feels his wife less beautiful.

(2) One must have the thinking that Allah has made her , his wife and nothing can happen without Allah's will. One has to be happy with the decisions of destiny. May Allah give us His guidance and make us from among His thankful slaves. Hazrat Thanvi (Ra) has said that the time in which a believer disobeys Allah

is very unlucky for him, for example, when he sees any non-*Mahram* woman–sees the illegal beauty of a woman other than his lawful wife. If ever he sees a woman unknowingly then he must remove his eyes saying there is none equal to his wife in beauty, so he should be happy in the happiness of Allah.

(3) Never expect something from someone other than Allah (though they are parents, wife, children or some near and dear) as one feel very bad when he is afflicted by his near and dear rather by unrelated persons. For example a man expects that his children will stand by his side in his old age and the children became disobedient or inspite of being obedient they do not give airs to you, certainly he will be embarrassed. Same is the case of husband and wife, so do not hope in your wife *Insha Allah* you will never be distressed, Allah forbid, if you are distressed, it will not last long.

## CHANGE THE STANDARD OF YOUR MENTALITY

What is the standard of wife's love? ............ Have you ever thought that the girl to whom you have brought as your wife will be according to your high standard, if she is not. Will you not love her? Will you not keep her happy? Will you not pay heed to her rights? Never, because in this way your marital life will become distasteful and you can't be peaceful, so change your thinking before moulding wife in accordance with your own standard.

There is a standard of love which you have decided in your mind or which is prevalent in your family or friend's circle and you feel it the basis of love. If your wife is not according to that, you at once decide that she does not love you. So don't be mistaken and change your thinking, then only you will get the desirous love from your wife *Insha Allah*.

May Allah create love between you and all Muslim couples so that both of them would work together according to *Shari'at-e-Islami* and be a source of spreading it in the whole world, Amen!

Now we are quoting the words of Maulvi Mohd Yousuf Ludhianvi which are the part of "Aapke Masaa'el Our Unkaa Hal", so that you can understand the standard of wife's love.

## STANDARD OF WIFE'S LOVE

**Question:**..............I am married to my cousin with whom I was in love before marriage, the sole reason of this love was her being veiled and well-behaved we have not talked to each other before marriage whereas she was also in love with me before marriage, this we knew both. Our parents had arranged this marriage, I was very happy when she came to my house, but she is not treating me like a loving wife, we are married for 7 years. It seems to me as if she is living with me under some compulsion and she has no attachment with me, she neither join me in my pleasure nor in my sorrow.

A distressed person wants that at least his wife should stand by his side while he is embarrassed or aggrieved moreover he wants her wife to welcome him cheerfully whenever he returns home. My matter is quiet different, she does not reply even my *Salaam*, there is little chatting between us, though she does all my work like a machine and wants to keep herself away from me as soon as possible.

A person marries to get a loving friend/ partner and to fulfil his natural demands, though my wife is of sound health but there is no love for me in her heart. If there is no sexual desire in a person, he / she can treat with love. Sir, though my wife wants to live with me but as a servant and not as a wife, I am an emotional man and remain thinking it, awaken in the nights but can't find its solution. Sir.... I also acknowledge veil and I had taken full care of all the necessities of my children through my lawful income. To understand a person, seven years are enough whereas if that person does not have love for the other, he /she can't be understood. Whenever I had asked my wife, do you have any problem with me everytime she replies, you do a second marriage. What does it mean when a woman herself asks her husband to remarry.

Sir....when I return home remaing busy the whole day I became more distressed due to my wife's behaviour and remain awaken the whole night, as a result I am feeling myself mentally disturbed.

Sir............guide me through *Shari'at* and tell me an incantation so that I would get homely respite, my wife would start loving me and pay attention to our children. Kindly pray for me and do *Istikhaara* (asking Allah for proper guidance in a certain matter). Sir....... I hope that you will guide me like your own son and tell me a suitable solution of this very mine distress and embarrassment.

**Answer:** You have married by your choice, inspite of this she is not up to your "high standard ". It is not her "the poor guy's " fault, rather it is a fault of your high standard as being a woman she has no complain from you. Its solution is that you have to lower your high standard.

(1) How the wife can't be connected with the sorrows and happiness of her husband but the way of its expression can be in accordance with one's own standard.

(2) When you return home you are not received enthusiastically, do you know how much she was busy in the house-hold work? Just take charge of the house for a day and experience yourself.

(3) She does all your work like a machine and you don't value a running machine just appoint a cook to prepare food ......, a servant to clean the house......., a launderer to wash clothes......, a wet-nurse to look after the children ......, a watchman to guard the house. Inspite of all these employees, your house will not be much disciplined as it is under the aegis of your wife but you don't value her services.

(4) In reality seven years, is a long period, but Alas! you had not seen the qualities which Allah has hidden in your wife, by lowering your high standard. If you

would have lowered your standard, you would have understand her.

(5) .........it doesn't matter how many times you get married, you will neither learn the way to live nor you will get mind satisfaction unless you lower your high standard.

(6) .........you neither need an incantation nor an amulet but you need to be a human by living in the company of a righteous man. When your ability to read the human mind will improve, you will know that Allah has given you an enormous blessing in the from of this very wife.

## MEN SHOULD RESPECT THEIR WIVES

Men should respect their wives for two reasons;

(1) being wives they are inferior to men and it is against the gallantry to trouble the inferiors.

(2) due to religion as both of you are Muslims. It is not necessary that the woman will always be inferior to man. She may either be equal or superior to man in the eyes of Allah the Almighty. Similarly one does not know who is more beloved for Allah in accordance with his/her religion. Therefore men should neither disdain nor disgrace their wives. (Kamaalaat-e-Ashrafiya-124)

## TWO QUALITIES OF WOMEN ARE PRAISE-WORTHY

Women are praise-worthy and pitiable as they have two good qualities which make them superior to men also.

These are service.......and chastity....... Their chastity is so much that, though the men are free of evils but won't be free of temptations, if you take 100 noble ladies they all might be free of temptations. Allah has recalled this only in the Holy Qur'an. "(Surah Nur - 23) "Chaste indiscreet"

(Kamaalaat-e-Ashrafiya-206)

## LOVE YOUR WIFE

When the disposition of some husbands and wives does not resemble the husband decides that now they can't live together, she can't move with me, she is not lovable– and remain counting her flaws only.

Before requesting these husbands, we prayAllah to forgive the sins all these spouses and bestow love and affection after finishing enmity in between them, Amen!

You also say Amen! on this prayer, offer 2 *Raka'at Nafil*, if you can, and pray Allah imploringly for such spouses, relatives and friends, so that Allah may bestow love in all these families, because if there is mutual love in all the spouses then only one can get the worldly and religious virtues.

### A high status of love

Its proof is that all the couples are made by Allah, this very wife is a gift of Allah for you, so love her and consider her the most beautiful woman of the world, saying you do agree with which your owner is agree.

## ONLY WAY TO BE SAVED FROM THE UNLAWFUL

Have faith, that your wife, given by Allah to you, is the most beautiful woman and she is the only way for you to be saved from fornication.

The Prophet (pbuh) has said, "Doing sexual intercourse with your wife is also a charity (*Sadaqah*)". The companions (mabawt) asked the Prophet (pbuh), "While a man is fulfilling his desire, how he can get the reward of doing charity?" The Prophet (pbuh) said "if he would have done fornication, he would have been punished ... or not? Therefore when he is using the legal way saving himself from the illegal way ... he is supposed to get reward."

Anyhow, Allah forbid, if you saw a non-*Mahram* woman or you listen her voice or some bad intentions come in your mind then first of all remove your eyes from her and be strong enough not to see her again praying Allah to save you from evil-doings. Try to remain content with the wife you have in order to be saved from fornication.

Just inagine that your daughter is of ordinary appearance and ill-tempered, while the son-in-law is handsome, will you wish that he would beat her, misbehave with her, taunt her, make her a psychological patient or will you wish from him to keep her in comfort. If he is treating her kindly then he will be best son-in-law for you and you will also try to please him in every possible way. Now think that your wife is also a daughter of someone and you are not treating her kindly as she should have been, so just for

Allah's pleasure treat her kindly. Allah also befriend those who treat their wives kindly and gives him His nearness.

There is a narration of Hazrat Shah Abul-Hassan Kharqaani (Ra), his wife was a surly woman, a person from Kharaasaan came to become his disciple and asked her about Shah Saheb. She replied, why are you saying Hazrat, Hazrat– he lives with me I know how big Hazrat is he.

He started weeping and told the onlookers that he had come from a far off place to become a disciple of Shah Saheb and his wife is saying that he is not a preceptor. The people told him, O fool! don't ask her as she won't ratify anyone's beneficence and asked him to go to the jungle in order to see his miracles. When he entered the jungle, he saw that Shah Saheb is coming to him seated on a lion having a snake in his hand instead of a whip. It became clear for Hazrat after seeing him that he is coming after listening bitter and stinging words from his wife. Hazrat said, I am enduring my wife's acrimony and due to this the lion is obeying me. I am living with her considering her a slave of Allah, if I divorce her she will harrass another Muslim brother. That's why I am accomodating her. I treat her kindly thinking that first of all she is a slave of Allah then she is my wife. If I would not have kept patience and tolerated her cursing, this lion would not have been in my service. I got this miracle by keeping patience on the trouble given by this very woman.

So, love your wife and remember if you love someone, he/ she will also love you. Every human (though you may see him disliking others) has a passion for love and affection. A person, who is desirous of being loved, when gets love and affection, starts feeling him an important and a proudy personality.

If a wife does not get the love of her husband, does not find respect or prestige or place in anybody's heart then a vaccum of deprivation is created in this unfortunate woman, which results in the prospering and rising of only the disturbed feelings.

Therefore, the Muslim husband should consider that her wife is also a human being who also has some human necessities, feelings and demands. His mere expressing some love and affection to her, accompanying her, fibbing with her and praising of her food can florish the decaying life of this unfortunate woman, it won't harm him. If the husband takes care of these things he will also get suitable reward from Allah the Almighty.

Imam Bukhari has made a separate chapter;

باب ادخال السرور فی قلب المؤمن (Insertion of happiness in the heart of a believer) pleasing a muslim person has a legal sensuous importance. Espesially a Muslim must please his wife as she is subordinate to him and all her happinesses are attached to him.

Though unwillingly, you just show love and affection to your wife, as we are asking you this, she will love you much more than you as it is the woman's nature, that whenever she gets some love she expresses double then what she gets.

In the end we ask you, that inspite of her curtness and unpleasantness, is it humanity to rebuke and scold her.....being your wife and a subordinate to you? Is there no importance of being her a slave of Allah, the daughter of Adam (pbuh), a follower of the Prophet (pbuh), the heart of her parent, the safeguarding device for your private parts and the mother of your children. If you consider, her any awkward reply, her frowning, excess salt in the food, or lesser sugar in tea, as a big reason to rebuke and scold her then in the light of the references given above feel mercy on her also.

# "*EHSAAN*" AND MARITAL LIFE

Doctor Mohd.Abdul Hai Arifi (Ra) was among those brilliant personalities of our time who passed their lives remaining away from publicity and ostentation, but their character and the way of life attract us to them. He was trained by Hakeemul-Ummat Maulvi Ashraf Ali Thanvi (Ra) and his spriritual successor in mysticism and Sufism. Therefore general people used to come to him for reformation and were getting benefit out of his directions. Once a man came to him and told him, Thank Allah , I have got the status of "*Ehsaan*".

("*Ehsaan*" is a Qur'anic term, which is explained in the traditions, to worship Allah in such a way as if the worshipper is seeing Allah the Almighty or at least in a way as if Allah is seeing the worshipper).

The man meant same by his this very saying that he has got the status of "*Ehsaan*" while worshipping.

Doctor Saheb (Ra) congratulated him and said *Ehsaan* is really a big blessing, but I want to ask you, whether you got this status only in prayers or you got this while dealing with your family or any other relatives and friends also...? He said as far as I knew *Ehsaan* is connected with prayers and other worships only, therefore I had practised it in prayers and by the grace of Allah I had got success in it but I did never thought of it in other social deals. Doctor Saheb (Ra) said, just to remove this misapprehension, I had asked you. No doubt it (Allah is seeing me) is sought in prayers and other worships rather it is needed in each and every field of life. A man should also take in his mind, that Allah is seeing him while dealing with general people, specially the relation of husband and wife is such that they live always together. There comes many ups and downs and unpleasant moments in their lives as a result the psyche of a human instigates him/her for injustice in retaliation to these unpleasant moments. At this juncture one must keep in his mind that Allah the Almighty is seeing him.

Afterwards Doctor Sb. (Ra) said that the Prophet (pbuh) had never scolded nor felt angry on any of his Holy Wives in his life, I also had practiced the same following this very *Sunnat* of him.

Hence, thanking Allah I acknowledge that I am living with my wife for 51 years and had never talked her with changed accent. Afterwards his wife said remembering him, "He never talked to me in an unpleasant accent or asked me to do any of his personal work, I used to do all his works pleasantly on my own."

While discussing the *Nikaah* sermon, I had said that piety (*Taqwa*) is necessary for a happy marital life. The practice of Doctor Sb. (Ra)was the result of this very piety and follow up of this very saying of the Prophet (pbuh) "Best among you are those who are best for their wives."

Verily, Allah has said in the Holy Qur'an that men are protectors and guardians of women (Nisa: 34) but the Prophet (pbuh) has clarified through his sayings and actions, this verse does not mean that the men are supposed to give them orders or treat them like servants or keep them under their dictatorship. Allah Himself has clarified this in another verse of Rum: 21 " And among His signs is this that He created for you mates from among yourselves, that you may dwell in tranquillity with them, and He has put love and mercy between your (hearts)". This verse means that the basic thing in the relationship between husband and wife is love while both of them are the means of tranquillity for each other.

Whereas, Islam has also taught us that whenever we do a collective work, there must be a leader (*Emir*) from among ourselves, so that the work is done systematically. Moreover, it is also commendable that, if two persons are going on a journey, though they are friends, one should be made *Emir*.This *Emir* is not supposed to give orders to others but he is to supervise the related necessities, to arrange for others' comfort and to take care of his companions. While the other members of that group are supposed to help and obey him.

Just like the *Emir* of an ordinary journey, Islam has made the men the *Emir* of marital life which is a bigger journey. Because the men are supposed to be more sound physically and has more ability to bear its responsibilities. This does not lessen the reality, their relationship is of love and mercy, while none is supposed to treat other like a servant. Likewise the husbands, being *Emir* of the house, should not consider that the wife is created just to obey his orders and every legal or illegal wishes. This supremacy of men given by Allah demands that he should use it to show kindness to his wife and to fulfil her legal wishes as far as possible.

Likewise, wives should use their Allah's gifted capabilities, rights and abilities in co-operating with their life-partners and keeping them happy . If both of them are acting accordingly then the house will become a sample of heaven (*Jannah*) moreover, it will be a worship for both of them and a real source of Jannah in the Hereafter also. That's why they are advised of piety (Taqwa) in the *Nikah* sermon and Doctor Abdul-Hai (Ra) has included it in *Ehsaan* (doing an act thinking that Allah is seeing him/her).

Dear husbands! you can live a happy married life only when you consider her a real life-partner, keep in mind this *Ehsaan*, give her dues, try to keep her happy within your capabilities and make her fully religious. When she will become happy, she will concentrate on obeying and fulfilling all of your wishes.

## ENLIVEN THE LEFT *SUNNAT*

Hazrat Ayesha (mabawh) says, whenever the Prophet (pbuh) used to come to the house, he used to enter with a smiling face inspite of having so much of grieves regarding his followers and different preoccupations such as welcoming delegations, preaching Islam and deciding different matters of Muslims etc.

This *Sunnat* has been left by us. The irreligious persons come as if they are Pharohs, showing anger to terrify their wives. While the religious persons come as if they are either Bayazeed Bustami (Ra) or Khwaja Moinuddin Chishti (Ra) or Baba Fariduddin Attar (Ra) with closed eyes in meditation as if they live in the Heaven and don't know anything about the earth. They won't see their wives affectionately but will scold them and remain sitting with a chaplet. Whereas their wives were waiting the whole day for their return to amuse themselves. The husband comes home and sits either with a chaplet in his hand or starts calling friends or thinking about business or asking different questions.

Both these methods are against the *Sunnat*. One must enter his house smilingly, ask her well-being and lend a helping hand in her work to enliven the *Sunnat* and please Allah the Almighty.

Giving their dues is more rewarding then telling beads and *Nafil* (Supererogatory) prayers. The Prophet (pbuh) has said "The best mannered man is one who is best with his wife". In another narration the words are as follows;

"The most complete in faith is one who is well-mannered and who is most lenient to his family."

(Mishkaat p. 282 Hadeeth No.35)

It is not fair for us to laugh and tell jokes in our friend circle but when we come to our wives, we would become serious or shrink our face as if we don't know laughing. Whereas, she is perplexed by seeing you, as she was waiting for you the whole day to be indulged in jokes with you and you are entering the house like a statue. You might have got the Islamic standard of piety and righteousness in the light of the Prophet's (pbuh) sayings. That is you should be polite with your wife, show patience and toleration in your house rather to show ettiquets in your office, shop, friend-circle, mosques or social life.

Indulging in jokes with wife, forgiving mistakes enduring anger, listening her complaints if these are making her happy, taking her out for amusement in Islamic veil and giving her pocket-money within one's capacity........etc. are worship. While offering supererogatory prayers the whole night and not talking with wife or sleeping separately is against the tradition of the companions of the Prophet (pbuh).

## WIVES HAVE THE RIGHT TO COOL DOWN A LITTLE, AFTER ALL IN WHOM THEY WOULD TAKE PRIDE OTHER THEN YOU

Have you ever noticed that sometime a child weeps uselessly so that his/her parents would love and fondle him/her more. While, sometimes you or any of your close friends cool down among themselves just to turn the other more towards him or perhaps he would say cheerfully, come let's have lunch in a restaurant or he would take you somewhere in his new car. If you cool down, they will neither move away from you after taunting nor they will be annoyed............nor they will stop talking to you.......

If your wife cools down and keeps quiet, will you go away from him after uttering some unpalatable words ... is this the only relation between you and your wife.

At this juncture, you have to bear with her caprices. As a child her parents used to pick her up leaving all their work whenever they saw her in the sulks, when she grew up her friends, brothers and sisters used to console her. Now, as she is with you leaving behind her parents friends, brothers and sisters, you have to bear with her caprices.

*Shari'at* has also given them the right to coquetry. The Prophet (pbuh) says, "O Ayesha! Whenever you cool down, I became conscious of your cooling down. She asked the messenger of Allah! May my parents be sacrificed on you, how you come to know of my cooling down? He (pbuh) said whenever you cool down you say " وَرَبِّ اِبْرَاهِيْمَ " (By the master/cherisher of Ibrahim), you don't call my name. While in a happy mood, you say "وَرَبِّ مُحَمَّدٍ صَلَّى اللّٰهُ عَلَيْهِ وَسَلَّمَ" (By the master /cherisher of Muhammad (pbuh)). Just imagine the respected Prophet (pbuh) bore her cooling down without becoming unpleasant, it means that they have the right to cool down and coquetry.

Some people consider themselves ruler over their wives and for this they quote a verse of Qur'an from Surah Nisa-34 "اَلرِّجَالُ قَوَّامُوْنَ عَلَى النِّسَاءِ" the men are protectors and guardian of women". An imminent Islamic scholar Shah Abrarul-Haque (Ra) said, you are supposed to rule them but in *Shar'ai* matters. If she wants to go against *Shari'at* such as she asks you to purchase a television or VCR or pictures and photographs to decorate the house or she wants to go to cinema then you must forbade her strictly. However, if she wants clothes, any edible item, to go to her mother's house then you can't forbade her as these are her rights. If you have authority over them, then you have to love them also. Putting a morsel in her mouth and seeing her with love are also *Sunnat* of our beloved Prophet (pbuh). His pious life is full of showing love to all his wives and he (pbuh) himself has said, " I love three things in the world namely prayer, scent and woman (Holy Wives).

( Munabbihat by Hafiz ibne Hajr)

It means that loving wives is also a tradition of our Prophet (pbuh). So we should enliven this *Sunnat*.

## SOFT TONE AND SWEET WORDS

The husbands must use soft tone and sweet words, without these two love is a mirage. If a husband and wife both are habitual of soft tone and sweet words, love and affection will be in abundance in that house and every member of that family will be full of love and affection.

Just try this easy procedure, *Insha Allah* , all of your embarrassments will be solved, the wife will start loving you heartily, your children will also use this very language whenever they will go outside , at the same time their passion for love and affection will also increase. Therefore, you must not leave soft tone and sweet words in any condition.Alah has said in the Holy Qur'an;

فَقُوْلَا لَهٗ قَوْلًا لَّيِّنًا لَّعَلَّهٗ يَتَذَكَّرُ اَوْ يَخْشٰى

*But speak to him mildly; perchance he may take warning or fear (Allah).* (Ta Ha -44)

In this verse a special direction is given to Hazrat Moosa and Haroon (pbut) to guide Pharoh. Hazrat Mufti Mohd. Shafi (Ra) has said in the exegesis of this verse, however much may the opposite be rebellious or having false believes and thoughts, the reformers should talk politely and in a sympathetic and friendly manner, only then he could be compelled to thinking and fearing Allah. Pharoh, who is tyrant , despot, claimant of divinity and murderer of thousands of Bani-Israel children for his own safety. When Allah the Almighty sent His selected Prophets (Moosa and Haroon (pbut) to him, He directed them to talk to him leniently, so that he might think and ponder. Though, he knew that Pharoh will not abstain himself from being rebellious and seduced, but He has to restrain His Prophets (pbuh) to this principle so that the creation of Allah (human and jinn) would fear Allah after due pondering. May the Pharoh be guided or not but the principle should be such that, it be a mean of guidance for the whole mankind.

(Ma'aariful-Qur'an vol. 9 pg.109&110)

Remember! Wives can easily be obedient to their husbands provided they (husbands) would become habitual of leniency while talking to them. The wives who don't care for their husband's mood remain dejected and grief stricken. If wives are provided with pleasant and joyous atmosphere and everything told to them leniently, then most of them will become habitual of their husband's mood and will obey them. This soft tone can easily generate the strong desire of service, love, selflessness, truthfulness, probity and nobility in the wife.

Remember! showing anger or shouting due to any fault of your children or wife is not a remedy for their faults and mischeives. If you want your house to be full of happiness, where you are being welcomed with smiles, received respectfully and get full sympathy then please start using sweet words and soft tone as soon as possible while dealing with your family members. Moreover, being a member of your home and Muslim society you are supposed to use joyous and peaceful tone while dealing with your family members and subordinates.

Remember! neither change your tone due to successive embarrassment and failures nor peevish your mood as these conditions usually comes in a man's life. One must neither be disappointed nor be in ecstasy over the befallen embarrassements and failures.

To give up affability, soft tone, smile, co-operation, forgiveness and connivence etc. are against the dignity of a true Muslim, so we have to be habitual of all these good qualities in order to keep our family joyous and pass a tension-free life.

**AN IDEA TO ACT UPON THIS**

One must think only thus far, that the deeds and words which I am going to use for my wife, if some other person says these words to me or treat me like this, will I not be grieved by these words and deeds.

If it is difficult, then just think if I were the wife what I would have liked for me. *Insha Allah*, this mere thinking will not necessiate a teacher even for the ignorant person. Alongwith this thinking pray Allah for sweet words, *Insha Allah* we will have all the good qualities.

Remember! a good way of talking is also an art, it is not necessary that a talkative person will talk well. At the same time, listenning others with patience and forbearance is also as hard as talking in a good way. So, if your wife wants to talk to you, listen her quietly and take care of her emotion, thinking and feeling.

Remember! soft tone and sweet words are just like a magic, it always effects the opposite person as sweet words keep all defects secret. If a man has all good qualities except sweat words then all his good qualities are useless.

The benefit of your using soft tone and sweet words will be that, she will feel its sweetness till you come back from your daily work, you will find her waiting eagerly for you and she will remain thinking of you the whole day. Otherwise she will offer thanks-giving prayer, that you have gone and will relax. While your children will also be happy and they will also pray for your going out.

Therefore remember! you have to take the invitiative for this good work. Adopt soft tone, good behaviour and conduct to see its effects at once.

## ADOPT A PREACHING WAY AND NOT A DIALECTIC WAY WITH WIFE

Remember one principle, the harmony of moods is found very rarely in the wordly relations, therefore taking notice of smaller things and deciding due to these is against the dignity of a Muslim.

So, forget the past, learn to live afresh and don't

convince your wife ever in a dialectic way. When you will have some painful things in your heart from your wife's side, your style will become dialectical unintentionally and you will think, that you have been fed up of convincing her and she is not listening to your words, then you will seek the help of other ways. Such as;

It would have been better, had I been married in my kin.....

It would have been better, had I been married to such and such girl..........

Would that my mother had not married me here.... etc.

Therefore remember! whatever you tell your wife tell in a soft and preaching way, the most successful husband is one who can convince his wife that he is a reformer, whatever he is telling is for reformation and not for taunting. For this, the husband should know that sympathy well-wishing and tolerance are the most important factors of preaching and reformation. The most difficult task is reformation, see the lives of the Prophets (pbut) and the reformers of nations,how much difficulties and embarrassments they have while preaching in the human.

A preaching husband will never be spiritless, short-sighted and status-seeker, rather after convicing the wife in every possible way, he leaves the result for Allah. He never becomes disappointed and keeps praying for the guidance. He has to pass a very cautious life. When reformation of a wife is sought, she is neither rebuked nor scolded nor taunted nor put to shame nor reminded about her previous mistakes rather she is seated close, convinced with love and reason accordingly, praised for her good work. May Allah give us all a perfect understanding of our religion, Amen!

Just think how much busy was our Prophet Muhammad (pbuh) he used to welcome the delegations of newly converts to Islam, prepare himself and others for a journey, send groups for preaching, solve individual's problems and make peace between two muslims etc. inspite of all these responsibilities and preoccupations, he run nine houses.

How unlucky we will be, if being a little religious and preacher, we could not run a single house. Alas! Today we have made religion invisible from our lives. May Allah guide us to the right path , make us to act according to the religion and to preach it, Amen!

## ONE SHOULD PRAISE HIS WIFE ALSO

This is an universal truth that, to whom one love, his/ her each and every action is loved, his/her flaws become agreeable and one not only praises him/her but also exeggerates in praising. So love your wife as much as possible, praise her often so that she may be encouraged and your love may deepen in her heart.

That's why, Dr. Abdul-Hai (Ra) used to say, the man who thinks that his wife is serving him by making food, it is due to her good conduct and behaviour, only such man will praise her food and encourage her.

But the man who thinks her wife a maid and thinks if she is making good, it is her duty so there is no need to praise her. Such a man will never praise his wife,will never forgive her even smaller mistakes such as, the sugar is more or salt is less, he will raise a tumult and start quarrelling.

The woman is kind hearted by nature, only a little praise makes her unable to contain herself and she tries her best to do it (praised work) better than earlier. So convince her positively praise whatever is done and if there is any shortcomimg or imperfection convince her in such a way that she don't do it again. From today make it your practice to say, جَزَاکِ اللّٰہُ خَیْرًا "May Allah give you best reward (for this act)", whenever she does any of your work. Be thankful to her by heart and tongue then see how much she appreciates and loves you thus you will see the model of a Hourie in the world itself and such house will become a model of the heaven.

Praise the works done by your wife and encourage her *Insha Allah* you will get full cooperation from her.

## ONE HIDDEN CRUELTY

In our society, the woman of the house whether she is a mother or a wife, though they are doing all the works properly and beautifully, are grieved by saying that these are the duties of a woman. If each husband and his children start thinking that it is the basic responsibility of a wife or a mother to wash their clothes, iron them, prepare good food for them or if they understand that their house becomes clean on its own. All the refuse and dirt are cleaned on their own, clothes are washed, cleaned and put in the almirahs on their own. All this decoration, bedecking and comfort are done without the skilful hands of a well-mannered woman then it will definitely be the mentality of an ingratitude man. May Allah save all of us from this (ingratitudeness), defend yourself and others from this.

Remember! It is the woman by whom all the house-keeping works are carried out and on whom the existence of a family depends. If one is not thanking her or giving her some words of indebtedness, then her heartbreaking can cause a number of tribulations and unpleasantness in the family.

You can guess what part, this thanklessness, ungratefulness and discouragement, is playing in creating the environment of commotion and depression in the families nowadays.

Suppose, you are working in an office, where neither anyone is praising you nor talking to you straight forwardly you are being discouraged and frightened, then you will break off all the connections by saying good-bye to this very service. Is it possible for your wife or mother to get rid off you easily, being comfortless and grievous due to your thanklessness and inattentiveness? … perhaps never.

However, who other than you can avert these unfortunate women from being comfortless due to your misbehavior, misconuct, ungratefulness and thanklessness? So make it a principle of your life from today that you will always praise your wife's good work , kindness & virtures.

From the *Ifaadaat* of Hakeemul-Ummat (Ra)

## DUE TO DISAGREEMENT OF WIFE SUFFERING IS ALSO AN ENDEAVOUR

A man writes to Hazrat Hakeemul-Ummat (Ra) relying on your eminent favour, I am seeking your help. Unfortunately I had been married to a woman whose nature is just opposite to mine. I am neither blaming my wife nor she is at fault in reality, rather I am of a strange nature. Due to difference in our nature there is a partition of unfriendliness and fear which is getting stronger day by day. It has effected my business also and an eternal depression has engulfed me. I was hoping a bright future for me since my childhood whereas, now my future is in complete darkness. This frustration and hopelessness has ruined my religion as well as my world while I am not finding any solution of this.

You are a venerable personality, pray Allah so that, He may save me from this embarrassment and give me peace of mind. I am in this agonizing torture since three years now and I pray for my death. Out of compulsion , now I had decided to lead a retired life but I am unable to find a candid person who can make me like himself so I want to come to you for some days to gain from your kindness.

**Ans**: I received your letter, *MaaShaa Allah* you are a bold person then why so much of impatience and inconstancy? This is the time to judge one's courage and determination, you have written to come to me, you are most welcome. The purpose, for which you have this idea (coming to me) depends on the endeavour whereas, the unpleasantness which you are facing is in itself a great endeavour. Have patience, *Insha Allah* all will become right and come after some time. (Tarbiyatus-saalik1/368)

## INCREASE IN LOVE WITH WIFE IS A SIGN OF *TAQWA* ( GOD FEARING )

Q: For sometime I am inclined towards my wife a little more, is it harmful for me?

A: It is a tradition, May Allah give both of you its best result. When *Taqwa* increases inclination towards wife also increases. (Tarbiyatus- Saalik 1/552)

## TO BE ATTACHED TO WIFE

Q. I am attached to my wife so much, that it had become a burden for me, I remain confused due to this great attachment, but whenever I am with her, I feel more love than earlier. Once she became very ill, my inner desire was her death, so that I could get rid of this violent attachment but I used to ward off this thinking intentionally to save myself from sin ... Now she has become healthy.

A: Yes! one should not think like this, sometimes this type of thinking can harm him much and increase Allah's anger.

Q: She loves me very much, since she is religious, well-mannered, educated and wise, therefore I am less afflicted. Otherwise, Allah knows what would have happened. She has full knowledge of *Bahishti Zevar* and *Tableegh-e-deen* and is acting upon them as much as possible.

A: O slave of Allah! you are embarrassed of such a blessing, which is called in the *Hadeeth* (tradition) the best possession.

**LOVING WIFE IS NOT HARMFUL**

Q:1 Hazrat! Nowadays I am suffering from a severe illness, that is, I had started loving my wife very much and due to this my daily routines (*Ma'moolaat*) are effected. Its treatment is compulsory, moreover I want this love to incline towards Allah. Though I am performimg daily routines (*Ma'moolaat*) but irregularly and its sole reason is love with wife.

A: Loving wife too much is neither blameworthy nor harmful but it should not be an obstacle in religion and its duties, that's why it is in one's power and related to courage.

Q:2 Thank Allah! All the daily routines are being done thoroughly. An issue is disturbing me and I remain thinking about it, what will be the end ? That is, my wife has died nearly 11 months ago but her thought is still there in my mind. If I died in between then what will happen, how I will present myself before Allah with a heart full of love for other than Him.

I have become more interested in her then in prayer. I go to her grave every Friday and don't want to return home. Once I went to the grave-yard, after seeking her absolution by reciting, I sat near her grave. A man called me but I did not replied. That man asked me later why I had not replied. After hearing him, I am more thoughtful now. Please, tell me a remedy as I am a worthless person, if I died in between what will happen, may Allah do the best.

A: If such concentration in lawful affection is unintentional, which is not disturbing the inevitable religious routines then it is completely unharmful and does not decrease the love of Allah. As this love is natural while the love of Allah is rational and both can be gathered in one heart (man's inner). If there was not love of Allah in the heart then such condition would not have happened. Have full confidence if death comes in between, there is no danger rather keeping other expediencies in view, remarrying will be more beneficial. (Tarbiyatus-Saalik1/748)

## CURE OF SHOCK DUE TO WIFE'S DEATH

Q: I was loving my wife very much, but she died nearly two year ago, I have children from her. The sorrow of her death could not be described in words, two years have gone by but I am still like a *Majnoon* (mad in love). All my routines have been left, though with great difficulty I am offering five time's prayer but there is no fear of Allah and humility in it. I have tried many methods but none is effective. I am very much helpless now as both my religion and worldly affairs are ruining, I have become a debtor also moreover I am afraid of the Hereafter. Please pray for me so that, either I get another woman like her or her thought would go away from me. Please do whichever of these two is better for me and tell me also.

A: May peace be with you, I pray for the betterment of you. Marrying will be beneficial, though she may not be like that, if there is no obstacle you should marry till then read *Tableegh-e-Deen*. (Tarbiyatus-Saalik 1/534)

Hazrat Thanwi (Ra) has said in his book *Malfoozaat Kamaalaat-e-Ashrafia* on page 46, that the contention of husband and wife is the bone of all contentions. Further on page 118, Hazrat (Ra) wrote, these wives will be more beautiful and esteemed than Houries, while seeking more beautiful is neither absurd nor untraditional so, praying to meet your wives is neither absurd nor untraditional.

# WIFE ..... A SINCERE FRIEND

Now, here is a gist of an article by Maulvi Abdullah (Teacher Daarul-Uloom, Karachi) published in "Al-Balaagh" magazine, with request to all our readers so as to remember us and Maulvi Abdullah in your prayers. While this prayer will also benefit you.

There are two sides of relation between husband and wife. First is, its delicateness and the second is, its depthness. If one sees its delicateness, then perhaps it is the most delicate relations.

This relation of years is so delicate that it can be broken in a moment just like a cobweb or a petal. Suppose there happens some sort of squabble or contention between them, the husband fires *Talaaq* three times and all is finished. The relation of the life ended in a moment, all the previous feelings, services and predilection, are undone and now feeling ashamed on his doing and repenting but nothing could be done now.

When bullet goes off a gun, it can't be retrieved. *Talaaq* has been given, now nothing could be done, as a result the children, the wife and the husband all are disturbed. What could be done now?

You have to think earlier–what would be the result of this very your doing? Perhaps, you might have thought that, now our relations are so old to be effected by *Talaaq* as you are living a married life since long, it is not the matter. In reality, your relations might have become strong but its delicateness is still there. Therefore *Talaaq* will have same effect as it would have in the earlier years of marriage. The difference is that your children will also suffer now, as they would have father on one side and mother on the other.

Anyhow, as a 100 years old infidle becoms a muslim after reciting *Kalimah*, likewise *Talaaq* would make the wife a stranger to her husband, though she might have lived with him for long.

Now let us see its depthness, only a wife can serve you in a perfect way, as the time passes her love and desire of service increases and the relation between them deepens.

Maulvi Ashraf Ali Thanvi (Ra) once said in one of his homilies "A man complained to Maulvi Fazlur-Rahman Ganj Moradabadi (Ra), that he is not enjoying *Zikr* (invocation of Allah) as earlier. Maulvi Saheb said, have you not heard that old wife becomes mother."

*Sub-haanallah*! What a wonderful example he has given. The theme of the reply is same that sensualism remains for sometime as the ardour of love with wife remains for sometime. It lessens as the time passes by but attachment increases while her love and affection effect the whole body. Same is the case of *Zikr* (invocation of Allah) that, after a long period though the ardour lessens but attachment increases.

In reality the wife of an old man becomes his mother as there remain no sensuality except immaculate love.

(Va'z Taqleelut-Ta'aam-68)

An incident is coming to my mind that is, once an old man intended to remarry after the death of his first wife, his sons and daughters-in-laws started cursing and reproaching him, saying that now this old man wants to marry. Here are we to serve you and for other works, then what is the need of marriage? But he did not heard anyone and got married.

After some time he became ill, vomiting and loose-motion got started. Now no one was coming near him leave alone serving him. His wife in his illness, used to serve, clean and give medicine to him, she looked after him in every way. The old man got the chance of saying that, you were preventing me from marrying, you have seen yourselves that nobody has served me except my wife. If I were up to you then I might be left unattended and perhaps might have died.

Anyhow! It is to be seen now, when the wife is ready to serve you fully, she co-oprates with you in poverty and misery, disaster and embarrassment, sickness and feebleness etc. how you are treating and keeping her?

Generally men want to keep their wives making them their subjects, treating them like servants and gave this verse as an argument, اَلرِّجَالُ قَوَّامُوْنَ عَلَى النِّسَاءِ "Men are the protectors and maintainers of woman". Verily this verse means that women are sub-ordinate to their husbands and its (sub-ordinatenss) classification is also there......wife, children, servant, attendant, cook, driver and guard etc. all are sub-ordinates, but it does not mean that you are supposed to treat them equal. Though, wife is subordinate to you but there is difference between her and others' subordination. Alongwith being sub-ordinate to you, she is not only your life partner but a sincere and intimate friend also. So it is wrong to treat her like servants.

Some lewd persons thinks that "girlfriend" should be other than the wife, as the duty of wife is house-keeping and bringing-up the children, while girlfriend is for amusement, enjoyment, sensualization and accompaniment in recreation. Although, the wives can comply with all these necessities of a man better than any other woman and that's too in a lawful way. It is clear that one can have peace and calmness in the lawful activities rather than in the unlawful way. It is possible only when you consider your wife not only a wife but also a sincere friend, life partner and treat her as you treat an intimate friend.

Just think can you overawe your friend like your servants? Never...... if you do, all your friends will leave you alone. A wise man will never treat his friends like servants. Then why you are treating your wife like a servant while no friend can be like her. It is tried that, all the friends, dear-ones and relatives desert man in embarsassment and poverty but only wife remains with her husband forever.

Now, it would have been clarifired that the best friend of a man is his wife and it is the peculiarity of this very connection that she takes pride in her husband and due to this very connection you can't overawe her like your servants, therefore it is not better to overawe her.

Due to this very connection the Holy Wives

(mabawt) used to behave the Prophet (pbuh) like a friend and take pride in him...........who can be like Muhammad (pbuh)? But he never overawed them..... rather treated them with subordination and friendliness. The effect of subordination was that they never went against the Prophet (pbuh) but used to respect him very much. Whereas the effect of friendliness was that, Hazrat Ayesha (mabawh) used to take pride in him and he never got angry with her.

When the *Ifk* incident occurred and the dissemblers calumniated Hazrat Ayesha (mabawh), the Prophet (pbuh) became sad so much that once he told her (while she was in her father's house).

"O Ayesha! If you are really exonerated then Allah the Almighty will definitely reveal your exoneration and if you are indeed wrong then seek Allah's forgiveness and turn to Him in repentence." Hazrat Ayesha (mabawh) became grieved of this and said, I don't know how to reply it , if I say that I am fully exonerated of this–Allah knows my exoneration then you people will never accept this and if I say yes I am mistaken while Allah knows my exoneration, you will accept this, now I am saying only what Yaqoob (pbuh) has said,

فَصَبۡرٞ جَمِيلٞۖ وَٱللَّهُ ٱلۡمُسۡتَعَانُ عَلَىٰ مَا تَصِفُونَ

*(for me)patience is most fitting: against that which you assert,it is Allah (alone) whose help can be sought".*

(Yousuf:18)

Saying this she fell down in the bed due to excessive grief and started weeping. At that very moment the signs of revelation appeared on the face of the Prophet (pbuh) and complete silence prevailed in the house. After sometime when the revelation finished, the first words which the Prophet (pbuh) spoke were; O Ayesha! Listen the good news, Allah has revealed your exoneration. Then the Prophet (pbuh) read out the recently revealed verses. All the family members become happy. Mother of Hazrat Ayesha (mabawt) told her; O Ayesha; stood up and thank the Prophet (pbuh). She replied, By Allah! I will not go to him, I praise only my Sustainer as he (pbuh) has considered me impure and Allah has exonerated me.

(Saheehul-Bakhari Hadith No. 2467 Kitabush-Shahadat)

We, the men should comprehend that Ayesha (mabawh) uttered these words as she took pride in the Prophet (pbuh) due to the friendly connection which she had with him. *Shari'at* has not penalized the women due to the words they utter in pride. If women were not having the right to take pride, the Prophet ( pbuh) would certainly have warned Hazrat Ayesha (mabawh) as the words were very harsh, while it is impossible for the Prophet (pbuh) to show partiality to anyone.

The connection between husband and wife is such that Allah and His Prophet (pbuh) have tolerated such harsh words from Ayesha (mabawh). Otherwise, either the Prophet (pbuh) would have objected or Allah would have revealed some verses. Hence, once the Holy Wives (mabawt) asked the Prophet (pbuh) for more money and he was against the worldly means, Allah the Almighty at once revealed these verses:

يٰاَيُّهَا النَّبِيُّ قُلْ لِّاَزْوَاجِكَ اِنْ كُنْتُنَّ تُرِدْنَ الْحَيٰوةَ الدُّنْيَا

وَزِيْنَتَهَا فَتَعَالَيْنَ اُمَتِّعْكُنَّ وَاُسَرِّحْكُنَّ سَرَاحًا جَمِيْلًا

*" O Prophet ! Say to your consorts: if it be that you desire the life of this world, and its glitter, –then come! I will provide for your enjoyment and set you free in a handsome manner,"* (Al-Ahzab-28)

Just see, Allah has prevented the Holy Wives (mabawt) from asking more money while He did not prevent these words of pride. So there is no evil in taking pride, but asking more expenses is bad and today's matter is quite opposite.

Some men want that women should be according to their self-made criteria and if they do any thing against it, they are punished severly. Whereas, it is a right of the women that their disgusting acts should be tolerated. It is in *Hadith*, that the women is born out of a crooked rib, so you will see crookedness in her is also like a rib. If you straighten a rib it will break, same is the case of the women. It means that the crookedness of a rib is in its beauty, likewise the beauty of a woman is in her crookedness.

If we consider, we will come to know that it is not strange, if some of the women are a little uncultured and impolite but these are homely women who are supposed to be more obedient and devoted to their husbands.

Anyhow, the women are sacrificing completely for the men while they are unconcerned and careless of them. As soon as the woman starts talking impudently, man starts beating and taking revenge leaving behind the kindness and friendship. This is not suitable for a man rather he should endure these as a reward of her wholetime services.

Such lewd persons must tell honestly, can they treat their "girlfriends" like this, to whom they have given the status of their "wives" without marriage which is unlawful and un-Islamic. How will you treat her? Will you ever beat her or rebuke her? Never as she is your friend. Is the status of the wife lesser than the "girlfriend"? No–the status of the "wife" is much higher than of " the girlfriend"?–then why you treat her like this. Making a "girlfriend" is in itself illegal and unlawful. Moreover it is strange that a man, who is having a wife, is making a "girlfriend", his wife can be the best girlfriend for him. The purpose for which a "girlfriend" is made can be attained by the wife, that's too in a legal and better way provided that you safeguard your eyes and consider her equal to you, a friend and a companion rather then your subordinate, servant and subject.

When you will start giving this right to your wife, certainly she will also love and serve you suavely. If you are having any complaint or unpleasantness with her, it will end as a result of this good behaviour. Just come out of this self-made carefreeness and self-respect to see the delicateness of this relation.

We have the best example of our Prophet (pbuh) which tells us how he (pbuh) treated his wives, how he showed love, affection and friendship for them. Hazrat Ayesha (mabawh) says!

During a journey, there was a competition of race on foot between me and the Prophet (pbuh) I won that race, later on, when I became heavy, we again competed but this time he won. He told me it is the reply of that very your triumph. (Ma'aariful-Hadeeth Vol 6 P.85)

In today's cultured age, racing with one's own wife is considered against the culture but if this race is with a strange person, it is not considered against the culture. We have the example of our Prophet ( PBUH) so we should take pride in it, though the people may consider it an uncultured action.

It is narrated, "Sometimes, when Ayesha (mabawh) drinks water, the Prophet (pbuh) used to sip from where she was sipping after taking the bowl from her".

Another narration,"Sometimes, when Ayesha (mabawh) eats meat from a bone, the Prophet (pbuh) used to eat from where she was eating by taking the bone from her".

Just compare these love-making actions of the Prophet (pbuh) with today's culture. Nowadays, if someone has left any edible in his/her plate or water in the glass, it is called left-over and its consumption is considered a causative of diseases, although it is a custom of Hindus. Whereas, to eat or drink the left-over is a *Sunnat* of our beloved Prophet (pbuh).

The Prophet (pbuh) has once said;

لا یفرک مومن مومنة، ان کره منها خلقا رضی منها آخر

*"A faithful husband must not detest his faithful wife, if any of her habit is offensive another might be pleasing."* (Muslim Kitaabur-Razaa' Hadeeth no 2672)

This *Hadeeth* means that one must not detest his wife and be indifferent due to any offensive habit of her rather he must look at her qualities and appreciate them. The same thing is also told in the Holy Qur'an.

وَعَاشِرُوْهُنَّ بِالْمَعْرُوْفِ فَاِنْ كَرِهْتُمُوْهُنَّ فَعَسٰىٓ اَنْ تَكْرَهُوْا
شَيْئاً وَّيَجْعَلَ اللّٰهُ فِيْهِ خَيْراً كَثِيْراً

*On the contrary live with them on a footing of kindness and equity. If you take a dislike to them it may be that you dislike a thing, and Allah brings about through it a great deal of good.* (Surah Nisa-19)

Another *Hadeeth* says;

عن عائشة رضى اللّٰه تعالىٰ عنها قالت قال رسول
اللّٰه صلى اللّٰه عليه وسلم ان من اكمل
المومنين ايما نا، أحسنهم خلقًا وألطفهم بأهله.

*H. Ayesha (mabawh) narrates the Prophet(*pbuh*) as saying, A true believer is one who is most ethical and most kind to his wife.* (Tirmizi kitaabul-Eimaan H.No.2537)

Another *Hadeeth* says;

عن عائشة رضى اللّٰه تعالىٰ عنها قالت قال
رسول اللّٰه صلى اللّٰه عليه وسلم خيركم
خيركم لأ هله و أنا خيركم لأ هلى.

*H. Ayesha (mabawh) narrates the Prophet (pbuh) as saying the most ethical (man) of you is one who is best of you for his wife while I am the best of you for my wives.* (Tirmizi, Kitaabul-Manaaqib H.No. 3830)

According to all these *Ahaadeeth,* the Prophet (pbuh) has fixed the criteria of a best man that he should be of best ethics for his wife, otherwise he is not the best.

Generally, a husband can be good for his wife, when he helps her in homely works, takes care of her comfort and ease, and consults her regarding children and homely affairs and gives her some powers and liberty within the limits of *Shari'at.* By treating this way, one will not become her slave rather he will win her heart and it is also a right of the wife because she has come to your house as your life partner...... she is your confidant .., your sincere friend ..., mother of your children..., queen of your home ..., companion of your public and private life..., your honour...., your heart's delight...., a mean of removing your tiredness..., to stand by your side in the time of poverty, destitution, illness, afflication, grief and hardships..., she knows all your perfections and imperfections..., moreover she is the best way for you to get peace of mind and tranquillity.

Tell honestly! A person who has tens of connections with you, will you become a slave of him/ her, if you agree with him/her? Never! Just think! If any of your fast friends ask you anything, will you deny him? you will not dare to deny him, as you have to keep the trust of friendship and you are supposed to be faithful in relations with that friend.

When one can't treat a friend like this, is the status of the wife less than a friend?

Is treating wife like this proper?

In the last sermon given at the time of *Hajjatul-Vadaa*', the Prophet (pbuh) has mentioned the summary of life and the gist of the whole *Shari'at*, in this sermon also, he (pbuh) had told specially about the women;

فاتقوا الله في النساء، فانكم اخذتموهن بامان الله
واستحللتم فروجهن بكلمة اللّٰه.

*O people! Fear Allah regarding your wives, as you have married tham under the protection of Allah and you have made them lawful ( for you) by the words of Allah.* (Muslim, Kitaabul-Haj P.No. 397)

Through this *Hadeeth*, the men are warned that though they are made the protectors of woman but they should not use this protection being negligent to Allah's penalization rather they should fear Allah regarding them.

Remember! Allah is between you and your wives as they have become your wives and lawful for you according to the rule of marriage made by Allah. They are made subordinate to you under the protection of Allah i.e. after becoming your wives they have got the protection of Allah. If you do injustice to them, then you are embezzling into the protection given to them by Allah and you are turning out to be a culprit of Allah.

Another *Hadeeth*;

عن أبی هريرة رضی اللّٰه تعالیٰ عنه قال،قال رسول اللّٰه صلی اللّٰه
عليه وسلم، لا تستقيم لک المرأة علی خليقة واحدة انما هی
کا لضلع ان تقيمها کسرتها وان ترکتها تستمتع بهاوفيها أود

*Hazrat Abu Hurairah (mabawh) narrates that the Prophet (pbuh) has said, a woman can't stick to one habit as she is like a rib–if you straighten it, it will be broken. If you left her as she is then you can savor her inspite of her crookedness.*

The crookedness found in the woman is natural and by birth, as it is told in another *Hadeeth*, that she is created from the upper rib, so you can't remove it.

If you want to take benefit from her, neither stand in the way of her crookedness nor try to straighten her, as it won't be removed rather divorce could take place.

If your wife is shrewish, foul-mouthed and shows stubbornness in each matters, then you are supposed to convince her patiently rather to put up a bold front. If she is convinced, it is better otherwise leave her alone. The only way to create a peaceful atmosphere in the house, is what the Prophet (pbuh) has taught us, if one chooses the other way he can't live peacefully. (Taken from al-Balaagh)

## SAVE YOURSELF FORM WHY....? WHAT....?

One important issue to which one must pay attention, that is in some homes there is prolonged tension between husband and wife, while its main reason is unreasonable interference in the wife's personal life or house-keeping matters by saying Why…?, What…..?, How….?, where…?, when…? These types of questions annoy her and she unwillingly becomes abusive, foul-mouthed and impudent while its reason is the mental peevishness due to excessive questioning of husband…

Why the husbands don't think that they enjoy the air of fans in the office also, while this poor fellow (wife) remains in the heat of stove, remains busy either in cleaning house or making food or keeping children neat & clean or attending phones or keeping children's whims when they return from schools. When a wife, who is busy in the works of children, husband and tens of other engagements, faces questions such as why…? What…? How…? etc. she will definitely become disgusted. If mother and sisters-in-law are living with her then she has to bear them also.

Don't ask incessantly such questions……Why this work has not been done? How it happened? When will food be prepared ? What had happened to the child? As she is tolerating so much of things waiting for her husband, who is her real sympathizer and comforter, to come and tell her some sweet words in order to lessen her grief and mental anguish …and that very husband, after entering the house, starts questioning Why…?, What….? When…..? How……? What will happen to that woman….

We are telling you, what will be its result?

1) If she is full of forbearance and patience then she

will pulverize herself and complain to Allah. Her mere seeing with tears and helplessness in her eyes towards the sky will be enough to bring worries and losses for you.

2) When she will be fed up of these sufferings, she won't tell you anything out of regard for you but retaliate either by beating or by abusing the children.

3) If she is not forbearing or the matter is unbearable then she will inevitably start replying you and will proclaim thus of her being foul-mouthed, while you will never think of your exceeding the limits. If you consult any of your friends or relatives to get rid of her this very habit, they all will blame her and none of them will pay attention to your fighting mood and hot-headedness.

Moreover, now you will start evaluating all her habits and actions with fault-finding sight, you will see her as inferior, impudent, unskilled and ill-mannered etc. While these thoughts, sometimes may lead to divorce.

4) She might show her anger, which is the result of your insignificant gossip, to your mother or sister in your absence. This will also become a reason of disturbance, as when you will return from work, your mother or sister will surely complain to you of her misbehaviour with some exaggeration and the dispute will increase. If you would have dealt with your wife cheerfully, kept yourself cool and checked

yourself, the matter would not have worsened so much.

5) When she will not find your sympathy and she has to vent her spleen anywhere, ultimately she will tell her story with some exaggeration to her friends or relatives and she will often go to her parental home by putting up false excuses. As a result this afflicted woman will be advised erroneously by her inexperienced mother, maternal aunt, friends and like minded sisters not to bow down, to put up a bold front against the husband, to remain firm and not to seek forgiveness to be the winner. The unfortunate woman will take such steps, under the influence of these wrong advices which will ruin her house.

So, my dear brother, for the sake of Allah, have mercy on you and your coming generation, consider cool-headedly that the solution of being saved from all these problems is with you only. As you have to change you conduct, the way of speaking...., avoid How...? Why...? What..? Where..? And don't dissociate yourself from your wife, who was busy in house-keeping the whole day. Because she has come only for you leaving behind every relations. Why are you creating hatred between you and your wife.....? In order to avoid all these, act upon our advices and see the result.

## IF THESE SHORTCOMINGS WERE IN YOUR SISTER OR DAUGHTER

Just imagine that the shortcomings, you are finding in your wife and due to these you are calling her unskilled and ill-mannered, are in your own sister and her parents-in-law are complaining to your parents of her shortcomings or these are in your daughter and you are told that you must have trained her in a proper way as she was supposed to go to their in-laws' house.

Certainly, their complaining would be unpalatable for you. As you are of the opinion that she is still of a tender-age, she has gone to a new house, she will take some time to be habitual of the new house, her husband seems to be a prince that he does not come under least obligation and he is complaining me of my dear sister or daughter.

Why don't you have this very opinion for your wife, that she just has come to your home, how she can make herself like us from the first day itself or she just has made a minor mistake etc....

Leave alone sister or daughter, just think! as you want to see all the good qualities in your wife and wants her to be free of all the shortcomings, in the same way if each father of the girls would have made a criteria for their would-be-sons-in-law that he should be like this and that.....then would you have been married.

When a father has given you his loving daughter, why have you become a fault-finding one only? If she is making a mistake why are you considering her action unpardonable? Why are you taunting her? Why are you abusing her family?

Now please, after due consideration to all these, treat your wife politely as she just has come to your home and as the time passes by, she will make herself as you want.

Just as you would have incited your son-in-law or sister's husband, that your daughter or sister will certainly make herself as you want but gradually, convince yourself also in the same way.

## AS YOU CLOSE YOUR SHOP LOCK ITS TENSIONS ALSO

There are some lucky persons who leave behind the tensions of their work whenever they intend to go home, thinking that they will see these the other day, *Insha Allah.* While some enter their houses having the blue funks on their faces due to different tensions at their respective working places.

Suppose, the whole day's fatigued wife waiting eagerly to receive you after making your favorite dishes, cleansing herself, children and house. While, after entering the house, you starts acting as if you are Hulagoo Khan or Changez Khan, what will she feel? Seeing your unpleasant conduct, she will not ask you even for an ordinary thing rather she will also fear to give you a good news even if it is connected to you. So please leave all the tensions of working place there only. A Muslim should be agree with his destiny, the decrees of Allah and keep praying Him.

Although such circumstances have natural effects, but it does not mean that its rage be vented on servants or wife and children. While due to your conduct they keep themselves away from you. Make yourself habitual of smile in every circumstances then only, *Insha Allah*, whosoever sees you will become cheerful.

# DON'T DISGRACE SOMEONE DUE TO OTHER

Suppose your opinion is not given heed in any office or department or the servants did not obey you or you are an employee, your salary is not increased or the privileges you were getting are withdrawn due to any of your shortcomings, naturally these things will hurt your feelings. Tell impartially is it not callousness and cowardice not to converse with concerned peoples and vent your spleen on your subordinates after returning home or to be rude towards family members' minor mistakes or to quarrel without any excuse. Such as (1) why you did not made so and so vegetable with so and so curry (2) The younger child is coming to you and you started crying 'why are you coming to me....?' (3) beating the door so loudly that the neighbour would gather around you and your wife, who also had come till then leaving the children frightened to ask what had happened ? As the door could not be opened alongwith your first bell.

When you have so much of confidence and courage, why don't you show these infront of your employer or sub-ordinates? So please show self-confidence, live with courage and boldness, have patience and decide not to oppress anyone especially your family (wife and children) for whom you are the only support. Try to be a kind friend to them, which is sought by the *Shari'at* also.

Its another harm is that the sorrow, from which you want to get rid of will increase–when your wife being fed up of your scolding and rebuking, Allah forbid, might counter attack you. As a result the brawling will increase while the children will become frightened and weep.

If the children are older, they might consider you an oppressor, their mother an oppressed one and might defend their mother. If any courageous boy starts abusing his mother by agreeing with your opinion then he will be guilty and factiousness will be created in the house. As some of them may be with their mother while others may be with their father, thus an awkwardness will engulf the house. This very scene and dialogue will disturb you the whole day while you are at your working place.

See! A little negligence by you or not using good tactics have disturbed your house as well as the working place–so it is sane not to vent your spleen, caused by any outsider's shortcoming, on your wife and children rather treat every one in accordance with his /her status.

## BEFORE GOING HOME

While working in *Daarul-Iftaa* (fatwa issuing office) we came across many incidents of mutual brawls of the husband and wife, then their legal (*Shara'i*) inquiries which clarify that, though most of the husbands love their wives, confess their loyalty, accept their service and good house-keeping still they quarrel with their wives and their marital lives are being ruined. When the reasons of their dissent were deliberated, it was found that most of these brawls were started either at office time or when the husband return from their work.

Some of the husband's expectations before reaching home…

1) She will be standing at the door, leaving all the work to receive me.

2) All the items in my room would be kept according to my direction.

3) Children will be sitting quietly in a corner with tape on their mouth.

4) She will come at the door as soon as the bell will ring rather after listening the horn when I will blow it in the street's corner.

5) She will neither tell me about her quarrel with my sister or mother or the neighbour nor will give me any sad news.

6) The food of my choice and a sweet dish will be ready.

Some time while the husband enters his house, he does not find its atmosphere according to his expectations and utters some harsh words without paying any regard to the wife's genuine excuse or helplessness. These harsh words of the husband incite futher brawls ……and then starts public ridicule, back-biting, taunting, accusing each other and reproaching. Whereas, in some cases mutual abuse or scuffle also takes place. Therefore, it will be better for a husband to move towards his house thinking that,

1) There may be any excuse that she had not acted on my directions.

2) She or the children might have felt the need of answering the call of nature and might have become late in opening the door after the bell rang.

3) Perhaps the house-maid not have come that's why the room is not cleaned or was cleaned but some relatives have come just before my coming and their children accompanied by mine have changed the places of some things so how can I taunt my wife of carelessness without listening the actual reason and excuse.

4) She may not have prepared the food of my choice or according to the number of friends coming with me–because as soon as I left the house in the morning, she felt headache and could not leave the bed for 2 hours. She was thinking that till evening she will complete the required work but could not or the younger baby had disturbed her unexpectedly and she could not complete the work inspite of the availability of all the necessary things or she had helped the child who had hurt himself and the curry is burnt, then in a hurry she made a light food ... or the oven had become faulty or the electricity had gone for a long period and the phone in the office or house has gone out of order otherwise she would have told me to bring some edibles for the guests.

There might be some other constraints also for her, so if you want your house to be free of daily brawls and your children may not become mentally ill you should mend your conduct.

Get used to tolerance and forbearance, you should select yourself a suitable excuse for each Muslim's mistakes especialy for your family members' mistakes and consider that Allah the Almighty has given them in your subordination, as your wife is your protection from the hell while your children are the blossoming flowers of your home. You should treat your wife and children in a fascinating way and in accordance with the *Shari'at* so that your house may become an ideal for others.

## DON'T MAKE YOUR WIFE SICK

Some youths have childish mentality, who are very much selfish, proudy, cruel, inexperienced and seduced by their irreligious mother or sister, show only fake love and sympathy to their wives just to achieve their object, they are the real cause of their wives' sickness.

Then these husbands are overburdened by spending huge money on their treatment, moreover they (sick wives) are blamed and made responsible for these expenses (though they are made sick by their husbands only). Just see the irony and the inexperience of the husband, whenever he goes to a religious scholar for councelling or *fatwa* (*Shara'i* verdict) he says, Maulvi Saheb,

> "Such an afflicted and sick wife was in my destiny only, I am fed up of her sickness and treatment. Maulvi Saheb, please give me either an amulet or an advice what should I do, I had taken her to the best doctors, physicians and homeopaths but to no avail".

Whereas, if considered thoroughly, atmosphere of the house is reviewed, the husbands would check themselves while talking to their wives from time to time, back-biting, jealousy and tale-bearing between different sisters-in-law are reviewed cool-headedly. Seeing your forgiveness and without making you angry, it will become clear that it is only you who had made her sick, older than her real age, ugly, lean and weak.

You can consult any just, wise, experienced and sincere friend or any religious physician regarding her sickness, they will certainly tell you that you are the only reason for her sickness. Don't forget, when love and affection mixes with youth and health it last long, even in old age one looks young and it immunizes against many a dangerous diseases. Leanness, weakness, cowardice, fear, non-confidence, mental anxiety and confusion etc. are terrified even from the shadow of such people.

When Hajjaj was asked, do you have to undergo much sufferings to fulfil your sexual desire from your wife? Then such a cruel person (it is said that he was the most cruel of the caliphs) replied," yes, even I had to kiss her feet to get my wife ready".

A man of ordinary sense, who has not lost his wits due to any mental disease and who is unfamiliar with the cunnings and wiles of different sisters-in-law (husband's sister / his elder or younger brothers' wives) can understand that a marriage would be successful, harmonious and a satisfying one for both (husband and wife) only when both are loving, caring for each other, forgiving each other just to please Allah, believing that Allah has given one eye to see other's excellence while another is to see his own faults and they should believe, if they are not loving each other in the beginning of their marital life, *Insha Allah*, after sometime Allah the Almighty will create love and affection among them provided that the husband should not allow a third person to interfere in their matter.

Allah forbid, if it does not happen then the marital pleasure will certainly become apathetic and both of them will become restless, unsatisfied, protesting, irritable, chattering, tumultive and enraged. Due to these, the wife will be afflicted by such sickness, treatment of which becomes compulsory. Especially, the women who are neither allowed to go to their parental house nor they can call their parents due to continuous watch over phone by mothers-in-law or husbands' sisters. Such women lead a miserable life as they can't explain what is happening to them and no medicine can heal their ailment. Such non-confidence or sexual unevenness or noncooperation between husband and wife will change the course of married life, which results in certain ailments either for wives or for husband. Some of these ailments are;

1) Pain in the nape
2) Throat infection
3) Pain or ulcer in the stomach
4) Pain in gall-bladder
5) Flatulence

6) Laziness and drowsiness

7) Headache

8) Palpitation and suffocation

9) Constipation

10) Depression and exhaustion

If you want your wife not to be a psychopathic or not to be afflicted by any of these ailments or may remain sound and healthy even in her senility or your children be intelligent and of higher qualification and ability then you must try not to aggrieve your wife rather she must have full confidence in you, so that she could tell you all her complexities without any hesitation.

You must create cheerfulness, hopefulness, magnanimity, courage and affection etc. in your wife and children by fulfilling their lawful demands (which Allah and His messenger (pbuh) have allowed). Don't trample your wife's confidence, listen her attentively and try to keep her happy as much as possible.

*Insha Allah*, she will repose confidence in you and will be saved of many a psychopathies and physical ailments as your health and happiness depend on her health and happiness.

Therefore, for Allah's sake! Have mercy on you, your wife and children (if they really have committed a mistake) by forgiving them to please Allah with the belief that, if I am having mercy on them, Allah will have mercy on me.

May Allah help us to act cautiously by using our wisdom and intelligence, Amen!

## AVOID CRITICISM

Some youths are of serious and gentle temperament having a cheerful and pleasant look. But after marriage the way of convincing or advising their wives becomes contradictive and critical, if they are living jointly. Sometimes, after listening the complaints of their elder brothers and sisters, such as;

Brother why don't you convince your wife.....

How stupid is she .............

Treat her harshly and see............

You don't know how to treat wife.......etc.

Now the brave husband vents his spleen by criticizing his wife and feels that he is convincing in the best way. Just consider his way of convincing....my such and such friend or relative scold their wives and beat them like wild animals while neither I do like them nor disgrace her before other women of the house. I do convince her either in an airconditioned room or during an outing and that's too after feeding her something, but this stupid, ungrateful and thankless woman neither obeys me nor is convinced. Whenever, I try to convince her, either she flies at me or splits her hair and does not accept her mistake etc. etc.

We are requesting such husbands, if you think cool-mindedly it is not the way of convincing, rather it is beating by besmeared shoes wrapped in beautiful clothes and asking her to accept the uncommitted faults on the basis of unverified complaints, for example;

My brother's wife has said "this" about you , you would have said "this", so accept your fault and apologise ...........

First of all, remember! That one can't be reformed by criticizing, objecting, finding faults, refuting, comparing, reproaching and rebuking not only open the door of debate and controversies but these will ruin the private life (of husband and wife) also and close the door of mutual understanding, obedience, admitting the mistakes and apologising on it.

Now we are giving you six contrivances to convince her politely, try to act upon these. May Allah help all of us to act accordingly, Amen!

1) Don't go ahead as soon as your parent or sisters or brothers' wives complain to you about your wife or you find anything in her against your wishes. Don't talk to her at-once, rather wait till the time of two prayers passes. Suppose you receive her complaint around *Zuhar* prayers, talk to her after *Maghrib* prayers. If you act upon this contrivance *Insha Allah* you will see a lot of changes in the house.

2) Your sister told you that ... yesterday in the feast, when our paternal aunt asked Zulekha why don't you

come to our house? Your wife told that, I don't get opportunity to go out as there are so many duties in the in-laws' house.

Don't believe on your sister and never ask your wife at-once, why you told this? Look! What sister is saying? You must not have told like this.....etc.

The Prophet's (pbuh) way of convincing was that he never took the name of a nation or a group in which any blemish was found rather he used to say;

مَا بَالُ النَّاسِ

*What had happened to people ( that they are doing like this).*

So, acting upon the brilliant way of our Prophet (pbuh), we also should not point out her mistake directly, rather we should talk to her in general way, for example.....

Dear Zulekha.... Do you know a bad habit of some women, that is they talk irrelevantly. It is an unbecoming act and I become irritated of such women, so you have to save yourself from this .... It is utmost stupidity to tell one's internal matters to others you must never do this.......I have full confidence in you...that you might not be doing this ...etc. etc.

3) Suppose you received four complaints of your wife or you felt unpleasantness due to some of her actions don't convince her by taking each actions and

complaints one by one, rather think the reason and try to end it. May Allah guide all of us to the accurate reason.

4) While convincing your wife neither repeat nor remind her of the bygone things as this will only create misunderstanding among you, your wife and children. May Allah protect all of us from this, Amen!

5) Choose an appropriate place and time to convince your wife so that the dispute may not get prolonged and she may mend her ways. Sometimes when she is convinced in an appropriate place and time she may even accept what she has not done and if it is not taken care of, then the issue becomes more and more complicated.

6) Neither convince nor disgrace her in the presence of other nor give her examples of other women. Remember it is not convincing rather it is disgracing her, in this way the issue will become much more complicated.

If one wants to reform someone, he must be full of sweet words, affection, tolerance, well-wishing and sympathy. While he must be far off from surliness and pinching words.

Alongwith these contrivances keep praying for you and your wife as well keep seeking forgiveness of your sins also because sometimes, due to ominousness of one's own sins, the wife becomes disobedient. May Allah create mutual affection between Muslim couples and mutual harmony in their nature, Amen!

## FAULT IS YOURS

Some husbands fret and fume at their wives' real mistakes in their hearts only neither they tell them anything nor try to reform nor pray Allah rather they curse themselves or shed tears on their parents' selection, this is fully wrong.

Here is an excerpt from the daily "JUNG" so that you may understand that being disappointed … or seeing anything through one angle …. or blaming the other only …or keep thinking the past is not suitable in anyway.

**Que**: Before three years I was sitting in a marriage function with some close-relatives and friends all of a sudden, the son of my wife's younger sister came and treated me rudely and unmannerly. The relatives and friends sitting with me, looked at me with furtive glances, I felt disgraced but remained silent and told the wife later on.

I remained silent for one year but was waiting for him to apologise of his rudeness. He and his mother kept coming to my house regularly but never greeted me, while my wife did not pay any attention to his rudeness.

One day the boy came when he was going back after having a conversation with my wife I asked him not to come ever to my house. He became infuriated, started talking non-sense and said no one can stop me from comong here. My wife was listening to him but kept silent. Once I fell ill and remained at home, his mother came and remained busy talking with her sister without paying any attention to me. In the evening the boy came to take her back, I became enraged seeing him and a hot argument ensued between us–the boy kept replying me but neither his mother nor my wife nor my son said anything. After going back to their home, the son called my wife on phone, but I could not hear what he told her. Afterwards my wife reviled me and asked for divorce, I told her that I won't divorce you, though you can take *Khula'* (divorce obtained on wife's initiative) and there was hot argument between us also. From that very time till now–which is nearly one year's time, there is no conversation between us, though I am giving her money which is obligatory for me, I am mentally disturbed now. Please tell me what is *Shara'i* decrees regarding this whole episode.

**Ans**: According to *Shari'at* both the wife and husband should live affectionately, should respect their conjugal rights, if they can't then separation is best. You have ruined your matter due to the son of your wife's sister. If he was ill-mannered then you should not have shown undue favor to him. Allah knows your matter in a better way, but your letter shows that you could not make room for yourself among your wife and children.

There is no conversation between you, your wife and children for one year but none of you asked its reason from the other. Though your wife is more sinful but the main fault is of your rigid nature, due to your nature you are not constant in relaitons with anyone. My advice is that start treating your family politely, mannerly and with a sound policy, then neither you will complain of your wife nor her sister nor her nephew. The Prophet (pbuh) has said, " best of you is one who is best for his family while I am the best for my family".

**Clarification**:- Our religion has asked us to hide ourselves from wife's sister and brother's wife, as after the death of wife one can marry her sister similarly one can marry his brother's wife after the death of brother, so they are non-*Mahram* for us and we should hide ourselves from them just like other non-*Mahram* woman. When we will displease Allah by disobeying Him, ultimately our all worldly affairs will be ruined. Though we consider someone's rudeness, pinching words, immorality, thanklessness or ingratitude shown to us but these are the result of our sins. Let us decide to hide ourselves from such woman as told by Allah, may the people say anything, we will not displease Allah. May Allah, make us to abide by His decrees and spread these, Amen!

## THOSE HAVING RELIGIOUS THOUGHTS..........

Some religious thinking people as is shown by their appearance come to us to ask about their wives' actions and the way of their living (infact they bring their complaints). Had these (men) convinced their wives according to the occasion, they would have understood and rectified their conduct. It would have been better, if such persons would have discussed the issue earlier with any preceptor and convinced their wives wisely and lovingly when needed then only she would have listened and given importance to them considering them as one of their well-wishers.

Now, to clarify this reality we are giving some examples.

1) The husband see that her wife, inspite of drawing her attention repeatedly, is erring in saying obligatory prayers. One way of convincing her is to say that your are regularly erring in offering obligatory prayers so you are sinful and such... keeping animosity with you is compulsory (these are certainly correct). I will not eat food made by you, so that you may know that Iam displeased with you. The husband could also say like this (it is much more better way).

   Whenever I enter my house, I feel suffocated, shocked and get the thoughts of being far away from religion. Last week, I took food at one of my religious friend's house and stayed there for some work, that night I invoked Allah's name at bed even said the *Tahajjud* prayers and there was no confusion. In my opinion both of us should check our actions, as it is possible that due to any of our unsuitable actions, Allah's help for us has been stopped as Allah is displeased with us, we are restless and there is no real comport inspite of having so many means of comfort.

   Most probably, the wife might think that, if the

husband had this very complaint again, either he will go to eat and sleep in any religious friend's house or will start living in mosque with the intention of *E'tikaaf* (retiring to the corner of a mosque for continued prayers) then there will be rumours about me, such as why Zulekha's husband does not give much time at home after coming back from work? Where does he go ? etc.., It is better for me to be regular at saying prayers instead of creating such situation.

2) While reading newspapers or magazines wife sees the photos and animated pictures (it is forbidden) and especially seeing the photos of non-*Mahram* gents ....is more ungraceful.

One way of telling her is that, I had confirmed this is much more sinful and forbidden, your eyes will be burnt in the Hell and you will be jammed together with these actors as seeing the photos and pictures of sinful persons is like enjoying with them.....

Another way of restraining her from this forbidden and sinful act is that, tell her, while going to work I had seen an advertisement (of a woman) by mistake. The bad woman of that advertisement is still coming in my mind and confusing me. when I was tired of removing that filthy thought during my duty hours, I started thinking of you, then only Igot peace of mind. I can't understand how men enjoy by seeing non-*Mahram* women or their photos and pictures. How bad it will be if due to this ominousness one does not like his/her spouse. I really hate such a person .........

3) If she is a back-biting woman. Don't tell her that you do back-biting and back-biters won't enter the Heaven, rather convince her in the following way. I don't know why some women convey the gossip of one person or place to others in such a way that the person hearing it, at once becomes mad with fury and there starts a quarrel in between two Muslims. The reason behind all these is the women who has back-bited. I have full confidence in you, that you will never like to talk to such women rather you will try to reform such women. In all probability, if you convince her in this way, *Insha Allah*, she will understand the harm of back-biting.

4) If she is abusing the children in anger and you have heard her abuses, don't tell her anything at that moment rather convince her later on or while going to bed like this. I was passing through the street, I heard an abuse. When I turned towards the voice, I was perplexed to see that it was a small child. I asked the people whose child is this ? They said he is the son of such and such person. He is taught abuses in his house as whenever his parents are angry they abuse him. Dear, I thought of our own son had he been in his place, what would have happened to us? ... How the parents dare to abuse before their children? May Allah show them the path of righteousness as they are being disgraced in the eyes

of Allah and ruining the new generation by abusing frequently before them. I think we never abuse before our children. Dear, if I ever make such mistake you are supposed to warn me.

If you start convincing her in these ways you will see positive consequence, so use these ways. The most important thing is that, never convince her while she is scolding the children, rather tell her these two things while the children are away and she is cool-minded;

Firstly while convincing the children neither use improper nor impolite words as they will also use these words if they become angry either with their friends or school colleagues or cousins or brother and sister. Tell me, will we get respect in this way? .... All will come to know that the atmosphere of our house is miserable. Remember, Allah has given these children to us, so that they may be an addition in the followers of the Prophet (pbuh) from our side, we should train them in such a way that they themselves be righteous, attract others to righteousness and should not forget their relation with the Prophet (pbuh). You should give up the habit of saying imprecatory words such as; may you die, may you be ruined, may you rue in your whole age, O the crying one like one who is without parents may Allah make you a waif in reality... we all have faith that as the blessings are accepted in the same way imprecations are also accepted. Just imagine the child had troubled you, being fed up you uttered an imprecatory word and that is accepted as it was the time of acceptance, then both of us will have to pass our lives weeping and rueing.

Dear husband! Don't make a noise to prevent the children from making a noise. If there is wrangling in the house, ask your wife about its reasons, but never ask before children and that's too politely.

Secondly, if you come to know a reason of wrangling between mother and children while you have a solution of it, then make a positive move. Suppose, while you came back from your work, you saw a child sitting displeased while your wife is scolding him / her. When inquired you came to know that the child wants to bring any of his/her favorite things and she has no money. Solution of this very problem is that bring some of their favorite things and keep it with your wife so that she can give to them as the need arises. Children are not controlled merely by the mother's words but they are supposed to be given something for amusement.

## PERILOUS MISTAKES

Neither quarrel nor rebuke the wife before children if you are very much irritated then went out of the house at once but never scold or rebuke her before children.

If the wife also started speaking and there is a brawl in between you then it will effect the children's psychology badly. If there is regular brawl, rude talk heated argument, mutual disdain and abasement etc. in a house, then not only that house will be ruined but generation will also be ruined.

The children are supposed to be senseless they do what they saw around them. You will see in such houses, the children are fighting rebuking, talking rudely among themselves and remain engaged in combat. While its ultimate result is that... each of them becomes self-conceited, proudy, restless, unmannerly, impatient and thinking of him / her only.

If the husbands are having brawl with their wives or scolding them in the presence of their own children regularly, then the wives will not respect them and make the children rebellious against their father, as a result, they will also not respect their father supporting their mother.

Sometimes, this afflicted mother resolves not to marry any of her children in her in-laws' family and declares openly that, it is better to keep my daughter in my house then marrying her with such person (pointing to her husband).

See how worst is the result of your incivility, rebuking or disgracing the wife in front of children and not respecting her virtues. Save yourself, your friends and relatives from this mistake.

## ANOTHER PERILOUS MISTAKE

Among the mistake committed by the husband while treating his wife, one is showing anger also. The person showing anger can't see its internal or external mortal effects himself while the person to whom he is showing anger can see these effects. Here we are giving some of the external effects; his whole body and face becomes reddish, he casts amorous glances, he has bloodshot eyes, his jaws become tight, his body starts shivering, he brandishes his fist, he starts roaring and his voice starts trembling etc. etc. While seeing these effects in any person one can easily guess that he is angry.

Whereas its internal mortal effects are more dangerous then the external effects. Some of these effects are; his blood starts boiling and effects his whole body, he is afflicted by several stomach ailments, heart's pulpitation increases, blood-pressure becomes high or low, heart attack becomes inevitable while sometimes due to fluctuation in his blood-pressure brain hemorrhage occurs and he dies, it is just like a suicidal death. Due to anger his heart's arteries are shrinked and he is afflicted by angina pectoris. All these ailments are for one who is showing anger. Whereas anger also effects those who are facing this anger, if they are his wife or children then it becomes firmly rooted in their minds, that her husband or their father is a cruel person and does not have love for us.

Therefore, we request you not to get angry as long as possible, if it is your nature then try to suppress it. Now we are giving some contrivances to reduce the anger, read it carefully and try to act upon these.

1) Learn and recite the prayers of entering the house. When you are entering the house, first read:

اَعُوذُ بِا للّٰهِ مِنَ الشَّيْطٰنِ الرَّجِيم

Then,

بِسْمِ اللّٰهِ الرَّحمٰنِ الرَّحِيم

Then Sura-e-Ikhlaas (قُلْ هُوَ اللّٰهُ اَحَدٌ) and Darood afterwards recite the following prayer with due concentration on its meaning;

اللّٰهُمَّ اِنِّي اَسْئَلُکَ خَيرَ الْمَوْلَجِ وَخَيرَ الْمَخرَجِ بِسْمِ اللّٰهِ وَلَجنَا
وَبِسْمِ اللّٰه خَرَجْنا وَعَلَى اللّٰهِ رَبِّنَا تَوَ كَّلْنَا

*O Allah ! I ask you the virtue and betterment of coming and going out of the house, in the name of Allah we enter and go out, we rely on Allah who is our Cherisher and Sustainer.* (Abu Dawood 2/339)

Remember! Prayers are not for recitation only but these are for seeking Allah's help also, that's why we should recite the prayers with full concentration on its meanings. If you are not seeking Allah's refuge from the Satan while entering the house, then the Satan will also enter with you and will try to stage disputes between the inmates of the house.

***Note:*** Keep the following books with you to know the prayers for different occasions. Learn these prayers and incite your family members also learn these prayers, the books are.

1) Masnoon Du'aain by Maulvi Ashiq Elahi (Ra).

2) Hisn-e-Haseen translated and explained by Maulvi Ashiq Elahi (Ra).

3) Mustanad Majmu'a-e-Wazaaif approved by Mufti Nizamuddin.

Whenever you feel anger, recite اَعُوْذُ بِاللّٰهِ مِنَ الشَّيْطَانِ الرَّجِيْمِ and drink water, *Insha Allah*, you will not get angry.

2) Whenever you feel angry make ablution as it will divert your mind, water lessens the heat and the Satan runs away while one makes ablution. It is clear that the Satan enrages anger, when the Satan will run away, anger will also end.

3) The Prophet (pbuh) has said;

من كظم غيظا وهو يستطيع ان ينفذ دعاه اللّٰه يو م القيامة على
رؤوس الخلائق حتى يخيره في اى الحور العين شاء

*A person who can show anger but suppresses it, Allah will call him before all the creations on Doomsday and will give him an option to choose a black-eyed hourie.* (Tirmizi 2/22, Abu Dawood 2/33)

At the time of anger, keep in mind the above mentioned excellence and suppress your anger in order to get the option of choosing a black-eyed hourie.

4) Allah the Almighty says in the Holy Qur'an;

وَجَنَّةٍ عَرْضُهَا السَّمٰوٰتُ وَالْاَرْضُ اُعِدَّتْ لِلْمُتَّقِيْنَ الَّذِيْنَ يُنْفِقُوْنَ فِى السَّرَّآءِ
وَالضَّرَّآءِ وَالْكَاظِمِيْنَ الْغَيْظَ وَالْعَافِيْنَ عَنِ النَّاسِ ؕ وَاللّٰهُ يُحِبُّ الْمُحْسِنِيْنَ ۝

*And for a garden whose width is that (of the whole) of the heavens and of the earth, prepared for the righteous,–those who spend (freely) whether in prosperity, or in adversity; who restrain anger, and pardon (all) men;– for Allah loves those who do good:* (Aal-e-Imraan 133&134)

Maulvi Mohd. Zakariyya (Ra) has written in *Fazail-e-Sadaqat* that, in this very verse one specific quality of the believers is given, that is they restrain anger and pardon men. The theologians have told if your wife or brother commits a mistake then search for excuses and convince yourself that when he/she is having so many excuses, I should pardon him/her. In case your heart is not accepting any of his/ her excuses then reproach yourself only as you are so rigid and adamant to accept their excuses. That's why the Prophet (pbuh) has said; if someone puts up an excuse before someone and he is not accepting it, he will be equal to an Octroi clerk in sin (who accepts illegal taxes from the people).

5) Imam Ahmed narrated that the Prophet (pbuh) has said; اذا غضب احدکم فلیسکت

*Whenever any of you got angry he should kept silence.* (Musnad Ahmed-Kitab Musnad Bani Hashim Hadith No.3029)

Therefore, whenever you got angry you should keep silence and retire to seclusion so that your mouth may remain shut.

6) One strange contrivance is that write this passage on a piece of paper and hang it in such a way that you could see it again and again.

"Allah has more power over them (wife, children & servants) then you have therefore, you should not punish more than their faults, otherwise you will be punished in the world and the Hereafter. On the Day of Judgment the fault and the punishment will be brought and weighed, if they are equal, one will be released otherwise he will be punished".

A man shows his anger to a person who is weaker than him or while he can't show his anger to a person who is stronger than him or has a stronger ally. Whereas a person who is seeing this passage repeatedly won't feel anger.

7. The Prophet (pbuh) has said if any of you feels anger while standing he should sit down and if he is sitting he should lie down. (Abu dawood 2/303)

Most probably it is the best contrivance as when a person is standing he is at a distance from the earth. while sitting he is nearer to the earth, and while laying down he touches it. Allah has kept meekness in its nature, it effects the man, while meekness is antagonistic to anger and arrogance.

# MEANING OF "WOMEN ARE BORN OUT OF CROOKED RIBS"

The Prophet (pbuh) has given a perfect simile while saying "woman is born out of a rib". It is a strange and sage-like simile. Some scholars have given its explanation that, first of all Allah had created Hazrat Adam (pbuh) then created Hazrat Hawwa (pbuh) out of his ribs. According to some scholars, the woman is like a rib whose soundness and beauty is in its crookedness, if one wants to straighten it, it will be broken. Similar is the case of woman as narrated by the Prophet (pbuh)

ان ذهبت تقيمها كسرتها

*If you want to straighten it, it will be broken*

(Muslim, Kitabur-Razaa' Hadith No.3669)

وإن استمتعت بها استمتعت بهاوفيها عوج

*If you want to reap benefit from her you can inspite of her crookedness.* (Bukhari,Kitabun-Nikah Hadith No.4786)

It is a very strange and sage-like simile given by the Prophet (pbuh) that her soundness is in her crookedness, if she is straight then she is sick and unsound.

## IT IS NOT A CONTEMPT OF THE WOMAN

Some people use this simile as a contempt and disgrace for woman that she is created out a crooked rib, therefore its base is crooked. Whereas it is not the motive of this very Prophet's (pbuh) saying.

## CROOKEDNESS OF WOMAN IS NATURAL

Allah has created men and women after giving them different qualities and there is a difference in their nature and temperament also. Due to this very difference, men think about women that they are against their nature and temperament. Whereas their being against the men's nature is not a vice rather it is the demand of their nature to be a crooked one. If someone says about the rib, that its crookedness is its vice, outwardly it is not a vice rather it is the demand of its nature. Therefore, the Prophet (pbuh) has said, "If you are finding anything in the woman which is against your nature and due to this neither consider her crooked nor reject her, rather consider it a demand of her nature, if you will try to straighten her, she will be broken and if you want to reap benefit from her you can inspite of her crookedness".

## "CARELESSNESS" IS THE BEAUTY OF A WOMAN

Nowadays time has reversed therefore, people's thinking and decrees have also changed, otherwise the real matter is that some things which are vice for men but these very vices are a beauty and virtue for a women. If we concentrate in the Holy Qur'an we will see that some thing which are vice for men but these very are beauty for the women and are called virtues. For example it is vice for men to be ignorant, careless and not having knowledge of the world, as Allah has given him the responsibility of worldly affairs. Whereas Qur'an has described the carelessness of the woman as their beauty, the Qur'an says;

إِنَّ الَّذِيْنَ يَرْمُوْنَ الْمُحْصَنَاتِ الْغَا فِلاَتِ الْمُوءْ مِنَاتِ

*Those who slander chaste indiscreet and believing woman (not well posted of the world)* (Nur-23)

The Qur'an has called, the indiscreetness of a woman from the worldly affairs, a beauty. We came to know by this verse, if a woman is not well-posted of the worldly affairs but in accordance with her duties then it is her good quality and virtue.

## DON'T TRY TO STRAIGHTEN FORCIBLY

Therefore, a thing which is a vice for a man and is not for a woman similarly the things which are not vice for a man can be a vice for a woman. Hence, if you find anything in them which is a vice for you and not for them, don't misbehave with them due to this, as the demand of being a rib is that she should be different in nature from you, so don't try to straighten her forcibly.

## ANY OF HER HABITS MIGHT BE PLEASING

Hazrat Abu Huraira (mabawh) has narrated;

عن أبي هريرة رضى الله عنه قال: قال رسول الله صلى الله عليه وسلم: لا يفرک مومن مومنة إن کره منها خُلقًا رضى منها آخر.

*Hazrat Abu Huraira has narrated, the Prophet (pbuh) has said " A faithful man should not keep animosity with a faithful woman, if he did not like any of her habit he might like another."*

(Muslim,Kitaabur-Razaa' H.No.2672)

In this Hadith the Prophet (pbuh) had made a marvellous principle that a faithful man should not keep animosity with a faithful woman completely by saying that there is no virtue in her or by considering her useless and silly. If any of her habits or actions are disliked some may be liked one.

The first principle told by the Prophet (pbuh) is that when two persons live together, some actions or habits of one of them are liked by another man while some other are disliked. If any habit is disliked it does not mean that he should be considered ungraceful rather his good virtues should be called in mind and thanks be given to Allah that he has that very good virtue. If one acts accordingly then he might not give much importance to that person's vices.

In reality human is ungrateful, if he dislikes some habits of a person he sticks to these and does not pay attention to that person's good virtues and misbehaves.

# EVERY THING IS A MIXTURE OF GOOD AND EVIL

In this world created by Allah, everything has a good and evil in itself. Neither anything in this mortal world is void of good virtue nor is void of vice. One can say that good and bad virtues are the two sides of a coin. In this world, good and bad virtues are intermingled, one is infidel or one is polytheist or one is a bad man but if a person tries to look good virtues in them also he will surely get some.

## AN ENGLISH PROVERB

There is an English proverb and our Prophet (pbuh) has said "wise-saying is the lost Property of a faithful, he should take it wherever he get it". Being an English proverb, it does not mean that it will certainly be wrong. The sage-like proverb is, "A watch or a clock which is out of order that also speaks truth twice daily". Suppose a clock is gone out of order at 12.05, it is apparent that it will not give right time the whole day but twice a day it will give right time. The meaning of this proverb is that, however may a thing be bad or useless, if one looks for a good virtue in it, he will surely get. Similarly there is not a single thing in this world which does not have any virtue.

## NONE IS BAD IN THE NATURE'S SYSTEM

Mufti Mohd Shafi' (Ra) often used to read this very couplet of Allama Iqbal;

نہیں ہے چیز نکمی کوئی زمانے میں     کوئی برا نہیں قدرت کے کارخانے میں

It means that Allah has created all the things in this world through his wish and raisondetre. If you consider, you will find the raisondetre and expedience in each of His creations. Whereas the man sees only its bad virtue and neglects good virtues because of this, being frustrated he undertakes cruelty and injustice.

## LOOK FOR GOOD VIRTUES OF THE WOMAN

Allah says in the Holy Qur'an;

فَإِنْ كَرِهْتُمُوهُنَّ فَعَسٰى أَنْ تَكْرَهُوا شَيْئًا وَّ يَجْعَلَ اللّٰهُ فِيهِ خَيْرًا كَثِيرًا ○

*"If you take a dislike to them (your wives) it may be that you dislike a thing and Allah brings about through it a great deal of good."* (Nisa-19)

So, we are asked to look for the good virtue of woman so that we would be satisfied and the ways of misbehavior would close down.

## A TEACHING INCIDENT OF A PRECEPTOR

Maulvi Ashraf Ali Thanvi (Ra) has written an incident of a preceptor that his wife was very quarrelsome. Whenever he enters the house, rebuking and quarreling gets started. Someone asked him, why are you tolerating this wrangling and fighting of day and night, get rid of her and divorce her. He replied, dear brother! giving divorce is very easy. I can divorce her any time. In reality this woman has so many flaws but there is one good virtue in her and due to that I will never divorce her. The only good virture in her is her loyalty given by Allah. Suppose I am arrested and sentenced for 50 years, I am confident that she will remain sitting in the corner where I will ask her to sit and will not dare to look at anyone.

In reality, this preceptor had acted upon this *Hadith* of the Prophet (pbuh):

ان کرہ منها خلقاً رضی منها آخر

*If you dislike any of habits, you may like another.*

(Muslim Kitabur-Razaa' H.No-2672)

One must take care of that very good virtue of her and treat her kindly. Evil starts by seeing the flaws only in the wives and neglecting their good virtues.

## MIRZA MAZHAR JAAN-E-JAANAN (RA) AND HIS TOUCHINESS

You would have heard about Mirza Mazhar Jaan-e-Jaanan (Ra) he was one of the greatest saints of Allah. He was such a touchy person that, if some one kept a glass unevenly on the earthen pot or he sees the bed-sheet wrinkled, he felt headache. But the wife he got was very ill-mannerred, ill-tempered, peevish and abusive as she used to murmur every now and then. Allah the Almighty tests His slaves through different ways in order to raise their status. It (getting such wife) was a test of him by Allah, he lived happily with her for the whole life, and used to say perhaps, Allah may forgive my sins in this way.

## WOMEN OF OUR SOCIETY ARE THE HOURIES OF THE WORLD

Hazrat Thanvi (Ra) used to say the women of our (India and Pakistan) society are the houries of the world as they have layalty in them. But since the westernization has effected them, it (loyalty) is also diminishing gradually. Inspite of all these, they are fully devoted to their husbands and they don't look at other than them.

## BEATING WIFE IS RUDENESS

عن عبد اللّٰہ بن زمعة رضی اللّٰہ عنہ انّہ سمع النبی صلی اللّٰہ علیہ وسلم یخطب ......ثم ذکر النساء فوعظ فیھن، فقال: یعمد احدکم فیجلد امرأتہ جلد العبد فلعلہ یضاجعھا من آخر یومہ

*Abdullah-bin-Zam'ah (mabawh) heard the Prophet (pbuh) while he was giving a speech ...... mentioning women he said, it is bad to beat one's own wife like a slave and at the end of the day lying down with her (to fulfill his sexual desire).*

(Bukhari- kitaabun- nikah Hadeeth no 5204)

How rude and shameless is the person who beats his wife like a slave .

# RELIGIOUS DECREE OF A DISOBEDIENT WIFE

Maulvi Mohd. Yousuf Ludhianvi (may his blessings last long) replies to a querry by a person.

**Que:-** A family is living in our neighbour. The husband is a noble person, the relation of husband and wife were very strong till one day when the wife insisted upon something. The husband got angry when she insisted again as it was an illegal insistence and slapped her. The wife uttered a dirty word "gipsy" for the husband and his parents and left for her parents' house. When her mother got angry knowing the reason of her coming, she returned to her house, but neither they are talking to each other nor she is trying to appease him. Please give your precious opinion in the light of the Holy Qur'an and traditions of the Prophet (pbuh).

**Ans:** Slapping on the face is strictly prohibited in the *Ahaadith* so the husband has exceeded the limits, he should not have been enraged like this. While replying the slapping by the wife with abuse is worse than his action.

## THREE STAGES OF WIFE'S REFORMATION

As told earlier, the Qur'an has dealt with every aspect of marital life, the strife between husband and wife starts when he dislikes any of her actions or habits. Its solution, as told by the *Shari'at* is to look for her good virtues. Even then if the husband feels that there are some unbearable habits in her which are reformable, he is supposed to try her reformation. The Qur'an has told us the ways to adopt for her reformation in this verse;

وَالّٰتِیْ تَخَا فُوْنَ نُشُوْزَهُنَّ فَعِظُوْ هُنَّ وَاهْجُرُوْهُنَّ فِی الْمَضَا جِعِ وَاضْرِبُوْهُنَّ

*As to those woman on whose part you fear disloyalty and ill-conduct, admonish them (first), (next), refuse to share their beds (and last) beat them (lightly);* (Nisa- 34)

The first stage of reformation is to advice and convince them politely, elegantly and amiably. If they are convinced then it is OK, other wise use the 2nd stage. That is, stop sleeping with them in their beds. If they will have a little common sense, they will abstain from their habits.

If the second stage is also not effective then use the 3rd stage, that is beating. The Prophet (pbuh) at the time of *Hajjatul-Vidaa'* had advised his followers about how and how much should be the beating in these words;

واضربوهن ضرباً غیرمبرح

*Beat them unviolently (it should not be vexing)*

(Bukhari Kitabun-Nikah Hadith No.4)

The beating should not be troubling, which leaves scars, rather it should be for admonition only.

## BEHAVIOUR OF THE PROPHET (PBUH) WITH WIVES

When our Prophet (pbuh) left this mortal word, he had 9 wives and these were not the angels descended from the Heaven, rather they were the members of this very our society and there were such affairs also which generally happen between co-wives and sometimes between husband and wife. Hazrat Ayesha (mabawh) said that the Prophet (pbuh) has never beaten any of his wife the whole life, rather he used to enter the house with smiling face.

## SUNNAT OF THE PROPHET (PBUH)

Not to beat the wife is the *Sunnat* of our Prophet (pbuh). Beating is allowed only when the matter turn inevitable otherwise it is an un-Islamic way. *Sunnat* is what Hazrat Ayesha (mabawh) has told that he used to enter the house smiling.

## A MIRACLE OF Dr. ABDUL-HAI (Ra)

Sometimes, our spiritual guide Dr. Abdul-Hai (Ra) used to tell us "I have been married for 55 years, but thank Allah! during this period I had not talked to her with a changed tone". If a man walks on the water or flies in the sky, people call it a miracle but according to me, the real miracle is this, that Dr. Abdul-Hai (Ra) spent 55 years with his wife, and it is a relation which contains many unpleasant incidents, but he is saying that he never talked to her in a changed tone. Moreover, his wife says, he never asked me a glass of water and never ordered me for any work rather I myself take care of his necessities considering it my duty and good fortune.

Hazrat used to say that I am here (in this world) to serve my wife, my children, my religious disciples and my dependents. The dignity of a slave is in being a servant, so I am a servant.

He used to say, that in reality, mystic way of life means serving the creation, when I deem my self a servant–I am not supposed to be served–How can a servant ask someone to do a certain work of him. He passed his whole life in such a way that whenever there emerged a need, he himself did that work and never asked anyone. This is the complete following of the Prophet's (pbuh) *Sunnat* we follow him in outwardly matters, whereas we should follow him completely.

## ONLY CLAIM IS NOT ENOUGH

Following the traditions of the Prophet (pbuh) is a strange thing in itself as it betters the worldly affairs and future life of a human while it also sets right his life. One can't get these just by claim. The man should take care of not hurting a person with whom he is connected in any way.

**Conclusion:-** The Prophet (pbuh) has explained the third stage of reforming the wife as told by Allah in the Holy Qur'an by not beating any of his wives, though he may have came across to most awkward situations and has proclaimed the people who beat their wives as the worst people.

عن عمرو بن الأحوص الجشمي رضى الله عنه انه سمع النبى صلى الله عليه
وسلم في حجة الوداع يقول بعد أن حمد الله تعالى وأثنى عليه و ذكر و وعظ،
ثم قال: ألا واستوصوا بالنساء خيراً، فإنما هن عوان عندكم، ليس تملكون
منهن شيئاً غير ذلك، إلا ان يأتين بفاحشة مبينة فان فعلن فاهجروهن فى المضاجع
واضربوهن ضرباغير مبرح فان اطعنكم فلا تبغوا عليهن سبيلا

(Tirmizi Kitabut-Tafseer Hadith No.3087)

In this hadeeth, an excerpt is given from the last sermon of the Prophet (pbuh), he had given at the time of *Hajjatul-Vadaa'*. In this sermon he had declared cleary, "Perhaps I may not see you here after this year", and he proclaimed the things which he feared might seduce or cause to err his followers. So that, it may become modus operandi for his followers till the day of Judgement and tried to cease all the possible seducing ways.

In this particular excerpt we are told to identify and take care of the mutual rights of men and woman. Now guess the importance of these rights by this fact that the Prophet (pbuh) dealt with these in the sermon of *Hajjtul-Vadaa'*, while he himself said that he may not get another opportunity of such discussion here after this. So we must take care of these very sayings of the Prophet (pbuh) which he has discussed in his last sermon and among these are the mutual rights of men and women.

## IMPORTANCE OF THE RELATION BETWEEN HUSBAND AND WIFE

We came to know through this very *Hadith*, the importance of the mutual rights of husband and wife, their relation in the life of a human and how much stress the Prophet (pbuh) has given to these. If husband and wife are not doing justice to their mutual rights, rather usurping these then it will not only effect the two families but also the children. As the civilization depends on the families and houses and due to this usurpation, it also ruins, that's why the Prophet (pbuh) has emphasized on it.

## WOMEN ARE PRISONERS WITH YOU

Hazrat Amr-bin al-Ahwas Jashmi (mabawh) says that after praising Allah and advicing in general, the Prophet (pbuh) said listen carefully "have the best intentions with the women, as they are captive with you". The Prophet (pbuh) has told such an epithet of women, if a man consider only this very epithet of women, he will never think of maltreating them.

## HAVE A LESSON FROM AN INNOCENT GIRL

Hazrat M.A. Thanvi (Ra) used to say "have a lesson from an innocent and ignorant girl who left her parents, brothers, sisters and her kith and kin after uttering just two words–one said I want to marry you while the other said I accepted–and become devoted to her husband". She protected the honor of these two words so much, that she became a captive in the hands of her husband, while you did not pay heed to what you have uttered for Allah i.e لا اله الا اللّٰه محمد رسول اللّٰه and did not become devoted to Him.

## HOW MUCH SACRIFICES HAD A WOMAN GIVEN FOR YOU

In this very *Hadith*, the Prophet (pbuh) is saying, look how big sacrifice she has given for you–on the contrary if you were told that, you are going to be married and you have to leave your family, parents, brothers and sisters how difficult it would have been for you–she became a captive in an unfamiliar atmosphere, house and man to pass her remaining life. Therefore, the Prophet (pbuh) is asking, won't you consider this sacrifice? Consider this (her sacrifice) and treat her kindly.

## YOU CAN'T CLAIM FROM THEM MORE THAN THIS

The Prophet (pbuh), then uttered a very harsh sentence, whenever this sentence is explained, the men became angry, the sentence is;

ليس تملكون منهن شيئاً غيرذلكم

You have this much right over them, that they are supposed to live in your home, more than this you don't have any claim from them according to *Shari'at*.

## SERVING PARENTS-IN-LAW IS NOT HER DUTY

One must understand it fully, that while making food for husband and children is not a duty of the wife then how serving or making food for parents-in-law or the husband's brothers and sisters can be her duty. It has become a custom in our society that when the son is married, his parents feel that we are more eligible to be served by the daughter-in-law than the son. In other words, whether she is serving her husband or not, she must serve her parents-in-law. Consequently, disputes and quarrels start between mother, sisters and daughters-in-law, that's what is seen in our day to day life.

## SERVING PARENTS-IN-LAW IS HER DUTIFULNESS

Understand well! if parents need to be served then it is the duty of the son to serve them himself. Whereas, if the wife of that son is serving her husband's parents happily considering it a rewarding act and her good fortune then it is her dutifulness. Neither the son nor the parents-in-law can compell her to serve them, if she is not agree to serve them happily. If daughter-in-law is serving her parents-in-law happily considering it her dutifulness then she will surely get its reward. She should serve in order to keep the environment of the house peaceful.

## APPRECIATE THE SERVICES OF DAUGHTER-IN-LAW

At the same time, the parents-in-law and the husband should consider her services as her good manners and etiquettes because it is neither an obligation nor a duty of her. Therefore, they should appreciate her services and try to give her its best reward. As we are not understanding these rights and issues many houses are being deserted.

The disputes of mother and daughter-in-law as well as disputes of husband's sisters and brother' wives are deserting many houses, its main reason is that none is keeping in his mind the definitions of different rights as told by our Prophet (pubh).

## ONE STRANGE INCIDENT

Once Dr. Abdul Hai Arifi (Ra) narrated a strange incident that, there was a person known to him. He and his wife used to come to his assemblies as they had reformatory connection with him also. Once they invited him for a feast, so he went to their house, took food and it was very tasty. It was the habit of Dr. Saheb that whenever he took his food, he used to praise the lady who had made it to encourage her. So, after the food was taken the lady came behind the curtain and saluted. Dr. Saheb told her, "you have prepared a tasty food and I really enjoyed it". When Dr. Saheb finished the sentence, she started crying and sobbing. Dr. Saheb became perplexed and began thinking what would have hurt her, so he asked, what happened? Why are you crying? The women replied, after controlling herself with great difficulty. Hazrat, I am living with this husband since last 40 years but I never heard him saying, "today's food is good" and when I heard this sentence today from you weeping came automatically".

## SUCH PERSON WILL NEVER PRAISE FOOD

Most of the times, Dr. Saheb after narrating this incident used to say a person can never do this (not praising good food). Who thinks that if the wife is making food, it is the matter of her good virtue, etiquettes and good manners towards me. But a person who considers his wife as his servant so she is supposed to make food–as it is her duty–if she is making good food, why should she be praised? Such a person will never praise his wife.

## THE HUSBAND SHOULD SERVE HIS PARENTS HIMSELF

If the parents are weak or sick–they need to be served, while in the house there are only son and his wife, what should be done now? In this situation also, according to *Shari'at* it is not obligatory for a daughter-in-law, to serve them rather it is her dutifulness, etiquettes and a cause of getting reward–if she serves, she will get rewarded *Insha Allah*. The husband should consider it (serving his ailing or weak parents) as his own duty. Either he would serve them himself or arrange a servant for them, but if the wife is serving he should consider it as her etiquettes and kindness.

## GOING OUT WITHOUT PERMISSION IS UNLAWFUL FOR WOMEN

Here is one more law to be taken care of, otherwise the matter will be reversed, because when people saw one side of a matter they try to take advantage of it illegally–As we have told you in detail that making food is not obligatory for a woman according to *Shari'at*. On the other hand the Prophet (pubh) has said that the women are captives in your home–it means that their going out without your permission is unlawful. Therefore, as the jurists (*Mufti*) have given detail of making food in the same way they have written this also, if a husband tells his wife that you can't go out, you can't meet your relatives–if he prevents her even to meet her own parents, she is not supposed to go out. Whereas, if the parents come to their daughter's home to meet her, then the husband con't prevent her. Rather the jurists have put a limit to it that is once a week–as it is her right. Allah the Almighty has balanced  between the two, that is–A woman is not bound to make food legally on the other hand it is also illegal for a wife to go out without husband's permission.

# BOTH OF THEM SHOULD CO-OPERATE WITH EACH OTHER

This was all about Islamic rules & jurisprudence, as for etiquettes and courtesy they should take care of each other's pleasure and happiness. Hazrat Ali (mabawh) used to do all the out-house works while Hazrat Fatima (mabawh) used to do all the in-house works and this is the tradition of our Prophet (pbuh), so all of us should do accordingly. Both the husband and wife should not split hairs of the Islamic jurisprudence every now and then, rather they should treat themselves elegantly.

In-house works are for the women and out-house works are for the men, it is a natural division of work so that their life may pass on peacefully.

## IF THEY COMMIT INDECENCY....THEN?

If they commit any kind of indecency in the house, it should not be born at any cost. In this situation, according to the decree of the Holy Qur'an, first of all advise them. If they don't abstain from it then separate your bed from them. If inspite of this also they don't abstain themselves from it, then beat them in a way that it does not hurt them. If after taking these steps, they start obeying you and abstain from the indecencies then don't try another way as there is no room for other than these three ways taught to us by Allah.

The right of these women towards you is that you should treat them well, take care of their clothes, fooding and their other needs which are obligatory to you.

## GIVE SEPARATE POCKET-MONEY TO YOUR WIVES

Now we are giving some points on which Hazrat M.A. Thanvi (Ra) has stressed in several of his exhortations while generally we don't pay attention to these. Alimony (*Nafaqa*) is not only giving food and clothes but one should give pocket-money also to his wife, which she could spend as she likes. Some people arrange only food and clothe but don't give pocket-money.

Hazrat Thanvi (Ra) said, pocket-money is also necessary as there are some needs of a human, he / she feel ashamed or confused in disclosing them. Because of this, the wife should have some money for these needs and it is also a part of alimony.

## SHOW GENEROSITY IN EXPENSES

Another point is that do favor in fooding, it means that either give her enough money or arrange food yourself in accordance with your income. Some people's anxiety is that on the one hand *Shari'at* has forbade prodigality while on the other hand, one is asked to spend generously in the expenses of house maintenance. Now the question is, what is the dividing line between the two? Which expenses come in prodigality and which don't?

## RESIDENCE AND COMFORT ARE LEGAL

Replying to this anxiety H.Thanvi (Ra) said " a house" is one which is residable for example, a hut or cottage. A man can live in a thatched house. It is the first category of residence which is fully legal. While the second category is that there are facilities alongwith residence, for example a firm house, one can live in it comfortably. If some work is done in the house to get more comfort, it is neither prohibited nor a prodigality. For example a man can live in a hut while another can't live as he wants a firm house and in that he need fans and lights to live comfortably, it is not prodigality.

## DECORATION IS ALSO LEGAL

Third category is that, there should be some decoration also in the house alongwith comfort. For example a man has a firm and plastered house with fan and electricity but it is not painted. One can live in this house also but decoration won't be there, if someone got his house painted, it is also legal.

Precisely, residence is legal, comfort is legal, decoration is legal while decoration means, a man does something in his house to please himself and get more comfort so that it looks good there is no harm in it and it is legal as well.

## SHOWING IS ILLEGAL

Now fourth category is of "showing". If a man is getting such works done which are neither aimed at getting comfort nor decoration. Whereas the aim of that work is either that the people would consider him a wealthy man or to show supremacy over others or self-ostentation. All these are the parts of "showing" which is illegal and prodigality.

## LIMIT OF PRODIGALITY

The four categories mentioned above are not only for residence or food or clothes but for all other needs also. Suppose if a man wears good-looking and costly clothes to comfort and please himself, his family members and relatives then there is no harm in it. Whereas, if a man wears a good-looking and of costly dress, so that he may be considered a wealthy man and of a high status, then it is showing and forbidden. That's why Hazrat Thanvi (Ra) had put a dividing line between need and prodigality. That is if a man spends money to fulfil his necessities or to get comfort or to please himself or for decoration then it is not prodigality, otherwise it is.

## IT IS NOT PRODIGALITY

Once I was in another city and I had to return to Karachi as it was summer, I gave money to a man and asked him to get a seat reserved for me in AC coach. A person sitting with me said at once, it is prodigality! Most of the people think that if someone is travelling in an a upper class, it is prodigality. Understand well, if the aim of travelling in the upper class is merely getting comfort–Suppose one can't bear the heat in summer and Allah the Almighty has given him ample wealth–travelling in AC coach is neither a sin nor prodigality. Whereas if the aim of travelling in AC coach is that people will consider him a wealthy man then it is illegal, showing and prodigality. Same is the case of clothes and food etc.

## BE GENEROUS ACCORDING TO YOUR INCOME

The needs and income of each and every men are different from another so, the standard of generosity should also be different and in accordance with the income of a particular man. If the income of a man is less, then his wife must neither think of copying the wealthy families nor make a request of buying things seen in their house, it is illegal. But the husband should be generous according to his resources and should not show miserliness to his wife's needs.

## WHAT ARE THE RIGHTS OF WIVES ON US?

عن معاويه بن حيدة رضى اللّٰه عنه قال: قلت، يا رسول اللّٰه ماحق زوجة احدنا عليه ؟قال :أن تطعمها إذا طعمت وتكسوها إذا كسيت ولا تضرب الوجه ولا تقبح، ولا تهجر الا فى البيت

*Hazrat Muaviya bin Hida (mabawh) says, I asked the Prophet (pbuh), what are the rights of our wives on us? He (pbuh) replied, when you eat feed her also, when you wear dress her also, don't slap, don't reproach her and don't leave her but within the house.* (Abu Dawood,Kitabun-Nikah H.No.2142)

## LEAVE HER BED

As mentioned earlier also, if you see any indecency in your wife then first of all convince her, if she is not abstaining herself then leave her bed and start sleeping somewhere else. The detail of leaving her bed is given in this tradition, that is don't go out of the house rather stay in the home itself and change either the room or the bed to maintain separation as a protest and to teach her a lesson.

## SUCH SEPARATION IS NOT LEGAL

Some theologians have said, while giving the details of this very tradition, separate the bed but neither stop talking nor it should be such that no one is saluting the other and if there is any important work no one is talking. Such separation between husband and wife is illegal.

## PERMISSION OF WIFE FOR A JOURNEY OF MORE THAN 4 MONTHS

Due to this very tradition, the jurists have said that if a man is living out of his house for more than 4 months without his wife's permission and willingness , it his illegal. As Hazrat Umar (mabawh) had circulated this order, in his whole dominion that, the warriors who are living out of their houses should not be away from their houses for more than 4 months. The jurists further say, if someone wants to go on a journey for less than 4 months, need not to take wife's permission. Whereas, if he is to go for more than 4 months, he should take her permission howsoever much blessed the journey may be. Until, if he is going for Haj and can return within 4 months he does not need to take his wife's permission otherwise he is supposed to take her permission, same decree is for the journeys of *Tableegh* (propagational journeys) and religious wars also. When permission of wife is necessary for these blessed journeys then her permission is also must for those who go to foreign countries for employment. If they are going without their wives' permission it is their usurpation, illegal and a sinful act.

## WHAT IS THE PERMISSIBLE DURATION OF LIVING AWAY FROM HOME?

**Que:** We are here (foreign country) for one year but what is the permissible duration of living away from our wives in Islam?

**Ans:-** Hazrat Umar (mabawh) had given this order to the religious warriors that they should not be away from their houses for 4 months. The persons who go to foreign countries for employment and leave their wives in their home, do great injustice to them. Moreover some of them unjustly order their wives to serve their parents and family members. These poor women are afflicted with two folded torture–separation from husband and insulting behaviors of the family members–while some of them get married again in the foreign country….. which sometimes ruin the family. If they had to leave these poor women in the centre, why they had married them?

(Taken from Aapke Masail our unka hal 5/198)

# WHO ARE THE BEST PERSONS?

وعن أبى هريرة رضى الله عنه قال: قال رسول الله صلى الله عليه وسلم:
أكمل المومنين إيما ناً أحسنهم خلقًا ، و خيا ركم خياركم لأ هله

Hazrat Abu Huraira (mabawh) narrates that the Prophet (pbuh) has said, the perfect man among the believers in his belief is one who is best mannered among them– the person who is well mannered will also be full of faith, therefore the demand of complete belief is that man should deal others with good manners. While the best among you are those who are best for their wives and treat them kindly.

(Tirmizi Kitabur Razaa' H. No. 1162)

## TODAY'S ETIQUETTES

Nowadays the meaning of each and everything have changed rather have reversed. Qari Tayyab (Ra) used to say nowadays everything has reversed in comparison to older days, until in the older days there used to be darkness at the lamp's base while nowadays it is over the bulb, furthermore each and every thing has changed.

Even the meaning of morality has changed nowadays, it is confined to some outwardly gestures only. For example, meeting someone with a smiling face and uttering some customary words, such as "glad to meet you "please to meet you" etc. One is uttering these words while concealing enemity and jealousy in his innerself and today it is called etiquettes.

Today it has become a regular and separate art to behave people in such a way that they would become attached to them. While separate books are being written on this topic dealing with different ways of making someone attached to someone. Today full stress is being given to make someone attached and impressed and it is being called etiquettes.

Understand well! It doesn't have any connection with what our Prophet (pbuh) has said about manners. It is not only deceit, ostentation and affection rather it is an excuse of attaching others and being surrounded by others. It is love of self-dignity and fame which are in itself a sickness and immorality while etiquettes are not connected to these.

## ETIQUETTE IS THE NAME OF INMOST-CONDITION

In reality morality is the name of a person's inmost-condition, which is shown by the body-parts. That is one must have well-wishing and love for the whole creation of Allah, whether he is an enemy or even an infidel. While one must also think that these are the creations of my Cherisher so I am supposed to love them and behave with them in a good way. First of all this feeling crops up in the heart then actions are performed accordingly. The smile which comes with this feeling will neither be artificial nor one which make others attached to him rather it is the result of one's inner feeling and desire. So there is great difference between today's etiquettes and those described by the Prophet (pbuh).

## THE WAY OF OBTAINING GOOD MANNERS

Neither mere reading of reformative books nor listening to homilies is enough for one who wants to obtain good manners rather it needs accompaniment of a reformer (*MUSLIH*) or a patron (*MURABBI*). The main aim of spiritual guidance is to obtain accomplished manners and to get away from bad manners. Anyhow, the most accomplished believers are those who are good mannered. May Allah the Almighty make all of us from amongst these accomplished believers, Amen!

# DON'T BEAT THE MAIDS OF ALLAH

وعن أيا س بن عبد اللّٰه رضى اللّٰه عنه قال: قال رسول اللّٰه صلى اللّٰه عليه وسلم: لاتضربوا إماء اللّٰه، فجاء عمر إلى رسول اللّٰه صلى اللّٰه عليه وسلم، فقال: ذئرن النساء على أزواجهن الخ"

*Hazrat Ayas bin Abdullah (mabawh) narrates, that the Prophet (pbuh) said while addressing the people, don't beat the maids of Allah i.e beating woman is not good, don't beat them. Then after some days Hazrat Umar (mabawh) came to the Prophet (pbuh) and said, these women have become disobedient to their husbands.*

(Abu Dawood kitabun-nikah Hadeeth no 2146 and Mishkaat page 282)

When the Prophet (pbuh) has forbade this (beating women) whosoever heard this directly from the Prophet (pbuh) it becomes absolutely forbidden for him and beating them can not be legal for him in any condition.

## CONJECTURAL (*ZANNI*) OR ABSOLUTE (*QAT'I*) *HADEETH*

Understand well! One *Hadeeth* is that which we read in the books or listen from a religious scholar or reaches us alongwith a long chain of narrators such *Hadeeth* is called a Conjectural *Hadeeth*. So we should act accordingly otherwise we will be guilty. Whereas if any of the companions of the Prophet (pbuh) had heard anything directly from the Prophet (pbuh) it is Absolute *Hadeeth*. If some one is disobeying it, then not only he will be guilty but an infidel also as he has declined the saying of the Prophet (pbuh).

## ONLY THE COMPANIONS (MABAWT) HAD THE ABILITY FOR THIS

Sometimes there comes this silly idea in our mind, would that we were born in the time of the Prophet (pbuh) and got the blessings of that time. It is the policy and sagacity of Allah the Almighty that He created us in this age. If we were born in that period, who knows, of how lowest status we would have been. May Allah save us, Amen! As in that period, the faith was so sensitive that the human would turn topsy turvy in a matter of moments.

The devotion shown by the companions (mabawt) to the Prophet (pbuh), it was their capacity and due to this they attained this status. If a person who is lazy and peace-loving like us would have been in that period then who knows what would have happened to him. It is the grace and kindness of Allah the Almighty, that he had saved us from this and created us in a period when there are so many facilities for us. Today we say about a *Hadeeth* that it is Conjectural if anyone denies it he will not be an infidel rather he will be guilty only. Whereas in the time of the companions (mabawt), if any person refused any decree after listening it from the Prophet (pbuh) he would have become infidel at once. May Allah save all of us, Amen!

## THE WOMEN HAVE BECOME DISOBEDIENT

When the Prophet (pbuh) asked not to beat women, so beating came to an end. As the companions (mabawt) were not such who would continue any action despite listening its prohibition from the Prophet (pbuh). When beating women ceased completely then, after some days Hazrat Umar (mabah) came to the Prophet (pbuh) and said,

ذئرن النساء على أزواجهن

*O the Prophet of Allah! The women have become disobedient to their husbands.*

As you have prevented us of beating, no one is beating his wife while due to this the women have become disobedient, have started usurping the rights of their husbands and maltreating them. Now tell us what should we do?

فرخص في ضربهن

So, the Prophet (pbuh) said, if they usurp your rights and there is no way accept beating then you are permitted to beat them. A few days later following this permission, women started coming to the Prophet (pbuh) saying you have permitted the husbands to beat us and they have gained its benefits wrongly.

## THESE ARE NOT THE BEST PEOPLE

فقال رسول الله صلى الله عليه وسلم: لقد طاف بآل محمد نساء كثيرة يشكون ازواجهن ليس أولئک بخيارکم

*The Prophet (pbuh) said by taking his name that many women came to the house of Muhammad (pbuh) complaining their husband's maltreatment towords them–they beat them badly. So listen attentively the people who are beating their wives are not the best as beating is not connected to a wise muslim.* (Mishkaat page No. 282)

The Prophet (pbuh) clarified that in inevitable circumstances, while there is no way out, *Shari'at* permits such beating which does not leave a sear or vex. Inspite of this permission, the Prophet (pbuh) wants that no man would beat his wife and it is his *Sunnat* also. Hence the mothers of the believers (mabawt) tell that the Prophet (pbuh) never beat a woman, it is the demand of *Sunnat* also.

## RECOMMENDATION OF ALLAH FOR THE PEEVISH WOMEN

Men should consider that how beautifully Allah the Almighty has recommended the women;

فَعسیٰ اَنْ تَكْرَهُوا شَيْئاً وَّ يَجْعَلَ اللّٰهُ فِيْهِ خَيراً كَثِرًا

*It may be that you dislike a thing, and Allah brings about through it a great deal of good.* (Nisa-19)

**CLARIFICATION:-**

Just imagine! Allah the Almighty is ordering us to live with them on a footing of kindness and equity without any restriction either of age or circumstances i.e in young or old age. Whether she is beautiful or not, she brings dowry or not, her relative are influential or not then also she has reputation and right over her husband's income. ولهن مثل الذی علیهن i.e. the women have right over their husband as they have over them because they are made for each other and their nature is same as proclaimed by Allah Himself in these words; وَاللّٰهُ جَعَلَ لَكُمْ مِنْ اَنْفُسِكُمْ اَزْوَاجاً

*And Allah has made for you mates of your own nature* *(Nahl, 72)*

Created from your own nature means her nature is yours. If you seek gold and silver, she also seeks these. If you want rest and comfort then her body also gets fatigued. If you got angry, she is also sensitive. If you seek respect and dignity she also can't be agree for being disgraced and insulted and if you want to rule, she is also not born for slavery only.

In short, she will also feel like you hunger and thirst, heat and cold, harshness and politeness, grief and happiness as the nature of all human whether men or women, is one and they are breeded from only one pair.

Hazrat Qari Tayyab (Ra) used to say that the man should not be so adamant that he would get angry with even the smallest unmannerliness of women. One should not be so overawed for his wife that he would become a bug bear for her and she may lost her senses as soon as he enters the house, the poor fellow uttered some words or asked something and scolding started.

The poor fellow left her mother, father and all the family–now she is fully dependent on her husband–if the husband is not hers then whoever will be hers. Humanity demands that such a loyal human should not be troubled. If any unmannerliness or rudeness is shown by her, it should be considered their coquetry as they are foolish, mannerless and don't know how to talk so their style troubles men, whereas its main reason is coquetry. Ultimately to whom will they show coquetry other than their husbands as they both are made for each other.

## CURE OF WOMEN'S UNMANNERLINESS AND IGNORANCE

If ignorance and unmannerliness of women hurts and annoys then its cure is also possible. Instruct them through religious books, let them listen the homilies of different theologians and preceptors in veil, send them to educating and preaching circles regularly, read out any book of *Hadeeth* at home daily by fixing a time while all the family members would listen to it. By adopting these they will become mannered as religious education corrects human's morality and ethics.

## DON'T TEASE WOMEN AS FAR AS POSSIBLE

*Shari'at* has taught us to comfort the woman as far as possible, not to trouble her, give her maintenance within our capacity and try to please them. If wife commits a mistake in real, forgive her. If one is keeping patience on the afflictions caused by the wife his status will be upgraded, so we must keep patience and keep the promise of reward by Allah in our mind.

Muslim husbands should treat their wives according to the Prophet's (pbuh) *Sunnat* and live with them on a footing of kindness and equity. Specially a religious husband must not tease his wife, otherwise she might think that if she would have been married to an irreligious man this nibbling would not have been. Such a husband has filled hatred in a Muslim's heart against the religion.

Don't get angry if there is more chilly or salt is less

in curry or she had not prepared a sweet-dish as when you will reproach her due to a religious negligence she will not pay heed to your reproaching, thinking that it is your habit.

May Allah guide us to the right path, Amen!

# AN ADVICE TO THE PARENTS OF GROOM

Every Muslim should turn towards Allah in his distress and anxiety. He must also contact the divine theologians to know what Allah or the Prophet (pbuh) has said in a certain matter, after knowing the religious decree of a certain matter he must not use his wisdom or come under the influence of social compulsion.

Once Qari Tayyab (Ra) said, "it is correct that one should recognize Allah using his wisdom but to say that we will also recognize the religious decrees using our wisdom is not correct".

We want to draw your attention towards a very important matter (may Allah help us to convince you and help you to understand it well) that is "separation of the groom & his wife from the groom's parents" just after their marriage. Our society feels it very bad and most of the parents do not agree while the son, thinking it usurpation of parent's right also do not agree. If the son agrees then our society reproaches him, as if they (son and his wife) had committed a big sin by living separately. You would have considered that there are so many people committing different sins openly and the society is not considering these sins as sins. Just like this, there are so many legal things, which are considered bad by the society, if someone is doing any of these, he is taunted and reproached.

If you consider cool-mindedly you will conclude that, to consider living with parents as compulsory and living separately as bad, these ideas are completely absurd and foolish. In our opinion these absurd and foolish ideas have crept into our mind by living with Hindus for years. That's why Maulvi Shahabuddin Nadvi has written that, "in accordance with the Hindu rules, the concept of joint family had crept into Muslims. Whereas if the wife does not want to live with her in-laws then the husband must arrange to keep her separately according to *Shari'at*".

Dear readers! Allah the Almighty and His messenger (pbuh) has not prevented rather they have allowed it (the son should live with his wife separately from his parents). In reality the *Shari'at* has liked and tried that there may not be any dispute between mother and daughter-in-law, while the husband and wife could live peacefully and lovingly.

It is seen that there used to be disputes more often in the joint families as a result, the husband and wife may remain uneasy most of the times.

Therefore, parents must not obstruct their son and daughter-in-law, if they want to live separately in order to act upon what *Shari'at* has liked (so that there may not be any dispute). The parents should allow them happily rather persuade them to live separately though in a rented house.

While serving in *Daarul-Iftaa'* (office of *Mufti*) we have come across to so many incidents that we can say, it is better not only for the son to live with his wife separately but for their families also and it is showing mercy to the son and favor to the daughter-in-law.

Hazrat Thanvi (Ra) has said on the topic;

a) In my opinion it is more suitable for the son and parents to live separately after the son's marriage.

(A gift for Muslim couple P.No.18)

b) If parents are preventing from living separately and wife is asking for it then the wife's demand will be accepted, as a Hadeeth says

لاطاعة لمخلوق فى معصية الخالق

While obeying the creator (Allah) one should not accept the creation's (man's) saying–though they are parents. Giving separate accommodation to wife is obligatory whenever she asks for it, otherwise it is a sin. If the parents are not accepting this demand, their decree won't be accepted.

(A Gift for Muslim couple P.No, 30)

c) In another place he says, nowadays it is better that the sons and the parents would live separately as there is relief in it for both the parties.

( Da'waat-e-Abdiyat 14/84 & Husnul-Azeez 2/359)

d) A person came to Hazrat Thanvi (Ra) to take an amulet as his daughter-in-law was disobedient. Hazrat said its amulet is that shift her alongwith her husband to a new house, she will become much obedient.

(A Gift for Muslim Couple P.18)

It is seen that the daughters-in-law love simple food with her husband more than the chicken and *Biryani* of the in-laws' house.

e) Hazrat Thanvi (Ra) once said, some people do not

live apart from their parents fearing disreputation and suffer the whole life by living with them. Comfort and reputation are two different things, but comfort is more essential than reputation. So, in this era one should live apart from parents after getting married and serve his parents as much as he can from his earnings.

## IT IS CRUELTY NOT TO ALLOW SON AND DAUGHTER-IN-LAW LIVE SEPARATELY

Once Hazrat said, one cruelty done to the daughter-in-law–many claimant of piety are involved in it–is that, if daughter-in-law wants to live separately along with her husband then she is not allowed saying it will take away the blessings of the house. The old women thinks like this only. Remember! Don't obey any while disobeying Allah the Almighty. By cooking in one pot, blessings will certainly come but hatred, jealousy, grudging and back-biting will also come into the house due to disputes between family members and it will keep the house away from the divine favor of Allah ........

If daughter-in-law wants to live separately with her husband it is her right and necessary rather this is the best way in this era because disputes occur while living jointly as most of these old women harrass their daughters-in-law.

These are the sayings of Hazrat Thanvi (Ra) who was well aware of the Qur'an and *Hadeeth* while he also has spent many years in the service and spreading of Islam. If you want that your son would love his wife, there would not be any disputes between them, the daughter-in-law would not stay at her parent's home, the son won't think to divorce his wife, there remain love & affection between you and your son and despite living separately they would serve you then its only solution, according to Hazrat Thanvi (Ra), is to allow them live separately.

Most of the time, the reason of not keeping them separately is that the parents think that she should serve us as we have brought up our son and now, we are old enough, should we not eat the food prepared by our daughter-in-law?

**The first Answer**

The first answer for the groom's father of this question is that when there will be disputes all through the day then your son and daughter-in-law can't live peacefully. When you will come back from your work, you won't get food first rather you will find your wife distressed and dejected and she will tell you replying to your querry;

The new bride has said this.........

She taunted me like this.............

She told her family members such and such ......

She treated my daughter like this ..............

After listening to your wife, you yourself will become dejected and distressed. So the best solution to avert your embarrassments is to keep the son and daughter-in-law away from you from the first night of marriage itself.

**The second Answer**

*Shari'at-e-Islami* has called it good manners and etiquettes if daughter-in-law is serving her parents-in-law but has not called it as obligatory or her duty while serving younger or elder brother is completely improper as there is every possibility of unveiling. When it is not her duty and are taking her service forcefully with this view only, this is the basis of disputes and the beginning of cruelty.

Remember! The women who has come after the marriage of your son is for her husband only. With lots of excuses we are saying that she has not come as a maid or a maid-servant.

The father has handed over his own daughter to your son, so that she may live with him as his wife, be pleased with him, serve him and be blessed with flower-like children otherwise her own old parents were more deserving of her services, from which you want to take benefit. The parent's of your daughter-in-law have married her with your son so that they (husband & wife) may pass their lives happily and peacefully while preparing themselves for the Hereafter.

Just consider yourself! Many husbands have told us that they took the supper with their wives only on the night of marriage and took the breakfast the day after, otherwise she is supposed to take her food with our mother, sisters and brothers' wives while we are supposed to take food with our father and brothers.

Do justice yourself! Though they are living their lives but is it a purposeful life or not, which is void of mutual love, affection, sympathy and harmony. They did not get the real peace of mind as they are passing their lives being separated from one another and could not know the mood of another, though they are living in a single house which results in mental and psychological disturbances for both of them.

The sole reason of this is that, she was supposed to be in the kitchen after a few days of her marriage, as soon as she got up in the morning if she becomes even a little late then elder or younger brother's wives would complain to their husbands and mother-in-law while husband's sisters to brother and mother-in-law to father-in-law....... the sun has risen and she is still sleeping, the van of husband's younger sister has come and her clothes are still not ironed.

Some husbands have told us that when they were going to their work, their wives were in the kitchen and when they came back in the night, they found them sleeping being tired of the works. Is this a life that the day would start with the breakfast after the *Fajr* prayers and the public-kitchen remain working till 11 O'clock in the night. Care is neither given to obligatory prayers nor to mid-morning prayer, nor to dawn prayer, nor to bring the local women to religionsness nor to be present in religious educational circles nor to free times for telling beads (Tasbeeh). Now you yourself decide the actual position of your daughter-in-law, who was a source of comfort and affection at the time of bewilderment for her husband but she fell asleep, thinking the comfort with which she passed her life in her parent's home being tired of workload of the in-law's house.

It is just like that there was a vacancy of a maid-servant in your home which she had filled up and after the completion of her duty she is slept. Then what is the use of the expenses you have done at her *Waleema* by preparing several varieties of food. Have you done all these for your own son, who would come in the night tired of the work to see that the wife , who would have received him with smiling face and some sweet words, is sleeping due to tiredness by being busy the whole day……where has gone the comfort and peace of your son?

What about that *Waleema*…? What about the sentence of the invitation card… our son and daughter of so and so are going to marry, beginning a new chapter of their lives…….

The "maid", who would have given your tired son a glass of cold water when he would enter the house, is sleeping after doing a full day's duty and listening unpalatable taunts or may be she would have slept waiting for her real master–husband, now who will ask your son for a glass of water and to warm the food……….?

Remember! If this husband is religious-thinking and caring for Allah's decrees then he will be choked thinking deprivations meted out to him by the destiny as he neither can say anything to his parents out of regards nor he can show anger to his wife due to his meekness and natural kindness. These inner thinkings, irregularities of unsystematic life can lead him to any nervous ailments, ulcer, cancer or bewilderment and his inner abilities will be ruined instead of being utilized.

Its other side is more dangerous and that is suppose, the son is non-pious and far from religion, associated with bad persons and does not give importance to safeguard his eyes, chastity and continence. Understand well, as is said regarding small children not to object them on each and every matter… not to rebuke them without any reason …. otherwise being fed up of this regular babblement and being deprived of parents' love and affection, they fell pray into the hands of lascivious people. Just like this when this very your son–the new groom–will be at a distance from his wife, will not get her love then why will the Satan not incite him–hungry of love towards either the office secretary or the sales-girl of a shopping centre or a model of an advertising company. If he fell into the traps of any Satan, then you yourself are beaten.

That is in such a way that one who has come in the name of the son to fulfil his longing and comfort him, this is not accomplished. Now being fed up with the coldness and peevishness of the tired wife, he fell in love with someone else….. As such an affair could not be concealed, the wife also got wind of it and she went to live with her parents … Everyone will talk about the house being ruined and they will say, who knows how tyrant her parents-in-law are that she went to live with her parents. Whereas her husband usually remain out of house the whole day. Understand well, these are neither suppositions nor touching idioms rather these are reality as many houses are being ruined due to these.

Therefore you are meekly requested that it will be better, safer and more advantageous to keep your son and his wife away from you so that she may get time to serve her husband, be ready to welcome, when he comes back in the evening after finishing all the necessary works and cleansing the children and would gift to you whatever she had cooked for her husband by adding some of your favourite things, whenever they (husband and wife) came to meet you. When the Prophet (pbuh) had persuaded us to increase the curry so as to give it to our neighbours, then how much rewarding would be such favour and pleasing behaviour shown by her to her parents-in-law. Mother-in-law will also become happy, give blessings, take care of her reputation herself. While the daughter-in-law, who is getting her mother-in-law's blessings, will mention her in a better way in her parent's house.

In comparison to this, we see and hear that though, the daughter-in-law become tired of cooking and serving her in-laws' family, her numerous flaws are being counted.

Therefore the best way of avoiding the disputes and establishing peace and tranquillity is that the son and his wife should live away from his parents............

As for the grand parents who want that there should be someone to accompany us in our old age and the house should be full of activities by the presence of paternal-grand-sons and daughters, one can keep a son and his wife whose disposition matches with that of his own and specially the disposition of daughter-in-law should match with that of mother-in-law, if there are more than one married sons. For example, Zaid has two married sons, namely Adnan and Salman. Adnan's disposition matches with that of Zaid's while the disposition of Salman's wife matches with that of Zaid's wife, then Zaid should keep Salman's family with him.

Take care of one more thing while keeping a son and his wife with you, that their room and kitchen should be separate if the house is big and she should feed her parents-in-law by cooking in that kitchen only to avoid the disputes of pots and stoves. If the kitchen could not be separated then we only can request the mother-in-law to keep patience and praying. While she also should not try to interfere in the matter or actions of daughter-in-law, that's too if she is not considering her rebuke or warning as that of her own mother's. Whereas the daughter-in-law must consider her mother-in-law as her own mother, similarly mother-in-law must consider her as her own danghter and not as her son's wife.

## DON'T KEEP TWO DAUGHTERS-IN-LAW TOGETHER AS FAR AS POSSIBLE

If you want to keep a son with you after his marriage as a measure of expediency and you already have one daughter-in-law in your house, then please arrange separate kitchens for the two. If possible, keep them maintaining a respectable distance. If inspite of controlling prodigality at the time of marriage you can't provide separate houses to the two, then keep one of them with you and arrange separate enterence and kitchen for the other, as the religious preceptor have said;

The best way of avoiding domestic disputes is that many families should not live in one house as presence of many women in a house motivates disputes.

(Malfoozat-e-Ashrafia P.27)

Remember! In some cases residing with mother-in-law is not as harmful as residing with husband's other brother's wives. Due to lack of religious atmosphere in the house, these poor fellows remain confused themselves and confuse other also.

For example, on a certain day the younger daughter-in-law prepared the food which was liked by the whole family and the elder daughter-in-law is abased and disdained. Now this lady, after listening her own abasement and disdain, either becomes restless or tries to vilify her calumniously.

If they are having good relations then mother-in-law and husband's sister think that these two are preparing a front against us. Whereas, if any of these two is having good relations with the mother-in-law, then the other thinks that they are preparing a front against her.

If, luckily both of them are saved from this then either their mother or house-maid will try to create disturbances between them by carrying different tales. May Allah save all Muslim families from these spiritual ailments, Amen !

Therefore, the best way is that they should meet each other again and again. May Allah give common sense to men so that they would keep woman as much busy in religious works as possible. So that they could not find time for irrelevant talks. They should take them in preaching delegations (*Tableeghi Jama'at*) from time to time and keep different religious books, in the house, so that they and their children would read these books. In this way our house will become a luminous spot, an exhilarating plot and a sample of heaven.

## IS THIS BETTER.............?

Is this better.... that there is a big bungalow or a big flat, in which three or four brothers are residing and sharing a single pot for cooking but all are malicious and engaged in back-biting of each other, the future of children and family is being ruined.... Or this is better that, every brother would live alongwith his family separately in accordance with his capacity but there is love, affection, intimacy and attachment among all the brothers, younger brothers are respecting their elders. On weekends they are arranging a get-together, sharing each other's pleasure and sorrows and praying for each other's prosperity. Their children are also showing love to their paternal cousins as they show to their maternal cousins. Now decision is yours and remember, when there is grudging, back-biting and enmity in between real brothers and sisters it will definitely run through the next generation.Therefore, please don't keep them together, as asking them not to quarrel or back-bite after keeping them together is just like asking a man not to wet his feet who is walking in the river.

If you don't believe then check yourself, nowadays generally neither daughter-in-law considers her mother-in-law as her own mother nor mother-in-law considers her daughter-in-law as her own daughter. We have seen so many houses in which the daughter-in-law is mother-in-law's real niece i.e. the mother-in-law is either her real paternal or maternal aunt, despite their relation, they quarrel on minor issues and ruin the peace of husband and wife.

Thousands of young women are living a restless life whose mothers-in-law are either their maternal or paternal aunts while the main reason of quarrels between them is telephone, the mother-in-law say, you call your mother too much that's why excess bills are coming, whereas this mother is either her own brother's wife or own sister. Sometimes they say the flour finishes speedily as you make more breads. On the other side, the husband says, I can't prevent my employee from calling in the office and my mother querrels with my wife, who is her neice also due to one call, my driver uses Air-condition whenever he drives the car while my mother raises tumult on making 2 extra breads.

Now do justice yourself! if you want that your son and daughter-in-law would live happily and be successful in the Hereafter also then it is better to keep them in separation from the first day itself.

Have you ever considered that your smaller grand children would see their grandmother and paternal aunts as cruel ones due to their frequent fighting with their mother and the resultant discord, unpleasantness and strained relations of husband and wife. Moreover they will become cowardice, frightened, liar, unadventurous and unambitious seeing the daily quarrels in the house while these bed qualities will remain in them forever.

These would-be-intelligent children pass their lives cowardly, restlessly and being afraid because they were not having confidence in their parents as children, they won't depend upon anyone in their whole life thinking when our own have not dealt with us properly then how can we expect for the better from strangers.

**SECOND HARM**

These daily discords between husband's younger or elder brothers' wives, disagreement between daughter and mother-in-law, complaints of husband's sister and daughter-in-law, turn the 25 years old lady into a 40 years old one. Thinking all these she becomes afflicted with several ailments such as heart problem, back-ache, headache and gastro problems etc. Thus this new bride becomes old before senility and the sinless children are not only deprived of motherly love but they have to bear her anger also. Sometimes, she vent her spleen on these children, reproach them, curse them and these very curses ruin the children's worldly and next world's affairs if it was the time of acceptance.

**WHY ALL THIS HAPPENED?**

All this happened because, you compelled your son to live with you against the teachings of Islamic *Shari'at* or you had not allowed him to save money as by living separately expenses might increase. While the child being deprived of motherly love becomes a thief or robber after being a vagabond.

**THIRD HARM**

If you are keeping the new bride with you while younger sons are also living with you, whereas generally husband's younger brothers don't hide themselves from elder brother's wife. As whole family lives and eats together so there will be the sin of unveiling also.

Once the Prophet (pbuh) has said that husband's younger brother is like death for a woman, which means, a woman must save herself from meeting him unvieled or joking with him as she saves herself from death. By living separately, the veiling will be taken care of and all will be saved from this sin. If due to piety, the groom avoids TV & VCR but by living jointly his wife and children can't be saved.

Briefly, as much you would consider this issue its vice will become clearer for you. If you would consider it positively you will get lots of religious and worldly advantages in keeping the son and his wife separately. Moreover you will find comfort for you and the whole family.

**FOURTH HARM**

As the number of families living with you increases, the anxieties for you and your wife will also increase. You have to be anxious about their ailments, deliveries of children etc. If the number of families will be lesser then your anxieties will also be lesser and you will feel comfortable.

In our opinion, if your are capable of giving a separate house or setting separate business for each of your sons as soon as they attain puberty, then you must arrange these. As much the distance will be between them as much they will love each other. If you are incapable then try fully that they would live comfortably and do not interfere in others' matters.

We are quoting a question and its answer from "Aapke Masaa'il Aur Unka Hal" by Maulvi Mohd. Yousuf Ludhianvi for the parents of the groom, so that they may consider seriously the need of keeping the son and his wife away from him. Therefore, read this excrept attentively cool-headedly praying Allah that He may help us acting upon this, Amen!

## A NUISANCE FOR YOU AND YOUR HUSBAND

**Que:** I have been married since 2 ½ year and there is regular discord between me and my-in-laws, until there is conflict between my husband and his parents. They have never treated me lovingly even they treat my daughter harshly and taunt me even on minor issues. They do business with us, while my husband does all the hard work. Praise be to Allah, there is abundance of subsistence in our business. During these 2 ½ years, I had lived with my parents many a times, everytime they promised not to repeat this, just to bring me back. Having regard for the elders and acting upon the advice of the parents, I would return to my in-laws' house seeking their pardon. For sometime, all would remain right then again same situation arises. At present I am living at my mother's house with my husband after a minor dispute between him and his father. Both of us want to take a separate house under the aegis of our parents without being separated from business so that we would remain in their service also. They are calling us again with same previous promise, nothing will happen now. Just tell me, when there will be conflicts in the house every now and then, how will there be abundance of subsistence? Please advice us, should we take a separate house, Allah will reward you for this, I will pray for you all through my life, I am extremely sorrowful.

**Ans:** I read your letter with due consideration. The conflict between mother and daughter-in-law has always been a confusing one. While it is experienced that usually both are at fault. The mother-in-law generally criticizes quite mean issues of her daughter-in-law and frown upon her.... While daughter-in-law who is tenderly nurtured at her home in genral, considers the kindly advices of her mother-in-law as her insult.......and this two-sided touchiness becomes a permanent court of conflict.

The solution of your matter is that, if you can bear each and every sayings or actions and touchiness of your mother-in-law cheerfully without uttering a faint cry then you must go back to her, whereas this will be your obedience and good fortune in this world and the Hereafter. If you are serving your husband's aged parents with such courage, guts and keeping patience then your future will become enviable while everyone will see its blessings clearly.

If you don't have so much of courage and guts then you should live with your husband in a separate house but your intention should not be to snap the ties with your husband's parents rather it should be;

To be saved from the annoyance and rudeness the parents were facing by our living with them. In short, you should be separated considering yourself at fault and not your husband's parents' fault.

While after separation one should consider serving them financially and physically his good fortune. It is not suitable to live with your husband in your parents' house as it is a disgrace of your husband's parents, while there is no harm in getting their help to arrange a separate house or business. I have given all the possible solutions of your embarrassment.

You can choose any of these according to your situation. If your husband becomes displeased, aggrieved and disgusted from his parents then both of you might face its nuisance.

Therefore you must try that the relations of your husband with his parents should be pleasant and he should be obedient to them, as obeying and serving parents is the key of success in the world and the Hereafter.

## MEANING OF GIVING SEPARATE HOUSE TO SON AND ITS EASY WAY

If someone is unable to arrange a separate house for his son and daughter-in-law, then either;

1) He should give them a closet in his house where they could lock their belongings, talk freely and relax in

solitude. Arranging this much is enough to discharge what is obligatory for him. (Separate kitchen though smaller in size is necessary as most of the quarrels start from here only). (Islah-e-Inqilab-e-Unmat 2/184)

2) One can arrange for rented accommodation by minimizing the expenses done at the time of marriage.

While marrying one should have the intention of safeguarding chastity, discharging the *Sunnat* of the Prophet (pbuh) and must believe in the promise of Allah;

إِنْ يَّكُونُوا فُقَرَآءَ يُغْنِهِمُ اللّٰهُ مِنْ فَضْلِهِ

*If they are in poverty, Allah will give them means out of His Grace.* (Nur, 32)

In short, neither refrain from marrying for being wealthy nor think that after the marriage expenses will increase as a wealthy person can also become an indigent or poor after the marriage. Because the real sustainer is Allah Himself, He can turn a wealthy person into an indigent and He only can take out a poor man from his indigence and poverty after his marriage.

Just imagine, that there is less dowry in a simple house for example it has neither a carpet nor a magnificent refrigerator nor costly couches nor sofas but there is love between husband, wife and the groom's mother, sister and elder brothers' wives are also being respected. The husband and wife are serving the parents as much as they can. If the house of the mother-in-law is nearer and the daughter-in-law is sending whatever she is cooking daily. This is a better house or the house where three married brothers are living and cooking together but each of them is hurting other's feelings whilst quarrels, jealousy and the greed among them are increasing day by day. When the brothers return from work their wives are sowing the seeds of enmity in between them (the real brothers) through back-biting and tale-bearing. The son or the brother is being kept away from parents or sisters and brothers. Then wife is asking either *Khula'* or divorce. The groom's mother is going to charmers to bring amulets for him. The groom is visiting either the different religious institutes to consult the *Muftis* of its *Daarul-iftaa* or the preceptors of religious monasteries or the heads of *Tableegh* movement or the psychologists. While the father of the bride is cursing after each prayer and her mother is proclaimimg thus the vices of the groom's parents with garbling in her kith and kin. If some tears of the woman are mixed with these saying then even the cruelest judge or the *Panchayat* chairman might decide in their favor kind heartedly though they may be far from truth.

## AT LEAST KITCHEN MUST BE SEPARATE

Therefore Hazrat Thanvi (Ra) has said, at least kitchen must be separate as most of the quearrels start from here only. Some people think that neither every man is capable of living separately nor their father can arrange for it just after the marriage. The simplest solution of it, is to take a house on rent or to separate just the kitchen only in the same house. Moreover he has said, the demand of today's human nature and circumstances is that, if a woman wants to live together and all the relative also wants her to live together then also as a matter of expediency she should be kept separately as there is a remedy and prevention for thousands of flaws and evils in it. For some days, the relatives will express their disgust, anger and reproach by saying, see this women, she could neither control her first daughter-in-law nor feed her. See the daughter of so and so, she could not live with her mother-in-law–How she will live with hers?

Her mother has not served her mother-in-law, how she will serve, her whole family is like this. But when they will see the benefits of living separately they will become happy. (Islah-e-Inqib-e-Ummat 2/188)

This is what we see daily in the *Darul-Iftaa*, we have came into contact with so many such people whose well settled houses have been ruined due to internal conflicts. Now the worldly as well religious matters of both the families are ruined as neither they might concentrate on prayers nor on business.

When the man become fed up with these daily quarrels, Allah forbid, by mistake he utters the word of *Talaaq* which is the worst word near Allah. The wife who is considered of unsound mind says, it is better to support myself by working in different houses and bring up the children by stitching clothes than to undergo troubles in the house and I could not live with a husband like you, your brother, sisters or mother. As a result the house breaks up and the innocents saplings of this society are deprived of either maternal or paternal love to become vagabond, enamoured of hotels and clubs, as a result not only their worldly affair but their Hereafter are also ruined by entangling themselves in fun and useless hobbies.

Now decide yourself which one is better of these two lives?–Whether, the one in which the house is well-furnished and all are living together but peace of mind and tranquillity are not there, or the one in which all are living separately and their houses are not well-furnished but peace of mind, mutual love and tranquillity are there .

We have described here for you the two lives, the tenor of *Shari'at-e-Islami,* their result and the *Fatwa* (verdict) of Hazrat Thanvi (Ra). Now choose yourself whichever you think is the best. For more details, please refer to "A Gift for Muslim Woman", "A Gift for Muslim Couple" etc.

In reality, the people consider any new thing in the society a sin, if someone is living separately after his marriage, he is considered a guilty and disobedient to his parents. Whereas it is neither bad according to *Shari'at* nor usurpation of their rights. On the contrary if there is loss of religion or risk of children & wife's religion or their morality is being ruined due to TV or unveiling and there are chances of disputes and abomination in between husband and wife, then one should live separately and one should deem it religion, moreover parents can be obeyed and loved by living separately in such situation. Since every parent want that their son and daughter-in-law may live loving each other and peacefully. If they knew that it is the tenor of *Shari'at* and only in it there is beneficence of this world and the Hereafter for them, then they might allow them with pleasure. Unfortunately, it is considered a sin in our society, howsoever much divorces may occur, houses or the lives of youth may be ruined, differences or quarrels may happen between brothers and sisters but our society boasts of cooking and eating together.

For Allah's sake, change this mode of life don't consider an issue bad which is not bad in the *Shari'at* don't restrict anything if *Shari'at* had allowed it and the son wants to live separately, let him live.

Its foremost example is seen in the Mammen Bantwa fraternity, that the parents of the girls used to give a cash turban of 1 or 2 lac Rupees to the groom, inspite of this there were so much of conflicts that they could not get respite from deciding these. Then they decided to give a furnished house to the girl instead of cash, so that she may live with her husband separately just after the marriage. The conflicts of mother-in-law and groom's sister ended with this, consequently, number of divorces started decreasing and the conflicts of many houses came to an end.

## PIETY OF WIFE

It is the dutifulness, obedience and good fortune of a daughter-in-law, if she is serving her parents-in-law, cooking food for them and considering them as her own parents. If the parents-in-law are old, weak, sick and need to be served–which is their son's responsibility, either to serve himself or to engage someone else (within the limits of *Shari'at*) if she is helping her husband, it is her morality and she will get its best reward in both the worlds.

If she is tolerating the taunts of her in-laws and forgiving them for the sake of Allah, she is indulging herself in getting their blessings all the time, then *InshaAllah*, she will also get a serving daughter-in-law. Allah knows, by the grace of whosoever's blessings she or her children may see lots of happiness in both the worlds or a saint is born to her.

If the daughter-in-law is having a small child then she is supposed to wake up for that child in the night whether it is winter or summer, she is sick or healthy, she is willing or not, in the same way if she is waking up for her mother-in-law, she must consider it as her good fortune because, Allah has shown His favor by giving her an opportunity to serve and please someone. If Allah is also pleased with this service then wonderful! It is said that, "through worship one gets heaven and through service one gets Allah".

## APPRECIATE THE SERVICES OF DAUGHTER-IN-LAW

At the same time, the parents-in-law and the husband should consider her services as her good manners and etiquettes because it is neither an obligation nor a duty of her. Therefore they should appreciate her services and try to give her its best reward.

As generally we are not understanding these rights & issues, many houses are being deserted. The disputes of mother and daughter-in-law as well as disputes of husband's sisters and brothers' wives have deserted many houses. Its main reason is that none is keeping in his mind the definitions of different rights as told by our Prophet (pbuh).

If anyone does not believe this, he must ponder over the reasons of divorces, incidents of *Khul'as* and separation between the husband and wife, he will find that in most of the cases these are due to either the disputes of mother and daughter-in-law or the disputes of husband's sisters and their brothers' wives only. These disputes lead to separation of husband and wife and to some perilous diseases–may Allah save all Muslim men and women from this, Amen!

# AIM OF WIFE

Allah the Almighty has described the aim of creating women (wife) in these words;

وَمِنْ اٰيَاتِهٖ اَنْ خَلَقَ لَكُمْ مِنْ اَنْفُسِكُمْ اَزْوَاجًا لِّتَسْكُنُوْا اِلَيْهَا وَجَعَلَ
بَيْنَكُمْ مَّوَدَّةً وَّرَحْمَةً ؕ اِنَّ فِيْ ذٰلِكَ لَاٰيٰتٍ لِّقَوْمٍ يَّتَفَكَّرُوْنَ

*And among His signs is this, that He created for you mates from among yourselves, that you may dwell in tranquillity with them–and He has put love and mercy between your (hearts): verily in that are signs for those who reflect.* (Rum-21)

Mufti Mohd. Shafi (Ra) said while commenting on this verse, the meaning of لِتَسْكُنُوْا اِلَيْهَا that you may get tranquillity by meeting them–if one considers the man's all requisites attached to women, he will find it is mere tranquillity, comfort and peace of mind. The Holy Qur'an has covered all these in a single word.

Thus, we came to know that the sole purpose of married life is tranquillity and peace of mind, if these are found in a house then the purpose is fulfilled otherwise, it (the purpose) is not fulfilled. It is also clear that peace of mind depends on good relation and understanding between husband and wife.

## AIM OF MARITAL LIFE IS TRANQUILLITY

This verse has fixed tranquillity as the aim of marital life of a woman and a man. It is possible only when both of them have the knowledge of their rights and both are fulfilling these otherwise disputes will destroy this tranquillity. One way of doing full justice to these rights was that certain rules and regulations would have been given as is done regarding other person's rights by making usurpation of the rights unlawful, proclaiming drastic threats, fixing chastisement and advising the selflessness and sympathy. But it is experienced that a nation could not be brought to moderation merely by rules without combining it with Allah's fear. That's why Allah has used the words اِتَّقُوااللّٰہَ and وَاخْشَوْا in the Holy Qur'an while describing the social matters.

The mutual affair of men and women are such that neither any rule can control nor any court can do justice in fulfilling these mutual rights. Therefore the Prophet (pbuh) has selected the verses which had persuasion to fear from Allah, the Hereafter and to be pious in the sermon of *Nikah* as only these can stand surety for the fulfillment of these mutual rights.

Moreover Allah has not only encircled these mutual rights in *Shari'at* but has made it natural and sensual. As Allah has put natural love in the hearts of parents for their children and they are supposed to love them and vice-versa, in the same way He has done in the case of husband and wife also. Therefore He has said, وَجَعَلَ بَيْنَكُمْ مَوَدَّةً وَّ رَحْمَةً which means that He has put not only the *Shar'ai* or legal relations in them but has transfixed love and mercy in their hearts also.

After this He said, اِنَّ فِیْ ذٰلِکَ لَاٰیٰتٍ لِّقَوْمٍ یَّتَفَکَّرُوْنَ which means there are many Signs in it for those who reflect. In this verse only one Sign is mentioned, while in the end He has said Signs. Its reason is that when one ponder over the marital relations, mentioned in this verse, he finds its different worldly and religious benefits, hence its is not a Sign but Signs. (Ma'aariful-Qur'an 6/736)

**Clarification :**

After reading the commentary of the aforesaid verse, you might have understood that the sole aim of wife's creation is that her husband might get mental and physical satisfaction from her. If you think that your daughter-in-law, while living in a house alongwith husband's sisters his elder and younger brother's wives i.e. living in such an environment where there are daily disputes, tribulation and taunting still she can whole-heartedly give love, affection, peace of mind, physical comfort and tranquillity to her husband then keep your son and his wife with you.

If this can't happen–as far as we think–the daughter-in-law can be in constant relations with her mother-in-law, as in some houses they live like mother and daughter. But the aim of wife, as told by the Qur'an, is lost if she is living with her husband's sister and elder or younger brothers' wives and become a reason of embarrassment. An embarrassed person can't be a source of tranquillity for others. Therefore it is upto you to choose cool-mindedly the best way, keeping in view your tranquillity and that of your son and daughter-in-law. May Allah help us to decide properly and to act upon it, Amen !

Now, for further clarification of this issue we are quoting some questions and their answers by Maulvi Mohd.

Yousuf Ludhianvi, published in the daily jung's columns "Aap ke Masaa'il Aur Unka Hal", hoping that the parents of the groom will take positive step, after reading this Questionnaire so as to check the internal disputes and make the environment of the house pleasant, while the son and his wife can pass their life with tranquillity and prepare themselves for the Hereafter.

## DEMAND FOR SEPARATE HOUSE BY THE WIFE

**Que 1)** How should a husband support his wife while he is not leaving any stone unturned in fooding and clothing. Moreover he is keeping aside all the money for their personal use and saying, whenever you are in need you can use this money.

**Ans:** Maintenance of wife is the responsibility of the husband and according to your question he is fulfilling it. What is the complaint of the wife then?

**Que 2)** Can a wife press down her husband for a separate house, while he is not capable of doing so, as he is still a student and saying have patience, after sometime all will be done. Is it necessary to give her separate house in this situation? Whereas if he is to arrange it, he will have to take a loan.

**Ans:** It is the bone of contention that the wife can't live with her mother-in-law and wants a separate house. It is the responsibility of the husband to settle her in such a place where no one can interfere in her matters. If he can't settle her in a separate house then a portion of that very house should be specified for her–where she can cook, eat and live without anyone's interference.

In short, this is a proper demand of the wife that her kitchen should be separate and there should not be anyone's interference in her residence, but this very her demand depend on husband's capacity. If he is unable then she can't demand a separate house.

**Que 3):** How a woman would respect her parents-in-law, please reply in the light the Qur'an and the *Ahadeeth*, while the mother-in-law is even pointing out to food cooked by her or the clothes washed by her, can she quarrel with her?

**Ans**: Her parents-in-law are just like her own parents, it is her moral responsibility to respect them as she respects her own, rather she should give them more respect than her own and they are also supposed to dignify her more than their own daughter. But Alas! it so happen that, neither they dignify her like their own daughter nor she considers them as her own parents. In this the mother of the bride and her mother-in-law are more at fault than the bride as due to mother's training and mother-in-law's surliness, the bride considers her mother-in-law a witch and her new house a hell. She does not find love and affection in her new house rather she finds abomination, surliness and taunts. It seems to her that she is taken out of heaven and put in the hell, at last she revolts against her mother-in-law and demands for a separate house.

The solution of their quarrel is that they must not be kept together and their kitchen should be separate. If the parents of the husband, specially his mother, are skilful they can easily and cheerfully take as much her services as they want, it is her good fortune and sign of their high morality. Whereas considering her a bond-maid and asking her to serve with the help of a stick is neither lawful in the *Shari'at* nor it is morally proper.

**Que 4)** Can a wife tell her husband while she is in her parent's house, first purchase a house–but he is unable–then only take me with you.

**Ans:** The demand of purchasing a house is wrong rather her demand of a separate kitchen and a hut void of anyone's interference is proper.

**Que 5)** Can a wife be impudent to her husband, in the light of these questions what should be the husband's way of treating his wife and is it necessary for a husband to take his wife to her parent's house once monthly.

**Ans:** Impudency is such a blemish of women which ruins all her memorable deeds and virtues. If a woman makes her main aim to serve and please her husband and keeps patience on some hardships then Allah opens the door of His blessings for her in both the worlds, whereas an egoist and stubborn woman who is impudenting before her husband ruins her both the worlds. Modern education has taken away the quality of having patience and confrontation of hardships to please Allah from the girls–therefore impudency is not considered a blemish–as a result the houses are not the sample of heaven.

**Que 6):** Is it legal or not in accordance with the *Shari'at,* that the groom's family would ask girl's family for the house etc.?

**Ans:** Asking anything from the girl's family is not legal according to the *Shari'at* .

**Que 7:** Is it right for a groom to live in the bride's house (given by her parents)?

**Ans:**If the parents of the bride had given a house to her (in her name) then she is the owner, if she allows its OK. But, if it is in the name of the groom on his demand, then it is oppression and living in it is illegal, rather it should be returned to the parents of the bride.

## A THINKING MOMENT

The environment of the in-laws' house for a new bride becomes heinous and dispersed if she is living with her husband's sisters and younger or elder brothers' wives, their predominance and controlling is understandable but being constant in relations with them is not easy, while their meddling with husband and wife proves to be dangerous in general. Due to this misconception and way of living thousands of families are being ruined.

When the mother brings her daughter-in-law after marrying her son.......she has many strange expectations which are ridiculously childish and foolish, whereas if the daughter-in-law had to deal with her husband's sisters also then a war front becomes ready, the daughters-in-law who are well-mannered, self-sacrificing, intelligent, sociable and sympathetic pass their life happily but this happens rarely.

Some wives, after being fed up of the curses by their mother-in-law, the taunts of husband's mischievous sisters and mischief-making of husband's elder or younger brothers' wives and maids, choose the only way that is they start controlling their husbands completely to make their lives peaceful and to save their children and themselves from such environments. While the husband who is your son is being crushed in between two millstones (on one hand he has his own mother, sisters and brothers' wives while on the other hand he has his own life-partner).

An unfortunate daughter-in-law, who could neither control her husband nor his family, goes to her paternal house time and again to find succor there.

All these disputes or ravages are in vogue in our society because each of us want to get his right though by usurpation of others' rights neglecting completely all the principles of nature and teachings of the Holy Qur'an and *Ahadeeth*.

While serving in *Darul-Iftaa* we receive several hurting complaints such as the wife says, "since I came in this house my husband neither loves me nor my children, he is under the influence of his mother and sisters and considers me worst than a bond-maid. Death is better than this life."

The mother-in-law says, "since this woman has come to our house, the peace and tranquillity of the house has eloped–she has full control over her husband–he listens to his wife only as we are his bond-man or bond-maid".

Other than these we used to read several heart-rending incidents in newspapers, such as a "woman committed suicide by pouring kerosene oil and setting herself on fire", "a mother-in-law, alongwith her daughter, beaten her daughter-in-law so much that she died," under the influence of wife a man strangulated his mother."

If we ponder over these complaints and incidents cool-mindedly, we will find its sole reason is the living of daughter-in-law with her in-laws' family. Therefore, we request you to try to keep your son and his wife away in any possible way from you for the prosperity of you, your son, your daughter-in-law and your grandsons, though it is a small cottage.

Just to satisfy you now we are quoting 2 questions with their answers by Maulvi Mohd. Yousuf Ludhianvi, published in the daily JUNG's column "Aap ke Masaa'il Aur Unka Hal". May Allah help us to understand it and act accordingly, Amen! After knowing the decree of *Shari'at,* it is improper to say that such is not the custom of our society, who will serve the mother ... May Allah give us proper understanding of the religion, Amen!

## ASKING WIFE TO SERVE THE MOTHER

**Que 1)** One can serve his father by obeying him and helping him in his work. If mother is aged and can't do household works, should not one ask his wife to help his mother? Whereas you have earlier told that, if the wife is not pleased with her mother-in-law then shift her to a separate house–in this way source of service will come to an end. Then how the mother will be served as merely obeying her is not serving her.

**Ans:** If the wife is serving her parents-in-law happily, then it is much more than better–a cause of her good fortune–but it is not legal rather it is moral. If wife wants to live away from her husband's parents, he can't compel her according to Islamic law.

## CAUSING DISRUPTION BETWEEN HUSBAND AND WIFE IS A MORTAL SIN

**Que 2)** How is it to cause split between husband and wife?

**Ans:** "He is not from us who incites a woman against her husband". (Abu Daud 1/296)

We came to know through this *Hadeeth* that creating hatred and dissension between husband and wife is a mortal sin. The Prophet (pbuh) has stated that such a person is not from amongst us. While the Qur'an has said that it is a habit of Jewish sorcerers.

**Clarification:** Just imagine what a strict threat has come in this *Hadeeth*! While it is done in our society by husband's elder or younger brothers' wives or by his sisters and mother, which is called by the Holy Qur'an as an action of Jewish sorcerers. You can check any society or country, if a son and his wife are living with mother, sisters and other brothers' wives then either there is difference of thought in between the husband and wife or the wife is living with her parents or divorce / *Khula'* had taken place or there are daily disputes.

# A REQUEST TO THE GROOM

All these advices were for your (groom's) parents, so you are requested not to take a step which would hurt your parents after reading these. You are not supposed to tell your mother, after reading these, you are such and such, you have harassed my wife in such and such way … etc. Remember! These advices are for your parents and it is not suitable for you to tell your parents such things specially don't tell a single word to your mother. Therefore we have advised you earlier also not to tell your mother anything after listening something from your wife. If you have to tell your mother something out of compulsion, tell her humbly as if you are enquiring only. Dear mother… was it like this …? If it was, then telling her (wife) this and that or scolding her without verification..... or disgracing her before other daughters-in-law is not suitable etc...........

Whereas the best and safest way is what we have told you earlier, convince your wife in the very first night itself, never tell me if you are hurt by my mother but keep patience considering her as your own mother, you will become more lovable to me and I will never annoy you. Serving mother is my duty but it will be your favor to me if you serve my mother as much as you can, keep patience if you are hurt and don't tell me. Similarly convince your mother that she is like your own daughter, if she hurts you tell her but don't tell me and please don't rebuke her without seeing any wrong in her.

If there are disputes between your wife and mother even after you had advised both of them. If your wife is telling you any vice of your mother, never tell a single word to your mother. Remember! We had given these advices to your parents and not to you, so don't ruin your worldly affairs and the Hereafter by using unsuitable and silly words.

If wife thinks that the mother does not need her services as you have sisters and other brothers' wives also, then arrange for separate residence before the marriage itself. If you are separating after the burst of quarrels then it will show signs of sorrow and distance while everyone will be displeased. If you are to separate from your family after the marriage don't separate as soon as your wife asks for it.

If your wife has got a separate kitchen where there is none to annoy her and she is to cook only for your parents, then also she is finding it difficult or someone has poisoned her ears or her mother would have told her to keep asking for a separate house. In this situation deliberate well before going ahead. Don't conclude this article "An advice to the parents of groom" wrongly to become a disciple of your wife and separate from your family as soon she asks for it without any deliberation rather ponder over the prevailing situation. In some cases it is seen that the wife is so guileless that she wants to serve her parents-in-law, while they are also happy that our grand-children are with us ...... but unfortunately, either her mother or sister seduce her to live separately or she sees her husband's other brothers' wives living separately so she is asking for it. Don't become as much hen-packed as you start searching for a rented accommodation whenever she asks for it. Sometimes this type of change becomes a reason of such incessant enmity that the children are deprived of not only their grand parents' paternal aunts' and uncles' love and affection but also of the family's good manners and etiquettes. Because, when you start living with your wife and children separately–it was not much needed–she will bring up your children according to her own family's customs and this may be against your own standard.... it is your harm.

Your parents will have to bear another harm, that is your wife started the mischief of living separately as she was seduced by her mother and sisters of mother as they told her, you will live comfortably, you will sleep or wake up by your own will and we will also come to see you time and again. So keep repeating your demand of living separately or ask him to live in your house which is full of all the facilities and is quiet bigger–leave your parents and start living either in our house or in any adjacent house. What about her coming as a bride, was it a hoax coming and her real aim was to separate you from your parents.

For Allah's sake, don't loose your senses in order to save your family as due to this very demand of your wife a happy family might be destroyed whereas they were living earlier like intimate friends. When your wife started mischief of living separately other brothers' wives may also ask for a separate house. Whereas they were living under the kind shadow and blessing of elders like a well-knit family.

Though living separately is better under certain circumstances, but don't decide for it unreasonably. If the husband acts sincerely in this situation and tries to convince his wife though with a little harshness after consulting his elders, then *Insha Allah* they might also get the blessings of the parents and the wife might also be happy.

Therefore we request you not to harrass your parents or younger brothers or sisters (specially if they are orphans) ever. If you have decided to live separately under certain circumstances then remember these are your parents and not hers, so you have to serve them. For example, meet your parents, brothers and sisters with gifts for them within your capacity and whenever you go to meet your parents, take your children also with you so that they also could meet their grand-parents, paternal aunts and uncles. Keep praying Allah with utmost humbleness and beseechment so that He may help you to serve your parents as they should be and He be pleased with you.

If you are unmarried then start offering 2 *Rak'ats* of *Nafil* and praying Allah so that He may give you such a pious wife, who would serve your parents alongwith you and give you His pleasure as a reward. If you are married then try as much as possible and pray Allah so that He may help you and your wife to serve your parents alongwith your wife while considering it as your good fortune.

We want to tell you that, if your wife is not helping you in serving your parents then you are not supposed to compel her for this rather you must continue to serve them. Because your parents won't feel so embarrassed if she annoys them as they will be embarrassed if you annoy them. Now we are telling you the importance of serving them and their status as told in the Qur'an and *Haadith*, and the summary of what the religious scholars have said regarding these. May Allah help us to act according to the decrees of the Qur'an and *Ahadeeth*, Amen!

Allah the Almighty has said in the Holy Qur'an;

اِمَّا يَبْلُغَنَّ عِنْدَکَ الْکِبَرَ اَحَدُهُمَآ اَوْ کِلَاهُمَا فَلَا تَقُلْ لَّهُمَآ اُفٍّ وَّلَا تَنْهَرْهُمَا
وَقُلْ لَّهُمَا قَوْلاً کَرِیْمًا وَاخْفِضْ لَهُمَا جَنَاحَ الذُّلِّ مِنَ الرَّحْمَةِ وَقُلْ رَّبِّ
ارْحَمْهُمَا کَمَا رَبَّیٰنِیْ صَغِیْرًا. رَبُّکُمْ اَعْلَمُ بِمَا فِیْ نُفُوْسِکُمْ ط اِنْ تَکُوْنُوْا
صٰلِحِیْنَ فَاِنَّهٗ کَانَ لِلْاَوَّابِیْنَ غَفُوْرًا.

*Whether one or both of them attain old age in your life, say not to them a word of contempt, nor repel them but address them, in terms of honour. And out of kindness, lower to them the wing of humility, and say; "My Lord! Bestow on them your mercy even as they cherished me in childhood." Your Lord knows best what is in your hearts: if you do deeds of righteousness, verily He is most Forgiving to those who turn to Him again and again (in true penitence).* (Bani-Israel, 23-25)

Hazrat Mujahid (Ra) has said while elucidating this very verse, if they attain old age and you have to wash or clean their urine and faecess, you are not supposed even to utter a faint cry as they had done the same for you in your childhood.

Hazrat Ali (mabawh) said, if there had been any lowly word then the "faint cry", then Allah would have forbidden that also. Someone asked Hazrat Hassan (mabawh), what is the magnitude of disobedience? He said, "to disappoint them from one's wealth, to leave meeting them and to see them frowningly." Another person asked him, “what is the meaning of قَوْلاً كَرِيْمًا (honorable address)”. He replied, don't call them by their names rather say "father or mother". Hazrat Zubair b Muhammad (Ra) has said, wherenever they call you, you should reply by these words, " I am at your service". Hazrat Qatada (Ra) said, “talk to them leniently”. Someone asked Sa’eed b al-Musayyab (Ra), he could not understand the meaning of قَوْلاً كَرِيْمًا He replied, as a hot-headed slave talks to his hot-headed master.

Hazrat Ayesha (mabawh) says, once a man came to the Prophet(pbuh) alongwith an aged man, Huzoor (pbuh) asked him about the man with him. He said, he is my father. Huzoor asked the man not to walk infront of him, not to sit before him, not to call him by his name and not to reproach him.

Someone asked Hazrat Urwa (Ra) what is the meaning of “lower to them the wing of humility” as told in the Holy Qur'an. He said, if they say some unpalatable words to you don't see towards them leeringly as unpalatability is first seen the eyes.

Hazrat Ayesha (mabawh) says that the Prophet (pbuh) has said “whosoever sees his father leeringly he is not obedient”.

Hazrat Abdullah-b-Mas'ood (mabawh) says, I asked the Prophet (pbuh) what is the most desirable action according to Allah, he said saying the prayers on their time.

I asked after this, he said, to treat parents kindly. I asked after this, he said, religious war. In another *Hadeeth* the Prophet (pbuh) has said, pleasure of Allah is in the pleasure of the father and displeasure of Allah is in the displeasure of the father. (Durre-Manthoor)

The author of "Mazahir-e-Haque" says, that one should serve and entertain his parents in such a way that they be pleased with him. One should obey them in legal activities, should not disrespect them and should not treat them haughtily though they are infidel. One should not raise his voice above theirs, or call them by their names, or precede them in any activity. One should be lenient in ordering what is right and forbidding what is wrong, say once if they do not accept then also keep treating kindly and seeking forgiveness for them and this he (author of Mazahir-e-Haque) has taken from the Holy Qur'an (Sura Maryam 42-48). Hazrat Ibrahim (pbuh) after advicing his father only once has said, I will seek Allah's forgiveness for you and keep praying for you. Some religious preceptors have said, obeying them in forbidden things is illegal but in dubious matters it is obligatory because being careful of dubious matters is piety, while fulfilling their wishes is obligatory. Therefore, if their wealth is dubious and they are displeased of your eating separately, you must eat with them.

Hazrat Talha (mabawh) says a man came to the Prophet (pbuh) and asked to participate in the religious war, the Prophet (pbuh) asked, Is your mother alive? He said, yes. The Prophet (pbuh) said, "serve her fully as the Heaven is under her feet", twice again he asked the same question. He (pbuh) repeated the same sentence.

Hazrat Anas (mabawh) says a man came to the Prophet (pbuh) and said, O the Prophet (pbuh)! I want to take part in the religious war but I could not. The Prophet (pbuh) asked, Is any of your parents alive? He says, 'my mother is alive'. The Prophet (pbuh) said keep fearing Allah regarding her (Always remain in her service) you will be like one who performs Haj, Umra and takes part in the religious wars, i.e you will get the rewards of these activities.

Hazrat Muhammad bin al-Munkadir (Ra) said that his brother Umar used to pass the nights offering prayers while I used to pass my nights pressing mother's feet but I never wished that I may get his night (reward of offering prayers) in place of my own night.

Hazrat Ayesha (mabawh) says I asked the Prophet (pbuh) who has more rights over a woman? The Prophet (pbuh) said her husband. Then I asked who has more rights over a man? The Prophet (pbuh) said, his mother. In another *Hadeeth*, the Prophet (pbuh) has said, be chaste with women–your women will also become chaste–treat your parents kindly–your children will treat you kindly.

(Durre Manthoor)

Hazrat Taa'oos (Ra) say, a sick person had four sons. One of these sons told the others, either you attend the father on the condition that you won't get anything from the legacy or I am ready to attend him on the same condition.

They all agreed that you only attend him on this condition while we won't. He attended his father well, but he died and according to the condition he didn't took anything. At night, he saw in the dream that a man is asking him to dig out 100 *Dinars* (Gold Coins) from a specific place. He asked him in the dream itself, is there prosperity in them? He said, 'no'. In the morning he told the dream to his wife, she insisted to dig out those *Dinars* but he didn't. In the second night he again saw a dream and was asked to dig out 10 *Dinars* from another place, he again asked about the prosperity in them, he replied, 'no'. In the morning he told the dream to his wife, she insisted to dig out but he didn't. In the third night he again saw a dream that a man is asking him to go to a certain place and dig out a solitary *Dinar*, he again asked about the properity in it, he replied, 'yes'. He went there, dug out the solitary *Dinar* and bought two fishes from the market. When he cut them, he found one unseen pearl in each of them. The ruler of that time purchased the pearls by giving him gold weighing 90 mules.

**Hadith :**

عَنْ اَبِیْ هُرَیَرَة قَالَ: قَال رَجُلٌ یَا رَسُوْلَ اللّٰهِ مَنْ اَحَقَّ بِحُسْنِ صَحَابَتِیْ قَالَ
اُمُّکَ ثُمَّ مَنْ قَالَ ثُمَّ اُمُّکَ قَالَ ثُمَّ مَنْ قَالَ ثُمَّ اُمُّکَ قَالَ ثُمَّ مَنْ قَالَ اَبُوْکَ
وفِی روایة قَالَ اُمُّکَ ثُمَّ اُمُّکَ ثُمَّ اُمُّکَ ثُمَّ اَبُوْکَ ثُمَّ اَدْ نَاکَ فَادْنَاکَ

*Hazrat Abu Haraira (mabawh) said some one asked the Prophet (pbuh) who is more entitled to my favor and kindness. The Prophet (pbuh) said your mother, he asked then who? He (pbuh) said your mother, he asked then who? He (pbuh) said your mother, he asked then who? He (pbuh) said your father. In another narration, he (pbuh) thrice says your mother, then your father, then who is more close to you and so on.*

(Bukhari, Kitabul-Adab Hadith No. 5514)

## SHOWING FAVOR TO PARENTS SPECIALLY IN THE OLD AGE

Serving and obeying parents is not limited to any specific age rather it is obligatory for us to serve and obey them during their whole life. Some circumstances usually come as obstacles in performing the duties and obligations, the way of the Holy Qur'an regarding these circumstances is that it trains us by different viewpoints so that it may become easy for us to act accordingly.

In the old age, the parents need to be served by their children and they feel themselves at the mercy of their children. If they feel though a little negligence from their children in this period they become dejected. Secondly some natural disorders of the old age make them peevish. Thirdly, in the old age when they become doated, their wishes and demands become such that these become difficult for their children to carry out. The Holy Qur'an while ordering us to console and comfort them, has reminded us of our childhood, when we were in more need of them than what they are now and has asked us to be sacrificed for them as they have done earlier for us. In the given verses the words كَمَا رَبَّيَانِى صَغِيرًا points to this only, after this some peremptory decrees are given, these are;

1) لَا تَقُلْ لَهُمَا أُفٍّ (say not to them a word of contempt) أُفٍّ means a word to which one can show his displeasure. Hazrat Ali (mabawh) narrates that the Prophet (pbuh) has said that, if there had been a word of causing less harm than that would have also been mentioned (Any thing which causes the least harm to the parents is prohibited).

2) وَلَا تَنْهَرْهُمَا (nor repel them) the meaning of نَهَرَ is scolding and rebuking.

3) وَقُلْ لَّهُمَا قَوْلاً كَرِيْماً (but address them in terms of honour). The first two orders were of negative nature in which orders of minimum unpleasantness of the parents are given. Whereas in this third order, the way of speaking to the parents is taught i.e. one should speak to his parents leniently and affectionately.

4) وَاخْفِضْ لَهُمَا جَنَاحَ الذُّلِّ مِنَ الرَّحْمَةِ (And out of kindness, lower to them the wing of humility) which means one should present himself before them meekly and humbly as a slave presents himself before his master. The word مِنَ الرَّحْمَةِ means that treating parents meekly should not be for show only rather it should be as a grace and respect to them, moreover it will bring forth the blessings.

5) وَقُلْ رَّبِّ ارْحَمْهُمَا (And say: My Lord! bestow on them your mercy) which means one can't give full comfort to his parents, but he should try his best and pray Allah to simplify their hardships and avert their sufferings. This last decree is so vast, that one can serve his parents even after their death.

**Mas'ala:** If the parents are Muslims then praying of mercy for them is obvious but if they are non-Muslims this prayer will also be legal so that they would get rid of worldly hardships and they might get the wealth of *Eimam* (faithfulness) but after their death this prayer will become illegal. (Tafseer-e-Qurtubi)

## A STRANGE INCIDENT

Qurtubi has narrated through Hazrat Jabir (mabawh) that a man came to the Prophet (pbuh) and complained that his father has taken his wealth. The Prophet (pbuh) asked him to bring his father. At the same time Hazrat Jibrail Ameen came and told the Prophet (pbuh) when his father comes to you, ask him the words he has said in such a way that he himself has not heard those words. When the man brought his father, the Prophet (pbuh) asked the father, what is the matter, your son is complaining of you, do you want to grab his wealth? The father said, ask him that where am I spending the money except on me, his paternal and maternal aunt? The Prophet (pbuh) said ایه which means (the reality is known, now there is nothing to explain) and asked the father about the words which even he had not heard but he had said. The father said, O the Prophet of Allah (pbuh) you increase our faith and belief in Allah in each matter (you got the knowledge of a gossip which none had heard, it is a miracle). Then the father said, really I had uttered some couplets in my heart and even I had not heard them. The Prophet (pbuh) said read out those couplets to us, he read out these couplets;

غَذَوْتُکَ مَولُودًا وَمُنْتُکَ یافعا　　　تُعلُّ بِمَا اَجْنِیْ عَلَیْکَ وَتُنْهَلُ

I fed you in the childhood and took care of you while you were a grown-up boy your feeding was from my earning.

اذا ليلة ضا فتک بالسقم لم ابت لسقمک الا ساهرا اتململ

If you got ill in any night, I passed the whole night in full wakefulness and restlessness due to your illness.

کأ نی انا المطر وق دونک بالذی طُرِقُتَ به دونی فعینی تهمل

As if I am ill and not you, due to this I remained weeping the whole night.

تخا ف الردٰی نفسی علیک وانها لَتَعلَم ان الموت وقت موٴجَّلُ

I remain fearing of your death though I know that the time of death is fixed and it can't be deferred.

فَلَمَّا بلغت السنَّ والغایة الَّتِی الیها مدی ماکنت فیک أو مِّلُ

When you attained the age and extremity I was hoping for.

جعلت جزائی غلظةً وفظاظة کانک انت المنعم المتفضِّلُ

You rewarded me with rudeness and bluntness as if you are doing a favor to me.

فَلیتکَ اذلم ترع حقَّ اُبوتی فعلتَ کما الجارُ المصاقب یفعل

If you could not do full justice to me being a father, at least you could have done what a noble neighbour does.

فَاَ و لَیتِنِی حَقَّ الجوارِ ولم تکن علیَّ بمال دونَ مالک تبخلُ

You would have given me at least the right of a neighbour and you would not have shown me miserliness out of my own wealth.

After listening the couplets, the Prophet (pbuh) collared the son and said انت و مالک لابیک i.e. go away you and your wealth is of your father. (Ma'aariful-Qur'an 5/468)

Therefore one must take full care of his aged parents and must remember that in this time of senility and weakness, all the emaciating ailments, which convert them into mere skeleton, are not organic ailments rather these are functional which tell the tales of loneliness, despair, hopelessness, sensitiveness, memories of the past and fears of future.

Suppose an old women is saying, Ah! What should I do now ..., I became alone ... I had only one sister and she too is died. I did not get an agreeable daughter-in-law, sons too have ignored me ....elder daughter too did not get relief etc... or an aged and weak man loses his loving and helping life-partner and as the life passes they lose their loving ones one after the other. These are the vicissitudes which are called ailments and disabilities of senility in general.

If these old men are pious, have the desire and fervor of meeting and seeing Allah, are engaged in preaching Islam, are thinking of driving out groups of preachers from the mosques of their area and sit in the company of preceptors then, All paises are for Allah, most of them will remain saved of these vicissitudes.

Anyhow, if your parents are becoming old then it is your as well as your wife's good fortune that you are a mean of confidence and encouragement for them. As you are bringing up your children, in the same way bear their unpalatable gossips, it will be your good-fortune.

## RECOGNIZE YOUR STATUS AND DON'T BE A HEN-PECKED

In different articles we have advised you to adopt

leniency towards your wife and to take care of her consolation moreover we have induced you not to abuse or taunt her while admonishing her due to any fault of hers. It does not mean that she is superior to you and can scold or rebuke you but you can't say anything or you are her slave. Therefore for Allah's sake don't be a hen-pecked rather be lenient to her and fulfil her legal demands. Here, it is necessary to remember this proverb, "provide all amenities but be a strict disciplinarian," said by our experienced elders.

Remember! Your position is of manliness, of being her husband and head of family while your slackness can upset your house, spoil the future of your children. When your daughters will see you agreeing with their mother's opinon and stooping before their mother then, Allah forbid, they will also be desirous of the same behaviour from their husbands and then several families will be ruined. So recognize your status and position in the family and be a domineering personality.

Deal your family members affectionately as the elders have also said, "Awe, found in an affectionate person, is not found in a person who keeps scolding and rebuking all the time". There is a good news in *Hadeeth* also, that there is a gate in the Heaven called *Babul-Farah* through which the persons, who keep their children laughing and please them (within the limits of *Shari'at*) will enter. Whereas the mother of the children–your wife–is also a dependent on you so please her also.

There is a good news for the Muslim couples, that is whenever they look towards each other with love , Allah the Almighty also looks towards them with love and mercy. The wives are not only dependent on their husbands rather they are committed to them like a prisoner as they can't go anywhere without your permission. And obviously a frail or dependant person should be treated kindly so she also should be treated kindly and leniently.

But adopting a behaviour which changes your status of a ruler into subjugation is also wrong. According to *Hadeeth* putting oneself to shame is also unlawful. The status, given to a man by Allah the Almighty being a male, losing it or disgracing it, is just like putting oneself to shame.

Another important thing is that, the woman is of unsound mind and religion as neither her leadership in the prayers nor her *Azaan* is legal, she can't travel legally without a *Mahram*. Offering prayers, in some days of every month (generally) is illegal for her, half share for her in the legacy, she has not been given the responsibility of earning, her maintenance is due on her father, husband, grand-father, son, brother and nephew according to the situation, evidence of two women is equal to a man's and during Haj she can't pronounce *Labbaik* loudly etc. One should remember that the dignity of woman is in these *Shar'ai* decrees only as Allah Himself has said in the Holy Qur'an; وَ مَا كُنَّا عَنِ الْخَلْقِ غٰفِلِيْنَ And We are never unmindful of (Our) creation. (almu'minoon-17)

Allah Himself is saying that He knows the needs and expendiencies of His creations very well.

Doing make-up is her second nature, using the means of make-up and arrogance is her habit. According to Hazrat Thanvi (Ra) it is the proof of her being deprived of perfection as the perfect persons do not use artificial means of adornment for example; doctors, engineers and artists live simply as they are expert in their respective fields and don't need any outward adornment. While the women hid their shortfalls in perfection by outward adornment...... moreover, they won't accept it........ We don't want to describe the women's religious position or worldly importance or its reasons, rather we want to tell you that, if your wife is overpowering you or you are becoming a yes-man then you are creating disturbance in the set-up of this Universe.

Just consider, you are sitting tired and simple food according to need is ready in the house, but your wife is compelling you either to take food in a restaurant... or to purchase a costly toy for any of your own children ... or to purchase a gift for her sister's marriage. You are having your own complications, such as you have to arrange for gas and electricity bills and for the marriage of your sister etc. from your salary. Now, you are perplexed because if you did not take your wife and children out for shopping or eating, then your wife will pull a long face for some days, treat you curtly and rebuke the children unnecessarily... Therefore, you are getting ready unwillingly by dressing up again and leaving the book or the newspaper or the preaching patrol (*Gasht*) of the mosque ... if you do not have your own vehicle, then there is extra burden of taxi fares.

Understand well ! don't become a stooge in the hands of your wives everytime, it will harm you forever, as you will have to accept their each and every demand though unwillingly and as a result they will get encouragement, when your daughters will see these, they will also try to overpower their husbands. Sometimes it so happen that the wives got the news that their husbands are planning for an outing with their friends… they become agitated, ask their husbands to take them to their maternal aunt or any other relative at once and say there is no planning for us, should we remain in our houses like orphans.

If the husband takes out her to any of her relatives then either the set-up of the house will be ruined or his own programme will get cancelled or postponed. In short, you should not bow down to her demands in such a way that she would overpower you and your programme may be cancelled … Rather live like a man and a head of the family, you are the king of the house so your orders must be effective and she is deputy to help in executing your orders while other members will reap its benefits. Don't be afraid of wife, remain devoted to Allah, read out religious books in the house, pray Allah in the night for the prosperity of your family, consult at times, with the family members of your wife for the reformation of your own house. If you have any complaints from your wife and it is not being reformed, you should tell her father this very complaint of hers.

Most of the times, the groom didn't tell his father-in-law anything. Whereas his wife gives garbled version to her sisters, maternal aunts and mother. These women give her wrong advices and consequently both the families have to bear its harm. When father of the bride comes to know that his wife has worsen the matter by misguiding the newly wed-bride. He regrets wringling his hands that, if he would have been told earlier, the matter would not have worsen so much. We have came across to many such matters therefore, we request all the grooms, if there is any complain try to solve it yourself otherwise talk to your father-in-law directly and in his absence either talk to your wife's elder brother or any *Mahram*. May Allah give proper understanding to all of us, Amen!

Undoubtedly live in your house like intimate friends with your family members while you must also keep them in awe so that all should be at your call. May Allah be your Guardian, Helper and may He put true love for you in her heart, so that she would obey you happily, Amen!

# FAMILY SYSTEM

The culture and civilisation of any society depends on the family life. If there is subversion and consternation in it then the life is deprived of peace though there may be lots of wealth. Today Europe and America are facing this very heinous problem, which are considered enviable by the politically, economically backward and developing countries. Consequently inspite of abundance of wealth and swift materialistic development, the people of these countries are restless. Due to inner anxiety some of them are joining yoga, some of them are becoming drug addict and some of them are committing suicide, if they are unable to avert their restlessness, as a result the number of suicides are increasing in these countries.

Before sometime I was on a visit to Switzerland, my hosts had arranged a car for me whose driver was an educationed Italian and fluent in English speaking. He was with me for quite some days and was an unmarried guy of 40 years. When I asked him the reason of not marrying, he replied that the marriage becomes aimless in our society as loyalty between husband and wife is rarely found because it is only a customary connection to reap financial gains. Most of the ladies get divorced just after their marriage to make their husband insolvent in accordance with the laws of our land. It is difficult to know which lady is marrying to take hold of her husband's property and which to pass her life with loyalty. He was talking wistfully, then he said that, in the Asian countries marriages are done aimfully which causes the emergence of a perfect family with full mutual understanding, but, Alas! We are deprived of such families. I asked him, did your parents, brother or sister not help you in finding a good wife? He listened this question with much surprise and said, I don't have parents but brother and sister are there–what is the relation of my marriage with them? Everyone of us solves his problems himself though we do meet occasionally.

These were the impressions of a driver, he may have exaggerated due to his personal circumstances but subversion of family system in the western countries is a reality which does not require much arguments as the whole world knows the reality. Intellectuals of western countries are trying to control it but it is deteriorating day by day.

The last president of the former USSR Mikhael Gorbachev is now fully out of world's politics, but his book "Perestroika" which he has written as president, still holds a status of courageous criticism on economic and social system of not only the USSR but also of the whole west. In this book he has discussed the dilapidation of family system under the heading, "women and family". In the beginning he has written that, undoubtedly this viewpoint of women liberation movement is laudable that men and women should get equal rights. Women should be able to work with man in each field so that our economy may grow. But later on he writes;

We have seen in the last few years that we were unable to draw our attention towards the rights and necessities of women which emerge due to their indispensible conduct as a mother, housewife and an instructor for children. But now they are unable to do house-keeping, to bring up their children and to create a suitable family atmosphere as they became busy in scientific research, productional services and other creative activities. Now we have come to know that so many of our problems, which are connected with the conduct of children or youth, our ethics, culture and productional activities have emerged as the family relations have weakend and a new irresponsible concept about the family obligations has prospered.

This is the contradictory result of our sincere and politically sound attempt to give men and women equal rights. Now we have taken steps to control this flaw during our reconstruction. For this we are organizing debates in press, public organizations, factories and door to door debates. While the main theme of these debates is, "which steps should we take to bring back woman to femality?"

(Perestroika p117 ed 1987)

These are the reviews of a political leader in whose society neither there is a concept of religious value of human and family rights nor these are deemed to be significant. Therefore his showing of woes on the subversion of family system is not due to any heavenly direction rather, it is due to those harms which he had seen himself in the materialistic life. Being a Muslim, we stand committed not only to outward and materialistic or worldly profit and loss but also to heavenly directions which are obligatory for us in the light of the Qur'an and *Sunnat*. Therefore subversion of the family system is not only a loss to our social and economical life but it is also against our religion, belief and ideal Muslim society.

Since the western thoughts have penetrated into our social and cultural lives, especially through TV, video and English films, we are accepting these social concepts without any hesitation.

Thank Allah! till now our family system has not deteriorated much but western culture is spreading among us, English movies had spread the western life-styles even in far off places. Our women are being taken out of house and they are being made factors of production by keeping Islamic instructions regarding house and families at a distance. These may be hazarduous for our family system in future. We must check it from today itself by following the Islamic moderate instructions which are neither eastern nor western but revealed by Allah and laid down by a person who was well-aware of human's nature, their present and future.

Hence we are not supposed to be impressed by it rather we have to decide if it is according to our religion or not in the light of the Qur'an and *Sunnat* so as our social life may remain intact.

## CONVINCE CHILDREN POLITELY

We humbly request you, if Allah has given you children then it is also a sort of thanksgiving to pay attention to them, patronize them, don't fly into passion over their mistakes, don't beat them but be careful to put your important things in such a place where they can't reach.

Just consider Newton was writing a book since 15 years he moved from his place for sometime at the same moment his dog's feet touched a nearby candle, it fell down and burnt many pages of the draft. He told his dog astonishingly "How should I treat you?" and started writing again. After some days' hard work he prepared a much better draft than the older one.

So, you should also forgive your children's minor mistakes with an open mind, should not make much noise over their mistakes. Similarly neither be disappointed nor distressed due to their illness, thinking that if there are children in a house, there will be cold, fever and some broken things while any of them will make a noise or disturb in sleeping etc. Accept all these perplexities and hardships laughingly and forget any thing else. Don't disturb yourself, your wife and children remembering the past perplexities.

Remember......if the frequently happening brawl and gabble between husband and wife ends, it will be a mercy to these innocent children as they will become confident for being grown up in a loving and peaceful atmosphere and will be far from psychological ailments and tensions.

The children who are brought up in a choked atmosphere, due to the quarrels between their parents, are deprived of self-confidence. They neither express their inner feelings infront of their mother considering her helpless….nor infront of their father considering him a cruel person.... who keep their mother crying won't listen them. While their God-gifted abilities and capabilities come to an end by seeing either their parents quarreling or their mother fearing from their paternal grand-mother and aunts.

We often come into contact with the children of diffrent national and international schools and madarsas as we ourselves are teachers. We have witnessed that the main reason behind some children's repeated failures, remaining absent from study, being dumb-founded in the class-rooms and non-participation in sports etc. Is that very ailment of fear, chokeness, deprivation of self-confidence and inferiority complex etc. caused by their quarreling parents.

In reality, if the slap of father and the flowing tears of mother are overtaking the mind of an innocent or brow-beating by father, paternal-grand mother and aunts… sobs of the mother weeping in the kitchen are echoing in the ears of an innocent or the scenes of mother weeping on the prayer-mat in seclusion are in the mind of an innocent……he can never be like other joyous children.

Therefore, for Allah's sake, show mercy to your own children, take care not to be angry due to any negligence or carelessness by your wife and children… if you got angry then for the sake of your own children's training and showing mercy to them please keep quiet and try to settle the matter amicably. At this moment think the goodness of keeping patience and forgiving, if you forgave them, Allah will also forgive you and convince your children politely and give them blessings for future.

## TAKE CARE OF CHILDREN'S RELIGIOUS TRAINING

Dear groom ….. *Nikah* is such a great blessing that both the husband and wife reap benefit from it by Allah's order. While its most important benefit rather its sole purpose is that both of them are not only saved from sins but they also fulfil their legal and natural desire in a lawful way and to get children as well. When a couple has got the blessing of children, but they could not take care of them as asked by the *Shari'at* or intellectually, this couple had not paid due regard to them. For example, a mother did not breast feed her child due to any certain reason or did not completed the *Shar'ai* suckling period.

The children's moral standard............way of talking, eating and drinking ......insisting unmannerly for a thing seen in another's possession deprave the goodwill of the whole family in such a way that the gossip of this scattered family remain on the theme of all nears and dears' discussion. When the tired husband hears such sentences, "the whole family is unreliable", "how they are bringing up their children" about his family he becomes more dejected. Have you ever pondered over the basic reasons of all these issues? One of the most important reasons is that we are far from our religion, so first of all we must try to create a religious atmosphere in our houses. May Allah guide all of us to abide by the true religion. Second important reason is that we do not pay suitable attention to them, we are not anxious about their bringing up, we do not shower our love or affection on them and we do not pray for them etc. Third reason is that, it is seen is some families that suitable gap is not maintained in between two children. Due to regular deliveries,the mother becomes weak, lean, tired and peevish. Generally it is seen in such house that the mother keeps beating and rebuking these children unnecessarily. She has no work except to suckle the youngest, give feeders to 3 of them ... give breakfast to her husband .... cook food ... bathe someone ... clean someone .... settle the dispute of someone.... curse someone and sometimes she even tell her husband angrily can't you even take care of any of these, you know only to speak ....as a result there is no trace of children's training.

The day starts with the breakfast at 7 am and the public-kitchen is continued up to 11 pm ...........The condition of the mother is that one child is still in suckling period & she again became pregnant, the milk became contaminated, the youngest is weaned as a result and is becoming thin. Husband's sisters or her own sisters won't prevent, the child who has just started walking on his own, from going to stove or the boiling saucepan while the mother being pregnant can't ascend or descend the steps in a hurry. Another big harm is that in such houses, neither obligatory prayers nor recitation of the Holy Qur'an nor reading the religious books nor bringing the women of the area to the religious fold are taken care of.

If we consider the reality, only having children is not desired rather existence of Allah's chosen slaves is desired. Teaching the children properly is the responsibility of all of us, we must spare some time from our work to train them religiously and read out *Hadeeth* books to them in the evening and try to put Allah's love, grandeur and thoughts of the Hereafter in their hearts.

Remember! to avoid deterioration in the religious training of the children and to keep the mother and baby healthy (baby would suck the mother for complete *Shar'ai* period and the mother would regain her lost health), keeping suitable gap with mutual consent of the couple is lawful ..... So take benefit of this very convenience and *Shar'ai* facility to show mercy to your family and yourself.

It this condition keeping suitable gap between two child is Mustahab (desirable);

وفي الفتاوى ان خاف من الولد السوء في الحرة يسعه العزل بغير رضاها لفساد الزمان فليعتبر مثله من الا عذار مسقطا لاذنها

*If there is a strong possibility of the children going out of gear due to deterioration and dissension in the milieu & surrounding (being irreligious)... then Azl (exterior ejection) is legal and it is not necessary to take the wife's permission.*

(Fatwa Alamgiri-1/235, Shami- 2/412 ,Fat-hul-Qadeer- 2/49)

Similarly, if there is any personal or individual excuse then also it is legal without any abhorrence. For example, the women is too weak to be pregnant or her health is being effected due to regular deliveries or the relations between husband and wife are not cordial and separation is inevitable or a religious and experienced doctor has advised for a certain gap due to caesarean birth, in such cases keeping suitable gap through temporary contraceptive methods is legal. But one should not think, while choosing any contraceptive method, that if the child is born from where he would feed him and from where his sustenance will be arranged, as this thinking is forbidden and against the outright decree of the Holy Qur'an. Allah the Almighty has said ;

وَلَا تَقْتُلُوٓا اَوْلَادَكُمْ خَشْيَةَ اِمْلَاقٍ نَحْنُ نَرْزُقُهُمْ وَاِيَّاكُمْ اِنَّ قَتْلَهُمْ كَانَ خِطْاً كَبِيراً

*Kill not your child for fear of want: we shall provide sustenance for them as well as for you. Verily the killing of them is a great sin.* (Isra-31)

Similarly giving it a national or social image is against the *Shari'at* and *Sunnat*. In the name of this "gap"causing an upheaval, shouting slogans such as 'from where sustenance will come', 'How the dowry of the girl will be arranged' and 'the country has become a debtor due to population' or shortening the family as fashion, all these are useless and absurd thoughts and due to any of these thoughts, keeping "gap" is not legal.

There is an admitted principle الامور بمقاصدها which means all the matters are in accordance with their intentions, that is if intention is correct then undoubtedly it is legal. If someone is keeping this gap sinisterly and with wrong intention which is not only wrong in *Shari'at* but also an interference in the system of Allah, then certainly it is illegal and forbidden. For more details please contact the religious scholars and *Muftiyan-e-Kiraam* (expounders of the irrevocable code of Islamic law) or consult any of these books; *'Zabt-e-wilaadat ki Aqli wa Shar'ai Haisiyat'* by Mufti Shafi' (Ra) & Mufti M.Taqi Usmani and *'Jadeed Fiqhi Mabahis'* Volume-1 by Maulvi Mujahidul Islam Qasmi.

## DIFFERENCES AND FIGHTS BETWEEN PARENTS

Differences and fights between parents are among the important reasons to keep a child away from the religion, to be an illiterate and a psychological patient. Hence, when a child is being brought up in any house and sees fights, he necessarily wants to be away from the obscure atmosphere of the house and wants to run away from this miserable family to live with his friends. If these friends are of inferior nature and ill-mannered then this child also becomes mannerless and criminal to be a danger for the whole nation and the country.

Islam has advised the Muslims, desirous of marriage, different ways of selecting a wife through its everlasting and full of wisdom rules and regulations, in the same way Islam has also guided the guardians of the girls to select a husband. The basic purpose of giving these guidelines is that they (husband and wife) should live with mutual consent, love and co-operation to be saved from day to day fights and embarrassments, we have started this book giving all the rules in detail.

## DIVORCE AND IRRELIGIOUSNESS ARISING OUT OF IT

The basic factors, which deviate and spoil a child in general are divorce and certain circumstances arising out of it because the divorce brings in separation and misunderstanding between the two families.

It is unanimously decided that, when a child opens his eyes and does not find an affectionate mother or father who would be a caring one, looking after him and fulfilling his wishes then he is necessarily inclined towards crime and other vices. This situation becomes more complicated when a divorced woman marries another man.

After the divorce, the poverty of a mother makes the situation more complicated as she is compelled to go to work in different houses and the children wander here and there in desolation. Vicissitudes of life and dormant troubles make them vagabond as there is none in the house to look after them. Now tell us, what one can hope from such children who neither got the love and care of father nor love, attention and sympathy of mother.

What one can hope from such a child who neither has bread to satiate him nor clothes to cover his body nor a cottage to cover his head or to take rest. In reality under these circumstances one can hope only profligacy or vagabondism from such a child. Only some of these children to whom Allah has shown His mercy, could be saved from being vagabond or profligate but such children are much less in number. He has ordered the husbands and wives to take full care of their obligations, duties and to discharge their mutual rights so that such a reproachable situation could not arise.

Among these rights, the husbands are responsible to bear the maintenance expenses of their wives and children, Allah has said in the Holy Qur'an;

وَعَلَى الْمَوْلُوْدِ لَهُ رِزْقُهُنَّ وَكِسْوَتُهُنَّ بِالْمَعْرُوْفِ

*"But he (father) shall bear the cost of their (children and wife) food and clothing on equitable terms".* (Baqra 233)

Imam Muslim (Ra) narrates that the Prophet (pbuh) has said;

اتقوا اللّٰه في النساء فإنكم أخذتموهن بأ مان اللّٰه واستحللتم فروجهن بكلمة اللّٰه ولهن عليكم رزقهن وكسوتهن بالمعروف

*O people! Fear Allah regarding your wives, as you have married them under the protection of Allah and you have made them lawful (for you) by the words of Allah so you are responsible for their food and clothes on equitable terms.*

(Sahih Muslim, Kitabul-Haj p-397)

One of these rights is that husband should consult his wife in domestic matters, the Prophet (pbuh) has said;

آمروا النساء في بناتهن

*Consult the woman (wives) about their daughters.*

(Abu Dawood, Kitabun-Nikah H.No.1793)

It means that before the marriage of the daughters, fathers should take permission from their mothers and consult them.

Another right is that the husband should overlook some of his wife's blemishes and faults especially if she has some virtues and good qualities which would compensate these faults and blemishes. The Prophet (pbuh) has said;

لایفرک مومن مومنة ان کره منها خلقا رضی منها آخر

*A faithful man should not keep animosity with a faithful woman, if he did not like any of her habits, he might like another.* (Muslim Kitabur-Razaa' H.No.2672)

Another right is that the husband should live with his wife happily, kindly and jestingly because Allah has said in the Holy Qur'an;

وَعَاشِرُوهُنَّ بِالْمَعْرُوفِ فَإِنْ كَرِهْتُمُوهُنَّ فَعَسَىٰ أَنْ تَكْرَهُوا شَيْئًا وَيَجْعَلَ اللَّهُ فِيهِ خَيْرًا كَثِيرًا

*On the contrary live with them on a footing of kindness and equity. If you take a dislike to them it may be that you dislike a thing, and Allah brings about through it a great deal of good.* (Nisa-19)

Another *Hadith*, quoted in Ibne-Maja (Hadith No. 1967) and by Hakim, say the Prophet (pbuh) has said;

خيركم خيركم لاهله وانا خيركم لا هلى

*"The most eithical man of you is one who is the best of you for his wife, while I am the best of you for my wives.*

Imam Bukhari (Ra) and Imam Muslim (Ra) narrates that the Prophet (pbuh) used to show Hazrat Ayesha (mabawh) the dramas going on in the field in front of the mosque. He (pbuh) used to put his palm on the door, while she used to put her face on his shoulder. Imam Tirmizi (Ra) has narrated the Prophet (pbuh) as saying;

اكمل المومنين إيما ناً أحسنهم خلقاً و ألطفهم بأ هله

*"A true believer is one, who is most ethical and kind to his wife".* (Tirmizi Kitabul-Eiman H.No.2537)

Hazrat Umar (mabawh), a strict and judicious man as he is known says that the man should be like a child for his wife in showing love and leniency but when he is with other men he should be a complete man.

Another right is that a man should help his wife in the household works following the Prophet's (pbuh) tradition. Tabrani has narrated that when Hazrat Ayesha (mabawh) was asked, what the Prophet (pbuh) used to do in the house? She replied," As you do in your home, put some thing in its place, help the family members even the servants, chop ment for them and dust the home etc.

These are the important rights of husband and wife prescribed by Islam. If both the husband and wife fulfil these, then unity and kindred will emerge instead of disagreement. The hatred and dislike will be changed into love and affection, the whole family will pass a peaceful, happy and better life. Moreover, it will be absolutely impossible that there may be an issue which would disturb the family or be offensive or hurt the husband and wife.

If due to immorality or rudeness of man or woman, unity and alliance is impossible and they could not live together then the husband must try to reform her before divorcing by adopting any of these ways;

1) Advising and counseling so that this verse is implemented, وَذَكِّرْ فَإِنَّ الذِّكْرٰى تَنْفَعُ الْمُؤْمِنِيْنَ. *"keep advising as it give benefit to the believers"*

(Zariyat-55)

2) Sleeping on a separate bed–it is a psychological punishment–she may come to the right way by it.

3) A little beating for admonition, if it is clear that beating will be useful. But one should neither beat badly nor on her face, chest and stomach nor as much that it would leave scars on her body. Beating with these conditions in mind will be a source of admonition rather than a source of hurting and annoying. Meanwhile, we should also keep in our minds that the Prophet (pbuh) has never beaten his wives. Hazrat ibne-Sa'ad (mabawh) narrates from Hazrat Ayesha (mabawh) that the Prophet (pbuh) of Allah had neither beaten a woman nor a servant nor any other person except when he was participating in a religious war.

Ibne-Sa'ad again narrates that when a women complained to the Prophet (pbuh) about her husband's beating. The Prophet (pbuh) told the husband;

يظل أحدكم يضرب امرأته ضرب العبد ثم يظل يعانقها ولا يستحي

*A man from amongst you beats his wife like a slave, then hugs her and does not feel ashamed.*

4) The last way is to make someone a judge (mediator) by selecting from amongst the intelligent, sensible and mild tempered relatives of both the families. Who should review the matter minutely and put up some practical suggestions to create unity, alliance and kindred among them.

These solution and suggestions can help in reaching the aim and saving the couple from the ignominy of divorce. Adopting these precautionary measures is necessary so that following verses of the Holy Qur'an would implement.

وَالّٰتِی تَخَافُونَ نُشُوزَهُنَّ فَعِظُوهُنَّ وَاهْجُرُوهُنَّ فِی الْمَضَاجِعِ وَاضْرِبُوهُنَّ ۚ
فَاِنْ اَطَعْنَكُمْ فَلَا تَبْغُوا عَلَيْهِنَّ سَبِيلًا ۗ اِنَّ اللّٰهَ كَانَ عَلِيًّا كَبِيرًا ○ وَاِنْ خِفْتُمْ شِقَاقَ
بَيْنِهِمَا فَابْعَثُوا حَكَمًا مِّنْ اَهْلِهٖ وَحَكَمًا مِّنْ اَهْلِهَا ۚ اِنْ يُّرِيْدَآ اِصْلَاحًا يُّوَفِّقِ اللّٰهُ
بَيْنَهُمَا ۗ اِنَّ اللّٰهَ كَانَ عَلِيمًا خَبِيرًا ○

*As to those women on whose part you fear disloyalty and ill-conduct, admonish them (first), (next) refuse to share their beds, (and last) beat them (lightly); but if they return to obedience, seek not against them means (of annoyance); for Allah is Most High, Great (above all). if you fear a breach between them twain, appoint (two) arbiters, one from his family, and the other from hers; if they seek to set things aright, Allah will cause their reconciliation: for Allah has full knowledge and is acquainted with all things.* (Nisa-34, 35)

If alliance is not possible even after acting upon these given measures then the husband should divorce the women during cleanliness (between two menses) in which he had not copulated with her so that they could return to conjugal life if situation arises.

# *TALAAQ* IS DISLIKED BY ALLAH AMONG LAWFULS

Now we are giving a little description of *Talaaq*, while praying Allah, that such grim situation may not come in the life of a Muslim couple .... Everyone knows how disliked is it ... if it is used wrongly then one can only weep and regret. Regarding this (*Talaaq*) we have two requests from all Muslims.

1) All should try that the matter should not reach to this extent under any circumstances.

2) If the situation worsens and there is no other way except *Talaaq* then for Allah's sake don't take a step hurriedly rather consult the religious scholars and expounders of the irrevocable code of Islamic law (*Mufti*) and act in accordance with what they advise you.

Now we are giving you an excerpt from an article by Mufti M. Taqi Usmani published in the "*Daily Jung*". May Allah give us proper understanding of our religion Islam, make us to act according to the Holy Qur'an and the *Sunnat* of our Prophet (pbuh) in each and every stage of our day to day life and make us to guide others also on the same, Amen!

## BEST WAY OF TALAAQ

I have been connected with family and specially marital disputes of Muslims in different capacities, it pains me to see that ignorance from Islamic teachings has increased so much in our society that the common issues which even children knew earlier but now even our elder do not know. I had seen that many misconceptions are in vogue about *Talaaq* because general people have become ignorant even of its primary decrees. Hence I am giving its detail so that all should know what Islamic *Shari'at* says about it.

The foremost and major mistake, most of the people think that *Talaaq* is a mode of venting one's spleen. As soon as there happened a difference between husband and wife and matter reached to provocation or spleen, the husband uttered the word *Talaaq*. Whereas *Talaaq* is not an abuse to be uttered in order to suppress one's anger rather it is the last step of terminating the marital bond. Its results are very harsh as not only the marital bond is terminated but several problems of family life are also created by it.

Not only Islam has allowed *Talaaq* but has claimed it to be ابغض المباحات also which means it is much disliked of the lawfuls by Allah. Since Islam is a natural religion it has not prevented *Talaaq* as sometimes the husband and wife can't live together and there is no other way except peaceful separation between the two because continuance of the marital bond in these circumstances can make their lives a nuisance. Therefore, Islam has neither proclaimed it illegal or unlawful nor fixed certain causes which could prevent them completely from being separated if the situation arises. Rather, first of all the Prophet (pbuh) has said clearly that *Talaaq* is much disliked of the lawfuls by Allah. Secondly, he (pbuh) has given such directions to us, if we act accordingly then *Talaaq* could become improbable. Thirdly if *Talaaq* becomes inevitable then he (pbuh) has told us a way which has least flaws. If today, the people would understand these directions and decrees properly, Allah knows, how many of these family disputes and problem would have been solved on their own.

As for the directions given to control *Talaaq*, the first of these is given by the Prophet (pbuh) that is, "if a husband dislikes any of his wife's action then he should consider her virtues also". Which means no one in this world is faultless, if there is any fault in someone he might be having numerous virtues also. One can't solve the problem by sticking to a fault of someone and neglecting his numerous virtues, moreover it is against the justice also. On the other hand the Holy Qur'an has also proclaimed against this decree in these words;

فَإِنْ كَرِهْتُمُوهُنَّ فَعَسَىٰ أَنْ تَكْرَهُوا شَيْئًا وَّ يَجْعَلَ اللّٰهُ فِيهِ خَيْرًا كَثِيرًا ○

*If you take a dislike to them it may be that you dislike a thing, and Allah brings about through it a great deal of good.* (Nisa; 19)

Another direction given by the Qur'an is that if a husband and wife could not settle their differences mutually and they had tried all the possible ways for it but in vain, then inspite of being separated at once, their families should make two arbiters form among themselves. These two arbiters should try to settle the issue after listening them cool-mindedly, moreover Allah says, if they seek to set things aright, Allah will cause reconciliation between them.

(Gist of verse No. 35 from Surah Nisa)

If all these efforts have become futile and there is no other way except *Talaaq*, then Allah has asked the husband in the Holy Qur'an to wait for a suitable time. The Prophet (pbuh) has said about "suitable time" that it is a time when wife is clean, (not menstruating) and after being clean the husband would not have copulated with her. Therefore, if the woman is not "clean" then divorcing her is a sin in the *Shari'at*. Moreover, if she is in such cleanliness that the husband has copulated with her then also divorcing her is a sin and the husband should wait for the next month in this situation.

There are many expediencies in this method one of these is, that *Talaaq* should not be the result of hatred or dispute. The husband has been asked to wait for a suitable time so that he may consider the whole situation properly. Just as the marriage was done with due consideration, *Talaaq* is also be given with due consideration. It is also possible that, due to this wait, their opinion regarding separation may be changed and *Talaaq* may not take place.

If the in tention of giving divorce is still there in the mind of husband and the suitable time has come then the best way is to utter the word *Talaaq* once only. It will be revocable (not definite) *Talaaq* which means that after the completion of *Iddat* (probationary period) marital bond will get terminatied on its own and both will be free to decide their future.

The benefit of this method is that if the husband, after giving *Talaaq* once, feels that he was mistaken and the situation can be better now, then he can revoke it within the probationary period with these words, "I revoke *Talaaq*" and the marital bond will get refreshed on its own. If the probationary period has elapsed and both of them think that they have learnt a lesson to live amicably in future, then they can remarry with mutual understading (but for this new proposal and consent, witness and dower are needed).

If reaping benefit of the given facility the husband and wife had remarried and again they started quarrelling then also the husband should not give *Talaaq* in a haste, rather act according to the given directions. If he decides to give *Talaaq* even after acting accordingly he should utter the word *Talaaq* once only this time also. Now the total number of *Talaaq* is two but the matter is still in the hands of husband and wife–the husband can revoke it during the probationary period and afterwards can marry third time by mutual understanding.

This is the method of giving *Talaaq* as told by the Qur'an and *Sunnat*. One can easily guess that how many ways are given is the Qur'an and *Sunnat* to keep the marital bond intact and to save it from being broken. If a person leaps across all the stages then marriage or *Talaaq* is not a game of hide and seek to be continued forever. Therefore, if someone gives third *Talaaq* also then there is no way to refresh the marriage in accordance with the *Shari'at*. Now neither the husband can revoke it nor they can remarry after mutual understanding and they will have to live separately.

A very wrong misconception about *Talaaq* is prevalent in our society and that is, we do not consider *Talaaq* as *Talaaq* if given less than thrice. Peoples' thinking in general is that if the word *Talaaq* is uttered or written once or twice then *Talaaq* won't happen. Whenever the time of *Talaaq* comes, people don't control themselves with less than three cousidering that it is necessary to use the word *Talaaq* at least thrice, though as told earlier divorce will happen if some, uses it once only.

According to *Shari'at*, the proper and best way of giving *Talaaq* is to utter or write the word "*Talaaq*" once only, though *Talaaq* will happen in this way also but the chance of refreshing the marital bond remain wide open if situation so arises, whereas using the word *Talaaq* thrice collectively is a sin according to *Shari'at*.

According to all the four schools of theology, i.e. *Malikite, Shafi'ite, Hanafite* and *Hanbalite*, the punishment of this sin is that there remains no room either for revoking the divorce or for remarrying. The people connected with these schools of theology have to face many difficulties after uttering the word *Talaaq* thrice.Therefore, first of all we have to avert this very misconception about *Talaaq* and proclaim that its best and proper way is to use the word *Talaaq* once only. If the right of husband, to revoke it, is to be withheld then use the word *Baa'in* (irrevocable) with the word *Talaaq* and that's too once only. Now the husband can't revoke it on his own but they can remarry with mutual understanding whenever they wish so.

There is no difference between different schools of theology regarding the word *Talaaq* to be uttered or written only once at a time. Therefore the religious scholars should clarify this *Mas'ala* to the general public.

# WILL

Every Muslim men or women should draw up his/her 'will', special emphasis has been given to it in *Hadith*. Especially if someone is answerable to some lapsed prayers or Haj or Zakat which he/she had not paid, in these conditions not drawing will is a sin. He/she will remain at fault till the 'will' is drawn. Therefore, we must draw our 'will' as early as possible.

To know how to draw a 'will' and its detail we can see the book *Tareeqa-e-Wasiyyat.* We are now giving a sample of a 'will' drawn by a husband for his wife and another by a wife for her husband. May Allah help us to take care of His rights (*Huqooqullaah*) and the rights of other people (*Huqooqul-Ibaad*) due on us and to prepare ourselves for death before its happening, Amen!

## 'WILL' OF A PIOUS HUSBAND FOR HIS WIFE

Ghazi Anwar Pasha is one of those glorious Turkish soldiers who spent their whole life fighting the enemies of Islam while in the end they were martyred fighting the Russian Bolsheviks. Just a day before his martyrdom he wrote a letter to his wife. It is so instructive and fervid that every youth should read it, summary of this letter is as follows;

Dear Bakhiya,

Allah the Almighty is your Protector–at the moment, your last letter is infront of me and believe me I will keep it embraced to myself forever–though I can't see your face, but I am seeing your fingers moving in between the words of this letter which used to play with my hair. In the twilight of the tent, I am seeing your shadow.

Ah! You have written that I had forgotten you, I had not cared your love as I am playing with blood and fire after breaking your loving heart and I had not cared that a woman is passing a sleepless night in my separation as I love only war and sword. But while writing these words, you would never have thought that how these words–you have written out of true love for me–will break my heart. How can I make you believe that I do not love anything in this world more than you, you are the extremity of my love and I had not loved any except you. Sweet heart! You can ask me precisely this question, then why I am separated from you?

Listen I am not separated from you because I want worldly wealth or ascend the throne as my enemies have proclaimed. I am separated from you as an obligation of Allah the Almighty has brought me here–there is no obligation bigger than *Jehad* (war) in the way of Allah–this is the obligation which can make a human entitled to the paradise. Thank Allah! I am performing this not merely having its intention. Though this separation is torturing me but I am very happy as only your love can become a trial for my determination and intention. Many many thanks to Allah that I have succeeded in my trial and given priority to the love and decree of Allah over my love and myself. You should also be happy and thank Allah for this.

*Jehad* with sword is not for you but still it is obligatory for you, no Muslim whether men or women is exempted from *Jehad*–your *Jehad* is to give priority to His love over your love and yourself and strengthen the real love of your husband.

Listen! Never pray that your husband would return to you from the battlefield in any way–it will be the prayer of selfishness and Allah will not like it–though you can pray that may Allah accept the *Jehad* of your husband and return him victorious or he would become a martyr.

Dear Bakhiya! How auspicious the moment will be when this head, you were describing it as a handsome one, will be separated from the body. The foremost desire of Anwar is to get martyred and be resurrected with Khalid-bin-Waleed (mabawh). This world is transitory and death is certain then why one would fear death?

When one has to die, why one should die lying on a bed. In reality the death of a martyr is not a death rather it is an eternal life. Bakhiya! Listen my will, if I got martyred then marry my younger brother Noori Pasha. After you he is more loving to me. I want that after my death, he may remain in your service faithfully.

My second 'will' is that you have to tell my life-story to all the children you bear and send them to the warfield to serve Islam and the country. If you had not done these, I will be displeased with you in the *Jannah*.

My third 'will' is that you are supposed to help and be a well wisher of Mustafa Kamal Pasha forever as Allah has given the liberation of the country in his hands. Well, dear Bakhiya, Good Bye! Allah knows, why I feel that, this is my last letter for you as I may be martyred tomorrow.... You have to keep patience...instead of lamenting on my martyrdom you are to be delighted as my being a martyr is a glory to you.

Bakhiya ! Good Bye. I embrace you in my thoughts.......... *Insha Allah* we will meet in the *Jannah* to live together forever.

Yours

ANWAR

(Taken from Turkan-e-Ahrar by A.M.Siddiqi 127-130, Lahore edition)

***Note:*** When this letter was written M.K. Pasha was known only as a warrior of Islam and he had not taken any anti-Islamic steps till then.

## 'WILL' OF A PIOUS WIFE FOR HER HUSBAND

A Muslim wife should apologize to her husband and try to please him as much as she has troubled or hurt him or fell short of his rights. As the Prophet (pbuh) has said, if a woman dies while her husband is agree with her, she will enter the paradise.(Tirmizi, Kitabur-Razaa' Tohfatul-Ahwazi 4/325)

Therefore, a Muslim wife should seek her husband's forgiveness for all the faults and shortfalls done in the earlier marital life and should try to please him fully. Whereas she is not supposed to obey him if he asks to do what the Prophet (pbuh) has prohibited and if he asks not to do what the Prophet (pbuh) has ordered to do. To know and fulfil the rights of husband, the Muslim wives should read Bahishti Zevar and Tohfa-e-Khawateen. Similarly each wife can use the following sentences while drawing her 'will' with certain changes according to her state of affairs.

1) Thank Allah, I am not habitual of nail-polish, if ever I had used it then I used to clean it either before bathing or making ablution. If I die and polish is still there, then clean it before giving me bath as neither the bathing will be correct nor the funeral prayer, therefore take special care of it.

(Ahsanul-Fataawa Babul-Janaa'iz 4/237)

2) A pious wife should try to make her sons and grand-sons Qur'an-conners and practicing religious scholars, while she also should try to make her daughters and grand-daughters religious and incite them to learn and teach the Arabic language. She must write this in her 'will'. If her sons and daughters are grown up, then she must point out in her 'will' that, I could not make you Qur'an-conners and religious scholars, it was my fault, but you are supposed to make your children Qur'an-conners, religious scholars, preachers of Islam and its true servant.

If she still has small sons, she must try to make them Qur'an-conners and draw up a 'will', when you grow up and I am not in the world then you must act according to my 'will' to be Qur'an-conner, religious scoholar, warrior and a preacher of Islam in the world.

3) Dear husband, please marry again after my death for the peace of mind, management of the house and specially to be saved from sins.

4) Keep praying for me.

5) Please waste my photos if there are any by mistake other than my passport and identity card, so that my sin may also perish with my death.

6) When the children attain the marriageable age, marry them simply after consulting our elders, taking care of children's approval and doing *Istikhara* specially while marrying daughters look for good-mannered boys. Remember! Our sons-in-law should be religious.

7) Remember to arrange separate house for the daughters-in-law just after their marriage, nowadays being constant in relation with real mother-in-law is difficult, if she is step-mother-in-law then what will happen, while the sufferer will be our son only.

8) Therefore, by organizing a simple marriage ceremony and by saving money from other needless customs, arrange a separate house for the son and his wife with the money saved thus. You would see its better results.

*Your life partner*

Note: Every Muslim either men or women must draw his / her 'will' after reading the book " *Tareeqa-e-Wasiyyat*".

## SUMMARY

Now we are giving the gist of this very book in points, so that you may read this book again and again to mould yourself accordingly

1) Husband and wife can't become one unless they are pious, so try to be pious and make your wife pious.

2) Try to marry with simplicity you will see a lot of blessings and happiness *Insha Allah*.

3) Settle for *Mahr-e-Fatmi* (131 *Tolas* & 3 *Mashas* which equals to 1530 grams approximately or its price) and try to pay it at once, it will be much better for you.

4) Never demand dowry, it is against the men's dignity to ask or long for financial assistance from the wife. Whatever you have to ask, ask from Allah.

5) Try your best to live separately, in today's era, living together didturbs the atmosphere of the house. We have seen so many houses where brothers were living with complete intimacy but after their marriages they don't like to see their brothers due to their wives' instigations. Therefore, it is better to live separately, though it is a small rented house, than to live together. Due to irreligiousness in our houses, the elder or younger daughters-in-law being involved in jealousy, hatred and back-biting create differences between brothers. When the new generation sees

unpleasant atmosphere of the house they become effected by different spiritual and psychological ailments.

6) The best amulet and remedy of creating love with wife is to safeguard your eyes. One, who sees those disliked by Allah, can never love his wife sincerely though she may be intelligent or beautiful, so you must safeguard your eyes.

7) Remember ! it is the nature of a woman that she is pleased whenever she is praised so praise her to enjoy a happy married life. Moreover, by praising her many internal problems and complaints will be dispelled.

8) When certain disputes of husband and wife were analysed, it was found that the disputes start when husband goes out for work and when he comes back. So take care of these two times and don't give *Satan* a chance to instigate you. Remember! disputes between two Muslims avert the blessings of Allah.

9) Ask your wife to give gifts to your mother from time to time and send cooked food also while living away from her. You also try not to meet her empty-handed. If you are living together, don't let your mother feel that you love your wife more than her.

10) Remember! Children are children don't consider them elder, don't quarrel over them with your wife. Assume the charge of the house for a day,

*Insha Allah* you will come to know how your children are. Similarly, for the sake of your children's training and caring for the health of mother and baby keep suitable gap between two children or elongate this gap due to any *Shar'ai* excuse.

# QUESTION PAPER

Dear husnbands! Read the following questions at least three times giving full concentration to these every time. Then reply the questions cool-mindedly. If your answer is in affirmative give ten numbers otherwise give zero. If you are a little doubtful then give 5 numbers. There is space for answers and number after each question.

**Que1:** Do you wake up your wife lovingly, after offering *Fajr* prayer, reciting the Holy Qur'an and telling beads to offer prayers alongwith your children? Do you take your elder children to the mosque to offer *Fajr* prayer with *Takbeer-e-Oola* (initial takbeer) and congregation?

**Answer:** ....................

**Numbers:** ....................

**Que2:** Do you accompany your wife with *Shar'ai* veil and according to your financial capacity for legal amusement in a month or two?

**Answer:** ....................

**Numbers:** ....................

**Que3:** Is there daily arrangement of *Ta'leem* (reading out any book of *Ahaadeeth*) in your house attended by all family members except non-*Mahram* women who either listen from behind the veil or the women would do *Ta'leem* separately?

**Answer:** ...................

**Numbers:** ..................

**Que4:** Do you take your wife to any religious gathering for women or to attend the reformal recountals of righteous preceptors?

**Answer:** ...................

**Numbers:** ..................

**Que5:** Do you ever convince your wife politely, lovingly and leniently after some time (period between two prayers) inspite of rebuking or scolding or Allah forbid beating at once, whenever your sister or mother complain of her to you?

**Answer:** ...................

**Numbers:** ..................

**Que6:** Have you ever told your wife the benefits and excellence of overlooking and having patience wisely and prudently whenever she complains about your mother or sister, inspite of saying any unsuitable words to them ? Have you told your wife to study '*Islaahi Khutbaat*' by M.T.Usmani?

**Answer:** ...................

**Numbers:** ..................

**Que7:** If your family is living jointly with your

parents, brothers and sisters and discords are happening each day. Have you ever tried to live separately though it is a rented house or to separate at least your kitchen?

**Answer:** ....................

**Numbers:** ..................

**Que8:** Do you send your wife and children, at times to see your parents, brothers and sisters? Do you send gifts to them?

**Answer:** ....................

**Numbers:** ..................

**Que9:** Have you drawn your own 'will' and persuaded your wife and parents to draw theirs? To draw the 'will' how many times have you read *Tareeqa-e-Wasiyyat* and *Ahkaam-e-Mayyat?*

**Answer:** ....................

**Numbers:** ..................

**Que10:** Do you give your wife monthly pocket-money according to your financial capacity without seeking its account from her?

**Answer:** ....................

**Numbers:** ..................

**Que11:** Are your children getting religious and worldly education in a religious atmosphere? If no, then think about it from today itself, pray Allah and consult the religions scholars.

**Answer:** ....................

**Numbers:** ...................

**Que12:** Do you take care of praying besides convincing your wife and children due to any fault of theirs in a preaching way instead of a dialectic way, so that Allah may make them a mean of satisfaction for you? How many times have you offered the prerequisite prayer *(Salaatul-Haajat)* for this?

**Answer:** ....................

**Numbers:** ...................

**Que13:** Do you ever praise your wife's make-up or good dressing or putting things in order or diligently cooked food, though unwillingly so that she may be encouraged and satisfied?

**Answer:** ....................

**Numbers:** ...................

**Que14:** If your marraiage is not much older, are you using any temporay contraceptive method to keep suitable gap between two children with these intentions, after cousulting some reliable religious scholars, such as;

a) baby and mother may remain healthy

b) parents may concentrate on each children individually.

c) the second may born when the first would complete his/her suckling period and starts doing some of his/her natural demands.

**Answer:** ...................

**Numbers:** ..................

**Que15**: If you have children, do you forgive their faults with the intention that;

a) Allah will also forgive yours

b) they will start loving you truly

c) they won't consider you a cruel. Similarly, if they really had done a harm then instead of rebuking or beating do you take such steps so that, such harm could not be done again?

**Answer:** ...................

**Numbers:** ..................

**Que16:** If you and your wife are fully faithful to each other then are you offering the thanks-giving prayers?

**Answer:** ...................

**Numbers:** ..................

**Que17:** If, Allah forbid, you airs with your wife then

do you intend to act according to the directions given in this book alongwith praying? Are you consulting the religious scholars regarding this?

**Answer:** ...................

**Numbers:** ..................

**Que18:** Have you intended not to tell your wife a secret either of your previous life or of your family members due to which a major dispute or discord can happen between you and your wife?

**Answer:** ...................

**Numbers:** ..................

**Que19:** Do you belive in this idiom, “provide all amenities but be a strict disciplinarian”? Which means are you having a special and necessary 'awe' over your wife and children to make them cultured, disciplined and act according to the decrees of Allah and His Prophet (pbuh) inspite of fulfilling their all legal wishes according to your financial capacity, enduring their coquetries and helping them in the house-keeping.

**Answer:** ...................

**Numbers:** ..................

**Que20:** قُوآ اَنْفُسَكُمْ وَاَهْلِيْكُمْ نَا رًاوَّ قُوْدُ هَا النَّاسُ وَالْحِجَارَةُ

*Save yourselves and your families from a Fire whose fuel is Men & Stones.* (Tahreem-6)

Are you trying to fulfil the responsibility incumbent on you in the wake of this verse (try fully to make your family religious by using your mental and physical power to raise the standard of their faith and ethics) in a better and preaching way?

**Answer:** ...................

**Numbers:** ..................

**Que21:** Dear husband ! Are you praying for us, for the people who have worked hard in preparing this book, for the preceptors from whose books we have taken advices and articles while compiling this book, so that Allah may help them in compiling more and more useful books in future also?

**Answer:** ...................

**Numbers:** ...................

**Que22:** Do you seek forgiveness of your wife while going on a Journey for your unnecessary scolding , surliness and heart breaking habits so that you may win her heart while she may pray for your well-being and pass the duration of your journey waiting eagerly for your safe return?

**Answer:** ...................

**Numbers:** ..................

**Que23:** If you think that your wife does not do certain works at time or she is not up to your expectations or you feel whatever your mother or sisters are complaining about your wife to be correct, have you ever taken the responsibility of all the works of the house (changing the clothes of younger children, readying the elders for the school, cleaning the house and working in the kitchen etc.) and found yourself according to your own high standard. If you have never taken the responsibility then do these house-keeping works for three days only and reply will you still ask your wife all these?

**Answer:** ....................

**Numbers:** ...................

Dear husband! Get this question paper electrostated and write the answers in a separate note-book, then count the numbers you obtained but think before answering, if your answers are wrong then you are deceiving yourself and not us. Therefore give correct answers thinking that, if you are asked these very questions after death, will your answers will be the same?

If your obtained marks are 230 then you are a successful husband, we pray Allah that He may bestow you peace and tranquillity in this world and the Hereafter and He may solve all the problems of your marital life. If your marks are less than 200 then you need not to worry as after some hardwork and patience *Insha Allah* you will also be counted among the best husbands in the eyes of Allah and His Prophet (pbuh).

If your marks are less than 100 then you should be annoyed and worried about your worldly life and the Hereafter. First of all pray Allah to ready you, so that you can reform the matters you are lacking in, then resolve not to hurt your wife and children in future and preach these among others. *Insha Allah*, Allah will avert these shortcomings in you.

Allah forbid, if your marks are less than 50 then offer the prayer of repentence (*Salaatut-Tawba*) at once and seek Allah's forgiveness imploringly of your shortcomings and mistakes. Resolve anew not to commit such mistakes in future and consult expert religious scholars and preceptors. While in the end, thank Allah as much as possible, as Allah has shown you the path of righteousness through this book and you got the opportunity of repenting.

This is our wish that, may Allah create much more sincerity, sympathy, love affection in between the Muslim couples of the whole world, Amen!

## About the Translator

This book (originally written in Urdu, Tohfa-e-Dulha, by Maulvi Haneef 'Abdul Majeed) has been rendered into English Language by Mohammad Saleem, eldest son of a renowned Islamic Scholar Late Maulvi Shameem Qasmi, Ex-Principal of Madrasatul Uloom Hussain Bakhsh, Delhi.

Having the religious background and curiosity to learn, he did M. Phil in Arabic language from University of Delhi, and was awarded Gold Medal for his Post Graduate Degree in Arabic. Later he joined Zakir Hussian College as part-time lecturer of Arabic.

Keeping in mind the need of the hour where a common man does not have enough time to consult the religious scholars to resolve the pity things in day today life, he has used very common and easy language to understand and resolve himself.

*Please pray for the writer, translator, publisher of the book and all those preceptors whose work or saying had been used in this book. May Allah the Almighty bless all of you for this.*

*Amen!*